OXFORD MEDICAL PUBLICATIONS

Science and Practice of
Cognitive Behaviour Therapy

Michael G. Gelder
W. A. Handley Professor of Psychiatry, Oxford University
1969–1996

Science and Practice of Cognitive Behaviour Therapy

Edited by

David M. Clark and Christopher G. Fairburn

Department of Psychiatry, University of Oxford

Oxford   New York   Tokyo
OXFORD UNIVERSITY PRESS
1997

Oxford University Press, Walton Street, Oxford OX2 6DP
Oxford New York
Athens Auckland Bangkok Bombay
Calcutta Cape Town Dar es Salaam Delhi
Florence Hong Kong Istanbul Karachi
Kuala Lumpur Madras Madrid Melbourne
Mexico City Nairobi Paris Singapore
Taipei Tokyo Toronto
and associated companies in
Berlin Ibadan

Oxford is a trade mark of Oxford University Press

Published in the United States
by Oxford University Press Inc., New York

A catalogue record for this book is available from the British Library

Library of Congress Cataloging-in-Publication Data
The science and practice of cognitive behaviour therapy / edited by
David M. Clark and Christopher G. Fairburn.
p. cm. – (Oxford medical publications)
ISBN 0-19-262726-0 (hardcover)
1. Cognitive therapy. 2. Gelder, Michael G. I. Clark, David M.
(David Millar), 1954– . II. Fairburn, Christopher G.
III. Gelder. Michael G. IV. Series.
RC489.C63S345 1997   96-8078
616.89'142–dc20   CIP
ISBN 0 19 262726 0 (hbk)
0 19 262725 2 (pbk)

Typeset by Dobbie Typesetting, Tavistock, Devon
Printed in Great Britain by
Biddles Ltd, Guildford and Kings Lynn

Foreword

Aaron T. Beck
Emeritus Professor of Psychiatry, University of Pennsylvania

This Festschrift is a fitting tribute to the enormous contributions that Michael Gelder has made to psychiatric research and training. As a medical student, he trained at Queen's College in Oxford from 1947 to 1951 and in University College Hospital, London, from 1951 to 1953. In Oxford, he became very interested in the anatomy and physiology of the nervous system, which were the strengths of these two departments at the time. After he qualified in medicine, he worked at University College Hospital preparing himself for a career in general medicine but became interested in psychiatry, largely through the influence of Sir Desmond Pond (now deceased) who was, at that time, a newly appointed consultant – and later became President of the Royal College of Psychiatrists and the Chief Scientist at the Department of Health. He therefore moved to the Maudsley Hospital where he learned much from Sir Aubrey Lewis, Michael Shepherd, and Dennis Leigh. At that time, Gwyn Jones in the Psychology Department was beginning to introduce early behavioural methods, which excited Michael Gelder's interest. He learned more about behaviour therapy during a Medical Research Council Training Fellowship from 1962 to 1963, particularly from Joseph Wolpe who was spending a sabbatical year in Oxford at that time and who was characteristically generous in helping a young research worker.

After the training fellowship, he became a lecturer at the Maudsley Hospital from 1965 to 1967 where he developed a programme of research on behaviour therapy. Isaac Marks was his first research assistant and took over the role and pursued it with great success. Michael Gelder was happily settled in a tenured post at the Maudsley when the invitation to come to Oxford arrived.

When he came to Oxford as Chairman of Psychiatry in 1969, there was a good clinical service and some clinical research organized mainly by Bertram Mandelbrote who was working with Geoffrey Harris, the Professor of Neuroanatomy, and one of the pioneers in neuroendocrinology. Gelder transformed the Department of Psychiatry into a world-class research and training centre. In Oxford, he set out to develop behavioural research and obtained a Medical Research Council Programme Grant which extended with only one brief interlude in the mid-1980s until prior to his retirement. This grant brought a number of highly talented researchers to the Department: Andrew Matthews, Derek Johnston, John Teasdale, David Clark, Paul Salkovskis, Gillian Butler, Melanie Fennell, Ann Hackmann, Adrian Wells, and a number of others. He has also encouraged and supported Christopher Fairburn's explorations of eating disorders and their treatment.

Concomitant with the behavioural research, Michael Gelder joined with Bertram Mandelbrote to develop further the work on neuroendocrinology that he had started. This led to the group which is now led by Philip Cowen and which now specializes in the clinical problems of 5-HT function. One of the first people to work on this grant was Peter Beaumont, now Professor of Psychiatry in Sydney, and others included Guy Goodwin, Michael Gelder's successor at Oxford, and several working in London with the PET facility. The third line of development at the Department was in general hospital psychiatry, and here people including John Bancroft, Keith Hawton, Richard Mayou, and Dennis Gath have built on the success of the department.

Although there were very few resources when Michael Gelder first came to Oxford, it seemed to him that there were great strengths in possible collaborations with other parts of the Medical School. He has had particularly fruitful collaborations with the Department of Obstetrics, with Clinical Pharmacology, and with the Department of Cardiology, but of course, the list does not end there, Michael Gelder has made significant contributions outside Oxford having served as Chairman of the Medical Research Council's Neuroscience Board, a member of the MRC Council, Chairman of the Wellcome Trust's Neuroscience Committee, and played a role in the Royal College of Psychiatrists where he served as Vice President.

My association with Michael Gelder, and through him with his very talented department, has been among the most enriching of my professional career. Our professional relationship extends back to 1971 when I first met him at the time of his visit to the University of Pennsylvania. We had frequent contact as he assumed the role of European Vice President of the Society for Psychotherapy Research, during my tenure as President of the Society.

Our collaboration extended to clinical research as his group expanded their work on the behavioural treatment of anxiety disorders to include cognitive interventions. His group then turned to research in cognitive therapy of depression. Starting with the visit of John Teasdale and Melanie Fennell to our Center for Cognitive Therapy, a stream of world-class clinicians and researchers came to Philadelphia for training in cognitive therapy and shared with us their expertise. With David Clark leading the way, we were fortunate to have Paul Salkovskis and Gillian Butler and, for a brief period, Ann Hackmann and Christopher Fairburn. In return, a number of our former fellows spent time at Oxford. Gary Emery and Mary Anne Layden were associated with the staff at Oxford and John Ludgate and Adrian Wells formally joined the Oxford Department. This exchange programme has been unique, I believe, in the recent history of psychotherapy.

Under Michael Gelder's inspiration and active participation, his group of cognitive therapists and researchers, has extended the application of cognitive therapy to a wide variety of disorders. One by one, major psychiatric problems have fallen to the impact of their customized cognitive strategies: depression, panic disorder, generalized anxiety disorder, bulimia nervosa, hypochondriasis, chronic fatigue syndrome, premenstrual syndrome, and social phobia. The work at Oxford has been remarkable in that basic work on the psychopathology and mechanism of these disorders has been conducted concomitantly with the clinical applications. The researchers were among the first to apply the more sophisticated tools of cognitive psychology in both experimental and correlational studies of psychopathology.

As he enters with an official retirement, Michael Gelder leaves a rich legacy of outstanding leader and scientist. He has been responsible for the development of a whole corps of scientist–clinicians and for adding substantially to our knowledge of the causes and treatment of various disorders.

Preface

The term cognitive behaviour therapy was first used in the scientific literature in the mid-1970s and the first controlled trials of the treatment were published towards the end of that decade. In the relatively short period of time since then, cognitive behaviour therapy has become a leading psychotherapy in most Western countries. Why? There is no single answer. However, we suspect part of the reason for the success of cognitive behaviour therapy is the close link between science and practice, which is characteristic of the cognitive behaviour therapy movement, and the demonstrated effectiveness of the treatment. Most cognitive behavioural treatments are based on detailed models of the cognitive and behavioural factors involved in maintaining the disorder in question. These models are tested with correlational and experimental studies, the results of which are used to modify both the models themselves and the treatment procedures derived from them. Once a promising treatment has been developed, it is usually only a short time before it is evaluated in controlled outcome trials. The results of the trials, and the experience gained in conducting them, are then used to further refine the treatment, in an attempt to make it more effective and/or more efficient.

This book illustrates many of the links between science and practice in modern cognitive behaviour therapy. It describes the leading cognitive behavioural models for a wide range of disorders and gives an account of their empirical standing. It also provides a description of the treatments themselves and the research on their effectiveness.

Cognitive behaviour therapy developed from early behaviour therapy. In Britain, Michael Gelder was one of the pioneers of behavioural treatment. With Gwyn Jones, Isaac Marks, and Jack Rachman he established the Maudsley Hospital as the pre-eminent research centre for behavioural treatments. Following his appointment as the first Professor of Psychiatry at Oxford, he went on to develop both an internationally respected programme of research on the psychological treatment of anxiety disorders and parallel research on the psychological treatment of many other conditions. He was one of the first to recognize the importance of incorporating cognitive models and procedures into behaviour therapy and as a result research on cognitive behaviour therapy has flourished. Many well-known investigators worked in the Oxford department during his chairmanship and others enjoyed productive periods of sabbatical leave in Oxford. As a token of appreciation for his leadership and encouragement, the chapters in this book have been written by these researchers.

The book is divided into two parts. Part One covers general issues and includes chapters on the evolution of cognitive behaviour therapy, the complementary interchange between science and practice, the relationship between cognition and affect, and the evaluation and dissemination of cognitive behavioural treatments. Part Two addresses specific disorders. Each chapter outlines the cognitive behavioural conceptualization of a disorder, reviews relevant research, and describes current cognitive behavioural treatment procedures.

Oxford   David M. Clark
April 1996   Christopher G. Fairburn

Contents

List of Contributors

JOHN BANCROFT
Director, The Kinsey Institute, Indiana University, Bloomington, USA

DAVID H. BARLOW
Distinguished Professor, Department of Psychology, State University of New York at Albany, USA

CHRISTOPHER BASS
Consultant Psychiatrist, Department of Psychological Medicine, John Radcliffe Hospital, Oxford, UK

GILLIAN BUTLER
Consultant Psychologist, Department of Clinical Psychology, Warneford Hospital, Oxford, UK

DAVID M. CLARK
Wellcome Principal Research Fellow, Department of Psychiatry, University of Oxford, Warneford Hospital, Oxford, UK

CHRISTOPHER G. FAIRBURN
Wellcome Principal Research Fellow, Department of Psychiatry, University of Oxford, Warneford Hospital, Oxford, UK

DENNIS GATH
Clinical Reader in Psychiatry, Department of Psychiatry, University of Oxford, Warneford Hospital, Oxford, UK

MICHAEL GELDER
W. A. Handley Professor, Department of Psychiatry, University of Oxford, Warneford Hospital, Oxford, UK

KEITH HAWTON
Consultant Psychiatrist and Senior Clinical Lecturer, Department of Psychiatry, University of Oxford, Warneford Hospital, Oxford, UK

STEFAN G. HOFMANN
Program Director, Center for Stress and Anxiety Disorders, State University of New York at Albany, USA

DEREK W. JOHNSTON
Professor, School of Psychology, University of St. Andrews, Scotland

JOAN KIRK
Consultant Psychologist, Department of Clinical Psychology, Warneford Hospital, Oxford, UK

ANDREW MATHEWS
Special Scientific Appointment, MRC Applied Psychology Unit, Cambridge, UK

RICHARD MAYOU
Clinical Reader in Psychiatry, Department of Psychiatry, University of Oxford, Warneford Hospital, Oxford, UK

LAURENCE MYNORS-WALLIS
Consultant Psychiatrist, Littlemore Hospital, Oxford, UK

STANLEY RACHMAN
Professor, Department of Psychology, University of British Columbia, Canada

PAUL M. SALKOVSKIS
Wellcome Trust Senior Research Fellow, Department of Psychiatry, University of Oxford, Warneford Hospital, Oxford, UK

MICHAEL SHARPE
Clinical Tutor, Department of Psychiatry, University of Oxford, Warneford Hospital, Oxford, UK

JOHN D. TEASDALE
Special Scientific Appointment, MRC Applied Psychology Unit, Cambridge, UK

ADRIAN WELLS
Senior Lecturer in Clinical Psychology, University of Manchester, Manchester Royal Infirmary, Manchester, UK

J. MARK G. WILLIAMS
Professor, Department of Psychology, University of Wales, Bangor, UK

PART I

General considerations

1

The evolution of cognitive behaviour therapy

Stanley Rachman

It is fitting that a book prepared in honour of Professor Gelder should include a chapter on the evolution of cognitive behaviour therapy. He was one of a small group of psychiatrists, most of them trained at the Institute of Psychiatry and the Maudsley Hospital, who took an active interest in the applications of psychology to psychiatry in the 1960s. During this period, important advances were made in the shaping of behaviour therapy, and Michael Gelder played a leading role in these developments, notably in the treatment of agoraphobia, and of sexual disorders. When he was appointed head of the Department of Psychiatry at Oxford, he used the opportunity to promote the development of psychological treatments and gathered a group of gifted research workers and clinicians. They were admirably prepared to play a key part in the growth of behaviour therapy and its expansion into cognitive behaviour therapy. The subject and the Department flourished and Oxford became the world's leading centre for cognitive behaviour therapy.

Professor Gelder prompted, encouraged, and directed these developments and yet found the time and energy to participate in the daily business of clinical research. Among his crucial abilities in fostering the remarkable achievements at Oxford, Professor Gelder successfully combines incisive thinking, a calmly balanced view of controversial problems, and a lucid writing and speaking style. Personally, I recall with pleasure and gratitude many enlightening and rewarding discussions with Professor Gelder.

The evolution of cognitive behaviour therapy (CBT) took place in three stages. Initially, behaviour therapy emerged in independent but parallel developments in the United Kingdom and United States, in the period 1950–70. The second stage, the growth of cognitive therapy, took place in the United States in the mid 1960s onwards. The third stage, the merging of behaviour and cognitive therapy into cognitive behaviour therapy, gathered momentum in the late 1980s and is now well advanced in Europe and North America. CBT is widely accepted and is practised by growing numbers of clinicians; in all likelihood, it is today the most broadly and confidently endorsed form of psychological therapy. Cognitive behaviour therapy dominates clinical research and practice in many parts of the world.

Stage 1: the evolution of behaviour therapy

It is impossible to give a precise date for the birth of a new form of psychological therapy but one can identify the period in which it emerged — even when as in this instance, the new therapy emerged independently, in two forms, in two countries.

The British form of behaviour therapy (BT), which emerged in the early 1950s, concentrated on neurotic disorders in adults and was derived mainly from the ideas of Pavlov, Watson, and Hull. The major contributors to the early growth of BT were Joseph Wolpe, whose laboratory research on the experimental induction of neurotic behaviour in animals laid the basis for his fear-reduction techniques (Wolpe 1958), and Hans Eysenck who provided a firm theoretical structure and rationale for the new therapy (Eysenck 1960). Unlike Wolpe, whose pioneering and even later work was conducted in relative isolation, Professor Eysenck was the dominating head of the largest graduate research department of psychology in Britain, a position which he deftly used to encourage research into and the teaching of behaviour therapy, at the Institute of Psychiatry at the University of London.

While these events were taking place, a group of American psychologists were pushing ahead with the application of Skinnerian ideas and techniques to clinical problems. Encouraged by Skinner, some of his students and colleagues attempted to replicate the effects of conditioning, so readily achieved with pigeons and other laboratory animals, in psychiatric patients. In one of the earliest attempts, by Lindsley (1956), a replica of a Skinner box, complete with lever and delivery chute, was constructed for research on psychiatric problems. The hope and intention was to shape and re-shape the behaviour of the affected patient by systematic operant conditioning in the 'box'. As in research with animals, attempts were made to deliver tangible rewards whenever the patient emitted a constructive response and withhold rewards after the emission of a disruptive response, such as incoherent rambling. The underlying ideas were that the 'abnormal' behaviour of the psychiatric patients is the result of an inappropriate conditioning history and secondly, that the 'abnormal' behaviour could be re-shaped into normal forms by arranging the correct 'reinforcement contingencies'. By arranging the patient's expressions of adaptive behaviour, such as appropriate speech, to be followed promptly by a reward, the psychologist could re-shape the patient's abnormal activities. It was merely a matter of ensuring that the rewarding contingencies followed appropriate behaviour, however elicited, and that non-rewarding consequences followed inappropriate behaviour.

The concepts of 'psychiatric disorder' and 'abnormal behaviour' were radically altered, and their value was firmly denied. The patient's predicament was redefined as a problem of behaviour, pure and simple, and the solution lay in providing a corrective programme of operant conditioning. The later introduction of the term 'behaviour therapy' to this American version of the new therapy was exquisitely accurate. As will emerge, the term was less precise when applied to the British version of therapy.

The American psychologists continued their research into and analysis of the behaviour of patients who were, in the conventional description, suffering from chronic psychiatric disorders. Some of these intrepid early researchers, such as Ayllon and Azrin (1968), nobly, and even defiantly insisted on working with the most severe cases, with patients who lived in the 'back' wards of large psychiatric hospitals. Much of their research was distinguished by its ingenuity and inventiveness.

For institutional reasons and more interesting theoretical reasons, the American and British clinicians turned their attention to different samples and different problems. The Americans continued to devote most attention to institutionalized patients with severe problems, believed by most other health workers to be chronic and indeed unchangeable, and the British group pursued their research into adult neurotic problems, working mainly with out-patient samples.

These differences can be illustrated by reference to some typical problems tackled by the two groups. The American group tried to improve the behaviour of people with severe psychiatric disorders, such as schizophrenia, manic-depressive disorders, and then branched out into other severe problems such as childhood autism, mental handicap, and self-injurious behaviour. The British clinical researchers worked on treatments for agoraphobia and other anxiety disorders among otherwise intact, functioning adult out-patients. For the sake of clarity and narrative flow, I am using the terms that were conventionally used for these disorders at the time; the American researchers particularly and insistently avoided using terms such as mental illness. Instead, the 'disorders' were re-described in purely behavioural terms, such as 'verbal behaviour deficits', or 'disruptive behaviour', etc. The noteworthy early attempts in the United States include Lindsley's (1956) re-shaping of verbal responses in psychiatric patients, Krasner's (1958) expansion of the scope of verbal conditioning, Lovaas' (1961) extraordinarily persistent work on the treatment of autism, and the ingenious techniques developed by Ayllon (1963) and Ayllon and Azrin (1968) for dealing with bizarre, psychotic behaviour. Ayllon and Azrin, helped by the research of Staats (1962 personal communication), laid the basis for what later became known as 'token economy systems', that is, systematic programmes of reinforcement for appropriate behaviour and the omission of reinforcements for inappropriate behaviour (tokens, originally plastic discs, were introduced as readily dispensable and usable markers of reinforcement which the patients were able to exchange for tangible material rewards, such as sweets, cigarettes, magazines, etc.). The earliest token economy systems were established in psychiatric institutions and later introduced into other institutions such as schools, homes for delinquent youths, hostels, and hospitals for mentally retarded people. In all of these endeavours the exclusive emphasis on behaviour was steadily maintained, and care was taken to use the new (behavioural) vocabulary and the new definition of all of these problems in behavioural terms. As with many radical changes, there was an insistence on using the newly correct vocabulary and an impatience with people and papers that continued to use the conventional terms. But this was not mere mannerism or awkwardness — the way in which a psychological problem is described can, of course, have profound implications.

In sum, the American psychologists were Skinnerian in training and outlook, radically behaviourist in their thinking and language, believed that all psychological/psychiatric disorders were problems of faulty learning, concentrated their efforts exclusively on behaviour, and worked mainly with people who resided in institutions and had severe, 'intractable' problems. They espoused an unqualified environmentalism, and tended to regard themselves as 'behavioural engineers'.

In Britain, the pioneering work on behaviour therapy was conducted by psychologists and psychiatrists, unlike in the United States where psychiatrists played little part. The British contributors were not associated with any specific theorist or theory, and certainly were critical of Skinner's ideas (1959) which they tended to reject as narrow and unhelpful. Among the psychologists there was a quiet reverence for the ideas and findings of Pavlov, and the two leading contributors, Hans Eysenck and Wolpe, both favoured the Hullian learning theory, a hypothetico-deductive theory which offered admirable precision and scientific formality, and was widely subscribed to at the time (Hull 1943). The potential extension of Hull's theory to clinical problems, and the hope of developing a quantitative hypothetico-deductive structure, of unquestionably scientific appearance, for abnormal as well as normal behaviour, were attractive possibilities. The selection of the clinical problems and samples arose partly out of the existing health care arrangements, with the large majority of psychiatrists and virtually all clinical psychologists working for the National Health Service. The concentration of clinical psychologists in the Maudsley Hospital (London), which is associated with the largest British training centre for psychologists and psychiatrists (the Institute of Psychiatry), ensured that the fledgling behaviour therapists encountered a goodly selection of psychiatric problems at this extremely active, major psychiatric establishment. The Maudsley Hospital did not cater for patients with chronic psychiatric problems, but provided a selective in-patient service and an extensive out-patient service. Many of the patients using these services had neurotic problems, notably anxiety and depression. Hence, the British concentration on the neurotic problems of adults was determined partly by circumstances and partly by intrinsic interest (Eysenck and Wolpe were deeply interested in the nature of neuroses).

The British also construed many psychological/psychiatric disorders as the product of faulty learning but did not neglect genetic contributions, as did their American counterparts (the terms 'genetic, heredity, inherited', found no place in contemporary publications in the United States). The British espoused a qualified environmentalism in which *neurotic* disorders were regarded as the product of environmental events, learning experiences, and conditioning in particular—but even these learning processes were thought to be influenced by inherited properties. All of the anxiety disorders were considered to be the result of unfortunate conditioning events. Traumatic conditioning or repeated sub-traumatic episodes were thought to be responsible for anxiety. As a result, the affected person experienced conditioned fear in response to conditioned stimuli that were adventitious and the conditioned responses were inappropriate. Particular attention was focused on agoraphobia which was regarded as a conditioned response that provided the basis and cause for the extensive avoidance behaviour which helped to define the disorder.

It is easy to see why agoraphobia was chosen as the prototypical neurotic disorder. The conditioned fear response was dependably provoked by broadly identifiable stimuli (public transport, shops, open spaces, etc.) and disturbed *behaviour* was a defining feature of the disorder. The British group too was preoccupied with the study and modification of behaviour; they too were behaviourists, albeit of a different hue. Most of the inspiration for the conditioning and other learning theories came from laboratory research on animal behaviour, and in particular the research on the induction of experimental neuroses in animals was of critical importance to the emerging theories of abnormal behaviour.

The results of work on experimental neuroses, beginning with Pavlov's original demonstrations, and strongly supported by the American research carried out by Gantt (1944), Liddell (1944), Masserman (1943), and others, provided a basis for thinking about human neuroses. It had been shown that many animals were vulnerable to neurotic behaviour and that conditioning techniques were dependably capable of producing such neurotic behaviour. Moreover this neurotic behaviour showed all of the characteristics of normal learning, conditioned processes—namely, stimulus generalization, extinction, second order conditioning, etc. Plainly, we were in possession of a nearly ideal experimental model.

There were, it is true, some limitations such as the relatively primitive behaviour of the animals, the absence of speech, and acknowledgment that the experimental analogue did not and could not prove that human neuroses developed in this way (i.e., by traumatic or sub-traumatic conditioning). The experiments showed that it was possible, and that in any event, the experimental product had so many features of normal learning as to permit legitimate speculation.

There was almost no human research to guide these moves, and as a result Watson and Rayner's (1920) famous demonstration of the genesis of a conditional fear reaction in young Albert was over-interpreted. It did however support the idea that human fears can be conditioned, and also inspired the invaluable research of Mary Cover Jones (1924) on the unlearning of children's fears. Her research, in particular, made the enterprise seem viable, and directly influenced the forms of behaviour therapy that were developed for children some 30 years later. The full value of her work emerged after a dormancy of three decades, an historical example that provides a spark of hope for clinical researchers who yearn for the recognition of their unjustly neglected gems.

It is an historical curiosity that the father of conditioning process and theory, having found a way to produce abnormal, neurotic behaviour in the laboratory did not take the logical next step and seek conditioning techniques to undo the artificial neuroses. Instead, Pavlov tried the predominantly pharmacological remedies that were in current use, and also prescribed prolonged rest. The first experimentalist to make systematic attempts to find a conditioning or learning cure was Masserman, and he certainly made useful progress by proving that it is possible to reduce an animal's fear and abnormal behaviour through conditioning techniques. Wolpe consolidated and expanded these findings and concluded that the most effective way to reduce the induced fear/abnormalities was to re-introduce the frightened animal to the fear-conditioning stimulus in a graded and gradual manner while feeding the animal at intervals, in order to inhibit the fear. These experiments provided a foundation of systematic desensitization, which in turn provided the basis for all modern, behaviourally based, procedures for reducing fear.

After some further experiments, and trial and error, Wolpe accomplished the successful transition from laboratory to clinic by making two changes in the method of systematic desensitization. For practical purposes, direct exposures to the fear stimuli were replaced by imaginal exposures, and relaxation replaced feeding as the means for inhibiting fear. On the basis of his findings Wolpe formulated the theory of reciprocal inhibition, according to which all or most therapeutic improvements (in anxiety disorders at least) were achieved by the repeated reciprocal inhibition of fear by the imposition of an incompatible response, such as relaxation. In his animal experiments the feeding of the hungry animals was incompatible with the expression of fear — the feeding response inhibited the fear. Repeated instances of such reciprocal inhibition of fear will give rise to the development of a permanent inhibition of the fear (so-called conditioned inhibition). In treating his patients Wolpe substituted relaxation for feeding as the main inhibitor of fear, but he was careful to argue that any inhibitor of fear would do as well.

Wolpe's theory had useful explanatory value and enabled clinicians to think constructively and systematically about therapeutic problems, but it proved difficult to subject the theory to definitive tests despite the clarity of Wolpe's statements. The theory continues to be helpful but even if it proves to be largely correct, it can no longer offer a comprehensive explanation for therapeutic effects in the anxiety disorders. In similar fashion, the conditioning theory of fear-acquisition, of which Wolpe was co-author, retains useful explanatory power but can no longer provide an account of the genesis of all fears. There appear to be at least two other pathways involved, vicarious acquisition and informational acquisition (Rachman 1978, 1990). Recent developments in conditioning theory (e.g., Mackintosh 1983; Rescorla 1988), emphasizing the informational quality of conditioning, may well prepare the way for a satisfactorily comprehensive new theory of fear and anxiety (Rachman 1991).

Theorists attempted to explain the persistence of anxiety and unadaptive behaviour in addition to its genesis. Here Mowrer's (1960) explanation of the 'neurotic paradox' proved to be extremely useful. He set out a two-stage model of fear and avoidance and argued that avoidance behaviour persists precisely because it is successful — at least in the short term. Any avoidant or other behaviour that reduces anxiety will be strengthened. This model was timely and fitting and behaviour therapists exploited its explanatory value to the full (its limitations became evident in the middle to late 1970s). By this means they were able to explain the genesis and maintenance of significant anxiety and of 'unadaptive' avoidance behaviour, notably agoraphobia.

Wolpe's desensitization method was placed on a firm experimental foundation by the pioneering research of Peter Lang (1963, 1968), who established the laboratory procedures that provided a model for the hundreds of experiments which validated the fear-reducing effects of desensitization and expanded our understanding of the nature of fear.

In addition to his didactic role, Hans Eysenck adroitly advanced behaviour therapy into the position of a leading form of psychotherapy. In his hands, behaviour therapy became important not only for what it asserted but also for what it rejected. In the aftermath of his famously severe criticism of the claims of interpretive psychotherapists, (Eysenck 1952), he went on to dispute the theoretical basis of psychodynamic therapy, and was able to present behaviour therapy as a constructive alternative. He rejected the theory that neuroses are caused by unconscious (sexual) conflicts and that the manifest symptoms are defences against distress that would otherwise be unendurable. In characteristically provocative style he asserted that if you get rid of the symptoms, you get rid of the neurosis (Eysenck 1960). Actually, he argued that the disturbed behaviour was not in fact symptomatic of anything, but rather, constituted the whole problem. Neurotic behaviour, it was argued, is *learned* behaviour and is therefore open to un-learning. The behaviour is the problem and the un-learning of the behaviour is the solution.

In common with other radical changes in thinking, the development of behaviour therapy was in part reactive. Eysenck, Wolpe, and their colleagues in Britain, and Skinner and the applied behaviourists in the United States, had scant regard for psychoanalysis and the associated ideas of therapy. It was argued that analysis and its derivatives lacked empirical support and that the analysts' claims were unfounded; other critics regarded the whole endeavour as irrelevant and indeed beyond the pale. Wolpe, Eysenck, and their colleagues were strongly influenced by the writings of Karl Popper (1959), and for most of this period Popper's view that psychoanalysis is unfalsifiable and hence outside of science, was accepted and propounded. (This view is now contested by Grunbaum (1984) who argues that psychoanalysis *is* falsifiable, and erroneous.) It is sometimes stated that theories do not fade away but are replaced by preferable, stronger ideas, and numbers of the early behaviour therapists felt the need to provide a replacement. Others were directly challenged to produce a superior form of treatment and set out to oblige. The period 1958–70 was extremely productive; there was movement in the air and an unmistakable sense of change. Enthusiasm reached un-British levels, and certainly a radically different and decidedly new theory and therapy did emerge at this time.

Common ground

In contrast to their counterparts in the United States, the British group were critical of Skinner's ideas and used broadly behavioural ideas and methods. They first tackled adult neurotic disorders and devoted little or no attention to chronic psychiatric illnesses or to the difficulties of people who were intellectually handicapped, until significant progress had been achieved in the United States. Both groups of workers concentrated on behavioural problems and both groups believed that it was necessary and usually sufficient to change the affected person's behaviour. Both groups regarded psychological problems as problems of faulty learning, but the British group was not dedicated to an unqualified environmentalism. Both groups were attempting to apply behavioural science to psychological/psychiatric problems, both espoused the use of strict scientific standards, and both were participants in the march of empiricism.

The separate development of early behaviour therapy in the United States and the United Kingdom was followed by a merging of the two approaches, at least in terms of aims and most methods. The strong adherence to a Skinnerian framework remained confined to the United States and eventually faded even there. In the period from 1970 to 1980 there was a consolidation of the early advances and a shift from innovative ideas and techniques to the less glamorous business of rigorously evaluating the claims of therapeutic efficacy. Outcome studies abounded, much to the subsequent delight of dedicated meta-analysts. Overall, the commitment to empirical, applied science led to the development of increasingly refined, stringent criteria methods for evaluating therapeutic effects. Behaviour therapists played a leading role in establishing these demanding standards, many of which have now become common coin.

In the course of following these scientific paths, and subsequently, large numbers of people benefited from the skilful and enthusiastic efforts of the new therapists. Greatest progress was achieved in reducing the anxiety disorders, overcoming a range of childhood disorders, such as aggressive and oppositional behaviour, and improving the quality of life of handicapped people. There were disappointments in this early stage, and little progress was made in dealing with depression or the so-called appetitive disorders such as alcoholism, eating disorders, sexual abnormalities, psychotic disorders. Attempts to analyse and treat depression by purely behavioural means had little success.

In the first decade of behaviour therapy there was a good deal of theorizing and grand designs were offered, but the emphasis gradually shifted to technical topics, notably to the assessment of therapeutic efficacy. The shift from theory to practice was natural, even healthy for the time, and marked a victory of sorts. The adoption of empiricism, one of the 'inward workings of the age', transformed the methods of clinical psychology, and behaviour therapy became one of its 'outward facts'.

The attractions of establishing behaviour therapy included the legitimacy of its foundations in academic–scientific psychology and its advocates' insistence on empirical standards (partly as a reaction to the frustrations of an elusive psychoanalysis). The establishment of behaviour therapy, mainly by psychologists, was a major factor in the advancement of the profession of clinical psychology, which had formerly been restricted to measurement and assessment. The introduction of a soundly based, effective psychological treatment provided psychologists with justification and tools.

Curiously, the specific connections with academic psychology, notably the dominating learning theories of the time, fell away, and now few seem to know and even fewer to care about those connections or their loss. The passionate debates over the strengths and flaws of the schemes of Hull, Skinner, and Guthrie gradually lost their appeal, and one cannot help wondering whether or not it was worthwhile — historical inevitability perhaps? Learning theory certainly played a critical role in the launch of behaviour therapy but then faded out of sight. Instead, we saw the development of an empirical and energetic behaviour therapy, which made valuable practical progress, but manifested a declining interest in theory-building. It shifted from science to technology (Wolpert 1992). The introduction of cognitive concepts has gone some way to filling the gap between technology and science, and the rapid acceptance of these ideas is, I believe, a reflection of dissatisfaction with an uncritical and undemanding form of empiricism.

The absence of progress in theorizing about behaviour therapy in the period 1970–90 gradually became a source of discontent. In addition, there was a second and more practical need to expand the search beyond the essentially behavioural techniques that characterized the first stage of this new type of psychological therapy. The early and considerable successes in reducing anxiety and overcoming unadaptive avoidance behaviour, as in agoraphobia for example, were not accompanied by successes in dealing with depression, the other major component of 'negative affect' (most adult patients complain of a mixture of anxiety and depression). The early attempts to treat depression, by rearranging the reinforcement contingencies for depressive *behaviour*, having made scant progress the door was opened to cognitive therapy. (Oddly, a renewed attempt at modifying such contingencies may now prove to be more successful than it was during the original attempt — particularly as the earlier unwillingness of behaviour therapists to encourage cognitive analyses and provide explanations and advice has disappeared.) The cognitive element in depression is large and obvious, and given the lack of behavioural success, it became the first target of cognitive therapy.

Stage 2: the emergence of cognitive therapy

Given the lack of progress in treating depression and the waning prohibition against using cognitive concepts, many behaviour therapists read Beck's work with growing interest, reassured in part by the inclusion of behavioural assignments in his programme. They were also impressed by his insistence on accurate and constant recording of events and the self-correcting nature of the programme itself. Setting aside whatever remaining suspicions they had about the acceptability of dabbling with these non-behavioural cognitive concepts, numbers of behaviour therapists began treating depressed patients with cognitive therapy. Early successes were reported and these helped to remove the remaining inhibitions about cognitive therapy, at least when used alongside behaviour therapy and with an emphasis on the behavioural component of cognitive therapy.

Two of the most productive and influential pioneers of cognitive therapy, Beck and Ellis, whose work provides the basis for this historical analysis, shared the view that most disturbances arise from faulty cognitions and/or faulty cognitive processing, and that the remedy is to be found in corrective actions. Both of their forms of therapy are directed at correcting these faulty processes/cognitions, both concentrate on present problems and present thinking in contrast to the historical dredging of earlier forms of psychotherapy, and both recommend the inclusion of behavioural exercises. It is worth mentioning that Ellis and Beck both started out as psychoanalytic-dynamic therapists, and even Wolpe's earliest clinical techniques were psychodynamic. Therapists had little choice in those days, so the likes of Beck, Ellis and Wolpe forged their own tools.

Both Beck and Ellis acknowledged the value of behaviour therapy (as well as its insufficiencies), and as a result behaviour therapists were sympathetic to the Beck/Ellis versions of cognitive therapy — which were regarded more as supplements than opponents. Beck writes that, in the mid 1960s: 'I became familiar with behavior therapy and incorporated many principles from this approach' (Beck 1993, p. 13). Beck and Ellis regarded the behavioural exercises as means of obtaining new, corrective, information and in this sense, they differed from the behaviour therapists who regarded the behaviour changes as the essence of therapy rather than one of several secondary methods of producing change. The debate about interactions between cognitions and behavioural change continues. For example, it is not yet clear exactly why behavioural exposure exercises are followed by such significant reductions in panic cognitions and panic episodes. Nor is it clear why this seemingly indirect exposure method should be followed by cognitive changes that sometimes equal those which follow from directly cognitive therapy.

Beck's form of cognitive therapy was based on the 'rationale that an individual's affect and behavior are largely determined by the way in which he structures the world' (Beck *et al.*, 1979, p. 3), and the therapeutic techniques were designed to 'identify, reality test, and correct distorted conceptualizations and the dysfunctional beliefs (schemas) underlying these cognitions' (p. 4). All of it distinctively cognitive and too diffuse for determined behaviour therapists, but the reported successes in treating depression could not be overlooked — and Beck's therapy had a respectably behavioural component.

Albert Ellis (1958, 1962) was an early and assertive advocate of a directive form of cognitive theory which he originally described as rational psychotherapy, a term which he later expanded into rational–emotive psychotherapy. He argued that 'emotional or psychological disturbances are largely a result of (the person) thinking illogically or irrationally; and that he can rid himself of most of his emotional or mental unhappiness...and disturbance if he learns to maximize his rational and minimize his irrational thinking' (Ellis 1962, p. 36). In Ellis' view, 'people are uniquely rational as well as uniquely irrational' (p. 36), and 'their difficulties largely result from distorted perception and illogical thinking'. The way to overcome their difficulties is to help them to improve their thinking and perceptions.

Early in his career, Ellis concluded that 'insight alone was not likely to lead an individual to overcome his deep-seated fears and hostilities; he *also* needed a large degree of fear-and-hostility-combating *action*' (original emphases, Ellis 1962, p. 10). He recognized that the need for professional psychological assistance arises largely from expressions of irrationality, particularly those in which emotional reactions/behaviour clash with the person's rational assessment of the circumstances. In company with Beck (see Beck 1993 for examples), he was early to recognize the impact which behaviour can have on a person's emotions and thinking, and he took care to include behavioural assignments and exercises in his treatment programmes. They were given a more important and more explicit role in therapy by Ellis than by Beck in his early writings, and Ellis acknowledged a direct debt to learning theory. In the early part of his career he explored ways of bringing about a convergence between psychoanalysis and learning theory, having received his original training as a psychoanalyst. He was also early to recognize that the crux of cognitive forms of therapy is the relationship between thinking and emotion. 'The theoretical foundations of rational therapy are based on the assumption that human thinking and emotion are *not* two disparate or different approaches, but they significantly overlap and are in some respects, for all practical purposes, essentially the same thing... and never can be seen wholly apart from each other' (Ellis 1962, p. 38).

Despite his prescience in identifying the interaction between cognition and emotion as the central question in cognitive approaches to therapy, his early recognition of the power of behavioural change, and his persistent and assertive advocacy of his form of rational therapy, the work of Ellis did not attract as much research and clinical attention as did that of Beck. The scientific status of Ellis' work lagged behind Beck's (Kendall *et al.* 1995). In part, no doubt, this difference can be traced to the form of their writings. In comparison with Beck's, the writings of Ellis were more anecdotal and loosely formulated. In addition, the thrust of Beck's early work was on understanding and treating depression, a clinical problem that remained essentially unsolved by behaviour therapists. It was understandable, therefore, that clinicians, even those who were using behavioural techniques for the management of other clinical problems, should turn to the work of Beck for guidance in trying to help people overcome depression. If Beck had carried out his initial investigations on anxiety disorders, in which behaviour therapy had already made significant progress, appreciation of his work may well have been delayed for a considerable period.

Beck's cognitive therapy for depression was based on the assumption that the affected people engage in faulty information processing and reasoning, and subscribe to schema that are self-defeating. In particular, depressed people are subject to what Beck called the 'cognitive triad' in which they have feelings of pessimistic helplessness about themselves, the world, and their future. The aim of the cognitive therapist is to identify and then help patients to correct these distorted ideas, and also to improve their information-processing and reasoning. The therapeutic procedures are highly structured and time-limited and begin with the recognition of the connections between cognitions and affect, careful recording of these connections, collection of evidence for and against the ideas, followed by the substitution of more adaptive and realistic interpretations. In addition to recording the dysfunctional thoughts and combating them, the patient is encouraged to engage in various homework assignments (a rudimentary form of behavioural therapy). The correct analysis and treatment of depression by these methods requires subtlety and skill which can only be achieved through supervised training.

Although cognitive therapy was developed during a time in which psychology as a whole was moving strongly in the direction of cognitive explanations, there was a curious gap between these two movements. The early claims of connections betwen cognitive behaviour therapy and cognitive psychology were statements of hope rather than fact. Teasdale recently observed that: 'The development of cognitive therapy for depression has proceeded largely in isolation from basic cognitive science' (Teasdale 1993, p. 341; see also Seligman 1988). The two most prominent forms of cognitive therapy share with basic cognitive science a general outlook, but there is little similarity in theorizing, terminology, or methodology. Moreover, both forms of cognitive therapy deal almost exclusively with attempts to correct conscious thoughts and to make them more rational by the collection of information, intellectual analysis, persuasion and encouragement, and behavioural changes. Cognitive therapists' tendency to refer 'solely to consciously experienced thoughts and images ... clearly diverges from the much wider use of the term in cognitive psychology. There, it is assumed that the majority of cognitive processing is not experienced as consciously accessible thoughts or images' (Teasdale 1993, p. 340).

The narrow use of the term 'cognition' and associated concepts, the neglect of 'non-conscious' processes and the absence of useful connections with cognitive science, have all given cause for concern. In addition, Teasdale (1993) has drawn attention to problems that have been encountered specifically by Beckian cognitive therapy. He argues that cognitive therapy is not uniquely more effective than other treatments for depression that do not deal with negative thinking directly, that improvements after medication are associated with changes in depressive thinking similar to those observed after cognitive therapy, that there has been a failure to demonstrate the persistence of dysfunctional attitudes in vulnerable people after the depression has remitted, that many patients experience emotional reactions without being able to identify proportionate negative thoughts, that rational argument is frequently ineffective in changing the emotions, and that cognitive therapy is too often ineffective. However, his deepest concern is the gap between cognitive therapy and cognitive science.

Accordingly, Teasdale and Barnard (1993) set out a comprehensive theoretical framework intended to accommodate contemporary cognitive science knowledge and the clinical cognitive theory exemplified by the work of Beck. This is not the place for a detailed description of their scheme, except to say that they proposed the existence of nine types of information, each representing a different aspect of experience. Each type of information is separately processed and has a separate memory store. Their model proposes that there are mental codes related to two levels of meaning, a specific and a more generic type. Patterns of propositional code represent specific meanings, whereas the implicational codes represent generic and holistic levels of meaning. It is this latter type that is most important in emotional experiences. These codes are 'directly linked to emotion' (Teasdale 1993, p. 345). The implicational level of meaning contains representations at a high level of abstraction, and the implicit knowledge encoded at the implicational level represents models of experience which capture regularities in the person's world. Sensory variables, such as gesture, make a direct contribution to these implicational meanings. The importance of the implicational codes lies in their direct connection with emotion. In contrast, the other type of representation, propositional, 'cannot, alone, elicit emotion' (p. 346). According to Teasdale, 'the central goal of therapy should be to replace implicational code patterns related to depressive schematic models with alternative patterns related to more adaptive higher level meanings or schematic models' (p. 349). The ultimate value of this ambitious and complex model will not become apparent until a good deal of research and debate has taken place, but the recognition by Teasdale and Barnard of the problems confronting cognitive therapy is timely. They are perhaps excessive in excluding the possibility that propositional representations can elicit emotion, and their theorizing is too exclusively concerned with Beck's theory and the clinical problem of depression. Some of their arguments are plausible with respect to depression, but less convincing when applied to the anxiety disorders such as panic.

The connections between early forms of cognitive therapy and cognitive psychology were sparse and even those were loose. However, it is now established that attentional biases do occur during emotional experiences, and that memories, at least those involving recall rather than recognition, often are mood-related, if not entirely mood-dependent (e.g., M. W. Eysenck 1982; Williams *et al.*, 1988). A small start has also been made in capturing the distortions of perception that are caused by, or at least related to mood disturbances. For example, feared objects, such as snakes, may appear to be larger or more active during periods of elevated fear than they do during periods of tranquillity. In fear, bridges loom larger, rooms shrink Alice-like (Rachman and Cuk, 1992).

So, fears and sadnesses, appear to influence what we attend to, they influence how we perceive what we attend to, and they influence our memories of what we have attended to and perceived in the past. This interplay of emotions and cognitions is fascinating and will occupy intense scientific curiosity in the coming decades. However, the very interconnectedness of emotions and cognitions that is so fascinating, will be a great challenge to researchers. The selection and isolation of the variable of interest, in a manner that allows one to maintain constancy in the rest of the interconnecting web, is difficult and will require the introduction of new methods to replace our presently superficial ones. Here ingenuity will be all.

Stage 3: the merging

The adoption of cognitive ideas and methods, such as Beck's, was facilitated, indeed promoted, by the major shift towards cognitive psychology that was taking place in psychology in general. Previously suspect cognitive concepts and language became allowable, even necessary, and steadily replaced such yawn-inducing concepts as fractional anticipatory goal responses. I suspect that a significant prompt to the shift from pure learning theory to cognitive science was a dissatisfaction with the overwhelming efforts devoted to laboratory animal research, especially the obliging white rat, and the priority assigned to this work; it became increasingly remote from the original aim of our scientific curiosity — human behaviour and experience.

The time was ripe for a cognitive behavioural form of therapy and the two streams, cognitive and behavioural, were welded together by the successful development of a treatment for panic disorder.

In the process of merging behaviour therapy and cognitive therapy, the behavioural emphasis on empiricism has been absorbed into cognitive therapy. The behavioural style of conducting outcome research has been adopted, with its demands for rigorous controls, statistical designs, treatment integrity and credibility, and the rest. The merging of the old (behaviour therapy), with the new (cognitive therapy) is not free of problems, and we have already discovered that behavioural changes are more accessible and easier to measure than evanescent cognitions and their fluctuations. Leaving these complexities aside for the moment, it is possible to discern an exchange, in which cognitive concepts were absorbed into behaviour therapy, and cognitive therapists attached increasing emphasis to behavioural experiments and exercises. Researchers and therapists are acutely interested in, and attuned to, the patients'/clients' explanations, understanding, wishes and fears, as never before. *Cognitive therapy is supplying content to behaviour therapy.* This development confirms the historical connection, seldom acknowledged, between *phenomenological psychopathology* (e.g., Jaspers 1963) and cognitive therapy.

Long before the infusion of cognitive ideas into this field, obsessions were regarded, indeed *defined*, as unwanted, intrusive thoughts (plus, of course, images and impulses). But the precise content of these unwanted thoughts was of little interest. Thanks to the influence of cognitive therapy, we now are intensely interested in this content, and can begin to hope that eventually we will be able to trace the content of these thoughts closer and closer to the true nature (and functions) of obsessions.

This is a specific and telling example, but the influence of cognitive therapy goes further and wider. It also offers the promise of greater explanatory power and deeper understanding of abnormal behaviour and its springs. The outstanding example here is, of course, the psychological theory of panic [theories actually (see Barlow 1988), but for present purposes Clark's theory (1986) will be used in exposition]. Despite the difficulties it has encountered, some of which are discussed below, Clark's theory has increased our understanding, removed some blurs, and made explicable, many facets of panic. The phenomenon now is seen to be coherent, to be psychologically understandable. In many cases, studies, and experiments, we are able to make good sense of the person's thoughts and fears, and how they connect. If anything, the danger now is that cognitive explanations are being fashioned too readily and that their evident plausibility can become a trap.

In short, cognitive concepts have widened the explanatory range of behaviour therapy and helped to fill in the picture. The most solid advances have been achieved in understanding and treating panic disorder, and these advances have spilled over and enlivened research and thinking on obsessive–compulsive disorder and on hypochondriasis, better now regarded as excessive health anxiety (Salkovskis and Warwick 1986). We can anticipate important developments in understanding these disorders, and indeed in the full range of anxiety disorders. Progress is underway in research on social phobias, generalized anxiety disorder, obsessive compulsive disorder, and post-traumatic stress disorder.

The nature and the treatment of depression are exceedingly complex subjects and will not be pursued here in any depth. Retrospectively, it has to be said that therapists were over-optimistic. Beck's (1967, 1976) ambitious, complex, and many-layered theory has a broad plausibility but is marred by internal problems (Teasdale and Barnard 1993), some moot assumptions and the unmanageability that often flows from complex and complicated explanations. At times it seems overdressed. Progress in coming to grips with this grand scheme has been slow, and the failure of the large-scale collaborative study to produce evidence of the superiority of cognitive therapy (Elkin 1994; Elkin and Shea 1989; Shea and Elkin 1992) was a disappointment, notwithstanding some flaws in that study. The elusiveness of evidence to support the claim that there are exclusive connections between specific cognitive changes and reductions in depression, is also troubling, and there is an echo of this problem even in the most recent research on panic.

The exhilarating advances in understanding anxiety inevitably raise fresh theoretical questions, some of which are discussed below.

There are prickly questions of causality, and the results of cognitive behaviour therapy are open to alternative interpretations: cause, consequence, or correlate? The decline in cognitions, and in bodily sensations, observed after successful treatment is open to more than a single interpretation (e.g., Seligman 1988). The decline in cognitions, and/or in bodily sensations, may produce the reduction of the panics. But it is possible that the decline in cognitions, and in bodily sensations, are consequences of the reduced episodes of panic, and not the cause. It is also possible that the decline of cognitions is a correlate of the reduction in the episodes of panic [some critics have suggested that the cognitions and their decline may be mere epiphenomena (e.g. Seligman 1988; Wolpe and Rowan 1988)].

One reason for giving serious consideration to these alternative explanations arises from the fact that in Margraf and Schneider's (1991) and Margraf's (1995) study of panic disorder, the patients who received pure exposure treatment without cognitive manipulations showed improvements as large and as enduring as the patients receiving pure cognitive therapy in which exposures were excluded. Moreover, the cognitions declined to the same extent in both groups. It appears that negative cognitions can decline after a direct attack or after an indirect attack. Indeed, a satisfactory cognitive explanation needs to account for the declining cognitions that occur after a non-direct treatment, such as exposure. The most obvious possibility is that with each exposure, the patient acquires fresh, disconfirmatory evidence (e.g., no heart attack, did not lose control). The accumulation of this personal, direct, disconfirmatory evidence weakens the catastrophic cognitions. However, one is nevertheless left to ponder why the direct assault on cognitions was not significantly more effective than the indirect, incidental effects of exposure in the studies by Margraf and by Ost. It remains possible that the longer-term effects of cognitive behaviour therapy are superior — even when differences in cognitions are not evident at post-treatment (e.g., Cooper and Steere 1995). Furthermore, there is evidence of a dose-responsiveness relationship between cognitive behaviour therapy and cognitive change. For example, in the important outcome study by Clark *et al.* (1994), panic patients who received added, direct cognitive therapy had a superior therapeutic outcome to those who received indirect treatments.

These complex theoretical matters will be sorted out over the next few years, but to return to the therapeutic mechanisms of cognitive therapy, we need to ascertain whether or not the reduction/elimination of key cognitions is the critical element in this form of therapy. We already know that the direct modification of cognitions can be a sufficient (or even superior, e.g. Clark *et al.* 1994) condition for treatment success, but we also know that direct modification is not a necessary condition for success (e.g., exposure alone can be as effective as cognitive therapy, imipramine and other medications produce therapeutic improvements, but presumably via different mechanisms, etc.).

In analysing the treatment of anxiety, as in the treatment of depression, one obstacle to severe tests of the theory arises from the need for control over the timing of events. If the reductions in negative cognitions are no more than correlates of panic reduction, or if the cognitive changes follow rather than precede the reduction of panic, we need to study the sequence of events with care. Reductions in fear are easier to observe and record, but they can occur slowly, over weeks rather than minutes. In cases of panic, the measures typically range over days or weeks (e.g., the number of panics recorded per week or even per month). So if the patient records a decrease in panics, say from four per week to one per week, when exactly did this decline take place?

Cognitive changes can be even more difficult to track. Major changes can occur suddenly (e.g., Ost 1989; Rachman and Whittal 1989), and are therefore easy to record. In many, perhaps most occurrences, clinical or experimental, the cognitive shifts are slow to develop, changing over weeks rather than minutes [e.g., the cognitive therapy group in the Booth and Rachman (1992) study]. To make matters worse, the changes in fear and in fearful cognitions can and undoubtedly often do occur even when the affected person is separated from and out of contact with the fear-provoking stimulus (Rachman 1990). It is not possible to determine precisely when the change occurred, assuming, of course, and there is a complete change in the first place. So we are left with the awkward task of timing the sequence of changes in the cognitions and in the episodes of panic, knowing that these changes may take place over an extended period and that the determination of a precise point of change will be difficult or impossible. We also have some evidence that cognitive shifts can initiate a process of change that becomes evident some time later.

The processes set in train during cognitive behaviour therapy reach a conclusion at some point between sessions; in this sense, CBT sessions *initiate* emotional processing (Rachman, 1980, 1990) that reaches completion only after an interval in which the fearful person has no contact with the phobic stimulus and usually cannot recall having made deliberate attempts to facilitate the fear reduction between sessions. This apparent delay in the effects of cognitive behaviour therapy was also encountered in the experimental reduction of claustrophobia described by Booth and Rachman (1992).

In Salkovskis' (1985) refreshing cognitive analysis of obsessive–compulsive disorders, the affected person's construal of the behaviour and urges was taken as the starting point and the conclusion of the problem. Salkovskis focused attention on the explanation which the affected person provides for his/her obsessive–compulsive urges, behaviour, and motives. In this way he succeeded in filling a previously unknown stage. Previously, the nature and significance of the specific *content* of the obsessions and compulsions remained unexamined. This is, I believe, an important advance and one that will absorb a great deal of thought and effort in the next few years.

Given their common ancestry (Salkovskis and Clark 1993), it is no surprise that the cognitive analyses of hypochondriasis and of panic disorder are similar. The cognitive theory of hypochondriasis shares the boldness that characterizes the theory of panic disorder. It is argued that 'bodily signs and symptoms are perceived as more dangerous than they really are, and that a particular illness is believed to be more probable than it really is' (Warwick and Salkovskis 1990, p. 110). In panic disorder, the affected person is assumed to make catastrophic misinterpretations of bodily sensations and hence panic (Clark 1986). Importantly, the panic theory pertains to expectations of imminent catastrophe (e.g., 'I am having a heart attack'). The hypochondriasis theory pertains to threats to one's health or well-being that can be equally catastrophic but are more remote (e.g., 'This bump on my skin will develop into a cancer'), but the underlying mechanisms are assumed to be common to both disorders.

The cognitive approaches to phobias, obsessive–compulsive disorder, and hypochondriasis and the emerging analyses of post-traumatic stress disorder (Ehlers, in prep.) have a common core that is derived mainly from the cognitive theory of panic. The future of cognitive behaviour therapy in the treatment of panic disorder will have major ramifications for the cognitive approaches to all of the anxiety disorders.

The advance of cognitive behaviour therapy, and especially the successes in treating panic, gave rise to the first and only major *psychological* alternative to the then widely accepted biological theory of panic (see Rachman and Maser 1988). The debate will rumble along and also incorporate competing explanations for obsessive–compulsive disorders. Importantly, the cognitive explanation for the results of cognitive therapy in treating panic is the best supported at present. *Indeed, there is no plausible alternative explanation for the effects of cognitive therapy at present.*

Predicted trends

As predicted in 1990, the advances in treating panic disorder triggered off a stimulating series of cognitive re-analyses of all of the anxiety disorders. The broad forward sweep is well under way and promises gold.

I wish to draw attention to another, less obvious development, namely the extension of cognitive analyses to non-psychiatric aspects of medicine. It was argued in 1975 (Rachman and Philips) that psychologists should expand the scope of their clinical work beyond the exclusive concern with psychiatric problems. To some extent an expansion did take place, most conspicuously in the increasingly successful application of psychology to clinical problems of pain. But progress on other medical topics has been slower than desired or expected.

We are now in a position to expedite the desired expansion by a systematic and inventive application of cognitive analyses to a wide range of medical–psychological problems. Some obvious and early subjects that will be tackled with increasing earnestness, in addition to pain, are the cognitive aspects of undergoing stressful medical procedures, doctor–patient communication, and the nature and efficacy of clinical reasoning. Even more deeply, we can expect subtle and enlightening cognitive analyses of the way people construe their health and illnesses, their construal of medical information and treatments, and so forth.

During the next few years we can also expect to see a forceful expansion of cognitive theory and therapy into a variety of non-psychiatric medical problems, in keeping with the fundamental expansion of clinical psychology itself. Before long, a fully cognitive clinical psychology will be established.

These changes, especially the expansion beyond psychiatric medicine, will involve institutional as well as scientific changes, and new inter-disciplinary arrangements will emerge. How will cognitive behaviour therapy fit into these changes?

Evidently and essentially, the collaborative interchange with cognitive psychology will improve. The relationship with psychiatry, recently strained by disagreements about the limits of exclusively biological explanations of psychopathology, probably will be restored by advances in neuroscience. Many medical scientists, not least Michael Gelder, will find the introduction of cognitive analyses into general medicine refreshing and illuminating. I envisage nothing short of a cognitive revolution in medical psychology, in which many aspects of health, illness, and treatment will be re-analysed in cognitive terms.

Growth points

To summarize, I anticipate that several growth points will emerge.

Within the traditional boundaries of cognitive behaviour therapy, we can expect important progress in understanding and treating the full range of anxiety disorders. Correspondingly, the explanatory use of the concept of emotional processing will be expanded to incorporate the new findings and successes. Look for the emergence of a theory of cognitive–emotional processing. The interplay between affect and cognition will be the critical topic for research.

Cognitive concepts and analyses will be extended into general medicine, beyond the traditional limits of psychiatric psychology. The wider use of cognitive concepts in the psychology of pain will have particularly important repercussions.

Attempts to link cognitive behaviour therapy to progress in neuroscience will continue, but with more success than in the past. The selective use of neuro-imaging techniques will begin to make a valuable contribution to our understanding of the cognitive psychology of abnormal behaviour and experiences, and how to remedy them. And, as ever, advances in clinical research will feed back to enrich the fundamental base, in this instance, cognitive psychology itself.

References

Ayllon, T. (1963). Intensive treatment of psychotic behaviour by stimulus satiation and food reinforcement. *Behaviour Research and Therapy*, 1, 47–58.

Ayllon, T. and Azrin, N. (1968). *The token economy*. Wiley, New York.

Barlow, D. H. (1988). *Anxiety and its disorders*. Guilford Press, New York.

Barnard, P. J. and Teasdale, J. D. (1991). Interacting cognitive subsystems: A systematic approach to cognitive–affective interaction and change. *Cognition and Emotion*, 5, 1–39.

Beck, A. T. (1967). *Depression*. Harper & Row, New York.

Beck, A. T. (1976). *Cognitive therapy and the emotional disorders*. International Universities Press, New York.

Beck, A. (1993). *Cognitive therapy of depression: A personal reflection*. Scottish Cultural Press, Aberdeen.

Beck, A., Rush, A., Shaw, B., and Emery, G. (1979). *Cognitive therapy of depression*. Guilford Press, New York.

Booth, R. and Rachman, S. (1992). The reduction of claustrophobia. *Behaviour Research and Therapy*, 30, 207–22.

Clark, D. M. (1986). A cognitive approach to panic. *Behaviour Research and Therapy*, 24, 461–70.

Clark, D. M., Salkovskis, P. M., Hackmann, A., Middleton, H., Anastasiades, P., and Gelder, M. (1994). A comparison of cognitive therapy, applied relaxation and imiprimine in the treatment of panic disorder. *British Journal of Psychiatry*, 164, 759–69.

Cooper, P. and Steere, J. (1995). A comparison of two psychological treatments for bulimia nervosa: Implications for models of maintenance. *Behaviour Research and Therapy*, 33, 875–86.

Ehlers, A. (in prep.). *A cognitive analysis of post-traumatic stress disorder.*

Elkin, I. (1994). The NIMH Treatment of Depression Collaborative Research Program: Where we began and where we are. In A. E. Bergin and S. L. Garfield (ed.), *Handbook of psychotherapy and behavior change*. Wiley, Toronto.

Elkin, I. and Shea, M. T. (1989). National Institute of Mental Health Treatment of Depression Collaborative Research Program: General effectiveness of treatments. *Archives of General Psychiatry*, 46, 971–82.

Ellis, A. (1958). Rational psychotherapy. *Journal of General Psychology*, 59, 35–49.

Ellis, A. (1962). *Reason and emotion in psychotherapy*. Lyle Stuart, New York.

Eysenck, H. J. (1952). The effects of psychotherapy: An evaluation. *Journal of Consulting Psychology*, 16, 319–24.

Eysenck, H. J. (ed.). (1960). *Behavior therapy and the neuroses*. Pergamon, Oxford.

Eysenck, M. W. (1982). *Attention and arousal, cognition and performance*. Springer, New York.

Gantt, W. H. (1944). Experimental basis for neurotic behaviour. *Psychosomatic Medicine*, 3, 82.

Grunbaum, A. (1984). *The foundations of psychoanalysis*. Berkeley, University of California Press.

Hull, C. L. (1943). *Principles of behaviour*. Appleton, Century, Crofts, New York.

Jaspers, K. (1963). *General psychopathology*, (trans. J. Honig and M. W. Hamilton). University of Chicago Press.

Jones, M. C. (1924). Elimination of children's fears. *Journal of Experimental Psychology*, 7, 382–97.

Kendall, P., Maaga, D., Ellis, A., Bernard, M., de Giuseppe, R., and Kassinove, H. (1995). Rational-emotive therapy in the 1990's and beyond. *Clinical Psychology Review*, 15, 169–86.

Krasner, L. (1958). Studies of the conditioning of verbal behaviour. *Psychological Bulletin*, 55, 148–70.

Lang, P. J. (1968). Appraisal of systematic desensitization techniques with children and adults. 2. Process and mechanisms of change, theoretical analysis and implications for treatment and clinical reseach. In C. M. Franks (ed.), *Assessment and status of the behavior therapies and associated developments*. McGraw-Hill, New York.

Lang, P. J. and Lazovik, A. D. (1963). The experimental desensitization of a phobia. *Journal of Abnormal and Social Psychology*, 66, 519–25.

Liddell, H. (1944). Conditioned reflex method and experimental neurosis. In *Personality and the behaviour disorders*, (ed. J. McV. Hunt). Ronald Press, New York.

Lindsley, O. R. (1956). Operant conditioning methods applied to research in chronic schizophrenia. *Psychiatry Research Reports*, 5, 118–39.

Lovaas, O. I. (1961). Interaction between verbal and non-verbal behaviour. *Child Development*, 32, 329–36.

Mackintosh, N. J. (1983). *Conditioning and associative learning*. Oxford University Press, New York.

Margraf, J. (1995). *Cognitive behavioural treatment of panic disorder: Three year follow-up*. Paper presented at the World Congress of Behavioural and Cognitive Therapies, Copenhagen.

Margraf, J. and Schneider, S. (1991). *Outcome and active ingredients of cognitive-behavioural treatments for panic disorder*. Paper presented at the AABT Conference, New York.

Masserman, J. H. (1943). *Behaviour and neuroses*. Chicago University Press.

Mowrer, O. H. (1960). *Learning theory and behavior*. Wiley, New York.

Ost, L. G. (1989). One session treatment for specific phobias. *Behaviour Research and Therapy*, 27, 1–8.

Popper, K. R. (1959). *The logic of scientific discovery*. Harper & Row, New York.

Rachman, S. (1977). The conditioning theory of fear-acquisition: A critical examination. *Behaviour Research and Therapy*, 15, 375–81.

Rachman, S. (1978). *Fear and courage*. Freeman, San Francisco.

Rachman, S. (1980). Emotional processing. *Behaviour Research and Therapy*, 18, 51–60.

Rachman, S. (1990). *Fear and courage* (2nd edn). Freeman, San Francisco.

Rachman, S. (1991). Neo-conditioning and the classical theory of fear acquisition. *Clinical Psychology Review*, 11, 155–73.

Rachman, S. and Cuk, M. (1992). Fearful distortions. *Behaviour Research and Therapy*, 30, 583–9.

Rachman, S. and Maser, J. D. (ed.). (1988). *Panic: Psychological perspectives*. Erlbaum, Hillsdale, NJ.

Rachman, S. and Philips, C. (1975). *Psychology and medicine*. Temple Smith, London.

Rachman, S. and Whittal, M. (1989). Fast, slow and sudden reductions in fear. *Behaviour Research and Therapy*, 27, 613–20.

Rescorla, R. A. (1988). Pavlovian conditioning. *American Psychologist*, 43, 151–60.

Salkovskis, P. M. (1985). Obsessional compulsive problems: A cognitive behavioral analysis. *Behaviour Research and Therapy*, 25, 571–83.

Salkovskis, P. M. and Clark, D. M. (1993). Panic disorder and hypochondriasis. *Advances in Behaviour Research and Therapy*, 15, 23–48.

Salkovskis, P. M. and Warwick, H. M. C. (1986). Morbid preoccupations, health anxiety and reassurance: A cognitive-behavioural approach to hypochondriasis. *Behaviour Research and Therapy*, 24, 597–602.

Seligman, M. E. P. (1988). Competing theories of panic. In *Panic: Psychological Perspectives*, (ed. S. Rachman and J. D. Maser), Erlbaum, Hillsdale, NJ.

Shea, M. T. and Elkin, I. (1992). Course of depressive symptoms over follow-up: Findings from the National Institute of Mental Health Treatment of Depression Collaborative Program. *Archives of General Psychiatry*, 49, 782–87.

Skinner, B. F. (1959). *Cumulative record*. Appleton Century, New York.

Teasdale, J. D. (1993). Emotion and two kinds of meaning. *Behaviour Research and Therapy*, 31, 339–54.

Teasdale, J. D. and Barnard, P. J. (1993). *Affect, cognition and change*. Erlbaum and Associates, Hove.

Warwick, H. D. and Salkovskis, P. M. (1990). Hypochondriasis. *Behaviour Research and Therapy*, 28, 105–18.

Watson, J. B. and Rayner, P. (1920). Conditioned emotional reactions. *Journal of Experimental Psychology*, 3, 1–14.

Williams, J. M. G., Watts, F. N., Macleod, C., and Mathews, A. (1988). *Cognitive Psychology and Emotional Disorders*. Wiley, Toronto.

Wolpe, J. (1958). *Psychotherapy by reciprocal inhibition*. Stanford University Press.

Wolpe, J. and Rowan, V. C. (1988). Panic disorder: A product of classical conditoning. *Behaviour Research and Therapy*, 27, 583–5.

Wolpert, L. (1992). *The unnatural nature of science*. Harvard University Press, Cambridge, MA.

2

The scientific foundations of cognitive behaviour therapy

Michael Gelder

From their beginning, claims have been made that the behavioural and cognitive therapies have a sound scientific basis and in this way are superior to other kinds of psychological treatment. Wolpe and Lazarus (1966) were among the first to emphasize this claim when they wrote that 'to obtain an adequate understanding of the techniques (of behaviour therapy) is scarcely possible unless the student has satisfied two minimum prerequisites. First, he should have a reasonable grounding in essential scientific method. Second, he should have acquired a knowledge of modern learning theory (especially Hull and Skinner)' (p. viii). Statements of this kind were intended to gain the interest of clinicians in the new methods of behavioural treatment at a time when they had rather modest effects. However, the claims could be sustained only by exaggerating the generality of theories of conditioning and learning based on mainly the results of animal experimentation, over-simplifying the psychopathology of the neuroses, and glossing over the difficulty of using learning principles to guide treatment. Clinicians were not unaware of these problems and many were sceptical of the early claims of behaviour therapy. This scepticism was not confined to clinicians, but extended to psychologists, such as Breger and McGaugh (1965) who wrote of behaviour therapy that 'many of the so-called principles of learning employed by workers with a behaviourist orientation are inadequate and not likely to provide useful explanations of clinical phenomena . . . . The behaviourists have traditionally assumed that principles established under highly controlled conditions, usually with animal subjects, form a scientific foundation for a psychology of learning. Yet when we come to apply these principles of human learning situations the transition is typically bridged by rather flimsy analogies' (p. 354). The literature concerned with attempts to apply principles with operant conditioning to the treatment of chronic schizophrenia, or of attempts to treat tics by negative practice confirms all the doubts expressed by Breger and McGaugh.

The first response to this scepticism about the scientific basis of behavioural treatment was a retreat from the study of patients with their complex clinical problems to the study of less serious forms of psychological dysfunction in healthy people, many of whom were college students. These 'pre-clinical' investigations were carried out to show that learning principles could be applied in an informative way to problems which bore some resemblance to clinical disorders, but their principal value was in establishing experimental methods that could be applied to actual clinical problems. Thus, instead of transferring by analogy findings from animal psychology to clinical problems, the experimental study of isolated symptoms such as simple phobias provided a more plausible basis on which to build the treatment of psychiatric disorders.

These studies of normal subjects were followed by a number of well-conducted clinical trials, mainly with phobic and obsessional disorders, which produced a better understanding of the value and limitations of the procedures. Increasing experience convinced many clinicians that the main limitation was the failure to take account of patients' attitudes and beliefs and a search began for ways of incorporating these important elements in treatment. Meanwhile, Beck was carrying out his studies of the cognitive component of emotional disorders from which he developed the new treatment for depression which he called cognitive therapy. This treatment was based on insightful clinical observation rather than on the findings of experimental psychology, and it was soon seen by clinicians as highly relevant to the problems of their patients. Clinical trials were carried out showing the value of cognitive therapy in depressive disorders, both as a treatment for acute depression of moderate severity and in preventing relapse. These findings prompted studies of the psychological abnormalities in depressive disorders and normal states of low mood. Thus, the claims for a scientific underpinning of cognitive therapy came later in its development than had been the case in the development of behaviour therapy.

In recent years cognitive behaviour therapy has been linked much more effectively with cognitive and behaviour science and this linkage has led to substantial advances in treatment. This chapter reviews some of these advances and for this purpose the experimental studies can be divided into three groups, designed to:

(1) characterize key cognitions in psychiatric disorders;
(2) test predictions about the role of these cognitions; and
(3) study factors that maintain cognitions.

The present account provides examples of the ways in which studies of these three kinds can be used to develop effective treatment. Some of the examples inevitably overlap with those used to illustrate different points in other chapters. In view of the theme of the book the examples that have been chosen are mainly from the work of the Oxford group. Before reviewing these three issues, it is appropriate to consider the kinds of theoretical frameworks within which experiments can be carried out.

Models, hypotheses, and clinical observations

Several theoretical schemes have been suggested for use with research on cognitive therapy. They are models, that is devices for ordering information which explain phenomena in a broad and comprehensive way but cannot easily be proved wrong. Beck's model is of schemata, that is stable mental representations of experience that are involved in the screening, coding, and evaluating of information (Beck 1964b). Beck proposed that in depression, schemata are abnormal and negative cognitions arise when a stressful event activates dysfunctional schema. The abnormal schema persists because people employ erroneous logic, for example they over-generalize from single instances, or abstract selectively the negative features in a situation instead of balancing positive and negative features. Beck's model suggests first that thinking becomes more negative when patients are depressed and that this negative thinking maintains the disorder; and second that some people who are not depressed have dysfunctional beliefs that make them prone to develop depression in the face of adverse circumstances. Beck's model, which is based on clinical observations, has been highly influential but it is necessarily less precise in its predictions than a more limited hypothesis would be.

A second model used widely in discussions of cognitive therapy is concerned with so-called emotional processing. This model was devised to account for the clinical observation that the recall of certain memories evokes an emotional response, and that this response diminishes with time and with repeating the recall. When the emotional response persists, emotional processing is said to have failed. The model links closely with Bower's (1981) associative network model which postulates that memory 'structures' are connected with 'structures' containing information about emotion, in such a way that a fear network results, and that in some way that is not closely specified, this network may fail to incorporate safety information.

Models of this kind are useful to the extent that they can incorporate new experimental findings. They are less good as sources of critical hypotheses so that it is more difficult to identify their weaknesses. They can, however, provide a framework for new experiments. For example, the idea that post-traumatic stress disorder is a failure of emotional processing suggests that it would be valuable to examine events taking place soon after the traumatic event, at the time when processing would be taking place.

In the view of the author, research on cognitive therapy is directed more usefully by low-level hypotheses which describe hypothetical links between sets of data that are more limited than those incorporated into a model. For example, the hypothesis that panic disorder is caused by abnormal catastrophic cognitions generates a series of hypotheses which can be tested experimentally (see p. 31–2). However, whether the guiding framework for experimental studies is a model or a more restricted hypothesis, the starting point for such research should be clinical observation. Beck's remarkable insights into the thinking and emotions of depressed patients provides one of the best examples of the value of listening carefully to patients as a way of gaining new ideas for research and clinical practice. His subsequent work on disorders involving anxiety (Beck 1976), and personality disorder (Beck *et al.* 1990) has been equally stimulating.

Characterizing cognitions

In cognitive therapy an attempt is made to reverse in a short time, patterns of thinking that have been established for many years. One way to achieve such rapid change is to focus treatment on as few as possible of the cognitions that are maintaining the disorder. Another approach is to use so-called broad spectrum therapy in which several cognitive and behavioural techniques are combined in an attempt to change a wider range of cognitions and symptoms. The difference can be illustrated by comparing the two approaches to the treatment of panic disorder. The treatment described by Clark (1989) was designed specifically to change catastrophic cognitions concerned with fears of impending physical illness. In contrast, the treatment developed by Barlow *et al.* (1989) combines cognitive procedures with exposure to interoceptive cues and relaxation training. In the treatment of Clark (1989) the largest part of treatment time is spent in modifying catastrophic cognitions on the grounds that change in these cognitions is the essential step in therapy. In the treatment devised by Barlow's group, time is divided between several procedures on the grounds that changes have to be effected in several aspects of the disorder. The question which of the two approaches to treatment is more effective can be answered only by comparing them. Nevertheless, I shall argue for the focused approach based on studies of psychopathology and particularly of abnormalities of cognition. Several aspects of cognition have been studied: thinking, attention, memory, visual imagery, worry, and meta-cognition.

Thinking

The study of abnormal thinking can be illustrated by the example of panic disorder. Patients with panic disorder generally describe fears that one or more of the physical symptoms of anxiety (such as palpitations) will lead to a medical emergency (such as a heart attack). This observation was reported many years ago by Freud (1895) and has been confirmed many times (see, e.g., Beck *et al.*, 1974; Hibbert 1984; Ottaviani and Beck 1987). Clinical observations have also shown the sequence in which symptoms and cognitions appear in panic disorder. Hibbert (1984) observed that 53% of patients became aware of autonomic symptoms before the fearful cognitions, while this sequence was described much less often by control patients.

Continuing with the example of panic disorder, two kinds of quantitative method have been used to follow up the clinical observation that fear of catastrophic consequences of physical symptoms is frequent in this disorder. The simplest method is to use a questionnaire to determine the frequency of the symptoms and cognitions in panic disorder and in other kinds of disorder. For example van den Hout *et al.* (1987) used a 14-item questionnaire to assess the interoceptive fears of patients with panic disorder, non-panic neurotic controls, and normal subjects. Panic patients scored higher than either of the other two groups, and there was no significant difference between the non-panic neurotics and the normal subjects. Panic patients also endorsed more fears of all anxiety symptoms except trembling, paraesthesiae, and feeling paralysed. If measurements of anxiety are made as well, it is also possible to relate differences between groups to possible confounding factors such as level of anxiety (see, e.g., Last and O'Brien 1985). Other associations can be examined by using more complex statistical techniques. For example, Marks *et al.* (1991) used a principal components analysis which showed a close relationship between cardiorespiratory symptoms and cognitions concerning physical illness and between depersonalization and cognitions concerning losing control. These quantitative methods have extended the clinical findings by demonstrating that this pattern of thinking is present in all panic disorder patients and distinguishes them from other anxious patients.

Questionnaires require patients to recall what they were thinking at times when symptoms were present. When these symptoms are continuous or frequently present, as in depressive disorder, patients can recall easily, but when symptoms are intermittent, as in most cases of panic disorder, accurate recall may be difficult. This difficulty can be reduced by attempting to recreate the thoughts in the patient's mind when the assessment is made. One method is to present patients with descriptions of situations in which symptoms usually appear and to ask them either to describe the thoughts that they would have experienced or to choose between examples of thoughts that they might have experienced at such a time. For example, in a study of panic disorder patients (Clark *et al.* submitted) were asked to imagine that they had just become aware of rapid heart action, and to say what thought they would think if they had this experience. After this they were asked to choose from three alternative ideas supplied by the investigator, the one that would be most likely to come to mind. For example, the three examples in relation to rapid heart action were: (1) I have been physically active; (2) there is something wrong with my heart (the catastrophic outcome); (3) I am excited. This method confirmed that concerns about catastrophic consequences of physical symptoms. Patients with panic disorder choose the catastrophic outcome more often than normal subjects. (In this example, (2) is endorsed more often by patients with panic disorder than by controls, Clark *et al.* submitted.)

Investigations of the above kind serve to confirm or deny the presence of abnormalities that have been suggested by clinical observations. Other techniques can be used to reveal abnormalities which cannot be observed readily with clinical methods. For example, Clark *et al.* (in prep. (a)) found that panic disorder patients respond differently from controls when making very rapid responses to certain stimuli, and do so in a way that suggests that the response to catastrophic cognitions is rapid and automatic. The subjects were required first to read an incomplete sentence presented on a television screen and then to read aloud as quickly as possible a single word presented soon after on the same screen. An example of the incomplete sentences is:'If I had palpitations I could be . . .'. Half the words presented after the sentence completed it in a way that expressed one of the catastrophic cognitions characteristic of panic patients (e.g., the word 'dying'); the other half of the target words completed the sentence in a way that was not threatening (e.g., the word 'excited'). All subjects responded rapidly to this task, delaying for only about a second before starting to read the word presented on the screen. Normal subjects responded at the same speed to words that completed the sentence in a threatening way and to the alternative words. However, panic patients responded significantly more rapidly to words that completed a threatening sentence. The greater speed with which panic patients make responses to threat words suggests that they already have in mind the idea expressed by the threatening sentence, and therefore anticipate the threatening word. Expressed in another way, they are primed to expect them. Since the responses are so rapid and the differences between them are measured only in milliseconds, the priming presumably takes place automatically.

Disorders of thinking have been studied extensively in depressive disorders. These investigations originate in Beck's classic papers on thinking and depression published in 1964 (Beck 1964*a*, *b*). He confirmed the traditional clinical descriptions of themes of low self-esteem, self-blame, and wishes to escape or die. However, he emphasized certain features that had been less clearly described by others, namely, intrusive thoughts concerned with self-commands and injunctions, as well as certain distorted ways of reasoning which he called arbitrary influence, selective abstraction, and over-generalization. In his early papers he drew parallels between the distorted reasoning of depressed patients and that found in other psychiatric disorders, and he suggested that the process of disordered thinking might be the same in many disorders, while the content of thinking might differ in each one (Beck 1964a, b). Later, he placed more emphasis on features specific to depressive disorder.

Subsequent experimental investigations have broadly confirmed Beck's original clinical observations, for example, by the use of an automatic thoughts questionnaire (Hollon and Kendall 1980) and a cognitive errors questionnaire (Lefebvre 1981). Also, Deutscher and Cimbolic (1990) found that depressed patients endorsed more dysfunctional attitudes than did non-depressed psychiatric patients. In other studies, depressed patients have been reported to be more likely than non-depressed controls to attribute the cause of failure to themselves rather than to external factors (see Coyne and Gotlib 1983) although not all studies have confirmed this (e.g., Deutscher and Cimbolic 1990). However, it is difficult to design experimental studies to produce convincing evidence that abnormal cognitions are vulnerability factors for depressive disorder by showing that they exist in people who are not depressed at the time and have not been depressed at some time before the tests. It remains possible, therefore, that the abnormal cognitions identified in anxiety and depressive disorders are a consequence of a current abnormal mood state. However, even if this is the case, they are highly likely to enhance and prolong the present and any future mood disorder, and are therefore an important target for treatment.

Attention

Anxiety and depressive disorders are characterized by complex abnormalities of attention which cannot be studied effectively without the use of experimental methods. In anxiety disorders, there is a general bias towards attention to anxiety-evoking stimuli rather than neutral stimuli, and there are more specific abnormalities in particular disorders (see Wells and Matthews 1994). For example, Ehlers and Breuer (1995) showed that both panic disorder patients and simple phobics have an attentional bias towards threatening physical stimuli but that panic disorder patients have a specific bias towards interoceptive cues, being more accurately aware of their heart rate than simple phobics.

Experimental studies of attentional focus have been particularly informative in social phobia. Patients with this disorder are afraid of scrutiny and criticism by others. Extending the general literature on anxiety and attentional bias to such patients, one might assume that they would attend selectively to the reactions of other people to their behaviour, focusing particularly on any signs of disapproval. Experimental studies suggest a different pattern of attention. Stopa and Clark (1993) studied social phobics, anxious patients of other kinds, and normal controls. All three groups of subjects took part in a conversation with a person who had been trained to behave in a reserved but not unfriendly way. The interchange was recorded on video. After the conversation they spoke their thoughts aloud, and afterwards completed a check list of possible thoughts. Focus of attention was assessed by testing recall and recognition memory of the other person's appearance, objects in the room, and the content of the conversation. Compared with the other two groups, social phobics had more negative self-evaluative thoughts about their social behaviour (e.g., I am boring), but not more thoughts about negative evaluation by the other person (e.g., he thinks I am boring). There is some evidence also that social phobic patients direct attention away from negative social cues (Clark and Yuen in prep.) and towards their own physiological responses (Johannson and Ost 1982). These findings suggest that it may be important for patients to be encouraged to direct their attention away from their own behaviour and physiological reactions and towards that of the other person so that they collect more accurate information about other people's responses.

The findings of an increased self-focus of attention in social phobia are parallelled by similar findings in other mood disorders suggesting that self-focus may be a feature common to several abnormal states. Compared with normal subjects, patients with anxiety disorders (Wells 1985), and depressive disorders (Ingram and Smith 1984; Smith and Greenberg 1981; Wood et al. 1990), and obsessional disorder (Gordon 1985) focus more attention on themselves and less on their surroundings. The findings are important because self-focus interferes with reality testing, and encourages withdrawal from threatening situations (Carver and Blaney 1977). Moreover, increased self-focus increases patients' awareness of the somatic components of their responses to stress and is associated with a tendency both to overestimate the intensity of this arousal (Mandler et al. 1958), and to report a greater emotional response (Scheier and Carver 1977). All of these behaviours would increase or prolong the emotional disorder.

Memory

Several experimental studies with depressed patients have been concerned with the effects of mood on autobiographic memory. Lloyd and Lishman (1975) were among the first to show that low mood is associated with more rapid recall of unhappy memories as opposed to happy memories.

This was a correlational study in depressed patients and the results could have arisen: (a) because depression facilitates the retrieval of negative experiences, (b) because people who become most depressed have had more unpleasant life experiences, or (c) because people in depressed mood evaluate memories differently, labelling as depressive, memories of events that were not sad at the time. The differential life experience explanation was ruled out by subsequent experiments in which memory was examined while mood was changed either by asking subjects to read statements capable of inducing depression, for example 'I wonder if I have accomplished anything really worthwhile' (Teasdale and Fogarty 1979), or to listen to sad music (Clark 1983). Induced mood produced retrieval biases similar to those reported by Lloyd and Lishman (1975). The possibility that change in mood simply alters the evaluation of memories was discounted by Teasdale *et al.* (1980), who asked people to recall memories while in an abnormal mood state and to categorize them when in normal mood. Memories categorized as depressive while in normal mood states were those recalled faster when in an induced low mood state. In a further study, Clark and Teasdale (1982) showed that these effects of mood on memory are not restricted to induced mood but can be demonstrated by comparing recall during more and less depressed phases of the diurnal cycle of mood in patients with depressive disorders.

This effect of mood on memory is important because it is likely to maintain low mood by setting up a vicious circle in which low mood leads to recall of unhappy memories which in turn lower mood further.

Visual imagery

Distressing visual imagery may occur in any psychiatric disorder; however clinicians have observed that it is particularly frequent in post-traumatic stress disorder. Quantitative studies have confirmed this observation, for example, Ehlers and Steil (1995) found that among victims of road accidents 65% reported intrusive visual images compared with only 45% who reported intrusive thoughts. Visual intrusions were rated as more distressing than intrusive thoughts. It has been suggested that such images are more persistent than the corresponding thoughts and that they dissipate sooner if the person talks or writes about them in a way that brings about verbal encoding (Pennebaker 1989). This last idea, although potentially important, has not been supported with convincing experimental evidence.

It has been suggested that visual images are more persistent because this kind of imagery is more difficult to process emotionally than are verbal recollections of the same events. Although expressed in terms of the emotional processing model, these statements do little more than repeat the clinical observation that visual intrusive memories tend to persist, and that they are often associated with strong emotions. Since visual imagery is an important component of several emotional disorders, further studies are required to investigate the conditions which provoke and maintain it, so that better forms of treatment can be developed.

Worry

In the present context, worry refers to repeated thoughts and images with anxiety-provoking themes. It is the continuing repetitious nature that distinguishes worry from the short-lived intrusive thoughts and images described above. Compared with normal thinking (Borkovec and Inz 1990) or obsessions (Wells and Morrison 1994), worry contains more thoughts than images. Worry is a characteristic feature of generalized anxiety disorders, a point which is recognized in the diagnostic criteria in DSM–IV. It has been suggested that worrying thoughts are associated with less emotional arousal than are visual images (Borkovec and Hu 1990) and that it may persist because it is a form of avoidance of imagery and therefore of anxiety (Borkovec and Inz 1990).

Worry has been considered in the context of theories of emotional processing. It is suggested that such processing is most effective when the person re-experiences the somatic components of emotional arousal at the same time as the cognitive components. If this is correct, then compared with imagery, worry should lead to less effective emotional processing and therefore to longer-term anxiety. Evidence consistent with this hypothesis was obtained by Butler *et al.* (1995) who showed a stressful film to subjects, half of whom were asked to worry about the content of the film immediately afterwards and half were asked to produce visual images of the film. The worry group were significantly less anxious immediately after the film. During the following three days they experienced more intrusive imagery about the film although, contrary to expectation, the ratings of the distress caused by the images was not greater in the worry group. Since worry is a prominent feature of generalized anxiety disorder, it is important to discover more about its causes, its effects, and the factors that maintain it. Attempts to define and measure and study worry are an important first measure but more experimental work is needed before the differences between intrusive thoughts, intrusive images, and worry become clearer.

Meta-cognition

The term 'meta-cognition' refers to beliefs and actions concerned with regulation and interpretation of a person's own cognitions (see Nelson and Nahrens 1990). Regulation includes, for example, switching between worry and visual imagery, or changing attentional focus. Interpretation includes, for example, the belief of obsessionals that thinking about an event makes it more likely to happen, and the belief of some people with post-traumatic stress disorder that the intrusive recollections indicate that they are going mad or that their brain has suffered damage. Clinical observation suggests that such ideas can both generate stress and maintain the disorder. Thus, Ehlers and Steil (1995) found that negative interpretations of intrusive recollections correlated with the distress caused by intrusions, and this effect remained significant when intrusion frequency was partialled out. In addition, Winton *et al.* (submitted) found that negative interpretation of initial post-traumatic stress disorder symptoms after sexual or physical assault distinguished patients with persistent versus transient post-traumatic stress disorder.

Clinical observations suggest also that such ideas are difficult to modify by discussion or questioning of a kind that might change other ideas. For this reason it is important to understand meta-cognitions better, but to date little progress has been made. Indeed, there have been few attempts even to describe meta-cognitions systematically or measure them reliably. As in the study of other cognitive abnormalities, progress will require increased knowledge of meta-cognitive processes in normal subjects before pathological states can be understood, while the study of meta-cognitions in abnormal states may direct attention to their mechanisms in normal mental processes.

Testing predictions

The experimental methods reviewed above can help to identify the cognitive and other psychological abnormalities that characterize a particular psychiatric disorder. The nature of these abnormalities will usually suggest hypotheses about the way in which they might be important in maintaining the condition. Stronger evidence can be obtained by arranging experiments to test predictions arising from these hypotheses. Experiments of this kind can be illustrated by work on panic disorder and depressive disorder.

The cognitive hypothesis of panic disorder predicts that panic attacks will occur when a person attends to this arousal, ascribes it to a physical cause, and fears that it will have a catastrophic outcome (e.g., that palpitations will lead to a heart attack). It follows from the cognitive hypothesis that autonomic arousal from any cause can lead to panic provided that the two conditions are fulfilled, a prediction different from that of the fear of fear hypothesis, which suggests that the autonomic arousal leads to panic only when it is part of a fear response. The cognitive hypothesis predicts also that panic will be produced if catastrophic cognitions are activated directly; and that autonomic arousal will give rise to less panic if the catastrophic cognitions are reduced in strength.

There is considerable evidence in support of the first prediction that panic will be induced by autonomic arousal arising from any cause. Panic can be induced by hyperventilation (Gorman *et al.* 1984), carbon dioxide (CO_2) inhalation (Woods *et al.* 1988), lactate infusion (Liebowitz *et al.* 1985), and yohimbine (Charney *et al.* 1984), all of which increase autonomic arousal directly. Moreover, each of these chemical agents induces more anxiety in panic disorder patients than in healthy people. The second prediction from the cognitive hypothesis is that panic will be induced if the catastrophic cognitions are activated directly. This prediction is supported by the work of Ehlers *et al.* (1988) who induced panic by providing false information that heart rate had increased (when in fact it had not), a procedure that could not have the effect of producing anxiety directly and must act through cognitive processes. Panic patients and controls responded similarly to true feedback. However, panic patients who were led to believe that the rate was higher than the true rate developed more anxiety than normal controls receiving the same false feedback.

A further prediction from the cognitive hypothesis is that panic attacks will not occur when cognitions are inactivated at the time when patients are exposed to a stimulus which produces panic. Three experimental approaches have been used. In the first approach the inhalation of CO_2-enriched air was used as a known stimulus of panic attacks in patients with panic disorder (Rapee *et al.* 1986). Compared with the usual response to this agent the effect of CO_2 was reduced substantially in patients who had been reassured that the autonomic arousal produced by CO_2 was a normal and transient reaction and not hazardous. (Social phobics who underwent the same procedure had few panic attacks in either condition.) In another experiment, panic responses to CO_2 inhalation were reduced by telling patients that they could control the amount of CO_2 that they were breathing, although, in fact, they had no control over the amount they received (Sanderson *et al.* 1989). In a third kind of experiment (van der Molen *et al.* 1985) lactate infusions caused fewer panic attacks in normal subjects when they had been told that the infusion would cause pleasant excitement than when they were told it would cause anxiety. Patients with panic disorder are many times more likely to develop panic attacks during a lactate infusion than are normal subjects, so it is important to determine whether they respond in a similar way. In a related experiment, Clark *et al.* (in prep. (b)) divided panic disorder patients into two groups, both of which received a standardized infusion of sodium lactate. One group received a detailed and reassuring explanation of the nature of the infusion and its normal effects on autonomic activity. The other did not receive this information. The group which had received the reassuring explanation developed significantly fewer panic attacks than the other group.

Another example of the use of experimental methods to test a prediction is concerned with depressive disorder. During the course of cognitive therapy with depressed patients, two sessions were identified for experimental study and measurements were made of mood and of target depressive cognitions (Teasdale and Fennell 1982). In one session, cognitive therapy procedures were used to change the target cognitions; in the other session the patient talked about the cognitions and there was no attempt to change them. The sessions were presented in balanced order to each of a group of patients. Cognitions changed more in the former condition and, as predicted, mood also improved more in those sessions, confirming the original prediction.

Other studies have explored the effects of distraction on the intrusive thinking which is a prominent aspect of depressive disorders. The results are important since distraction is used as part of cognitive therapy for depression, on the basis that intrusive thoughts lower mood. Fennell *et al.* (1987) showed that when the level of depression was low, distraction had the desired effect of reducing the frequency of depressive thoughts and of producing an associated improvement of mood. However, when the severity of the depressive disorder was high and the pattern more 'endogenous', distraction produced less reduction of thought frequency, and no significant change in depressed mood. These findings point to the hazards of generalizing from studies of mild degrees of depression in healthy subjects to the more severe depressive disorders found in patients. There are three reasons why distraction may be less effective in more severely depressed patients. First, since low mood increases self-focus (Wood *et al.* 1990) there may be a greater difficulty in shifting focus from the intrusive thoughts when mood is lower. Secondly, clinical observations suggest that low mood increases the intensity of the intrusive thoughts and it seems plausible that it could be more difficult to switch attention away from more intense intrusive thoughts. Third, 'endogenous' disorders may have an aetiology different from the other depressive cases.

Distraction has been studied also during exposure treatment for anxiety disorders. There is evidence that it has the immediate effect of reducing anxiety but that in the long term there is less improvement in the disorder. For example, Sartory *et al.* (1982) found that following rapid exposure ('flooding'), anxiety was greater when subjects were distracted from the phobic situation immediately after the exposure than when subjects were required to think about the phobic situation at that time. Grayson *et al.* (1986) obtained a similar result when distraction was combined with exposure in patients with compulsive symptoms: in the distraction condition, anxiety was less during exposure but was greater subsequently. It seems likely that the effects of distraction depend on the meaning that the patient attaches to it at the time. If it is thought of as a form of escape from anxiety it may prolong the disorder. If it is thought of as part of a strategy to cope positively with anxiety it may have beneficial effects. This idea is considered further in the next section.

Factors that maintain cognitions

Experimental studies not only help to identify the cognitive abnormalities present in a psychiatric disorder, they can also suggest ways of changing them. Cognitions can be changed in two main ways. First, they can be altered directly by questioning their logical basis, presenting contrary arguments, or arranging experiences that show that they are unfounded — these methods are used, for example, in Beck's cognitive therapy for depression. Second, cognitions can be modified indirectly by removing factors that are preventing the changes that normally take place when people are confronted with information and experiences that are incongruent with their beliefs. (In practice, the two approaches overlap since removing maintaining factors results in change which helps, in turn, to disconfirm beliefs.) The second approach has as its starting point the question why abnormal cognitions are so resistant to change and are not modified by the kind of information and experiences that change normal beliefs. For example, panic disorder patients continue to fear that their symptoms will end in a heart attack even though none of their many panic attacks has ever ended in this way. The explanation for this paradox seems to be that certain of the coping strategies used by patients to reduce their immediate feelings of anxiety, have the additional and unintended effect of preventing longer-term cognitive change (Salkovskis 1991). Escape and avoidance are two obvious examples of such coping strategies; they prevent anxiety but at the same time deprive people of the opportunity to find out what would have happened had they stayed in the feared situation. Patients who expect that they will faint in a crowded shop and who always avoid or escape from such places, are never able to test the belief that they would have fainted had they remained in the shop, and so they continue to fear that this would happen were they to remain.

Escape and avoidance are two examples of a class of 'safety behaviours', that is, actions which bring about immediate relief from anxiety but have the long-term effect of maintaining abnormal cognitions. Other safety behaviours have been described in relation to panic disorder, agoraphobia, and social phobia, and these are related in an understandable way to patients' fearful cognitions. For example, people who fear fainting often use the safety behaviours of holding on to objects or tensing muscles, while people who fear a heart attack tend to employ the safety behaviours of relaxing and keeping still. These clinical observations have been confirmed by Salkovskis *et al.*

(1996) who examined the association between particular fears and particular behaviours and by Wells *et al.* (1995) who studied the role of safety behaviours in social phobia. In this condition, commonly used safety behaviours are avoiding eye contact, gripping objects tightly to avoid tremor, and taking deep breaths in an attempt to keep calm. Wells *et al.* (1995) exposed social phobic patients to an anxiety-provoking situation under two conditions: while continuing to use their usual safety behaviours during exposure, and while attempting to decrease these behaviours as much as possible. Measures of patients' beliefs in the feared catastrophes diminished significantly more in the group that had reduced their safety behaviours than in the group that had maintained them, a finding that is consistent with the hypothesis that safety behaviours maintain the fearful cognitions. Anxiety also fell more in the first group than in the second, confirming the link between cognition and emotion in these patients.

Another maintaining factor has been identified in studies of the intrusive thoughts. Salkovskis *et al.* (in press) asked subjects either to attempt to neutralize or simply to count intrusive thoughts provoked by a tape recording of that person's usual thoughts spoken aloud. Compared with the control group, the group which attempted to neutralize experienced more discomfort after the tape had stopped as well as a greater urge to continue suppressing the thoughts. Two other studies have demonstrated that attempts to suppress thoughts lead, after a short delay, to an increase in the frequency of the previously suppressed thoughts (Clark *et al.* 1991, 1993), although not all studies have confirmed this observation (e.g., Lavy and van den Hout 1990, who found an immediate enhancement but no delayed rebound after suppression). These findings are of interest because they suggest that thought suppression could set up a vicious circle which could maintain intrusive thoughts.

Attempts to suppress intrusive thoughts may play a part in the maintenance of post-traumatic stress disorder. Patients are more likely to suppress intrusions when the content is highly distressing, so it is possible that the more troublesome the thought the more they attempt to suppress and the greater the urge to keep on doing so. The amount of distress caused by an intrusive thought depends on the content, the meaning, and the person's feeling of responsibility. In keeping with this idea, intrusive memories in post-traumatic stress disorder are more frequent when the traumatic experience was thought of as uncontrollable and unpredictable (Foa *et al.* 1989, 1992; Baum *et al.* 1993). The meaning attached to an event at the time of the trauma, can change afterwards. An observation reported by Foa *et al.* (1989) makes the point: a rape victim developed post-traumatic stress disorder only after hearing that the rapist had killed the next victim. In obsessive–compulsive disorder, the patient's feeling of responsibility for the thoughts may increase the distress it causes: for example, thoughts with violent content will be more distressing if patients think that they are responsible for these thoughts, and if they think that they could act on them. If thoughts persist because they are repeatedly suppressed, and the amount of suppression depends on the distress they generate, which in turn depends on their meaning, and the person's feeling of responsibility for them then it would seem likely that to be effective, treatment should be directed not just to reducing suppression but also to changing meaning and feeling of responsibility.

These and similar findings indicate the potential importance of maintaining factors in preventing cognitive change. They also suggest that, in treatment, it could be more effective to modify maintaining factors than to attempt to change cognitions directly by reasoning or questioning.

Conclusions

Although selective and incomplete this review has shown some of the ways in which the experimental study of normal and abnormal cognitive processes can inform the development of cognitive treatment. Also, the study of factors that bring about change in abnormal states provides a useful focus for studies of cognitive processes. Abnormal states of mind can draw attention to key features of normal cognitive processes in the same way that abnormalities of the cardiac or renal function focus attention on key aspects of the normal working of the heart or kidney.

Despite the advances that have been made in experimental cognitive psychology in recent years, there are many unanswered questions about the processes involved in abnormal states. In particular, we lack information about visual imagery and worry, two prominent and persistent features of abnormal emotional states. For this reason, cognitive therapy cannot be based solely on the results of scientific investigations of normal subjects, nor can they derive exclusively from experimental studies of psychopathological states. Instead, scientific findings have to be combined with clinical observations, although scientific methods can be used to sharpen and test these clinical observations. When experimental methods are used in this way, it is generally more fruitful to construct low-level hypotheses about the relationship between variables than to use more ambitious models of mental functioning. This use of the scientific method can help to identify features of abnormal states that enhance or maintain the basic disorder. It seems likely that it will be fruitful to focus on factors that maintain these key features as well as attempting to change them directly.

Whether the focus of treatment is mainly on changing cognitions, or mainly on removing maintaining factors, the therapist's time is likely to be used more effectively if it is employed in bringing about change in a few target cognitions and behaviours, and not diffused by employing a wide spectrum of techniques directed to a range of target behaviours and cognitions. An analogy might be drawn between the advances in psychopharmacology that follow when drugs with a wide spectrum of actions can be replaced by newer compounds with targeted actions on specific receptors. This advance in psychopharmacology has resulted from a combination of basic research and studies with patients, and it seems likely that progress in cognitive therapy will be achieved most rapidly if knowledge from basic cognitive psychology is combined with experimental studies of patients of the kind that have been illustrated here.

References

Barlow, D. H., Craske, M. G., Cerny, J. A., *et al.* (1989). Behavioural treatment of panic disorder. *Behaviour Research and Therapy*, 20, 261–82.

Baum, A., Cohen, L., and Hall, M. (1993). Control and intrusive memories as possible determinants of chronic stress. *Psychosomatic Medicine*, 55, 274–86.

Beck, A. T. (1964a). Thinking and depression. I. Idiosyncratic content and cognitive distortions. *Archives of General Psychiatry*, 9, 324–33.

Beck, A. T. (1964b). Thinking and depression. II. Theory and therapy. *Archives of General Psychiatry*, 10, 561–71.

Beck, A. T. (1976). *Cognitive therapy and the emotional disorders*. International Universities Press, New York.

Beck, A. T., Laude, R., and Bohnert, M. (1974). Ideational components of anxiety neurosis. *Archives of General Psychiatry*, 31, 319–325.

Beck, A. T., Freeman, A. *et al.* (1990). *Cognitive therapy of personality disorders*. Guilford Press, New York.

Borkovec, T. D. and Hu, S. (1990). The effect of worry on cardiovascular response to phobic imagery. *Behaviour Research and Therapy*, 28, 69–73.

Borkovec, T. D. and Inz, J. (1990). The nature of worry in generalized anxiety disorder: a predominance of thought activity. *Behaviour Research and Therapy*, 28, 153–8.

Bower, G. H. (1981). Mood and memory. *American Psychologist*, 36, 129–48.

Breger, L. and McGaugh, J. L. (1965). Critique and reformulation of "learning theory approaches" to psychotherapy and neurosis. *Psychological Bulletin*, 63, 338–58.

Butler, G., Wells, A., and Dewick, H. (1995). Differential effects of worry and imager after exposure to a stressful stimulus. *Behavioural and Cognitive Psychotherapy*, 23, 45–56.

Carver, C. S. and Blaney, P. M. (1977). Perceived arousal, focus of attention and avoidance behaviour. *Journal of Abnormal Psychology*, 86, 154–162.

Charney, D. S., Heninger, G. R., and Breier, A. (1984). Noradrenergic function in panic anxiety. *Archives of General Psychiatry*, 41, 751–783.

Clark, D. M. (1983). On the induction of depressed mood in the laboratory: evaluation and comparison of the velten and musical procedures. *Advanced Behaviour Research and Therapy*, 5, 27–49.

Clark, D. M. (1989). Anxiety states: panic and generalized anxiety. In *Cognitive behaviour therapy for psychiatric problems* (ed. K. Hawton, P. M. Salkovskis, J. Kirk, and D. M. Clark), pp. 97–128 Oxford University Press.

Clark, D. M. and Teasdale, J. D. (1982). Diurnal variation in clinical depression and accessibility of memories of positive and negative experiences. *Journal of Abnormal Psychology*, 91, 87–95.

Clark, D. M. and Yuen, P. K. (in prep.). Social anxiety and an attentional bias away from negative faces.

Clark, D.M., Ball, S., and Pape, D. (1991). An experimental investigation of thought suppression. *Behaviour Research and Therapy*, 29, 253–7.

Clark, D. M. Winton, E., and Thynn, L. (1993). A further experimental investigation of thought suppression. *Behaviour Research and Therapy*, 31, 207–10.

Clark, D. M., Salkovskis, P. M., Ost, L.-G., Westling, B., Koehler, K. and Gelder, M. G. (submitted). Assessing misinterpretation of bodily sensations in panic disorder: the body sensations interpretations questionnaire.

Clark D. M., Salkovskis, P. M., Martin, H., Koehler, K., and Gelder, M. G. (in prep. *a*). Psychological priming in panic disorder.

Clark, D. M., Salkovskis, P. M., Middleton, H., Anastasiades, P., Hackmann, A. and Gelder, M. G. (in prep. *b*). Cognitive mediation of lactate induced panic.

Coyne, J. C. and Gotlib, I. H. (1983). The role of cognition in depression: a critical appraisal. *Psychological Bulletin*, 94, 472–505.

Deutscher, S. and Cimbolic, P. (1990). Cognitive processes and their relationship to endogenous and reactive components of depression. *Journal of Nervous and Mental Disease*, 178, 351–9.

Ehlers, A. and Breuer, P. (1992). Increased cardiac awareness in panic disorder. *Journal of Abnormal Psychology*, 101, 371–82.

Ehlers, A. and Breuer, P. (1995). Selective attention to physical threat in subjects with panic attacks and simple phobias. *Journal of Anxiety Disorders*, 9, 11–31.

Ehlers, A. and Steil, R. (1995). Maintenance of intrusive memories in post-traumatic stress disorder: A cognitive approach. *Behavioural and Cognitive Psychotherapy*, 23, 217–49.

Ehlers, A., Margraf, J., Roth, W. T., Taylor, C. B. and Birbaumer, N. (1988). Anxiety produced by false heart rate feedback in patients with panic disorder. *Behaviour Research and Therapy*, 26, 1–11.

Fennell, M. J. V., Teasdale, J. D., Jones, S., and Damle., A. (1987). Distraction in neurotic and endogenous depression: An investigation of negative thinking in major depressive disorder. *Psychological Medicine*, 17, 441–52.

Foa, E. B., Steketee, G., and Rothbaum, B. O. (1989). Behavioural/cognitive conceptualizations of post-traumatic stress disorder. *Behaviour Therapy*, 20, 155–76.

Foa, E. B., Zinbarg, R., and Rothbaum, B. O. (1992). Uncontrollability and unpredictability in post-traumatic stress disorder: An animal model. *Psychological Bulletin*, 112, 218–38.

Freud, S. (1895). Über die Berechtigung, von der Neurasthenie einen bestimmten Symptomcomplex als "Angstneurose" abzutrennen. *Neurologische Zentralblatt*, 14, 50–66.

Gordon, P. K. (1985). Allocation of attention in obsessional disorder. *British Journal of Psychiatry*, 47, 517–23.

Gorman, J. M., Askanazi, J., Liebowitz, M. R., Fyer, A. J., Stein, J., Kinney, J. M., and Klein, D. F. (1984). Response to hyperventilation in a group of patients with panic disorder. *American Journal of Psychiatry*, 141, 857–61.

Grayson, J. B., Foa, E. B., and Steketee, G. S. (1986). Exposure *in vivo* of obsessive–compulsives under distracting and attention-focusing conditions: Replication and extension. *Behaviour Research and Therapy*, 24, 475–79.

Hibbert, G. A. (1984). Ideational components of anxiety: their origin and content. *British Journal of Psychiatry*, 144, 618–24.

Hollon, S. D. and Kendall, P. C. (1980). Cognitive self-statements in depression: Development of an automatic thoughts questionnaire. *Cognitive Therapy and Research*, 4, 383–95.

Ingram, R. E. and Smith, T. W. (1984). Depression and internal versus external focus of attention. *Cognitive Therapy and Research*, 8, 139–52.

Johannson, J. and Ost, L. G. (1982). Perception of autonomic reactions and actual heart rate in phobic patients. *Journal of Behavioural Assessment*, 4, 133–43.

Lavy, E. and van den Hout, M. (1990). Thought suppression induced intrusions. *Behavioural Psychotherapy*, 18, 251–8.

Last, C. G. and O'Brien, G. T. (1985). The relationship between cognition and anxiety. *Behaviour Modification*, 9, 235–41.

Lefebvre, M. F. (1981). Cognitive distortion and cognitive errors in depressed psychiatric and low back pain patients. *Journal of Consulting and Clinical Psychology*, 49, 517–25.

Liebowitz, M. R., Fyer, A. J., Gorman, J. M., Dillon, D., Davies, S., Stein, J. M., *et al.* (1985). Specificity of lactate infusions in social phobia versus panic disorders. *American Journal of Psychiatry*, 142, 947–50.

Lloyd, G. G. and Lishman, W. A. (1975). Effects of depression on the speed of recall of pleasant and unpleasant experiences. *Psychological Medicine*, 5, 173–80.

Mandler, G., Mandler, J. M., and Uviller, E. T. (1958). Autonomic feedback: The perception of autonomic activity. *Journal of Abnormal and Social Psychology*, 56, 367–373.

Marks, M. P., Basoglu, M., Alkubaisy, T., Sengun, S., and Marks, I. M. (1991). Are anxiety symptoms and catastrophic cognitions directly related? *Journal of Anxiety Disorders*, 5, 247-254.

Nelson, T.O. and Narens, L. (1990). Metamemory: A theoretical framework and some new findings. In *The psychology of learning and memory*, (ed. G Bower). Academic Press, New York.

Ottaviani, R. and Beck, A. T. (1987). Cognitive aspects of panic disorders. *Journal of Anxiety Disorders*, 1, 15–28.

Pennebaker, J.W. (1989). Confession, inhibition and disease. *Advances in Experimental Social Psychology*, 22, 211–44.

Rapee, R., Mattick, R., and Murrell, E. (1986). Cognitive mediation in the affective component of spontaneous panic attacks. *Journal of Behaviour Therapy and Experimental Psychiatry*, 17, 245–53.

Salkovskis, P. M. (1991). The importance of behaviour in the maintenance of anxiety and panic: a cognitive account. *Behavioural Psychotherapy*, 19, 6–19.

Salkovskis, P. M., Clark, D. M., and Gelder, M. G. (1996). Cognitive-behaviour links in the persistence of panic. *Behaviour Research and Therapy*, 34, 453–458.

Salkovskis, P. M., Westbrook, D., Davis, J., *et al.* (in press). Effects of neutralizing on intrusive thoughts: an experiment on the aetiology of obsessive–compulsive disorder. *Behaviour Research and Therapy*.

Sanderson, W. C., Rapee, R. M., and Barlow, D. H. (1989). The influence of an illusion of control on panic attacks induced via inhalation of 5.5 per cent carbon dioxide enriched air. *Archives of General Psychiatry*, 46, 157–62.

Sartory, G., Rachman, S., and Grey, S. J. (1982). Return of fear: The role of rehearsal. *Behaviour Research and Therapy*, 20, 123–34.

Scheier, M. F. and Carver, C. S. (1977). *Scripts, plans, goals and understanding*. Erlbaum, Hillsdale, NJ.

Smith, T.W. and Greenberg, J. (1981). Depression and self-focused attention. *Motivation and Emotion*, 5, 323–33.

Stopa, L. and Clark, D. M. (1993). Cognitive processes in social phobia. *Behaviour Research and Therapy*, 31, 255–67.

Teasdale, J. D. and Fennell, M. J. V. (1982). Immediate effects of cognitive therapy interventions. *Cognitive Therapy and Research*, 6, 343–52.

Teasdale, J. D. and Fogarty, S. J. (1979). Differential effects of induced mood on retrieval of pleasant and unpleasant events from episodic memory. *Journal of Abnormal Psychology*, 88, 248–57.

Teasdale, J. D., Taylor, R., and Fogarty, S. J. (1980). Effects of induced elation-depression on the accessibility of memories of happy and unhappy experiences. *Behaviour Research and Therapy*, 18, 339–46.

van den Hout, M. A., van der Molen, G. M., Griez, E., and Lousberg, H. (1987). Specificity of interoceptive fear to panic disorders. *Journal of Psychopathology and Behavioural Assessment*, 9, 99–106.

van der Molen, G. M., van den Hout, M. A., Vroemen, J., Lousberg, H., and Griez, E. (1985). Cognitive determinants of lactate induced anxiety. *Behaviour Research and Therapy*, 24, 677–80.

Wells, A. (1985). Relationship between private self-consciousness and anxiety scores in threatening situations. *Psychological Reports*, 57, 1063–66.

Wells, A. and Matthews, G. (1994). *Attention and emotion*. Erlbaum, Hove, UK.

Wells, A. and Morrison, A. P. (1994). Qualitative dimensions of normal worry and normal obsessions: a comparative study. *Behaviour Research and Therapy*, 32, 867–70.

Wells, A., Clark, D. M., Salkovskis, P., Ludgate, J. Hackman, A., and Gelder, M. G. (1995). Social phobia: The role of in-situation safety behaviours in maintaining anxiety and negative beliefs. *Behaviour Therapy*, 26, 153–61.

Winton, E., Clark, D. M., and Ehlers, A. (Submitted). Cognitive factors in persistent versus transient post-PTSD following sexual or physical assault.

Wolpe, J. and Lazarus, A. (1966). *Behaviour therapy techniques: A guide to the treatment of neurosis*. Pergamon, Oxford.

Wood, J. V., Salzberg, A., and Goldsamt, L. A. (1990). Does affect induced self-focussed attention? *Journal of Personality and Social Psychology*, 58, 899–908.

Woods, S. W., Charney, D. S., Goodman, W. K., and Heninger, G. R. (1988). Carbon dioxide-induced anxiety. *Archives of General Psychiatry*, 45, 43–52.

3

Information-processing biases in emotional disorders

Andrew Mathews

The nature of information-processing in cognition and emotion

'I know that nothing terrible is going to happen, but I can't stop worrying about it'. How are we to understand the mental process being described in this comment? There are several subsidiary questions that need to be clarified before a full answer can be given, including the following: (1) how can there be a contradiction between knowledge that nothing will happen and the feeling that it will? (2) what makes worrying thoughts come into mind 'out of the blue'?; (3) why can we not stop worrying whenever we want?

The information-processing approach to cognition and emotion does not directly answer such questions, but it does provide two very useful tools for their investigation: a general framework for generating specific hypotheses; and a set of experimental methods for testing them. A number of core assumptions are made in this approach, some of which are briefly mentioned below. First, it is assumed that the mental operations in both cognition and emotion depend on the acquisition, transformation, and storage of information, about the world and ourselves, in various specialized modules that are themselves interconnected. Because the potential amount of information available is extremely large, while the capacities of the modules must be limited, only some information can be fully processed, and the rest will be partially processed, or not at all. As a result, it is assumed that there must be mechanisms to determine the selection of information, such as attention.

Different modules within the system are assumed to be able to handle information in parallel, so that different aspects of an event may be processed simultaneously. However, there are some processes that must depend on sequential operations, because a later process cannot begin until it receives output from an earlier one. For present purposes, perceptual pick-up of information from the environment can be considered as one stage in a sequence, interpretation of meaning as another, and storage of the resulting meaning as yet another, although these stages may often follow complex cycles. The first stage in reading the word 'palm', for example, is the 'bottom-up' perceptual resolution of lines on paper; access to memory for possible words then directs further 'top-down' attentional search to provide confirmation of a likely match; but final interpretation of meaning might depend on integration with input from other words close by (e.g., palm–tree vs. palm–hand).

The information-processing framework assumes that many of these operations can proceed without awareness: indeed, most routine or well-practised mental operations are presumed to be automatic and non-conscious. Certain products of these routine processes may then reach awareness, and allow the operation of consciously controlled processes, such as intentional search for a wanted object, or reflective thought about a problem. Unlike automatic processes that can operate in parallel, these controlled processes seem to draw on limited resources, such that we can only do one such task at a time. So, for example, I can perform a relatively automated procedure such as driving without it interfering too much with my thinking about what I will do at work. But if someone engages me in conversation about something else, then I will have to stop thinking about work for the time being.

A critical hypothesis underlying the research to be discussed here, and elsewhere in this book, is that emotions arise from the operation of cognitive processes. It may seem obvious that some normal emotions, such as pride, depend in part on conscious thoughts (e.g., about my self-worth or achievements): but it is less obvious that *all* emotional states do so, let alone emotional disorders. It is quite possible, however, that all normal emotions arise from cognitive evaluations of events, but that the processes involved in generating them are often automatic and non-conscious. Only after becoming aware of the outcome of automatic emotion-generating processes, in the form of conscious thoughts and feelings, are we able to exert some degree of intentional control over these outcomes. If so, then emotional disorders could also be understood as a product of similar non-conscious evaluations, which have become sufficiently strong to overcome our conscious attempts to control them.

Returning then to the problem described at the beginning of this chapter: what hypotheses would the information-processing approach suggest to account for reports of persistent worry, despite claims of knowing that nothing will really happen? One possibility is that these two cognitive products represent the output of different processing modules. Propositional knowledge of low actuarial risk may be the product of controlled thought, but other forms of knowledge in memory, that are accessed more automatically, could influence the thoughts and feelings that reach awareness. Tentative answers to the questions posed earlier might therefore be as follows: (1) contradictions between propositional knowledge and feelings can arise because they are the product of different types of cognitive process; (2) worrying thoughts can seem to come 'out of the blue' because the generating process is non-conscious; and (3) we cannot always stop worrying because of the limited nature of conscious control. Such speculative descriptions are clearly inadequate, however: the information-processing approach demands that we formulate such hypotheses in testable form, and submit them to experiment. It is to this research that we now turn.

Biases in information-processing

Because some degree of selection among varieties of available information is inevitable, decisions have to be taken as to what is to be processed, and what is discarded. Bias is used here to describe any systematic preference in the priorities used in making such decisions, particularly those influencing the selection or rejection of information having emotional meaning. The speculations above would lead us to suppose that individuals prone to negative emotional states such as anxiety or depression should be more likely to select information congruent with negative mood. Selection of this sort can occur at many points in the processing of emotional information, and for purposes of convenience, the relevant findings will be grouped under the headings of perceptual encoding, interpretation, and memory.

Perceptual encoding

The simplest way of investigating perceptual encoding is to present emotional stimuli, such as words or pictures, and assess the ease with which different subject groups can identify them. For example, Powell and Hemsley (1984) found that depressed patients recognized a higher proportion of negative to neutral words than did controls, when these were presented very rapidly (7–100 milliseconds). Similar findings were reported more recently by von Hippel et al. (1994), who also found that the more accurate identification of negative words in depressed students applied only to words given extreme ratings by that individual on a self-description task. Equivalent effects emerged when the students were divided according to their score on a measure of trait (but not state) anxiety, suggesting that some enduring characteristic is involved.

One problem with drawing definite conclusions from tasks that require identification of emotional stimuli is that subjects may vary in their willingness to report them. MacLeod et al. (1987) argued that the above data may not reflect a perceptual encoding difference so much as a response bias. That is, after perceiving partial cues as to the nature of a word, depressed or anxious subjects may be more (or less) willing to guess at negative candidates. This should apply less to some other tasks, such as lexical decisions, in which subjects do not have to say the word, but simply decide if a letter string is a legitimate word or not. In lexical decision tasks, group differences have typically not been found (Clark *et al.* 1983; MacLeod *et al.* 1987).

Although response bias may thus account for some effects, it does not seem sufficient to account for all of them, since significant effects in a mood-congruent direction were found when two stimuli were presented simultaneously in a lexical decision task (Macleod and Mathews 1991; Mogg *et al.* 1991). Rather, it may be that whether or not encoding differences are found between groups depends critically on competition among processing options. That is, when the task forces subjects to choose among several possible targets or responses that differ in their emotional significance, then individual differences in emotionality are likely to influence which is selected. When only one target or response is available, then there is no scope for selective processes to influence the outcome.

Another method of investigating perceptual encoding is to present briefly competing stimuli, and use detection latencies for probes in positions corresponding to these stimuli to assess the allocation of attention. For example, if two words are presented simultaneously for 500 milliseconds, and then one of them is replaced by a probe dot that subjects are to detect, anxious patients are quicker to detect the probe if it replaces a threatening rather than a neutral word (MacLeod *et al.* 1986). The implication is that clinically anxious patients are more likely to attend to an emotional stimulus in a perceptual array than are non-anxious control subjects. This selective attention effect is stronger when there is a match between the stimuli presented and the current concerns (e.g., worries) of the individual (Mogg *et al.* 1992). Thus, panic disorder patients attend to physically threatening words (e.g., collapse, death) but less so to socially threatening words (e.g., failure, stupid; Asmundson *et al.* 1992). Selective attention is not always directed outwardly, but can be self-focused, if the individuals perceive their own reactions to be the source of threat. Panic patients not only attend to physically threatening words, but are particularly attentive to bodily sensations, and are more accurate at detecting them (Ehlers and Breuer 1992). Similarly, socially phobic patients may be very attentive to their own behaviour in social situations because they fear that their reactions (e.g., trembling hands) may be visible to others (Clark and Wells 1995).

A third method of investigating selective encoding is to use tasks in which emotional stimuli are present as distractors, so that if they attract attention this will cause interference with the other task. For example, when searching for a neutral target among distractor words, anxious patients are slowed more by threatening than by neutral distractors, presumably because their attention is captured by the former (Mathews *et al.* 1990, 1995). By far the most commonly used interference task, however, is colour naming, in which subjects are required to call out the colours in which words are displayed while ignoring their meaning. Words whose meaning matches the emotional concerns of the individual concerned typically cause slowed colour-naming performance. This finding has been reported in patients with anxiety disorders, depression, and eating disorders; and is probably present in many others (for a review, see Williams *et al.* in press).

Although it is not certain that the three approaches briefly reviewed here share a common mechanism, the tasks that have revealed encoding differences all involve selection among processing options. The implication is that emotionality is not associated with differences in the speed or efficiency of processing emotional events *per se*, but with the allocation of priority to such events when choices become necessary. This distinction is revealed most clearly in experiments where a similar task is performed with or without competing options. Thus, although anxious patients were never faster than controls on lexical decisions for single threatening words, they were relatively speeded in decisions for threatening words when these were presented simultaneously with other non-threatening stimuli (Macleod and Mathews 1991; Mogg *et al.* 1991).

Rather than consider hypotheses about these allocation mechanisms in greater detail, the present focus will be on the probable consequences of such selection. The most obvious generalization is that selective encoding favours emotional information when it matches current emotional concerns. Thus, if emotionally disordered individuals are particularly worried about a specific threat, then they will attend to cues (internal or external) that are associated with it, or will be distracted by the same cues when performing other tasks. In so doing, they are presumably accumulating information in memory about threatening aspects of events, at the expense of other aspects. Selective encoding processes may thus have the potential for maintaining or exacerbating emotional states, or if reversed, for reducing them.

Interpretation of meaning

A different sort of selection is made when encountering ambiguous events: many alternative meanings may be accessed, of which one will become dominant while others are suppressed. Many real-life social situations have considerable potential for ambiguity; for example, a friend or partner who seems to be ignoring you may really disapprove of something you have done, or may merely be distracted by his/her own problems. Equally, physical sensations are often ambiguous in meaning. The way in which such ambiguous events are interpreted often seems to play an important part in anxiety disorders. For example, someone with hypochondriacal anxiety expressed the fear that her dry throat meant she had cancer. When told by her doctor no treatment was needed, she interpreted this as meaning that she was beyond help and about to die.

The resolution of ambiguity has been studied with a variety of verbal material, ranging from single words to complex texts. In two studies, Eysenck *et al.* (1991) had anxious patients listen to ambiguous sentences such as 'The Doctor checked little Emily's growth', and then later rate disambiguated versions such as 'The Doctor measured little Emily's height' or 'The Doctor examined little Emily's cancer'. Relative to controls, anxious patients were more likely to endorse the more threatening version as having the same meaning as the sentence that they had heard previously. Subjects who had recovered from an earlier anxiety disorder were similar to, or even more positive than, the normal controls. In an attempt to rule out response bias, additional foil sentences that were not possible interpretations of an original were included in a second experiment. Anxious patients did not differ from controls in rejecting threatening foils, and a signal detection analysis confirmed that the group differed only in sensitivity to possible threatening versus neutral interpretations.

A similar conclusion was drawn in a study of interpretations made by panic patients as they were reading (Clark *et al.* 1988). Subjects read incomplete sentences, such as 'If my thinking were unusual I could be . . .', immediately followed by single words that they were to pronounce out loud as fast as they could. The panic patients were faster when pronouncing threatening completion words (such as 'insane') than neutral or positive words (such as 'clever'), but only when preceded by the appropriate incomplete sentence. The implication is that a threatening inference had been made by panic patients as they read the incomplete sentence, and that this speeded their recognition of the threatening, but not the neutral, target word.

We are currently working on experiments that extend these findings to inferences about complex events, in which the implied threat is inherent in the whole situation rather than single words or sentences, such as an interview for a job. Anxious and non-anxious subjects were asked to imagine themselves as the candidate as they read descriptions of interviews, and at various points of uncertainty in the text, made speeded decisions about words that matched either possible threatening or benign inferences. For example, just after reading: 'As the interviewer asks you the first question, all your preparation is . . . ', subjects might be asked to decide if 'forgotten' is a real word or not.

Anxious subjects were speeded when making such decisions for words matching threatening inferences, but only when the words were placed in the text at the point where such inferences were possible (Hirsch and Mathews, submitted). We believe that this constitutes convincing evidence that anxious individuals spontaneously make inferences about uncertain emotional events, which tend to confirm their perception of these events as personally threatening.

The evidence that anxious patients, relative to normal controls, are inclined towards threatening interpretations of ambiguous information is thus fairly strong. Several questions need to be addressed in future work, such as whether this bias is specific to current concerns, as seems to be the case with attentional selection. None the less, the research so far suggests that similar biases operate on the selection of interpretations as has been established for attention. Again, the congruence between the interpretations that are favoured and the emotional state of the individual suggests a causal link between them. That is, anxiety states may increase the probability of making threatening interpretations of ambiguous events, but these interpretations seem likely to maintain or further elevate anxious mood.

Implicit and explicit memory

The research already described on biases in attention and interpretation suggests that patients with emotional disorders will select congruent information from their experience and store it in memory. Thus, whether or not they have experienced more objectively negative events in real life, they may well recall more of them. Indeed, there is good evidence from tests of autobiographical memory, that when asked to recall past events both depressed and anxious patients will produce more negative examples in a limited time than will normal controls (Teasdale 1983; Burke and Mathews 1992). But does this represent a bias in memory, or simply a greater number of actual negative events in memory to choose from? To resolve this difficulty, researchers have presented positive and negative words to subject groups, and then tested for differential memory under experimental conditions.

Depressed patients consistently show a memory bias in that they recall fewer positive words, and (relatively) more negative words, than do normal mood controls. However, there appear to be definite limiting conditions to this phenomenon. The effect is stronger for words describing negative personality traits (Clark and Teasdale 1985) and disappears when subjects encode the words by judging whether the words describe someone else (Bradley and Mathews 1983). More problematic is the failure to find consistent effects in anxiety: some studies find evidence of a bias in favour of better recall for threatening words (McNally *et al.* 1989), while others find the reverse (e.g., Mogg *et al.* 1987). Such a mixed pattern could be due to clinical characteristics of the various groups, or it could reflect the variable use of different strategies. For example, some subjects might choose to use negative self-descriptors (or some other category) as an aid to recall, and thus generate many words of that type, while others may use different strategies, or none at all. Thus, Mogg and Mathews (1990) noted that although their anxious subjects did recall more negative words, they also produced more intrusion errors of the same type, as might be expected if they were using a generate-and-recognize strategy.

An alternative approach in memory research has been to use so-called implicit memory tasks, in which memory is indirectly assessed, without the explicit request to use recall or recognition. If subjects have been exposed to a word list, and are then asked to complete letter stems (e.g., wor..?) with the first word that comes to mind, they are more likely to complete stems with previously seen words, even if they fail to recognize them as such. (For example, readers may have thought of word, or worry, rather than work, world, worm, worn, worse, or worship.) Similarly, recently seen words are more likely to be accurately identified when exposed very briefly (e.g., for 33 milliseconds before being masked). In this way, it is claimed, non-conscious aspects of memory can be assessed using facilitation or priming effects, while avoiding the influence of intentional strategies. In some studies of this type, stronger priming effects on threatening words have been reported for anxious subjects (Mathews *et al.* 1990; MacLeod and McLaughlin 1995; but see Mathews *et al.* 1995, for negative results). In depressed samples, results have been more negative (Watkins *et al.* 1992; Denny and Hunt 1992) but again there are some contrary positive findings (Watkins *et al.* 1996). It is possible that priming effects in anxiety are stronger with perceptually-driven tasks, such as word identification (e.g., Macleod and Maclaughlin 1995), and in depression with conceptually driven tasks, such as word association (Watkins *et al.* in press). However, it is too early to come to any firm conclusions about this confusing pattern of evidence with implicit tasks.

In explicit memory tasks, however, it is possible to conclude that depressed patients consistently show a recall bias favouring negative trait descriptors which have been related to themselves. Another interesting finding in depression (Williams 1992) is that personal emotional memories tend to be general ('When I lived alone') rather than specific ('Driving home last night'). It is likely that both these findings reflect a habitual style of thinking in terms of generic emotional categories (e.g., 'Things that are wrong with me') rather than of specific episodes. Such an encoding style may make it difficult to later reinterpret events as having any meaning other than that originally imposed on them.

Automatic and controlled processing

Fully automated processes have several distinguishing features: they are unintended, uncontrollable once begun, and require neither awareness nor limited-capacity resources. As Bargh (1989) has pointed out, however, these features do not always coexist, so that partially automated processes may have some but not all of them. Bargh and Tota (1988) showed that in depressed (but not normal) subjects, negative judgements about oneself are not slowed by having to perform another task simultaneously. Because these judgements are therefore judged to be independent of limited-capacity resources, they are in a sense automatic, but they cannot be completely unintended, since they were produced on request. Similarly, Nolan-Hoeksema (1991) has shown that ruminative thinking in depressives causes prolongation of negative mood, although subjects do not appear to be aware of the connection. Despite being unaware of the process, it is clearly not uncontrollable, since it is possible to start and stop ruminating if motivated to do so. This mixture of automatic and controlled features seems to be characteristic of some emotional effects, such as the memory bias in depression described above.

It is commonly assumed that biases which persist despite subjects being able to report on the presence of the eliciting stimuli, must be strongly automatic. That is, if you do not even know that an emotional cue is present, how could you intend or control your reactions? Accordingly, interference due to emotional words that are not attended, or are presented out of awareness, is taken as evidence that selective biases are automatic. In one such study, Mogg *et al.* (1993) presented different kinds of emotional words under two conditions: either they were clearly visible, or were shown for only 16 milliseconds before being covered by a pattern mask. In the latter condition, subjects were unable to guess above chance levels whether the mask had concealed a word or not. In both cases, the background to the word was coloured, and anxious, depressed, or control subjects named the colour as rapidly as possible. Anxious, but not depressed, patients were significantly slowed by negative words, even when they were presented out of awareness.

Although awareness of specific words was clearly absent, the interference observed in colour naming does indicate that the non-conscious detection of an emotional word resulted in demands being placed on limited resources. That is, even if the detection of an emotional stimulus is automatic, it can initiate other processes that take up attentional capacity. We suggest that all valenced stimuli are evaluated non-consciously, and if the relevant decision mechanism is sufficiently activated, further resources will then be directed to analyse it more fully. Such a fuller analysis would presumably involve attention being directed to the relevant location and meaning, thus interrupting other ongoing tasks. In this way, the early automatic detection of potential threat can eventually lead to more controlled processes being deployed, and appropriate action being taken. The experimental results described here therefore suggest that the decision mechanism initiating attentional processes is too readily activated in anxious patients.

The conditions used in the above experiment are obviously artificial, and it does not seem likely that such brief stimulus displays are reproduced very often in everyday life. However, a very similar pattern of results emerges from experiments in which stimuli are neither very brief nor masked, but simply occur while subjects are preoccupied with another task. In a dichotic listening study, for example, threatening (but not neutral) words played in one ear caused slowed performance in anxious patients, although they were attending to the other ear, and denied hearing any of the critical words (Mathews and McLeod 1986). It is not a great leap from this result to the suggestion that fleeting events, thoughts, sensations, and so on, occurring under the conditions of divided attention that are very common in real life, would also be selectively processed. In this way, threatening cues might be partially encoded even though the person concerned would not be fully aware of their source. Such a process might provide an explanation for vague feelings of anxiety that are experienced despite people being unable to explain how they arose.

Although the data discussed above strongly suggests that emotional encoding is partly automatic, it must be emphasized that controlled processing is also involved, and the two probably interact. That is, even if the early detection of threat is automatic, this will typically direct attention towards the relevant location, leading to awareness of it. Thereafter, the observer may choose to search for and fixate such stimuli and thus add to the original effect (see D. E. Broadbent and M. Broadbent 1988, for an example). The final result may thus depend on a complex product of early automatic selection, followed by either further controlled processing of the same information, or deliberate avoidance.

Content specificity

In studies of attention to emotional words it is commonly found that the strongest effects occur when the meaning of the words matches the main concern or worry of the subjects tested. If patients are asked to describe their main worry, then interference in colour naming, and attention to word location, are more marked for words describing those worries (Mogg *et al.* 1989, 1992). Even positive words can apparently cause interference, if they are semantically associated with these emotional concerns (Martin *et al.* 1991; Mathews and Klug 1993). Furthermore, even normal subjects show similar effects, if words are specifically chosen to describe the individuals' current concerns (Rieman and McNally 1995). It is of interest that, at least on the basis of the results of Mogg *et al.* (1993) using masked presentations, content specificity effects are less marked at the earliest stages of processing. Anxious patients were slowed by all negative words, including those chosen to be more relevant to depression. This suggests that the first non-conscious evaluation of stimuli simply classifies them as negative or positive, and a more detailed appraisal of specific content follows later.

Memory tasks can also reveal content-specificity effects. As indicated earlier, memory bias in depression is most marked for negative trait-adjectives that have been encoded in relation to oneself. While replicating this effect, Watkins *et al.* (1992), found that depressed patients showed no signs of preferential recall for physically threatening words (that hold attention in anxiety). Thus, in tasks sensitive to later stages, beyond the mere classification of emotional valence, it seems that selection becomes progressively more specific, homing in on the topics of most pressing emotional concern. Under most circumstances this would be an adaptive way of focusing limited resources on the topic of greatest importance to that individual. However, in vulnerable individuals it may also lead to a specific focus on the very information most associated with anxiety or depression, making these feelings difficult to control.

Differences among disorders

The foregoing review has highlighted two apparent differences across emotional disorders. One of these is the variations in the cognitive content of worries or concerns typically reported by the various diagnostic groups, and correspondingly in the type of material that produces the most marked biases. Depressed patients ruminate about personal inadequacies and past failures, and memory bias is present only for events relevant to these topics, rather than for all negative information. Panic patients show attentional bias effects for physically threatening stimuli matching their fears, but not for socially threatening stimuli. The concordance between self-report and information-processing measures is reassuring, and has even prompted some researchers to suggest using the latter as clinical assessment tools in cases where self-report is suspect. Thus far, however, content differences across disorders have been most useful in evaluating psychological theories. Both the differential activation model of depression (Teasdale 1988) and the catastrophic misinterpretation model of panic (Clark *et al.* 1988) have found support from findings that the strongest bias effects occur for material matching the domain postulated to be the critical maintaining feature of that disorder.

The second apparent difference across disorders is in the type of *process* that reveals the bias most reliably. Explicit memory biases are more consistently found in depression than in anxiety. On the other hand, perceptual encoding effects seem more reliably found in anxiety disorders than in depression. This is not to say that exceptions to this rule cannot be found: in fact there are several. None the less, the overall pattern seems striking (see Mathews and MacLeod 1994, for a review). Equally striking is the data from patients with mixed diagnoses. An additional diagnosis of depression seems to block masked interference effects in patients who are just as anxious as those with the single diagnosis of anxiety, and who show these effects clearly (Bradley *et al.* 1995). An additional diagnosis of anxiety in depressed patient seems to similarly block memory bias (Bradley and Mathews 1983).

If future research continues to support these trends, they are likely to be important in constraining cognitive theories of emotional disorders. Models linking cognition and emotion via schemata (Beck and Clark 1988) or memory networks (Bower 1981, 1992) provided the inspiration for much of the research discussed so far. But if emotional states do indeed differ in the cognitive processes involved, as well as content, these models will need to be modified or replaced. Neither the schema account nor the memory network model offer any obvious explanation for a process difference; both predict equivalent biases across all attention and memory tasks.

What sort of theories are needed?

At a descriptive level the process differences observed seem to make some intuitive sense. Anxiety is closely related to fear, and the function of fear is the early detection and avoidance of danger. Giving greater priority to perceptual vigilance would thus be more relevant to anxiety than to depression. By the same argument, depression is related to sadness, and is more concerned with past events already in memory, than with future danger. According to Oatley and Johnson-Laird (1987), emotions have evolved to determine priorities when conflicts arise in ongoing plans and goals. Fear/anxiety, for example, results when a background goal of ensuring survival and safety is violated, or sadness/depression by failure of a major plan, or loss of a goal. Emotions impose a relatively stereotyped mode of operation on the cognitive system, consistent with the nature of the plan or goal involved. For example, anxiety should impose a configuration on the cognitive system which facilitates the operations that are helpful in avoiding danger, while inhibiting processes relevant to other goals.

It is not clear how the suggested function and process differences among emotional states could be represented in existing single network models of memory. One way forward may be to consider the possibility that emotions vary in how they are represented in the cognitive system. Johnson and Multhaup (1992) suggest that emotional information may be stored in several different perceptual or higher-level conceptual modules, with basic biological emotions such as fear arising mainly from the former, and complex emotions such as remorse being more dependent on the latter. The apparent differences between the bias seen in anxiety and depression could thus be a function of the modules primarily responsible for processing the relevant emotional information.

Teasdale and Barnard (1993) propose an alternative multi-level system in which a central 'implicational' module integrates emotional information derived from other specialized modules. Because both models allow that emotions can draw on quite different types of information (e.g., verbal-propositional, perceptual, body sensations, etc.), they can account for variations in the cognitive operations that are biased in different emotions. Multi-level systems can thus overcome some of the difficulties encountered by single network models, although the problem may be that they explain too much, without making precise and testable predictions. Within the general framework provided, however, more specific hypotheses can be developed about the type of process or content most likely to show evidence of bias in different emotions, and these hypotheses may then be subjected to experimental test (e.g., Teasdale *et al.* 1995).

The distinction between normal and abnormal mood

It is clear that variations in the tendency to feel anxious or depressed are distributed throughout the population, and self-report scales measuring negative emotionality (Watson *et al.* 1988) generally reveal a roughly normal distribution. Similarly, many of the emotional biases that have been documented above may sometimes appear in normal subjects with high scores on these scales, although the association between bias and emotionality is probably far from linear. In a study of unselected normal students, for example, D. E. Broadbent and M. Broadbent (1988) found that selective attention to threat was not apparent at all in subjects with low to moderate trait-anxiety scores; but with subjects having progressively more extreme scores, attentional bias increased disproportionately.

In another study of normal subjects, medical students varying in their trait-anxiety scores were found not to show any evidence of attentional bias on initial testing, but immediately before a stressful examination the high trait-anxious students became more attentive to relevant threatening words (MacLeod and Mathews 1988). Thus, normal students with high negative emotionality scores can behave somewhat like anxious patients, but perhaps only when under stress. Neither stress nor anxious mood alone can account for this effect, however, since the low-emotionality students also became more anxious, but were if anything *less* attentive to threatening words when under stress. One could summarize the findings as showing that the examination stress elicited an anxiety-elevating attentional style from high-trait individuals, but a more protective style from the less anxiety-prone group.

A similar situation exists as regards the interaction between mood state, individual differences, and memory bias. It has been established in many experiments that a negative bias in recall can be produced in normal subjects by inducing a transient depressed mood state (e.g., Bower 1981; Teasdale and Russell 1983). However, such memory effects are not the same for all subjects, but are more marked in those with high scores on measures of negative trait-emotionality (Martin 1985), and may be absent in so-called 'defensive' subjects (Davis 1987). In this way, depressed mood can elicit differential degrees of negative memory bias, depending on more enduring individual differences in cognitive style and/or emotionality.

Despite the evidence of continuity in negative emotionality across the normal population, the belief that emotional disorders are qualitatively different from normal emotions (the 'disease model') is quite prevalent, based on features such as severe and unusual emotional symptoms, and subjective loss of control over mental state. From the present perspective, however, there is no real contradiction between the continuous and discontinuous accounts of emotional disorder. The evidence just reviewed suggests that in vulnerable individuals, increasing stress or negative mood elicits selection of emotionally congruent information. It is assumed that some aspects of this selection are automatic, although they may be opposed by intentional control processes, such as selective ignoring, distraction, or focusing on positive alternatives. However, as stress or negative mood state increases, the automatic selection of congruent information will also increase, making intentional control more difficult and demanding of effort. Finally, because control processes draw on limited resources, a point will be reached when their capacity is exceeded. At this point, the individual will be simultaneously aware of a sudden elevation in distressing thoughts, and of their own inability to control them. It is this breakdown in cognitive control, and the resulting discontinuity in subjective experience, that is claimed to constitute the onset of an emotional disorder.

Are biases really causal?

The central thesis proposed here is that variations in cognitive bias can account for why vulnerable individuals develop emotional disorders when they come under severe and prolonged stress, while others do not. Individuals with high pre-existing levels of neuroticism and negative emotionality are more likely to experience problems following life events or natural disasters (Ormel and Wohlfarth 1991; Nolen-Hoeksema and Morrow 1991). However, this research does not establish that it is the way in which stressful events are processed that causes emotional distress. Research showing that cognitive bias scores predict later distress is more direct, although similarly inconclusive. Colour naming interference scores in women undergoing a stressful diagnostic procedure were correlated with subsequent self-reports of adverse emotional reactions following a diagnosis of malignancy (MacLeod and Hagan 1992). Interference due to threatening words presented out of awareness predicted later distress, and did so more accurately than trait-anxiety scores.

Although intriguing, the capacity of automatic cognitive bias to predict later distress remains correlational, and cannot demonstrate causality. An alternative approach is to show that emotional reactions can be manipulated by selective processing. For example, panic attacks in patients can be induced by rehearsal of phrases corresponding to key emotional concerns (such as 'palpitations–coronary'), or can be prevented by the provision of alternative and more reassuring explanations for alarming bodily symptoms (Clark *et al.* 1988). Another related approach is to train normal subjects to process information in a biased manner, without making the purpose of the training obvious. Prolonged training of this sort, in which subjects selectively attend to threatening words, leads to increased subjective anxiety when faced with experimental stressors (MacLeod 1995). Although this work is at a preliminary stage, results so far are encouraging, and show that it may be possible to demonstrate a causal relationship between selective processing and emotional reactions in the laboratory.

Linking research to treatment

It is not the primary purpose of this chapter to consider treatment methods, and these are discussed extensively elsewhere. None the less, research on processing bias is motivated by the hope that it will lead to new or better methods for treating and preventing emotional disorders. Have we made any progress towards this goal?

The idea that processing biases maintain anxiety and depression, both justifies and is supported by the successful use of cognitive therapy. At least some of the processes identified can be brought under intentional control, provided that the person realizes that it is his/her own responses that are responsible. As discussed earlier, depressed people often do not realize that rumination is prolonging their negative mood, thinking instead that it helps them develop insight into their problems (Nolan-Hoeksema 1991). Being personally involved in gathering evidence in cognitive therapy is likely to lead to such misunderstandings being corrected, so that the individual can use control strategies effectively. Such methods have been developed, however, quite independently of the detailed evidence discussed here.

One possible direction indicated by this research is to include training procedures to modify biases that patients cannot control, even when made aware of them. In the earlier account of how abnormal emotional states develop (see also Mathews and MacLeod 1994), it was suggested that effortful control eventually fails because it depends on capacity-limited resources. In this light, what is required is to automate the processes that *oppose* the selective intake of negative information, in order to reduce the load placed on vulnerable individuals when under stress. In the experiments mentioned above, a number of training sessions were required before signs of automation appeared, such as changes in the probe detection latencies attributable to masked emotional words. It may take even longer to reverse the well-established attentional bias in anxious clients, by training them to select the more positive of the available options. If some degree of automation can be achieved, however, then the benefits may include the ability to ignore minor emotional triggers without effort, even when preoccupied or when under stress.

We are beginning to explore a similar procedure in which experimental subjects are provided with clues biasing them towards either the threatening or non-threatening meaning of ambiguous words. Again, the idea is to see if accessing the negative (or positive) aspects of events can be automated by extensive practice. Although it is often possible to find alternative meanings of ambiguous information just by looking for them, anxious or depressed clients sometimes seem to have difficulty even seeing that alternative interpretations are possible. Instead, what is in fact an inference derived from the interpretation of ambiguity is experienced as an 'automatic thought', and accepted as accurate. Guided practice in discovering alternative interpretations, although a part of existing cognitive therapy, could perhaps be supplemented by more systematic training if initial experimental investigations are encouraging.

Needless to say, these ideas are little more than speculations at this stage, and a good deal more evidence will be needed before therapeutic applications can be expected. None the less, there are signs that one phase of research, in which the existence and nature of information-processing biases have been firmly established, is complete; and will be replaced by a second phase, in which methods for modifying these biases will become the new target for our research efforts.

Epilogue

A short while ago I was invited to give a talk on research on cognition and anxiety, and decided to start by explaining why I got interested in this area in the first place. As I thought about it, however, the reasons were not entirely obvious, even to me. Then I started to think about the people who influenced me early on, and just three or four came readily to mind. Michael Gelder was one of them.

He was a leading figure at the Institute of Psychiatry when I got my first research job (with him). When he moved to Oxford, he invited me to join his first programme grant there, on behavioural treatments for severe anxiety disorders. With his direction and support, we carried out several major evaluative studies, and continued on to develop improved methods of treatment. Although a real advance, it was the very limits to the effectiveness of these treatments that directed our attention towards cognitive processes that could be involved in maintaining anxiety.

Throughout this time, Michael Gelder was an unfailing source of inspiration and encouragement. He never imposed an approach on us, but was always a perceptive and balanced critic. When our ideas were badly thought out, he quickly spotted the weak links; but if they were sound, he was the first to recognize and support them. My time in the Oxford department was exciting, formative and rewarding, due in no small measure to his influence.

References

Asmundson, G. J. G., Sandler, L. S., Wilson, K. G., and Walker, J. R. (1992). Selective attention toward physical threat in patients with panic disorder. *Journal of Anxiety Disorders*, 6, 295–303.

Bargh, J. A. (1989). Conditional automaticity: varieties of automatic influence in social perception and cognition. In *Unintended thought*, (ed. J. S. Uleman, J. A. Bargh) pp. 3–51. Guilford Press, New York.

Bargh, J. A. and Tota, M. E. (1988). Context-dependent automatic processing in depression: Accessibility of negative constructs with regard to self but not others. *Journal of Personality and Social Psychology*, 54, 925–39.

Beck, A. and Clark, D. A. (1988). Anxiety and Depression: An information-processing perspective, *Anxiety Research*, 1, 23–36.

Bower, G. H. (1981). Mood and memory. *American Psychologist*, 36, 129–48.

Bower, G. H. (1992). How might emotions affect learning. In *Handbook of emotion and memory*, (ed. S. A. Christianson) pp. 3–31. Erlbaum: Hillsdale, NJ.

Bradley, B. P. and Mathews, A. M. (1983). Negative self-schemata in clinical depression. *British Journal of Clinical Psychology*, 22, 173–81.

Bradley, B. P., Mogg, K., Millar, N., and White, J. (1995). Selective processing of negative information; effects of clinical anxiety, concurrent depression, and awareness. *Journal of Abnormal Psychology*, 104, 532–36.

Broadbent, D. E. and Broadbent, M. (1988). Anxiety and attentional bias: State and trait. *Cognition and Emotion*, 2, 165–83.

Burke, M. and Mathews, A. M. (1992). Autobiographical memory and clinical anxiety. *Cognition and Emotion*, 6, 23–35.

Clark, D. M. and Teasdale, J. D. (1985). Constraints on the effects or mood on memory. *Journal of Personality and Social Psychology*, 48, 1595–608.

Clark, D. M. and Wells, A. (1995). A cognitive model of social phobia. In *Social phobia: diagnosis, assessment and treatment* (ed. R. G. Heimberg, M. Liebowitz, D. Hope, and F. Schneier), pp. 69–93. Guilford Press, New York.

Clark, D. M., Teasdale, J. D., Broadbent, D. E., and Martin, M. (1983). Effect of mood on lexical decision. *Bulletin of Psychonomic Science*, 21, 175–8.

Clark, D. M., Salkovskis, P. M., Gelder, M., Koehler, C., Martin, M., Anastasiades, P., *et al.* (1988). Tests of a cognitive theory of panic. In *Panic and phobias*, (ed. I. Hand and H-U. Wittchen), pp. 149–58. Springer, Berlin.

Davis, P. (1987). Repression and the inaccessibility of affective memories. *Journal of Personality and Social Psychology*, 53, 585–93.

Denny, E. B. and Hunt, R. R. (1992). Affective valence and memory in depression: Dissociation of recall and fragment completion. *Journal of Abnormal Psychology*, 101, 575–80.

Ehlers, A. and Breuer, P. (1992). Increased cardiac awareness in panic disorder. *Journal of Abnormal Psychology*, 101, 371–82.

Eysenck, M. W., Mogg, K., May, J., Richards, A., and Mathews, A. (1991). Bias in interpretation of ambiguous sentences related to threat in anxiety. *Journal of Abnormal Psychology*, 100, 144–50.

Hirsch, C. and Mathews, A. Inferences when reading about uncertain emotional events. Submitted for publication.

Johnson, M. K. and Multhaup, K. S. (1992). Emotion and MEM. In *Handbook of emotion and memory* (ed. S. A. Christianson), pp. 33–60. Erlbaum, Hillsdale, NJ.

MacLeod, C. (1995). *Training selective attention: a cognitive-experimental technique for reducing anxiety vulnerability?* Paper presented at the World Congress of Behavioural and Cognitive Therapies, Copenhagen.

MacLeod, C. and Hagan, R. (1992). Individual differences in the selective processing of threatening information, and emotional responses to a stressful life event. *Behaviour Research and Therapy*, 30, 151–61.

MacLeod, C. and Mathews, A. (1988). Anxiety and the allocation of attention to threat. *Quarterly Journal of Experimental Psychology: Human Experimental Psychology*, 38, 659–70.

MacLeod, C. and Mathews, A. (1991). Biased cognitive operations in anxiety: accessibility of information or assignment of processing priorities. *Behaviour Research and Therapy*, 29, 599–610.

MacLeod, C. and McLaughlin, K. (1995). Implicit and explicit memory bias in anxiety: a conceptual replication. *Behaviour Research and Therapy*, 33, 1–14.

MacLeod, C., Mathews, A., and Tata, P. (1986). Attentional bias in emotional disorders. *Journal of Abnormal Psychology*, 95, 15–20.

MacLeod, C., Tata, P., and Mathews, A. (1987). Perception of valenced information in depression. *British Journal of Clinical Psychology*, 26, 67–68.

Martin, M., Williams, R. M. and Clark, D. M. (1991). Does anxiety lead to selective processing of threat-related information? *Behaviour Research and Therapy*, 29, 147–60.

Mathews, A. and Klug, F. (1993). Emotionality and interference with colour-naming in anxiety. *Behaviour Research and Therapy*, 31, 57–62.

Mathews, A. and MacLeod, C. (1986). Discrimination of threat cues without awareness in anxiety states. *Journal of Abnormal Psychology*, 95, 131–8.

Mathews, A. and MacLeod, C. (1994). Cognitive approaches to emotion and emotional disorders. *Annual Review of Psychology*, 45, 25–50.

Mathews, A., May, J., Mogg, K., and Eysenck, M. (1990). Attentional bias in anxiety: Selective search or defective filtering? *Journal of Abnormal Psychology*, 99, 166–73.

Mathews, A., Mogg, K., Kentish, J., and Eysenck, M. (1995). Effect of psychological treatment cognitive bias in generalized anxiety disorder. *Behaviour Research and Therapy*, 33, 293–303.

McNally, R., Foa, F., and Donnell, C. (1989). Memory bias for anxiety information in patients with panic disorder. *Cognition and Emotion*, 3, 27–44.

Mogg, K. and Mathews, A. (1990). Is there a mood-congruent recall bias in anxiety? *Behaviour Research and Therapy*, 28, 91–92.

Mogg, K., Mathews, A. M., and Weinman, J. (1987). Memory bias in clinical anxiety. *Journal of Abnormal Psychology*, 96, 94–98.

Mogg, K., Mathews, A. M., and Weinman, J. (1989). Selective processing of threat cues in anxiety states: A replication. *Behaviour Research and Therapy*, 27, 317–23.

Mogg, K., Mathews, A., Eysenck, M., and May, J. (1991). Biased cognitive operations in anxiety: Artefact, processing priorities or attentional search? *Behaviour Research and Therapy*, 5, 459–67.

Mogg, K., Mathews, A., and Eysenck, M. (1992). Attentional bias to threat in clinical anxiety states. *Cognition and Emotion*, 6, 149–59.

Mogg, K., Bradley, B., Williams, R., and Mathews, A. (1993). Subliminal processing of emotional information in anxiety and depression. *Journal of Abnormal Psychology*, 102, 304–311.

Nolen-Hoeksema, S. (1991). Responses to depression and their effects on the duration of depressive episodes. *Journal of Abnormal Psychology*, 100, 569–82.

Nolen-Hoeksema, S. and Morrow, J. (1991). A prospective study of depression and posttraumatic stress symptoms after a natural disaster: The 1989 Loma Prieta earthquake. *Journal of Personality and Social Psychology*, 61, 115–21.

Oatley, K. and Johnson-Laird, P. (1987). Towards a cognitive theory of emotions. *Cognition and Emotion*, 1, 29–50.

Ormel, J. and Wohlfarth, T. (1991). How neuroticism, long-term difficulties, and life situation change influence psychological distress: A longitudinal model. *Journal of Personality and Social Psychology*, 5, 744–55.

Powell, M. and Hemsley, D. R. (1984). Depression: a breakdown of perceptual defence? *British Journal of Psychiatry*, 145, 358–62.

Riemann, B. C. and NcNally, R. J. (1995). Cognitive processing of personally relevant information. *Cognition and Emotion*, 9, 325–40.

Teasdale, J. D. (1983). Negative thinking in depression: cause, effect, or reciprocal relationship? *Advances in Behaviour Research and Therapy*, 5, 3–25.

Teasdale, J. D. (1988). Cognitive vulnerability to persistent depression. *Cognition and Emotion* 2, 247–74.

Teasdale, J. D. and Barnard, P. J. (1993). *Affect, cognition and change*. Erlbaum, Hove, UK.

Teasdale, J. D. and Russell, M. L. (1983). Differential effects of induced mood on the recall of positive, negative and neutral words. *British Journal of Clinical Psychology*, 22, 163–71.

Teasdale, J. D., Taylor, M. J., Cooper, Z., Hayhurst, H., and Paykel, E. S. (1995). Depressive thinking: shifts in construct accessibility or in schematic mental models? *Journal of Abnormal Psychology*, 104, 500–8.

von Hippel, W., Hawkins, C., and Narayan, S. (1994). Personality and perceptual expertise: individual differences in perceptual identification. *Psychological Science*, 5, 401–406.

Watkins, P., Mathews, A. M., Williamson, D. A., and Fuller, R. (1992). Mood congruent memory in depression: Emotional priming or elaboration? *Journal of Abnormal Psychology*, 101, 581–86.

Watkins, P. C., Vache, K., Verney, S. P., Muller, S., and Mathews, A. (1996). Unconsicous mood-conguent memory bias in depression. *Journal of Abnormal Psychology*, 105, 34–41.

Watson, D., Clark, L. A., and Tellegen, A. (1988). Development and validation of brief measures of positive and negative affect: The PANAS scales. *Journal of Personality and Social Psychology*, 54, 1063–70.

Williams, J. H. G. (1992). Autobiographical memory and emotional disorders. In *Handbook of emotion and memory* (ed. S. A. Christianson), pp. 451–77. Erlbaum, Hillsdale, NJ.

Williams, J. M. G., Mathews, A., and MacLeod, C. (in press). The emotional Stroop task and psychopathology. *Psychological Bulletin*.

4

The relationship between cognition and emotion: the mind-in-place in mood disorders

John D. Teasdale

Cognitive behavioural approaches to treating emotional disorders are based on the assumption that emotional responses are mediated through the interpretations, or meanings, that we give to experience. This idea appears relatively clear and straightforward, and has proved enormously heuristic in guiding the development of effective treatments for a range of emotional disorders. However, if we look more closely, it becomes clear that this basic idea has to be elaborated and qualified in many ways.

First, the simple assumption that certain types of cognition are the *antecedents* to emotional reactions has to be elaborated to include recognition of the fact that those same cognitions may be so powerfully influenced by affective state that cognition often appears to be a *consequence* of emotional state. For example, in the case of depression, a considerable experimental literature now demonstrates that depressed mood states can powerfully influence cognitive processes intimately involved in the interpretation and evaluation of experience (e.g., Blaney 1986; Morris 1989). Consequently, once depressed, a powerful influence affecting the production of the negative interpretations of experience that, it is suggested, are antecedents to depression will be the depressed state itself. Relatedly, the patterns of negative thinking characteristically shown by depressed patients largely disappear when their mood improves following treatments, such as antidepressant medication, that make no attempt to modify cognition (e.g., Simons *et al.* 1984). Such observations are consistent with the suggestion that negative depressive cognition may often be a consequence of depressed emotional state.

We can get round such difficulties by suggesting that there is a *reciprocal* relationship between cognition and emotion; certain types of interpretation or meaning are antecedents to emotional states, but those emotional states,

Note. This chapter is based on a keynote address delivered to the World Congress of Behavioural and Cognitive Therapies, Copenhagen, 15 July 1995.

themselves, increase the likelihood of those very same cognitions (Teasdale 1983; Ingram 1984). Such a proposal seems to do more justice to the available evidence (e.g., Teasdale 1993). However, this proposal, itself, needs to be qualified by the recognition that apparently similar mood states can have quite different effects on cognitive processes, that apparently related cognitions can have quite different effects on emotion, and that the actual distinction between mood states and cognition may not be as clear as we at first thought. Let me elaborate each of these assertions.

The possibility that apparently similar mood states can have very different effects on affect-related cognition is suggested most forcefully by research on mood incongruent memory (Parrott and Sabini 1990). Typically, studies investigating the effects of induced mood states on memory have used verbal or musical mood inductions and found mood *congruent* memory; in depressed moods, compared to happy moods, subjects are less likely to recall positive experiences and are more likely to recall negative experiences (Blaney 1986). Using such typical mood induction procedures, Parrott and Sabini (1990) also observed a pattern of mood congruent recall. However, when these workers studied the effects of moods induced by other means (the weather, background music, or succeeding vs. failing an examination) a pattern of mood *incongruent* memory was observed; in depressed moods, compared to happy moods, subjects were *more* likely to recall positive memories and *less* likely to recall negative memories. Such findings suggest that one depressed mood state is not necessarily equivalent to another depressed mood state in terms of its effect on cognition. More generally, any analysis of emotional disorders in terms of reciprocal relationships between cognition and emotion will have to take account of the detailed nature of the mood state and the way it affects cognitive processes (Teasdale and Barnard 1993, Chapter 10).

A related conclusion emerges when we look at the effects of cognition on emotion; here, also, it seems that we have to distinguish between the effects of qualitatively different cognitive representations of the same topic in order to understand the way that cognition affects emotion (Teasdale, 1993).

A clinical example will serve to illustrate what this means. Imagine a depressed patient with a profound sense of worthlessness and inadequacy. We could ask them to repeat self-statements such as 'I'm OK, really'. Or, we could review with them evidence of their successes, achievements, and positive personal qualities so that they will agree, at the level of 'intellectual belief', that they are not a total failure or without any positive attributes. Alternatively, we could aim for changes at the 'gut' level of 'emotional belief' in their 'sense' of worthlessness.

Clinical experience suggests that, frequently, the first two types of procedure, alone, may be quite ineffective in producing emotional change. Often, it seems that such change depends on modifying 'emotional belief'. And yet, each of these three levels of representation can be regarded as 'cognitions' with similar content. In other words, in considering the effect of cognition on emotion, it seems that it may be necessary to qualify the attractive simplicity of the original idea that cognitions with particular types of content mediate emotional reactions. It seems that we have to make distinctions between qualitatively different *kinds* of cognition related to the same topic, each kind of cognition having a different relationship to emotion.

A similar conclusion has emerged from more systematic attempts to make sense of the detailed pattern of findings of empirical studies of the relationship between cognition and emotion. A consistent emerging trend across a number of theoretical analyses within this area has been the recognition of the need for multiple levels of cognitive representation of the same topic, each kind of representation having its own distinct relationship to emotion (e.g. Leventhal 1984; Barnard and Teasdale 1991; Johnson and Multhaup 1992; Teasdale and Barnard 1993; Power and Dalgleish in press).

The suggestion that changing 'emotional belief' may be the necessary precondition to changing emotion obviously raises the question of whether cognition and emotion, while they may be conceptually separable in some contexts, can actually be so clearly distinguished in relation to moods and mood disorders. For example, one researcher in the area of cognitive–affective interaction went so far as to entitle a paper, 'Mood affects memory because feelings *are* cognitions' (Laird 1989). Such a possibility suggests that it may be overly simple to frame our analyses in terms of the effects of distinct 'cognitions' and 'emotions' on each other.

As a final example of the complexities that arise as we look more closely at the simple assumption with which we began this chapter, we can note issues related to the maintenance of emotional disorders. It is not difficult to see how the immediate emotional reactions to ongoing environmental events might be mediated by the interpretations made of those events. However, mood disorders, such as depression, often seem to involve affective states that persist for long periods in the absence of any related ongoing environmental input. How is the persistence of such mood states to be explained? We could suggest that ongoing streams of negative automatic thoughts act to maintain depression in these situations, but we then have to explain the maintenance of those thought streams—yet another set of problems to be addressed.

Clearly, investigating these complexities is likely to provide a happy occupation for large numbers of academics and researchers, but do these issues really matter to clinicians concerned with treating patients? There is evidence to suggest that they do, and that the need to go beyond the simple assumptions of the first sentence of this chapter are well recognized by experienced cognitive therapists. As just one example, consider what Chris Padesky, one of the most highly respected clinicians and teachers of cognitive therapy, had to say in a keynote address on Socratic questioning, one of the central components of cognitive therapy: 'Theoretically, I can't accept that the goal of Socratic questioning is to change client's beliefs'. Anticipating the surprise such a statement might elicit, she goes on: 'Why not? Isn't change in beliefs one of the primary goals of cognitive therapy? Yes . . . and no' (Padesky 1993).

That 'Yes . . . and no' suggest a recognition of the complexities of the issues we face in attempting to understand the relationship between cognition and emotion. In this chapter, I shall suggest that, if we are to do justice to those complexities, we are forced to frame our analysis beyond the simple level of the effects of thoughts and beliefs on emotion. Rather, I will suggest that, particularly in the case of mood disorders such as depression, our analyses have to be at the level of integrated, motivated, patterns of information-processing, that continue over extended periods of time, and that involve multiple levels of information and cognitive representation. These are not easy ideas to convey, and I shall start with a 'reader-friendly' level of description, using the heuristic metaphor of 'mind-in-place' suggested by Robert Ornstein (1992).

I shall consider three basic ideas in relation to this metaphor. The first is that we do not have one mind, but many — at any one time, one of these many minds may be dominant, and can be thought of as the current mind-in-place.

The second basic idea is that mood disorders can be thought of in terms of the persistence of particular minds-in-place. Normally, one mind-in-place will give way to another as circumstances change, so that we move in and out of a variety of different minds. In contrast, in mood disorders, it is as if an individual gets 'stuck' in one mind. Interactions between 'cognition' and 'emotion', play a central role in the persistence of such minds.

The third idea is that cognitive behaviour therapies for mood disorders work by helping clients shift out of the mind-in-place in which they have got stuck and into other minds. Long-term effects of such treatments depend on helping clients avoid getting stuck in these minds in the future.

Let us now look at the first of these ideas in more detail.

We do not have one mind but many

One of the most widely accepted and far-reaching conclusions of cognitive neuroscience is the idea of modularity (Fodor 1983) — the idea that we need to think of ourselves as having a number of distinct 'minds', each specialized for certain functions, and each having its own evolutionary and developmental history.

Robert Ornstein has neatly captured the essence of this notion in his concept of 'the mind-in-place'. The idea is that, at any one time, circumstances will call up one of our minds and this mind will be 'wheeled in' to occupy the position of mind-in-place, just as we access a particular computer module to perform a specific specialized function. As circumstances change, and the existing mind-in-place is no longer the most appropriate to respond to current needs, that mind will be 'wheeled out', and another, more relevant mind will be 'wheeled in'.

In his book, *The evolution of consciousness*, Ornstein (1992, p. 79) dramatically illustrates the notion of separate minds and mind-in-place through the story of an incident that happened to a psychiatrist friend of his:

> The psychiatrist received an emergency call from the local police department to let him know that his patient, Alfred, was currently standing on the edge of a cliff threatening to jump off. The psychiatrist ran to his car and drove up the hill.
>
> There was Alfred on the ledge, over the canyon. The psychiatrist tried asking Alfred if he knew what this would do to his mother, how hurt she would be? But Alfred knew. The psychiatrist asked him to think of the effects on his children, how they would be scarred for life. But Alfred knew. What about his robotics company, just about to make a breakthrough? And what about his relationship with his wife — weren't things improving there so that there was a real chance of their being reunited? But nothing the psychiatrist said had any effect. He walked away, desolate.
>
> But Alfred did not jump. As the psychiatrist walked away, another police officer, on patrol, pulled his car up to the site, unaware of the drama. He took out his loudhailer and blared sharply to the group of people on the cliff: 'Who's the idiot who left that Pontiac station wagon double-parked out there in the middle of the road? I almost hit it. Move it *now* whoever you are'. Alfred heard the message, and he got down at once from his perch, dutifully shuffled out to his car, parked it precisely on the side of the road and then went off, without a word, in the policeman's car to Stanford Hospital.

This is a particularly dramatic example of a shift of the mind-in-place. Alfred had worked out, in his rehearsal and consideration of his suicide, all the reasons and all the answers why, despite the effects on his family, he should kill himself. But, Ornstein points out, he had rehearsed in one mind only. Alfred's other minds had their own priorities. His suicidal resolution was not worked through. It was simply overcome, moved out of place by the automatic shifting of his mind, which replaced the suicidal fanatic with a simple reflexive law-abiding citizen.

As this example illustrates, it is as if, as the pattern of external information changes, a different set of buttons is pressed—the old mind-in-place is wheeled out and a new mind-in-place is wheeled in. All this happens relatively automatically, in response to the pattern of environmental input, rather than in any willed, intended, or deliberate way.

Ornstein's story provides intuitively convincing anecdotal evidence for a very pronounced automatic cognitive shift. Research in social cognition, using sensitive experimental paradigms, has revealed the pervasiveness of a range of much more subtle automatic shifts. Initially, this work focused on effects that were interpreted in terms of changes in the accessibility of individual cognitive constructs or concepts. So, for example, in an early classic study, Srull and Wyer (1979), under the guise of a sentence construction task, presented subjects with words related to the concepts of either hostility or kindness, and examined the effects on a subsequent impression formation task. In this task, subjects read descriptions of a person's behaviour that were ambiguous with respect to hostility or kindness, and then rated their impressions of the target person. Ratings of the target's hostility increased with the number of times that hostile concepts had been activated in the sentence construction task.

Such findings were accommodated very comfortably within the suggestion that exposure to hostile words in the sentence construction task automatically primed into readiness related constructs or cognitive categories and so made it more likely that they would be used in subsequent social judgements. The suggestion here is not so much an automatic shift of a 'mind', as an automatically triggered adjustment of thresholds for the use of particular constructs.

More recent work within this tradition has produced further evidence of wide-ranging automatic activation effects, for example, effects on motivational states and goals. However, the results of these studies cannot so easily be reduced to effects on construct accessibility.

For example, using procedures very similar to those of Srull and Wyer, John Bargh and his colleagues (Bargh *et al.* 1994) have demonstrated convincing evidence that prior presentation of words related to achievement (e.g., *strive*, *success*) increases measures of related goals and motives. In one experiment, some subjects were primed with achievement-related words, the remainder with neutral words. Subjects participated three at a time, with partitions between them so that they could not see each other. After completing the priming task, and under the instructions that it was a separate 'language ability' measure, subjects were given seven Scrabble letter tiles and told to make as many words with those letters as they could in the next three minutes, writing their answers on a piece of paper. The experimenter explained that she had to leave to run another experiment, and if she could not get back by the end of three minutes she would give the signal to 'stop' over the room's intercom. Unknown to the subjects, they could all be seen by a hidden video camera that recorded the experimental session. The experimenter did not, in fact, return, and subjects received the instruction to stop over the intercom, in the apparent absence of any observer. In reality, of course, they were closely monitored via the hidden video camera.

The measure of interest was the proportion of subjects who continued to work on finding the words after the signal to stop had been given. It was assumed that persistence on the task in this way reflected the level of achievement motivation at that time. The results provided convincing evidence for the automatic priming of an achievement-related motivational state: 55% of subjects in the achievement priming condition, but only 22% of those in the neutral priming condition persisted on the task after being told to stop — a clear indication that the mere presentation of achievement words had automatically triggered a related motivational state.

Findings such as these are very difficult to explain in terms of simple construct accessibility models. Rather, they are much more consistent with the suggestion that, just as Ornstein's notion of the mind-in-place suggests, changing environmental stimuli can automatically switch in and out of operation complex, integrated, patterns of interpretation, motivation, and behaviour.

When we look at developments in attempts to understand the biases in interpretation, attention, and memory associated with mood states such as depression, an interestingly similar conclusion to that in social cognition emerges.

Mood-related cognitive biases as shifts of mind-in-place

As is well known, depression is associated with a tendency to interpret experience more negatively (Haaga *et al.* 1991). A continuing line of research, which began in the University of Oxford Department of Psychiatry in parallel with studies of cognitive therapy, has investigated the ways in which such negative cognitive biases can be understood as effects of depressed mood on information-processing. The starting point for this work was Lloyd and Lishman's (1975) seminal demonstration that clinical depression was associated with an increase in the relative accessibility of unpleasant, relative to pleasant, autobiographical memories; with increasing levels of depression, the latency to retrieve unpleasant memories decreases, whereas that for pleasant memories increases.

Using the same paradigm, we were able to show related results in normal subjects in whom depressed mood had been temporarily induced (Teasdale and Fogarty 1979). These findings suggested that it might be fruitful to conceptualize depressive cognitive biases as transient effects of mood state on information-processing, rather than as enduring characteristics of individuals prone to depression. Subsequent studies showing similar effects of induced moods (Teasdale *et al.* 1980; Teasdale and Taylor 1981) and of natural, diurnal variations in depression in hospitalized patients (Clark and Teasdale 1982) on the relative probability of recall of pleasant and unpleasant autobiographical memories, together with demonstrations of related effects of induced moods on recall of positive and negative verbal material (Teasdale and Russell 1983), supported this view.

Initial attempts to understand these effects were essentially construct accessibility accounts, similar to those developed within social cognition. So, for example, Bower's (1981) associative network theory suggested that depressed mood selectively increased the accessibility of negative interpretative concepts, or constructs, priming them into readiness. In other words, depressed mood puts these negative constructs 'on a hair trigger', so that they are more likely to be used to interpret experience, producing the negative interpretative biases so characteristic of depression. This construct accessibility account provided an attractively simple explanation of negative depressive thinking that was also heuristic in stimulating a novel view of cognitive vulnerability in depression (Teasdale 1983, 1988; Teasdale and Dent 1987).

More recently, just as in social cognition, it has become clear that simple construct accessibility accounts cannot do justice to the phenomena of mood-related cognitive biases, and accounts focusing on higher levels of representation have been developed. For example, the Interacting Cognitive Subsystems (ICS) framework (Barnard and Teasdale 1991; Teasdale 1993; Teasdale and Barnard 1993) suggests that mood effects operate, not at the level of individual constructs, but at a more generic level of representation. At this level, high order *interrelationships* between patterns of constructs are represented in schematic mental models.

The ICS analysis suggests that depression is associated with a shift in schematic models, for example, those concerned with the *relationship* between personal worth and social approval, or success. On this view, normal mood is characterized by functional mental models, in which personal worth is relatively independent of whether or not one is liked by others, or whether one succeeds or fails at tasks. But, it is suggested, once depressed, patients switch to different, dysfunctional models. These models, as well as encoding more globally negative views of self, also imply a much closer dependence of personal worth on approval or task outcome. Interpreted through these dysfunctional models, failure or disapproval will be interpreted more catastrophically in depression because such events imply global personal worthlessness. On the other hand, and at first sight counter-intuitively, this view suggests that, although depressed patients may regard success or social approval as unlikely, if such events do occur, they will be interpreted more *positively* than in the non-depressed state. Again, this is a reflection of the closer *relationship* between personal worth and success/failure or approval/ disapproval in the models operating in depression, compared to the non-depressed state.

In a recent study (Teasdale *et al.* 1995*b*), my colleagues and I took advantage of this counter-intuitive aspect of the ICS analysis to contrast predictions from this approach with predictions from the view that depressive thinking reflects increased accessibility of individual negative constructs. The easiest way to understand the logic of this experiment is to consider one of the specially constructed sentence stems used in this study. Subjects were asked to fill in with 'the first word that comes to mind' the stem: 'For everyone to look to me for guidance and advice would make me _____ .' This sentence stem, like all the others used in the study, was constructed so that dysfunctional models, implying a close dependence of personal worth on attention and approval from others, would lead to positive completions, such as 'happy'. In contrast, more functional, realistic, models, implying a less close dependence of worth on approval, would lead to negative completions, such as 'exhausted'. The simple construct accessibility view, of course, suggests that, other things being equal, depression will be associated with a tendency to give more negative completions.

By using these sentences, a situation was created in which the construct accessibility view, focusing on the activation of individual constructs, predicts that depressed patients will make more negative sentence completions than non-depressed controls, and this tendency will reduce with recovery. In contrast, the view that depression is associated with changes in schematic mental models, representing the *interrelationships* and *dependencies* between *patterns* of constructs, predicts, counter-intuitively, that depressed patients will give more positive completions than controls, and that this tendency will decrease with recovery.

The results, shown in Fig. 4.1, clearly supported the schematic models view: at initial testing, depressed patients gave significantly more positive completions than non-depressed controls. At three-month follow-up, patients whose mood had improved showed a significant decrease in positive completions, whereas patients whose mood had deteriorated further showed a significant increase in positive completions. These results, which have been replicated in two subsequent studies (Sheppard and Teasdale, in press; Teasdale *et al.* in prep.) clearly support the view that negative depressive thinking is better explained in terms of changes in representations that reflect the *relationships* between key aspects of experience, rather than in terms of changes in the accessibility of individual cognitive constructs.

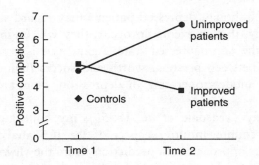

FIG. 4.1. Positive sentence completions in depressed patients who improved and who deteriorated over the three-month interval from Time 1 to Time 2, and in non-depressed controls (Time 1 only). (Data from Teasdale *et al.* 1995*b*.)

The findings of this study can be appreciated most readily by inspection of Table 4.1, which shows the changes in an individual recovered patient who demonstrated quite strongly the effects predicted from the schematic mental models view. From Table 4.1, it is clear that the changes in thinking that occurred with recovery were not simply a reflection of the patient retaining the same view of herself in relation to the world, while generally reducing the accessibility of negative constructs. Rather, these changes seem to reflect a radical shift in the mental model of self-in-relation-to-the-world, so that it is not too far-fetched to talk of the patient actually living in two different alternative mental realities in the depressed and recovered states. This, of course, is wholly consistent with the idea that the depressed state is characterized by a quite different mind-in-place to that which prevails in normal mood states.

TABLE 4.1. Sentence completions at Time 1 and Time 2 in a mood-improved patient

Sentence stem	Time 1 Completion (Depressed)	Time 2 Completion (Recovered)
Always to put others' interests before your own is a recipe for_____.	'success'	'disaster'
If I could always be right then others would _____ me.	'like'	'hate'
For everyone to look to me for guidance and advice would make me_____.	'important'	'frightened'
Always seeking the approval of other people is the road to_____.	'happiness'	'disaster'

Mood disorders as the persistence of mind-in-place

Normally, the mind-in-place changes over time, old minds being 'wheeled out' and new minds being 'wheeled in' as circumstances change. In contrast, in mood disorders, such as depression, patients seem to get stuck in one mind, so that their thinking seems to be dominated by a limited number of recurring themes. How is this persistence of mind-in-place to be explained?

In order to answer this question, it is necessary to articulate the concepts of separate minds and mind-in-place more precisely. One way to do this is through the Interacting Cognitive Subsystems (ICS) approach.

The Interacting Cognitive Subsystems (ICS) framework

ICS is a comprehensive information-processing framework that provides a vehicle for developing accounts of a wide range of phenomena. Originally developed within mainstream cognitive science by Barnard, he and I have collaborated to develop this approach and to apply it to understanding depression. ICS is a complex approach, described in detail in a book (Teasdale and Barnard 1993) and a number of papers (Barnard and Teasdale 1991; Teasdale 1993, in press; Teasdale *et al.* 1995*a*). Here, I shall only sketch out aspects of direct relevance to the current topic.

ICS is based on a few, basically simple, ideas. The first is that, in order to do justice to what we know about the way the mind works, we have to recognize that there are qualitatively different kinds of information, or mental codes. Each of these codes represents a distinct aspect of experience. So, in ICS, certain codes represent the information of relatively 'raw' 'undigested' sensory experience, such as patterns of light, shade, and colour, the pitch, timbre, and temporal patterns of sounds, and the patterns of proprioceptive stimulation arising from the musculature, and other internal sensory organs.

Other codes represent recurring regularities that have been extracted from the patterns of sensory codes created by an individual over the course of their life experience. So, for example, a speech-level code captures the features that are common to particular words, irrespective of the loudness or accent with which they are spoken, so that only the essential 'wordness' is retained, and other, more superficial, sensory features are discarded. Similarly, a visual object code captures underlying patterns that have recurred in the patterns of visual sensory codes. This code would represent, for example, 'sphericity' or 'behindness'.

Recurring patterns in speech-level and visual object codes are, themselves, represented by codes that represent meanings. ICS distinguishes between two kinds of meaning: relatively specific, low-level meanings, and more generic, high-level meanings, or schematic mental models. As this distinction is particularly important when considering the relationship between cognition and emotion, it will be considered in greater detail later.

The second basic idea of ICS is that there are processes that transform information from one kind of code to another. The conversions performed by these transformation processes are 'learned' on the basis of regularities and covariations in the patterns of information codes previously encountered. So, for example, one process, when it receives a particular pattern of sound sensory information as input, will produce a pattern of speech-level code corresponding to the word 'good' as output. The same process, on receiving a different pattern of sound sensory information, will produce as output a pattern of speech-level code corresponding to the word 'live'. Similarly, another process, when it receives a pattern typical of previous loss-related situations in the information code representing high-level meanings, will produce, as output, patterns of effector code that will produce components of the depressive emotional reaction.

The third basic idea of the ICS approach is that all the patterns of information codes created are stored in memory, there being separate memory systems for each of the different mental codes. For example, following a conversation, multiple records of that event will exist; in the speech-level store there will be representations corresponding to the words uttered during the conversation, in the specific meaning store, there will be representations corresponding to the specific meanings derived from sentences including those words during the conversation, and in the high-level meaning store there will be representations corresponding to the high-level interpretations (e.g., of threat, attraction, or 'hidden agendas') created in relation to the total conversation experience. The information stored in memory records is accessed not only at times of obvious 'remembering', but also in the course of extended processing operations, such as those involved in understanding a current situation or in predicting future states of affairs.

A final basic idea of the ICS approach is that emotion-related high-level meanings play a central role in emotion production. From situations eliciting a given emotion, recurring themes and patterns will be extracted into affect-related schematic mental models encoding relevant high-level meanings. So, for example, schematic models encoding themes such as 'globally negative view of self' or 'hopeless, highly aversive, uncontrollable situation that will persist indefinitely' will be extracted as prototypical of depressing situations. When, subsequently, high-level meanings related to these themes are synthesized, a depressive emotional response will arise.

High-level meanings may include substantial contributions from sensorily derived elements. Consequently, sensory inputs can make a *direct* contribution to the synthesis of high-level affect-related meanings, and so to the production of emotion. For example, patterns of loss-related low-level meanings that may create depressogenic ('hopeless-self-devaluative') schematic models in conjunction with bodily feedback indicating sluggishness, bowed posture, and frowning expression, might create more coping models (meanings) in conjunction with feedback indicating bodily alertness, erect, dignified posture, and a half-smiling expression.

In the ICS cognitive architecture, the transformation processes that convert patterns of information in one code to patterns of information in another code, and the code-specific memory stores, are arranged in nine cognitive subsystems. Each subsystem is specialized for processing input in a given information code; all the transformation processes that take input in that code are included in the subsystem, as are the memory records that store representations of all the information entering the subsystem in that code.

Within ICS, information-processing involves the transformation of patterns in one information code into patterns in another information code. Extended information-processing involves a continuing flow and exchange of data between subsystems, in the course of which the nature of the information processed is repeatedly modified as a result of the actions of transformation processes and the contributions from memory stores. Such processing will often involve reciprocal transformations that, for example, create high-level meanings from patterns of low-level meanings and then create new low-level meanings from those high-level meanings. Information-processing can take as input either 'externally' derived patterns of sensory information originating in environmental events, or 'internally' derived patterns of information arising from previous processing or from access to memory.

The patterns of interaction between subsystems, and the content of the information flowing between them, will differ from one mental function to another. We can think of 'minds' as recurring 'alliances' or linked patterns of subsystems processing related material. Changes in mind-in-place correspond to shifts in these patterns of interaction, and changes in the content of the circulating information.

Having completed this brief primer in ICS, let us now apply this approach to understanding the persistence of minds-in-place in mood disorders.

A self-perpetuating depressive mind

ICS suggests that synthesis of an emotion-related schematic model, or high-level meaning, is the immediate antecedent to the production of an emotional response (Teasdale and Barnard 1993, chapter 7). If that emotional response is to be sustained, the relevant emotion-related schematic model has to be repeatedly re-synthesized. It follows that maintenance of a depressed state depends on the continuing production of depressogenic schematic models from patterns of specific meanings and patterns of sensorily derived input.

What keeps the production of depressogenic models going? In some situations, a continuing stream of severe loss events or difficulties from the environment may lead to repeated synthesis of depression-maintaining schematic models. However, often it appears that depression is maintained by more minor negative events that, if encountered in a non-depressed state, would not elicit much of a depressive response. At other times, depression seems to be maintained, not so much by negative environmental events, as by persistent streams of negative, ruminative, thoughts. ICS suggests that, in all these situations, any contribution to the production of depressogenic schematic models from environmental events is substantially enhanced, prolonged, or even supplanted by cognitive processes that support the 'internal maintenance' of depression. The ICS analysis suggests that such internal maintenance depends, to a considerable extent, on the establishment of self-perpetuating processing configurations that continue to regenerate depressogenic schematic models. Figure 4.2 illustrates a sketch of such a configuration, or 'mind' (see Teasdale and Barnard 1993, for a more detailed

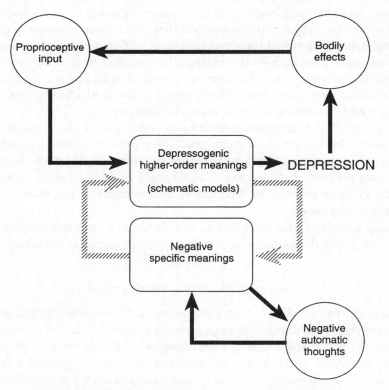

FIG. 4.2. Sketch of the Interacting Cognitive Subsystems (ICS) analysis of a self-perpetuating depressive 'mind'.

specification of the actual transformation operations involved and for a discussion of relevant evidence).

Let us focus on a number of key features of this 'mind'. First, there are two cognitive subsystems handling meaning. One subsystem handles specific meanings, the other handles higher order meanings, or schematic mental models of experience. These models represent recurring patterns, themes, and 'deep' interrelationships extracted from experience.

Second, depression is produced by the processing of schematic models encoding depressogenic themes or patterns. Specific meanings only contribute indirectly, through their influence on high-level meanings. Similarly, 'internal speech' in the form of 'negative automatic thoughts' only contributes indirectly to the production of depression, through the possibility of their influencing specific meanings, and thence high-level meanings.

Third, the system is dynamic. The maintenance of depression depends on the continuing regeneration of depressogenic schematic models. If this is blocked, for example by distraction tasks that take over the limited cognitive resources required for model regeneration, depression will lift (Fennell *et al.* 1987; Teasdale and Barnard 1993, chapter 13).

Fourth, the processing configuration or 'mind' shown is actually motivated to reduce depression, by reducing discrepancies between current and highly desired states of affairs [cf. self-awareness models of depression (Pyszczynski and Greenberg 1987; and see Teasdale and Barnard 1993, chapter 14) and self-discrepancy theory (Higgins 1987)]. However, the cognitive strategies directed to achieve that goal in this mind are dysfunctional: not only do these strategies fail to achieve the desired goal, they actually produce patterns of negative specific meanings that contribute to the synthesis of further depression-related schematic models.

Three aspects of this processing configuration contribute to the tendency to become stuck in this particular depressive 'mind-in-place'. The first is the feedback loop through which depression-related schematic models produce patterns of specific meanings that act to regenerate further depressogenic models (this loop is shown hatched in Fig. 4.2). Here, depressogenic schematic models output negative specific meanings (negative predictions for the future, attributions of failures to personal inadequacy, negative evaluations of interpersonal interactions, retrieval cues to access memories of previous failures or difficulties, etc.). These outputs will often be components of motivated processing routines, directed (ineffectually) at obtaining highly valued goals that can neither be attained nor relinquished (see Teasdale and Barnard 1993, chapter 14; and cf. Pyszczynski and Greenberg 1987). Because they encode specific negative meanings, these outputs, after further processing, may act to regenerate further depressogenic schematic models, similar to those from which the outputs were derived.

For example, a schematic model related to the theme ('self as a worthless, useless, incompetent person whose actions will probably fail but who has to keep seeking others' approval'), might output specific meanings related to attributions of personal inadequacy for a particular recent failure experience. Such specific meanings [e.g. 'It's because I'm no good as a person that I failed at X (or that Y dislikes me)'] are, of course, likely to fuel further synthesis of 'globally negative self' models on the next processing cycle. These negative specific meanings may also (but not necessarily) be experienced, downline, in 'inner speech' as streams of 'negative automatic thoughts' as a result of the operation of transformation processes that generate patterns of speech-level code from patterns of specific meanings (Fig. 4.2).

The second aspect contributing to the persistence of the depressive mind-in-place is a feedback loop through which sensory feedback from the bodily effects of depression also contributes to the regeneration of depressogenic schematic models. Here, depressogenic schematic models produce the bodily components of a depressive emotional response, such as reduced arousal and activation, bowed and stooped posture, tearful, sad, frowning expression, etc. These responses lead to sensorily derived (body-state) informational elements that, because they have been associated with the synthesis of depressogenic schematic models and the production of depression in the past, can contribute to the current synthesis of further depressogenic schematic models.

The third aspect acting to maintain the depressive mind-in-place can be referred to as 'cognitive imperialism': the tendency of depressogenic schematic models to set processing priorities for access to limited processing resources so that information that is likely to maintain depression is given preferential treatment to the exclusion of information related to other minds competing for the same cognitive resources. A range of experimentally demonstrated cognitive biases support the existence of such cognitive imperialism in depression (Teasdale and Barnard 1993, chapter 9).

The motivated processing configuration illustrated in Fig. 4.2, with its interconnected feedback loops, can be thought of as a 'mind'. Continuing occupation of the 'mind-in-place' by this mind will be associated with the maintenance of the depressed state, even in the absence of continuing experiences of aversive environmental events. Being 'stuck' in such a depressogenic mind seems to characterize a proportion of depressive disorders.

So, having described a more detailed analysis of a depressive mind-in-place, what does this view have to say about the relationship between cognition and emotion in terms of the issues raised in the introduction to this chapter?

The relationship between cognition and emotion revisited

The analysis presented suggests that the 'internal' maintenance of depression often depends on the integrity of a total self-perpetuating processing configuration, or 'mind'. To the extent that any one component of this total configuration can be isolated as 'causal' it would be the synthesis of depression-related high-level meanings, or schematic models. These meanings could be regarded as the immediate antecedent to the elicitation of a depressive emotional response. However, as we have indicated, the continuing production of such depressogenic models, itself, depends on, and is powerfully influenced by, the other components of the total configuration, including those that might normally be regarded as aspects of emotion or mood state. To that extent, depressogenic cognitions could be seen as dependent on, and consequences of, emotional state.

In fact, if we accept that, in practice, analyses will often have to be at the level of total, motivated, processing configurations, or 'minds', questions of antecedents, consequences, or even of reciprocal relationships between cognition and emotion considered in isolation cease to represent the key issues. Rather, we have to change our level of analysis to think in terms of more comprehensive patterns of information processing, extending through time. [Interestingly, Beck, Young, and their colleagues, working from a more clinical perspective, have recently arrived at a very similar conclusion in their concept of cognitive 'mode' (e.g., Beck, in press)]. Naturally, the details of this analysis are likely to vary from one clinical condition to another. Here, we shall continue to focus on those forms of (neurotic) depression to which the analysis presented seems most applicable, and examine the implications of this analysis for the cognitive behavioural treatment of such depressions. This will also provide an opportunity to consider a further issue raised at the beginning of this chapter — the distinction between different types of cognition in relation to emotion production, and the implications of this for treatment.

So, how can we assist someone who has become stuck in a depressive mind-in-place to shift out of this mind and into one that will allow them to recover from depression?

Changing the mind-in-place

As before, Robert Ornstein describes an incident that usefully focuses the mind on some key issues — this time the incident is from a social psychological study (Ornstein 1992, p. 203):

Imagine that you are at home on a quiet Sunday afternoon. The doorbell rings. It is a cordial and concerned couple. They show you a

10 cm × 15 cm card that they hope you will display in a window of your home. It says 'Keep California Beautiful'. You accept it and put the card in your window.

Two weeks later, another couple rings the doorbell. This time they are wearing 'Driver Safety' buttons and are lugging with them a 2 m × 3 m sign. It says 'DRIVE CAREFULLY' in big black letters. They ask if you would put it on your front lawn, even though it would block your view of the street and darken the whole house.

As Ornstein notes, one would imagine that few people would agree to such a request. And indeed, in the study from which this incident comes, almost nobody who had not been visited by the 'Keep California Beautiful' couple agreed. However, of those people who had been visited by this couple, an extraordinary 60% agreed to put up the huge sign!

It appears that the experience of agreeing to the original minor request to put a card in the window created an 'acquiescent mind' that could later be reinstated by the related, but much more substantial, request to put up the huge notice.

More generally, it seems we have a 'memory for minds': having once had a particular mind occupy the position of mind-in-place in a particular context, there is a tendency for that mind to be reinstated, subsequently, in similar contexts. Within ICS, a key aspect of this phenomenon is the storage and retrieval of schematic mental models.

ICS suggests that all the schematic models created in situations are stored in a specialized memory system, from which they can be accessed by retrieval cues, much as any other form of information. From this perspective, the initial experience with the 'Keep California Beautiful' couple in Ornstein's story led to storage of a model related to themes of agreeing to help with socially useful projects. In subjects with this prior experience, the visit by the second couple was sufficiently similar to the original experience to access this stored model, which, applied in the later context, led to their agreement, even though the request was now more outrageous.

So how is this analysis relevant to depression? If someone has been stuck in a depressive mind-in-place for any length of time, there will be many recent examples of depressogenic schematic models stored in memory. These models can be accessed automatically in appropriate contexts. It follows that, even if a depressed individual manages to switch temporarily to another mind, for example in a distraction task (e.g., Fennell *et al.* 1987), once the distraction task is over, there will be a tendency for stored depressogenic models to be accessed from memory. Having been accessed, these depressogenic models will, in their imperialistic way, impose their own self-perpetuating processing priorities, and so reinstate a depressive mind-in-place.

This reinstatement could be prevented by creating a stock of alternative schematic models related to depression. These alternative models will need to be sufficiently similar to depressogenic models that they will be accessed from memory by the same cues or contexts that would otherwise access depressogenic models. On the other hand, these alternative models will need to differ from depressogenic models so that they will not, themselves, elicit depression.

On this view, the task of psychological treatments is to create a store of alternative depression-related models associated with a wide variety of possible eliciting contexts.

Psychological treatment of depression

Ornstein's story illustrates very powerfully how a single experience led to the storage, in memory, of a representation of a related schematic model. This model, subsequently accessed in a related context, altered dramatically the response that would otherwise have occurred. Extrapolating to depression, this analysis suggests that arranging situations in which patients approach symptoms of depression, and related experiences, with a different 'mind-set' or mind-in-place, will create a store of modified depression-related models. These alternative models can then be accessed, subsequently, in similar contexts, pre-empting access to depressogenic models and the re-establishment of the depressive mind-in-place.

This analysis suggests that structured psychological treatments for depression, both cognitive therapy and behavioural approaches, achieve their long-term effects through the creation of a store of memories of alternative depression-related models (Teasdale and Barnard 1993, chapter 16; Teasdale *et al.* 1995*a*). Homework assignments are important because they ensure that these modified models are created in association with a wide range of contexts. Consequently, the chances of these contexts subsequently accessing these alternative models are increased.

Clinical observation suggests that cognitive therapy often leads to a shift in perspective, sometimes referred to as 'decentring' or 'disidentification'; patients move to a wider perspective on their symptoms and problems in which, rather than simply 'being' their emotion, or identifying personally with negative thoughts and feelings, patients relate to negative experiences as mental events in a wider context or field of awareness. In terms of the present analysis, this shift involves the creation of alternative schematic models; patients create models related to themes such as: depression-as-a-psychological-state-in-which-I-see-myself-as-worthless, in contrast to models related to depressogenic themes such as: the reality-of-my-worthlessness-and-the-hope-lessness-of-the-current-situation.

On this view, an important aspect of answering negative automatic thoughts may be that, in addition to any effects arising directly from changes in specific thoughts, the thought-answering exercise, itself, implicitly creates a modified mind-set or model. This alternative model embodies a different view and relationship to depressive experience in general: 'thoughts and feelings as mental events that can be considered and examined', rather than 'thoughts as self-evident facts'. Similarly, an important feature of behaviour experiments in cognitive therapy may be that, in addition to the actual 'evidence', in the shape of specific facts, that they yield, they implicitly create a 'set' or 'mind' which involves a different relationship to difficult experiences; 'problems to be considered, approached, and investigated', rather than 'further evidence of my inadequacy and the hopelessness of my position'.

We recently had the opportunity to make a preliminary test of these ideas in the context of the Cambridge/Newcastle collaborative study of residual depressive chronicity. In this controlled treatment trial, cognitive therapy, combined with antidepressant medication and clinical management, is compared with antidepressant medication and clinical management alone. The principal investigators in this trial are Professors Gene Paykel, Jan Scott, and myself.

Previous clinical trials that have compared cognitive therapy with antidepressant medication in the treatment of depression have provided encouraging evidence for an enduring prophylactic effect of cognitive therapy; relapse rates are lower in patients who have received cognitive therapy, after treatment has been completed, than in patients who have received antidepressants, after medication has been withdrawn (see Teasdale *et al.* 1995*a*, for relevant evidence). These are particularly exciting findings, as it is increasingly recognized that the major challenge in the treatment of depression is the prevention of relapse and recurrence following recovery from the treated episode. However, the mechanisms through which any preventative effects of cognitive therapy are achieved remain unclear. The Cambridge/Newcastle collaborative study provided an opportunity to explore these mechanisms further.

In order to test the idea that the long-term effects of cognitive therapy are mediated through access to a store of alternative depression-related models in memory, Richard Moore, Hazel Hayhurst, and I devised a new assessment instrument. Patients were presented descriptions of scenarios involving depression-related themes. They were instructed to put themselves into the situations and to feel the feelings described. For each scenario, they were asked to remember a particular experience from their lives brought to mind by the feelings evoked by the description.

The aim of this measure was to create an analogue of the experience in which an individual is exposed to a situation involving depression-related themes, and to infer the kind of schematic models automatically accessed from memory by that situation. In particular, we were interested in the extent to which the models accessed from memory involved a wider perspective on thoughts and feelings as mental events in the field of awareness, rather than as phenomena with which patients identified personally as aspects of themselves. We called this dimension meta-awareness.

Patients gave detailed descriptions of the situations brought to mind by the scenarios. From these descriptions, judges rated the extent of meta-awareness shown at the time of the original event on a 1–5 scale, higher scores representing greater meta-awareness. Ratings were made blind to treatment condition.

A preliminary analysis of the results from the first 36 patients to complete treatment showed that patients receiving cognitive therapy in addition to antidepressants showed a significantly greater increase in meta-awareness than patients receiving antidepressants alone. The easiest way to illustrate this difference is in terms of the percentage of memories that were rated at 4 or above on the meta-awareness scale. In these memories, 'at some point, the subject saw their thoughts and feelings in a wider perspective; there was a discrimination of self from thoughts and feelings'. In other words, patients decentred.

Very few memories (approximately 5%) showed evidence of this level of meta-awareness prior to treatment. On post-treatment measures, cognitive therapy was associated with a substantial increase in the percentage of memories showing evidence of decentring (to 25%). This was significantly greater than the change in the medication only group, where very little change occurred.

These findings are particularly interesting because, in the treatment of depression generally, it has been difficult to show, on any cognitive measure, modality-specific effects of cognitive therapy that are not simply attributable to post-treatment differences in severity of depression. These preliminary findings also provide encouraging support for the analysis described. The really interesting question, of course, is whether the specific effects of cognitive therapy revealed by the measure of meta-awareness actually mediate any long-term effects of cognitive therapy in preventing relapse in the future. To answer that question we shall have to wait until we have completed treatment on the total sample of 160 patients in the trial and followed them to one year.

Two kinds of meaning and cognitive therapy

The suggestion that cognitive therapy acts through changing schematic models is distinct from, on the one hand, the idea that patients simply learn a specific set of coping techniques, and, on the other hand, the idea that cognitive therapy works by changing schemas conceived as dysfunctional rules or beliefs. These distinctions can be amplified by further consideration of the two kinds of meaning touched on earlier (see Teasdale 1993 for a fuller discussion).

The Interacting Cognitive Subsystem (ICS) recognizes two qualitatively distinct kinds of meaning, a specific and a more generic, and suggests that emotion is linked directly only to the more generic form of meaning.

In ICS, specific meanings are represented by patterns of Propositional code, and refer to specific concepts and the relationships between them, as in, for example, 'the cat sat on the mat'. Meaning at this level is not difficult to grasp, and corresponds fairly closely to the meanings conveyed by single sentences in language. Such meanings have a truth value that can be assessed, and the examination of such meanings by the collection of data, consideration of evidence, and the like, is, of course, the focus of much activity in cognitive therapy.

ICS also recognizes a more generic level of meaning, corresponding to schematic mental models of experience, and represented in patterns of Implicational code. Such meanings represent deep regularities, themes, interrelationships, and prototypical features extracted from the patterns of specific meanings and sensory features that recur across experiences that share deep similarities, even though they may be superficially different. These higher-order meanings are much more difficult to convey than specific meanings as there is no direct correspondence between this level of representation and language. Implicational meanings do not have a truth value that can be evaluated or tested by the collection of evidence. Sensory features, such as tone and loudness of voice, or proprioceptive feedback (e.g., from bodily sensations related to posture or facial expression), can make a direct contribution to Implicational meaning.

Implicational meanings are associated with intuitive, holistic, 'felt senses' or feelings (cf. Laird's suggestion, noted at the beginning of this chapter, that 'feelings *are* cognitions'). For example, a sense of confidence marks the creation of schematic models associated with themes of competence, worth, optimism, and positive expectancy. In relation to the self, Propositional meanings refer to aspects of the self-as-object, whereas Implicational meanings are associated with different experiences of self-as-subject. From this perspective, the same words 'I am worthless' can refer to two, qualitatively distinct meanings; at the specific Propositional level the meaning is 'there is nothing of worth about me as an object'; at the Implicational level, the feeling 'I am worthless' marks the processing of a much more generic representation related to themes extracted from experiences in which an individual has been humiliated or rejected.

As far as treatment is concerned, the important points are: (1) only generic meanings are directly linked to emotion; (2) generic and specific meanings are qualitatively different so that one cannot simply be reduced to another; and (3) different forms of intervention are likely to be required for these two kinds of meaning.

The relation between specific and generic meanings is analogous to the relationship between the letters that make up a sentence and the meaning of the sentence. A sentence conveys a specific meaning that is qualitatively different from and greater than the sum of its individual letters. In the same way, the generic meaning of a schematic model is qualitatively different from and greater than the sum of the patterns of specific meanings that contribute towards it.

Poetry provides a good illustration of this qualitative distinction between forms of meaning. The extract of a poem shown below conveys a sense of melancholy and abandonment, marking the synthesis of a related schematic model. The alternative version of the poem retains the same sequence of specific meanings, but, expressed in different words, with different sounds, rhythms, and imagery, the effect is very different. It is clear that the Implicational meaning of the schematic model created by the first version cannot be reduced simply to the sum of its constituent specific meanings.

The suggestion that there are qualitatively different forms of meaning, only one of which is directly linked to emotion, has profound implications for our understanding of therapeutic change (Teasdale 1993; Teasdale and Barnard 1993, chapter 16). It suggests that the primary aim of treatment should be to change schematic mental models. Sometimes, this may be achieved by changing the individual specific meanings that contribute to these models, using procedures such as gathering evidence for and against beliefs, but often that will not be enough (c.f. Padesky's 'Isn't change in beliefs one of the

TABLE 4.2. Poetry as Implicational meaning. The original poem in the upper part of the table and the alternative version in the lower part have the same sequence of propositional meanings. However, only the original version conveys a coherent Implicational 'sense'. (From Teasdale and Barnard 1993)

O what can ail thee, knight-at arms,
Alone and palely loitering?
The sedge has wither'd from the lake,
And no birds sing.

What is the matter, armed old-fashioned soldier,
standing by yourself and doing nothing with a pallid expression?
The reed-like plants have decomposed by the lake
and there are not any birds singing.

primary goals of cognitive therapy? Yes . . . and no' noted in the introduction to this chapter). The ICS analysis suggests that such procedures, although they may be appropriate for changing meanings at the specific level, may not be appropriate when cognitive therapy is attempting to achieve change at the schematic level. In this respect, the ICS analysis differs from the view that regards schemas primarily as dysfunctional proposition-like beliefs. Taken at face value, the schemas-as-dysfunctional-beliefs approach suggests that essentially similar approaches will be appropriate for changing beliefs, whether they are at a specific or more schematic level—the difference between these two levels is essentially one of degree rather than kind.

In contrast, the ICS analysis suggests that, in order to achieve change at the level of schematic models, it is not sufficient simply to gather data *about* experience, and evaluate beliefs against this evidence. Rather, it is necessary to arrange for actual experiences in which new or modified models are created. As far as self-related models are concerned, this would mean changes in patient's actual way of *being*, rather than the detached consideration of evidence for or against beliefs related to self-as-object, described in some accounts of schema change procedures in cognitive therapy. For example, although dispassionately reviewing evidence of previous successes might be an appropriate way to invalidate the specific propositional belief 'I am a total failure as a person', this would probably not be an effective way to create alternative self-related schematic models. The recall of previous success experiences that might be involved in such reviews achieve change in affect-related models, but only if recall was associated with re-experience of success-related positive affect, marking access to the related positive self-models stored in memory. Alternatively, enactive procedures could be used to create, on-line, success- or mastery-related schematic models. On the other hand, it might also be important to help clients, at times when they they feel total failures, to relate to themselves more gently and kindly, in that way creating a store of alternative models related to failure.

Use of enactive procedures, either in reality or imagination, is, of course, the bedrock of behaviour therapy. It is often asserted that therapeutic change is mediated cognitively, but the most effective way to change cognition is to change behaviour. The present analysis extends this position by suggesting that enactive procedures may not simply be a more powerful way of achieving changes in meaning that can be achieved more slowly by purely cognitive techniques. Rather, it suggests that enactive and 'rational' approaches may be particularly relevant to different kinds of meaning. Equally, the current analysis suggests that the important aspect of enactive procedures may not be simply that a particular behaviour is performed so much as the mind-set or schematic model that is in place as the deed is done; it is not what is done but the way that it is done that is of critical importance.

Conclusions

Attempts to understand the relationship between cognition and emotion, and to treat mood disorders, push us towards recognizing the importance of higher levels of cognitive representation and organization. These higher levels can be usefully thought of in terms of 'minds'. The task of psychological treatments is to change the 'mind' that gets automatically switched on by particular contexts, and, ultimately, to give individuals, themselves, greater control over the switching in and out of different minds-in-place.

Over the years, and over an impressive range of problem areas, the University of Oxford Department of Psychiatry has had an enormous, and widely respected, influence in furthering an undogmatic, applied science approach to the development, evaluation, and investigation of behaviour and cognitive behaviour therapies. The world-wide impact of this work is eloquent testimony to the vision that Michael Gelder showed, from the very inception of the Department that he created, and to the care with which, over many years, he has fostered and nurtured research in psychological treatment. May he be delighted with the fruits of his labours.

References

Bargh, J. A., Barndollar, K., and Gollwitzer, P. M. (1994). *Environmental control of behavior*. Unpublished manuscript, New York University. Cited in Bargh, J. A. and Barndollar, K. (1995). Automaticity in action: the unconscious as repository of chronic goals and motives. In *The psychology of action* (ed. P. M. Gollwitzer and J. A. Bargh) Guilford Press, New York.

Barnard, P. J. and Teasdale, J. D. (1991). Interacting cognitive subsystems: A systemic approach to cognitive-affective interaction and change. *Cognition and Emotion* 5, 1–39.

Beck, A. T. (in press). The concept of mode. In P. M. Salkovskis (ed.), *Frontiers of cognitive therapy*, Guilford Press, New York.

Blaney, P. H. (1986). Affect and memory: A review. *Psychological Bulletin*, 99, 229–46.

Bower, G. H. (1981). Mood and memory. *American Psychologist*, 36, 129–48.

Clark, D. M. and Teasdale, J. D. (1982). Diurnal variation in clinical depression and accessibility of memories of positive and negative experiences. *Journal of Abnormal Psychology*, 91, 87–95.

Fennell, M. J. V., Teasdale, J. D., Jones, S., and Damlé, A. (1987). Distraction in neurotic and endogenous depression: An investigation of negative thinking in major depressive disorder. *Psychological Medicine*, 17, 441–52.

Fodor, J. (1983). *The modularity of mind. An essay on faculty psychology*. MIT Press/Bradford, Cambridge, MA.

Haaga, D. A. F., Dyck, M. J., and Ernst, D. (1991). Empirical status of cognitive theory of depression. *Psychological Bulletin*, 110, 215–36.

Higgins, E. T. (1987). Self-discrepancy: A theory relating self and affect. *Psychological Review*, 94, 319–40.

Ingram, R. E. (1984). Toward an information-processing analysis of depression. *Cognitive Therapy and Research*, 8, 443–78.

Johnson, M. K. and Multhaup, K. S. (1992). Emotion and MEM. In *Handbook of emotion and memory research and theory* (ed. S. A. Christianson), pp. 33–66. Erlbaum, Hillsdale, NJ.

Laird, J. D. (1989). Mood affects memory because feelings *are* cognitions. *Journal of Social Behavior and Personality*, 4, (special issue), 33–8.

Leventhal, H. (1984). A perceptual-motor theory of emotion. In *Advances in experimental social psychology*, Vol. 17, (ed. L. Berkowitz), pp. 117–82. Academic Press, New York.

Lloyd, G. G. and Lishman, W. A. (1975). Effect of depression on the speed of recall of pleasant and unpleasant experiences. *Psychological Medicine*, 5, 173–80.

Morris, W. N. (1989). *Mood. The frame of mind.* Springer, New York.

Ornstein, R. (1992). *The evolution of consciousness.* Simon & Schuster, New York.

Padesky, C. A. (1993). *Socratic questioning: changing minds or guiding discovery?* Keynote address to European Congress of Behavioural and Cognitive Therapies, London.

Parrott, G. W. and Sabini, J. (1990). Mood and memory under natural conditions: Evidence for mood incongruent recall. *Journal of Personality and Social Psychology*, 59, 321–36.

Power, M. J. and Dalgleish, T. I. (in press). *Cognition and emotion: from order to disorder*, Erlbaum, Hove, UK.

Pyszczynski, T. and Greenberg, J. (1987). Self-regulatory perseveration and the depressive self-focusing style: A self-awareness theory of reactive depression. *Psychological Bulletin*, 102, 122–38.

Sheppard, L. C. and Teasdale, J. D. (in press). Depressive thinking: changes in schematic mental models of self and world. *Psychological Medicine*.

Simons, A. D., Garfield, S. L., and Murphy, G. E. (1984). The process of change in cognitive therapy and pharmacotherapy for depression: Changes in mood and cognition. *Archives of General Psychiatry*, 41, 45–51.

Srull, T. K. and Wyer, R. S. (1979). The role of category accessibility in the interpretation of information about persons: some determinants and implications. *Journal of Personality and Social Psychology*, 37, 1660–72.

Teasdale, J. D. (1983). Negative thinking in depression: Cause, effect or reciprocal relationship? *Advances in Behaviour Research and Therapy*, 5, 3–25.

Teasdale, J. D. (1988). Cognitive vulnerability to persistent depression. *Cognition and Emotion*, 2, 247–74.

Teasdale, J. D. (1993). Emotion and two kinds of meaning: Cognitive therapy and applied cognitive science. *Behaviour Research and Therapy*, 31, 339–54.

Teasdale, J. D. (in press). Clinically relevant theory: integrating clinical insight with cognitive science. In *Frontiers of cognitive therapy* (ed. P. M. Salkovskis). Guilford Press, New York.

Teasdale, J. D. and Barnard, P. J. (1993). *Affect, cognition and change: re-modelling depressive thought.* Erlbaum, Hove, UK.

Teasdale, J. D. and Dent, J. (1987). Cognitive vulnerability to depression: an investigation of two hypotheses. *British Journal of Clinical Psychology*, 26, 113–26.

Teasdale, J. D. and Fogarty, S. J. (1979). Differential effects of induced mood on retrieval of pleasant and unpleasant events from episodic memory. *Journal of Abnormal Psychology*, 88, 248–57.

Teasdale, J. D. and Russell, M. L. (1983). Differential effects of induced mood on the recall of positive, negative and neutral words. *British Journal of Clinical Psychology*, 22, 163–71.

Teasdale, J. D. and Taylor, R. (1981). Induced mood and accessibility of memories: An effect of mood state or of induction procedure? *British Journal of Clinical Psychology*, **20**, 39–48.

Teasdale, J. D., Taylor, R., and Fogarty, S. J. (1980). Effects of induced elation depression on the accessibility of memories of happy and unhappy experiences. *Behavior Research and Therapy*, **18**, 339–46.

Teasdale, J. D., Segal, Z. V., and Williams, J. M. G. (1995*a*). How does cognitive therapy prevent depressive relapse and why should attentional control (mindfulness) training help? *Behaviour Research and Therapy*, **33**, 25–39.

Teasdale, J. D., Taylor, M. J., Cooper, Z., Hayhurst, H., and Paykel, E. S. (1995*b*). Depressive thinking: shifts in construct accessibility or in schematic mental models? *Journal of Abnormal Psychology*, **104**, 500–7.

Teasdale, J. D., Taylor, M. J., and Lloyd, C. A. (in prep.). *Dysfunctional schematic mental models in depression*. Unpublished data, MRC Applied Psychology Unit, Cambridge, UK.

5

Efficacy and dissemination of psychological treatments

David H. Barlow and Stefan G. Hofmann

Professionals and policy-makers around the world have now concluded that effective psychological treatments exist. Although those now entering the mental health professions may not be surprised by this conclusion, the full realization that a number of procedures are available with specific effectiveness for identifiable disorders has only occurred in the past five years (Barlow 1994a). Furthermore, these psychological procedures are, in most instances, more effective than credible alternatives and/or pharmacological approaches based on the results of current clinical trials (Barlow 1994a; Andrews *et al.* submitted).

Although psychotherapy has been practised for centuries, it was not until Hans Eysenck (1952) issued his then heretical challenge on the ineffectiveness of psychotherapy that a general realization slowly emerged of the need for the development of a database in this area. It was only in the 1960s, beginning with the pioneering work of Michael Gelder and others (e.g., Gelder and Marks 1966; Gelder *et al.* 1967; Meyer and Gelder 1963) that controlled systematic study of the effectiveness of psychotherapeutic interventions began.

The ensuing 30 years, which spans most of the length of the very productive career of Michael Gelder, has seen no less than a revolution in conceptions of the development, evaluation, and dissemination of psychological procedures. This resolution has culminated in the current general acceptance on the part of policy-makers and professionals alike that we have effective psychological procedures for specific problems. But progress has not been the linear over the decades, and much work still remains. From the perspective of the present it is useful to review, briefly, current thinking on the process of developing and evaluating psychological treatments.

In 1980, Agras and Berkowitz (1980) published a model of clinical research that is still useful in ascertaining the effectiveness of specific psychological procedures (see Fig. 5.1). The first stage involves assessing the current status of interventions in the context of a specific disorder or problem, as well as

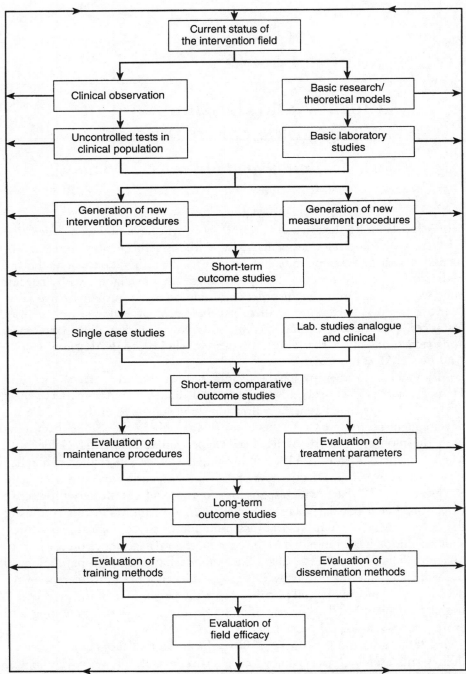

FIG. 5.1. A progressive model of clinical research for psychological procedures. (From Agras and Berkowitz 1980, with permission.)

examining the various sources of ideas on the development of new procedures or the enhancement of existing procedures for the disorder or problem in question. Some of these sources include basic research, new theoretical developments, or innovations by creative clinicians working in the area. Once a potentially useful procedure is developed or discovered, the next step typically involves short-term clinical trials to determine the effectiveness of the procedure compared to no treatment. In evaluating pharmacological interventions, this stage would be similar to the 'open label' study in which a medication is compared to customary and usual treatment, or to no treatment, without appropriate experimental controls in place. If efficacy of a psychological procedure is established in these initial stages, this process then continues with a component analysis of the treatment approach and/or short-term comparative outcome studies comparing the treatment to other alternative interventions for a specific problem. The alternative interventions in the context of evaluating therapies are most often attention placebo controls or credible existing psychological procedures. This strategy is roughly parallel to the double-blind placebo control strategy for evaluating pharmacological agents. If effectiveness of a psychological procedure is further established, additional goals include establishing the long-term effects of treatment as well as determining the most efficient way of disseminating and delivering the treatment. A final step is what Agras and Berkowitz (1980) then called 'field efficacy', which refers to ascertaining the feasibility and generality of the experimental treatment when applied in typical clinical settings.

With the growing realization that we have effective psychological treatments, as well as effective drug treatments for a number of disorders, there has emerged, among policy-makers, a new strategy called 'best practices' or 'clinical practice guidelines' (Barlow 1994a). In the United States, Congress created a new federal agency in 1989 called the Agency for Health Care Policy and Research (AHCPR). The sole purpose of this agency is to determine the effectiveness of treatments for specific disorders and to promulgate appropriate treatment guidelines for specific disorders based on this information. The overriding goal of these types of efforts is to correct the enormous variability in treatment delivery wherein any number of patients might receive ineffective treatments, or treatments with no proven efficacy for a given disorder, despite the fact that effective treatments exist. These clinical practice guidelines, which had their origins in medical disorders, have now rapidly spread to the full range of psychological disorders. In a variety of subtle ways, these guidelines are assuming the force of law. For example, in several states within the United States, practitioners who can demonstrate that they followed relevant clinical practice guidelines would be immune from malpractice litigation. Conversely, those practitioners who strayed too far from these guidelines would be subject to costly litigation in the event of some adverse outcomes.

Since the development of clinical practice guidelines is so crucial, a Task Force appointed by the American Psychological Association (APA) and chaired by one of the authors (DHB) recently developed a template for constructing and evaluating guidelines for clinical interventions in the area of behavioural health care (APA 1995). This template requires that clinical practice guidelines for behavioural health care be constructed on the basis of two simultaneous considerations or 'axes'. The first is that guidelines take into consideration a rigorous assessment of scientific evidence with the goal of measuring the efficacy of any given intervention. The second axis specifies that guidelines consider the applicability and feasibility of the intervention in the local setting where it is to be proffered as well as a determination of the generalizability of an intervention of established efficacy. In recent years, the terms 'internal validity' or 'efficacy' have most often been used to describe data emanating from studies on the first axis, while the terms 'external validity' or 'effectiveness' have sometimes been used to describe the second axis. However, the term chosen by the Task Force for this second axis is 'clinical utility'.

The purpose of this template (see Table 5.1) is to provide a 'road map' for constructing and evaluating clinical practice guidelines which are currently proliferating and coming from various sources (both public and private).

However, this template also extends the model of Agras and Berkowitz (1980) by updating and elaborating on the concept of 'field efficacy'. Specifically, the current status of psychological interventions, as reviewed briefly below, reflects the fact that we have accumulated sufficient studies on the internal validity or efficacy axis to state that we now have effective treatments. However, we know less about the feasibility and generalizability of these treatments when delivered in the very settings for which they were devised, such as clinics, hospitals, and rural health centres. Thus, determining the clinical utility of psychological interventions with proven efficacy, modifying these interventions to be the most efficacious in the variety of settings in which they will be utilized, and discovering how best to disseminate these relatively new approaches to reach the widest number of practitioners and patients is the challenge ahead of us.

In the remainder of this chapter we will review briefly the current status of the efficacy of psychological interventions, as well as current evidence pertaining to the effectiveness of combined psychological and drug treatments. This will be followed by a review of efforts to disseminate treatments to those who need them.

Efficacy of psychological treatments

Clinical research has demonstrated that psychological treatments, as practised in out-patient settings, are clearly effective for a number of mental disorders

TABLE 5.1. Overview of the template for constructing psychological intervention guidelines

Internal validity (efficacy)	External validity (clinical utility)

1. Better than alternative therapy (randomized controlled trials — RCTs)
2. Better than non-specific therapy (RCTs)
3. Better than no therapy (RCTs)
4. Quantified clinical observations
5. Strongly positive clinical consensus
6. Mixed clinical consensus
7. Strongly negative clinical consensus
8. Contradictory evidence
 	
Note. Confidence in treatment efficacy is based on both: (a) the absolute and relative efficacy of the treatment; and (b) the quality of the studies on which the judgement is made, as well as their replicability.
	1. Feasibility
	  A. Patient acceptability (cost, pain, duration, side-effects, etc.)
	  B. Patient-choice in face of relatively equal efficacy
	  C. Probability of compliance
	  D. Ease of disseminability, (e.g., number of practitioners with competence, requirements for training, opportunities for training, need for costly technologies, or additional support personnel, etc.)
	
	2. Generalizability
	  A. Patient characteristics
	    (i) cultural background issues
	    (ii) gender issues
	    (iii) developmental issues
	    (iv) other relevant patient characteristics
	  B. Therapist characteristics
	  C. Issues of robustness when applied in practice settings with different time frames, etc.
	  D. Contextual factors regarding setting in which treatment is delivered
	
	3. Costs and benefits
	  A. Costs of delivering intervention to individual and society
	  B. Costs of withholding intervention to individual and society of effective intervention
	
	Note. Confidence in clinical utility as reflected on these 3 dimensions should be based on systematic and objective methods and strategies for assessing these characteristics of treatment as they are applied in actual practice. In some cases, randomized controlled trials will exist. More often, data will be in the form of quantified clinical observations (clinical replication series) or other strategies such as health economic calculations.

(From APA 1995, copyright by the American Psychological Association. Reprinted with permission.)

compared to credible interventions characterized as placebo (e.g., Andrews *et al.* submitted). For example, Andrews *et al.* utilizing a meta-analytic methodology identified average effect sizes and subject numbers associated with studies carried out on pharmacological treatments during the 1980s (e.g., data from the Quality Assurance Project 1983, 1985). These effect sizes and the studies that produced them were designated by the World Health Organization (WHO) as sufficient such that the drug treatment included in these studies were placed on the WHO list of essential drug treatments. The identified effect sizes of these successful pharmacological treatments were then compared to the effect sizes of psychological treatments in published studies. In addition, the authors used a series of stringent inclusion criteria before determining that an effective treatment exists. Those criteria included: (1) the existence of at least three independent studies; (2) sufficient specification of the psychological treatment to allow replication; (3) clear diagnoses of the targeted clinical disorder; and (4) the ability to calculate the effects and standard deviations compared to a well-matched 'placebo' psychological treatment. Using these criteria, the authors identified 29 trials across six disorders that were included in the meta-analysis. As evident in Fig. 5.2, cognitive behaviour therapy was effective for a number of mental disorders, including alcohol abuse and dependence, major depressive disorder, panic disorder, generalized anxiety disorder, obsessive–compulsive disorder, and even schizophrenia (in combination with medication). The solid line in Fig. 5.2 identifies the effect sizes of successful pharmacological treatments and marks the threshold for satisfactory treatment.

Recently, the Division of Clinical Psychology of the APA created a Task Force on Promotion and Dissemination of Psychological Procedures (APA 1993). Recognizing that evidence now exists for the efficacy of psychological treatments, the goal of the Task Force was to identify effective treatments for particular disorders based on current evidence, and make recommendations on more effective ways to disseminate these approaches. The Task Force first summarized some of the literature on the efficacy of different psychotherapeutic approaches. Although the initial list of treatments was not the product of an exhaustive review of the literature, the list provided documentation, at a glance, of the current status of psychological treatment. Using strict methodological criteria, the Task Force then classified treatments into the categories 'well-established treatments', 'probably efficacious treatments', and 'experimental treatments'. A particular treatment was classified into the category 'well-established' if either one of the following two criteria were met: (1) at least two experimental clinical trials, conducted by different investigators, demonstrating the efficacy of treatment (the treatment must have been either equivalent to an already established treatment or superior to pill, psychological placebo, or to another treatment); or (2) a large series of

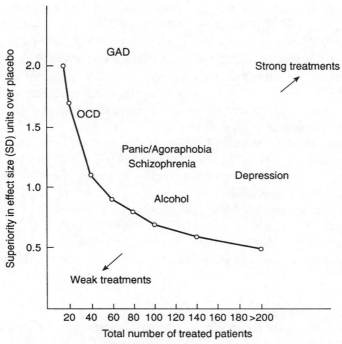

FIG. 5.2. Threshold for a satisfactory treatment: superiority of various cognitive behaviour therapy treatments in effect (SD) units over placebo. (GAD, generalized anxiety disorder; OCD, obsessive–compulsive disorder.) From Andrews *et al.* (submitted), with permission.

single-case design studies demonstrating efficacy of the treatment. These single case studies must have used adequate experimental designs and must have compared the intervention to other treatments. Furthermore, the intervention has to be specified in treatment manuals, and characteristics of the client samples must have been clearly delineated.

The Task Force identified a number of effective psychological techniques for the treatment of various mental disorders, including depression (DiMascio *et al.* 1979; Dobson 1989; Lewinsohn *et al.* 1989), somatic problems (Blanchard *et al.* 1987; Keefe *et al.* 1992; Kupfersmid 1989; Wright and Walker 1978), sexual dysfunctions (Auerbach and Kilmann 1977; LoPiccolo and Stock 1986), eating disorders (Fairburn *et al.* 1993; Wilfley *et al.* 1993), marital problems (Azrin *et al.* 1980; Jacobson and Follette 1985; Johnson and Greenberg 1985), various childhood disorders (Matson and Taras 1989; Kupfersmid 1989; Wright and Walker 1978; Wells and Egan 1988; Walter and Gilmore 1973), obsessive–compulsive disorder (Marks and O'Sullivan 1988; Steketee *et al.* 1982), generalized anxiety disorder (Butler *et al.* 1991; Borkovec *et al.* 1987; Chambless and Gillis 1993), panic disorder with and without agoraphobia (Barlow *et al.* 1989; Clark *et al.* 1994; Mattick *et al.* 1990; Öst 1988; Öst and Westling 1991; Trull *et al.* 1988), specific phobia (Kazdin and Wilcoxin 1976), post-traumatic stress disorder (Foa *et al.* 1991), social phobia (Heimberg *et al.* 1990; Mattick and Peters 1988), schizophrenia (in combination with medication; Hogarty *et al.* 1986; Falloon *et al.* 1985; Liberman 1972), and borderline personality disorder (Linehan *et al.* 1991). Table 5.2 gives an overview of some of the most effective psychological treatments for common mental disorders.

In an important development, Roth and Fonagy (1995) reviewed the status of psychological treatments in a commissioned report to the UK National Health Service (NHS) in order to create a policy for the delivery of psychological treatments within the service. Similar to the APA Task Force, the NHS report underscored the effectiveness of a number of psychological interventions, particularly of cognitive behaviour therapy and interpersonal psychotherapy (IPT), for a variety of mental disorders, including anxiety disorders, depression, eating disorders, psychotic disorders, and personality disorders.

Psychological treatments, pharmacotherapy, or both?

The comparative effectiveness of psychological and pharmacological treatments, as well as combination treatments, has been explored in a limited fashion, particularly with anxiety disorders. Frequently prescribed drugs for treating anxiety disorders include benzodiazepines, tricyclic antidepressants, and monoamine oxidase inhibitors (MAOIs). In treating panic disorder, some studies suggest that approximately 60% of patients are panic-free as long as they stay on an effective drug (e.g., Ballenger *et al.* 1988; Klosko *et al.* 1990). However, relapse rate is relatively high once patients stop taking medication. Studies reported relapse rates between 20% and 50% after stopping tricyclic antidepressants (Telch 1988; Telch *et al.* 1983) and between 50% and 60% after discontinuation of benzodiazepines (Marks *et al.* 1993; Spiegel *et al.* 1994). Each class of drugs has advantages and disadvantages in the treatment of anxiety disorders. For example, imipramine produces adverse side-effects such as dizziness, dry mouth, and on occasion sexual dysfunction. For that reason, many patients refuse to stay on it for very long. However, if patients can become accustomed to the side-effects or wait until they wear off, they may often find the drug to be very helpful. On the other hand, high-potency benzodiazepines (BZs), such as alprazolam, have a rapid effect, but are difficult to stop taking due to psychological and physical dependence and addiction (Rickels *et al.* 1990; Schweizer *et al.* 1990; Noyes *et al.* 1991). Furthermore, BZs may create some interference with both cognitive and

TABLE 5.2. Examples of empirically validated psychological treatments

Well-established treatments	Study
Cognitive behaviour therapy for panic disorder with and without agoraphobia	Barlow et al. (1989) Clark et al. (1994)
Cognitive behaviour therapy for generalized anxiety disorder	Butler et al. (1991) Borkovec et al. (1987)
Exposure treatment for phobias (agoraphobia, social phobia, simple phobia) and post-traumatic stress disorder	Mattick et al. (1990) Trull et al. (1988)
Group cognitive behaviour therapy for social phobia	Heimberg et al. (1990) Mattick and Peters (1988)
Systematic desensitization for simple phobia	Kazdin and Wilcoxin (1976)
Exposure and response prevention for obsessive–compulsive disorder	Marks and O'Sullivan (1982) Steketee et al. (1982)
Beck's cognitive therapy for depression	Dobson (1989)
Klerman and Weissman's interpersonal therapy for depression	DiMascio et al. (1979) Elkin et al. (1989)
Interpersonal therapy for bulimia	Fairburn et al. (1993) Wilfey et al. (1993)
Cognitive behaviour treatment for bulimia	Fairburn et al. (1993)
Behaviour therapy for marital problems	Azrin et al. (1980) Jacobson and Folletto (1985)
Behaviour therapy for female orgasmic dysfunction and male erectile dysfunction	LoPiccolo and Stock (1986) Auerbach et al. (1977)
Parent training programmes for children with oppositional behaviour	Wells and Egan (1988) Walter and Gilmore (1973)
Cognitive behaviour therapy for chronic pain	Keefe et al. (1992)
Behaviour therapy for headache and irritable bowel syndrome	Blanchard et al. (1987) Blanchard et al. (1980)
Behaviour modification for enuresis and encopresis	Kupfersmid (1989) Wright and Walker (1978)
Family education programmes for schizophrenia	Hogarty et al. (1986) Falloon et al. (1985)
Token economy programmes	Liberman (1972)
Behaviour modification for developmentally disabled individuals	Matson and Taras (1989)

(From APA 1993, copyright by the American Psychological Association. Reprinted with permission.)

motor functioning (e.g., Petursson and Lader 1981; Tyrer and Owen 1984; O'Hanlon et al. 1982; Hindmarch 1986, 1990; Ray et al. 1992). Therefore, the optimal use of BZs is generally believed to be for the short-term relief of anxiety that may be associated with a temporary crisis.

Recent studies demonstrated that certain types of psychological interventions are not only more effective than credible placebo or no treatment, but are at least as good if not better than existing pharmacological approaches immediately following treatment. For example, Klosko et al. (1990)

demonstrated that panic control treatment (PCT), a form of cognitive behaviour therapy, was superior to either the waiting list controls or drug placebo as well as alprazolam in the treatment of panic disorder (Barlow and Brown 1995). More importantly, however, other studies indicate that the psychological intervention is long-lasting, with patients retaining their gains at follow-ups of up to two years (e.g., Craske *et al.* 1991). More recently, Clark and his colleagues in England have produced similar data (Clark *et al.* 1994). These authors showed that cognitive behaviour intervention abolished panic attacks more quickly than imipramine and was more effective at the 15-month follow-up (see Chapter 7).

As part of a large-scale four-site study on treatment of panic disorder, M. Katherine Shear at the University of Pittsburgh, Jack M. Gorman at Columbia University, Scott Woods at Yale University, and the authors' centre at Albany are currently conducting a randomized controlled trial designed to determine the comparative efficacy of medication (imipramine or placebo), psychological intervention (PCT), and their combination in the treatment of panic disorder. A total of 480 panic disorder patients with no more than mild agoraphobia are being randomly assigned to one of five treatment conditions: PCT alone, imipramine alone, pill placebo alone, a combination of PCT and pill placebo, and a combination of PCT and imipramine. Each treatment condition consists of a 3-month acute treatment phase and a 6-month maintenance phase. The acute treatment phase consists of 11 weekly sessions with a psychiatrist and/or psychologist, followed by 6-monthly sessions of the maintenance phase. This study was begun in 1990, with the hypothesis that these treatments may combine to produce a superior effect compared to either treatment offered in isolation. Preliminary data support this hypothesis, although confirmation will have to await full analyses of the results. The outcome of the study is likely to have important policy implications.

Previous studies indicated that psychological treatments for panic disorder with agoraphobia, such as exposure *in vivo*, combine very well with tricyclic antidepressants. For example, results indicate that imipramine enhances the effects of exposure-based psychological treatments, and psychological treatments enhance the effects of imipramine. Even when imipramine is discontinued, the effects of psychological interventions are maintained at follow-up periods, at least if the treatment was delivered in a structured manner, as opposed to simply prescribing a self-help book (Barlow 1988; Mavissakalian 1993). On the other hand, it appears that some of the high-potency benzodiazepines (e.g., alprazolam) may interfere with the effects of exposure treatments over the long term. Whereas initial improvement was approximately equal after cognitive behaviour therapy with or without medication, at follow-up periods; patients who received drugs showed substantial relapse (Marks *et al.* 1993). Findings from the authors' centre also indicate that benzodiazepines may interfere with the effects of panic control treatment (Brown and Barlow 1995). These findings build on results from animal models indicating that benzodiazepines may interfere with the types of learning that would be important in psychological procedures (Wardle 1990; Barlow 1988).

Important results on drug–psychological treatment comparisons have also been reported from a large collaborative study on the treatment of social phobia, carried out under the direction of Richard Heimberg at the authors' centre and Michael Liebowitz at the New York State Psychiatric Institute (e.g., Barlow 1994b, Heimberg 1993). In this study, cognitive behavioural group treatment was compared with phenelzine, an MAOI. Preliminary results show that psychological treatments and pharmacotherapy have approximately equal effectiveness. Both are significantly more effective than either a drug placebo or a credible educational support treatment. Preliminary follow-up data during the maintenance drug treatment phase show continuing comparability. However, when medication is discontinued, psychological treatment retains its effectiveness while individuals on medication begin to relapse.

Very similar results were reported from clinical trials on depression. The meta-analysis by Dobson (1989) suggested that cognitive therapy is more effective than either no treatment or non-specific treatment, and at least as effective as alternative psychological and pharmacological interventions in the treatment of unipolar depression (e.g., Blackburn et al. 1981; Bowers 1990; Hollon et al. 1992; Miller et al. 1989; Murphy et al. 1984; Rush et al. 1977; Thase et al. 1991). Furthermore, follow-up studies suggest that cognitive therapy reduces the risk of future episodes following treatment termination (Blackburn et al. 1986; Evans et al. 1992; Kovacs et al. 1981; Shea et al. 1992; Simons et al. 1986). These studies found that responders to cognitive therapy were only half as likely to relapse or seek further treatment following termination than responders to pharmacotherapy alone (Hollon et al. 1991). Furthermore, there seems to be no indication that combined treatment significantly enhances the effect of cognitive therapy or pharmacotherapy alone (Hollon et al. 1991). These studies suggest that cognitive therapy is an effective treatment for depression and may reduce risk following treatment termination (Hollon and Beck 1994).

In summary, there is a large body of evidence on the effectiveness of a variety of psychological interventions across a number of severe disorders. The hypothesis that all psychotherapies are of equal effectiveness with 'placebo' factors or reassurance as a mechanism of action is no longer viable for the majority of disorders. In most instances, psychological treatments are not only better than no treatment but also as good as or better than effective drug treatments. In particular, psychological therapy is superior following drug withdrawal. Thus, more data on the cost-effectiveness of the different treatments are likely to strengthen the case for psychological interventions.

Despite the impressive results of studies on the effectiveness of psychological interventions, when out-patient treatment is considered, pharmacological approaches are often emphasized and recommended in clinical practice plans and by policy-makers, to the exclusion of psychological approaches. As detailed below, the reason why certain psychological treatments are still not completely accepted is not one of effectiveness. Rather the problem is related to public relations, accessibility, and dissemination.

The problem of accessibility and dissemination of effective psychosocial treatments

Given the consistent findings on the effectiveness of psychological therapy, why is it that policy-makers are all but ignoring these data? One major problem seems to be accessibility. In other words, most procedures are simply not available to the majority of individuals who would benefit from them. Therefore, the majority of individuals suffering from these problems are not even aware that effective psychological treatments exist. In the case of phobic disorders, for example, psychotherapists from all theoretical persuasions have concluded that structured exposure-based exercises are a necessary part of effective treatment; subsequent evidence has borne this out (Barlow 1988). Nevertheless, as indicated in Table 5.3, three recent surveys report that a large percentage of phobic individuals in three major cities in the United States received counselling, hospitalization, or medication, but only 15–38% were being treated with exposure-based procedures (Breier *et al.* 1986; Taylor *et al.* 1989; Goisman *et al.* 1993). Moreover, national probability samples indicate that only three out of four individuals with panic disorder are receiving any treatment at all, let alone an effective one (NIH 1991).

One possible reason for this state of affairs is that at least some of these psychological treatments require highly skilled administration of a type only available from senior mental health professionals with a broad and deep knowledge of psychological processes and treatments. Although the evidence supporting this contention is sparse (Christensen and Jacobson 1994), more recent evidence suggests that the quality of treatment impacts on treatment outcome. After reviewing studies on therapists' contribution to treatment outcome, Roth and Fonagy (1995) concluded that experience is less relevant than expertise. A number of studies have shown that treatment outcome is correlated with therapist's competency and protocol adherence (Crits-Cristoph *et al.* 1991; DuRubeis and Feeley 1990; Frank *et al.* 1991). For

TABLE 5.3. Utilization of effective psychological treatments in panic and phobic disorders

Study	No.	Patients receiving effective treatment (%)
Taylor *et al.* (1989)	794	15% (counselling and hospitalization: 50%)
Breier *et al.* (1986)	60	16%
Goisman *et al.* (1993)	231	38% (medication: 93%)

(From Barlow 1994*a*, with permission.)

example, Frank and her colleagues assessed the relationship between the quality of interpersonal therapy (IPT) as determined by objective ratings, and the prevention of recurrence of depressive episodes in patients with recurrent unipolar depression. Those patients who received high-quality interpersonal therapy delivered in a skilled manner were far more likely to remain stable than a comparable group receiving lower quality therapy. In fact, patients of therapists scoring above the median in quality of therapy survived an average of two years without recurrence of a depressive episode compared to five months for patients of therapists scoring below the median. These data indicate that the delivery of psychological therapy requires sophisticated skills. And yet, the prevailing attitude in many mental health settings is that anyone who is capable of forming a good relationship with the patient can practise psychotherapy.

As denoted earlier, the APA (1993) Task Force has collected data indicating that relatively few students in organized clinical psychology programmes are being taught these interventions. Table 5.4 shows the percentage of American Psychological Association doctoral programmes that offer training in empirically validated treatments. Ten out of the 18 treatments listed in Table 5.4 are taught in courses or supervised during clinical work in less than 50% of the programmes. Less than 30% of the programmes offer training in some of the well-established treatments, such as family education programmes for schizophrenia, cognitive behaviour therapy for social phobia, and interpersonal therapy. Only Beck's cognitive therapy for depression (Beck *et al.* 1979) reaches 80%. Furthermore, these data are likely to be an overestimate based on reporting biases. There is no reason to think that the data would be different in training programmes for the other mental health professions.

In order to facilitate dissemination of effective psychotherapy, the APA Task Force outlined an ambitious programme with 19 recommendations. For example, the Task Force suggested promotion of the development of clinicians' competence to practise new procedures via continuing education programmes that combine structured didactic learning with supervised clinical work. Educating third-party payers and the public about the health benefits

TABLE 5.4. Percentage of APA doctoral programmes that offer training in empirically validated treatments

Well-established treatments	Taught in course (%)	Supervised clinical work (%)
Cognitive behaviour therapy for panic disorder with and without agoraphobia	64.4	69.6
Cognitive behaviour therapy for generalized anxiety disorder	69.6	77.0
Exposure treatment for phobias (agoraphobia, social phobia, simple phobia) and post-traumatic stress disorder	64.4	59.3
Group cognitive behaviour therapy for social phobia	24.4	19.3
Systematic desensitization for simple phobia	68.9	62.2
Exposure and response prevention for obsessive–compulsive disorder	58.5	48.1
Beck's cognitive therapy for depression	89.6	80.0
Klerman and Weissman's interpersonal therapy for depression	25.9	16.3
Interpersonal therapy for bulimia	20.7	31.9
Behavioural marital therapy	57.0	60.7
Behaviour therapy for female orgasmic dysfunction and male erectile dysfunction	38.5	27.4
Parent training programmes for children with oppositional behaviour	57.8	60.0
Cognitive behaviour therapy for chronic pain	47.4	46.7
Behaviour therapy for headache and irritable bowel syndrome	38.5	40.7
Behaviour modification for enuresis and encopresis	45.2	40.0
Family education programmes for schizophrenia	24.4	22.2
Token economy programmes	45.2	25.2
Behaviour modification for developmentally disabled individuals	34.1	36.3

(From APA 1993, with permission.)

and effectiveness of psychotherapy, and encouraging the government-funding agencies to finance research on long-term treatments for populations that may require such approaches will also be important. Many of the recommendations can be implemented without financial cost and in very little time. For example, committees accrediting mental health training programmes should make training in empirically validated treatments high priority in their review — a policy recently adopted by the American Psychological Association. New treatment procedures with proven efficacy should be taught in workshops for continuing education credit, and regular information on data-based treatment approaches should be published in professional newsletters.

Investigators receiving federal support for research on psychological procedures typically develop detailed and clinically useful treatment manuals which are excellent resources for training students. However, many are, as yet, unpublished documents, and their existence is not widely known. Only a few effective psychological treatments are currently available in the form of published manuals and workbooks (e.g., Barlow and Craske 1994). These treatments can be easily disseminated, are highly cost-effective, and they can be 'prescribed' much like a medication in the context of competent general psychological care and attention to idiosyncratic problems that arise during the course of treatment. Evidence is accumulating supporting the viability of this type of approach to specific psychological disorders, even with minimal therapist contact, at least in less severe cases (e.g., Craske *et al.* 1995; DiBartolo *et al.* 1995). Other studies have indicated that structured interventions can be delivered in briefer format than has been customary with beneficial results for a number of patients (e.g., Craske *et al.* 1995; Swinson *et al.* 1992). For example, even a very brief and unstructured intervention for patients presenting to an emergency room with panic attacks may be effective if delivered early enough to less severe patients (Swinson *et al.* 1992). Considering the high prevalence rates of clinical and subclinical mental disorders in primary care settings (Fifer *et al.* 1994; Shear *et al.* 1994; Yingling *et al.* 1993), such interventions are clearly cost-effective (cf. Hofmann and Barlow, in press).

The cost-effectiveness and dissemination of psychological treatments can be further enhanced by utilizing new technologies as treatment tools. For example, C. B. Taylor and his colleagues at Stanford are currently investigating the effects of utilizing a palm-top computer as part of cognitive behaviour treatment for anxiety disorders. Preliminary data suggest that this method can lead to a significant reduction in therapist contact. Furthermore, Rothbaum *et al.* (1995) successfully used virtual-reality technology in combination with graded exposure in the treatment of height phobia.

These examples illustrate the flexibility of effective psychological treatments in an environment that focuses on the cost-effectiveness of mental health care. Considering the current developments of the mental health care system in the United States and the United Kingdom, it seems likely that in the future, psychologists and other behavioural health care professionals will no longer carry out most treatments directly because of the cost of delivering empirically based treatment (Van den Bos 1993). These professionals will then triage patients with less severe psychological disorders and/or symptoms of anxiety into cost-effective self-help programmes and/or programmes administered largely by para-professionals working under the supervision of psychologists. This, however, may not be the final state of affairs. Once we start monitoring treatment effectiveness and include these data in the cost-effectiveness analyses, there might be again a greater emphasis on therapy delivered by suitably qualified therapists based on the assumption that outcomes will be superior with more highly trained therapists.

Conclusion and the emerging role of clinical practice guidlines

Given the overwhelming cost advantage of out-patient services, compared to in-patient or other models, and the effectiveness of out-patient psychological interventions, mental health professionals should be in the position to make valuable contributions to behavioural health care. And yet, we find ourselves in the paradoxical position where the importance of psychological interventions is greatly diminished and, under some proposals, in danger of being excluded from many health care systems. Therefore, it is essential that we demonstrate to policy-makers and the public at large that we can offer effective treatments. It is also essential that we convey to policy-makers the cost-effectiveness of delivering these interventions early, and on an out-patient basis. Furthermore, we need to challenge the general assumption of many clinicians that most findings from research trials have little or no 'clinical utility' because trials use standardized treatment protocols and are based on a highly selected group of patients. Preliminary data indicate that the methods developed and evaluated in research trials can, in fact, be very successfully incorporated into everyday clinical practice (Kirk 1983). One study even found that standardized therapy was more successful than the same treatment adapted by therapist to clients and settings in ways they thought important (Schulte *et al*. 1992).

As noted above, clinical practice guidelines are an emerging reality in the delivery of behavioural health care in the United States. Guidelines are being developed by managed care companies, government agencies, such as the Agency for Health Care Policy and Research in the United States, the National Health Service in the United Kingdom, and professional societies, such as the American Psychiatric Association and the American Psychological Association. It is very likely that these clinical practice guidelines will have a substantial influence in the years to come. Already, elements of these guidelines are being adopted by state legislatures in the United States in an attempt to ensure that currently effective assessment and intervention procedures are practised by the widest number of clinicians for both medical and behavioural disorders (cf. Barlow 1993). This trend will only increase.

By properly evaluating not only the efficacy of psychological and drug treatments, as derived from tightly controlled clinical trials, but also the effectiveness or clinical utility of these procedures in the practice situation in which they are applied, we can obtain a true picture of the worth of our interventions. The template referred to earlier (Table 5.1) provides the structure for collecting this type of information. In view of the evidence reviewed in this chapter, it would seem clear that psychological interventions should be an essential component of any health care system.

References

Agras, W. S. and Berkowitz, R. (1980). Clinical research and behavior therapy: Halfway there? *Behavior Therapy*, **11**, 472–87.

APA (American Psychological Association) (1993). *Task Force on promotion and dissemination of psychological procedures. A report to the Division 12 Board of the American Psychological Association.* (Available from the Division 12 of the American Psychological Association, 750 First Street, NE, Washington, DC 20002–4242, USA)

APA (American Psychological Association) (1995). *Template for developing guidelines: Interventions for mental disorder and psychological aspects of physical disorders.* (Available from the American Psychological Association, 750 First Street, NE, Washington, DC 20002–4242, USA)

Andrews, G., Crino, R., Hunt, C., Lampe, L., and Page, A. (submitted). *A list of essential psychotherapies.*

Auerbach, R. and Kilmann, P. R. (1977). The effects of group systematic desensitization on secondary erectile failure. *Behavior Therapy*, **8**, 330–9.

Azrin, N. H., Bersalel, A., Bechtel, R., Michalicek, A., Mancera, M., Carroll, D., et al. (1980). Comparison of reciprocity and discussion-type counseling for marital problems. *American Journal of Family Therapy*, **8**, 21–8.

Ballenger, J. C., Burrows, G., DuPont, R., Lesser, I., Noyes, R., Pecknold, J., et al. (1988). Alprazolam in panic disorder and agoraphobia: results from a multi center trial: I. Efficacy in short term treatment. *Archives of General Psychiatry*, **45**, 413–22.

Barlow, D. H. (1988). *Anxiety and its disorders: The nature and treatment of anxiety disorder.* Guilford Press, New York.

Barlow, D. H. (1993). Presidential Column — Clinical practice guidelines: The next chapter. *Clinical Psychologist*, **46**, 163–4.

Barlow, D. H. (1994a). Psychological interventions in the era of managed competition. *Clinical Psychology Science and Practice*, **1** (2), 109–22.

Barlow, D. H. (1994b). Comorbidity in social phobia: Implications for cognitive-behavioral treatment. *Supplement to the Bulletin of the Menninger Clinic*, **58**, A43–57.

Barlow, D. H. and Brown, T. A. Correction to Klosko et al. (1990). *Journal of Consulting and Clinical Psychology*, **63**, 830.

Barlow, D. H. and Craske, M. G. (1994). *Mastery of your anxiety and panic II.* Graywind, Albany, NY.

Barlow, D. H., Craske, M. G., Cerny, J. A., and Klosko, J. S. (1989). Behavioral treatment of panic disorder. *Behavior Therapy*, **20**, 261–82.

Beck, A. T., Rush, J., Shaw, B., and Emery, G. (1979). *Cognitive therapy of depression.* Guilford Press, New York.

Blackburn, I. M., Bishop, S., Glen, A. I. M., Whalley, L. J., and Christie, J. E. (1981). The efficacy of cognitive therapy in depression: A treatment trial using cognitive therapy and pharmacotherapy, each alone and in combination. *British Journal of Psychiatry*, **139**, 181–9.

Blackburn, I. M., Eunson, K. M., and Bishop, S. (1986). A two-year naturalistic follow-up of depressed patients treated with cognitive therapy, pharmacotherapy and a combination of both. *Journal of Affective Disorders*, **10**, 67–75.

Blanchard, E. B., Andrasik, F., Ahles, T. A., Teders, S. J., and O'Keefe, D. (1980). Migraine and tension headache: A meta-analytic review. *Behavior Therapy*, **11**, 613–31.

Blanchard, E. B., Schwarz, S. P., and Radnitz, C. (1987). Psychological assessment and treatment of irritable bowel syndrome. *Behavior Modification*, **11**, 348–72.

Borkovec, T. D., Mathews, A. M., Chambers, A., Ebrahimi, S., Lytle, R., and Nelson, R. (1987). The effects of relaxation training with cognitive or nondirective therapy and the role of relaxation-induced anxiety in the treatment of generalized anxiety. *Journal of Consulting and Clinical Psychology*, **59**, 883–8.

Bowers, W. A. (1990). Treatment of depressed in-patients. Cognitive therapy plus medication, relaxation plus medication, and medication alone. *British Journal of Psychiatry*, **156**, 73–8.

Breier, A., Charney, D. S, and Heninger, G. R. (1986). Agoraphobia with panic attacks: Development, diagnostic stability, and course of illness. *Archives of General Psychiatry*, **43**, 1029–36.

Brown, T. A. and Barlow, D. H. (1995). Long-term outcome of cognitive-behavioral treatment of panic disorder: Clinical predictors and alternative strategies for assessment. *Journal of Clinical and Consulting Psychology*, **63**, 754–65.

Butler, G., Fennell, M., Robson, P., and Gelder, M. (1991). Comparison of behavior therapy and cognitive behavior therapy in the treatment of generalized anxiety disorder. *Journal of Consulting and Clinical Psychology*, **59**, 167–75.

Chambless, D. L. and Gillis, M. M. (1993). Cognitive therapy of anxiety disorders. *Journal of Consulting and Clinical Psychology*, **61**, 248–60.

Christensen, A. and Jacobson, N. S. (1994). Who (or what) can do psychotherapy: The status and challenge of nonprofessional therapies. *American Psychological Society*, **5**, 8–14.

Clark, D. M., Salkovskis, P. M., Hackman, A., Middleton, H., Anastasiades, P., and Gelder, M. (1994). A comparison of cognitive therapy, applied relaxation, and imipramine in the treatment of panic disorder. *British Journal of Psychiatry*, **164**, 759–69.

Craske, M. G., Brown, T. A., and Barlow, D. H. (1991). Behavioral treatment of panic disorder: A two-year follow-up. *Behavior Therapy*, **22**, 289–304.

Craske, M. G., Maidenberg, E., and Bystritsky, A. (1995). Brief cognitive-behavioral versus non-directive therapy for panic disorder. *Journal of Behaviour Therapy and Experimental Psychiatry*, **26**, 113–20.

Crits-Cristoph, P., Baranackie, K., Kurcias, J. S., Beck, A. T., Carroll, K., Perry, K., *et al.* (1991). Meta-analysis of therapist effects in psychotherapy outcome studies. *Psychotherapy Research*, **1**, 81–91.

DiBartolo, P. M., Hofmann, S. G., and Barlow, D. H. (1995). Psychosocial approaches to panic disorder and agoraphobia: Assessment and treatment issues for the primary care physician. *Mind/Body Medicine*, **1**, 1–12.

DiMascio, A., Weissman, M. M., Prusoff, B. A., Neu, C., Zwilling, M., and Klerman, G. L. (1979). Differential symptom reduction by drugs and psychotherapy in acute depression. *Archives of General Psychiatry*, **36**, 1450–56.

Dobson, K. S. (1989). A meta-analysis of the efficacy of cognitive therapy for depression. *Journal of Consulting and Clinical Psychology*, **57**, 414–19.

DuRubeis, R. J. and Feeley, M. (1990). Determinants of change in cognitive therapy for depression. *Cognitive Therapy and Research*, **14**, 469–82.

Elkin, I., Shea, M. T., Watkins, J. T., Imber, S. D., Sotsky, S. M., Collins, J. F., Glass, D. R., Pilkonis, P. A., Leber, W. R., Docherty, J. P., Fiester, S. J., and Parloff, M. B. (1989). National Institute of Mental Health Collaborative Research Program: General effectiveness of treatments. *Archives of General Psychiatry*, **46**, 971–82.

Evans, M. D., Hollon, S. D., DeRubeis, R. J., Piasecki, J. M., Grove, W. M., Garvey, M. J., *et al.* (1992). Differential relapse following cognitive therapy and pharmacotherapy for depression. *Archives of General Psychiatry*, **49**, 802–8.

Eysenck, H. J. (1952). The effects of psychotherapy. *Journal of Consulting and Clinical Psychology*, **16**, 319–24.

Fairburn, C. G., Jones, R., Peveler, R. C., Hope, R. A., and O'Conner, M. (1993). Psychotherapy and bulimia nervosa: Longer-term effects of interpersonal psychotherapy, behavior therapy, and cognitive behavior therapy. *Archives of General Psychiatry*, **50**, 419–28.

Falloon, R. H., Boyd, J. L., McGill, C. W., Williamson, M., Razani, A., Moss, H. B., *et al.* (1985). Family management in the prevention of morbidity of schizophrenia: Clinical outcome of a two-year longitudinal study. *Archives of General Psychiatry*, **42**, 887–96.

Fifer, S. K., Mathias, S. D., Patrick, D. L., Mathias, S. D., Patrick, D. L., Mazonson, P. D., *et al.* (1994). Untreated anxiety among adult primary care patients in a health maintenance organization. *Archives of General Psychiatry*, **5**, 740–50.

Foa, E. B., Rothbaum, B. O., Riggs, D. S., and Murdock, T. B. (1991). Treatment of posttraumatic stress disorder in rape victims: A comparison between cognitive-behavioral procedures and counseling. *Journal of Consulting and Clinical Psychology*, **59**, 715–23.

Frank, E., Kupfer, D. J., Wagner, E. F., McEchran, A. B., and Cornes, C. (1991). Efficacy of interpersonal psychotherapy as a maintenance treatment of recurrent depression. *Archives of General Psychiatry*, **48**, 1053–59.

Gelder, M. G. and Marks, I. M. (1966). Severe agoraphobia: A controlled prospective trial of behaviour therapy. *British Journal of Psychiatry*, **112**, 309–19.

Gelder, M. G., Marks, I. M., and Wolff, H. H. (1967). Desensitization and psychotherapy in the treatment of phobic states: A controlled inquiry. *British Journal of Psychiatry*, **113**, 53–73.

Goisman, R. M., Rogers, M. P., Steketee, G. S., Warshaw, M. G., Cuneo, P., and Keller, M. B. (1993). Utilization of behavioral methods in a multi center anxiety disorders study. *Journal of Clinical Psychiatry*, **54**, 213–18.

Heimberg, R. G. (1993). *Psychosocial treatment of social phobia*. Paper presented at the annual meeting of the Anxiety Disorders Association of America, Charleston, SC.

Heimberg, R. G., Dodge, C. S., Hope, D. A., Kennedy, C. R., and Zollo, L. J. (1990). Cognitive behavioral group treatment for social phobia: Comparison with a credible placebo control. *Cognitive Therapy and Research*, **14**, 1–23.

Hindmarch, I. (1986). The effects of psychoactive drugs on car handling and related psychomotor ability: A review. In *Drugs and driving*, (ed. J. F. O'Honlon and J. J. Gier), pp. 71–9. Taylor & Francis, London.

Hindmarch, I. (1990). Cognitive impairment with anti-anxiety agents: A solvable problem? In *The anxiolytic jungle: Where next?*, (ed. D. Wheatley), pp. 49–61. Wiley, Chichester, UK.

Hofmann, S. G. and Barlow, D. H. (in press). The costs of anxiety disorders: implications for psychosocial interventions. In *Psychotherapy: Costs and benefits; a guide for practitioners, researchers and policymakers* (ed. The National Institute of Mental Health, Division of Clinical and Treatment Research). NIH, Rockville, MD.

Hogarty, G. E., Anderson, C. M., Reiss, D. J., Kornblith, S. J., Greenwald, D. P., Javna, C. D., *et al.* (1986). Family psychoeducation, social skills training, and maintenance chemotherapy in the aftercare treatment of schizophrenia: I. One-year effects of a controlled study on relapse and expressed emotion. *Archives of General Psychiatry*, **43**, 633–42.

Hollon, S. D. and Beck, A. T. (1994). Cognitive and cognitive-behavioral therapies. In *Handbook of psychotherapy and behavior change* (ed. A. E. Bergin and S. L. Garfield), pp. 428–66. Wiley, New York.

Hollon, S. D., Shelton, R. C., and Loosen, P. T. (1991). Cognitive therapy and pharmacotherapy for depression. *Journal of Consulting and Clinical Psychology*, **59**, 88–99.

Hollon, S. D., DeRubeis, R. J., Evans, M. D., Wierner, M. J., Garvey, M. J., Grove, W. M., *et al.* (1992). Cognitive therapy and pharmacotherpy for depression: Singly and in combination. *Archives of General Psychiatry*, **49**, 774–81.

Jacobson, N. S. and Follette, W. C. (1985). Clinical significance of improvement resulting from two behavioral marital therapy components. *Behavior Therapy*, **16**, 249–62.

Johnson, S. M. and Greenberg, L. S. (1985). Differential effects of experiential and problem-solving interventions in resolving marital conflict. *Journal of Consulting and Clinical Psychology*, **57**, 175–84.

Kazdin, A. E. and Wilcoxin, L. A. (1976). Systematic desensitization and non-specific treatment effects: A methodological evaluation. *Psychological Bulletin*, **83**, 729–58.

Keefe, F. J., Dunsmore, J., and Bunett, R. (1992). Behavioral and cognitive-behavioral approaches to chronic pain: Recent advances and future directions. *Journal of Consulting and Clinical Psychology*, **60**, 528–36.

Kirk, J. W. (1983). Behavioural treatment of obsessional-compulsive patients in routine clinical practice. *Behaviour Research and Therapy*, **21**, 57–62.

Klosko, J. S., Barlow, D. H., Tassinari, R., and Cerny, J. A. (1990). A comparison of alprazolam and cognitive-behavior therapy in treatment of panic disorder. *Journal of Clinical and Consulting Psychology*, **58**, 77–84.

Kovacs, M., Rush, A. J., Beck, A. T., and Hollon, S. D. (1981). Depressed out-patients treated with cognitive therapy or pharmacotherapy: A one-year follow-up. *Archives of General Psychiatry*, **38**, 33–9.

Kupfersmid, J. (1989). Treatment of nocturnal enuresis: A status report. *The Psychiatric Forum*, **14**, 37–46.

Lewinsohn, P. M., Hoberman, H. M., and Clarke, G. N. (1989). The coping with depression course: Review and future directions. *Canadian Journal of Behavioural Science*, **21**, 470–93.

Liberman, R. P. (1972). Behavioral modification of schizophrenia: A review. *Schizophrenia Bulletin*, **1**, 37–48.

Linehan, M. M., Armstrong, H. E., Suarez, A., Allmon, D., and Heard, H. L. (1991). Cognitive-behavioral treatment of chronically parasuicidal borderline patients. *Archives of General Psychiatry*, **48**, 1060–64.

LoPiccolo, J. and Stock, W. E. (1986). Treatment of sexual dysfunction. *Journal of Consulting and Clinical Psychology*, **54**, 158–67.

Marks, I. M. and O'Sullivan, G. (1988). Drugs and psychological treatments for agoraphobia/panic and obsessive–compulsive disorders: A review. *British Journal of Psychiatry*, **153**, 650–8.

Marks, I. M., Swinson, R. P., Basoglu, M., Kuch, K., Noshirvani, H., O'Sullivan, G., *et al.* (1993). Alprazolam and exposure alone and combined in panic disorder with agoraphobia: A controlled study in London and Toronto. *British Journal of Psychiatry*, **162**, 776–87.

Matson, J. L. and Taras, M. E. (1989). A 20 year review of punishment and alternative methods to treat problem behaviors in developmentally delayed persons. *Research in Developmental Disabilities*, **10**, 85–107.

Mattick, R. P. and Peters, L. (1988). Treatment of severe social phobia: Effects of guided exposure with and without cognitive restructuring. *Journal of Consulting and Clinical Psychology*, **56**, 251–60.

Mattick, R. P., Andrews, G., Hadzi-Pavlovic, D., and Christensen, H. (1990). Treatment of panic and agoraphobia: An integrative review. *Journal of Nervous and Mental Disease*, **178**, 567–76.

Mavissakalian, M. G. (1993). Combined behavioral and pharmacological treatment of anxiety disorders. In *Review of Psychiatry*, Vol. 12, (ed. J. M. Oldham, M. B. Riba, and A. Tasman), pp. 565–84. American Psychiatric Press, Washington, DC.

Meyer, V. and Gelder, M. G., (1963). Behaviour therapy and phobic disorders. *British Journal of Psychiatry*, **109**, 19–28.

Miller, I. W., Norman, W. H., Keitner, G. I., Bishop, S. B., and Dow, M. G. (1989). Cognitive-behavioral treatment of depressed in-patients. *Behavior Therapy*, **20**, 25–47.

Murphy, G. E., Simons, A. D., Wetzel, R. D., and Lustman, P. J. (1984). Cognitive therapy and pharmacotherapy, singly and together, in the treatment of depression. *Archives of General Psychiatry*, **41**, 33–41.

NIH (National Institutes of Health) (1991). *Treatment of panic disorder. NIH Consensus Development Conference Consensus Statement*, **9** (2). (Available from the U.S. Department of Health and Human Services. National Institutes of Health Public Health Service. Office of Medical Applications of Research. Federal Building, Room 618, Bethesda, MD 20892, USA)

Noyes, R., Garvey, M. J., Cook, B., and Suelzer, M. (1991). Controlled discontinuation of benzodiazepine treatment for patients with panic disorder. *American Journal of Psychiatry*, **148**, 517–23.

O'Hanlon, J. F., Haak, J. W., Blaauw, G. J., and Riemersma, J. B. J. (1982). Diazepam impairs lateral position control in highway driving. *Science*, **27**, 79–81.

Öst, L-G. (1988). Applied relaxation vs. progressive relaxation in the treatment of panic disorder. *Behaviour Research and Therapy*, **26**, 13–22.

Öst, L-G. and Westling, B. E. (1991). *Treatment of panic disorder by applied relaxation versus cognitive therapy*. Paper presented at the meeting of the European Association of Behaviour Therapy, Oslo.

Petursson, H. and Lader, M. H. (1981). Withdrawal from long-term benzodiazepine treatment. *British Medical Journal*, **283**, 643–5.

Quality Assurance Project (1983). Treatment outlines for depressive disorders. *Australian and New Zealand Journal of Psychiatry*, **17**, 129–48.

Quality Assurance Project (1985). Treatment outlines for the anxiety states. *Australian and New Zealand Journal of Psychiatry*, **19**, 138–51.

Ray, W. A., Gurwitz, J., Decker, M. D., and Kennedy, D. L. (1992). Medications and the safety of the older driver: Is there a basis for concern? Special issue: Safety and mobility of elderly drivers: II. *Human Factors*, **34**, 33–47.

Rickels, K., Schweizer, E., Case, W. G., and Greenblatt, D. J. (1990). Long-term therapeutic use of benzodiazepines. I. Effects of abrupt discontinuation. *Archives of General Psychiatry*, **47**, 899–907.

Roth, A. and Fonagy, P. (1995). *National Health Service report on research on the efficacy and effectiveness of the psychotherapies.* (Available from the National Health Service, Department of Health, Wellington House, 135–155 Waterloo Road, London SE1 8UG, UK)

Rothbaum, B. O., Hodges, L. F., Kooper, R., Opdyke, D. O., Williford, J. S., and North, M. (1995). Effectiveness of computer-generated (virtual reality) graded exposure in the treatment of acrophobia. *American Journal of Psychiatry*, 152, 626–8.

Rush, A. J., Beck, A. T., Kovacs, M., and Hollon, S. D. (1977). Comparative efficacy of cognitive therapy and pharmacotherapy in the treatment of depressed out-patients. *Cognitive Therapy and Research*, 1, 17–38.

Schulte, D., Kunzel, R., Pepping, G., and Schulte-Bahrenberg, T. (1992). Tailor-made versus standardized therapy of phobic patients. *Advanced Behavioral Research and Therapy*, 14, 67–92.

Schweizer, E., Rickels, K., Case, W.G., and Greenblatt, D. J. (1990). Long-term use of benzodiazepines. II. Effects of gradual taper. *Archives of General Psychiatry*, 47, 908–15.

Shea, M. T., Elkin, I., Imber, S. D., Sotsky, S. M., Watkins, J. T., Collins, J. F., *et al.* (1992). Course of depressive symptoms over follow-up: Findings from the National Institute of Mental Health Treatment of Depression Collaborative Research Program. *Archives of General Psychiatry*, 49, 782–7.

Shear, M. K., Schulberg, H. C., and Madonia, M. (1994). *Panic and generalized anxiety disorder in primary care.* Paper presented at a meeting of the Association of Primary Care, Washington, DC.

Simons, A. D., Murphy, G. E., Levine, J. L., and Wetzel, R. D. (1986). Cognitive therapy and pharmacotherapy for depression: Sustained improvement over one year. *Archives of General Psychiatry*, 43, 43–8.

Spiegel, D. A., Bruce, T. J., Gregg, S. F., and Nuzzarello, A., (1994). Does cognitive behavior therapy assist slow-taper alprazolam discontinuation in panic disorder? *American Journal of Psychiatry*, 151, 876–81.

Steketee, G., Foa, E. B., and Grayson, J. B. (1982). Recent advances in the behavioral treatment of obsessive–compulsives. *Archives of General Psychiatry*, 39, 1365–71.

Swinson, R. P., Soulios, C., Cox, B. J., and Kuch, K. (1992). Brief treatment of emergency room patients with panic attacks. *American Journal of Psychiatry*, 149, 944–6.

Taylor, C. B., King, R., Margraf, J., *et al.* (1989). Use of medication and *in vivo* exposure in volunteers for panic disorder research. *American Journal of Psychiatry*, 146, 1423–6.

Telch, M. J. (1988). Combined pharmacological and psychological treatments of panic sufferers. In *Panic: Psychological perspectives* (ed. S. Rachman and J. D. Maser). Erlbaum, Hillsdale, NJ.

Telch, M. J., Tearnan, B. H., and Taylor, C. B. (1983). Antidepressant medication in the treatment of agoraphobia: A critical review. *Behaviour Research and Therapy*, 21, 505–27.

Thase, M. E., Bowler, K., and Harden, T. (1991). Cognitive behavior therapy of endogenous depression: Part 2. Preliminary findings in 16 unmedicated in-patients. *Behavior Therapy*, 22, 469–77.

Trull, T. J., Nietzel, M. T., and Main, A. (1988). The use of meta-analysis to assess the clinical significance of behavior therapy for agoraphobia. *Behavior Therapy*, 19, 527–38.

Tyrer, P. J. and Owen, R. (1984). Anxiety in primary care: Is short-term drug treatment appropriate? *Journal of Psychiatric Research*, 18, 73–9.

Van den Bos, G. R. (1993). U.S. Mental Health Policy — Proactive evolution in the midst of health care reform. *American Psychologist*, 48, 283–90.

Walter, H. I. and Gilmore, S. K. (1973). Placebo versus social learning effects in parent training procedure designed to alter the behavior of aggressive boys. *Behavior Therapy*, 4, 361–77.

Wardle, J. (1990). Behaviour therapy and benzodiazepines: Allies or antagonists. *British Journal of Psychiatry*, 156, 163–8.

Wells, K. C. and Egan, J. (1988). Social learning and systems family therapy for childhood oppositional disorder: Comparative treatment outcome. *Comprehensive Psychiatry*, 29, 138–46.

Wilfley, D. E., Agras, W. S., Telch, C. F., Rossiter, E. M., Schneider, J. A., Cole, A. G., *et al.* (1993). Group cognitive-behavioral therapy and group interpersonal psychotherapy for the nonpurging bulimic individual: A controlled comparison. *Journal of Consulting and Clinical Psychology*, 61, 295–305.

Wright, L. and Walker, C. E. (1978). A simple behavioral treatment programme for psychogenic encopresis. *Behaviour Research and Therapy*, 16, 209–12.

Yingling, K. W., Wulsin, L. R., Arnold, L. M., and Rouan, G. W. (1993). Estimated prevalences of panic disorder and depression among consecutive patients seen in an emergency department with acute chest pain. *Journal of General and Internal Medicine*, 8, 231–5.

Part II

Specific problems and disorders

6

Panic disorder and social phobia

David M. Clark

Historically, some of the most effective psychological treatments for emotional disorders have been developed by constructing a model of the development and maintenance of the disorder and then devising a set of treatment procedures that focus on the core pathology and reverse the maintaining factors. In the early days of behaviour therapy this approach was applied with success to the treatment of phobias and obsessive-compulsive disorders. Both disorders were considered to be the result of conditioning. In phobias, it was hypothesized that one of the major maintaining factors was avoidance of the feared stimulus. This led to the development of exposure therapy, which was subsequently shown to have a specific effect in most phobic disorders (Rachman and Wilson 1980; Marks 1987). In obsessive–compulsive disorder, it was hypothesized that the compulsive behaviour (checking, washing, and other-putting-right acts) prevented the fear associated with the obsessional thought from extinguishing. This led to the development of the exposure and response prevention treatment approach (Meyer *et al.* 1974), which was also shown to have a specific effect (Rachman *et al.* 1979), and to be superior to exposure alone (Foa *et al.* 1984). This chapter shows how the same general strategy has been, and is being, used to develop effective and specific cognitive treatments for anxiety disorders. Two contrasting anxiety disorders—panic disorder and social phobia—are chosen as examples. In the case of panic disorder, the approach is well developed and the resulting treatment has been extensively evaluated. In the case of social phobia, the work is at an early stage and the treatment, although promising, has yet to be extensively evaluated. As this book is in honour of Professor Gelder, particular emphasis is placed on studies that were conducted in Oxford. These studies benefited greatly from Michael Gelder's enthusiastic support and from his incisive and constructive criticism.

   The plan of the chapter is as follows. First, panic disorder and social phobia are described. Second, the treatments that were available before the advent of cognitive therapy are outlined along with their strengths and weaknesses. Third, detailed cognitive models of panic disorder and social phobia that specifically address the maintenance of the disorders are outlined. Fourth, the correlational and experimental studies that have been used to test the models are reviewed. Fifth, the specialized cognitive treatments that have been derived from the models are described and illustrated. Finally, studies investigating the effectiveness of the specialized cognitive treatments are reviewed.

The clinical features of panic disorder and social phobia

The clinical features of panic disorder and social phobia have been recognized for many years. However, it was not until the advent of the *Diagnostic and Statistical Manual of Mental Disorders* (DSM–III: APA 1980) that the two conditions were recognized as specific syndromes. Klein's (1964, 1967) claim that patients with recurrent panic attacks respond to imipramine but not benzodiazapines, and vice versa for anxious patients without recurrent panic attacks, was particularly influential in establishing panic disorder as a separate diagnostic entity, although some aspects of this claim were not supported by subsequent investigations (see Margraf *et al.* 1986, for a review). The term 'social phobia' was introduced by Marks and Gelder in 1966 and their demonstration that it had a different age of onset to other phobias (Marks and Gelder, 1966) was particularly influential in establishing it as a separate disorder. Since 1980, the DSM has undergone two revisions (APA 1987, 1994), and the essential features of the two disorders have been defined more clearly.

Panic disorder

The essential feature of panic disorder is the occurrence of panic attacks. DSM–IV (APA 1994) defines a panic attack as a sudden onset period of intense fear or discomfort associated with at least four symptoms that include: breathlessness, palpitations, dizziness, trembling, a feeling of choking, nausea, de-realization, chest pain, and paraesthesias. Defined this way, occasional panic attacks are common in all anxiety disorders (Barlow *et al.* 1985). The diagnosis of panic disorder, however, is reserved for a subset of individuals who experience *recurrent* panic attacks, at least some of which come on unexpectedly. That is to say, the attacks are not always triggered by entering phobic situations or by anticipating doing so. Individuals diagnosed as having panic disorder with agoraphobia can identify certain situations in which they think attacks are particularly likely to occur, or would be especially catastrophic, and tend to avoid these situations. Individuals diagnosed as having panic disorder without agoraphobia tend not to be able to identify such situations and show no gross situational avoidance.

Social phobia

The essential feature of social phobia is a marked and persistent fear of social or performance situations due to the individual's belief that he/she will act in a way which will be embarrassing or humiliating. Typically, feared situations are avoided whenever possible and otherwise endured with considerable discomfort. For some individuals only a small number of specific performance situations (such as writing in public or speaking to an audience) are feared. Others fear a wide range of public performance and social interaction situations. In either instance, social phobia is only diagnosed if the fears interfere significantly with the individual's daily routine, occupational, or social functioning.

Previous treatment approaches

Exposure therapy was the first psychological treatment that was shown to be effective in patients who would now be diagnosed as panic disorder or social phobia. In the case of panic disorder, the treatment specifically focused on the subgroup of patients who were agoraphobic. By the mid 1970s, repeated *in vivo* exposure to feared situations had been shown to be an effective treatment for agoraphobic fear and avoidance. In an impressive programme of research which extended throughout the 1970s Michael Gelder and colleagues (Mathews *et al.* 1981) made this treatment more efficient by placing more emphasis on self-exposure and by recruiting patients' partners as helpers. As a consequence, the gains which initially required 20 hours of therapist contact could be achieved with only 7 hours of home-based treatment. However, the treatment had a number of limitations. First, it was only suitable for panic patients who were also agoraphobic. Second, although these patients reported a reduced frequency of attacks in agoraphobic situations, a substantial proportion (up to 45%) continued to experience panic attacks at home (Michelson *et al.* 1985). The research on exposure therapy as a treatment for social phobia has also revealed that although it is effective when compared to no treatment (Butler *et al.* 1984), it has limitations. In particular, a sizeable proportion of patients either fail to respond or show only partial improvement. For example, Mattick and Peters (1988) found that at the end of treatment only 30% of exposure treated patients had achieved high end-state function and 47% felt they were still in need of treatment. Similar figures are reported by Butler *et al.* (1984).

In summary, although exposure to feared situations proved an effective treatment, it was not suitable for a substantial proportion of panic disorder patients and many of the panic disorder and social phobic patients for whom it was, in principle, suitable showed only a partial response with significant residual symptomatology being common. It was these limitations which provided the impetus for the development of alternative, cognitive approaches to the conceptualization and treatment of these two disorders.

Cognitive models of panic disorder and social phobia

The cognitive models which are used to account for different anxiety disorders share a number of common features. First, it is assumed that individuals become anxious in response to certain stimuli because they interpret the stimuli as much more dangerous than they really are. Second, these unrealistic interpretations persist because patients engage in cognitive and behavioural strategies that are intended to prevent the feared events from occurring. As the fears are unrealistic, the main effect of these strategies is to prevent patients' from disconfirming their negative beliefs. Third, in many anxiety disorders, the symptoms of anxiety are additional sources of perceived danger, producing a series of vicious circles which further contribute to the maintenance of the disorders.

Panic disorder

The cognitive model of panic disorder states that:

> Individuals who experience recurrent panic attacks do so because they have a relatively enduring tendency to interpret certain bodily sensations in a catastrophic fashion. The sensations that are misinterpreted are mainly those involved in normal anxiety responses (e.g., palpitations, breathlessness, dizziness, paresthesias) but also include some other sensations. The catastrophic misinterpretation involves perceiving these sensations as much more dangerous than they really are and, in particular, interpreting the sensations as indicative of *immediately* impending physical or mental disaster—for example, perceiving a slight feeling of breathlessness as evidence of impending cessation of breathing and consequent death, perceiving palpitations as evidence of an impending heart attack, perceiving a pulsing sensation in the forehead as evidence of a brain haemorrhage, or perceiving a shaky feeling as evidence of impending loss of control and insanity. (Clark 1988, p. 149).

The sequence of events that it is suggested occurs in panic attacks is shown in Fig. 6.1. External stimuli (such as a department store for an agoraphobic)

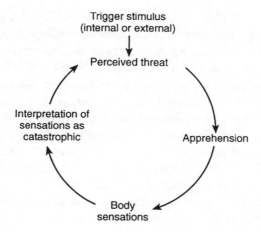

Trigger stimulus
(internal or external)

Perceived threat

Interpretation of
sensations as
catastrophic

Apprehension

Body
sensations

FIG. 6.1. The suggested sequence of events in a panic attack. (From Clark 1986, p. 463.)

and internal stimuli (body sensations, thoughts, images) can both provoke panic attacks. The sequence that culminates in an attack starts with the stimuli being interpreted as a sign of impending danger. This interpretation produces a state of apprehension, which is associated with a wide range of bodily sensations. If these anxiety-produced sensations are interpreted in a catastrophic fashion (impending insanity, death, loss of control, etc.) a further increase in apprehension occurs, producing more bodily sensations, leading to a vicious circle which culminates in a panic attack.

Once an individual has developed a tendency to interpret catastrophically bodily sensations, two further processes are said to contribute to the maintenance of panic disorder. First, because they are frightened of certain sensations, patients become hypervigilant and repeatedly scan their body. This internal focus of attention allows them to notice sensations which many other people would not be aware of. Once noticed, these sensations are taken as further evidence of the presence of some serious physical or mental disorder. Second, various safety behaviours tend to maintain patients' negative interpretations (Salkovskis 1988, 1991). For example, a panic patient who is preoccupied with the idea that he may be suffering from cardiac disease might avoid exercise and believe that this avoidance helps prevent him from having a heart attack. However, as he has no cardiac disease, the real effect of the avoidance would be to prevent him from learning that the symptoms he is experiencing are innocuous.

The cognitive model accounts both for panic attacks that are preceded by elevated anxiety and for panic attacks that are not and instead appear out of the blue. For both types of attack, it is argued that the critical event is the misinterpretation of certain bodily sensations. In attacks preceded by heightened anxiety, the sensations are often a consequence of the preceding anxiety, which in turn is due either to anticipating an attack *or* to some other anxiety-evoking event which is unrelated to panic. In attacks that are not preceded by heightened anxiety, the misinterpreted sensations are initially caused by a different emotional state (anger, excitement, disgust) or by innocuous events such as exercising (breathlessness, palpitations), drinking too much coffee (palpitations), or standing up quickly after sitting (dizziness). In such attacks patients frequently fail to distinguish between the triggering bodily sensations and the subsequent panic and so perceive the attack as having no cause and coming out of the blue.

When applying the cognitive model to individual patients, it is often useful to distinguish between the first panic attack and the subsequent development of repeated attacks and panic disorder. Community surveys (Wilson *et al.* 1991; Norton, Dorward, and Cox, 1986; Margraf and Ehlers, 1988; Brown and Cash, 1990) indicate that between 7% and 28% of the normal population will experience an occasional unexpected panic attack. It is unlikely that there is a single explanation for these relatively common, but occasional, autonomic events. Stressful life events, hormonal changes, illness, caffeine, drugs, and a variety of transient medical conditions could all produce occasional perceived autonomic changes. However, the cognitive model assumes that individuals only go on to develop the rarer condition of repeated panic attacks and panic disorder (approximately 3–5% of the general population; Wittchen and Essau, 1991) if they develop a tendency to interpret these perceived autonomic events in a catastrophic fashion. Such a tendency could either be a consequence of learning experiences that predate the first attack (e.g., observing parents panicking or modelling illness-related behaviour; Ehlers, 1993) or arise as a consequence of the way the patient, physicians, and significant others respond to the first attack.

Social phobia

A cognitive model of social phobia was recently outlined by Clark and Wells (1995*a*). Figure 6.2 summarizes the processes which this model assumes occur when a social phobic enters a feared social situation. On the basis of early experience, social phobics are said to develop a series of assumptions about themselves and social situations. For example: 'Unless someone shows that they like me, they dislike me. Unless I am liked by everyone, I am worthless. If I show I am anxious people will think I am odd/will reject me.' These assumptions lead them to interpret normal social interactions in a negative way, viewing them as signs of danger. For example, if a social phobic is talking to someone at a party and the other person briefly looks out of the window the social phobic may think 'I'm being boring'. This interpretation triggers an 'anxiety programme' that can be usefully divided into three interlinked components.

The first component is the somatic and cognitive symptoms of anxiety that are *reflexively* triggered by the perception of danger. These include blushing, trembling, racing heart, palpitations, difficulty concentrating, and mental blanks. Each of these symptoms can become a further source of perceived danger, creating a vicious circle which maintains the anxiety. For example, blushing may be taken as an indication that one has made a fool of oneself, leading to further embarrassment and blushing; a shaking hand may be taken as an indication of impending loss of control leading to more anxiety and shaking.

The second component is the safety behaviours which patients engage in to try to reduce social threat and prevent feared outcomes from occurring. Common examples include: trying not to attract attention, avoiding eye contact, censoring what one says, avoiding pauses in speech, and making an effort to come across well. Often, there are quite precise links between safety behaviours and specific feared outcomes. For example, a patient who was concerned about the possibility that her hand might shake while drinking would half fill her wine glass and then grip the glass very tightly while drinking. A patient who was concerned that others might think what he was saying was stupid would try to recall what he had just said and compare it with what he was about to say while in the middle of a conversation. A patient

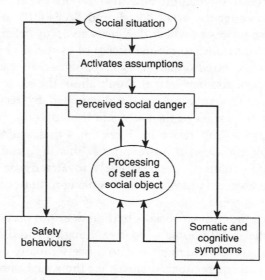

FIG. 6.2. The processes that, it is hypothesized, occur when a social phobic enters a feared situation. (After Clark and Wells, 1995*a*).

who was concerned that people would think he was anxious and evaluate him negatively if he paused during a speech rehearsed the speech in great detail and spoke quickly. As in panic disorder, the safety behaviours prevent patients from disconfirming their unrealistic beliefs and, in some instances, also increase their feared symptoms. For example, the woman who grasped her wine glass very tightly discovered during therapy that this made her hand more likely to shake. In addition, some safety behaviours adversely affect other people's response to the social phobic. For example, the patient who was constantly trying to recall what he has just said, appeared bored with the conversation and as a consequence elicited less warm responses from other people.

The third, and crucially important, component is a shift in attention. When social phobics think they are in danger of negative evaluation by others, they shift their attention to detailed monitoring and observation of themselves. They then use the interoceptive information produced by self-focus to construct an impression of themselves which they assume reflects what other people actually notice and think about them. In this way, they find themselves in a closed system in which belief in danger of negative evaluation is strengthened by internally generated information and opportunities for disconfirmation are neglected or avoided.

Figure 6.2 concerns the processes which occur during a social interaction. However, social phobics' distress is not restricted to times when they are in a social situation. Many social phobics experience considerable anxiety when anticipating a social interaction and also report experiencing a range of negative emotions after the event. Clark and Wells (1995a) have outlined a series of cognitive processes which they assume occur before and after social interactions and contribute to the maintenance of social phobia.

Prior to entering a feared situation, social phobics review in detail what they think might happen. As they start to think about the situation, they become anxious and their thoughts tend to be dominated by recollections of past failures, by negative images of themselves in the situation, and by predictions of poor performance and rejection. Sometimes these ruminations lead the phobic to completely avoid the situation. If this does not happen and the phobic enters the situation, he/she is likely to already be in a self-focused processing mode, expect failure, and be less likely to notice any signs of being accepted by other people.

Leaving or escaping from a social situation does not necessarily bring to an immediate end the social phobic's negative thoughts and distress. There is no longer an immediate social danger and so anxiety rapidly declines. However, the nature of social interactions is such that the social phobic is unlikely to have received from others unambiguous signs of social approval, and for this reason it is not uncommon for him or her to conduct a 'post-mortem' of the event. The interaction is reviewed in detail. During this review, the patient's anxious feelings and negative self-perception are likely to figure particularly prominently as they were processed in detail while the patient was in the situation and hence would have been strongly encoded in memory. The unfortunate consequence of this is that the patient's review is likely to be dominated by his/her negative self-perception and the interaction is likely to be seen as much more negative than it really was. This may explain why some social phobics report a sense of shame that persists for a while after the anxiety has subsided. A further aspect of the 'post-mortem' is the retrieval of other instances of perceived social failure. The recent interaction is then added to the list of past failures, with the consequence that an interaction which may have looked entirely neutral from an outside observer's perspective will have strengthened the patient's belief in his/her social inadequacy.

Empirical status of the cognitive models

In this section we consider some of the correlational and experimental studies which have investigated the cognitive models of panic disorder and social phobia that were outlined above.

Panic disorder

Misinterpretations of bodily sensations and their role in panic disorder
A key prediction of the cognitive model of panic is that individuals with panic disorder will be more likely to interpret bodily sensations in a catastrophic fashion than individuals who do not experience panic attacks. The first direct test of this prediction was reported by McNally and Foa (1987). A modified version of a questionnaire originally developed by Butler and Mathews (1983) was used to compare DSM–III agoraphobia with panic patients and non-patient controls in terms of the extent to which they interpreted ambiguous events in a negative way. Two classes of ambiguous events were included. 'Internal stimuli' consisted of descriptions of bodily sensations that the cognitive theory predicts will be more likely to be misinterpreted by panic patients (e.g., 'You notice your heart beating quickly and pounding. Why?'). 'External stimuli' consisted of potentially threatening external events (e.g., 'You wake with a start in the middle of the night, thinking you heard a noise, but all is quiet. What do you think woke you up?'). Subjects were asked to write down the first explanation that came to mind for each event. After writing their response to the open-ended question, subjects turned the page and rank-ordered three explanations with respect to the likelihood of their coming to mind in a similar situation. One explanation was negative and the remaining two were neutral or positive. Analysis of both open-ended responses and

rank-order data indicated that agoraphobia with panic patients were more likely than controls to interpret both internal and external stimuli in a negative fashion.

In a subsequent study, Harvey *et al.* (1993) administered McNally and Foa's (1987) questionnaire to DSM–III–R panic disorder patients, social phobics, and non-patient controls. The comparison between panic disorder patients and non-patient controls replicated McNally and Foa's finding of a significant difference for both internal and external events. The comparison between panic disorder patients and social phobics revealed evidence for a more specific cognitive abnormality. In particular, panic patients were significantly more likely to choose negative interpretations of internal events than social phobics but the two patient groups did not differ in the likelihood of choosing a negative interpretation for external events. This pattern of results suggests anxiety disorders may have a general effect on threat interpretation and, in addition, panic disorder is associated with a specifically enhanced tendency to interpret internal events in a negative fashion.

Clark *et al.* (submitted) replicated and extended Harvey and colleagues' findings. The interpretations questionnaire was modified to exclude anxiety responses (e.g., 'I am having a panic attack') from the experimenter-provided interpretations, and belief ratings were included. Consistent with the first prediction, patients with panic disorder were more likely to interpret ambiguous autonomic sensations as signs of immediately impending physical or mental disaster, and were more likely to believe these interpretations, than other anxiety disorder patients (social phobics and generalized anxiety disorder) and non-patients. In addition, the likelihood of interpreting ambiguous autonomic sensations as signs of immediately impending disaster reduced with successful treatment and the degree of change in interpretations discriminated between treatments which varied in their impact on panic.

The above studies indicate that panic disorder patients misinterpret bodily sensations. However, demonstrating that patients think as required by the theory does not in itself establish that the thinking plays a causal role in the production of attacks. Logically, the negative thinking could be just an epiphenomenon. To illustrate this point, consider epilepsy. Epileptic attacks are an alarming experience. After having suffered an attack many epileptics develop a characteristic set of fearful thoughts about the attacks. However, no one would argue that these thoughts have a primary causal role in epilepsy. Instead, the epileptic attacks are the result of spontaneously occurring neural activity. Some biological theorists would make similar statements about the cognitions that accompany panic attacks. If one wants to discount the epiphenomenon argument one must go beyond correlational observations and manipulate the putative cause. If the cognitive model is correct, manipulations which increase or decrease misinterpretations of body sensations should have the effect of respectively increasing or decreasing panic.

Ehlers *et al.* (1988) used a false heart rate feedback task to test the prediction that conditions which are likely to activate patients' catastrophic interpretations of bodily sensations will lead to increase in anxiety in panic patients. During the course of a laboratory experiment, panic disorder patients and normal controls were given false auditory feedback indicating a sudden increase in heart rate. Because patients are prone to misinterpret cardiac changes, it was predicted that panic patients would show a greater increase in anxiety during the false feedback, and this is what happened. Compared to normal controls, panic disorder patients showed significantly greater increases in self-reported anxiety, heart rate, skin conductance, and blood pressure.

Clark *et al.* (1988) used another cognitive manipulation to activate catastrophic misinterpretations and obtained essentially similar results to those reported by Ehlers *et al.* (1988). Panic patients and normal controls were asked to read out loud a series of pairs of words. In the crucial conditions, the pairs of words consisted of various combinations of body sensations and catastrophes (e.g., palpitations–dying, breathless–suffocate, numbness–stroke, dizziness–fainting, chest tight–heart attack, unreality–insane). As these combinations represent the sort of thoughts that panic patients are prone to have and believe during attacks, it was predicted that panic patients would show a greater increase in anxiety and panic while reading the pairs of words. This is indeed what happened. Panic disorder patients, recovered panic disorder patients (treated with cognitive therapy), and normal controls were asked to rate their anxiety before and after reading the cards and also to rate whether they experienced an increase in any of the 12 DSM–III (APA 1980) panic symptoms. On the basis of this information, it was determined that 10 out of 12 (83%) panic patients, but no recovered patients or normal controls, had a panic attack while reading the cards.

Several studies have tested the prediction that reducing patients' tendency to misinterpret body sensations will prevent panic attacks. Early research in panic established that a range of pharmacological agents (sodium lactate, yohimbine, carbon dioxide, isoproterenol, caffeine) can reliably induce a state that is perceived as similar to natural panic attacks in panic disorder patients but rarely does so in non-panic patients or normal controls. Biological theorists interpreted these findings as evidence that panic can be directly induced by biochemical changes and that panic disorder is due to a neurochemical disturbance. In contrast, cognitive theorists have argued that these pharmacological agents do not have a direct panic-inducing effect but, instead, induce panic because patients misinterpret the pharmacologically induced body sensations. To distinguish between the cognitive and biological accounts of pharmacological panic inductions, Rapee *et al.* (1986), Sanderson, *et al.* (1989), and Clark *et al.* (in preparation) investigated whether or not purely cognitive manipulations could block pharmacologically induced panic.

Rapee *et al.* (1986) used a pre-inhalation instructional manipulation to influence patients' interpretation of the sensations induced by a single inhalation of 50% carbon dioxide/50% oxygen. One-half of the panic disorder patients were allocated to a no explanation condition in which minimal information about the procedure was provided. The other half were given a more detailed explanation in which all possible sensations were described and attributed to the effects of the gas. A manipulation check confirmed that the detailed explanation group had less catastrophic cognitions during the inhalation than the no explanation group. As predicted by cognitive theory, the detailed explanation group also reported significantly less panic than the no explanation group.

Sanderson *et al.* (1989) studied carbon dioxide (CO_2) inhalation. Prior to receiving a 20-minute inhalation of 5% CO_2 in air, panic disorder patients were shown a dial and told that turning this dial would reduce CO_2 flow if a nearby light was illuminated but not otherwise. In fact, the dial had no effect on CO_2 flow. During the infusion, the light came on for half the patients (illusion of control group) but was not illuminated for the remaining subjects (no illusion of control group). As predicted, patients in the illusion of control group were significantly less likely to panic, even though they did not use the dial and received as much CO_2 as the no illusion group.

Clark *et al.* (in preparation) studied sodium lactate infusions. Panic disorder patients were randomly allocated to one of two pre-infusion instruction sets (experimental or control). The experimental instructions were designed to prevent patients from misinterpreting lactate-induced sensations. Consistent with cognitive theory, patients' self-reports, physiological monitoring, and judgements by a blind assessor indicated that patients given the experimental instructions were significantly less likely to panic than patients given the control instructions, even though the amount of lactate infused was the same in both groups.

A further prediction which can be derived from the cognitive model is that sustained improvement after the end of any treatment (whether psychological or pharmacological) will depend on cognitive change having occurred during the course of therapy. Clark *et al.* (1994) tested this prediction by examining end of treatment and follow-up data in a trial of psychological (cognitive therapy or applied relaxation) and pharmacological (imipramine) treatments for panic disorder. Two analyses provided support for the prediction. First, when the data from all patients was examined, misinterpretation of bodily sensations at the end of treatment was a significant predictor of panic/anxiety at follow-up, and this relationship remained significant when panic/anxiety at the end of treatment was partialled out. Second, within patients who were panic-free at the end of treatment, there was a significant correlation between misinterpretation of bodily sensations at the end of treatment and subsequent relapse.

The above studies provide strong support for the proposed causal role of misinterpretations of body sensations in panic disorder. Other studies have focused on the processes which, it is hypothesized, normally prevent cognitive change and so maintain panic disorder.

Factors which prevent cognitive change in the absence of treatment

Ehlers and colleagues have reported a series of studies that provide support for the role of interoception in the maintenance of panic disorder. In one study (Ehlers and Breuer 1992, experiment 2) subjects were given a heartbeat perception task in which they had to silently count their heartbeats without taking their pulse. Consistent with the hypothesis that panic disorder is characterized by enhanced awareness of bodily sensations, panic disorder patients were more accurate in their heartbeat perception than infrequent panickers, simple phobics, or normal controls. In a subsequent study (Ehlers 1995), a longitudinal design was used to determine whether or not enhanced cardiac awareness contributes to the persistence of panic disorder. Patients who had a history of panic disorder but were in remission when tested in the laboratory were followed-up one year later and asked whether or not they had experienced any further panic attacks during the follow-up period. As predicted, patients who reported a re-occurrence of their panic attacks had demonstrated significantly better heart rate perception during the initial laboratory test than patients who did not experience a re-occurrence.

Salkovskis *et al.* (1996) provided evidence that panic patients engage in safety behaviours of the sort which *could* maintain their negative beliefs. Panic disorder patients completed the Agoraphobic Cognitions Questionnaire (Chambless *et al.* 1984), which assesses thoughts experienced during a panic attack, and a Behaviours Questionnaire, which assessed their behaviour during a panic attack. Correlational analyses revealed a series of meaningful links between cognitions and behaviour. For example, patients who reported thinking that they might be having a heart attack rested and slowed down their breathing during a panic. Patients who thought they might be about to faint leaned against solid objects, and patients who thought they might be going insane made strenuous efforts to control their thinking.

To determine whether these safety behaviours prevent disconfirmation of panic patients' negative beliefs about bodily sensations, it is necessary to manipulate experimentally the safety behaviours. Salkovskis (1995) has recently reported preliminary results from a study in which patients with panic disorder and agoraphobia had equivalent periods of exposure to a feared situation while either maintaining their usual safety behaviours or dropping them. As predicted, the dropping-safety behaviours condition lead to a significantly larger decrease in negative beliefs and produced a significantly greater improvement in anxiety in a subsequent behaviour test.

Social phobia

The nature of negative thinking in social phobia

The cognitive model assumes that social phobics interpret social situations in a more threatening fashion than non-social phobics. Clark and Stopa (in preparation) used modified versions of the ambiguous events questionnaire developed by Butler and Mathews (1983) to investigate this assertion. Social phobics, other anxiety disorder patients, and non-patient controls completed two questionnaires. One questionnaire contained ambiguous social situations (e.g., 'You have visitors round for a meal and they leave sooner than expected'), and ambiguous non-social situations (e.g., 'A letter marked urgent arrives at your home'). Social phobics were significantly more likely to choose negative interpretations of the ambiguous social situations than either other anxious patients or non-patient controls but did not differ from these two groups in their interpretation of non-social ambiguous situations. The second questionnaire contained mildly negative social events (e.g., 'You have been talking to someone for a while and it becomes clear that they're not really interested in what you're saying'), and was used to assess catastrophic interpretations. Consistent with the cognitive model, social phobics were more likely to choose catastrophic interpretations of mildly negative social events (e.g., 'It means I am a boring person') than other anxious patients or non-patient controls.

Investigations of thoughts in actual social situations using various thought-listing procedures have produced results consistent with the questionnaire data on hypothetical social situations. Stopa and Clark (1993) reported an experiment in which social phobics, other anxious patients, and non-patient controls were asked to have a brief conversation with an attractive, female stooge. The stooge was instructed to behave in a reserved but not unfriendly manner. After the conversation, subjects listed their thoughts and gave ratings of the extent to which they had shown a variety of positive and negative behaviours. Independent assessors rated the same behaviours. Analysis of the thoughts data revealed that social phobics reported more negative self-evaluative thoughts than both the other anxious patients and the non-patient controls.

The cognitive model assumes that social phobics' negative evaluations of their performance are at least partly distorted. To investigate this, Stopa and Clark (1993) compared self and observer ratings of performance following a conversation with a stooge. When compared to the observers' ratings social phobics underestimated their performance while other anxiety disorder patients and non-patient controls were relatively accurate. Other investigators have also found that high socially anxious individuals underestimate their performance (Rapee and Lim 1992), and overestimate how anxious they appear to others (Bruch et al. 1989; McEwan and Devins 1983).

In-situation safety behaviours

Wells *et al.* (1995) tested the hypothesis that in-situation safety behaviours play a role in maintaining social phobia by comparing one session of exposure to a feared social situation with one session of similar exposure accompanied by the intentional dropping of safety behaviours. Although the two procedures did not differ in patients' credibility ratings, exposure and dropping of safety behaviours produced significantly greater reductions in anxiety and belief ratings for feared outcomes in a behaviour test administered before and after the intervention.

Self-focused attention and the use of interoceptive information to construct an impression of oneself as a social object

A key component of Clark and Wells' (1995a) model is the idea that social phobics use interoceptive information to construct an impression of themselves which they assume reflects what other people observe and that this information is relatively more important than observation of others' actual behaviour. A number of studies have reported findings which are consistent with various aspects of this hypothesis.

First, several studies have suggested that social phobics' belief that others are evaluating them negatively is not based on detailed information about others' responses to them. Stopa and Clark (1993) found that social phobics reported more negative self-evaluative thoughts (e.g., 'I'm boring') than controls during a conversation with a stooge, but did not report more negative thoughts which explicitly mentioned evaluation by the stooge (e.g.,'She thinks I'm boring'). Winton *et al.* (1995) investigated accuracy in detecting negative emotion in briefly presented slides of different emotional expressions. Slides of negative and neutral facial expressions were presented for 60 milliseconds, followed by a pattern mask. Students scoring high on Fear of Negative Evaluation (FNE: Watson and Friend, 1969) correctly identified more negative facial expressions than low FNE students, but a signal detection analysis revealed that this was due to a negative response bias. That is to say, high FNE students were more likely to rate a briefly presented face as negative in the absence of having abstracted more affective information from the face.

Second, a number of studies have suggested that social phobics have reduced awareness of the details of a social interaction. Clark *et al.* (in preparation) used a modified dot probe paradigm to compare attention to social cues (faces) or non-social cues (furniture and other everyday objects). On each trial subjects were simultaneously presented with a picture of a face and a picture of an object. The pictures were presented for 500 milliseconds and then followed by a single letter which appeared at the location where the face or object had been. Time to classify the letter was used to assess attentional bias. Compared to low FNE students, high FNE students showed an attentional bias away from faces. As one might expect from this finding, Kimble and Zehr (1982), Daly *et al.* (1989), and Hope *et al.* (1990) all found that, compared to low socially anxious subjects, high socially anxious subjects had poorer memory for the details of a recent social interaction. However, Stopa and Clark (1993), using a slightly different methodology, failed to replicate this effect.

Third, Arntz *et al.* (1995) and Mansell and Clark (submitted) have reported results which suggest social phobics' estimates of the dangerousness of social situations are partly based on the perception of their own emotional response. Arntz *et al.* (1995) presented subjects with scripts describing hypothetical social situations in which they were participants. The scripts varied along two dimensions: the presence of objective danger or safety information and whether the subject felt anxious or non-anxious. After imaging being in the scripted situation subjects were asked to rate how dangerous they viewed the situation to be. Controls' estimates of danger were only influenced by the presence of objective danger information, but social phobics' estimates were also influenced by anxiety response information. Mansell and Clark (submitted) asked high and low FNE students to give a speech. After the speech they completed a check-list of anxious feelings and rated how anxious they thought they appeared. An independent assessor also rated how anxious the subject appeared. As in previous studies, high FNE subjects overestimated how anxious they appeared. In addition, within high FNE subjects, the degree of overestimation was significantly correlated with the intensity of their anxious feelings.

Anticipatory anxiety and selective memory
Mansell and Clark (submitted) have recently provided support for the hypothesis that socially anxious individuals will selectively retrieve negative information about how they may appear to others when anticipating a social interaction. High and low FNE students rated positive and negative trait words in one of three ways: public self-referent ('How well does the word describe what someone who knows you or had just met you would think of you?'); private self-referent ('How well does the word describe you?'); and other referent ('How well does the word describe your nextdoor neighbour?'). Half the subjects were then told that they would shortly have to give a speech. Recall for all the trait words was then tested. Compared to low FNE subjects, high FNE subjects showed a bias towards recall of negative, rather than positive, public self-referent words but only when both groups were anticipating giving a speech. There were no differences between high and low FNE subjects in their recall of private self-referent or other-referent encoded words.

To summarize this section, recent studies have provided encouraging preliminary support for several aspects of the cognitive model of social phobia.

Description of the specialized cognitive treatments

Clark, Salkovskis, Hackmann, Wells, and colleagues have devised specialized forms of cognitive therapy based on the cognitive models described in this chapter. The treatments for panic disorder and social phobia both involve a mixture of cognitive and behavioural techniques which are intended to help patients identify and modify their distorted, anxiety-related thoughts and beliefs. Particular emphasis is placed on reversing the maintaining factors identified in the models. The two treatments share a number of common features including detailed exploration of patients' idiosyncratic evidence for their negative beliefs and the modification of safety behaviours. However, because the key abnormalities in each disorder are different, many of the treatment procedures are disorder-specific. A brief overview of each treatment is given below. Readers interested in a more detailed description of the panic treatment are referred to Clark (1989) and Salkovskis and Clark (1991). Further details of the social phobia treatment can be found in Clark and Wells (1995a).

Panic disorder

Treatment starts by reviewing with the patient a recent panic attack and identifying the main sensations and the negative thoughts associated with the sensations. Careful questioning about the sequence of events is used to derive an idiosyncratic version of the panic vicious circle. An example is shown in Fig. 6.3. Once patient and therapist agree that the panic attacks involve an interaction between bodily sensations and negative thoughts about the sensations, a variety of procedures are used to help patients challenge their misinterpretations of the sensations.

Identifying the triggers for an attack
Many patients interpret the unexpected nature of some of their panic attacks as an indication that they are suffering from a cardiac or other physical abnormality. For these patients, it can be helpful to identify the triggers for unexpected attacks. Diaries and in-session discussions usually reveal that the trigger for their unexpected attacks is a slight bodily change caused by a different emotional state (excitement, anger, disgust) or by some innocuous event, such as rapid circadic eye movement (world seems to move), exercise

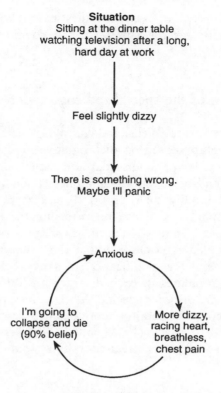

Situation
Sitting at the dinner table
watching television after a long,
hard day at work

Feel slightly dizzy

There is something wrong.
Maybe I'll panic

Anxious

I'm going to
collapse and die
(90% belief)

More dizzy,
racing heart,
breathless,
chest pain

FIG. 6.3. A specific panic attack.

(breathlessness, palpitations), suddenly standing up after sitting (dizziness), or drinking too much coffee (palpitations).

Cognitive procedures
One of the most useful cognitive procedures involves helping patients to understand the significance of past events which are inconsistent with their negative beliefs. For example, the telephone may have rung while a patient was sitting at home experiencing palpitations, breathlessness, and a tight chest, and thinking he/she was having a heart attack. Answering the telephone momentarily distracted the patient from the negative thoughts and as a consequence the physical symptoms and panic ceased. Questions such as 'Do you think answering the telephone is a good treatment for heart attacks?' and 'If answering the telephone isn't stopping a heart attack, what is it doing?', can be used to help the patient see the significance of this observation.

Education about the nature of anxiety can also be helpful, especially if it is tailored to patients' idiosyncratic concerns. For example, patients who are concerned that they might faint in a panic attack are often helped by being told that blood pressure increases during a panic and fainting is associated with a drop in blood pressure (see Clark 1989, p.76 for an illustrative transcript). Similarly, patients who report predominantly left-sided pain and take this as evidence for a cardiac abnormality often benefit from being shown the results of an investigation (Beunderman *et al.* 1988) which compared the location of chest pain in patients seen in a cardiology clinic. Predominantly left-sided pain was more characteristic of anxious patients *without* cardiac abnormalities than of patients who had suffered myocardial infarctions or had angina pectoris.

Images of feared outcomes (such as fainting, dying, or going mad) often accompany panic attacks. Often these images can be treated as equivalent to a negative thought (e.g., 'I'm about to faint') and dealt with in the same way. However, it is sometimes necessary to directly modify the image by transforming it into a less threatening and more realistic image. This is particularly likely to be necessary if the intrusive image is repetitive and stereotyped. The images that accompany a panic attack invariably stop at the worst moment. Encouraging the patient to visualize what in reality would happen next can therefore be helpful. For example, a patient who sees herself collapsed on the floor after fainting may be encouraged to visualize slowly coming round, getting to her feet, and leaving. In instances where continuing the image would not be helpful, the visual and auditory components of the image are transformed into something less threatening.

Behavioural experiments
Most of the behavioural experiments used with panic patients fall into one of two categories: (1) inducing feared sensations in order to demonstrate possible causes of the patients' symptoms; and (2) stopping safety behaviours in order to help patients disconfirm their negative beliefs about the consequences of the sensations. Some of the most commonly used procedures for inducing feared sensations include: focusing attention on the body, reading and dwelling on pairs of words representing feared sensations and catastrophes (e.g., palpitations–dying, breathless–suffocate, numbness–stroke, racing thoughts–insanity), and reproducing the way patients breathe in a panic attack, if it seems likely that they normally over-breathe. For patients who interpret the dizziness that accompanies attacks as a sign that they might faint, the dropping-safety-behaviours manoeuvre might involve inducing dizziness (by entering a feared situation and/or over-breathing) and then not holding on to solid objects or tensing the legs. For patients who are concerned that they might have something wrong with their heart and who avoid exercise because of this concern, the safety behaviours manoeuvre might involve encouraging the patient to exercise, particularly when feared sensations are present.

Usually, this manoeuvre would first be practised in a therapy session and then set as homework.

Social phobia

Treatment of social phobia starts by reviewing several recent episodes of social anxiety. As with panic, careful questioning is used to develop an idiosyncratic version of the cognitive model. An example is shown in Fig. 6.4. The model should include a comprehensive list of the patient's safety behaviours and a description of the interoceptive information which the patient becomes aware of when he/she is self-focused. As in Fig. 6.4, this typically includes bodily sensations and a felt sense of how the person might appear to others. Sometimes the felt sense is also accompanied by an image in which the patient sees him/herself as if viewed from an observer's perspective. The image contains visible (or audible) distortions which are derived from the interoceptive cues. For example, the patient in Fig. 6.4 felt that the muscles around her mouth tensed when she was the focus of attention. This feeling was transformed in the image into a visibly contorted mouth which she thought everyone must be able to see. Similarly, a warm forehead and a slight sweating sensation can be transformed into a picture of rivulets of sweat running down the forehead.

Safety behaviours experiment
Once patient and therapist have agreed a working version of the cognitive model, key elements of the model are manipulated. We found that changing safety behaviours is often the best way to start. During a treatment session the patient is asked to role play a feared social interaction under two conditions. In one condition, they are asked to use all their normal safety behaviours. In the other condition, they are asked to drop their safety behaviours and focus their attention on the other person(s) in the interaction, rather than on themselves. After each role play patients rate how anxious they felt, how anxious they thought they appeared, and how well they thought they performed. By comparing these ratings several points can be established. First, to patients' considerable surprise, the habitual safety behaviours often make the patient feel more anxious rather than less anxious. Second, ratings of how anxious patients think they appear and how well they think they performed closely follow the ratings of how they felt, indicating that they are using their feelings to infer how they appear to others.

Video and audio feedback
Once it is established that patients are using their interoceptive cues to infer how they appear to others the next step is to obtain realistic information about how they actually appear. One way of doing this is to ask the stooge(s)

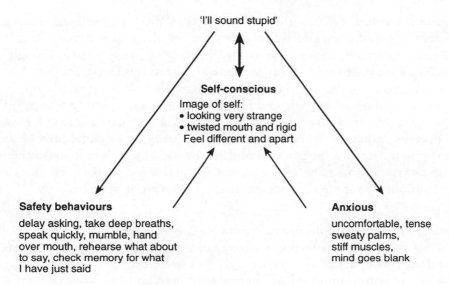

FIG. 6.4. Elements of the cognitive model for a social phobic.

in the safety behaviours experiment to give the patient feedback. The feedback usually indicates that the patient appeared less anxious than he/she estimated, establishing that feelings are not a good indicator of how one appears. Video and audio feedback are another particularly good way of making this point. Normally, we would videotape the safety behaviours experiment and show the patient the video during the next session. Before viewing the video, patients are asked to visualize how they think they will appear. This constructed image is then compared with how they actually appear. The actual appearance is invariably better than patients expect.

In order to maximize the amount of cognitive change produced by each treatment session, we audiotape sessions and ask patients to listen to the tape as part of their homework. In this way they can consolidate and develop further answers to their negative thoughts which were identified in the session. The audio record also gives patients' invaluable information about how they sound, again correcting their distorted impressions. For example, a professional woman talked quietly in meetings. She did this in order not to attract attention. However, the consequence was that other people had to strain to hear what she was saying, and hence stared at her more. It was agreed that she would experiment with speaking louder in meetings. While practising this in the session, it became evident that the patient systematically overestimated the volume of her own voice, thinking she was shouting when she was not. This was easily corrected by playing back the tape and comparing the volume of the patient's 'shout' with the therapist's normal speech. To the patient's surprise, her 'shout' was quieter than the therapist's usual voice. Further discussion revealed a probable basis for the misperception. Because the patient normally spoke very quietly, speaking up initially felt as though it required a lot of effort, and this feeling was mistaken for volume.

At this point in therapy, homework assignments would typically involve encouraging the patient to drop safety behaviours and to shift to an external focus of attention during social interactions. The explicit rationale for this manoeuvre is that the evidence the patient normally uses to infer how he/she appear to others (i.e., the contents of their self-awareness) is inaccurate and it is necessary to focus more on the interaction and other people's responses in order to obtain a more accurate impression of how one appears.

Testing predictions about negative evaluation by others

Normal social interactions provide only limited opportunities to test patients' distorted beliefs about the consequences of behaving in ways which they perceive as inept. This problem can be partly overcome by asking patients to perform intentionally behaviours that they falsely believe will lead to negative evaluation. For example, a secretary feared that if she spilt her drink in a local bar people that she knew would think that she was an alcoholic and would reject her. The first step in challenging this belief was to ask her how she thought the other people would react if they thought spilling her drink meant she was an alcoholic. She said that they would stare at her and start whispering. This was then tested by intentionally spilling a drink in a conspicuous fashion. To her amazement no one showed any interest apart from the barman who briefly glanced in her direction but hardly paused in his conversation. Similarly, patients can be asked to experiment with introducing boring topics into conversations, pausing while speaking, stammering, or expressing opinions that they know others will disagree with. Surveys are another useful way of collecting information about how others respond. For example, a social phobic who stuttered and was concerned other people would think she was stupid, was greatly reassured by a survey in which fifteen people were asked what they thought of someone who stutters. To her surprise, nobody thought it was a sign of stupidity and respondents provided a wide range of non-threatening explanations for why someone might stutter.

Dealing with the 'post-mortem'

Because normal social interactions rarely provide patients with unambiguous feedback on how well they have performed and how others perceived them, social phobics often conduct a post-mortem of their social interactions. In these post-mortems, the patients' anxious feelings and negative self-perceptions figure particularly prominently and so the post-mortem provides further, incorrect, evidence of social failure. This point is discussed with the patient and then the post-mortem is banned.

Modifying assumptions

The assumptions which lead social phobics to interpret social situations in a threatening fashion can be modified by the use of Socratic questioning. For example, the assumption: 'If someone doesn't like me, it means I am inadequate' can be modified by questions such as: 'How do you know that someone does not like you?' 'Are there any reasons why someone might not respond well to you other than your adequacy, for example, their mood, you reminding them of someone else, their mind being elsewhere, etc.?', 'Can you think of any examples of where someone was not liked yet they were not inadequate, for example, Jesus and the Pharisees?' 'If one person doesn't like you and another does, who is right?' 'If one person doesn't like you, does that write you off as a person?'

Efficacy of the cognitive treatments

Panic disorder

Five controlled trials have investigated full cognitive therapy for panic disorder. Beck *et al.* (1992) allocated panic patients to 12 weeks of cognitive therapy or 8 weeks of supportive therapy. When assessed at comparable time points (4 and 8 weeks), patients given cognitive therapy had improved significantly more than those given supportive therapy, indicating that the effectiveness of cognitive therapy is not entirely attributable to non-specific therapy factors. In addition, the gains achieved in treatment were maintained at one-year follow-up.

Clark *et al.* (1994) compared cognitive therapy with an alternative active psychological treatment and with a pharmacological intervention. Panic disorder patients were randomly allocated to cognitive therapy, applied relaxation, imipramine (mean 233 mg/day), or a 3-month wait followed by allocation to treatment. During treatment patients had up to twelve sessions in the first 3 months and up to three booster sessions in the next 3 months. Imipramine was gradually withdrawn after 6 months. All treatments included homework assignments involving self-exposure to feared situations. Comparisons with waiting list controls showed all three treatments were effective. Comparisons between treatments showed that at 3 months cognitive therapy was superior to both applied relaxation and imipramine. Between 3 and 6 months imipramine-treated patients continued to improve while those who had received cognitive therapy or applied relaxation showed little change. As a consequence, at 6 months cognitive therapy did not differ from imipramine and both were superior to applied relaxation. Imipramine was gradually withdrawn after the 6-month assessment. Between 6 and 15 months, 40% of imipramine patients relapsed compared with only 5% of cognitive therapy patients. At 15 months cognitive therapy was again superior to both applied relaxation and imipramine.

Öst, the originator of applied relaxation, has also compared cognitive therapy and applied relaxation (Öst and Westling 1995). Assessments were at pre-, post-treatment, and one-year follow-up. Pre- to post-treatment comparisons indicated that cognitive therapy and applied relaxation were both associated with substantial improvements in panic frequency, panic-related distress/disability and generalized anxiety. In the initial report (Öst and Westling 1995) there were no significant differences between the treatments. However, Öst (personal communication, December 1995) has pointed out that each of the four therapist's initial training case in cognitive therapy was included. Only 1/4 (25%) of the training cases became panic-free but 13/15 (87%) of subsequent cognitive therapy cases became panic-free and achieved high end-state function at the end of treatment. When the data are re-analysed, excluding the four cognitive therapy training cases, there is a significant difference between cognitive therapy and applied relaxation in terms of the percentage of patients achieving high end-state function at post-treatment: 13/15 (87%) for cognitive therapy versus 8/17 (47%) for applied relaxation. For both treatments the gains made during therapy were maintained at the one-year follow-up.

Arntz and van den Hout (1996) have recently reported an independent evaluation of cognitive therapy and applied relaxation. Their group was not involved in the development of either treatment. Therapists were given specialist training in cognitive therapy from Clark and Salkovskis and specialist training in applied relaxation from Öst. Assessments were at pre-, post-treatment, and 1-month and 6-month follow-ups. A significantly greater proportion of cognitive therapy patients achieved panic-free status at the end of treatment and this difference was maintained at both follow-ups.

Finally, Margraf and Schneider (1991) conducted a component analysis of cognitive therapy. The full cognitive treatment (which combines cognitive and behavioural procedures) was compared with an intervention involving cognitive procedures alone and an intervention involving situational and interoceptive exposure without explicit cognitive restructuring. Comparison with a waiting list control group indicated that all three treatments were highly effective. On most measures, there were no significant differences although combined treatment was superior to exposure on an intention-to-treat analysis of the percentage of patients who became panic-free. In all three groups, treatment gains were fully maintained at one-year follow-up. Change in panic-related cognitions was a significant predictor of immediate improvement in all three treatments, suggesting that the cognitive and behavioural procedures both have their effects through the common mechanism of cognitive change.

Table 6.1 summarizes the five trials reviewed above. In each trial the therapists were provided with some training from the Oxford group. Taken together, the five trials indicate that properly conducted cognitive therapy is a highly effective treatment for panic disorder, with intention-to-treat analyses indicating 74–94% of patients becoming panic-free and these gains being maintained at follow-up. It is also clear that the effects of the treatment are not entirely due to non-specific therapy factors as three studies (Arntz and van den Hout 1996; Beck *et al.* 1992; Clark *et al.* 1994) have found cognitive therapy to be superior to an equally credible alternative psychological treatment and re-analysis of a fourth (Öst and Westling 1995) indicates a similar pattern of results. One study (Clark *et al.* 1994) compared cognitive therapy with imipramine in adequate dose. Cognitive therapy was superior to imipramine early in treatment and again at one-year follow-up. Finally, the treatment seems to travel well as the results obtained with cognitive therapy are remarkably consistent across five countries (England, Germany, the Netherlands, Sweden, and the United States).

The excellent results obtained with the full cognitive therapy package have encouraged researchers to investigate whether it might be possible to obtain similar results with a briefer form of the treatment. If so, more patients could potentially benefit from the treatment. The studies of full treatment described above had a total of 12–16 sessions. The first group to report an evaluation of a briefer version was Black *et al.* (1993). These investigators devised their own brief (8 sessions) version of cognitive therapy which included additional psychological procedures specifically devised by the investigators (Bowers, personal communication). The Oxford group had no involvement in therapist training or in the modification of treatment content. Panic disorder patients were randomly allocated to brief cognitive therapy, fluvoxamine, or placebo medication. Main assessments were at pre-treatment and eight weeks later. No follow-up was reported. Response to fluvoxamine was superior to brief cognitive therapy on a number of measures in a completers analysis. However, the unusually high drop-out rate (40% for brief cognitive therapy compared to between 0% and 5% in the studies of full cognitive therapy reviewed above) suggests that the investigators' modifications severely interfered with treatment acceptability.

Clark *et al.* (1995) have recently reported a more successful attempt to produce a brief version of cognitive therapy. The total number of sessions was reduced to seven by devising a series of self-study modules covering the main stages in therapy. Patients read the self-study modules and completed the homework outlined in the modules before discussing an area with their

TABLE 6.1.   Controlled trials of (full) cognitive therapy for panic disorder: intention-to-treat analyses

| Study | Treatment | Per cent (number) of panic-free patients | |
		Post-treatment	Follow-up
Beck et al. (1992)	1. CT	94 (16/17)	77 (13/17)[b]
	2. ST	25 (4/16)[a]	–
Clark et al. (1994)	1. CT	86 (18/21)	76 (16/21)[c]
	2. AR	48 (10/21)	43 (9/21)[c]
	3. IMP	52 (11/21)	48 (10/21)[c]
	4. WL	7 (1/16)	-
Öst & Westling (1995)[d]	1. CT	74 (14/19)	89 (17/19)[c]
	2. AR	58 (11/19)	74 (14/19)[c]
Arntz & van den Hout (1996)	1. CT	78 (14/18)	78 (14/18)
	2. AR	47 (9/19)	47 (9/19)
	3. WL	28 (5/18)	–
Margraf & Schneider (1991)	1. Combined (CT)	91 (20/22)[e]	–
	2. Pure Cog	73 (16/22)[e]	–
	3. Pure Exp	52 (11/21)[e]	–
	4. WL	5 (1/20)	–
Total across all studies for CT		85 (82/97)	80 (60/75)

Note. Intention-to-treat analysis includes drop-outs as well as completers. Drop outs are coded as still panicking. CT, cognitive therapy. ST, supportive therapy. AR, applied relaxation. IMIP, imipramine. Exp, interoceptive and situational exposure; WL, waiting list.

[a]At 8 weeks, which is the end of supportive therapy. At this time 71% of CT patients were panic-free.

[b]One year follow-up.

[c]Percentage of patients panic-free at follow-up and who received no additional treatment during the follow-up period.

[d]The figures for cognitive therapy are conservative as they *include* the therapists' four training cases.

[e]Four-week follow-up.

therapist. In this way, the therapist was able to devote more attention to misunderstandings and problems. Panic disorder patients were randomly allocated to brief cognitive therapy, full cognitive therapy, or waiting list. Brief and full cognitive therapy were both superior to no treatment and did not differ from each other. In addition, the substantial improvement observed with both treatments was as large as that obtained in the Oxford group's previous trial (Clark *et al.* 1994), which used similar selection criteria.

Barlow's panic control treatment

At the same time as cognitive therapy for panic was being developed, Barlow and colleagues were independently developing another cognitive behaviour therapy (panic control treatment, PCT), which also focused on panic patients' fears of bodily sensations. Although differing in some respects, cognitive therapy and PCT share many common procedures. Five studies have investigated the effectiveness of Barlow and colleagues' treatment. As one might expect from the similarity in procedures, these studies have established that it is also a highly effective treatment for panic disorder. Barlow *et al.* (1989) compared PCT with another cognitive treatment, with progressive muscle relaxation, and a waiting list control. Both cognitive treatments were consistently superior to the waiting list control, and were more effective than relaxation at reducing panic frequency. Klosko *et al.* (1990) compared PCT with alprazolam, placebo, and a waiting list control. PCT was superior to alprazolam, placebo, and waiting list control. The percentages of patients who became panic-free on alprazolam and placebo were similar to those found in the Cross-National Collaborative Panic Study (1992), but alprazolam was not significantly different from placebo, perhaps because of the very small sample size in the latter condition.

Shear *et al.* (1994) compared PCT with a specially devised non-prescriptive treatment. PCT appeared to be slightly less successful than in the preceding two studies and did not differ significantly from non-prescriptive treatment. In discussing the study, Shear *et al.* (1994) point out that PCT may not have been delivered optimally as therapist adherence ratings were lower than expected. An additional possible explanation for a lack of difference between treatments is a design confound. The first three sessions in the non-prescriptive treatment were identical to those in PCT and may have accounted for much of the common outcome variance. Unfortunately, it is not possible to assess this suggestion as the investigators did not conduct an assessment after the third session.

Finally, Craske *et al.* (1995) investigated a brief (four-session) version of PCT. Panic disorder patients were randomly allocated to four sessions of PCT or four sessions of non-directive supportive therapy. Brief PCT was more effective than non-directive supportive therapy in reducing panic and phobic fear, suggesting that it has a specific effect. However, the overall panic-free rate at the end of treatment (53%) was relatively low, suggesting that a number of patients would have benefited from more sessions of treatment.

Social phobia

Several cognitive behavioural treatments for social phobia have been developed by investigators using earlier cognitive behavioural models. These treatments include Butler and colleagues' anxiety management training (AMT), Heimberg's cognitive behavioural group treatment (CBGT), and Mattick and Peter's combined group exposure and cognitive restructuring treatment. Controlled trials involving comparison psychological interventions (Butler *et al.* 1984; Heimberg *et al.* 1990; Mattick and Peters, 1988; Mattick *et al.* 1989) indicate that each of these treatments has a specific effect in social phobia. Butler *et al.* (1984) and Mattick and colleagues (Mattick and Peters 1988; Mattick *et al.* 1989) also found that their treatments were superior to exposure alone. However, inspection of the percentage responder data suggests there is still room for substantial improvement in treatment effectiveness. Heimberg *et al.* (1990) found that 65% of CBGT patients were improved at the end of treatment. Mattick and Peters (1988) used a more stringent improvement criterion and found that only 38% of the combined exposure and cognitive restructuring treatment group achieved 'high end-state function'. Analysis of the degree of change in fear of negative evaluation (Watson and Friend 1969) tells a similar story. Although patients show improvement on this measure, the post-treatment mean for treated patients remains well above the mean for the general population. It is hoped that the new version of cognitive therapy which we have recently developed on the basis of the cognitive model outlined in this chapter will produce a further improvement in treatment effectiveness. A preliminary indication that this might be the case was provided by a recent study (Clark and Wells 1995*b*) in which 12 consecutively referred social phobics were given the treatment. The mean change in fear of negative evaluation was between 1.5 and 2 times greater than that reported in trials of the three alternative cognitive behavioural treatments described above.

It is now necessary to see whether these encouraging preliminary results are confirmed in larger scale controlled trials.

Summary and conclusions

This chapter has illustrated a particular strategy for developing an effective psychological treatment for an anxiety disorder. Careful interviews with patients, correlational and experimental studies are used to identify the core cognitive abnormality in the disorder and the factors that normally prevent cognitive change. A specialized form of cognitive therapy which focuses on the core abnormality and its maintaining factors is then developed and evaluated in controlled trials. Throughout the exercise there is a close interplay between the experimental studies and the treatment development work. For example, in panic, our experimental studies of safety behaviours arose from clinical observations during treatment development and the results of the experiments led to the current major emphasis on dropping safety behaviours during treatment. Similarly, in the social phobia treatment our emphasis on patients' erroneous use of interoception to infer how they appear to others was strongly influenced by unexpected findings in an experimental study of negative thinking during social interactions (Stopa and Clark 1993).

The strategy has been applied to two contrasting, severe anxiety disorders. In the case of panic disorder, the strategy is well developed, the resulting treatment has been extensively evaluated, and is highly effective. In the case of social phobia, work is at an earlier stage and the treatment, although promising, has yet to be extensively evaluated.

Acknowledgements

Most of the Oxford studies described in this chapter were supported by grants from the Medical Research Council (Gelder and Clark) and the Wellcome Trust (Clark and Ehlers). The programme of research was very much a team effort and I have been fortunate to have many excellent collaborators including: Michael Gelder, Paul Salkovskis, Ann Hackmann, Adrian Wells, Anke Ehlers, Hugh Middleton, John Ludgate, Carolyn Fordham-Walker, Melanie Fennell, and Gillian Butler.

References

APA (American Psychiatric Association) (1980). *Diagnostic and Statistical Manual of Mental Disorders*, (3rd edn). APA, Washington DC.

APA (American Psychiatric Association) (1987). *Diagnostic and Statistical Manual of Mental Disorders*, (3rd edn, revised). APA, Washington, DC.

APA (American Psychiatric Association) (1994). *Diagnostic and Statistical Manual of Mental Disorders*, (4th edn). APA, Washington, DC.

Arntz, A. and Van den Hout, M. (1996). Psychological treatments of panic disorder without agoraphobia: cognitive therapy versus applied relaxation. *Behaviour Research and Therapy*, 34, 113–21.

Arntz, A., Rauner, M., and Van den Hout, M. A. (1995). "If I feel anxious, there must be danger": ex-consequentia reasoning in inferring danger in anxiety disorders. *Behaviour Research and Therapy*, 33, 917–25.

Barlow, D. H., Vermilyea, J., Blanchard, E. B., Vermilyea, B. B., Di Nardo, P. A., and Cerny, J. A. (1985). The phenomenon of panic. *Journal of Abnormal Psychology*, 94, 320–328.

Barlow, D. H., Craske, M. G., Cerny, J. A., and Klosko, J. S. (1989). Behavioural treatment of panic disorder. *Behavior Therapy*, 20, 261–82.

Beck, A. T., Sokol, L., Clark, D. A., Berchick, B., and Wright, F. (1992). Focused cognitive therapy for panic disorder: a crossover design and one year follow-up. *American Journal of Psychiatry*, 147, 778–83.

Beunderman, R., Van Dis, H., Koster, R. W., Boel, E., Tiemessen, C., and Schipper, J. (1988). Differentiation in prodromal and acute symptoms of patients with cardiac and non-cardiac chest pain. In *Advances in theory and practice in behaviour therapy* (ed. P. M. G. Emmelkamp, W. T. A. M. Everaerd, F. Kraaimaat, and M. J. M. van Son). Swets & Zeitlinger, Amsterdam.

Black, D. W., Wesner, R., Bowers, W., and Gabel, J. (1993). A comparison of fluvoxamine, cognitive therapy, and placebo in the treatment of panic disorder. *Archives of General Psychiatry*, 50, 44–50.

Brown, T. A. and Cash, T. F. (1990). The phenomenon of non-clinical panic: parameters of panic, fear, and avoidance. *Journal of Anxiety Disorders*, 4, 15–29.

Bruch, B. A., Gorsky, J. M., Collins, T. M., and Berger, P. A. (1989). Shyness and sociability reexamined: a multicomponent analysis. *Journal of Personality and Social Psychology*, 57, 904–15.

Butler, G. and Mathews, A. (1983). Cognitive processes in anxiety. *Advances in Behaviour Research and Therapy*, 5, 51–62.

Butler, G., Cullington, A., Munby, M., Amies, P. L., and Gelder, M. G. (1984). Exposure and anxiety management in the treatment of social phobia. *Journal of Consulting and Clinical Psychology*, 59, 167–75.

Chambless, D. L., Caputo, G. C., Bright, P., and Gallagher, R. (1984). Assessment of fear of fear in agoraphobics; the Body Sensations Questionnaire and the Agoraphobia Cognitions Questionnaire. *Journal of Consulting and Clinical Psychology*, 52, 1090–7.

Clark, D. M. (1986). A cognitive approach to panic disorder. *Behaviour Research and Therapy*, 24, 461–70.

Clark, D. M. (1988). A cognitive model of panic. In *Panic; psychological perspectives* (ed. S. J. Rachman and J. Maser). Erlbaum, Hillsdale, NJ.

Clark, D. M. (1989). Anxiety states: panic and generalized anxiety. In *Cognitive therapy for psychiatric problems: A practical guide* (ed. K. Hawton, P. M. Salkovskis, J. Kirk, and D. M. Clark), pp. 52–96. Oxford University Press.

Clark, D. M. and Wells, A. (1995a). A cognitive model of social phobia. In *Social phobia: diagnosis, assessment and treatment* (ed. R. Heimberg, M. Liebowitz, D. A. Hope and F. R. Schneier). Guilford Press, New York.

Clark, D. M. and Wells, A. (1995b). *Treatment implications of a cognitive model of social phobia*. Paper presented at the World Congress of Behavioural and Cognitive Therapies, Copenhagen, Denmark.

Clark, D. M., *et al.* (1988). Tests of a cognitive theory of panic. In *Panic and phobias*, Vol. 2 (ed. I. Hand and U. Wittchen). Springer-Verlag, Berlin.

Clark, D. M., Salkovskis, P. M., Hackmann, A., Middleton, H., Anastasiades, P., and Gelder, M. G. (1994). A comparison of cognitive therapy, applied relaxation and imipramine in the treatment of panic disorder. *British Journal of Psychiatry*, 164, 759–69.

Clark, D. M., Salkovskis, P. M., Hackmann, A., Wells, A., and Gelder, M. G. (1995). *A comparison of standard and brief cognitive therapy for panic disorder*. Paper presented at the World Congress of Behavioural and Cognitive Therapies, Copenhagen, Denmark.

Clark, D. M., Salkovskis, P. M., Ost, L. G., Westling, B. E., Koehler, C., Jeavons, A., and Gelder, M. G. (submitted). Misinterpretation of body sensations in panic disorder.

Clark, D. M., Mansell, W., Chen, Y. P., and Ehlers, A. (in preparation). *Social anxiety and attention for faces*.

Clark, D. M., Salkovskis, P. M., Middleton, H., Anastasiades, P., Hackmann, A., and Gelder, M. G. (in preparation). *Cognitive mediation of lactate induced panic*.

Craske, M. G., Maidenberg, E., and Brystritsky, A. (1995). Brief cognitive-behavioural versus nondirective therapy for panic disorder. *Journal of Behavior Therapy and Experimental Psychiatry*, 26, 113–20.

Cross-National Collaborative Panic Study (1992). Drug treatment of panic disorder: comparative efficacy of alprazolam, imipramine and placebo. *British Journal of Psychiatry*, 160, 191–202.

Daly, J. A., Vangelisti, A. L., and Lawrence, S. G. (1989). Self-focused attention and public speaking anxiety. *Personality and Individual Differences*, 10, 903–13.

Ehlers, A. (1993). Interoception and panic disorder. *Advances in Behaviour Research and Therapy*, 15, 3–21.

Ehlers, A. (1995). A one year prospective study of panic attacks: clinical cause and factors associated with maintenance. *Journal of Abnormal Psychology*, 104, 164–72.

Ehlers, A. and Breuer, P. (1992). Increased cardiac awareness in panic disorder. *Journal of Abnormal Psychology*, 101, 371–82.

Ehlers, A., Margraf, J., Roth, W. T., Taylor, C. B., and Birbaumer, N. (1988). Anxiety induced by false heart rate feedback in patients with panic disorder. *Behaviour Research and Therapy*, 26, 1–11.

Foa, E. B., Steketee, G., Graspar, J. B., Turner, R. M., and Latimer, R. L. (1984). Deliberate exposure and blocking of obsessive–compulsive rituals: immediate and long-term effects. *Behavior Therapy*, 15, 450–72.

Harvey, J. M., Richards, J. C., Dziadosz, T., and Swindell, A. (1993). Misinterpretation of ambiguous stimuli in panic disorder. *Cognitive Therapy and Research*, 17, 235–48.

Heimberg, R. G., Dodge, C. S., Hope, D. A., Kennedy, C. R., and Zollo, L. J. (1990). Cognitive behavioural group treatment for social phobia: Comparison with a credible placebo control. *Cognitive Therapy and Research*, 14, 1–23.

Hope, D. A., Heimberg, R. G., and Klein, J. F. (1990). Social anxiety and the recall of interpersonal information. *Journal of Cognitive Psychotherapy*, 4, 185–95.

Kimble, C. E. and Zehr, H. D. (1982). Self-consciousness, information load, self-presentation, and memory in a social situation. *Journal of Social Psychology*, 118, 39–46.

Klein, D. F. (1964). Delineation of two-drug responsive anxiety syndromes. *Psychopharmacologia*, 5, 397–408.

Klein, D. F. (1967). Importance of psychiatric diagnosis in prediction of clinical drug effects. *Archives of General Psychiatry*, 16, 118–26.

Klosko, J. S., Barlow, D. H., Tassinari, R., and Cerny, J. A. (1990). A comparison of alprazolam, and behaviour therapy in the treatment of panic disorder. *Journal of Consulting and Clinical Psychology*, 58, 77–84.

Mansell, W. and Clark, D. M. (submitted). How do I appear to others? Biased processing of the observable self in social anxiety.

Margraf, J. and Ehlers, A. (1988). Panic attacks in nonclinical subjects. In *Panic and phobias* (ed. I. Hand and H. U. Wittchen), pp. 103–16. Springer, Berlin.

Margraf, J. and Schneider, S. (1991). *Outcome and active ingredients of cognitive-behavioural treatments for panic disorder*. Paper presented at the Annual Conference of Association for Advancement of Behaviour Therapy, New York.

Margraf, J., Ehlers, A., and Roth, W. T. (1986). Biological models of panic disorder and agoraphobia: a review. *Behaviour Research and Therapy*, 24, 553–67.

Marks, I. M. and Gelder, M. G. (1966). Different ages of onset in varieties of phobia. *American Journal of Psychiatry*, 123, 218–21.

Marks, I. M. (1987). *Fears, phobias and rituals*. Oxford University Press.

Mathews, A., Gelder, M. G., and Johnston, D. W. (1981). *Agoraphobia: nature and treatment*. Tavistock, London.

Mattick, R. P. and Peters, L. (1988). Treatment of severe social phobia: effects of guided exposure with and without cognitive restructuring. *Journal of Consulting and Clinical Psychology*, 56, 251–60.

Mattick, R. P., Peters, L., and Clarke, J. C. (1989). Exposure and cognitive restructuring for social phobia: a controlled study. *Behavior Therapy*, **20**, 3–23.

McEwan, K. L. and Devins, G. M. (1983). Is increased arousal in social anxiety noticed by others? *Journal of Abnormal Psychology*, **92**, 417–21.

McNally, R. J. and Foa, E. B. (1987). Cognition and agoraphobia: bias in the interpretation of threat. *Cognitive Therapy and Research*, **11**, 567–81.

Meyer, V., Levy, R., and Schurer, A. (1974). The behavioural treatment of obsessive–compulsive disorder. In *Obsessional states* (ed. H. R. Beech). Methuen, London.

Michelson, L., Marchione, K., and Mavissakalian, M. (1985). Cognitive and behavioural treatments of agoraphobia: clinical, behavioural and psychophysiological outcome. *Journal of Consulting and Clinical Psychology*, **53**, 913–26.

Norton, G. R., Dorward, J., and Cox, B. J. (1986). Factors associated with panic attacks in nonclinical subjects. *Behavior Therapy*, **17**, 239–52.

Öst, L. G. and Westling, B. (1995). Applied relaxation vs. cognitive therapy in the treatment of panic disorder. *Behaviour Research and Therapy*, **33**, 145–58.

Rachman, S. J. and Wilson, G. T. (1980). *The effects of psychological treatment*. Pergamon, Oxford.

Rachman, S. J., Cobb, J., Grey, S., MacDonald, R., Mawson, D., Sartory, G., and Stern, R. (1979). The behavioural treatment of obsessive–compulsive disorders with and without clomipramine. *Behaviour Research and Therapy*, **17**, 462–78.

Rapee, R. M. and Lim, L. (1992). Discrepancy between self- and observer ratings of performance in social phobics. *Journal of Abnormal Psychology*, **101**, 728–31.

Rapee, R., Mattick, R., and Murrell, E. (1986). Cognitive mediation in the affective component of spontaneous panic attacks. *Journal of Behaviour Therapy and Experimental Psychiatry*, **17**, 245–53.

Salkovskis, P. M. (1988). Phenomenology, assessment and the cognitive model of panic. In *Panic: psychological perspectives* (ed. S. J. Rachman and J. Masser). Erlbaum, Hillsdale, NJ.

Salkovskis, P. M. (1991). The importance of behaviour in the maintenance of anxiety and panic: a cognitive account. *Behavioural Psychotherapy*, **19**, 6–19.

Salkovskis, P. M. (1995). *Cognitive approaches to health anxiety and obsessional problems: some unique features and how this affects treatment*. Paper presented at the World Congress of Behavioural and Cognitive Therapies, Copenhagen, Denmark.

Salkovskis, P. M. and Clark, D. M. (1991). Cognitive therapy for panic disorder. *Journal of Cognitive Psychotherapy*, **5**, 215–26.

Salkovskis, P. M., Clark, D. M., and Gelder, M. G. (1996). Cognition-behaviour links in the persistence of panic. *Behaviour Research and Therapy*, **34**, 453–8.

Sanderson, W. C., Rapee, R. M., and Barlow, D. H. (1989). The influence of an illusion of control of panic attacks induced via inhalation of 5.5% carbon dioxide-enriched air. *Archives of General Psychiatry*, **46**, 157–62.

Shear, M. K., Pilkonis, P. A., Cloitre, M., and Leon, A. C. (1994). Cognitive behavioural treatment compared with non-prescriptive treatment of panic disorder. *Archives of General Psychiatry*, **51**, 395–401.

Stopa, L. and Clark, D. M. (1993). Cognitive processes in social phobia. *Behaviour Research and Therapy*, **31**, 255–67.

Watson, D. and Friend, R. (1969). Measurement of social-evaluative anxiety. *Journal of Consulting and Clinical Psychology*, **33**, 448–57.

Wells, A., Clark, D. M., Salkovskis, P. M., Ludgate, J., Hackmann, A., and Gelder, M. G. (1995). Social phobia: The role of in-situation safety behaviours in maintaining anxiety and negative beliefs. *Behaviour Therapy*, **26**, 153–61.

Wilson, K. G., Sandler, L. S., Asmundson, G. J. G., Derrick, K., Larsen, B. A., and Ediger, J. M. (1991). Effects of instructional sets on self-reports of panic attacks. *Journal of Anxiety Disorders*, 5, 43–63.

Winton, E., Clark, D. M., and Edelman, R. J. (1995). Social anxiety, fear of negative evaluation and the detection of negative emotion in others. *Behaviour Research and Therapy*, 33, 193–6.

Wittchen, H. A. and Essau, C. A. (1991). The epidemiology of panic attacks, panic disorder and agoraphobia. In *Panic disorder and agoraphobia* (ed. J. R. Walker, G. R. Norton, and C. A. Ross). Brooks/Cole, Pacific Grove, CA.

7

Generalized anxiety disorder

Adrian Wells and Gillian Butler

In comparison with anxiety disorders such as panic and social phobia, there is little theoretical understanding of generalized anxiety disorder (GAD), and those treatments developed or adapted specifically for GAD (Borkovec *et al.* 1983*a*; O'Leary *et al.* 1992; Borkovec and Costello 1993; Barlow 1995; Ladouceur *et al.* 1995), have not been clinically evaluated or are still at an exploratory stage of development. This chapter argues for an improved conceptual understanding of GAD, based on experimental and clinical observations. It starts with a description of the nature of the problem and an outline of the development of psychological treatments so far. It then focuses on some recent experimental and theoretical work on generalized anxiety and on worry. An assumption implicit in the approach presented here is that worrying is one of the main causes of distress in GAD. A new cognitive model of GAD is outlined, and its treatment implications are discussed. Finally, some of the concepts used in constructing models of vulnerability to stress in general, and of GAD in particular, are discussed in relation to models of cognition in disorders such as obsessive–compulsive disorder and schizophrenia.

The nature of generalized anxiety disorder (GAD)

Generalized anxiety disorder was first defined in DSM–III (APA 1980). In order to fulfil the original diagnostic criteria of DSM–III patients had to have symptoms lasting at least one month from three of the following four categories: (1) motor tension; (2) hyperactivity; (3) apprehensive expectation (defined as anxiety, worry, fear, rumination and anticipation of misfortune to self and others); (4) and vigilance and scanning. The specification for the disorder was revised in 1987, making worry the predominant feature, (DSM–III–R; APA 1987), and this revision has been maintained in DSM–IV (APA 1994). The main defining feature of the disorder is 'excessive anxiety and worry (apprehensive expectation), occurring more days than not for at least 6 months, about a number of events or activities (such as work or school performance)' (p. 435). The other diagnostic features include three out of six cognitive, affective or somatic symptoms: (1) restlessness or feeling keyed up or on edge; (2) being easily fatigued; (3) difficulty concentrating or mind going blank; (4) irritability; (5) muscle tension; and (6) sleep disturbance. For GAD to be present, the anxiety, worry, or physical symptoms must lead to significant distress or impairment in important areas of functioning, and the focus of the anxiety or worry should not be confined to features of another Axis I disorder (such as the precipitants or effects of panic attacks, or phobic reactions).

From retrospective data it appears, as indeed would be expected, that the onset of GAD is gradual in comparison to disorders such as panic (Anderson *et al.* 1984; Rapee 1985). The average age of people presenting for treatment is 39 (Rapee 1989) and Rapee (1991) notes that the average period between onset of the disorder (mid teens) and presentation at a clinic is approximately 25 years. Although it is not possible to know whether patients currently with GAD also fulfilled diagnostic criteria for the disorder many years ago, it is likely that GAD in adulthood reflects a long-standing susceptibility to anxiety, or tendency to worry, that may have been present since childhood.

The persistence of GAD has important implications for understanding its nature. Between 60% and 80% of patients report having been worried or anxious all their lives (Butler *et al.* 1991; Rapee 1991; Barlow 1988), reflecting a consistently high level of trait anxiety. Indeed, patients often think of anxiety or worry in terms of a personality characteristic. Nearly 50% of patients with GAD have a comorbid personality disorder (Sanderson *et al.* 1994*a,b*). The most common Axis II diagnoses of patients with GAD are the avoidant or dependent type. In addition GAD, in common with other long-standing disorders, is associated with secondary problems. Butler *et al.* (1987*a*; 1991), found that patients who fulfilled DSM–III–R criteria for GAD were frequently also socially anxious, unconfident, demoralized, and depressed (the mean Beck Depression Inventory score on referral of the patients in the latter study was just over 20). The implication in this context is that people suffering from GAD may have a number of related difficulties, any of which may trigger a bout of worrying, and the whole process is likely to leave them feeling vulnerable and confused. They cannot predict when they will be free of symptoms, and without help it is hard to distinguish primary from secondary aspects of the problem.

GAD has been described as the basic, or 'core' anxiety disorder (e.g., Barlow 1988; Rapee 1991). Although it is not clear exactly what this means, it may be true in the sense that the disorder reflects in a relatively pure form basic cognitive processes involved in vulnerability to anxiety states, such as self-referent negative rumination, dysfunctional self-knowledge, and particular styles of processing (Wells and Matthews 1994). Beck *et al.* (1985) suggest that anxiety arises when the number or cost of perceived threats outweighs the perceived ability to cope with them, with the result that people feel at risk and vulnerable — or anxious. Patients with GAD feel that this balance has shifted, or might shift, against them even in the absence of identifiable situational cues. The part that worry plays in this process is not yet fully understood, but it is nevertheless possible that a better understanding of GAD, and of the part played in it by worry, could contribute significantly to our understanding of the mechanisms underlying other anxiety states as well as to our ability to develop more effective treatments for GAD.

Developing psychological treatments for GAD

The seemingly complex nature of GAD has made it difficult to treat as well as difficult to conceptualize. Reviews by Barrios and Shigetomi (1979) and by Rachman and Wilson (1980), written before the disorder was so clearly defined, recognized this problem, giving the overall impression that only about a third of patients appeared to benefit from the treatments then available and that there was nothing much to choose between them. Early attempts to develop more effective treatments were based on three main ideas. First, generalized anxiety is maintained by individual reactions to anxiety, which feed back into the anxiety in a vicious circle. Therapy should therefore aim to identify, and modify, individual maintaining factors so as to break the vicious circle. Exposure and relaxation, the main behavioural and physiological ways of doing this, had been used successfully in the treatment of phobic anxiety, but cognitive methods had not been widely used at this time and should have potential given the prominent cognitive aspects of the disorder. Second, exposure, the main strategy developed for treating other anxiety disorders, is unlikely to be helpful because environmental triggers of anxiety, and behavioural avoidance of them, are not obvious: 'exposure is of little or no use to those with generalized anxiety disorder . . . since they avoid nothing to begin with' (Barlow *et al.* 1984). Third, as anxiety is a normal response to uncertainty about the future, and because people's coping resources are necessarily limited, the emphasis in treatment should be on finding ways of mobilizing these resources more effectively. Cognitive methods may help to keep problems (and worries) in perspective and help to change expectations and beliefs about vulnerability. They are also potentially valuable for dealing with secondary aspects of the problem such as social anxiety, depression, low self-confidence, and low self-esteem. An overview of relevant studies will illustrate how these ideas have been put into practice.

Early studies using cognitive interventions showed small or inconclusive effects and also used rather simplistic versions of the approach in small samples (e.g., Ramm *et al.* 1981; Woodward and Jones 1980). One problem was that insufficient attention was given to the identification of individual thoughts, assumptions, and beliefs, and more attention was given to providing people with and helping them to use more constructive or positive ways of thinking. Another was that more sophisticated cognitive methods were used in conjunction with behavioural interventions (e.g., Butler *et al.* 1987*a*; Barlow *et al.* 1984), and the effects of the various components are therefore confounded. The combination of cognitive and behavioural methods, in the form of behavioural experiments used to re-examine thoughts or beliefs, is now generally accepted. In the early 1980s the two types of methods were applied more separately, without necessarily using a single unifying rationale (Butler and Booth 1991). Lastly, little was known about specific cognitive processes in anxiety, so cognitive interventions were based predominantly on ideas derived from work on depression (Beck *et al.* 1979).

The study by Butler *et al.* (1987*a*), demonstrated that significant, durable, and internally replicable gains can be achieved using a multi-component, cognitive and behavioural treatment which they called 'anxiety management'. Individualized and collaborative cognitive methods were combined with exposure, relaxation, and methods to increase confidence. Anxiety management, compared with a waiting list control group, produced significant change in measures of depression and the frequency of panic attacks as well as in measures of anxiety, and the gains persisted for up to two years. Just under two-thirds of the patients had no further contact with their general practitioners, because of anxiety, during this period. This study represented an advance on previous findings, and it also provided more information about the nature of GAD. Contrary to previous assumptions, and consistent with Borkovec's subsequent theory of worry, they found that 64% of their patients reported non-phobic types of avoidance and 80% of them reported some situational anxiety (Butler *et al.* 1987*b*). Much of this avoidance took subtle, cognitive or affective forms which might maintain anxiety if not reversed. Despite these encouraging results response to treatment was still highly variable. Up to one-third of the patients appeared to gain little from treatment, and similar rates were also observed by Durham and Turvey (1987) and Borkovec and Mathews (1988).

In order to improve on these results it seemed essential to find out more about the nature of cognition in anxiety. In a series of studies, Butler and Mathews (1983, 1987; Butler 1990) observed that, relative to depressed patients and normal control subjects, patients with GAD overestimate the likelihood of unpleasant events happening to themselves. Estimates of subjective risk and measures of anxious mood were found to be consistently and significantly related to each other. This relationship varied according to: (a) the level of anxiety; (b) the amount of worry; (c) the enduring nature of anxiety or trait anxiety; and (d) a person's predominant concerns, in particular concerns about threats to the self. At the same time, patients with GAD rated the subjective cost of threatening events more highly than did controls, and were found consistently to interpret ambiguous material as threatening.

These findings suggested that it would be beneficial to identify and examine patients' predictions during cognitive therapy for GAD, or to learn how to deal more effectively with the perceived cost of potential threats and with the misinterpretation of ambiguous information. Both Butler (1993) and Clark *et al.* (1994) have found that the degree to which patients interpret ambiguous material as threatening contributes to the outcome of treatment. The people who continue to interpret events in this way tend to do worse or relapse. Theoretically, cognitive treatments should either target faulty interpretations and probability/cost appraisals specifically during treatment or they should target the source of these processes. Possible sources in GAD include the beliefs that drive worry, attentional processes, thought control strategies, and the effects of worry on information-processing (Wells 1994*a*, 1995).

Although early studies using cognitive methods did not focus on possible source components, they demonstrated some superiority for cognitive methods over other forms of treatment (e.g., Durham and Turvey 1987; Borkovec *et al.* 1987; Power *et al.* 1989). However, the gains achieved by non-specific treatments appeared to be substantially similar (e.g., Borkovec and Mathews 1988; Rapee *et al.* 1988), and it was not until 1991 that a cognitive intervention (CBT, cognitive behaviour therapy) was shown to have a clear and consistent advantage over another form of treatment, in this case behaviour therapy (Butler *et al.* 1991). The latter study has been described as 'a model for how comparative research ought to be conducted' (Hollon and Beck 1994). The therapists involved were experienced and had good training in both methods; the quality of the treatment was rated by assessors working in another centre, and a wide range of cognitive measures were included. CBT was found to produce greater cognitive change and more stable gains than behaviour therapy. Group differences were greater six months after treatment ended than they were initially, and at this time 42% of the patients receiving CBT met operationally defined criteria for 'good outcome' compared with 5% of those receiving behaviour therapy. CBT was apparently equally helpful for patients who were depressed as well as anxious, while behaviour therapy was not. In addition to standard cognitive work on assumptions and beliefs, tackling the various forms of avoidance present in GAD using cognitive methods and related behavioural experiments, enabled therapists applying this treatment to work on more subtle, cognitive, and affective types of avoidance which might otherwise maintain the problem. This work led to changes in thoughts, expectations, and beliefs.

Evidence for a relative advantage of cognitive therapy over other treatment methods continues to grow. Borkovec and Costello (1993) compared applied relaxation with cognitive behaviour therapy, both treatments being adapted to tackle the specific behavioural, cognitive and somatic features of GAD that distinguish it from other anxiety disorders. These treatments were demonstrably more effective than a non-directive control, and it is therefore likely that they contain ingredients that are active independent of non-specific factors. Long-term follow-up results suggest a further advantage of the cognitive method, with 57.9% of cognitive behaviour therapy patients reaching high end-state functioning compared with 37.5% of patients receiving relaxation. However, the difference was not statistically significant. Durham *et al.* (1994) have also reported substantial advantages for cognitive therapy, this time in comparison with analytic psychotherapy, and once again the advantages appear to become greater over the year following treatment, gains made with cognitive methods being sustained in 72% as opposed to 31% of patients (Durham 1995).

In summary, there is a growing body of research showing that treatment of GAD using cognitive behaviour methods produces both durable and consistent effects. The more we have learned about the cognitive features of anxiety, and the greater the attempt to adapt these methods to what is known about anxious cognitions and worry (e.g., Butler *et al.* 1991; Borkovec and Costello 1993), the clearer the effects seem to be. Better functioning at the end of treatment is now achieved in about half as opposed to one-third of patients. It would be helpful if we knew precisely which aspects of cognition had been targeted by the more successful treatments. However, only general comments are possible based on accounts in the literature. Cognitive treatments were predominantly based on Beck's cognitive model of vulnerability reflected in the balance between perceived threats and perceived resources. More specifically, it was recognized that the focus of worry shifts in GAD and that a strategy that applies only to a specific concern will have limited use. Ways out of this dilemma included focusing on commonalities such as ways of dealing with uncertainty, or ways of identifying and controlling worry; and working with underlying assumptions, beliefs, and meaning (Butler 1994). As will become clear below, these treatments may not have focused on primary aspects of problem maintenance and it may be particularly helpful to focus on worry about worry and other specific meta-cognitive dimensions (Wells 1994*a*, 1995).

Although treatments for GAD have become more effective they still lag behind those of other anxiety disorders such as simple phobias and panic disorder. This may partly be an artefact of the measures used, as criteria for the absence of phobic anxiety or panic attacks are relatively easy to develop, whereas those for the absence of generalized anxiety have not been so clear.

Unlike phobias or panic attacks, modest degrees of worry and anxiety appear to have advantages for all of us (Davey *et al.* 1992; Borkovec and Roemer 1995), and it is not therefore reasonable, or even advisable, to expect to remove them totally. However, later in this chapter a cognitive model of GAD is presented that provides a clear perspective on differences between normal and abnormal worries, and has implications for what we should measure and modify. There is undoubtedly room for improvement in the treatment of GAD. A more specific model for GAD, and a better understanding of worry within it, should provide a new source of hypotheses about the development of more specific and more effective treatments.

The concept of worry

The term 'worry' occurs in common everyday language but this does not negate the need for detailed definitions of the process. Detailed specification of the nature of worrying is necessary for distinguishing worry from other types of thought. Borkovec *et al.* (1983*b*) defined worrying as a predominantly verbal, conceptual activity aimed at problem-solving. Worry occurs as a chain of thoughts which have a negative affective content. It is concerned with future events where there is uncertainty of outcome. Davey (1994) also emphasizes the problem-solving nature of worrying, and proposes that worrying is a manifestation of 'thwarted problem solving'.

Evidence from a number of sources supports a distinction between worry and other types of thought, and suggests that a distinction may be useful in creating a model of anxiety disorders (e.g., Wells 1994*a*). Turner *et al.* (1992) reviewed the literature on two types of thought — worry and obsessions — and concluded that there were several differences between them. In particular, worry usually occurs as a thought while obsessions can occur as thoughts, images, or impulses. Worry is perceived as less intrusive than obsessions. The content of worry is not perceived as unacceptable as is typical of the content of obsessions. Wells and Morrison (1994) conducted an empirical study comparing normal worries and intrusive thoughts reported by subjects over a two-week period. Subjects in the study were asked to complete a diary by recording their first two worries and first two intrusive thoughts (obsessions) and to rate these thoughts on a number of important dimensions. The results of the study showed a number of significant differences between normal worry and normal obsessions. Worry was reported to have more verbal content than obsessions, and obsessions were reported as more imaginal. Worry was rated as significantly more realistic, less involuntary, harder to dismiss, more distracting, and of longer duration than intrusive thoughts. An unexpected finding was that worry was associated with greater compulsion to act than obsessions.

Wells (1994a) suggests that it will be useful to clarify the distinctions between worry, obsessions, and automatic thoughts. Automatic thoughts (Beck 1967) occur rapidly and are apparently unbidden and they take a verbal, or imaginal shorthand form. The telegraphic nature of negative automatic thoughts contrasts with the extended ruminative appraisals thought to characterize worry. The content of automatic thoughts is considered to be specific to a disorder (Beck *et al.* 1987), thus in panic, thoughts concern misinterpretations of bodily or mental events as a sign of an immediate physical, mental or psychosocial catastrophe (Clark 1986; Ottaviani and Beck 1987; Hibbert 1984). In social phobia, negative automatic thoughts concern fear of negative evaluation by others, and actual negative self-evaluation (Stopa and Clark 1993; Clark and Wells 1995; Wells and Clark in press). The content of worries in GAD is probably more variable than the content of automatic thoughts in other anxiety disorders. The differences between worry and automatic thoughts is suggestive of associations between these thoughts and specific types of information processing (Wells and Matthews 1994). In particular, automatic, thoughts seem more reflexive, while the more sustained execution of worrying requires a greater input of attention. Wells and Matthews (1994) argue that it is useful to distinguish the elicitation of negative thinking from its execution. Although the initiation of worrying may be relatively automatic the complex and demanding nature of worry-routines, and their modification by internal and external feedback in GAD, imply that maintenance of worry requires the individual's sustained attention.

Normal worry and problematic worry do not show reliable differences in content. Craske *et al.* (1989) compared the worries of 19 GAD patients with 26 non-anxious controls in a self-monitoring study. Worries were classified by independent judges into five predetermined categories: (1) family/home/ interpersonal relationships; (2) finances; (3) work/school; (4) illness/injury/ health; (5) miscellaneous. GAD subjects reported a significantly greater proportion of worries about illness/health/injury than control subjects. However, the controls reported a significantly larger proportion of financial worries than GAD subjects. Worries in GADs and controls did not differ in terms of the maximum anxiety or maximum aversiveness associated with them; the degree to which the content was likely, or the level of anxiety aroused by attempting to resist worrying. In a forward regression with grouping (GAD vs. control) as the dependent variable only perceived control was a significant predictor. Vasey and Borkovec (1992) examined the content of a catastrophizing sequence in chronic worriers and non-worriers and found few differences in worry content: only 4 out of 34 comparisons showed a difference. Similarly, Borkovec *et al.* (1983b) found no differences between self-labelled 'worrier' and 'non-worrier' college students in the frequency of particular worry content.

A number of investigators have reached the conclusion that a central feature of problematic worry is its uncontrollability (Craske *et al.* 1989; Borkovec *et al.* 1991; Rapee 1991; Wells 1994*a*). In one study, Kent and Jambunathan (1989) showed that uncontrollability of worry accounted for the greatest amount of variance in anxiety change in medical students across a 4 to 5-week period preceding final exams.

The uncontrollability of worry

The evidence reviewed above suggests that uncontrollability of worry is a central feature of GAD. Theoretical descriptions of worry and GAD have accounted for perceived uncontrollability in different ways. Barlow (1988) presents a model in which narrowing of attention on apprehensive concerns and consequent hypervigilance for threat in anxiety is thought to lead to 'intense worry that individuals are unable to shut-off or control in any effective way' (p. 259). The model accounts for the uncontrollable nature of worry in terms of attentional narrowing, but as Wells and Matthews (1994, p. 161) point out, the mechanism by which this occurs is not specified. It is conceivable that such narrowing may deplete attention available for processing worry-incongruent information, or it may sap attention needed for control operations such as shifting attention away from worry. It seems unlikely, however, that attention narrowing leads to hypervigilance. Here, attention narrowing refers to a restricted focus on worrying thoughts whereas hypervigilance involves increasing sensitivity to external threat. It is more likely that attentional-narrowing follows hypervigilance after a threat has been detected (Eysenck 1992).

Borkovec and colleagues offer a different perspective on worry in relation to GAD. They propose that worry represents avoidance of other types of thought, such as imaginal processes, that are more closely associated with negative affect (e.g., Borkovec and Inz 1990; Borkovec *et al.* 1991). In essence, GAD patients may be using worry as a form of cognitive avoidance. According to this perspective, worrying creates its own problems. It is likely to be reinforced because it has the effect of reducing or averting negative emotion, and it may also block emotional processing by preventing the full accessing of fear information in memory (e.g., Foa and Kozak 1986). In this way the immediate anxiety-reducing, or anxiety-controlling, properties of worry will lead to a loss of control of the activity as it is reinforced, and over a longer course worry will maintain anxiety through blocked emotional processing. Borkovec and Hu (1990) present evidence in support of the emotionally suppressing effects of worry. Speech-anxious subjects who worried just prior to imaging a phobic scene demonstrated significantly reduced heart rate responses compared with subjects instructed to engage in neutral or relaxed thinking. However, the worry group reported significantly greater subjective fear to the images than the neutral group.

It is possible, therefore, that worrying has a self-exacerbating effect or increases other types of intrusive thought. Following the reasoning of Borkovec and colleagues (e.g., Borkovec and Inz 1990; Borkovec *et al.* 1991), that worry could block emotional-processing, Butler *et al.* (1995) conducted a pilot study of the effects of worrying following exposure to a stressful stimulus. In the study, three groups of student volunteers watched a short, silent, film about a gruesome workshop accident. Subjects were then asked to worry in verbal form about the events in the film and their implications, to image the events in the film, or to settle down for four minutes afterwards. Subjects were asked to keep a diary of the number of intrusive images about the film experienced in the next seven days. These diary data showed that most of the intrusions occurred in the three days after the film. Comparison of the number of intrusions for this time period demonstrated that subjects who had worried reported significantly more intrusions than subjects who had imaged or control subjects.

In a subsequent study, Wells and Papageorgiou (1995) tested a hypothesized co-joint mechanism underlying the incubation effect of worry on intrusive images following stress. It was hypothesized that worry both blocks emotional processing and leads to a 'tagging' of representations of the stressor in memory. Tagging refers to elaborative processing of the stressor in a way that increases the range of potential retrieval cues for stress-related material by association. In order to test this hypothesis, a variety of post-stress mentation manipulations were used. The manipulations varied in their hypothesized ratio of blocked emotional processing and tagging effects. Five groups were tested. The control group were told that they had time to 'settle down' after watching a gruesome film. The other groups were given one of the following manipulations: to image the events in the film; to perform a simple distraction task; worry in verbal form about the things they normally worried about; or worry in verbal form about the events in the film. It was assumed, based on the co-joint mechanism model, that imaging would facilitate emotional-processing while producing small degrees of tagging. Distraction should block emotional processing partially, but not produce much tagging. Worry about usual concerns should block emotional processing quite extensively, since it is attentionally demanding and diverts attention away from images, but it should produce little tagging. Worrying about the film should both block emotional processing and lead to high tagging. A linear incremental trend in frequency of intrusive images was predicted across these groups. A significant linear trend was obtained, consistent with the operation of a co-joint mechanism. The results of these two studies are consistent with the view that under some circumstances worrying can lead to an incubation of intrusive images. Clearly, individuals who are prone to worry, in particular those that use worry as a coping strategy, perhaps to avoid images, are likely to engage in an activity that pollutes the stream of consciousness with an increasing frequency of intrusive thoughts. An effect of this type could be interpreted by an individual as evidence of diminished control over worrisome thought, although it actually reflects a symptom of the use of worry as a processing strategy rather than an actual control deficit.

In a different line of research on thought suppression, counter-productive effects have been found when subjects attempt 'not to think' certain thoughts (e.g., Clark *et al.* 1991). The implication of this is that individuals, such as GAD patients and obsessionals, who try to control their thoughts may be engaged in an activity that contributes to subjective uncontrollability. For example, Wegner *et al.* (1987) asked subjects not to think of a 'white bear' but to report their stream of thought for five minutes and ring a bell each time the target thought occurred. Subjects were unable to suppress the thought as instructed. When they were subsequently asked to think about a white bear for five minutes they reported significantly more thoughts about the white bear than subjects who were asked to think about the bear from the outset. Wenzlaff *et al.* (1988) showed that college students with high depression scores, although initially successful at suppressing negative material, showed a delayed resurgence of unwanted negative thoughts. Paradoxical suppression effects have also been demonstrated for naturally occurring intrusive thoughts (Salkovskis and Campbell 1994).

Wells and Davies (1994) developed the Thought Control Questionnaire (TCQ) to measure individual differences in strategies used to control unwanted/unpleasant thoughts. The TCQ subscales include five subtypes of strategy: (1) distraction; (2) social control; (3) worry; (4) punishment; and (5) reappraisal. Several measures of emotional vulnerability (trait anxiety, neuroticism, impaired control over mental events, private self-consciousness) are positively correlated with use of worry and punishment strategies but not with the other control strategies. Although these data support the contention that individuals use worry to control unwanted thought and this strategy is associated with heightened perceptions of impaired control, the direction of causality in this association remains unknown. However, combined with the results of the suppression and worry-incubation studies reviewed, there is evidence both that attempts to control thoughts and worry contribute to increased intrusions. GAD patients may be particularly prone both to using worry as a processing strategy and to trying to control their thoughts, which is likely to contribute to intrusions and enhanced perceptions of uncontrollability.

In conclusion, the best candidate mechanisms underlying heightened uncontrollability of worry are: (1) use of worry as a processing strategy or coping behaviour; and (2) thought control attempts. To these we should also add faulty appraisals of control arising from other sources such as dysfunctional beliefs about one's own cognition. Perceived uncontrollability could be a function of attempted *over-control*. Over-control exists in at least two forms: (a) controlled execution of demanding worry routines, believed to aid coping; and (b) expending effort in thought-suppression activities. The concept of motivated use of worry as a processing strategy, and use of thought control attempts is a component of Wells' (1995) cognitive model of GAD, discussed later.

The multi-dimensional nature of worry

Three questionnaire instruments have recently been developed to measure worry: the Penn State Worry Questionnaire (PSWQ, Meyer *et al.* 1990), the Worry Domains Questionnaire (WDQ, Tallis *et al.* 1992) and the Anxious Thoughts Inventory (AnTI, Wells 1994*b*). Each measure reflects a different conceptual approach to worry measurement. The PSWQ is a general undifferentiated measure of proneness to worry and includes items such as 'Many situations make me worry', whereas the WDQ measures different domains of worry that are discriminable by content. The WDQ consists of five content dimensions, tapping worry about: relationships, lack of confidence, aimless future, work, and finances. The AnTI is a multi-dimensional measure of worry that assesses process characteristics of worrying in addition to worry content. It has three subscales that measure *social*, *health*, and *meta-worry*. Meta-worry consists of worrying about worry, and includes negative appraisals of thought as uncontrollable and intrusive. Meta-worry is likely to be an important dimension of worrying since the appraisal of worries as uncontrollable, disruptive, and less successfully reduced by control attempts differentiates the worry of people with GAD from the worry of non-anxious individuals (Craske *et al.* 1989).

A cognitive model of generalized anxiety disorder

The similarity between the content of worry in normal and GAD populations indicates that attempts to explain the problematic nature of worry in GAD in terms of differences in surface content are unlikely to prove useful. Wells (1995) proposed that two types of worry should be distinguished in constructing a theoretical model of GAD: type 1 and type 2 worry. Type 1 worry is concerned with external events and internal non-cognitive events such as the social and health worries measured by two of the AnTI subscales. Type 2 worry, or '*meta-worry*', is concerned with the negative appraisal of one's own cognitive events, particularly the occurrence of worry. Examples of meta-worry themes are: 'worrying will make me crazy'; 'I can't control my worries'; 'it's abnormal to worry', and 'worrying thoughts can make bad things happen'. An initial empirical study demonstrated that meta-worry proneness (measured in terms of the extent of 'worry about worrying thoughts') predicted the degree to which normal subjects rated worry as a problem when proneness to type 1 worries and trait-anxiety were controlled. However, type 1 worry did not predict problem-rating in this equation (Wells and Carter, in prep.).

A conceptualization of GAD in terms of meta-worry accounts for the lack of difference in type 1 worry content found across GAD and normal samples. It also presents a new framework for modelling GAD and for developing more effective treatments. Moreover, treatment based on challenging the content of type 1 worry, such as questioning the evidence for social worries or health worries in GAD, is likely to be of small effect if type 2 worries are central.

An adequate cognitive model of GAD must explain a set of phenomena. Primarily, it must be able to accommodate the similarities and differences that exist between normal and GAD worries while proposing a pathological mechanism. It must also account for the perceived uncontrollability of worry in GAD.

Wells (1995) has proposed such a model. Generalized anxiety disorder patients are viewed as in a state of cognitive dissonance in which positive and negative beliefs about worry coexist. The development of these beliefs may be viewed over a time course in which positive beliefs are formed first and pre-date the development of negative beliefs. Once negative beliefs about worry develop the individual is prone to appraise worry in a negative way (meta-worry), and the individual is likely to exercise particular attempts to control worry. Thus, non-problematic worry becomes problematic when meta-worry develops. Wells (1995) proposes that a greater incidence of meta-worry distinguishes GAD worries from normal worries. Once negative beliefs and meta-worry are established the individual is motivated to avoid the appraised negative consequences of worrying. This can be accomplished by suppressing or avoiding worry, but total abandonment of worry is likely to be too threatening since this is discrepant with positive worry beliefs. Examples of positive worry beliefs include: 'worrying helps me cope with future problems'; 'if I worry everything will turn out fine'; 'if I think of all the bad things that could happen I'll be prepared to prevent them'; 'worrying helps me to get my work done'; 'it's bad not to worry'; 'I'll be tempting fate'. In consequence, GAD patients are prone to engage in worrying as a coping strategy and when they do, this activates fears concerning the process of worrying. The best strategy is to attempt to avoid the need for worry in the first instance, (e.g., by avoiding anxiety-provoking situations). However, since this is not often possible because of the wide range of potential triggers, individuals with GAD use subtle safety behaviours to circumvent the need for worrying, or if worry is used, engage in behaviours intended to prevent the negative appraised consequences of worrying. These safety behaviours include reassurance seeking, distraction, and use of thought control strategies.

Worrying of the type 1, and type 2 variety is associated with 'threat monitoring'. That is, individuals show heightened vigilance for information associated with their worries. In some instances this is a voluntary strategy aimed at early detection of threat so that avoidance or safety responses can be initiated. However, monitoring may also be an involuntary strategy. Involuntary monitoring is likely to result from worry priming automatic processing units responsible for detection of threat (e.g., Wells and Matthews 1994) such that threat-related information is likely to intrude into consciousness. The type 1 versus type 2 worry distinction implies that monitoring can be directed at external threat or internal threat. Internal threat is represented by the occurrence of worrying thought itself.

There are a number of pathways to the development and maintenance of meta-worry in Wells' (1995) model. First, information concerning the dangerous consequences of worrying may be available from a number of sources. For example, someone with a history of worrying may be observed later to develop a mental disorder, or media information on the ill-effects of stress may contribute to meta-worry. Second, popular western culture reflects the idea that it is bad to worry or that worrying is abnormal in some way and a sign of a 'neurotic personality', bringing with it connotations of social unacceptability. Third, through social comparison processes the individual who uses worry routines for coping may discover that this is not the norm for coping with possible threats to the self. Fourth, repeated worrying contributes to greater accessibility of negative information for predicting unwanted outcomes, contributing to a proliferation of worrying to prevent or avert these outcomes. Thus, worrying becomes more extensive and harder to manage. Fifth, avoidance, safety behaviours, thought control attempts, and threat monitoring keep the individual 'locked-in' worry mode, as intrusive thoughts are incubated, threat is more readily detected, and dysfunctional beliefs fail to be disconfirmed. Finally, the emotional consequences of worrying, such as the anxiety associated with contemplating catastrophes aroused by worrying, and blocked emotional processing, maintain anxious affect and arousability which may also contribute to worry. For example, cognitive and somatic symptoms of anxiety, and symptoms of blocked emotional processing can be misinterpreted as evidence of loss of control thus contributing to meta-worry.

Avoidance in GAD

The model has implications for the nature of avoidance in GAD. Traditionally, avoidance was thought not to play a central role in the disorder but avoidance may be more subtle (Butler *et al.* 1987*b*). The type 1 versus meta-worry analysis suggests that GAD individuals avoid external threat and affective arousal in an attempt to avoid the activation of worry itself. A range of behaviours may be used to avoid worry. Avoidance of types of media material, requests for certain types of behaviour from others, such as frequent telephone contact, avoidance of certain topics in conversation, and avoidance of ill people, are some examples that represent attempts to avoid the activation of worrying.

An analysis of avoidance and safety behaviours in GAD is rather more complex than it first appears. Worrying in Wells' (1995) model is itself used as a form of avoidance and as a safety behaviour. The use of worry as a safety and avoidance strategy is linked to positive beliefs held about the benefits of worrying and rumination. For example, individuals with GAD may worry as a means of coping with anticipated threat. They believe that worrying prepares them to deal with negative events should they occur. Thus, worrying serves the function of avoiding failures of coping in the future. When worry strategies are negatively appraised (meta-worry) they become problematic.

Treatment implications of a meta-cognitive model

Constructing a model of problematic worry in terms of meta-worry, and underlying positive and negative beliefs about worrying, shifts the emphasis of cognitive therapy of the disorder. We have seen how early non-worry, and non-meta-cognitive-driven treatments such as anxiety management and generalized cognitive therapy have produced relatively modest results. It is hoped that treatment based on the specific meta-cognitive model will lead to the development of more effective treatments.

A detailed account of the nature of treatment based on the meta-cognitive model is beyond the scope of this chapter. For more detailed discussion the reader is referred to Wells (1995, in prep.). Briefly, the central aim of meta-cognitive therapy is the modification of dysfunctional beliefs about worrying. Typically, meta-worry should be challenged initially. This is achieved through a combination of behavioural experiments targeted at challenging negative beliefs that drive meta-worry. For example, if the individual fears loss of control of worry, an experiment may involve deliberate attempts to increase worry and lose control of the activity. Beliefs in uncontrollability are challenged by experiments involving worry postponement strategies which requires development of a 'detached letting go' of worrisome thought. This is presented so that it *does not* become a paradoxical control strategy, and it is directed at belief change. The modification of meta-worry and negative beliefs relies on the modification of behavioural responses, such as avoidance and thought control attempts, that prevent disconfirmation of beliefs. Thus, an important aspect of therapy is the reversal or abandonment of avoidance and worry control behaviours in a way that facilitates belief change. Once meta-worry and associated beliefs have been effectively challenged positive beliefs that motivate the use of worry as a coping strategy can be modified. In some cases, work on positive beliefs is conducted in conjunction with negative belief work in order to facilitate progress in cognitive behaviour change. A component of treatment consists of practice in generating alternative positive endings to worry scenarios. It should be noted that these strategies *are not* introduced as strategies for avoiding appraised harmful effects of worrying or as worry control techniques, but are intended to broaden the range of available appraisal strategies if required.

The model and treatment reviewed here shifts the emphasis of intervention away from traditional anxiety management and cognitive therapy. Teaching control over worrying and challenging the content of type 1 worries are likely to be only moderately effective on their own. Although focus on type 1 worries is likely to be necessary in many GAD cases in which there are concurrent concerns, such as social-evaluative worries, this should not be at the expense of modifying meta-cognition.

The function of worrying

The meta-cognitive model reviewed here implies that individuals are motivated to use worrying as a coping strategy. Borkovec assumes that GADs use worry to distract from, or avoid provoking, more upsetting thoughts, and Wells (1994*a*,1995) assumes that chronic worriers hold a range of beliefs about the benefits of worrying. Beliefs about the advantage of worrying also seem to exist in a subgroup of health-anxious patients (Wells and Hackmann 1993) who assume that worrying about their health has a protective function.

In two studies, Borkovec and Roemer (1995) examined six reasons for worrying (commonly reported by GAD patients) held by college students meeting self-report criteria for GAD. In the first study these subjects were compared with non-anxious control subjects, in the second study a third group of non-worried but anxious subjects was also used. The most highly endorsed reasons for all subjects in both studies were: motivation; preparation for events; and avoidance/prevention. In both studies, GAD subjects showed significantly higher ratings for the use of worry as 'distraction from more emotional things'. In the second study GAD subjects showed significantly higher ratings on distraction from emotional topics than the non-worried anxious subjects. They also gave significantly higher ratings for using worry for superstitious reasons and for problem solving than did non-anxious subjects.

Cartwright-Hatton and Wells (submitted) developed the Meta-Cognitions Questionnaire (MCQ) to measure dimensions of beliefs about worrying and intrusions, and individual differences in monitoring of mental events and in self-reported cognitive efficiency that could contribute to problems of intrusive thoughts. In a series of factor analytic studies a reliable five-factor measure was obtained. Four factors represented beliefs: (1) *positive beliefs about worry*; (e.g., 'worrying helps me cope'); (2) *beliefs about uncontrollability of thoughts* ('when I start worrying I cannot stop'); (3) *cognitive confidence* ('I have a poor memory'); (4) *general negative beliefs* about thoughts including themes of superstition, punishment, and responsibility ('not being able to control my thoughts is a sign of weakness').

The fifth factor represented a meta-cognitive process; *cognitive self-consciousness*, this is a dimension of meta-awareness or a tendency to be aware of and monitor thinking ('I pay close attention to the way my mind works').

One of the central aims in the development of the MCQ was to assess the correlates of worry as predicted by the meta-cognitive model. In particular, the model predicts that meta-cognitive dimensions of positive and negative beliefs should correlate positively with problematic worry and intrusions. All MCQ subscales were significantly positively correlated with worry proneness assessed by the Anxious Thoughts Inventory, and with the impaired control of mental events subscale of the Padua Inventory. Moreover, hierarchical regression controlling for covariances of the MCQ subscales and trait anxiety showed that positive beliefs about worry, belief that one cannot control one's thoughts, and low cognitive confidence uniquely predicted worry proneness in a sample of 104 undergraduate and graduate students.

Predictions of the meta-cognitive model

Preliminary studies discussed in the preceding sections are consistent with the meta-cognitive model. It is encouraging that the model is also able to explain the lack of differences found between normal and GAD types of worry in earlier studies. Strong validation of the model depends on studies aimed at testing its central predictions. These are:

1. Compared to anxious patients whose primary problem is not one of intrusive thoughts, and compared to normal controls, patients suffering from GAD should show a higher incidence of meta-worry.
2. Independent of the frequency of type 1 worries, meta-worry should contribute to the distress/anxiety associated with worrying.

3. GAD patients should show positive beliefs about worrying or rumination as well as negative beliefs.
4. Treatments which fail to modify meta-worry and beliefs that drive the use of worry routines should have higher relapse rates than treatments that modify these dimensions.

Meta-cognition and self-regulation: implications for constructing models of cognition in other emotional disorders

Worrying is a component of most emotional disorders. Wells and Matthews (1994) have developed a model of general vulnerability to emotional dysfunction in which self-focused active worry plays a central role. The model accounts for cognitive phenomena associated with emotional disorders such as attention and memory biases, cognitive deficits, dysfunctional beliefs, and processing configurations typified by self-focused attention and active worry (rumination). These phenomena are conceptualized within a cognitive architecture of three interacting levels: (1) self-beliefs; (2) on-line controlled processing; and (3) lower-level automatic processing. The interaction of primary concern in modelling emotional disorder is that involved in self-relevant processing. This type of processing configuration is termed the self-regulatory executive function (SREF) since its primary aims are the analysis and reduction of discrepancies between current status and predetermined and acquired standards for the self. This process is aimed at reducing unpleasant emotions through cognitive, physiological, and behavioural self-regulation. In this context the SREF not only determines the content of attention in emotional disorder, it serves a wider meta-cognitive function of modifying and modulating aspects of the processing system. In the SREF model the processing configurations engaged by the individual are determined by self-beliefs. These are not only beliefs in declarative form (e.g. 'I'm vulnerable') as specified by schema theory of emotional disorder (Beck 1967, 1976), but are procedural beliefs which guide the processing system in its activities. Thus, self-regulatory processing has a meta-cognitive function. For example, some beliefs specify active rumination on a topic, or monitoring for particular types of stimuli. Other procedural beliefs guide processing to strengthen existing beliefs, or to assimilate new information thereby changing beliefs. Some procedures regulate activity at the automatic processing level. In this model, active worry or self-focused rumination is a particularly problematic processing configuration in emotional disorder. It maintains activation of dysfunctional beliefs, primes lower level processing units for detection of threat, and drains attentional resources for processing information capable of disconfirming dysfunctional knowledge. Ruminative configurations interfere with the use of other on-line processing strategies. The model implies that on-line SREF processing should be managed in a way that optimizes belief change. This involves abandoning ruminative strategies and increases the flexibility of control of processing with procedures such as attentional training (e.g., Wells 1990; Wells *et al.* in prep.) and 'detached mindfulness' (Wells and Matthews 1994, p. 305–307).

Dysfunctional meta-cognition is likely to be a central element in all disorders in which problematic intrusive thoughts are involved (Wells and Matthews 1994). In obsessive–compulsive disorder, negative beliefs about intrusions and rumination, beliefs relating to confidence in one's cognitive skills, such as memory and thought control strategies, are likely to be important. Salkovskis' (1985) model of obsessional problems presents a key role of appraisal of intrusive thoughts based on dysfunctional beliefs such as: 'having a thought about an action is like performing the action; not neutralizing when an intrusion has occurred is similar or equivalent to seeking or wanting the harm involved in that intrusion to happen' (p. 579). Meta-cognition is implicated here but the model is developed in terms of appraisals of subjective responsibility rather than in terms of meta-cognition. Other investigators, for example, D. A. Clark and Purdon (1993), have begun to examine meta-cognition in obsessional problems in more detail.

In schizophrenia, positive and negative beliefs about the meaning of intrusions and positive symptoms will influence affective and behavioural responses to them. Moreover, some beliefs are likely to be tied to 'meta-monitoring', in which the individual is hypervigilant for occurrences of positive symptoms such as hallucinations. Activation of hypervigilance may increase detection of a variety of normal experiences that are misinterpreted as hallucinations. Meta-monitoring could even activate these symptoms. Moreover, positive and negative beliefs about such symptoms are likely to increase the individual's engagement with them. Positive beliefs may be associated with efforts to maintain particular symptoms.

Wells and Matthews (1994) propose that meta-cognitive dysfunction manifested as the use of self-ruminatory processing configurations may constitute a basic core vulnerability to emotional disorder. In parallel with this it is interesting to note that Rapee (1991) suggests that GAD, which we argue is a disorder of worry, may be the basic anxiety disorder highly similar to the concept of trait anxiety. Further analyses of worry and of meta-cognitive dimensions could improve our understanding of vulnerability to emotional dysfunction.

Conclusion

Generalized anxiety disorder is now recognized as a disorder of chronic worry. To date, treatment approaches have used techniques that have been effective with other anxiety disorders, but without a coherent conceptual focus in GAD. The characteristics and effects of worry reviewed in this chapter offer valuable insights into important issues in GAD such as the controllability of worry. Wells' (1994a,1995) cognitive model of chronic worry and GAD was outlined. The model presents a specific perspective for treatment that shifts emphasis away from teaching worry control and symptom-management skills towards conceptualizing and modifying the beliefs and processes that contribute to problematic types of worrying. In summary, GAD is not a disorder of uncontrollable worry, it is a disorder of worry about worry and the over-use of worry as a processing strategy.

Finally, a meta-cognitive approach is likely to illuminate our understanding of other disorders of intrusive mental experience such as schizophrenia and obsessional problems. Meta-cognitive dimensions have already been implicated in some approaches (e.g., Salkovskis 1985; Clark and Purdon 1993; Frith 1992), but further developments are likely to require a more comprehensive formulation of interactions between types of thought and the causes and effects of meta-cognitive processing (e.g., Wells 1995). Future advances in cognitive therapy are likely to result from an inclusion of meta-cognitive analysis and intervention alongside the more traditional cognitive approaches. On this basis new interventions can be generated and old strategies can be re-tuned for optimal effects.

The research described in this chapter owes a great deal to the support of Professor Michael Gelder and we have benefited from his encouragement throughout. We offer him our sincere thanks.

References

APA (American Psychiatric Association) (1980). *Diagnostic and Statistical Manual of Mental Disorders* (3rd edn). APA, Washington, DC.

APA (American Psychiatric Association). *Diagnostic and Statistical Manual of Mental Disorders* (3rd edn, revised). APA, Washington, DC.

APA (American Psychiatric Association) (1994). *Diagnostic and Statistical Manual of Mental Disorders* (4th edn). APA, Washington, DC.

Anderson, D. J., Noyes, R., and Crowe, R. R. (1984). A comparison of panic disorder and generalised anxiety disorder. *American Journal of Psychiatry*, 14, 572–5.

Barlow, D. H. (1988). *Anxiety and its disorders: The nature and treatment of anxiety and panic*. Guilford Press, New York.

Barlow, D. H. (1995). *The development of worry control treatment for generalized anxiety disorder*. Paper presented at the World Congress of Behavioural and Cognitive Therapy, Copenhagen.

Barlow, D. H., Cohen, A. S., Waddell, M. T., Vermilyea, B. B., Klosko, J. S., Blanchard, E. B., and Di Nardo, P. A. (1984). Panic and generalized anxiety disorders: nature and treatment. *Behavior Therapy*, 15, 431–9.

Barrios, B. A. and Shigetomi, C. C. (1979). Coping-skills training for the management of anxiety: a critical review. *Behavior Therapy*, **10**, 491–522.

Beck, A. T. (1967). *Depression: Causes and treatment*. University of Pennsylvania Press, Philadelphia, PA.

Beck, A. T. (1976). *Cognitive therapy and the emotional disorders*. International Universities Press, New York.

Beck, A. T., Rush, A. J., Shaw, B. F., and Emery, G. (1979). *Cognitive therapy of depression*. Guilford Press, New York.

Beck, A. T., Emery, G. and Greenberg, R. (1985). *Anxiety disorders and phobias: A cognitive perspective*. Basic Books, New York.

Beck, A. T., Brown, G., Steer, R. A., Eidelson, J. I. and Riskind, J. M. (1987). Differentiating anxiety and depression: A test of the cognitive content specificity hypothesis. *Journal of Abnormal Psychology*, **96**, 179–83.

Borkovec, T. D. and Costello, E. (1993). Efficacy of applied relaxation and cognitive-behavioral therapy in the treatment of generalized anxiety disorder. *Journal of Consulting and Clinical Psychology*, **61**, 611–19.

Borkovec, T. D. and Hu, S. (1990). The effect of worry on cardiovascular response to phobic imagery. *Behaviour Research and Therapy*, **28**, 69–73.

Borkovec, T. D. and Inz, J. (1990). The nature of worry in generalised anxiety disorder: A predominance of thought activity. *Behaviour Research and Therapy*, **28**, 153–8.

Borkovec, T. D. and Mathews, A. M. (1988). Treatment of nonphobic anxiety: a comparison of nondirective, cognitive, and coping desensitization therapy. *Journal of Consulting and Clinical Psychology*, **56**, 877–84.

Borkovec, T. D. and Roemer, L. (1995). Perceived functions of worry among generalized anxiety disorder subjects: distraction from more emotionally distressing topics? *Behaviour Therapy and Experimental Psychiatry*, **26**, 25–30.

Borkovec, T. D., Wilkinson, L., Folensbee, R., and Lerman, C. (1983*a*). Stimulus control applications to the treatment of worry. *Behaviour Research and Therapy*, **21**, 247–51.

Borkovec, T. D., Robinson, E., Pruzinski, T., and De Pree, J. A. (1983*b*). Preliminary exploration of worry: Some characteristics and processes. *Behaviour Research and Therapy*, **21**, 9–16.

Borkovec, T. D., Mathews, A. M., Chambers, A., Ebrahimi S., Lytle, R, and Nelson, R. (1987). The effects of relaxation training with cognitive therapy or nondirective therapy and the role of relaxation-induced anxiety in the treatment of generalized anxiety. *Journal of Consulting and Clinical Psychology*, **55**, 883–8.

Borkovec, T. D., Shadick, R. N. and Hopkins, M. (1991). The nature of normal and pathological worry. In *Chronic anxiety: Generalised anxiety disorder and mixed anxiety-depression* (ed. R. M. Rapee and D. H. Barlow). Guilford Press, New York.

Butler, G. (1990). *Anxiety and subjective risk*. Unpublished D.Phil. thesis. Open University, UK.

Butler, G. (1993). Predicting outcome after treatment for GAD. *Behaviour Research and Therapy*, **31**, 211–13.

Butler, G. (1994). Treatment of worry in generalised anxiety disorder. In *Worrying: Perspectives on theory, assessment and treatment* (ed. G. Davey and F. Tallis), pp. 209–28. Wiley, Chichester, UK.

Butler, G. and Booth, R. (1991) Developing psychological treatments for generalized anxiety disorder. In *Chronic anxiety and generalized anxiety disorder* (ed. R. M. Rapee and D. H. Barlow), pp. 187–209. Guilford Press, New York.

Butler, G. and Mathews, A. (1983). Cognitive processes in anxiety, *Advances in Behaviour Therapy and Research*, **5**, 51–62.

Butler, G. and Mathews, A. (1987). Anticipatory anxiety and risk perception. *Cognitive Therapy and Research*, **11**, 551–65.

Butler, G., Cullington, A., Hibbert, G., Klimes, I., and Gelder, M. (1987*a*). Anxiety management for persistent generalised anxiety. *British Journal of Psychiatry*, **151**, 535–42.

Butler, G., Gelder, M., Hibbert, G., Cullington, A., and Klimes, I. (1987*b*). Anxiety management: developing effective strategies. *Behaviour Research and Therapy*, **25**, 517–22.

Butler, G., Fennell, M., Robson, P., and Gelder, M. (1991). A comparison of behavior therapy and cognitive behavior therapy in the treatment of generalised anxiety disorder. *Journal of Consulting and Clinical Psychology*, **59**, 167–75.

Butler, G., Wells, A., and Dewick, H. (1995). Differential effects of worry and imagery after exposure to a stressful stimulus: A pilot study. *Behavioural and Cognitive Psychotherapy*, **23**, 45–56.

Cartwright-Hatton, S. and Wells, A. (submitted). Beliefs about worry and intrusions: The Meta-Cognitions Questionnaire and its Correlates.

Clark, D. A. and Purdon, C. (1993). New perspectives of a cognitive theory of obsessions. *Australian Psychologist*, **28**, 161–7.

Clark, D. M. (1986). A cognitive model of panic. *Behaviour Research and Therapy*, **24**, 461–70.

Clark, D. M. and Wells, A. (1995). A cognitive model of social phobia. In *Social phobia: Diagnosis, Assessment and Treatment* (ed. R. G. Heimberg, M. Liebowitz, D. Hope, and F. Schneier), pp. 69–93. Guilford Press, New York.

Clark, D. M., Ball, S., and Pape, D. (1991). An experimental investigation of thought suppression. *Behaviour Research and Therapy*, **29**, 253–7.

Clark, D. M., Salkovskis, P. M., Hackmann, A., Middleton, H., Anastasiades, P., and Gelder, M. (1994). A comparison of cognitive therapy, applied relaxation and imipramine in the treatment of panic disorder. *British Journal of Psychiatry*, **164**, 759–69.

Craske, M. G., Rapee, R. M., Jackel, L., and Barlow, D. M. (1989). Qualitative dimensions of worry in DSM-III-R generalised anxiety disorder subjects and non-anxious controls. *Behaviour Research and Therapy*, **27**, 397–402.

Davey, G. C. L. (1994). Pathological worrying as exacerbated problem solving. In *Worrying: Perspectives on theory, assessment and treatment* (ed. G. C. L. Davey and F. Tallis), pp. 35–59. Wiley, Chichester, UK.

Davey, G. C. L., Hampton, J., Farrel, J., and Davidson, S. (1992). Some characteristics of worrying: evidence for worrying and anxiety as separate constructs. *Personality and Individual Differences*, **13**, 133–47.

Durham, R. C. (1995). *Cognitive therapy, analytic psychotherapy and anxiety management training for generalised anxiety disorder: relative efficacy at one year follow-up and determinants of outcome*. Paper presented at the World Congress of Behavioural and Cognitive Therapy, Copenhagen.

Durham, R. C. and Turvey A. A. (1987). Cognitive therapy vs behaviour therapy in the treatment of chronic general anxiety: outcome at discharge and at six month follow-up. *Behaviour Research and Therapy*, **25**, 229–34.

Durham, R. C., Murphy, T., Allan, T., Richard, K., Treliving, L. R. and Genton, G. (1994). Cognitive therapy, analytic psychotherapy and anxiety management training for generalised anxiety disorder. *British Journal of Psychiatry*, **165**, 315–23.

Eysenck, M. W. (1992). *Anxiety: The cognitive perspective*. Erlbaum, Hillsdale, NJ.

Foa, E. B. and Kozak, M. J. (1986). Emotional processing and fear: Exposure to corrective information. *Psychological Bulletin*, **99**, 20–35.

Frith, C. (1992). *The cognitive neuropsychology of schizophrenia*. Erlbaum, Hove, UK.

Hibbert, G. A. (1984). Ideational components of anxiety: Their origin and content. *British Journal of Psychiatry*, 144, 618–24.

Hollon, S. D. and Beck, A. T. (1994). Cognitive therapy and cognitive behaviour therapy: a review. In *Handbook of cognitive therapy and cognitive behaviour therapy* (ed. Garfield and Bergin). Wiley, New York.

Kent, J. and Jambunathan, P. (1989). A longitudinal study of the intrusiveness of cognitions in test anxiety. *Behaviour Research and Therapy*, 27, 43–50.

Ladouceur, R., Dugas, M. J., and Freeston, M. H. (1995). *Intolerance of uncertainty in normal and excessive worry*. Paper presented at the World Congress of Behavioural and Cognitive Therapy, Copenhagen.

Meyer, T. J., Miller, M. L., Metzger, R. L., and Borkovec, T. D. (1990). Development and validation of the Penn State Worry Questionnaire. *Behaviour Research and Therapy*, 28, 487–95.

O'Leary, T. A., Brown, T. A., and Barlow, D. H. (1992). *The efficacy of worry control treatment in generalized anxiety disorder: a multiple baseline analysis*. Paper presented at the annual meeting of the Association for the Advancement of Behavior Therapy, Boston, MA.

Ottaviani, R. and Beck, A. T. (1987). Cognitive aspects of panic disorder. *Journal of Anxiety Disorders*, 1, 15–28.

Power, K. G., Jerrom, D. W. A., Simpson, R. J., Mitchell, M. J., and Swanson, V. (1989). A controlled comparison of cognitive behaviour therapy, diazepam and placebo in the management of generalised anxiety. *Behavioural Psychotherapy*, 17, 1–14.

Rachman, S, and Wilson T. (1980) *The effects of psychological therapies*. Pergamon, Oxford and New York.

Ramm, E., Marks, I. M., Yuksel, S., and Stern, R. S. (1981). Anxiety management training for anxiety states: Positive compared with negative self statements. *British Journal of Psychiatry*, 140, 367–73.

Rapee, R. M. (1985). Distinctions between panic disorder and generalized anxiety disorder: clinical presentations. *Australian and New Zealand Journal of Psychiatry*, 19, 227–32.

Rapee, R. M. (1989). *Boundary issues: GAD and somatoform disorders; GAD and psychophysiological disorders*. Paper prepared for the generalized anxiety disorder subcommittee for DSM–IV.

Rapee, R. M. (1991). Generalized anxiety disorder: A review of clinical features and theoretical concepts. *Clinical Psychology Review*, 11, 419–40.

Rapee, R. M., Adler, C., Craske, M., and Barlow, D. (1988). *Cognitive restructuring and relaxation in the treatment of generalized anxiety disorder: a controlled study*. Paper presented at the Behaviour Therapy World Congress, Edinburgh.

Salkovskis, P. M. (1985). Obsessional-compulsive problems: A cognitive behavioural analysis. *Behaviour Research and therapy*, 23, 571–83.

Salkovskis, P. M. and Campbell, P. (1994). Thought-suppression in naturally occurring negative intrusive thoughts. *Behaviour Research and Therapy*, 32, 1–8.

Sanderson, W. C., Wetzler, S., Beck, A. T., and Betz, F. (1994a). Prevalence of personality disorders in patients with anxiety disorders. *Psychiatry Research*, 51, 167–74.

Sanderson, W. C., Beck, A. T., and McGinn, L. K. (1994b). Cognitive therapy for generalized anxiety disorder: significance of comorbid personality disorders. *Journal of Cognitive Psychotherapy*, 8, 13–18.

Stopa, L. and Clark, D. M. (1993). Cognitive processes in social phobia. *Behaviour Research and Therapy*, 31, 255–67.

Tallis, F., Eysenck, M. W., and Matthews, A. (1992). A questionnaire for the measurement of non-pathological worry. *Personality and Individual Differences*, 13, 161–68.

Turner, S. M., Beidel, D. C. and Stanley, M. A. (1992). Are obsessional thoughts and worry different cognitive phenomena? *Clinical Psychology Review*, 12, 257–70.

Vasey, W. W. and Borkovec, T. D. (1992). A catastrophizing assessment of worrisome thoughts. *Cognitive Therapy and Research*, 16, 505–20.

Wegner, D. M., Schneider, D. J., Carter, S. R., and White, T. L. (1987). Paradoxical effects of thought suppression. *Journal of Personality and Social Psychology*, 5, 5–13.

Wells, A. (1990). Panic disorder in association with relaxation induced anxiety: An attentional training approach to treatment. *Behavior Therapy*, 21, 273–80.

Wells, A. (1994a). Attention and the control of worry. In *Worrying: Perspective on theory, assessment and treatment* (ed. G. C. L. Davey and F. Tallis). Wiley, Chichester, UK.

Wells, A. (1994b). A multi-dimensional measure of worry: Development and preliminary validation of the Anxious Thoughts Inventory. *Anxiety, Stress and Coping*, 6, 289–99.

Wells, A. (1995). Meta-cognition and worry: A cognitive model of generalised anxiety disorder. *Behavioural and Cognitive Psychotherapy*, 23, 301–20.

Wells, A. (in prep.). *Cognitive therapy of anxiety disorders: A practical guide*. Wiley, Chichester, UK.

Wells, A. and Carter, K. (in prep.). Predictors of problematic worry: Tests of a meta-cognitive model.

Wells, A. and Clark, D. M. (in press). Social phobia: A cognitive perspective. In *Phobias: A handbook of description, treatment and theory* (ed. G. C. L. Davey). Wiley, Chichester, UK.

Wells, A. and Davies, M. (1994). The Thought Control Questionnaire: A measure of individual differences in the control of unwanted thoughts. *Behaviour Research and Therapy*, 32, 871–78.

Wells, A. and Hackmann, A. (1993). Imagery and core beliefs in health anxiety: Content and origins. *Behavioural and Cognitive Psychotherapy*, 21, 265–73.

Wells, A. and Matthews, G. (1994). *Attention and emotion: A clinical perspective*. Erlbaum, Hove, UK.

Wells, A. and Morrison, T. (1994). Qualitative dimensions of normal worry and normal obsessions: A comparative study. *Behaviour Research and Therapy*, 32, 867–70.

Wells, A. and Papageorgiou, C. (1995). Worry and the incubation of intrusive images following stress. *Behaviour Research and Therapy*, 33, 579–83.

Wells, A., White, J. and Carter, K. (in prep.). Attention training treatment: Effects on anxiety and belief in panic and social phobia.

Wenzlaff, R. M., Wegner, D. M. and Roper, D. W. (1988). Depression and mental control: the resurgence of unwanted negative thoughts. *Journal of Personality and Social Psychology*, 53, 882–92.

Woodward, R. and Jones, R.B. (1980). Cognitive restructuring treatment: A controlled trial with anxious patients. *Behaviour Research and therapy*, 18, 401–7.

8

Obsessive–compulsive disorder

Paul M. Salkovskis and Joan Kirk

Obsessive–compulsive disorder (OCD) is a severely disabling anxiety disorder which tends to be regarded as an intractable condition requiring lifelong treatment; a problem to be lived with and adapted to rather than to be 'cured'. Drastic measures, such as psychosurgery, are still considered appropriate in the most severe cases, justified by the desperation of sufferers rather than by evidence of effectiveness. Until a decade ago, clinicians could console themselves with the belief that OCD is an almost vanishingly rare disorder. This notion has been dispelled by more recent epidemiological data from community surveys which indicate a prevalence between 1% and 3% of the general population. Michael Gelder encouraged both of us, in different ways, to challenge therapeutic nihilism in the area of OCD. His strong support of behavioural treatments in the clinical setting encouraged the widespread application of cognitive behaviour therapies (CBT) in OCD (Kirk 1983), and he actively encouraged the development of the theoretical formulations described below as part of a specific research programme focused on the further development of CBT in obsessional problems. This programme has concerned the better understanding of the cognitive processes in obsessive–compulsive disorder in general to allow the refinement of existing behavioural treatments by the addition of cognitive elements, and the development of effective treatments for obsessional ruminations.

The nature of the problem

Obsessive–compulsive disorder is a problem characterized by recurrent intrusive thoughts, images, and impulses or compulsive 'behaviours'. Compulsions can include both overt rituals (such as handwashing and checking behaviours) and covert rituals; both will be referred to here as 'neutralizing'. DSM–IV (APA 1994) defines obsessive–compulsive disorder as recurrent and persistent intrusive cognitions of the above type which are not simply excessive worries about real-life problems (to distinguish obsessions from worries more typical of generalized anxiety disorder). In order to distinguish obsessions from psychotic phenomena, it is required that the person recognize the intrusion as being the product of their own mind. By definition, people suffering from obsessions attempt to ignore, suppress, or neutralize their intrusive thoughts. Compulsions are defined as repetitive behaviours which the person either performs in response to an obsessional intrusion or according to rules which they believe must be applied rigidly. To be defined as obsessional, these behaviours have to be aimed at preventing or reducing distress or some dreaded outcome (but without being connected in a *realistic* way with what they are designed to neutralize).

In addition to the specific definitions of obsessions and compulsions, it is essential that the obsessions and/or compulsions cause a degree of social/ occupational impairment and cause marked distress. This aspect of the definition of OCD is crucial, given that intrusive thoughts are commonplace among people who do not have any clinical problems.

Prevalence

Obsessive–compulsive disorder has, until recently, been regarded as a rare clinical problem, with rates of less than 0.1%. The relatively high frequency of obsessional problems in the clinic has often been regarded as a consequence of the natural history of the disorder. Spontaneous remission is relatively rare, and it has always been regarded as a disorder that is highly resistant to treatment. It may be that these factors lead to a relatively small number of patients taking up a statistically disproportionate amount of clinic time. However, recent epidemiological studies suggest that OCD may also be much more common in the general population than had previously been believed (Robins *et al*, 1984). Community rates in the range of 1.9–3.2% have recently been reported.

In contrast to OCD itself, the prevalence of the *basic phenomena* involved in OCD is extremely high. Rachman and de Silva (1978) found that intrusive thoughts, indistinguishable from obsessional thoughts, in terms of their content were reported by almost 90% of a non-clinical sample. This robust and frequently replicated finding (e.g., Freeston *et al.* 1991; Parkinson and Rachman 1980; Salkovskis and Harrison 1984) has more recently been supplemented by work indicating that 'normal compulsions' are also common in non-clinical subjects. These findings are of particular interest to those working with behaviour and cognitive-behaviour approaches, and it is hypothesized that the origins of obsessional problems are to be found in normal intrusive cognitions (see below).

The development of current treatments

The origins of current cognitive behavioural treatment are to be found in learning theory. Mowrer (1947, 1960) described a two-factor model of fear and avoidance behaviour in anxiety disorders. He suggested that fear of specific stimuli is acquired through *classical* conditioning, and maintained by *operant* conditioning processes, as the organism learns to reduce aversive stimuli initially by escaping, and later by avoiding, the fear-associated conditioned stimuli. Solomon and Wynne (1960) made the further important observation in animal experiments that if stimuli had become classically conditioned by previous association with strongly aversive stimuli, then avoidance responses to the conditioned stimuli were extremely resistant to extinction. That is, they demonstrated that avoidance responses continued unabated long after any pairing of conditioned stimuli with aversive consequences had ceased. The avoidance behaviour observed under these circumstances tended to become stereotyped in a fashion analogous to the behaviour of obsessional patients. Only when the avoidance behaviour was blocked did high levels of anxiety reappear; these animals would persistently attempt to continue the avoidance/escape behaviour for a considerable time after the behaviour was blocked, although these efforts eventually ceased.

In the first application of learning theory approaches to obsessional problems, Meyer (1966) reported the successful behavioural treatment of two cases of chronic obsessional neurosis, followed by a series of successful case reports. Meyer's work heralded the application of psychological models to obsessions and the development of effective behavioural treatments. Meyer seems to have drawn the idea for what he described as 'atoreptic therapy' from animal models of compulsive behaviour such as that of Metzner (1963). It is notable that attempts to generalize systematic desensitization (as used by Wolpe in the treatment of phobias) to obsessional rituals had been unsuccessful. Meyer argued that it was necessary to tackle avoidance behaviour directly by ensuring that rituals did not take place within or between treatment sessions. He emphasized the role of the expectations of harm in obsessions and the importance of invalidating these expectations during treatment in a way reminiscent of current cognitive behavioural theories. Rachman *et al.* (1971) adapted and developed this treatment method, combining specific *in vivo* exposure to feared situations with response prevention.

The behavioural theory

Behavioural treatment of obsessive–compulsive disorder is based on the hypothesis that obsessional thoughts have become associated, through conditioning, with anxiety which has subsequently failed to extinguish. Sufferers have developed escape and avoidance behaviours (such as obsessional checking and washing) which have the effect of preventing extinction of the anxiety (Rachman and Hodgson 1980). This view leads simply and elegantly to the behavioural treatment known as exposure and response prevention (ERP), in which the person is (a) exposed to stimuli which provoke the obsessional response; and (b) helped to prevent avoidance and escape (compulsive) responses (Steketee and Foa 1985; Salkovskis and Kirk 1989).

Rachman and his associates (see Rachman and Hodgson 1980 for a detailed review) also conducted a series of key experimental studies with obsessional patients to examine the applicability of this model. As predicted by their adaptation of the two-process theory they found that: (1) elicitation of the obsession was associated with increased anxiety and discomfort; (2) if the patient was then allowed to ritualize, anxiety and discomfort almost immediately decreased; (3) if the ritualizing was delayed, anxiety and discomfort decreased ('spontaneously decayed') over a somewhat longer period (up to one hour); and (4) when the patient refrains from ritualizing, the anxiety level on the next trial is relatively lower, and this does not occur if the ritualizing takes place. The success of behavioural treatments of obsessional disorders has in large part been due to the combination of and interaction between empirically grounded theoretical work, well-conducted research studies, and the creative clinical application of theory and research.

Behaviour therapy in practice

Behavioural treatment was initially carried out in in-patient or other intensive therapy settings (Marks *et al.* 1980), and tended to be relatively expensive. The practice of ERP treatment has been extended to its logical conclusion by Edna Foa's group (Riggs and Foa 1993), with maximal levels of exposure combined with continuous (24 hour) response prevention in some studies. Typically such programmes report 'success rates' of 75% or better (Abel 1993; Christensen *et al.* 1987), and there is evidence that those patients who do not respond to treatment may be predicted by the presence of depressed mood or very distorted beliefs (Foa *et al.* 1983). Recent research suggests that the more generally adopted clinical practice of out-patient treatment emphasizing homework ('self-exposure') can be at least as effective in some settings (Marks *et al.* 1988).

Behavioural treatments are difficult to apply to patients who ruminate and have no overt ritualistic behaviour, and treatment refusals and drop-outs are relatively common. Success in the treatment of OCD usually means the patients are 'much improved' or 'improved'; the proportion of patients fully relieved of their obsessional problem is considerably less. Treatment refusal and early drop-outs are also common, reducing the figure obtaining the reported improvement to 50%, or less, of those suitable for inclusion and seeking treatment in clinical trials. The significant residual levels of social and occupational impairment at the end of treatment persist to longer-term follow-up, with little sign of further improvement (Kasvikis and Marks, 1988). Thus, despite extension of ERP to its fullest, there is considerable room for improvement both in the response rate for those offered treatment and the extent to which patients are completely cured at the end of treatment.

The limitations of behavioural treatment suggest the need for an alternative approach to the conceptualization and therapy of OCD while retaining the best features of behaviour treatment. Given that obsessional problems are, by definition, driven by unusual and distorted patterns of thinking, a cognitive approach was developed by Salkovskis (1985; 1989*a,b*), and used to devise cognitive elaborations of existing behavioural-based therapy approaches (see also Rachman 1976, 1993). Before considering the cognitive behavioural approach in detail, general deficit models will be briefly considered. Psychological deficit models (where a general impairment of cognitive functioning is hypothesized) have strong similarities to biological theories, which hypothesize that neurological problems result in the failure of normal cognitive functioning.

Deficit theories and cognitive factors

Obsessive–compulsive disorder readily lends itself to cognitive deficit and biological disease theorizing. Thoughts intrude uncontrollably; repetitive, stereotyped, and sometimes bizarre behaviour is prominent and pervasive; patients report problems with their memory and with decision-making and generalized disturbances of mood are frequently evident. It is therefore not surprising that several writers and researchers have proposed that there may be a general cognitive deficit (Reed, 1985), possibly related to structural/and or neurochemical disturbances (Goodman *et al.* 1992; Insel 1992).

Cognitive *deficit* theories of obsessional disorders have been based on one of two main views: (1) that obsessional patients are experiencing a general failure in cognitive control; or (2) obsessional patients have poor general memory and decision-making abilities. These approaches both represent radical departures from behaviour therapy, and no attempt has thus far been made to use these views to account for the effectiveness of exposure and response prevention treatment. In contrast, the much more specific cognitive behavioural hypothesis is related to the previously described behavioural theory, in that it proposes that the problem is a highly specific one related to normal functioning rather being a function of some general deficit. According to this cognitive behavioural view, obsessional problems arise from a pattern of specific responses to key stimuli to which the sufferer has acquired emotional sensitivity. Other problems, such as reported memory and decision-making difficulties and 'failures of inhibition', are regarded as secondary to the emotional arousal and particularly to counter-productive coping strategies deployed by the sufferer. In other words, obsessional patients tend to try too hard to control their own cognitive functioning and other cognitive functions suffer as a result of competition for processing resources. Some recent research provides support for this view; Maki *et al.* (1994) found that (non-clinical) checkers performed similarly to non-checkers on tests of inhibitory control of cognition. However, checkers *perceived themselves* to be more prone to failures of cognitive control, consistent with the hypothesis that, even in the absence of actual failures of control, these people will try to exert control over their perceived shortcomings in this area.

Paradoxically, then, one of the main problems with general deficit theories is their inability to account for key aspects of the phenomenology of OCD: sufferers do appear to have memory and decision-making problems. However, these are highly specific. Although they will check many times that the door of their house is locked, the same patient seldom has problems locking a broom cupboard door. The presence of a trusted other (e.g., therapist or spouse) also removes the urge to check (Rachman 1993). Similarly with contamination, there is a degree of specificity involved in the experience of an object as contaminating (e.g., by particular people or classes of people) which is difficult to account for as a general problem of deciding what is clean and what is contaminated. A similar situation holds for memory. The main evidence for memory problems has come from the work of Sher and colleagues (e.g., Sher *et al.* 1989), who have correlated Maudsley Obsessive–Compulsive Inventory (MOCI) checking scores with the Weschler Memory Scale (WMS), and report that both non-clinical and clinical 'checkers' have lower WMS scores than subjects scoring low on the checking scale. Curiously, obsessional patients do not have such memory impairment, nor indeed do such patients show any signs of problems with their memory *outside areas directly linked to their obsessional problems.* However, if people are *concerned* about their memory, they may check because of this concern. This means that at least two types of people will report checking: those who have a memory problem and make attempts to compensate for it; and those who are *unduly* concerned about their memory and attempt similar compensation. The possible explanation of the findings of Sher *et al.* (1989) is, therefore, that people who actually have general problems with poor memory tend to check more than those who do not. The evidence from clinical *obsessional* checkers indicates that there is not a generalized memory deficit; the cognitive behavioural hypothesis suggests that in these instances checking may arise from undue and highly focused concern about memory for particular things. Checking may also develop in other people who *know* that they tend to have a poor memory; these probably constitute Sher's 'non-obsessional clinical checkers'.

Finally, there is the matter of the effectiveness of therapy. For a general deficit theory to be truly viable as an explanation of OCD, it must be able to account for the effectiveness of existing psychological treatment (i.e., exposure and response prevention). Such an account directly leads to testable predictions concerning changes that should occur in the course of treatment. It seems most unlikely that a procedure that cuts down repetitions of checking and washing will enhance memory *per se*. Despite their evident simplicity and the apparent face validity, general deficit theories do not currently add to the understanding of clinical obsessional problems. To be useful, cognitive or biological deficit theories must both account for the phenomenology of OCD, and support this with specific experimental evidence evaluating theoretically derived predictions (for a more detailed critique of simple biological models, see Salkovskis, 1996*a*, *b*). At this point, only the behavioural and cognitive behavioural theories can provide comprehensive and testable accounts of the phenomenology of OCD.

Cognitive behavioural theory

It is hypothesized (Salkovskis 1985) that clinical obsessions are intrusive cognitions, the occurrence *and* content of which patients interpret as an indication that they might be responsible for harm to themselves or others unless they take action to prevent it. This interpretation results in attempts to both suppress and to *neutralize* the thought, image, or impulse. Neutralizing is defined as voluntarily initiated activity *which is intended to have the effect of reducing the perceived responsibility* and can be overt or covert (compulsive behaviour or thought rituals). As a consequence of neutralizing activity, intrusive cognitions become more salient and frequent, they evoke more discomfort, and the probability of further neutralizing increases. By the same token, attempts to suppress the thought increase the likelihood of recurrence.

The hypothesis is that it is the *interpretation* of obsessional thoughts as indicating increased responsibility explains a number of important effects in people suffering from OCD: (1) increased discomfort, anxiety and depression; (2) greater accessibility of the original thought and other related ideas; and (3) behavioural 'neutralizing' responses which constitute attempts to escape or avoid responsibility. These may include compulsive behaviour, avoidance of situations related to the obsessional thought, seeking reassurance (thus diluting or sharing responsibility), and attempts to get rid of or exclude the thought from his/her mind (see p. 188). Each of these effects contributes not only to the prevention of extinction of anxiety but also to a worsening spiral of intrusive thoughts leading to maladaptive affective, cognitive, and behavioural reactions. For example, an obsessional patient may believe that the occurrence of a thought, such as 'I will kill my baby,' means that there is a risk that she will succumb to the action unless she does something to prevent it, such as avoiding being left alone with her child or by seeking reassurance from people around her, by trying to think positive thoughts to balance the negative ones, and so on.

The cognitive hypothesis, therefore, suggests that the problem in obsessions is not poor mental control. Instead, it is hypothesized that obsessional patients tend to *misinterpret* aspects of their own mental functioning, including memory for actions, intrusive (obsessional) thoughts and doubts, and as a result then try too hard to exert control. The *discomfort* experienced is due to the patient's appraisal of the content and occurrence of intrusive thoughts. The increased *frequency* of intrusions relative to non-obsessional subjects is in large part due to the behaviours (overt and covert) that are motivated by the appraisal made. These appraisals in obsessional patients centre on distorted beliefs about responsibility. The distorted sense of responsibility which the sufferer attaches to his/her activities (including intrusive thoughts and memories as well as overt behaviour) leads to mental effort characterized both by *over-control* and preoccupation.

'Responsibility' means, here, that the person believes that he/she may be, or come to be, the cause of harm (to self or others) unless he/she takes some preventative or restorative action. The 'responsibility' appraisals of obsessionals can be defined as:

'The belief that one has power which is pivotal to bring about or prevent subjectively crucial negative outcomes.' (Salkovskis *et al.* 1992).

The appraisal of intrusive thoughts as having implications for responsibility for harm to self or others is therefore seen as important, because appraisal links the intrusive thought with both distress *and* the occurrence of neutralizing behaviour. If the appraisal solely concerns harm or danger without an element of responsibility, then the effect is more likely to be anxiety or depression, which may become part of a mood-appraisal spiral (Teasdale 1983), but would not result in clinical obsessions without the additional component of the responsibility-neutralizing link. Hearing someone else making blasphemous statements or talking about harming one's children might not be upsetting in itself. However, if one perceives what is said as personally significant (e.g., 'perhaps this person wants to harm my children') some emotional response (anxiety or anger) would be expected. Without the specific appraisal of *responsibility*, an obsessional episode would not result.

An obsessional pattern would be particularly likely in vulnerable individuals when intrusions are regarded as self-initiated (e.g., resulting in appraisals such as 'these thoughts might mean I want to harm the children; I must guard against losing control'). This is similar to the difference between effects of asking an obsessional checker to lock a door himself or to watch someone else locking the same door. This responsibility effect is clearly demonstrated by the experiments conducted by Roper and Rachman (1975) and Roper *et al.* (1973), in which situations which usually provoked checking rituals in obsessional patients (such as locking the door) produced little or no discomfort or checking when the therapist was present, in sharp contrast to the effects of having to deal with such situations when alone (see Rachman 1993 for a detailed description of responsibility/checking links).

Thus, the core of the cognitive formulation is to be found in the occurrence of neutralizing behaviour elicited by the appraisal of responsibility. That is, 'if the automatic thoughts arising from the intrusion do not include the possibility of being in some way responsible . . . then neutralizing is very unlikely to take place, and the result is likely to be heightened anxiety and depression rather than an obsessional problem' (Salkovskis 1985, p. 579). Part of this appraisal arises from the occurrence of the intrusion itself linked with beliefs about thoughts themselves, such as those described by Salkovskis (1985, p. 579); for example, 'not neutralizing when an intrusion has occurred is similar or equivalent to seeking or wanting the harm involved in the intrusion to happen' or 'thinking something is as bad as doing it . . .'. Under these circumstances, appraisal will then tend to be of the form 'my thinking this thought means . . .'. In this way, an appraisal which is regarded as sensible is based on a thought which is itself regarded as senseless. It is, of course, quite common to be told by anxious patients that 'I must be crazy because I have crazy thoughts, and I know that they are crazy thoughts . . .'.

According to the cognitive behaviour hypothesis, patients are seen as being especially concerned about their memory and the process of decision making; as a consequence, *they try too hard to exert control over mental processes and activity* in a variety of counter-productive and therefore anxiety-provoking ways. Efforts at over-control increase distress because: (1) direct and deliberate attention to mental activity can modify the contents of consciousness; (2) efforts to deliberately control a range of mental activities meet with failure and even opposite effects; (3) attempts to prevent harm and responsibility for harm increase the salience and accessibility of the patients' concerns with harm; and (4) neutralizing directed at preventing harm also prevents the patient from discovering that the things he/she is afraid of will not occur. This means that exaggerated beliefs about responsibility and harm do not decline.

Recent experimental studies of normal intrusive thoughts

Measurement of responsibility

Two main measures of responsibility appraisals have been developed by the authors' group. First, we have devised a measure of the extent to which patients held *general attitudes and beliefs* that are likely to predispose to the interpretation of intrusive thoughts as indicating inflated responsibility (e.g., 'If I think bad things, this is as bad as *doing* bad things; If I can have even a slight influence on things going wrong, then I must act to prevent it'). Preliminary analyses of results in obsessional patients and control subjects indicates that scores on this scale are significantly higher in obsessional patients compared to both non-clinical controls and non-obsessional anxious patients, consistent with the hypothesis that general beliefs concerning responsibility may predispose to OCD.

Secondly, a *specific measure of self-reported responsibility interpretations* was devised, in which patients were asked to rate how often particular ideas occurred when the person was bothered by intrusive thoughts, impulses, or images and how much they believed them (e.g., 'It would be irresponsible to ignore these thoughts', 'Thinking this could make it happen'). Clinical obsessional patients not only scored significantly higher on this measure, but they did not overlap with non-clinical controls and had minimal overlap with anxious control patients. This measure has the advantage of assessing a 'state' type of variable and is sensitive to clinical change. In therapy development work it has proven useful in helping the therapist target specific beliefs for modification, and to assess the extent of change within and between sessions.

Laboratory and field experiments on the response to intrusive thoughts

If the cognitive hypothesis is true, then it should be possible to show that intrusive thoughts in non-clinical subjects follow predictable patterns under specified conditions in which the person uses particular strategies to deal with his/her intrusive thoughts. For example, deliberate efforts to suppress or neutralize intrusive thoughts should increase the frequency and discomfort associated with them. Wegner (1989) describes a series of experiments on factors influencing mental control of emotionally neutral stimuli, particularly focusing on thought suppression. The results of these studies suggested that efforts to suppress thoughts did not result in an initial enhancement, but that suppression was achieved in the short term. In contrast, during the immediately subsequent period, an enhancement (described as a 'rebound') *was* observed. However, another group (Lavy and van den Hout, 1990; Merckelbach *et al.* 1991) did find the expected paradoxical enhancement of emotionally neutral stimuli, and did not find a rebound. Subsequently, Clark *et al.* (1991) and Clark *et al.* (1992) again failed to find an immediate enhancement effect, using vivid emotionally neutral stimuli (green rabbits) from a previously heard taped story. Clark and colleagues suggested that studies which found enhancement had failed to control for the effects of the frequency with which the to-be-suppressed target was mentioned prior to the suppression task.

There are major methodological differences between such studies which present major problems of interpretation. For example, some studies used a thought-counting procedure, whereas others used 'streaming', in which subjects are asked to verbalize their stream of consciousness which is later coded, often with the 'target' thought being represented as a percentage of total thoughts. Target stimuli have varied in terms of how commonplace and relevant they are, ranging from green rabbits to kitchen utensils; most did not concern 'intrusive' thoughts as usually defined, and did not focus on naturally occurring thoughts. Salkovskis and Campbell (1994) targeted personally relevant and naturally occurring negative intrusive thoughts which subjects reported that they normally attempt to suppress to some extent. Thus, a characteristic of such intrusions is that subjects find them personally unacceptable and are self-motivated to remove or suppress such intrusions. In the study, 75 non-clinical subjects were allocated to one of five experimental conditions: thought suppression, mention control, and suppression under three different distraction conditions. This initial experimental period was followed by a standard 'think anything' period. The design therefore allowed assessment both of suppression and rebound effects. Thought frequency was measured by means of a counter. This study showed that the subjects asked simply to suppress experienced significantly more intrusive thoughts during *both* first and second experimental periods when compared to the mention control group. Distraction instructions significantly decreased frequency only when a specific engaging task was provided. Effects on evaluative components of the intrusive thought (discomfort and acceptability) were observed only in the condition which involved the specific distracting task.

Clearly, laboratory studies involving brief suppression periods (typically a few minutes) need to be generalized to obsessions in which subjects describe struggling to exclude thoughts *most of the time*. In a study designed to investigate the longer-term impact of thought suppression in naturally occurring intrusive thoughts, Trinder and Salkovskis (1994) asked subjects to record intrusions only, to suppress, or to 'think through' over a period of four days. Again, suppression was found to enhance intrusion. This study serves to bridge the phenomenology of OCD and thought-suppression experiments. We have now begun to apply these findings to clinical populations. First, suppression over a period of days was investigated in a single-case series using an alternating treatments design, where patients were asked to use a diary to record intrusive thoughts for a few days, then to either continue to record or to record and suppress on randomly alternating days. The first four patients show a clear differentiation of 'suppress' days from 'record days', with an approximate doubling of intrusions when suppression is used as a thought control strategy. In a group design, which was subjected to a preliminary analysis for a conference presentation (Salkovskis *et al.* 1995), suppression, thinking through, and recording alone were compared in OCD and non-clinical individuals. Results for 30/45 obsessional patients and 40/45 controls indicate that suppression increases intrusion in both OCD and non-clinical subjects compared to both sets of control instructions, but that the obsessional patients continue to experience an increased frequency of intrusions in a subsequent 'think anything' period, while the non-clinical subjects show a substantial decrease in intrusive thinking.

Other studies have shown the importance of responsibility appraisal in the emotional reaction to negative intrusive thoughts (Freeston and Ladouceur, 1993; Freeston *et al.* 1991; Purdon and Clark 1994). The cognitive model suggests that, in the more severe problems characteristic of people suffering from emotional disorders, the basis of such appraisals can be found in 'thinking errors' (Beck 1976). Thinking errors are characteristic distortions which influence whole classes of reactions, and which reflect general assumptions about the world and the person's relationship with it.

Distorted thinking: the origins of negative appraisals

Thinking errors are not of themselves pathological; in fact, most people make judgements by employing a range of 'heuristics', many of which can be fallacious (Nisbett and Ross 1980). The cognitive hypothesis suggests that OCD patients show characteristic thinking; probably the most typical and important is the idea that:

Any influence over outcome = Responsibility for outcome

An interesting area is the relationship between responsibility through action as opposed to inaction. Salkovskis (1985) suggests that the belief that: 'Failing to prevent (or failing to try to prevent) harm to self or others is the same as having caused the harm in the first place', may be a key assumption in the generation of obsessional problems. Clinical experience (and recent pilot work by the authors' group) suggests that obsessional patients may be unduly sensitive to omissions compared to non-obsessionals. Initially, it seemed that this sensitivity was a generalized characteristic, so that people suffering from OCD seemed be much more careful than non-clinical subjects about the possible harmful consequences of things which they neglected to do. However, closer investigation suggested an alternative explanation. There are at least two circumstances under which people not suffering from obsessional problems can be sensitive to omission: first, when they believe that they have a specific *duty* to be aware of the consequences of omission (i.e., it is their responsibility); and second, when they have actually foreseen negative consequences arising from the omission. The omissions which concern people suffering from OCD concern areas where they tend to over-conscientiousness, and it is clear that they perceive a duty. More importantly, foreseeing disaster can include experiencing an intrusive thought. If a person spots a piece of glass on the pavement and, for no obvious reason, experiences the intrusive thought that a child might fall and cut an eye on that piece of glass, they are nevertheless confronted by a decision: 'Do I leave this glass here and walk on, or do I pick it up?' Without the occurrence of the intrusive thought, no decision would have been involved. Thus, intrusive thoughts about harm transform situations where no decision is required into situations requiring a specific decision concerning harm. By definition, OCD patients are likely to experience such thoughts more frequently than non-clinical subjects. In an experimental investigation, we have found that non-clinical subjects react like obsessionals in omission when an intrusive thought concerning harm is introduced. That is, one of the characteristics of obsessional patients is that they frequently foresee a wide range of possible negative outcomes; intrusive thoughts often concern things which could go wrong unless dealt with (such as passing on contamination, having hurt someone accidentally, having left the door unlocked or the gas turned on). Sometimes it is not even permissable for an obsessional patient to avoid foreseeing problems/disasters, because this would mean that he/she had deliberately chosen this course, increasing the sense of responsibility. As a result, some patients regard it as a *duty* to try to foresee negative outcomes. If a negative outcome *is* foreseen even as an intrusive thought, responsibility is established: to do nothing, the person would have had to decide not to act to prevent the harmful outcome. That is, deciding *not* to act despite being aware of possible disastrous consequences becomes an active decision, making the person a causal agent in relation to those disastrous consequences. Thus, the occurrence of intrusive/obsessional thoughts transforms a situation where harm can only occur by omission into a situation where the person has 'actively' chosen to allow the harm to take place. This might mean that the apparent absence of omission bias in obsessionals is mediated by the occurrence of obsessional thoughts.

Deciding not to do something results in a sense of 'agency'; thus, a patient will not be concerned about sharp objects he/she has not seen, and will not be concerned if he/she did not consider the possibility of harm. However, if something is seen and it occurs to the person that he/she could or should take preventative action, the situation changes because NOT acting becomes an active decision. In this way, the actual occurrence of intrusive thoughts of harm and/or responsibility for it come to play a key role in the perception of responsibility for their contents. Suppression, as described on p. 00 will further increase this effect by increasing the thoughts in precisely the situations that the obsessional most wishes to exclude any intrusion. Thus, having locked the door, the person tries not to think that it could be open, experiences the thought again, and is therefore constrained to act or risk being responsible through having chosen not to check. The motivation to suppress will increase, but it is very difficult to suppress a thought which is directly connected to an action just completed, so the action serves as a further cue for intrusion/ suppression, and so on.

Treatment implications of the cognitive behavioural theory: an overview

Given the success of exposure and response prevention, cognitive approaches initially emphasized techniques for identifying and modifying the thoughts and beliefs which prevented patients from engaging in or benefiting from exposure treatment (Salkovskis and Warwick 1985), and in the modification of anxious or depressed mood concurrent with the obsessions (Salkovskis and Warwick 1988). Increasingly, treatment has developed in a way in which the cognitive approach allows a different conceptualization of the process of change in the treatment of OCD (Salkovskis and Warwick 1985, 1988; Salkovskis, 1996a, 1989c) and therefore suggests new treatment techniques which go beyond exposure (Salkovskis, 1996b).

The principal aim of cognitive behavioural *treatment* for obsessional problems therefore follows directly from the theory. Therapy aims to help the patient conclude that obsessional thoughts, however distressing, are irrelevant to further action. Teaching the patient to control the occurrence of intrusive thoughts will be beneficial only if it alters the way in which their occurrence is interpreted, such as by convincing the patient that intrusive thoughts are at least partially under their own control and therefore of no special significance. Thus, the key to the control of obsessional thoughts may be to learn that the exercise of control is unnecessary.

The cognitive theory predicts that, for treatment to be successful, the patient needs to be helped to modify beliefs involved in, and leading to, the misinterpretation of intrusive thoughts as indicating increased responsibility and of the associated behaviours involved in the maintenance of these beliefs. Prior to treatment, the obsessional patient is distressed because they have a particularly threatening perception of their obsessional experiences; for example, that their thoughts mean that they are a child molester, or that they are in constant danger of transmitting disease to other people, and so on. The essence of treatment is helping the sufferer to construct and test a new, less threatening model of their experience. The obsessional washer is helped to shift their view of their problem away from the idea that they might be contaminated and therefore must ensure that they do not transmit this to someone else (or come to harm themself) to the idea that they have a specific problem which concerns their *fears* of contamination. That is, the patient is helped to understand their problem as one of *thinking* and deciding rather than the 'real world' risks which they fear.

For example, some patients believe that, if one imagines performing an act (such as stabbing one's children), this increases the probability that they will carry out the action. The patients would be encouraged to test that belief by finding out directly whether thinking about things really can make them happen. For example, the therapist might say: 'Let's see if I can make myself die by thinking of it. I wish I would die right now, with no delay [Pause]. Can you do that? What happens when you did?'; or, if the patient is unable to: 'What went through your mind right then when I asked you to do that, and when you thought about doing it?'. The same patient might be later encouraged to actively bring about the feared consequence by adopting particular thinking patterns in order to fully demonstrate the limits of their responsibility (e.g., 'Is it possible to commit suicide by thinking about it? Could you try your hardest to think yourself dead before the next session, and record what happens when you do it, what comes into your mind...'). This type of sequence is designed to help the patient reappraise their obsessional problem as being an understandable result of trying too hard to control their mental activity, rather than as one of being dangerously out of control and liable to act on their thoughts and therefore cause harm. In cognitive therapy the patient is thus helped to understand and test the way their beliefs and related efforts to prevent harm are not only unnecessary but also create the problems which they experience. The aim is to allow them to see the problem as one of thinking rather than one of actual danger of harm.

This style of therapy is particularly powerful in patients who are afraid of fully committing themselves to exposure and response prevention (ERP) because the cognitive elements target the beliefs that produce distress as well as initiate and motivate compulsive behaviour. Rather than simply asking patients to stop carrying out their compulsive behaviour, cognitive therapy seeks to identify and challenge the misinterpretations which lead the patient to ritualize, so that stopping compulsive behaviour is perceived by the patient as less dangerous and therefore irrelevant. The early development of cognitive therapy was in fact carried out with patients refusing and failing to respond to ERP (Salkovskis and Warwick, 1985). Direct modification of the misinterpretation of intrusive thoughts and related beliefs should also bring about a more complete and thorough change, as well as being more likely to engage the patient in treatment with a consequent reduction in treatment refusal and drop-out.

Apart from the specific development of cognitive behavioural treatment for OCD in patients resistant to ERP (Salkovskis and Warwick 1985), and as a fuller treatment strategy in its own right (Salkovskis and Warwick 1988), the cognitive behaviour theory has also been applied to the development of an effective treatment for patients suffering from obsessional ruminations. Given the emphasis on the maintaining role of *compulsive behaviour* in behavioural theory and treatment, patients who do not appear to ritualize are theoretically anomalous and difficult to treat using traditional methods. No behavioural treatment has been shown in controlled trials to be effective in the treatment of pure ruminators. Only 46% of patients treated in previous studies experienced at least a 50% reduction in rumination frequency, and only 12% experienced a 50% reduction in distress (reviewed in detail in Salkovskis and Westbrook 1989). The cognitive approach incorporates the findings that *covert* compulsions are almost invariably present, and need to be tackled in therapy. For example, a patient who pictures his child dead neutralizes this thought by thinking of the child alive, and mentally prays that this should not come about. Such covert compulsive behaviour is rapid and difficult to identify and control, unlike handwashing or checking. The use of the cognitive conceptualization and procedures, such as those outlined above for OCD, provide a framework for the therapist to help the patient to detect, understand, and gain control over the mental compulsions. The covert nature of these rituals makes them difficult to stop without dealing with the patient's appraisal of the intrusions (and of the feared harm which could arise from *not* ritualizing). Cognitive behavioural treatment both targets appraisal and uses an audiotape loop in order to maximize exposure and make response prevention easier for the patient. As an additional focus, an audiotape loop is used to provoke obsessional thoughts; subsequent within-session discussion identifies both the disturbing interpretations made by the patient and any impulses to control or neutralize these thoughts (Salkovskis 1983; Salkovskis and Westbrook 1989). Patients are taught to identify neutralizing (compulsive) behaviour by attention to its effortful nature (in contrast to obsessional intrusions, which occur automatically). Cognitive techniques are used to modify the interpretation and hence reduce distress and facilitate the patients' attempts to stop mentally controlling or neutralizing obsessional thoughts. The use of the tape and cognitive procedures is then extended outside therapy sessions both as a specific focus for homework exercises, and as an accessible way of taking the exposure and belief change exercises into target (obsession-provoking) situations (by means of personal stereos with headphones). Early in treatment, homework involves daily tape-assisted exercises and thought-answering at preset times. Subsequently, the same procedures are used in situations which are identified as usually provoking the obsessional thoughts. Later in treatment, patients will be helped to apply these techniques at times when the obsessional thoughts occur unexpectedly in the course of the day. The aim is to ensure complete emotional processing in the sense that the obsessional comes to see intrusive thoughts as a harmless (and potentially useful) aspect of normal psychological functioning. In a series of single-case experiments, we found that a combination of cognitive procedures and exposure aided by an audio tape loop were effective where more traditional habituation and thought-stopping techniques were not (Salkovskis and Westbrook 1989). The cognitive behavioural version of this treatment is described in greater detail below.

Cognitive behavioural treatment in obsessional problems: special considerations

The cognitive hypothesis allows a clear understanding of both the origin and the maintenance of anxiety problems in general. A particularly powerful component of cognitive behaviour therapy involves techniques directed at bringing about disconfirmation of danger (Salkovskis 1991, 1996a,b). However, OCD poses some special difficulties in this respect. Attention to the details of obsessional beliefs illustrates where the difficulty lies and how it may best be resolved. In obsessions, it is often the case that the danger which is feared is judged as likely to occur *at some relatively distant future time*. For example, the obsessional patient may believe that their failure to control their blasphemous thoughts mean that they will suffer eternal torment after their death. Manoeuvres which are intended to show the person that their feared consequences did not come about are likely to fail. It has long been known that this type of obsession does not respond well to reassurance (Marks 1981).

Fortunately, it is fundamental to the practice of good cognitive therapy that the therapist and patient work together to reach a shared understanding (conceptualization) of the way the patient's problem works. The most effective way of changing a misinterpretation (whether it be of a symptom, a situation or a thought) is to help the person suggest an alternative less threatening interpretation of their experience. Subsequent therapy (including discussion, behavioural experiments, and exercises in disconfirmation) are then all directed at helping the person distinguish between the different interpretations that they have. In every instance, the alternative explanation is going to be highly idiosyncratic, based on the particular pattern of symptoms and interpretations experienced by that person.

The cognitive hypothesis also specifies that different types of psychological problem will show certain broad consistencies within categories. Thus, the concerns of the person experiencing repeated panic attacks are particularly likely to focus on the way in which that person interprets bodily and mental sensations as a sign of *imminent* catastrophe; the social phobics' concerns are particularly likely to focus on ideas of being humiliated, scorned, or rejected. The more specific models of particular psychological problems provide the clinician and researcher with general guidance which allow them then to focus their interventions in a more accurate way. Cognitive treatment thus emphasizes the negotiation of a shared understanding of the patient's problems combined with subsequent manoeuvres designed, where possible, to help the patient achieve a disconfirmation of their negative interpretation as well as bolstering the less threatening alternative. Because the feared catastrophes in OCD tend to lie further in the future than in other problems, disconfirmation is much less useful as a strategy. This increases the relative importance of both the patient's and the therapist's understanding of the non-threatening explanation of the patient's problem (i.e., the cognitive model as is idiosyncratically applied to the patient's symptoms and situation).

General strategies of treatment in OCD

Engagement

It is crucial that treatment of obsessional problems involves reaching a shared understanding with the patient concerning the psychological basis of the problem. This is because at the beginning of therapy, the patient believes that the problem is that they are in danger of some terrible catastrophe. If this belief is held very strongly, the patient is unlikely to engage properly in psychologically (or psychiatrically) based treatment. For example, if the obsessional patient believes that his thoughts mean that he is a potential child molester, a potential murderer, a blasphemer, and so on. Given such beliefs it is not surprising that he seeks to deal with the situation by fighting his thoughts and neutralizing any consequences of their occurrence in attempts to ensure that he cannot be responsible for any harm or be otherwise blamed. It is therefore necessary that in the early stages of treatment the patient is helped to see that there may be an alternative explanation of the difficulties they are experiencing which offers a quite different and less threatening account of the problem. For example, it could be that the crux of the problem is that the patient is *worried about and believes* that they might be a child molester (rather than being one) and that these worries mean that they are therefore plagued by the very intrusive thoughts which they seek to exclude. For treatment to be effective, it follows that it is crucial that the patient agrees that therapeutic strategies should be aimed at reducing such worries rather than the fruitless attempts to reduce risk.

Specific elements of cognitive behavioural treatment

Once the patient is engaged in treatment in a collaborative relationship, the main elements of treatment are focused on using guided discovery to develop and evaluate a comprehensive cognitive behaviour model of the maintenance of their obsessional problems.

Helping the patient to consider evidence for the alternative account

The two possible explanations for the patient's problems are considered alongside each other rather than as mutually exclusive alternatives, and therapy then proceeds as an evaluation of the relative merits of these two views. The patient is invited to consider how the two alternative views match up to their experience. Evidence for and against each is reviewed and discussed in detail. Often, discussion reaches the point where further information which is not currently available to the patient has to be sought. Behavioural experiments are used as information-gathering exercises to help patients reach conclusions about the beliefs which they hold. For example, an obsessional patient can see from discussion that trying not to think a thought might increase the frequency of that thought. However, she may also consider it possible that her thoughts of harming her children may not follow this pattern, and it may be that she is only managing to control the thoughts by pushing them away and distracting herself. To test this out the patient keeps a diary record of the frequency of occurrence of the thoughts and on some days attempts to distract herself from the thoughts as hard as she possibly can and on other days tries to allow the thoughts to come and not fight them. In doing so she discovers that the thoughts occur more frequently and upset her more on those days when she chooses to resist the thoughts. In this way there is a constant interplay between the cognitive behavioural formulation drawn up by patient and therapist, discussion of how the patient's experience fits with that formulation, and generation of new experiences (using behavioural experiments) further to illuminate the model. Cognitive and behavioural elements are interwoven in order to allow patients to consider and adopt a more helpful and less frightening belief than the one they have previously accepted.

Detailed identification and self-monitoring of obsessional thoughts and patient's appraisal of these thoughts is combined with exercises designed to help the patient to modify their responsibility beliefs on a minute-by-minute basis outside therapy sessions (e.g., by using the daily record of dysfunctional thoughts). Discussion techniques are extensively used to challenge appraisals and basic assumptions on which these are based. The therapist aims to help the patient modify their negative beliefs about the extent of their own personal responsibility. For example, a patient felt that he caused a colleague to lose his job, and constantly sought reassurance about this from people around him. The therapist asked him to list all possible contributory factors in the loss of his colleague's job, beginning the list by with the comment he had made to the department manager which the patient feared had caused his colleague to be made redundant. Other factors were then listed by the patient (his colleague being near retirement, his department's financial problems, antagonism between the colleague and manager, and so on). The therapist then drew a blank pie chart, and invited the patient to allocate segments beginning with the bottom of the list (and therefore ending with the top of the list, which are the patient's comments to another colleague that may have been repeated to the manager). This exercise has the advantage of not involving reassurance (all factors are identified by the patient) and is effective in challenging 'black and white thinking' such as 'If it is possible that I may have influenced a bad outcome, I am probably responsible for it': 0–100 ratings of belief in personal responsibility are taken before and after an exercise of this kind.

Behavioural experiments are explicitly focused on helping the patient to draw conclusions concerning some aspect of the view that their problem is worry about being responsible for harm rather than actually being responsible for harm. Behavioural experiments are carried out both within sessions (in order to clarify some part of that session's discussion) and between sessions as homework either to gather entirely new evidence or to consolidate what was elicited during the therapy session. Most of the strategies used fall into two broad categories: (1) behavioural experiments designed to assess the extent to which a particular process may be playing a role in maintaining the patient's fears; a key feature of these experiments is the elicitation of processes which may be increasing symptoms themselves (such as intrusive thoughts) or the fear and distress associated with these symptoms; and (2) exposure exercises, where feared stimuli are repeated elicited in the absence of any neutralizing behaviour.

There are a range of behavioural experiments which allow the patient and therapist to test directly processes hypothesized to be involved in the patient's obsessional problems. For example, it can be demonstrated that attempts to suppress a thought lead to an increase in the frequency with which it occurs. This might be done first with a neutral thought during the session ('try right now not to think of a giraffe'), then with the person's own obsessional thought. For some patients it is helpful to demonstrate the longer-term effects of suppression by having them keep a diary (or use a counter) for longer periods between sessions (e.g., several hours or even a day at a time); for some of the pre-identified periods patients are asked to suppress as much as they can (and rate this effort), for others they are asked only to record occurrence and the degree of effort directed to suppression. At the following session, the two types of time-period are plotted on one graph as two series of points. Once this is graphed, the patient is asked what they think of the result. This is a particularly powerful way of demonstrating the counter-productive effects of thought suppression efforts.

Carefully planned exposure exercises may be helpful in examining evidence for the negative appraisals made when disconfirmation is an option (e.g. in a patient who believes that thinking a particular thought will bring about specific consequences, the therapist wishes himself dead at that instant by saying this out loud, followed by the patient doing the same thing). Even if disconfirmation is not possible, exposure is a useful demonstration that anticipation of discomfort is almost invariably considerably worse than actual discomfort, and that discomfort decreases rapidly when compulsions are prevented. These observations are evaluated against the two possible explanations of the person's problems previously identified: (1) is the problem one of actual harm and one's responsibility; or (2) of worry about that harm and an excessive concern about one's possible responsibility for its prevention. Thus, although emphasis may be placed on exposure and response prevention as a treatment strategy, it is embedded in the overall framework of the cognitive approach. In the treatment of obsessional ruminations, the exposure component is best conducted with the use of a tape loop, where the patient is given the opportunity to discover that repetition of their intrusive thoughts or eliciting stimuli (with reduced levels of negative appraisal of responsibility) results in a decrease in the discomfort experience. This is described in greater detail below.

Each behavioural experiment is idiosyncratically devised within a framework devised to help the patient test their previous (threatening) explanation of their experience against the new (non-threatening) explanation worked out with their therapist. The patient is also helped to identify and modify underlying general assumptions (such as 'not trying to prevent harm is as bad as making it happen deliberately') which give rise to their misinterpretation of their own mental activity. When planning and conducting behavioural experiments, it is crucial to bear in mind that the fundamental basis of obsessional problems lies in the way that the patient interprets or appraises intrusive thoughts and related mental phenomena, and therapy strategies aim to help the patient reach a new understanding of the basis of their problem. The best way to decrease belief in misinterpretations (e.g., interpreting the occurrence and content of an intrusive thought as a sign of personal responsibility for harm), is to provide the person with a less threatening alternative explanation. The alternative explanation is, of course, based on the cognitive behavioural formulation agreed with the patient. Thus, the patient is continually reminded that there are really two possible explanations for the problems they are experiencing: (1) it could be that they really are in danger of causing harm or failing to prevent harm and that they therefore have to do everything they possibly can to avert such harm; or (2) it could be that they are someone who is worried about such harm and that his problems are coming from this particular anxiety and concern rather than from any actual reality of harm. It is also emphasized at every opportunity that these two different views make contradictory predictions about what would be helpful. In particular, it is emphasized that constant effort to prevent something that one is concerned about is inevitably going to have the effect of increasing preoccupation.

The way in which these treatment strategies are implemented in the treatment of obsessional ruminations will be described next. As described above (p. 194), the treatment of obsessional ruminations presented particular problems in behaviour therapy which are in part dealt with by a more precise division of ruminations into intrusive thoughts and neutralizing thoughts. This is integrated into the cognitive conceptualization to allow an integrated cognitive behavioural approach.

Cognitive behavioural treatment strategies in obsessional ruminations

Stage 1: assessment and goal-setting

In the assessment stage, the therapist focuses on getting a description of a recent episode of rumination and identifying within that episode the specific sequence that occurred. Considerable emphasis is placed on identifying the way in which intrusive thoughts or other intrusive cognitions were interpreted in terms of responsibility and the impact that this interpretation had on subsequent efforts to neutralize, suppress, or otherwise control the intrusive thoughts. The impact of such control attempts on the occurrence of thoughts is also then highlighted. By the end of this phase, two targets should have been reached. The first of these is that a formulation or shared understanding of the problem should be agreed and secondly that the goals of therapy should have been negotiated. These goals should include short-term, medium-term, and long-term goals. It is very important to emphasize with patients suffering from obsessional ruminations that the type of goal being considered does not include getting rid of the thoughts entirely.

Stage 2: normalizing and considering non-threatening alternative explanations

This stage involves further clarification of the formulation and helping the patient to understand the mechanisms by which their problem with intrusive thoughts is being maintained. Several strategies are employed in this phase in order to help the patient to understand the significance of their intrusive thoughts. These include:

1. Discussing the normal function of intrusive thoughts; are there ever circumstances where intrusive thoughts are helpful (e.g., positive intrusive thoughts, good ideas)? Could negative intrusive thoughts be helpful (e.g., when occurring in moderation, making one more aware of possible dangers)? Could even extreme and violent intrusive thoughts be helpful in some circumstances (e.g., as a member of your family is about to be attacked by a stranger)? Is it possible to dictate that intrusive thoughts only intrude when one wants them?

2. Further discussion of the link between the occurrence and content of intrusive thoughts and their appraisal (and how that can generate neutralizing activity). Circumstances where normal neutralizing takes place are identified (e.g., going over plans and precautions when one is going on holiday, given the extra sense of responsibility involved then; worries which are provoked when another person suggests things which could go badly wrong as a result of something a person does).

3. The way in which someone suffering from obsessional thinking provides their own ideas about what could go wrong is examined (see p. 191).

4. The way in which a positive intrusive thought could be evaluated negatively were it to occur in an inappropriate context is considered, further demonstrating the importance of appraisal of the occurrence and content of thoughts as opposed to the thought itself. For example, the thought of having a really good, relaxing, enjoyable holiday might be relished most of the time, but not at the moment that the person begins see his best friend's coffin lowered into the grave.

5. Discussing who it is who would experience particular types of intrusive thoughts and what that means about that person. What would happen if a Satanist had the thought 'God is bad'?

6. Identifying the link between problem-solving/creativity and the occurrence of intrusive thoughts, whether they be positive, negative, or neutral. This latter strategy would also involve identifying the usefulness of having negative intrusive thoughts in unusual situations (e.g., thoughts of being violent when one is physically attacked in a dark alleyway).

7. The patient is asked to consider what it would be like if no intrusive thoughts were ever to occur. How would it be if you had to decide on the next

thing you were going to think before you thought it? What kind of thoughts would you have? Would it be at all boring?

By the end of this phase, the patient should have been helped to see that intrusive thoughts are not merely normal, but are also a crucial part of daily life. Aspects of these discussions are re-referred to throughout therapy.

Stage 3: reconsidering the problem

The patient is invited to contrast directly the two alternative views of their problem. The differences and similarities are highlighted and the requirement to be able to experience the thoughts without experiencing distress is discussed in detail. It is emphasized that prevention of intrusive thoughts is not only not an option, it is not even slightly desirable. The use of the audiotape procedure and the importance of identifying ideas about responsibility (so they can be modified and any kind of neutralizing behaviour prevented) are explained.

Stage 4: audiotaped exposure and belief modification

A tape loop is used to elicit the patient's intrusion; emphasis is placed on identifying responsibility appraisals and how they link to urges to neutralize identified at this point. Response prevention is initiated with a cognitive rationale, usually by helping the patient to challenge their appraisal of the intrusions. In session, habituation is begun with recording of discomfort and any further difficulties in response prevention identified and dealt with. Homework is set up with charts and full instructions. Belief modification continues during this phase at every opportunity, drawing on the discussion techniques and behavioural experiments, described earlier (pp. 193, 198–200).

The patient is asked what they think of any changes which occur in the course of the exposure sessions and how these fit with each of the two alternative accounts of the problem previously agreed. Subsequent sessions may target different thoughts on the tape. The patient is asked to use the tape regularly in their own home at set times; subsequently, a portable personal stereo is used to allow the tape to be played over in situations where the intrusive thoughts tend to spontaneously occur. Finally, the tape is carried around and used *in response* to the occurrence of actual intrusions wherever they occur.

Stage 5: further behavioural experiments in vivo

The next stage, again using tape, is using the natural occurrence of intrusive thoughts as a cue for the use of the tape. During the latter stages of the tape's sequence, self-directed exposure and response prevention for other thoughts is initiated and recorded. Part of the response prevention recording is picking-up on particular beliefs and modifications of these. Throughout this period, the responsibility and interpretations questionnaire is used to monitor particular beliefs which may need tackling.

The formulation and the patient's beliefs about their thoughts should be very clear at this stage, and guide the further conduct of therapy. Discussion and behavioural experiments should weave together the notion of the alternative explanation ('my problem is worry') and behavioural experiments designed to reinforce this idea. Examples would be imagery or thought restructuring, catastrophizing imagery, or verbal exercises as a demonstration of the way in which these ideas worsen, discomfort, and distress; pie charts which tackle the idea of responsibility; thought experiments in which the person thinks of ways of bringing about the event they fear they may be responsible for; pros and cons of being obsessional and not being obsessional; cumulative probability–downward arrows.

In the treatment of obsessional thinking, the idea is that the factors which previously triggered anxiety and discomfort may continue to occur. However, therapy has the effect of modifying the meaning of intrusive thoughts to the kind of level experienced by almost everybody. No direct attempt is made to decrease the number of intrusive thoughts experienced, and any intention on the part of the patient to bring about such a reduction is challenged on the basis of the beliefs which drive it. However, a fortunate and desirable side-effect of cognitive therapy is that there is usually an actual decrease in intrusions. Note that the 'normal' person does not constantly seek to control thoughts; control tends to be indirect, because there are no serious negative consequences of failing to control symptoms.

Final stage: relapse prevention

Possible future difficulties are identified and a set-back pack compiled by the patient. The patient, throughout therapy, should have been recording a 'what I have learned during therapy'. The questionnaires described earlier (p. 000) are used to identify: (1) any remaining tendency to make responsibility appraisals when intrusive thoughts occur; (2) the extent to which more positive appraisals are now held; and (3) any general assumptions concerning responsibility which may lead to future problems. Discussion and behavioural experiments are again used to help the patient to modify any problems identified. At this stage, the emphasis is placed on the patient's own efforts to bring about such changes, with the therapist playing a minimal monitoring role as far as possible. This helps to maximize the extent to which the patient takes responsibility for their own thoughts and actions.

The effectiveness of treatment

There have been a number of published case reports and case series describing the effectiveness of this type of cognitive behavioural treatment of obsessional thinking (e.g., Headland and Macdonald 1987; Salkovskis 1983; Salkovskis and Westbrook 1989; Roth and Church 1994). More recently, Freeston (1994) reported the results of a controlled trial in which full cognitive behaviour treatment (including both reappraisal strategies and revised habituation training) was compared to a waiting list control condition. Treatment resulted in a substantial reduction in both self-report and assessor-rated obsessional symptoms. It is especially encouraging to note that there treatment effects persisted at the six-monthly follow-up, with no evidence of relapse after the cessation of active psychological treatment. The authors' group is currently comparing cognitive behavioural treatment to both a waiting list control and to a high-credibility stress-management package.

The application of cognitive therapy procedures in obsessive–compulsive disorder has, until recently, been confined to investigations of rational emotive therapy (RET) compared to exposure. Interestingly, Emmelkamp *et al.* (1988) found that RET was as effective as exposure and response prevention. More recently, van Oppen *et al.* (1995) compared cognitive therapy, based on an earlier version of the cognitive theory of OCD (Salkovskis 1985) and on a relatively limited set of cognitive manoeuvres (Salkovskis and Warwick 1988; Salkovskis, 1989*a*), with exposure and response prevention. It was found that cognitive therapy with almost no exposure was at least as effective as exposure and response prevention, and there was some suggestion that, in limited respects, cognitive therapy may be superior to exposure. Although this type of comparison has some theoretical value, in the authors' view the more crucial clinical comparisons involve habituation-based exposure and response prevention compared to cognitively based therapy involving similar amounts of exposure and response prevention. If the cognitive theory is correct, more rapid and complete improvement would be expected with the cognitive behavioural approach.

Future directions

The effectiveness of cognitive therapy has now been established. Current work in the authors' group is underway to investigate the relative effectiveness of exposure and response prevention with a habituation rationale compared to cognitive behavioural treatment (emphasizing not only changing responsibility and threat beliefs but also the explicit development of the cognitive conceptualization as an alternative to the fears held by patients about the meaning of their obsessional thoughts). Both shorter- and longer-term effectiveness of these two approaches need to be evaluated. It is also predicted that both treatment outcome and relapse will be related to the extent to which the appraisal of intrusive thoughts as a sign of inflated responsibility has been modified in the course of treatment. The effectiveness of pharmacotherapy raises interesting questions about the mode of action of drugs such as the selective serotonin re-uptake inhibitors. Given that obsessional problems can be conceptualized as a set of interconnected responses and processes (such as the occurrence of intrusive thoughts, their evaluation, inflated responsibility appraisals, neutralizing), the extent to which treatments affect (or fail to change) the different components will be of great interest in terms of understanding the likely mechanisms of change. This type of information should also suggest ways in which treatments which are partly or transiently effective may be improved. Apart from therapy, further experimental investigations are required concerning the pathways to inflated responsibility, how best to manipulate responsibility in both the short and long term, and specific investigations into ways in which the psychological formulation accounts for what appear to be general deficits, but which the theory suggests are the results of the sufferer trying too hard.

Acknowledgement

The first author is grateful to Elizabeth Forrester, Candida Richards, Sue Thorpe, Charlotte Wilson, and Abigail Wroe who have been involved in the development of the ideas in this Chapter.

References

Abel, J. L. (1993). Exposure with response prevention and serotonergic antidepressants in the treatment of obsessive–compulsive disorder: a review and implications for interdisciplinary treatment. *Behaviour Research and Therapy*, 31, 463–78.

APA (American Psychiatric Association) (1994). *Diagnostic and Statistical Manual of Mental Disorders* (4th edn). APA, Washington, DC.

Beck, A. T. (1976). *Cognitive therapy and the emotional disorders*. International Universities Press, New York.

Christensen, H., Hadzi-Pavlovic, D., Andrews, G., and Mattick, R. (1987). Behavior therapy and tricyclic medication in the treatment of obsessive–compulsive disorder: a quantitative review. *Journal of Consulting and Clinical Psychology*, 55, 701–11.

Clark, D. M., Ball, S., and Pape, D. (1991). An experimental investigation of thought suppression. *Behaviour Research and Therapy*, 29, 253–57.

Clark, D. M., Winton, E., and Thynn, L. (1993). A further experimental investigation of thought suppression. *Behaviour Research and Therapy*, 31, 207–10.

Emmelkamp, P. M. G., Visser, S., and Hoekstra, R. J. (1988). Cognitive therapy vs exposure *in vivo* in the treatment of obsessive–compulsives. *Cognitive Therapy and Research*, 12, 103–14.

Foa, E. B., and Goldstein, A. (1978). Continuous exposure and strict response prevention in the treatment of obsessive–compulsive neurosis. *Behaviour Therapy*, 9, 821–29.

Foa, E. B., Steketee, G., Grayson, J. B., and Doppelt, H. G. (1983). Treatment of Obsessive–compulsives: when do we fail? In *Failures in behaviour therapy* (ed. E. B. Foa and P. M. G. Emmelkamp), New York, Wiley.

Freeston, M. H., and Ladouceur, R. (1993). Appraisal of cognitive intrusions and response style: replication and extension. *Behaviour Research and Therapy*, 31, 185–91.

Freeston, M. H., Ladouceur, R., Gagnon, F., and Thibodeau, N. (1991). Cognitive intrusions in a non-clinical population. I. Response style, subjective experience and appraisal. *Behaviour Research and Therapy*, 29, 285–97.

Freeston, M. (1994). Characteristiques et traitement de l'obsession sans compulsion manifeste. Unpublished thesis. Université Laval, Québec.

Goodman, W. K., McDougle, C. J., and Price, L. H. (1992). The role of serotonin and dopamine in the pathophysiology of obsessive–compulsive disorder. *International Clinical Psychopharmacology*, 7 35–8.

Headland, K. and McDonald, R. (1987). Rapid audio-tape treatment of obsessional ruminations: a case report. *Behavioural Psychotherapy*, 15, 188–92.

Insel, T. R. (1992). Neurobiology of obsessive–compulsive disorder: a review. *International Clinical Psychopharmacology*, 7, 31–4.

Kirk, J. (1983). Behavioural treatment of obsessional–compulsive patients in routine clinical practice. *Behaviour Research and Therapy*, 21, 57–62.

Kasvikis, Y. and Marks, I. M. (1988). Clomipramine, self-exposure, and therapist-accompanied exposure in obsessive–compulsive ritualizers: two year follow-up. *Journal of Anxiety Disorders*, 2, 291–8.

Lavy, E. and van den Hout, M. (1990). Thought suppression induces intrusions. *Behavioural Psychotherapy*, 18, 251–8.

Maki, W. S., O'Neill, H. K., and O'Neill, G. W. (1994). Do nonclinical checkers exhibit deficits in cognitive control? *Behaviour Research and Therapy*, 32, 183–92.

Marks, I. M. (1981). *Cure and care of neurosis*. Wiley, New York.

Marks, I. M., Lelliott, P., Basoglu, M., and Noshirvani, H. (1988). Clomipramine, self-exposure and therapist aided exposure for obsessive–compulsive rituals. *British Journal of Psychiatry*, 152, 522–34.

Marks, I. M., Stern, R. S., Mawson, D., Cobb, J., and McDonald, R. (1980). Clomipramine and exposure for obsessive rituals: I. *British Journal of Psychiatry*, 136, 1–25.

Merckelbach, H., Muris, P., van den Hout, M. A., and de Jong, P. (1991). Rebound effects of thought suppression: instruction-dependent. *Behavioural Psychotherapy*, 19, 225–38.

Meyer, V. (1966). Modification of expectations in cases with obsessional rituals. *Behaviour Research and Therapy*, 4, 273–80.

Mowrer, O. H. (1947). On the dual nature of learning—a reinterpretation of "conditioning" and "problem solving". *Harvard Educational Review*, 17, 102–48.

Mowrer, O. H. (1960). *Learning theory and behaviour*. New York, Wiley.

Metzner, R. (1963). Some experimental analogues of obsession. *Behaviour Research and Therapy*, 1, 231–6.

Nisbett, R. E., and Ross, L. (1980). *Human inference: strategies and shortcomings of social judgement*. Prentice Hall, Englewood Cliffs.

Parkinson, L. and Rachman, S. J. (1980). Are intrusive thoughts subject to habituation? *Behaviour Research and Therapy*, **18**, 409–18.

Purdon, C. and Clark, D. A. (1994). Obsessive intrusive thoughts in non-clinical subjects: II. Cognitive appraisal, emotional response and thought-control strategies. *Behaviour Research and Therapy*, **32**, 403–10.

Rachman, S. J. (1976). The modification of obsessions; a new formulation. *Behaviour Research and Therapy*, **14**, 437–43.

Rachman, S. J. and de Silva, P. (1978). Abnormal and normal obsessions. *Behaviour Research and Therapy*, **16**, 233–38.

Rachman, S. J. (1993). Obsessions, responsibility and guilt. *Behaviour Research and Therapy*, **31**, 149–54.

Rachman, S. J., de Silva, P., and Roper, G. (1976). The spontaneous decay of compulsive urges. *Behaviour Research and Therapy*, **14**, 445–53.

Rachman, S. J. and Hodgson, R. (1980). *Obsessions and compulsions*. Prentice Hall, Englewood Cliffs, NJ.

Rachman, S. J., Hodgson, R., and Marks, I. M. (1971). The treatment of chronic obsessional neurosis. *Behaviour Research and Therapy*, **9**, 237–47.

Reed, G. F. (1985). *Obsessional experience and compulsive behaviour*. Academic Press, London.

Riggs, D. and Foa, E. B. (1993). Obsessive–compulsive disorders. In *Clinical handbook of psychological disorders* (ed. D. H. Barlow). Guilford, New York.

Robins, L. N., Helzer, J. E., *et al.* (1984). Lifetime prevalence of specific disorders in three sites. *Archives of General Psychiatry*, **41**, 949–58.

Roper, G. and Rachman, S. J. (1975). Obsessional–compulsive checking: replication and development. *Behaviour Research and Therapy*, **13**, 25–32.

Roper, G., Rachman, S. J., and Hodgson, R. (1973). An experiment on obsessional checking. *Behaviour Research and Therapy*, **11**, 271–77.

Roth, A. D., and Church, J. A. (1994). The use of revised habituation in the treatment of obsessive–compulsive disorders. *British Journal of Clinical Psychology*, **33**, 201–4.

Salkovskis, P. M. (1983). Treatment of an obsessional patient using habituation to audiotaped ruminations. *British Journal of Clinical Psychology*, **22**, 311–13.

Salkovskis, P. M. (1985). Obsessional-compulsive problems: a cognitive–behavioural analysis. *Behaviour Research and Therapy*, **25**, 571–83.

Salkovskis, P. M. (1989c). Cognitive-behavioural factors and the persistence of intrusive thoughts in obsessional problems. *Behaviour Research and Therapy*, **27**, 677–82.

Salkovskis, P. M. (1989a). Obsessions and compulsions. In *Cognitive therapy: a clinical casebook* (ed. J. Scott, J. M. G. Williams, and A. T. Beck). Croom Helm, London.

Salkovskis, P. M. (1989b). Obsessions and intrusive thoughts: clinical and non-clinical aspects. In *Anxiety disorders: Annual series of European research in behaviour therapy*, vol. 4 (ed. P. Emmelkamp, W. Everaerd, F. Kraaymaat, and M. van Son). Swets, Amsterdam.

Salkovskis, P. M. (1991). The importance of behaviour in the maintenance of anxiety and panic: a cognitive account. *Behavioural Psychotherapy*, **19**, 6–19.

Salkovskis, P. M. (1996a). The cognitive approach to anxiety: threat beliefs, safety seeking behaviour and the special case of health anxiety and obsessions. In *Frontiers of cognitive therapy: the state of the art and beyond* (ed. P. M. Salkovskis). Guilford Press, New York.

Salkovskis, P. M. (1996b). Avoidance behaviour is motivated by threat beliefs: a possible resolution of the cognition-behaviour debate. In *Trends in cognitive and behavioural therapy*, Vol. 1 (ed. P. M. Salkovskis). Wiley, Chichester.

Salkovskis, P. M. (1996c). Cognitive-behavioural approaches to the understanding of obsessional problems. In *Current controversies in the anxiety disorders* (ed. R. Rapee). Guilford Press, New York.

Salkovskis, P. M. and Campbell, P. (1994). Thought suppression in naturally occurring negative intrusive thoughts. *Behaviour Research and Therapy*, 32, 1–8.

Salkovskis, P. M. and Harrison, J. (1984). Abnormal and normal obsessions: a replication. *Behaviour Research and Therapy*, 22 549–52.

Salkovskis, P. M. and Kirk, J. (1989). Obsessional disorders. In *Cognitive-behavioural treatment for psychiatric disorders: a practical guide* (ed. K. Hawton, P. M. Salkovskis, J. Kirk and D. M. Clark). Oxford University Press.

Salkovskis, P. M. and Warwick, H. M. C. (1985). Cognitive therapy of obsessive–compulsive disorder—treating treatment failures. *Behavioural Psychotherapy*, 13, 243–55.

Salkovskis, P. M. and Warwick, H. M. C. (1988). Cognitive therapy of obsessive–compulsive disorder. In *The theory and practice of cognitive therapy* (ed. C. Perris, I. M. Blackburn and H. Perris). Springer, Heidelberg.

Salkovskis, P. M. and Westbrook, D. (1989). Behaviour therapy and obsessional ruminations: can failure be turned into success? *Behaviour Research and Therapy*, 27, 149–60.

Salkovskis, P. M., Rachman, S. J., Ladouceur, R., and Freeston, M. (1992). *Proceedings of the Toronto Cafeteria*.

Sher, K. J., Frost, R. O., Kushner, M., Crews, T. M., and Alexander, J. E. (1989). Memory deficits in compulsive checkers: replication and extension in a clinical sample. *Behaviour Research and Therapy*, 27, 65–9.

Solomon, R. L. and Wynne, L. C. (1960). Traumatic avoidance learning: the principles of anxiety conservation and partial irreversibility. *Psychological Review*, 61, 353–85.

Steketee, G. and Foa, E. B. (1985). In *Clinical handbook of psychological disorders: a step by step treatment manual* (ed. D. H. Barlow), (1st edn). Guilford Press, New York.

Teasdale, J. D. (1983). Negative thinking in depression: Cause, effect or reciprocal relationship? *Advances in Behaviour Research and Therapy*, 5, 3–25.

Trinder, H. and Salkovskis, P. M. (1994). Personally relevant intrusions outside the laboratory: long term suppression increases intrusion. *Behaviour Research and Therapy*, 32, 833–42.

van Oppen, P., de Haan, E., van Balkom, A. J., Spinhoven, P., Hoogduin, K., and van Dyck, R. (1995). Cognitive therapy and exposure in vivo in the treatment of obsessive–compulsive disorder *Behaviour Research and Therapy*, 33, 379–90.

Wegner, D. M. (1989). *White bears and other unwanted thoughts: suppression, obsession and the psychology of mental control*. Viking, New York.

9

Eating disorders

Christopher G. Fairburn

This chapter is dedicated to Michael Gelder. In his 27 years as Head of the Department of Psychiatry at Oxford he developed a broad-based department of international repute. Not surprisingly, his particular research interests flourished (as this book testifies), but it is to his great credit that he also fostered research in other areas, eating disorders being just one example. Without his encouragement and thoughtful input, the Oxford programme of research on eating disorders would never have started, let alone thrived. I am extremely grateful to Michael for his unfailing support over the years. The rigour with which he addressed clinical and research problems will always be an inspiration.

In 1981 the first report was published concerning the use of cognitive behaviour therapy to treat eating disorders (Fairburn, 1981). It described the promising effects of a cognitive behavioural treatment for bulimia nervosa, a disorder which had previously been regarded as 'intractable' (Russell, 1979). Since then, this specific form of cognitive behaviour therapy has been the subject of much research, the results of which show that it is the most effective treatment for the disorder. Today, bulimia nervosa is one of the strongest indications for cognitive behaviour therapy. Cognitive behavioural treatments have also been devised for anorexia nervosa and 'binge eating disorder'.

The aim of this chapter is to review the scientific standing and practice of cognitive behaviour therapy as applied to eating disorders. It has several sections. The first describes the rationale for this use of cognitive behaviour therapy. The second is concerned with its effectiveness. In the third, the treatments themselves are described. Finally, the utility of the cognitive behavioural approach is considered. The main emphasis is on the cognitive behavioural treatment of bulimia nervosa since it is this application of cognitive behaviour therapy that is supported by most research.

Rationale for using cognitive behaviour therapy to treat eating disorders

The maintenance of anorexia nervosa and bulimia nervosa

Cognitive distortions are a prominent feature of anorexia nervosa and bulimia nervosa. Indeed, they have long been regarded as their 'core psychopathology'. In the 1970s, the psychotherapist Bruch (1973) wrote of the 'relentless pursuit of thinness' of patients with anorexia nervosa, and Russell (1979), in the original report on bulimia nervosa, described their 'morbid fear of becoming fat'. The cognitive distortions concerning shape and weight are pathognomonic of these two disorders and their variants; indeed, their presence is required to make either diagnosis (see Table 9.1). It can be argued that anorexia nervosa and bulimia nervosa are essentially cognitive disorders.

TABLE 9.1. DSM–IV diagnostic criteria for anorexia nervosa and bulimia nervosa (italics added by the author)

Anorexia nervosa
A. Refusal to maintain body weight at or above a minimally normal weight for age and height (e.g., weight loss leading to maintenance of body weight less than 85% of that expected; or failure to make expected weight gain during period of growth, leading to body weight less than 85% of that expected).
B. *Intense fear of gaining weight or becoming fat, even though underweight.*
C. *Disturbance in the way in which one's body weight or shape is experienced, undue influence of body weight or shape on self-evaluation, or denial of the seriousness of the current low body weight.*
D. In post-menarchal females, amenorrhoea, i.e., the absence of at least three consecutive menstrual cycles. (A woman is considered to have amenorrhoea if her periods occur only following hormone e.g., oestrogen, administration.)

Bulimia nervosa
A. Recurrent episodes of binge eating. An episode of binge eating is characterized by both of the following:
    (1) eating, in a discrete period of time (e.g., within any 2-hour period), an amount of food that is definitely larger than most people would eat during a similar period of time and under similar circumstances;
    (2) a sense of lack of control over eating during the episode (e.g., a feeling that one cannot stop eating or control what or how much one is eating).
B. Recurrent inappropriate compensatory behaviour in order to prevent weight gain, such as self-induced vomiting; misuse of laxatives, diuretics, enemas, or other medications; fasting; or excessive exercise.
C. The binge eating and inappropriate compensatory behaviours both occur, on average, at least twice a week for three months.
D. *Self-evaluation is unduly influenced by body shape and weight.*
E. The disturbance does not occur exclusively during episodes of anorexia nervosa.

(From APA 1994, with permission.)

The central cognitive disturbance in anorexia nervosa and bulimia nervosa is a characteristic set of attitudes and values concerning body shape and weight. Thinness and weight loss are idealized and sought after, and there are strenuous attempts to avoid weight gain and 'fatness'. At the heart of this psychopathology is the tendency to judge self-worth largely or even exclusively in terms of shape and weight. Whereas it is usual to judge one's self-worth on the basis of one's performance in a variety of domains (e.g., the quality of one's relationships; one's performance at work; one's abilities at sport and other pastimes), people with anorexia nervosa or bulimia nervosa evaluate themselves primarily in terms of their shape and weight. In cognitive terminology, they have characteristic 'weight-related self-schemata' (Vitousek and Hollon 1990).

Many of these patients have a second core cognitive characteristic, namely long-standing negative self-evaluation (a 'general self-schema' (Vitousek and Hollon 1990)). While the great majority have significant depressive symptoms at presentation, including negative self-evaluation, only in some is it a long-standing trait. In such patients insecurity about their performance in a variety of domains leads them to evaluate themselves largely in terms of their shape and weight. In part this is because appearance, and more especially weight, seem more controllable than many other aspects of life, and in part because dieting and weight loss are socially reinforced. These patients hope that they will feel better about themselves if they are thinner. However, their fundamentally negative view of themselves leads them to be perpetually dissatisfied with their appearance and weight with the result that they show a particularly intransigent pursuit of thinness and weight loss.

The cognitive behavioural treatment of anorexia nervosa and bulimia nervosa is based on a cognitive view of their maintenance (Fairburn 1985; Fairburn et al. 1986; Garner and Bemis 1985)—see Fig. 9.1. According to this view, the characteristic concerns about shape and weight are a central feature, since most other features can be understood as being secondary to them. The dieting and resultant weight loss are obvious secondary features, as is the preoccupation with thoughts about food, eating, shape, and weight. The same applies to the self-induced vomiting, overexercising, and laxative misuse.

Binge eating is the only component of the characteristic psychopathology that cannot easily be seen as a direct expression of the concerns about shape and weight. It is present in all patients with bulimia nervosa (by definition) and a subgroup of those with anorexia nervosa. It is likely to be the result of these patients' particular type of dieting. Patients with anorexia nervosa or bulimia nervosa severely restrict their food intake and are therefore under continuous physiological pressure to eat, but it is the form of their dieting that makes them particularly prone to binge eat. Rather than having general guidelines about how they should eat, they impose on themselves multiple

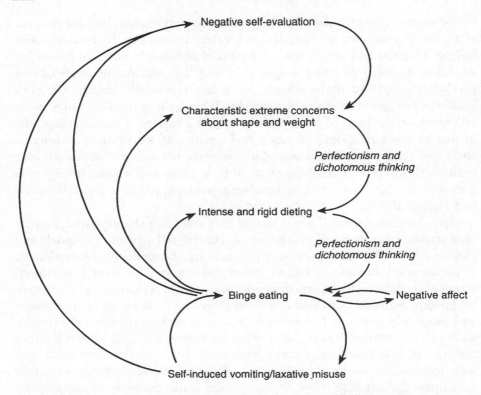

FIG. 9.1. The cognitive view of the maintenance of bulimia nervosa.

specific dietary rules. These rules concern *when* they should eat (or rather when they must not eat; e.g., not before six in the evening), exactly *what* they should eat (or rather, what they must not eat; thus most patients have a large list of 'forbidden foods'), and the overall *amount* of food they should eat (e.g., less than 1000 kcal daily). Most attempt to follow many such rules and as a result their eating is stereotyped and inflexible.

The intensity and rigidity of the dieting seen in anorexia nervosa and bulimia nervosa can be understood as an expression of the combined influence of two additional general cognitive characteristics, perfectionism and dichotomous thinking (thinking in black and white terms). Patients with eating disorders tend to be perfectionist by nature. They set themselves extremely high standards and are profoundly dissatisfied when they do not meet them. This perfectionism is seen in many aspects of their lives, and it is applied to their dieting thereby accounting for its intensity. Their dichotomous style of thinking is also imposed on their dieting. It accounts for the presence of dietary rules rather than guidelines and, in conjunction with the perfectionism, it also accounts for their response to the breaking of these rules. Even after minor dietary transgressions, these patients view themselves as having 'broken' their diet, and they respond by temporarily abandoning their attempts to restrict their food intake since they regard anything other than perfect control as being virtually worthless. Such dietary lapses are inevitable, however, given the large number of strict rules that they are attempting to follow. The result is a brittle pattern of eating in which attempts to restrict food intake are interrupted by repeated episodes of overeating.

The dietary lapses that tend to precipitate binges are particularly likely to occur at times of negative affect. All types of negative affect seem to undermine these patients' ability to maintain strict control over their eating. Conversely, binge eating tends to moderate negative affect. This is due to several processes, including the sense of release that accompanies starting to binge, the positive connotations of eating certain foods, the drowsiness that follows eating large quantities of carbohydrate, and in those who vomit, the release of tension that follows self-induced vomiting. Of course, these effects are short-lived and are gradually replaced by mounting regret and self-disgust and heightened fears of weight gain and fatness. By the time the binge has finished the patients are determined to redouble their efforts to diet, thereby establishing a vicious circle. (See Polivy and Herman 1993, for a detailed account of the psychological processes associated with binge eating.)

A second vicious circle links the binge eating and compensatory 'purging' (the American term for self-induced vomiting and the misuse of laxatives or diuretics). Since these patients (mistakenly) view these forms of behaviour as effective means of compensating for overeating, once they have been adopted a barrier to overeating is removed. In the case of self-induced vomiting this process is further encouraged by the fact that it is easier to vomit if the stomach is full. As shown in Fig. 9.1, once this vicious circle is established, the loss of control over purging becomes an additional source of self-condemnation.

In patients with anorexia nervosa, certain of the psychological and physiological effects of starvation (see Garner et al. 1996) also serve to maintain the eating disorder. For example, the ritualistic eating slows down the act of eating and encourages inflexibility; the reduction in gastric motility results in a sense of fullness, even after eating modest amounts of food; the preoccupation with thoughts about food and eating exaggerates concerns about eating; the lowering of mood intensifies the negative self-evaluation and thereby the dependence on shape and weight to judge self-worth; and the social withdrawal magnifies self-preoccupation and the focus on shape and weight. Thus, two sets of processes maintain the eating disorder, the core cognitive psychopathology, as in bulimia nervosa, and the effects of starvation.

There is also a third maintaining factor in anorexia nervosa, namely the fact that many of these patients do not view themselves as having a problem. As Vitousek and Orimoto (1993) put it: 'Individuals with anorexia nervosa do not regard their disorder as an affliction but as an accomplishment.' Whereas most patients with bulimia nervosa find their binge eating aversive and are therefore keen to receive help, there is little about the anorectic state that is 'egodystonic'. This is because these patients' behaviour (dieting and other weight loss behaviour) and its effects (weight loss and increasing thinness) are entirely consonant with their goals (the pursuit of weight loss and thinness; the avoidance of weight gain and fatness) with the result that they see little need to change, and when they do present for treatment they often do so reluctantly.

Implications for treatment

The cognitive account of the maintenance of anorexia nervosa and bulimia nervosa has important implications for treatment. The main implication is that, for there to be lasting change, treatment must not only result in the normalization of eating habits and weight but it must also address the concerns about shape and weight since these concerns drive the disturbed eating. The account also suggests that treatment must rectify negative self-evaluation. In many patients this happens by default merely as a result of regaining control over eating, but this is not true of those with long-standing negative self-evaluation.

Evidence for the cognitive view on maintenance

There is a sizeable body of research that indirectly supports this cognitive view on the maintenance of anorexia nervosa and bulimia nervosa. This includes controlled descriptive studies of the cognitive characteristics of these patients (see Mizes and Christiano 1995), and the research on dietary restraint and 'counter-regulation' (a possible analogue of binge eating)—see Polivy and Herman (1993). However, it is the research on the effects of treatment that provides the strongest support for the cognitive view.

Treatment studies, if properly designed, provide an excellent opportunity to test theories about the maintenance of disorders. Thus, the strongest evidence in support of the cognitive account comes from the research on the treatment of bulimia nervosa. Indirect support is provided by the large body of research indicating that cognitive behaviour therapy has a major and lasting impact on the disorder (see below). Further support comes from the finding that 'dismantling' the treatment by removing those procedures designed to produce cognitive change attenuates its effects and results in patients being markedly prone to relapse (Fairburn et al. 1993a). The most direct support comes from the finding that, among patients who had recovered in behavioural terms, the severity of concerns about shape and weight at the end of treatment was directly related to the likelihood of relapse: 9% of the patients with the least concern about shape and weight relapsed, compared with 29% of those with a moderate level of concern, and 75% of those with the greatest level of concern (Fairburn *et al.* 1993*b*). This important finding needs to be replicated. It is also of note that some (but not all) studies have found that the level of self-esteem at presentation predicts response to treatment with those patients with the lowest self-esteem doing least well (Fairburn *et al.* 1987, 1993*b*). This finding provides some support for the view that negative self-evaluation, when not simply a secondary depressive symptom, ought also to be a target of treatment.

The maintenance of binge eating disorder

Binge eating disorder is a recently described eating disorder characterized by recurrent binges in the absence of the extreme weight-control behaviour that characterizes anorexia nervosa and bulimia nervosa (namely, self-induced vomiting, the misuse of laxatives or diuretics, overexercising, and intense dieting) (Fairburn and Walsh 1995). As yet, relatively little is known about its psychopathology and treatment. Most patients with binge eating disorder are concerned about their shape and weight (and many are significantly overweight) but their concerns generally do not have the same intensity and personal significance as those of patients with anorexia nervosa or bulimia nervosa, and in those who are overweight they are more understandable. Unlike patients with anorexia nervosa or bulimia nervosa whose binge eating occurs against a background of extreme dieting, patients with binge eating disorder eat relatively normally outside their binges—indeed, if there is an abnormality, it is a tendency to overeat rather than undereat. Their binge eating seems to be more a habitual response to negative affect than a breakdown of rigid dietary restraint. The cognitive account of the maintenance of anorexia nervosa and bulimia nervosa appears to have limited relevance to binge eating disorder.

The effectiveness of the cognitive behavioural approach

Bulimia nervosa

The cognitive behavioural approach to the treatment of bulimia nervosa is well established and widely accepted. It was developed by the author in the 1970s in response to the emergence of this seemingly new eating disorder. Two of its features seemed of particular relevance to treatment. First, there were cognitive distortions similar to those found in anorexia nervosa. Often, the form of the eating disorder had altered over the years (with about a third of the patients having previously had anorexia nervosa) but the extreme concerns about shape and weight had persisted largely unchanged. Since these concerns appeared to be driving the disorder (as described above), one major goal of treatment had to be to moderate them. The cognitive techniques developed by Beck and colleagues (Beck *et al.* 1979) appeared well suited for this purpose. The second feature was the profound loss of control over eating. Certain of the behavioural techniques developed for the treatment of obesity (Mahoney and Mahoney 1976) seemed relevant in this regard. The preliminary versions of the new treatment were essentially an amalgam of these two approaches. However, subsequent clinical experimentation showed that other procedures were needed and that the order in which they were applied was also important. By 1979, a relatively standard treatment had been developed.

The results of a case series were published in 1981 (Fairburn 1981) and a detailed manual was published in 1985 (Fairburn 1985). The treatment has subsequently been modified in various ways but it is essentially the same treatment as that developed in the 1970s. Other research groups have developed their own versions of the treatment, but with multicentre trials necessitating the adoption of a standard approach, most investigators have adopted the latest version of the Oxford manual (Fairburn *et al.* 1993c) as the method of choice.

The treatment has been the subject of much research with over 20 controlled trials having been completed. The findings have been reviewed by Fairburn *et al.* (1992), Mitchell *et al.* (1993) and, most recently, by Wilson and Fairburn (in press). Three main findings have emerged.

1. *Cognitive behaviour therapy has a major beneficial effect on all aspects of the psychopathology of bulimia nervosa.* There is a marked reduction in the frequency of binge eating and associated purging, a decrease in dietary restraint and reduction in the intensity of the concerns about shape and weight. Associated with these changes is a decrease in the level of general psychiatric symptoms and an improvement in self-esteem and social functioning. 'Abstinence' or 'remission' rates are often quoted for binge eating and purging. These refer to the proportion of patients who are not engaging in the behaviour concerned. Craighead and Agras (1991) pooled the results of 10 controlled studies and obtained a mean reduction in the frequency of purging of 79%, with 57% of the patients being abstinent. Wilson (1996a) obtained similar figures for eight subsequent studies (86% and 55%, respectively).

Although of interest, abstinent rates should be interpreted with caution since many patients have an excellent outcome despite not being fully abstinent. Outcome needs to be considered in various ways (e.g., raw frequencies of key behaviours, their percentage change from recruitment levels, abstinence rates) using a variety of indices (e.g., dietary restraint, concerns about shape and weight, actual weight, general psychiatric symptoms, self-esteem and quality of social adjustment), rather than focusing exclusively on binge eating and purging.

2. *The changes obtained with cognitive behaviour therapy appear to be well maintained.* Although there is a definite need for further studies on the medium to long-term outcome following cognitive behaviour therapy, the available data suggest that the changes are robust. Between a half and two-thirds have an excellent outcome which is well maintained over the following 6 to 12 months. The one study of longer-term outcome [mean ($\pm$SD) length of follow-up = 5.8 $\pm$ 2.0 years] found that two-thirds (63%) had no eating disorder, the great majority of whom were functioning extremely well (Fairburn *et al.* 1995). This is an impressive outcome given the brevity of the cognitive behavioural treatment (19 sessions over 18 weeks), the fact that only 37% of the patients had received any further psychiatric treatment (for any problem) over the intervening period, and the chronicity of the eating disorder at presentation (the mean duration at presentation was almost seven years).

3. *Cognitive behaviour therapy has been found to be superior to all, bar one, of the treatments with which it has been compared.* Cognitive behaviour therapy has been compared with treatment with antidepressant drugs (and with antidepressant drugs and cognitive behaviour therapy combined), behavioural versions of cognitive behaviour therapy, exposure with response prevention, supportive expressive psychotherapy and interpersonal psychotherapy (IPT). With the exception of IPT, it has been found to be superior to all these treatments. Antidepressant drugs are the leading alternative, but they are less readily accepted by these patients and relapse commonly follows. Combining cognitive behaviour therapy and antidepressant drugs conveys no clear benefit (see Wilson (1996a)).

Interpersonal psychotherapy (IPT) is the one treatment that appears to be as effective as cognitive behaviour therapy. It is a short-term focal psychotherapy designed by Klerman and colleagues as a treatment for depression (Klerman *et al.* 1984). The adaptation devised for the treatment of bulimia nervosa pays little attention to the eating disorder *per se*; rather, it focuses on the identification and modification of current interpersonal problems (Fairburn 1993; Fairburn 1996). The one trial to have investigated its effects found that at the end of treatment it was less effective than cognitive behaviour therapy (Fairburn *et al.* 1991) but during follow-up the difference between the two treatments disappeared due to continuing improvement among the patients who received IPT (Fairburn *et al.* 1993a, 1995). At 12-month follow-up the proportion of patients who met strict criteria for a good outcome was equivalent (see Fig. 9.2) and a fine-grain analysis of the effects of the two treatments showed them to be equivalent. However, it should not be concluded that cognitive behaviour therapy and IPT operate in the same way given the temporal differences in their pattern of response. Rather, it seems that there is more than one way of influencing the processes involved in the maintenance of bulimia nervosa.

Clinical experience suggests that IPT operates by improving interpersonal functioning and thereby self-evaluation. This results in a moderation of these patients' dependence on shape and weight to evaluate their self-worth. As a result weight control becomes of less importance to them, they diet less intensely, and the eating disorder gradually erodes. If this is its mode of action, it is not surprising that IPT takes longer to act than cognitive behaviour therapy, since it requires interpersonal change (which generally involves others changing too) and since it has a less direct effect on the eating disorder. On the other hand, this is not likely to be its only mode of operation (Fairburn 1996); for example, any reduction in the frequency and severity of interpersonal stressors might be expected to lead directly to a decrease in the frequency of binge eating.

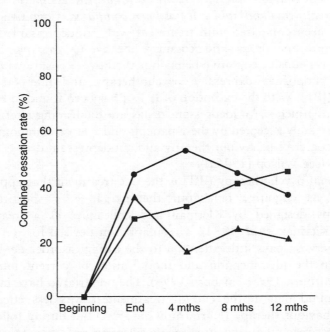

FIG. 9.2. Proportions of patients who received cognitive behaviour therapy (CBT) (●), behaviour therapy (BT) (▲), or interpersonal psychotherapy (IPT) (■) who were in complete remission. (From Fairburn *et al.* 1993*a*, with permission).

Before IPT can be accepted as an established alternative to cognitive behaviour therapy its effects need to be evaluated in further controlled trials. For the present, cognitive behaviour therapy must be regarded as the leading treatment for bulimia nervosa.

Anorexia nervosa

The value of cognitive behaviour therapy in the treatment of anorexia nervosa remains to be established. There is no agreed procedure and there has been just one treatment trial (Channon *et al.* 1989). Unfortunately, the findings from this trial are difficult to interpret in view of the small number of patients studied, the use of a weak assessment protocol, and concerns about the treatment itself (Pike *et al.* 1996).

There are several reasons why the cognitive behavioural treatment of anorexia nervosa has been relatively neglected. First, anorexia nervosa is much more difficult to study than bulimia nervosa since it is considerably less common and treatment takes much longer. Second, as will be discussed later, many of these patients are difficult to engage in treatment and entering them into a treatment trial is even more problematic. Third, nothing approaching a treatment manual is available, whereas in the case of bulimia nervosa a detailed manual was in circulation by the early 1980s. Nevertheless, it is lamentable that so few investigators have risen to this challenge given the strong rationale for using the approach.

Other eating disorders

It often gets forgotten that more than a third of those who present for the treatment of an eating disorder have neither anorexia nervosa or bulimia nervosa (Fairburn and Walsh 1995). Instead, they have an 'atypical eating disorder' or an 'eating disorder not otherwise specified'. These eating disorders have been poorly characterized and their treatment has not been studied. The one exception is binge eating disorder which has been the focus of several preliminary studies.

Investigators have shown most interest in testing those approaches that have been shown to benefit patients with bulimia nervosa. Thus, anti-depressant drugs, cognitive behaviour therapy and IPT have all been evaluated. As in the treatment of bulimia nervosa, relapse appears to be problem with the use of antidepressant drugs (McCann and Agras 1990). The outcome with cognitive behaviour therapy and IPT also seems disappointing, possibly because the treatment has been administered in a group rather than individual format (Telch *et al.* 1990; Wilfley *et al.* 1993). Much better results are being reported from a study from Pittsburgh in which cognitive behaviour therapy and a behavioural weight control programme were compared, both treatments being administered on a one-to-one basis (Marcus *et al.* 1995). Substantial and sustained changes were obtained with both interventions and in the case of the behavioural weight control programme there was also significant weight loss. If this finding is confirmed, it would indicate that dietary/behavioural techniques alone may be sufficient when treating binge eating disorder, whereas their use is associated with relapse in bulimia nervosa (Fairburn *et al.* 1993*a*). It is also of note that preliminary data from a trial evaluating a self-help treatment for binge eating problems (Fairburn 1995) suggest that a simple intervention of this type may also benefit many patients with binge eating disorder (Carter and Fairburn in prep.). Taken together, these findings reinforce the doubts already expressed about the relevance to binge eating disorder of the cognitive account of the maintenance of anorexia nervosa and bulimia nervosa.

The cognitive behavioural treatment of bulimia nervosa

The treatment derives from the cognitive account of the maintenance of bulimia nervosa and the primary goal is therefore to modify not just these patients' disturbed eating habits but also their extreme concerns about shape and weight. In addition, the treatment addresses general cognitive distortions including perfectionism, dichotomous thinking and, when relevant, negative self-evaluation. The treatment is out-patient-based and generally involves about 20 sessions over 20 weeks, each session being approximately 50 minutes in length. A recent development has been to complement the treatment sessions with the reading of a cognitive behavioural self-help book such as *Overcoming binge eating* (Fairburn 1995) or *Bulimia nervosa and binge eating* (Cooper, 1995). These books are designed to provide an accessible account of our current understanding of binge eating problems (from a cognitive behavioural perspective) together with a self-help manual based on the cognitive behavioural approach to treatment. They have been written in part to be an adjunct to therapist-administered cognitive behaviour therapy.

Three stages in the treatment may be distinguished. In the first, the main emphasis is on presenting the cognitive account of the maintenance of bulimia nervosa since this underpins the entire treatment. In addition, behavioural techniques are used to replace the binge eating with a stable pattern of regular eating. In the second stage, further attempts are made to establish healthy eating habits with particular emphasis on the elimination of dieting. It is at this stage that cognitive procedures are most extensively used, the focus being on the thoughts, beliefs, and values that are maintaining the problem. The final stage is concerned with the maintenance of change following treatment. The treatment is additive, with procedures being added to previous ones rather than being introduced and then withdrawn. Although the precise timing of the introduction of techniques is not critical, the order is important since they are designed to build upon each other.

There follows an outline of the treatment. Readers who would like a more detailed account should refer to the latest version of the cognitive behaviour therapy manual (Fairburn *et al.* 1993) together with a related chapter on its implementation (Wilson *et al.* in press).

Stage one

There are two major aims. The first is to explain the rationale underpinning the treatment, and the second is to replace binge eating with a stable pattern of regular eating.

In the original form of the treatment, the appointments in stage one were twice a week. Subsequent experience suggests that such frequent appointments are generally only needed for those patients whose eating habits are severely disturbed; in particular, those who overeat many times each day. These patients need to be seen more often than once a week, otherwise the gains made following one session tend not to endure until the next. On the other hand, the majority of patients may be managed successfully with weekly sessions.

Explaining the cognitive view of the maintenance of bulimia nervosa
This is done in the first session. The therapist draws out Fig. 9.1 incorporating the patient's own experiences and terms. Once the figure has been fully discussed, the therapist reviews its implications. The major point to be stressed is that there is more to the patient's eating problem than just binge eating. Although most patients present complaining of binge eating (and possibly purging), they need to appreciate that they must make changes in other areas if they are to make a lasting recovery. Tackling binge eating in isolation is likely to produce only temporary gains since the factors that promote binge eating will still be in place. There needs to be a reduction in dietary restraint, otherwise the patients will be prone to binge eat, and for this to be achieved their concerns about body shape and weight (and possibly self-esteem) will also need to be addressed. Thus, the treatment needs to focus on both their behaviour (e.g., the binge eating and purging) and their thoughts and feelings (e.g., their concerns about shape and weight). The therapist explains that the treatment tends to work from the bottom of Fig. 9.1 upwards (see p. 212). The initial focus is on the patient's presenting complaint of binge eating, but later on the emphasis extends to tackling dieting and concerns about shape and weight.

To supplement this account, the therapist may recommend that the patient reads the relevant sections from *Overcoming binge eating* (chapters 4 and 7).

Self-monitoring
In the first session, patients are also asked to start monitoring their eating. The rationale for monitoring should be clearly explained: first, it greatly helps the examination of patients' eating habits and the circumstances under which problems arise; and second, and more importantly, between sessions it helps patients identify, question, and, where appropriate, change their behaviour, thoughts, and feelings. To help patients monitor, they are given detailed instructions describing what is involved together with an example monitoring sheet (see Fig. 9.3). (These are provided in *Overcoming binge eating*). Session 2 and all subsequent sessions open with a review of the monitoring sheets that have been completed since the previous session.

Monitoring body weight
With this form of treatment patients are not weighed by the therapist (except at the initial assessment appointment and perhaps also at the end of treatment). This is in part because in-session weighing can result in sessions becoming dominated by the subject of weight at the expense of other more pertinent issues, and in part because advantages come from having patients weigh themselves between sessions. Instead, early in stage one, patients are asked to start weighing themselves once a week on a morning of their choice. Weighing at weekly intervals is an important part of treatment. Since these patients' eating habits will be changing markedly, and since certain of the behavioural interventions are designed to activate their concerns about shape and weight, it is reasonable that they monitor their weight. Indeed, it is essential for subsequent behavioural experiments. However, in view of their tendency to draw major conclusions on the basis of trivial short-term weight fluctuations, they are advised against making inferences about their weight on the basis of less than four consecutive weekly readings (i.e., they should only draw conclusions on the basis of longer-term trends).

Weekly weighing is a good example of how a simple behavioural instruction, in combination with educational and cognitive interventions, can highlight an underlying psychopathological feature and bring about its change.

Education
An important element of the treatment is the education of patients about their weight and eating since many harbour misconceptions that maintain the eating disorder. For example, most of those who practise self-induced vomiting believe that it is a more effective means of retrieving food than is really the case. The topics that need to be covered are listed in Table 9.2. All the relevant information is provided in *Overcoming binge eating* (chapters 4 and 5). The patient and therapist must review this material in detail and discuss its implications for the patient.

Day . *Wednesday* . . . .   Date . . *April 8* . . . .

Time	Food and drink consumed	Place	*	V/L	Context and comments
8:15	(Weighed myself)				Can't write down my weight — it's gross.
5:50	Glass water	Kitchen			Thirsty after yesterday.
10:10	Diet coke	At work			Determined not to binge today.
11:30	10-20 Graham crackers Water	At work	*		Started by just eating a couple, and then, before I knew what I was doing, I was out of control.
12:05	Water			V	
6:50	Piece of apple pie ½ gallon ice cream 4 slices toast with peanut butter Diet pepsi 6 cupcakes 1 raisin bagel 2 pints ice cream Diet pepsi		* * * * *	V V	Started to eat as soon as I got home. Out of control immediately.
7:50	Two glasses water				Feel very lonely.
9:45	Glass water				Went to bed early.

FIG. 9.3. A typical monitoring sheet. (From Fairburn 1995, with permission.)

Advice regarding eating, vomiting, and the misuse of laxatives and diuretics
This advice is central to the regaining of control over eating. It is introduced gradually over stage one.

1. *The prescription of a pattern of regular eating.* This needs considerable emphasis. Patients are asked to restrict their eating to three planned meals

TABLE 9.2. Topics to be covered when educating the patient

---

1. Body weight and its regulation
    The body mass index and its interpretation
    Calculating the patient's own body mass index
    Natural weight fluctuations and their misinterpretation
    A goal weight range that does not necessitate dieting
    The effects of treatment on weight
2. The physical effects of binge eating, self-induced vomiting, laxatives, and diuretics
    Fluid and electrolyte abnormalities
    Oedema
    Salivary gland enlargement
    Dental damage
    Menstrual irregularities
    Effects on hunger and fullness
3. The ineffectiveness of vomiting, laxatives, and diuretics as means of weight control
    Many patients survive on the residue of their binges
    Vomiting only retrieves a proportion of what has been eaten
    Laxatives have little or no effect on calorie absorption
    Diuretics have no effect on calorie absorption
4. The effects of dieting
    The types of dieting that promote binge eating
    The three types of dieting
    Dietary rules versus dietary guidelines (and dichotomous thinking)

---

each day, plus two or three planned snacks. These meals and snacks must not be followed by vomiting or any other compensatory behaviour, and there should rarely be more than a three-hour interval between them. This pattern of eating should take precedence over other activities; irrespective of their circumstances and appetite, patients should not skip the meals or snacks. Conversely, between the meals and snacks they should do their utmost to refrain from eating. Thus, their days should be structured by this pattern of eating.

The introduction of this eating pattern has the effect of displacing the alternating overeating and dietary restriction that characterizes these patients' eating habits. Obviously, the pattern must be tailored to suit the patient's daily commitments, and usually it needs to be modified to accommodate weekends. If particular days are unpredictable, patients should plan ahead as far as possible and identify a time when they can plan the remainder of the day. Patients whose eating habits are severely disturbed should be asked to introduce this pattern in gradual stages. First, they should concentrate on the part of the day when their eating is least disturbed, which is usually the mornings; then they should gradually extend the pattern until it encompasses the entire day.

Some patients are reluctant to eat meals or snacks since they think that this will result in weight gain. They can be reassured that this rarely occurs since the introduction of this pattern of eating will result in a decrease in their frequency of binge eating with the result that their energy intake will decline. Despite such reassurances, it is common for patients to select meals and snacks that are low in energy. At this stage there need be no objection to this practice since the focus is on establishing a pattern of regular eating rather than on tackling what they eat.

The introduction of this eating pattern may be presented in part as a behavioural experiment designed to demonstrate to patients that they can eat meals and snacks without gaining weight.

2. *The use of alternative behaviour to displace or delay binges.* To help patients adhere to the pattern of regular eating, they are asked to identify activities that are likely to protect them from binge eating. Such activities are used to cope with times when they have an urge to overeat. It is especially important to encourage patients to keep 'one step ahead of the problem'. They should try to predict when difficulties are likely to occur and devise plans for dealing with them, including the use of activities incompatible with binge eating. Typical examples of such activities include telephoning friends or visiting them, taking some form of exercise, and having a bath or shower.

3. *Advice regarding vomiting.* In the great majority of cases vomiting does not need to be addressed since it ceases once the patient has stopped overeating. Nevertheless, it is important to ask patients to select meals and snacks which they are prepared not to vomit. Those patients who have strong urges to vomit after eating are asked to distract themselves for the following hour or so until the urge has passed.

4. *Advice regarding laxatives and diuretics.* Having explained the ineffectiveness of these drugs at preventing food absorption, the therapist asks patients to cease taking them and throw away their supplies. It is surprising how many can do so with no further help. Those who find this advice impossible to follow are given a fixed withdrawal schedule during which the drugs are gradually phased out. A small number of regular users experience a temporary period of weight gain following their discontinuation (lasting one to two weeks) which is the result of rebound fluid retention. It is worth warning patients of this possibility.

Interviewing key friends or relatives
Towards the end of stage one, the therapist should consider arranging one or two joint interviews with the patient and any key friends or relatives. These interviews serve three functions. First, they encourage patients to bring the eating problem into the open, thereby removing the secrecy that typically accompanies and maintains it. 'Coming out' makes it more difficult for

patients to revert to secretive binge eating and purging. Second, having patients describe the treatment to these friends and relatives gives the therapist an opportunity to check that its principles have been fully understood. Third, by educating key friends or relatives, and answering their questions, patients can be helped to provide an environment which will facilitate their own efforts at overcoming the problem.

Stage two

This stage in treatment generally consists of eight weekly appointments. There is continuing emphasis on regular eating, the use of alternative behaviour, and weekly weighing, but in addition the focus broadens to tackle all forms of dieting, concerns about shape and weight, and more general cognitive distortions. The techniques consist of a combination of behavioural and cognitive procedures.

Tackling dieting

A major goal of treatment is to reduce, if not eliminate altogether, the strong tendency of these patients to diet, since (as discussed earlier) their particular form of dieting makes them prone to binge eat. Most patients are afraid that ceasing to diet will result in weight gain. This is rarely the case since much of their energy intake will have come from their binges and they will be much less vulnerable to binge once they have ceased to diet.

In stage one, one form of dieting will have been addressed, the tendency to avoid eating for long periods of time. Early in stage two is the time to address the two other forms, avoiding specific types of food and attempting to maintain a low energy intake. To tackle food avoidance, the first step is to identify the foods being avoided. A good way of doing this is to ask patients to visit a local supermarket and note down all foods that they would be reluctant to eat because of their possible effect on their shape or weight. They should then be asked to rank the avoided foods in order of the degree of reluctance that they would have eating them and then categorize them into four groups of increasing difficulty. Over the following weeks the therapist asks patients to introduce progressively these foods into their diet, starting with the easiest category and gradually moving on to the most difficult. These foods should be eaten as part of their planned meals or snacks and only at times when they feel that they have a reasonable degree of control over eating. At first, the amount of the food eaten is not important, although the eventual goal is that patients should be capable of eating conventional quantities. The systematic introduction of avoided foods should continue until patients are no longer anxious about eating them. Thereafter, patients may choose to eat a narrower diet.

The elimination of the third form of dieting, the restriction of the total amount eaten, is achieved in a similar fashion. By direct questioning and detailed scrutiny of the monitoring sheets, it should be possible to determine whether patients are eating too little. If this is the case, they should be asked to eat more until they are consuming at least 1500 kcals each day, and preferably nearer 1800 kcals.

Patients are asked to relax other controls over eating. For example, patients who are highly calorie-conscious dislike eating foods whose calorie content is uncertain. They may insist on preparing all their own food so that they know its exact composition. Such patients should be encouraged to eat foods whose calorie content is difficult to determine. All patients should practise eating in a wide variety of circumstances (e.g., restaurants, buffets, dinner parties, picnics, etc.) and they should eat as varied a diet as possible.

Enhancing problem-solving skills

Once patients are binge eating on an intermittent rather than regular basis, the therapist and patient together should attempt to identify the precipitants of individual episodes of overeating. Although the immediate antecedents can usually be identified as specific thoughts and affects, these are generally provoked by external problems of an interpersonal nature. Training patients in formal problem-solving enhances their ability to deal with such problems. The procedure used is similar to that developed by Goldfried and Goldfried (1975) (see Table 9.3) and it becomes a component of each subsequent treatment session.

Addressing concerns about shape and weight

To address the extreme concerns about shape and weight, cognitive and behavioural procedures are used in tandem. The cognitive procedures follow the principles devised by Beck and colleagues for the treatment of depression (Beck et al. 1979).

When training patients in cognitive restructuring, the first step is to identify a representative problematic thought (i.e., one that is likely to be contributing to the problematic behaviour). Usually, many such thoughts will have emerged during the course of treatment, in which case a typical example should be chosen. If no suitable thought is available, then it is often possible to elicit one, for example, by asking patients to think exactly what would go through their mind if they got on their weighing scales and discovered that their weight had increased by two pounds. Once a suitable thought has been identified, then it should be examined using the following four steps:

1. *The thought itself should be noted down.* It is most important that it is the actual thought that passed through the patient's mind and not a distillation of it.

TABLE 9.3.   The seven steps of problem-solving

Step 1. The problem should be identified and specified as soon as possible after it has occurred. It may emerge that there are two or more coexisting problems, in which case each should be addressed separately. Rephrasing the problem is often helpful.

Step 2. All ways of dealing with the problem should be considered. The patient should generate as many potential solutions as possible. Some solutions may immediately seem nonsensical or impracticable. Nevertheless, they should be included in the list of possible alternatives. The more solutions that are generated, the more likely a good one will emerge.

Step 3. The likely effectiveness and feasibility of each solution should be considered.

Step 4. One alternative should be chosen. This is often an intuitive process. Sometimes a combination of solutions is best.

Step 5. The steps required to carry out the chosen solution should be defined.

Step 6. The solution should be acted upon.

Step 7. The entire problem-solving process should be evaluated the following day in the light of subsequent events. This is a crucial step since the goal is not simply to resolve the problem in question: rather, it is to become skilled at problem-solving. The patient should therefore review each of the seven steps and consider how the process could have been improved.

(Adapted from Fairburn *et al.* 1993.)

2. *Arguments and evidence to support the thought should be marshalled.* For example, if the patient has gained weight, this fact could be said to support the thought 'I am getting fat' (or more accurately, 'I have gained weight'), although it does not justify the thought that 'I am fat'.

3. *Arguments and evidence which cast doubt on the thought should be identified.* Here it is important to examine what the thought means to the patient. For example, the thought 'I feel fat' may have various different meanings including 'I am overweight' or 'I look overweight', or it may refer to unpleasant affective states which make the patient feel unattractive. The notion of 'feeling fat' should be distinguished from 'being fat', and 'being fat' should be distinguished from being overweight from a health perspective and also from gaining weight. Problematic thoughts are typically pejorative and undermining, and not truly applicable to the situation that provoked them, yet because they tend not to be scrutinized they are believed and acted on. Using the example above, if the patient had gained a few pounds, this cannot be equated with imminent obesity. Using a Socratic style of questioning the therapist should encourage the patient to consider such issues as: 'At what stage does one become "fat"?' 'Can "fatness" be equated with a specific shape or weight (for example, clothes size)?', and if so, 'Am I actually approaching this shape or weight?'

Once the true meaning of the thought in question has been identified (and in many cases this is straightforward), patients should consider what other people would think given the circumstances. Would others conclude they were 'fat' if they had gained a few pounds in weight? Patients should ask themselves whether they are applying one set of standards to themselves while applying another, less rigorous, set to others. They should check that they are not confusing subjective impression (e.g., feeling fat) with objective reality (e.g., being statistically overweight). They should also look out for errors of attribution: for example, could the weight gain be due to premenstrual fluid retention rather than overeating? In addition, it is essential that they check for logical errors in their thinking, by far the most common being dichotomous reasoning.

4. *Patients should reach a reasoned conclusion which should then be used to govern their behaviour*. On the basis of the analysis of the appropriateness of the thought in question, patients should decide what is reasonable to think under the circumstances. They should remind themselves of their reasoned conclusion each time that the problematic thought occurs. At this stage it is not to be expected that they will necessarily 'believe' the reasoned conclusion: instead, it is sufficient that they know that this is the appropriate thing to think and they use it to govern their behaviour.

Having illustrated the four steps of cognitive restructuring using a typical thought and ensured that patients understand them, the therapist asks them to practise the procedure between sessions. The therapist then reviews at each session their attempts at cognitive restructuring. Most patients have a limited repertoire of problematic thoughts triggered by a range of different circumstances. By repeatedly examining these thoughts and the circumstances that trigger them, their potency and 'automatic' character gradually declines.

Underpinning the problematic thoughts are certain characteristic attitudes and assumptions. Typical examples include the view that all the patient's problems will be solved once she reaches her goal weight; that all her difficulties are a result of her eating (or weight) problem; that people who are thin are happy, successful, and content with their appearance; and that people who are overweight are unhappy and unsuccessful. Clearly, such beliefs are extreme forms of widely held views. It is their strength, personal significance, and inflexibility that makes them problematic.

The techniques used to question these problematic attitudes resemble those used with other disorders—see Hawton *et al.* (1989). These attitudes cannot be identified using the approach used to identify problematic thoughts. This is because attitudes do not tend to pass fully articulated through one's mind. They are implicit, unarticulated underlying rules. Indeed, they are so much a part of one's conceptual scheme that it is difficult to step back and analyse them. For this reason they have to be inferred from the patients' behaviour (e.g., the avoidance of weighing) and the nature of their problematic thoughts (e.g., those equating fatness with being a failure) rather than identified directly. When examining problematic attitudes, the principles are similar to those used when addressing problematic thoughts, although most of the work has to take place in treatment sessions.

In tandem with the cognitive restructuring, the therapist employs relevant behavioural techniques. As with dieting, these mostly involve the principle of 'exposure'. For example, some patients actively avoid others seeing their shape and so never wear tight clothes and always undress in private. This avoidance of others seeing their body can extend even to themselves with the result that in extreme cases patients dress and undress in the dark, avoid mirrors, wear shapeless clothes, and bathe or shower wearing a chemise. Treatment of these patients involves helping them seek out opportunities to reveal themselves (e.g., by wearing more revealing clothes, by going to swimming baths and exercise classes). The obverse is also seen with some patients expressing their concerns about their appearance by paying minute attention to possible changes in their shape. Patients who frequently monitor their shape should be helped to limit this behaviour. All patients should be encouraged to inspect other women's bodies to put their own in perspective. Swimming baths and exercise classes are particularly helpful in this regard. Patients should be asked to identify a seemingly attractive woman and then scrutinize her body paying particular attention to the appearance of her stomach, hips, and thighs. Typically they will discover that even attractive women have 'imperfections', be they flesh that is dimpled or areas that wobble.

All these behavioural techniques should be dovetailed with cognitive work. The exposure exercises will almost invariably provoke problematic thoughts which should be examined there and then and reviewed with the therapist at the next treatment session.

Addressing other cognitive distortions

With a minority of patients, progress is limited by the severity of the general cognitive distortions (usually extreme perfectionism and profound low self-esteem). In such cases, the focus of the cognitive work needs to be broadened and treatment may need to be extended (see below).

Stage three

This, the final stage in treatment, consists of three appointments at two-week intervals. The aim is to ensure that progress is maintained in the future. With patients who are still symptomatic (the majority) and who are concerned at the prospect of finishing treatment, reassurance should be given that it is usual for there to be continuing improvement in the months following the end of treatment.

Preparing for difficulties in the future ('relapse prevention')
It is important to ensure that patients have realistic expectations regarding the future. A common problem is that many patients hope never to binge again. This expectation makes them vulnerable to relapse since it reinforces the tendency to view any setback as a full-scale 'relapse' rather than a 'lapse'. The result is that they view themselves as having returned to square one which in turn leads them to abandon their attempts to control their eating. All patients should be told to expect setbacks. Their eating problem is an Achilles' heel with overeating being their response to stress. They should be reminded that during treatment they developed skills for dealing with the eating problem and that they should be able to use these skills again. It is useful to help them prepare a written plan for use at times of difficulty.

The cognitive behavioural treatment of anorexia nervosa

In principle, it ought to be possible to treat anorexia nervosa using an adaptation of the cognitive behavioural treatment for bulimia nervosa. This is because the maintaining mechanisms are very similar as are the cognitions and behaviours. Two main adaptations are required: those needed to address the poor motivation of these patients; and those needed to reverse the effects of starvation. In practice, however, there is no established treatment procedure. Helpful guidelines have been provided by Garner and Bemis (1982, 1985) and Pike *et al.* (1996), but there is nothing approaching a treatment manual. Below are some suggestions as to how the treatment for bulimia nervosa may be modified.

Enhancing motivation to change
The poor motivation of these patients needs to be addressed from the outset. It is important that therapists make it absolutely clear that they are working on behalf of the patients and not their relatives or concerned others. Garner and Bemis (1982) have described various ways of motivating the patients. They emphasize the importance of establishing a sound therapeutic relationship, accepting the patient's beliefs and values as genuine for her, and adopting an experimental approach in which the therapist and patient together explore the use of various different treatment strategies. In addition, it is worthwhile reviewing from the patient's standpoint the relative advantages and disadvantages of change. When doing so, it is especially important to draw a distinction between the short-term and long-term consequences of change since these patients tend to focus on the immediate present rather than the future.

To help motivate the patient, the therapist also needs to identify clinical features that the patient regards as a problem. In Oxford, the author and colleagues have found it helpful to have patients read about anorexia nervosa and its characteristics. Good accounts have been written by Palmer (1988) and Bruch (1978). Initially, many patients are reluctant to accept the diagnosis but once they have read about the disorder most find that they identify with it. It is particularly important to educate them about the physiological and psychological effects of starvation, especially the impaired concentration, preoccupation with food and eating, sleep disturbance, sensitivity to cold, and enhanced fullness secondary to delayed gastric emptying. Most patients have these features and once they understand their origin, they are more willing to countenance weight gain. It also needs to be explained how starvation tends to perpetuate the eating disorder. The issue of motivation is less problematic with those anorectics who binge eat since the loss of control is usually a source of distress.

Restoring a healthy weight

The second problem is the need for weight gain. Unless the weight loss is rapid or extreme, or the patient's health is endangered by physical complications, procedures for weight restoration can be incorporated into the out-patient regime. Before emphasizing the need for weight gain, however, it is best to devote several sessions to the establishment of a collaborative working relationship. Thereafter, weight gain must become a non-negotiable part of treatment. It is best to decide on a target weight range in excess of a body mass index of 19.0. Patients should be reassured that care will be taken to ensure that they do not exceed this weight range. The weight gain should be gradual and controlled (about 1 kilogram per week) and should occur within the context of other components of the cognitive behaviour therapy programme. In effect, this means that they must eat high-calorie foods as part of their planned meals and snacks. Alternatively, some patients find it easier to drink energy-rich supplements, labelling them as 'medicine'. This is acceptable at this stage in treatment, but once the target weight range has been reached, patients must maintain their weight without relying on the supplements. If weight gain does not occur, the therapist and patient must consider whether other treatment approaches are indicated including partial or full hospitalization. On the other hand, if the patient succeeds in gaining weight and reaches the target weight range, treatment can thereafter proceed much as for bulimia nervosa.

A disadvantage of out-patient weight restoration is that it is a lengthy process. Treatment can be accelerated by starting with an initial period of hospitalization during which weight is restored relatively rapidly and following this with treatment on an out-patient basis. This is the procedure being used in two ongoing treatment trials. The relative merits of the two approaches (including their cost-effectiveness) need to be studied.

The treatment approach outlined by Garner and Bemis (1982, 1985) and Pike *et al.* (1996) is broader in its cognitive focus than the cognitive behavioural treatment for bulimia nervosa. To quote Pike *et al.* (1996): 'a schema-based cognitive therapy is applied to address the variety of developmental, interpersonal, and intrapsychic factors that may be implicated in the disorder.' Whether this broadening of the focus of treatment is necessary needs to be established.

The cognitive behavioural treatment of other eating disorders

The cognitive behavioural approach to the treatment of bulimia nervosa can be regarded as modular in form since it contains groups of procedures directed at particular facets of the specific psychopathology of the disorder. Thus, there are techniques for addressing binge eating, the various forms of dieting, concerns about shape and weight, and the risk of relapse. These techniques may be used within a cognitive behavioural framework with patients who show just some of these features. As a result, the treatment has a wide application since, as mentioned earlier, there are many patients who have a clinically significant eating disorder yet do not meet all the diagnostic criteria for anorexia nervosa or bulimia nervosa. Included among these patients are those with binge eating disorder. A cognitive behavioural approach to the treatment of this disorder has been described by Fairburn *et al.* (1993). It is an adaptation of the treatment for bulimia nervosa which involves more emphasis on the amount that the patient is eating as well as the addition of measures designed to encourage weight loss, namely, moderate calorie restriction and an increase in activity level. However, as discussed earlier, the findings of the Pittsburgh study suggest that a simple dietary/behavioural treatment may be just as effective.

Disseminating the cognitive behavioural treatment for bulimia nervosa

Bulimia nervosa is a common disorder which affects at least 1–2% of young adult women (Fairburn and Beglin 1990). Although a proportion of these women do not want treatment (Fairburn 1995), it is still the case that it is unlikely that there will ever be sufficient specialist resources for the patients who do want treatment. A priority for research is, therefore, to develop a treatment that can be widely disseminated.

The cognitive behavioural treatment for bulimia nervosa is a specialist treatment. It has been tested on specialist patient samples; it uses specialist treatment techniques; and it is labour-intensive. The question therefore arises as to whether it can be adapted so that it can be used more widely. Three sets of findings suggest that this may be possible. First, it is common clinical experience that some patients respond extremely rapidly to cognitive behaviour therapy (Jones *et al.* 1993), well before the more complex cognitive procedures (of stage two) have been introduced. Second, Olmsted *et al.* (1991) have shown that brief didactic educational groups (based on cognitive behavioural principles) help a proportion of these patients, at least in the short term. Third, there is mounting evidence that some patients respond to cognitive behavioural self-help interventions (see Carter and Fairburn 1995).

In Oxford, the author and colleagues have developed three simplified versions of the cognitive behavioural treatment for bulimia nervosa: brief cognitive behaviour therapy, self-help, and guided self-help.

Brief cognitive behaviour therapy

The author, in collaboration with Deborah Waller, an Oxford general practitioner, has developed a simplified and condensed version of cognitive behaviour therapy for use in primary care. It is administered in eight weekly sessions of approximately 20 minutes in length. It retains the main educational and behavioural components of the cognitive behavioural treatment, but it does not include formal cognitive restructuring. In a pilot study, it was administered to a series of 11 women seen in primary care (Waller *et al.* 1996). The therapists, four general practitioners and a practice nurse, attended two introductory training workshops and were provided with a simple treatment manual. On reassessment at the end of treatment, six of the patients were found to have improved substantially, of whom only three needed all eight treatment sessions. Of the five patients who did not benefit, two were unable to commit themselves to treatment due to major external events, two had a coexisting personality disorder, and one obese patient was more concerned with losing weight than overcoming the eating problem.

These findings suggest that a subgroup of patients with bulimia nervosa may be helped in primary care using brief cognitive behaviour therapy. However, it must be noted that even this treatment requires some degree of training since it is a therapist-directed approach.

Self-help and guided self-help

The other two adaptations of cognitive behaviour therapy have centred on the use of cognitive behavioural self-help books (Cooper 1995; Fairburn 1995). These books include a self-help programme based directly on the cognitive behavioural treatment for bulimia nervosa. The programme may be used either on its own ('pure self-help') or with guidance from a non-specialist therapist ('guided self-help'). The latter approach involves six to eight 20- to 30-minute sessions over three to four months. Pure self-help clearly has the potential to be readily disseminated. However, our experience suggests that some sufferers have difficulty persevering on their own, whereas with guided self-help compliance is generally better. From the perspective of dissemination, guided self-help is preferable to brief cognitive behaviour therapy since it is programme-led rather than therapist-led and therefore requires less expertise on the part of the therapist.

The author and his colleague Jacqueline Carter have been evaluating the relative effectiveness and utility of these two forms of cognitive behavioural self-help. To date, we have focused on the treatment of binge eating disorder. Our findings indicate that both approaches produce substantial change in the short term with guided self-help being somewhat more effective (Carter and Fairburn in prep.). However, before firm conclusions can be drawn, maintenance of change needs to be studied since binge eating problems tend to run a chronic course. Maintenance of change is especially pertinent in this context given the finding from the second Oxford trial that, unlike full cognitive behaviour therapy, a simplified behavioural version of the treatment was associated with a high rate of relapse (Fairburn *et al.* 1993*a*). Simplifying cognitive behaviour therapy to make it suitable for administration in a self-help format therefore runs the risk of creating a treatment which has only short-lived effects and therefore little overall utility.

When cognitive behaviour therapy fails

The cognitive behavioural treatment for bulimia nervosa is far from being a panacea. In research trials (generally using secondary or tertiary referrals) between a half and two-thirds of patients obtain a substantial and lasting benefit, the remainder responding either partially or not at all. It is not known how this figure compares with the response rate in routine clinical practice. It cannot be assumed that the response rates in the two settings are comparable in view of likely differences in both the patient populations and the implementation of the treatment. Whatever the actual response rate in routine practice, the author is convinced that it could be higher. Having conducted a great many training workshops, it is evident that the treatment is rarely implemented as well as it could be, the most common problem being that therapists stray from the manual. Wilson (1995, 1996*b*) has argued persuasively that better results would be obtained if therapists adhered to empirically-based treatment manuals, an argument that certainly appears to apply to the treatment of bulimia nervosa.

Nevertheless, there is an undoubted need to develop improved methods for the treatment of bulimia nervosa. A starting point would be to determine whether non-responders have any distinctive features. This is important for two reasons: first, the identification of such features might provide clues both as to why these patients have not responded and, one hopes, how their treatment might be improved; and second, were it possible to identify these patients at assessment or early on in treatment, it might be possible to allocate them directly to a more effective approach — of course, this presupposes that such a treatment exists or can be developed.

Unfortunately, no consistent predictors of response to cognitive behaviour therapy (or any other form of therapy) have been identified (Wilson 1996a). The factors implicated include the severity of eating disorder features at presentation (Maddocks and Kaplan 1991; Fahy and Russell 1993; Olmsted et al. 1994), low self-esteem (Fairburn et al. 1987, 1993b), comorbid personality disorder particularly of a borderline type (Johnson et al. 1990; Herzog et al. 1991; Fahy and Russell 1993; Fahy et al. 1993; Rossiter et al. 1993; Steiger et al. 1993; Fairburn et al. 1993b), low weight (Fahy and Russell, 1993; Fahy et al. 1993) and a history of having been underweight or anorectic (Lacey 1983; Wilson et al. 1986; Davis et al. 1992). Premorbid obesity (i.e., childhood obesity) and paternal obesity have been implicated as predictors of poor long-term outcome (Fairburn et al. 1995). These findings provide few clues as to what treatments might benefit non-responders.

Wilson (1996a) has reviewed the main alternatives to cognitive behaviour therapy. Antidepressant drugs and interpersonal psychotherapy (IPT) are obvious options since both are established treatments in their own right. However, there is no *a priori* reason why they should benefit patients who do not respond. Other alternatives include psychodynamic psychotherapy and family therapy. Once again, there is no reason to think that these treatments will succeed where cognitive behaviour therapy has failed. There has been just one controlled study of a psychodynamic treatment, supportive expressive psychotherapy, and the results indicated that it was less effective than cognitive behaviour therapy (Garner et al. 1993). Similarly, the one study of family therapy obtained disappointing results (Russell et al. 1987). It is sometimes argued that psychodynamic psychotherapy would be a particularly good option since it is well suited to the treatment of those cases in which there is a coexisting personality disorder. It is certainly true that patients with severe personality disorders seem to be over-represented among cognitive behaviour therapy non-responders, but on the other hand there is no evidence to suggest that psychodynamic psychotherapy will be any more effective with this patient group than cognitive behaviour therapy.

Rather than replacing cognitive behaviour therapy with a different form of treatment, it is the author's view that there might be more to be gained by adapting the treatment to suit these particular patients. Several possibilities suggest themselves. As mentioned earlier, one is to broaden the focus of the treatment to address more general issues such as self-esteem and interpersonal functioning (Hollon and Beck 1993; Vitousek and Orimoto 1993). However, as Wilson (1996a) points out, there is no evidence that 'broad' cognitive behaviour therapy is superior to a more focused approach, with respect to either this disorder or any other. Another possibility would be to incorporate features of Linehan's cognitive behavioural treatment of borderline personality disorder (Linehan 1993). A third possibility would be to intensify the treatment in such a way as to ensure that compliance with key procedures was enhanced. It is common clinical experience that many cognitive behaviour therapy non-responders have either failed to follow key assignments (such as eating at regular intervals and introducing avoided foods) or have followed them only to a limited extent. If their compliance were somehow improved, this might improve their outcome. To this end, the Oxford manual suggests that therapist-assisted exposure be used with those patients who do not succeed in introducing avoided foods (Fairburn *et al.* 1993). This principle is taken a step further in the in-patient programme of Tuschen and Bents (Tuschen and Bents 1996; Bents 1995) which involves intensive therapist contact and sustained exposure. A similar programme could be instituted on a day-patient or out-patient basis. This would have the advantage of allowing the patient to remain in at least partial contact with the circumstances under which problems arise while also being less costly.

The treatment of cognitive behaviour therapy non-responders is an important topic which needs to be researched. However, it is not an easy one to study since most patients with bulimia nervosa respond to cognitive behaviour therapy.

Acknowledgements

The author is grateful to the Wellcome Trust for their support (grant 13123). Zafra Cooper made helpful comments on the first section of the chapter and Patricia Norman helped with a review of the outcome studies.

References

APA (American Psychiatric Association) (1994). *Diagnostic and Statistical Manual of Mental Disorders* (4th edn). APA, Washington, DC.

Beck, A. T., Rush, A. J., Shaw, B. F., and Emery, G. (1979). *Cognitive therapy of depression*. Guilford Press, New York.

Bents, H. (1995). Exposure therapy for bulimia nervosa: Clinical management at the Christoph-Dornier-Center for Clinical Psychology in Munster. In *Current research in eating disorders* (ed B. Tuschen and I. Florin), pp. 99–107. Verlag für Psychotherapie, Munster.

Bruch, H. (1973). *Eating disorders: Obesity, anorexia nervosa and the person within.* Basic Books, New York.

Bruch, H. (1978). *The golden cage.* Open Books, Shepton Mallet.

Carter, J. C. and Fairburn, C. G. (in prep.). Self-help and guided self-help in the treatment of binge eating disorder: A controlled study.

Carter, J. C. and Fairburn, C. G. (1995). Treating binge eating problems in primary care. *Addictive Behaviors,* 20, 765–72.

Channon, S., de Silva, P., Hemsley, D., and Perkins, R. (1989). A controlled trial of cognitive-behavioural and behavioural treatment of anorexia nervosa. *Behaviour Research Therapy,* 27, 529–35.

Cooper, P. J. (1995). *Bulimia nervosa and binge eating.* Robinson, London.

Craighead, L. W. and Agras, W. S. (1991). Mechanisms of action in cognitive-behavioral and pharmacological interventions for obesity and bulimia nervosa. *Journal of Consulting and Clinical Psychology,* 59, 115–25.

Davis, R., Olmsted, M. P., and Rockert, W. (1992). Brief group psychoeducation for bulimia nervosa. II: Prediction of clinical outcome. *International Journal of Eating Disorders,* 11, 205–11.

Fahy, T. A., Eisler, I., and Russell, G. F. M. (1993). Personality disorder and treatment response in bulimia nervosa. *British Journal of Psychiatry,* 162, 765–70.

Fahy, T. A. and Russell, G. F. M. (1993). Outcome and prognostic variables in bulimia nervosa. *International Journal of Eating Disorders,* 14, 135–45.

Fairburn, C. G. (1981). A cognitive behavioural approach to the management of bulimia. *Psychology and Medicine,* 11, 707–11.

Fairburn, C. G. (1985). Cognitive-behavioral treatment for bulimia. In *Handbook of psychotherapy for anorexia nervosa and bulimia* (ed. D. M. Garner and P. E. Garfinkel), pp. 160–92. Guilford Press, New York.

Fairburn, C. G. (1993). Interpersonal psychotherapy for bulimia nervosa. In *New applications of interpersonal psychotherapy* (ed. G. L. Klerman and M. M. Weissman), pp. 353–78. American Psychiatric Press, Washington, DC.

Fairburn, C. G. (1995). *Overcoming binge eating.* Guilford Press, New York.

Fairburn, C. G. (1996). Interpersonal psychotherapy for bulimia nervosa. In *Handbook of treatment for eating disorders* (ed. D. M. Garner and P. E. Garfinkel). Guilford Press, New York.

Fairburn, C. G. and Beglin, S. J. (1990). Studies of the epidemiology of bulimia nervosa. *American Journal Psychiatry,* 147, 401–8.

Fairburn, C. G. and Walsh, B. T. (1995). Atypical eating disorders. In *Eating disorders and obesity: A comprehensive handbook* (ed. K. D. Brownell and C. G. Fairburn), pp. 135–40. Guilford Press, New York.

Fairburn, C. G., Cooper, Z., and Cooper, P. J. (1986). The clinical features and maintenance of bulimia nervosa. In *Handbook of eating disorders: physiology, psychology and treatment of obesity, anorexia and bulimia* (ed. K. D. Brownell and J. P. Foreyt), pp. 389–404. Basic Books, New York.

Fairburn, C. G., Kirk, J., O'Connor, M., Anastasiades, P., and Cooper, P. J. (1987). Prognostic factors in bulimia nervosa. *British Journal of Clinical Psychology,* 26, 223–4.

Fairburn, C. G., Jones, R., Peveler, R. C., Carr, S. J., Solomon, R. A., O'Connor, M. E., *et al.* (1991). Three psychological treatments for bulimia nervosa: A comparative trial. *Archives of General Psychiatry* 48, 463–9.

Fairburn, C. G., Agras, W. S., and Wilson, G. T. (1992). The research on the treatment of bulimia nervosa: practical and theoretical implications. In *The Biology of feast and famine: Relevance to eating disorders* (ed. G. H. Anderson and S. H. Kennedy), pp. 317–40. Academic Press, San Diego.

Fairburn, C. G., Jones, R., Peveler, R. C., Hope, R. A., and O'Connor, M. (1993*a*). Psychotherapy and bulimia nervosa: The longer-term effects of interpersonal psychotherapy, behaviour therapy and cognitive behaviour therapy. *Archives of General Psychiatry*, 50, 419–28.

Fairburn, C. G., Peveler, R. C., Jones, R., Hope, R. A., and Doll, H. A. (1993*b*). Predictors of twelve-month outcome in bulimia nervosa and the influence of attitudes to shape and weight. *Journal of Consulting and Clinical Psychology*, 61, 696–8.

Fairburn, C. G., Marcus, M. D., and Wilson, G. T. (1993*c*). Cognitive-behavioral therapy for binge eating and bulimia nervosa: A comprehensive treatment manual. In *Binge eating: Nature, assessment and treatment* (ed. C. G. Fairburn and G. T. Wilson), pp. 361–404. Guilford Press, New York.

Fairburn, C. G., Norman, P. A., Welch, S. L., O'Connor, M. E., Doll, H. A., and Peveler, R. C. (1995). A prospective study of outcome in bulimia nervosa and the long-term effects of three psychological treatments. *Archives of General Psychiatry*, 52, 304–12.

Garner, D. M. and Bemis, K. M. (1982). A cognitive-behavioral approach to anorexia nervosa. *Cognitive Therapy and Research*, 6, 123–50.

Garner, D. M. and Bemis, K. M. (1985). A cognitive-behavioral approach to anorexia nervosa. In *Handbook of psychotherapy for anorexia nervosa and bulimia* (ed. D. M. Garner and P. E. Garfinkel), pp. 107–46. Guilford Press, New York.

Garner, D. M., Rockert, W., Davis, R., Garner, M. V., Olmsted, M. P. and Eagle, M. (1993). Comparison of cognitive-behavioral and supportive-expressive therapy for bulimia nervosa. *American Journal of Psychiatry*, 150, 37–46.

Garner, D. M., Rockert, W., Olmsted, M. P., Johnson, C. and Coscina, D. V. (1996). Psychoeducational principles in the treatment of bulimia and anorexia nervosa. In *Handbook of psychotherapy for anorexia nervosa and bulimia* (ed. D. M. Garner and P. E. Garfinkel), pp. 513–72. Guilford Press, New York.

Goldfried, M. R. and Goldfried, A. P. (1975). Cognitive change methods. In *Helping people change* (ed. F. R. Kanfer and A. P. Goldstein). Pergamon, New York.

Hawton, K., Salkovskis, P. M., Kirk, J., and Clark, D. M. (1989). *Cognitive behaviour therapy for psychiatric problems. A practical guide*. Oxford University Press.

Herzog, T., Hartman, A., Sandholz, A., and Stammer, H. (1991). Prognostic factors in outpatient psychotherapy of bulimia. *Psychotherapy and Psychosomatics*, 56, 48–55.

Hollon, S. D. and Beck, A. T. (1993). Cognitive and cognitive-behavioral therapies. In *Handbook of psychotherapy and behavior change: An empirical analysis* (ed. S. L. Garfield and A. E. Bergin). Wiley, New York.

Johnson, C., Tobin, D. L., and Dennis, A. (1990). Differences in treatment outcome between borderline and nonborderline bulimics at one-year follow-up. *International Journal of Eating Disorders*, 9, 617–27.

Jones, R., Peveler, R. C., Hope, R. A. and Fairburn, C. G. (1993). Changes during treatment for bulimia nervosa: A comparison of three psychological treatments. *Behaviour Research and Therapy*, 31, 479–85.

Klerman, G. L., Weissman, M. M., Rounsaville, B. J., and Chevron, E. S. (1984). *Interpersonal psychotherapy of depression*. Basic Books, New York.

Lacey, J. H. (1983). Bulimia nervosa, binge eating, and psychogenic vomiting: a controlled treatment study and long term outcome. *British Medical Journal*, 286, 1609–13.

Linehan, M. M. (1993). *Cognitive-behavioral treatment of borderline personality disorder.* Guilford Press, New York.

Maddocks, S. E. and Kaplan, A. S. (1991). The prediction of treatment response in bulimia nervosa. A study of patient variables. *British Journal of Psychiatry*, 159, 846–9.

Mahoney, M. H. and Mahoney, K. (1976). *Permanent weight control.* Norton, New York.

Marcus, M. D., Wing, R. R., and Fairburn, C. G. (1995). Cognitive treatment of binge eating vs. behavioral weight control in the treatment of binge eating disorder. *Annals of Behavioral Medicine*, 17, S090.

McCann, U. D. and Agras, W. S. (1990). Successful treatment of nonpurging bulimia nervosa with desipramine: a double-blind, placebo-controlled study. *American Journal of Psychiatry*, 147, 1509–13.

Mitchell, J. E., Raymond, N., and Specker, S. (1993). A review of the controlled trials of pharmacotherapy and psychotherapy in the treatment of bulimia nervosa. *International Journal of Eating Disorders*, 14, 229–47.

Mizes, J. S. and Christiano, B. A. (1995). Assessment of cognitive variables relevant to cognitive behavioral perspectives on anorexia nervosa and bulimia nervosa. *Behaviour Research and Therapy*, 33, 95–105.

Olmsted, M. P., Davis, R., Garner, D. M., Eagle, M., Rockert, W., and Irvine, M. J. (1991). Efficacy of a brief group psychoeducational intervention for bulimia nervosa. *Behaviour Research and Therapy*, 29, 71–83.

Olmsted, M. P., Kaplan, A. S., and Rockert, W. (1994). Rate and prediction of relapse in bulimia nervosa. *American Journal of Psychiatry*, 151, 738–43.

Palmer, J. L. (1988). *Anorexia nervosa.* Penguin, London.

Pike, K. M., Loeb, K., and Vitousek, K. (1996). Cognitive-behavioral therapy for anorexia nervosa and bulimia nervosa. In *Eating disorders, obesity and body image: A practical guide to assessment and treatment* (ed. J. K. Thompson). American Psychological Association, Washington.

Polivy, J. and Herman, C. P. (1993). Etiology of binge eating: psychological mechanisms. In *Binge eating: Nature, assessment and treatment* (ed. C. G. Fairburn and G. T. Wilson), pp. 173–205. Guilford Press, New York.

Rossiter, E. M., Agras, W. S., Telch, C. F., and Schneider, J. A. (1993). Cluster B personality disorder characteristics predict outcome in the treatment of bulimia nervosa. *International Journal of Eating Disorders*, 13, 349–57.

Russell, G. F. M. (1979). Bulimia nervosa: an ominous variant of anorexia nervosa. *Psychology and Medicine*, 9, 429–48.

Russell, G. F. M., Szmukler, G. I., Dare, C., and Eisler, I. (1987). An evaluation of family therapy in anorexia nervosa and bulimia nervosa. *Archives of General Psychiatry*, 44, 1047–56.

Steiger, H., Leung, F., Thibaudeau, J., and Houle, L. (1993). Prognostic utility of subcomponents of the borderline personality construct in bulimia nervosa. *British Journal of Clinical Psychology*, 32, 187–97.

Telch, C. F., Agras, W. S., Rossiter, E. M., Wilfley, D., and Kenardy, J. (1990). Group cognitive-behavioral treatment for the non-purging bulimic: an initial evaluation. *Journal of Consulting and Clinical Psychology*, 58, 629–35.

Tuschen, B. and Bents, H. (1996). Intensive brief inpatient treatment of bulimia nervosa. In *Eating disorders and obesity: A comprehensive handbook* (ed. K. D. Brownell and C. G. Fairburn), pp. 354–60. Guilford Press, New York.

Vitousek, K. B. and Hollon, K. B. (1990). The investigation of schematic content and processing in eating disorders. *Cognitive Therapy and Research*, 14, 191–214.

Vitousek, K. B. and Orimoto, L. (1993). Cognitive-behavioral models of anorexia nervosa, bulimia nervosa, and obesity. In *Psychopathology and cognition* (ed. K. S. Dobson and P. C. Kendall), pp. 191–243. Academic Press, San Diego.

Waller, D., Fairburn, C. G., McPherson, A., Kay, R., Lee, A., and Nowell, T. (1996). Treating bulimia nervosa in primary care: A pilot study. *International Journal of Eating Disorders*, **19**, 99–103.

Wilfley, D. E., Agras, W. S., Telch, C. F., Rossiter, E. M., Schneider, J. A., Cole, A. G., *et al.* (1993). Group cognitive-behavioral therapy and group interpersonal psychotherapy for the nonpurging bulimic individual: a controlled comparison. *Journal of Consulting Clinical Psychology*, **61**, 296–305.

Wilson, G. T. (1995). Empirically validated treatments as a basis for clinical practice: Problems and prospects. In *Scientific standards of psychological practice: Issues and recommendations* (ed. S. C. Hayes, V. M. Follette, R. D. Dawes, and K. Grady), pp. 163–96. Context Press, Reno, NV.

Wilson, G. T. (1996a). Treatment of bulimia nervosa: When CBT fails. *Behaviour Research and Therapy*, **34**, 197–212.

Wilson, G. T. (1996b). Manual-based treatments: The clinical application of research findings. *Behaviour Research and Therapy*, **34**, 295–314.

Wilson, G. T. and Fairburn, C. G. (in press). Treatment of eating disorders. In *Treatments that work* (ed. P. E. Nathan and J. M. Gorman). Oxford University Press, New York.

Wilson, G. T., Rossiter, E., Kleifield, E. I., and Lindholm, L. (1986). Cognitive-behavioral treatment of bulimia nervosa: a controlled evaluation. *Behaviour Research and Therapy*, **24**, 277–88.

Wilson, G. T., Fairburn, C. G., and Agras, W. S. (in press). Cognitive-behavioral therapy for bulimia nervosa. In *Handbook of treatment for eating disorders* (ed. D. M. Garner and P. E. Garfinkel). Guilford Press, New York.

10

Sexual problems

John Bancroft

During the past 20 years the most important influence on sex therapy has been the work of Masters and Johnson (1970). Their first writings on methods of treatment were fundamentally eclectic, with no real attempt to base their approach explicitly on any theoretical model. Partly as a consequence, their descriptions conveyed, by default, a predominantly behavioural approach in which the couple was instructed to follow a carefully described programme of behavioural steps. Not surprisingly, this approach became the inspiration for many behaviourally oriented therapists. Subsequent writing by Masters and Johnson (e.g., 1979) revealed that there was much more to their treatment method than they had originally described; their reluctance to define the principles of their therapeutic method had perhaps made it easier for them to leave these gaps.

Before long, many therapists exploring sex therapy came to the conclusion that whereas the behavioural programme outlined by Masters and Johnson was indeed helpful, more often than not other psychotherapeutic procedures were required to enable the couple or the individual to overcome the behavioural blocks that the programme uncovered. The fact that sex therapy had started with an empirical basis, and had attracted therapists from a variety of ideological backgrounds, resulted in a variety of approaches being used to fill this psychotherapeutic gap. Kaplan (1974), for example, recognized the merits of Masters and Johnson's behavioural approach and incorporated explanatory models from her own psychoanalytic background. In my account of sex therapy (Bancroft 1989) I described a variety of psychotherapeutic procedures which, although comparable to current cognitive therapy, were not so specifically defined, and which perhaps fell more comfortably into a 'common sense' approach to conflict resolution. Hawton (1989), when describing sex therapy in a textbook dedicated to cognitive behavioural methods, paid scant attention to cognitive therapy principles in describing his treatment approach, although he acknowledged the need for 'counselling techniques' to combine with the behavioural programme.

This developmental sequence, whereby the use of a behavioural model produces limited success and reveals the need for an additional complementary approach, has not been restricted to sex therapy. Similar trends have occurred in other areas of behaviour therapy leading eventually to the emergence of cognitive methods and the combination of 'cognitive behavioural' principles of treatment. The theoretical underpinning of this development was in part provided by the proposal of Lang, Rachman, and others that psychological problems could be conceptualized in terms of three interrelated but essentially independent systems: behavioural, cognitive, and physiological (Hawton *et al.* 1989). Much of the relevant research has been carried out in the University of Oxford Department of Psychiatry under the leadership of Michael Gelder. Effective treatment required that the interrelationships between such systems be both understood and taken into account in the treatment approach. This has perhaps been most convincingly illustrated in the development of cognitive behavioural methods of treating anxiety. The role of cognitions in interpreting, exaggerating, or misinterpreting the physiological changes that typically accompany the emotional state of anxiety has become an effective focus of cognitive treatment (see Chapter 6). The psychophysiological interrelationship between the three, although not yet completely understood, is being usefully investigated, providing a steadily emerging and strengthening rationale for the cognitive behavioural treatment approach (Clark 1989), and leading to a reasonably convincing improvement in therapeutic efficacy. The cognitive approach to depression has received even more research attention, although the main focus has been on the interrelationship between cognition and affect, with physiological mechanisms as yet playing a minor role (see Chapter 11).

When we turn our attention to the treatment of sexual problems, we find a rather different developmental history. Having started with considerable optimism, sex therapists now acknowledge the considerable variability in prognosis, and in most respects long-term outcome is difficult to predict (Hawton 1992). There has been little attempt to evolve the treatment method on the 'three-system' model that has proved so effective in the treatment of anxiety. The exceptions have been those of Barlow and his colleagues who have reported a series of experiments in which cognitive and affective processes have been manipulated, and the effects on male genital response measured (reviewed by Barlow 1986; Cranston-Cuebas and Barlow 1990). This has led to a theoretical model which could be relevant to treatment. However, Barlow's group has not been particularly active in exploring the treatment of sexual problems, and so far this body of experimental knowledge has had little impact on the field of sex therapy. Other researchers, in particular Everaerd's group in Amsterdam (Janssen and Everaerd 1993), have been exploring information-processing as it relates to sexual response, and there is now a large body of evidence from which to consider treatment implications, which is one of the principal aims of this chapter. My objective is to convince the reader that whereas the understanding of cognitive processes takes us a certain distance in understanding sexual dysfunctions, and hence their treatment, there remain some crucial gaps in our understanding of the mechanisms which mediate between cognitions and sexual response. And yet, of the three types of clinical problem I have mentioned, anxiety, depression, and sexual dysfunction, the physiological response system and the means by which it can be aroused or inhibited is probably of most fundamental importance in the sexual domain. Sexual function hinges, probably to a unique extent, on the capacity to show specific physiological responses rather than behaviours. For a long time, sex therapists have turned a blind eye to the fact that the most relevant mechanisms underlying sexual dysfunction have not been understood, and for the most part have not been investigated.

In pursuing this case, I will first describe a fairly typical approach to sex therapy, and indicate the extent to which the needs of such treatment are understood and can be met by a cognitive behavioural approach. I will then review the experimental evidence relating cognitive and affective processes to sexual response (evidence that is largely confined to erectile response in the male) and consider the extent to which this provides us with a rationale for treatment. Finally, I will offer some questions which need to be addressed before the treatment of sexual dysfunction, using a cognitive behavioural approach, can be placed on a sufficiently comprehensive rational basis.

The sex therapy approach

I will not attempt to provide all the details of this treatment approach. These have been adequately addressed previously (Masters and Johnson 1970; Bancroft 1989; Hawton 1985). The essence of the approach, however, is that the couple is asked to carry out precisely defined behaviours as a series of homework assignments. Typically, these start with non-genital touching, often referred to as 'sensate focus', and progress to involve genital touching and eventually intercourse, as obstacles to carrying out the behavioural assignments are overcome. The behavioural assignments thus have two crucial functions. They provide a graduated behavioural programme which may, in some cases, be sufficient in itself to lead the couple toward mutually enjoyable sexual interaction. In such cases, the programme probably succeeds by its behaviourally graduated 'desensitizing' and anxiety-reducing approach, as well as providing 'permission' from the therapist to explore alternative behavioural patterns. In the majority of cases, however, the behavioural programme is more crucial in uncovering the relevant inter- and intrapersonal issues which appear to block effective sexual interaction. When uncovered, these blocks then have to be overcome, and that is when a complementary psychotherapeutic approach becomes important. The behavioural programme is therefore a combination of behavioural change and discovery.

The issues that are tackled in the course of such therapy can be considered under four broad headings: (1) improving communication and understanding between the couple; (2) the learning by the couple of new methods of conflict resolution and the expression of negative feelings; (3) 'cognitive restructuring' of sexual meanings; and (4) modification of sexual responses *per se*. We can consider the relevant mechanisms of change in each case.

1. *Improving communication and understanding between the couple.* Sex therapy can have a powerful effect on the communication between the couple. The negotiation of a behavioural programme in which each partner seeks ways of giving the other pleasure whilst at the same time allowing the clear assertion of what is regarded as unpleasant or threatening often results in a substantial improvement in mutual understanding. Whereas the treatment involves considerable discussion of such issues between the therapist and the couple of a type that might occur in any type of couple therapy, there is no doubt that the behavioural programme, particularly in its use of small behavioural steps, and the initiation of sexual interaction by one specific partner at a time, is also very effective in this respect. This is not a particularly 'cognitive' approach, but a combination of behavioural direction and 'common sense' interpretation. In some couples, this process is the most important in bringing about relevant change.

2. *Learning new methods of conflict resolution.* Apart from facilitating greater understanding between the couple, sex therapy often identifies maladaptive patterns of coping or conflict resolution within the relationship. One of the advantages of working with the couple is that the therapist often observes these maladaptive patterns being manifested in the course of treatment. An additional, and sometimes crucial, objective is to enable the couple to learn alternative and more adaptive patterns of conflict resolution. This may be particularly important in focusing on how each partner deals with anger or other negative emotions. Here, we see a combination of education and behavioural training, with feedback from the therapist playing a central role. Such objectives, although often crucially important in allowing the redevelopment of rewarding sexual interaction, are not confined to sex therapy, and are often of primary importance in general marital therapy.

3. *Cognitive restructuring of sexual meanings.* An important aspect of sex therapy, particularly when it reaches the stage in the behavioural programme when genital touching is involved, is the appraisal and reappraisal of the

meanings of specific types of sexual act or response. In some cases, negative meanings to certain types of sexual activity are acquired during childhood often maintaining a primitive, 'childlike' form into adulthood. The emotional cathexis associated with such meanings may remain as the key determinant in shaping or inhibiting sexual responses as the individual gets older. By reappraising these meanings in an adult light, their emotional impact may change and they cease to have the same effect on current behavioural responses. For example, as a result of early childhood experiences and parental disapproval, a woman might have incorporated the view that any form of direct genital stimulation is wrong and unacceptable and a cause for guilt. Alternatively, a woman who was sexually abused as a child might have established feelings of guilt at experiencing pleasure during the abusive experiences such that she blames herself for the abuse, and sees any pleasurable responses she experiences as wrong. Such a pattern of emotional response may persist even without the specific sexual meaning being acknowledged, so that, subsequently, such women react adversely to any form of direct genital stimulation with feelings of guilt and consequent inhibition of sexual arousal and pleasure. The process of taking them through the behavioural programme, by gradual changes in the behavioural assignments and appropriate guidance from the therapist, may enable them to recognize that the original meanings of such behaviours are still determining their emotional responses to situations which are now occurring in a fundamentally different context. By reappraising such meanings, each woman is able to view the interaction with her partner in a new, more adult light, with a lessening of the negative emotional reactions.

Such a process may be seen to be involved in a variety of psychotherapeutic approaches, including psychoanalysis. However, there is no doubt that it lends itself particularly well to the cognitive behavioural approach. In this aspect of sex therapy, therefore, cognitive behavioural techniques have a lot to offer the therapist.

4. *Direct modification of sexual responses.* When we consider how the therapist deals directly with the various specific types of sexual dysfunction, the analysis of mediating mechanisms of change becomes much more difficult. In certain respects, techniques based on principles of learning have proved their worth. Thus, the 'stop-start' or 'squeeze' techniques for treating premature ejaculation, which are moderately effective, can be seen as training in the control of autonomic responses. Often, the ability to exploit such training depends on other difficulties in the sexual relationship being resolved first. Thus, if the man continues to experience anxiety during sexual interactions with his partner, then his ability to make use of this training approach will be limited. The notion of 'discriminative learning' by which the

man improves his ability to recognize when he is approaching 'ejaculatory inevitability' so that he can delay further stimulation and postpone the 'inevitable', is a plausible rationale for this treatment approach, although its validity has not as yet been clearly demonstrated.

Another behavioural technique which is often successful is graded dilation of the perivaginal muscles in the treatment of vaginismus. As yet we understand very little about why some women develop these reflex muscle spasms, which make vaginal entry virtually impossible. Whereas in some cases there is a clear history of trauma, either from sexual assault or from insensitive vaginal examination, in the majority of cases there is no clear reason why such spasms are so readily elicited. It remains a possibility that some women are constitutionally prone to such perivaginal spasm. Vaginismus, as one of the categories of sexual dysfunction, probably has the best prognosis, with many cases requiring only graduated dilatation training to overcome the problem. Some cases, on the other hand, may be among the most resistant of any to treatment. This reflects the extent to which vaginismus can become a psychosomatic expression of complex personality problems.

It is when we turn to the most common types of sexual dysfunction, erectile problems in the male, and difficulties with sexual arousal or orgasm in the female, that we are least certain about the relevant mediating mechanisms. Whereas during the earlier stages of treatment, when issues related to communication and meaning are addressed, progress is relatively easy to predict, once the stage of genital responsiveness is reached prediction becomes much more difficult. In the male, although there are many forms of organic pathology which can interfere with normal erectile function, psychological factors still predominate in the majority of cases. Yet how psychological factors result in erectile failure remains largely a mystery. There has been a tendency, in identifying the association between erectile dysfunction and a variety of psychological, interpersonal or intrapersonal problems, to assume that the occurrence of such problems is a sufficient explanation for this specific failure of physiological response. At the same time it is well recognized that such psychological problems often coexist with perfectly normal erectile function. A somewhat more sophisticated approach is to assume that certain emotional states, such as anxiety, interfere with normal sexual response, perhaps by the activation of sympathetic mechanisms which may block genital response. I shall consider the evidence for this shortly. In so far as sex therapy has been based on a rationale for behavioural change, the rationale has depended on such assumptions: for example, that failure of sexual response results from the occurrence of anxiety or the preoccupation with 'goal orientation' in the sexual situation and treatment therefore aims to reduce anxiety or the striving for sexual goals. Let us consider whether such assumptions have any validity.

For some time there has been evidence that negative emotional states, such as anxiety or anger, have a varied and somewhat unpredictable association with sexual response (Bancroft 1970; 1980). Only recently has there been any attempt to test these assumptions experimentally.

Experimental evidence in the male

Barlow and his colleagues in the United States (for reviews see Barlow 1986; Cranston-Cuebas and Barlow 1990) have used a cognitive or information-processing approach involving measurement of erectile response to erotic stimuli in men with and without erectile dysfunction, in conditions which manipulate specific cognitive or affective aspects of the experience. Their key results can be summarized as follows:

(1) By inducing states of anxiety, sexual response can be enhanced in functional and impaired in dysfunctional subjects.
(2) Imposing 'performance demand', requiring the subject to respond to an erotic stimulus with an erection, and measuring the response, can again enhance the response in functional and impair it in dysfunctional subjects.
(3) Increasing arousal, in a non-specific way, leads to a similar discrimination.
(4) In contrast, distraction with some non-erotic cue impairs response in the functional subjects and may have no effect or even enhance response in the dysfunctional subjects.
(5) Functional subjects either correctly perceive their degree of response, or exaggerate it; dysfunctional subjects tend to underestimate it.

Barlow (1986) has focused on two particular aspects of these findings. First, the distraction: the negative effect of distraction in the functional men he sees as evidence of the fundamental importance of 'attention to the sexual cues' for normal sexual response. The paradoxical effect of distraction in dysfunctional men, he suggests, is because they are otherwise distracted by non-erotic cues which are even more negative in their effects on sexual response than the experimental ones. Second, he draws attention to the amplifying effect of arousal, whether it be negative, such as that associated with anxiety, or otherwise non-specific. Thus, arousal will enhance the focus of the information-processing — if it is focused on sexual cues, then the sexual response will be enhanced, whereas if it is focused on non-erotic or anti-erotic cues, such as worrying thoughts about failure, then the anti-erotic effect will be enhanced. In this way he explains the discrepancy between the functional and dysfunctional men in his experiments. In considering the implications for therapy, Barlow reasonably concludes that attempts to reduce arousal non-specifically are unlikely to be helpful. Apart from that he sees his findings and his model of functional and dysfunctional arousal as more or less supporting the prevailing objectives of the sex therapist — focusing on positive aspects and avoiding distraction by concerns over failure. Although these findings are undoubtedly relevant and important for sex therapists, they beg a number of questions which have not yet been addressed. In particular, are these differences in information-processing between functional and dysfunctional subjects related to the cause of the dysfunction or are they the consequence of the dysfunction becoming established, or perhaps both? Second, how are these different physiological patterns of response to information-processing mediated?

Apart from the extent to which autonomic arousal is seen to amplify the effects of whichever response pattern predominates, the key to Barlow's model is distraction, a 'process which is the mechanism of action through which many experiences act to inhibit sexual responsivity' (Cranston-Cuebas and Barlow 1990, p. 141). My clinical impression of erectile dysfunction is that whereas distraction from erotic cues may well be contributory, it is inadequate to explain the often complete failure of erectile response which occurs despite adequate direct physical stimulation. Some other inhibitory mechanism of a more direct physiological nature would appear to be involved. But clinical impressions are not enough. Let us consider some experimental evidence that raises questions about the adequacy of the Barlow model. As it happens, the most interesting examples are from Everaerd's group in Amsterdam and from Barlow's own work.

Janssen and Everaerd (Janssen 1995; Janssen and Everaerd 1993) compared the erectile response, in functional and dysfunctional men, to two types of stimulation, vibration applied to the penis, and vibration combined with an erotic film. With the vibration alone, the dysfunctional men showed significantly less response than the functional men. But when the vibration was combined with the film, the two groups did not differ. Once again information-processing must have been involved; but how does one explain the lack of response to tactile vibration in terms of information-processing alone? It is, of course, possible and indeed likely that information-processing amplifies the response to such a stimulus by invoking other excitory mechanisms. Those who rely on information-processing for their explanatory model would go further and say that the processing of the tactile experience, with its labelling as a positive sexual stimulus, is necessary for it to have the erotic effect. That would imply that the impaired erectile response to the vibration alone, in the dysfunctional men, was the consequence of receiving peripheral tactile stimulation which was labelled or 'processed' as less positively sexual than in the functional men, but must have been labelled 'sexual' to some extent, otherwise no erection would have occurred. There is an alternative and, to me, more persuasive explanation. Vibration alone may well be capable of producing erection without any specific cognitive mediation. However, the processing of the information in the dysfunctional men receiving vibration alone, with the connotation of 'need to respond to this direct stimulus', invoked an inhibitory mechanism which reduced the erectile response. The effect of adding the erotic film was to distract the dysfunctional man from this anti-erotic thinking and hence switch off (or reduce) the inhibitory mechanism. Thus, what I am postulating is a particular pattern of information-processing leading to the recruitment of a central neurophysiological inhibitory mechanism.

The second example involves the interesting use of misattribution. The idea is that you give someone a pill, which in fact is inactive, but tell him that it will increase his sexual response while he looks at erotic stimuli. He will attribute any response that occurs to the pill and consequently minimize his own arousal. Conversely, if you give him an inactive pill and tell him that it will *decrease* his response, he will be impressed by any response that does occur and hence report greater subjective sexual arousal. Cranston-Cuebas and Barlow (1990) examined this possibility and to their surprise demonstrated the effect strikingly in functional men, but with the effect showing itself in the actual erectile responses and not in their report of subjective arousal. With dysfunctional men, however, the findings were different. When told that the pill would decrease their response, that is what in fact happened, again in the erectile and not in their subjective responses. The response-enhancing pill, on the other hand, was no different to placebo. Thus, there was a further difference between functional and dysfunctional men which again raises the question of whether it is a cause or an effect. Janssen and Everaerd (1993) went on to replicate these findings, although they looked only at functional and not dysfunctional men. They commented, however, on the remarkable difference between the clear effect of the misattribution procedure on the physiological response, the erection, and the lack of effect on the subjective response, the self-rating of arousal.

Although information-processing was undoubtedly involved in these procedures, if it was the only relevant mechanism it is difficult to account for the lack of effect on the subjective experience. An alternative explanation is that the altered expectation produced by the misattribution effect was associated, in the functional men, with a reduction in the usual level of inhibitory tone, an effect of which the subject was presumably unaware and which did not lead to any revision of his subjective state. In contrast, the dysfunctional men processed the information differently and in a way which either did not reduce inhibitory tone, or actually increased it.

The role of central inhibition

My interpretation of these interesting experiments, whilst recognizing the fundamental role of information-processing, also requires some other mediating mechanism to explain the occurrence of erectile failure. The most likely candidate is a central inhibitory mechanism which reduces or impairs genital response. If this is a correct interpretation, it implies that, for an effective rationale of treatment, we need to understand more about this inhibitory process and how it is recruited by cognitive mechanisms. Are some individuals more prone to inhibitory responses and hence more vulnerable to dysfunction? Are patterns of inhibition learnt? To what extent can the degree of inhibition be explained by the pattern of information-processing that invokes it? Are such inhibitory mechanisms relevant to dysfunctional responses in women as well as men, and to ejaculatory and orgasmic problems as well as impaired genital response? Needless to say, we have hardly started to address such questions, let alone answer them. However, although the concept of central inhibition has been on the agenda for some time (e.g., Bancroft 1970), only recently have opportunities to study it experimentally, at least in men, become available. I will briefly describe some of the recent evidence of this kind.

It has been known for more than 30 years that spontaneous erections occurring during sleep, so called nocturnal penile tumescence (NPT), are largely confined to REM or 'paradoxical' sleep. Remarkably, little attention has been paid to why this might be so. However, recent developments in our knowledge of REM sleep and its relevance to autonomic function present us with some interesting possibilities.

A characteristic of REM is that noradrenergic and serotonergic neurones in the locus coeruleus are effectively switched off as if to allow REM to occur (Parmeggiani and Morrison 1990). The locus coeruleus is the relay station in an extensive network within the central nervous system, which is linked to the peripheral autonomic nervous system. Although there may be species variability, certain parts of the peripheral sympathetic nervous system are switched off together with the locus coeruleus, and these parts are likely to include those that control the erectile tissues of the penis (Parmeggiani & Morrison 1990). This provides us with an obvious, at least partial, explanation for why NPT occurs during REM—noradrenergic tone in the smooth muscle of the sinusoids in erectile tissue, which normally keeps the penis flaccid, is 'switched off' permitting erections to occur. This immediately suggests a neurophysiological basis for our inhibitory system, although we should not be too simplistic—other neurotransmitters (e.g., 5-HT) may also be involved. Studies of NPT and its relationship to REM offer exciting possibilities for investigating inhibitory mechanisms.

Now let us move 'downstream' to the penis. Another recent development which is starting to provide relevant information is the injection of smooth muscle relaxant drugs into the corpus cavernosum to induce erection. This is a pharmacological method for overcoming the local noradrenergic constrictor tone, which I am postulating plays a crucial part in the inhibition of erection. Various drugs have been injected in this way — some of them specific noradrenergic alpha-1 antagonists, others pharmacologically different, such as prostaglandin E_1 or papaverine. They all have in common the ability to relax the smooth muscle of the sinusoidal spaces of the corpus cavernosum. A widespread tendency among clinicians, at least until recently, has been to see this as a peripheral target organ effect, which has nothing to do with psychological mechanisms. We and others have shown, however, that a substantial proportion of men with assumed psychogenic erectile dysfunction respond poorly to these injections, as if some psychologically induced 'inhibitory mechanism' was counteracting the effects of the injection (Buvat *et al.* 1990; Bancroft and Malone 1995). Buvat *et al.* (1990) postulated that this inhibition was a result of increased circulating levels of noradrenaline that resulted from anxiety induced by the injection. Such an explanation is consistent with the traditional model of the autonomic nervous system and its relationship to emotional states, mentioned earlier.

Two studies so far have investigated this possibility. Granata *et al.* (1995) compared men with and without evidence of inhibited erectile response to the intracavernosal injection, and measured a number of psychological and psychoendocrine parameters. Circulating noradrenaline was in fact lower in the inhibited group. Kim and Oh (1992), in a comparable study, measured noradrenaline in the penile blood and found this to be significantly higher in the inhibited group. Together, this evidence makes it unlikely that the inhibition of penile erection is part of a generalized anxiety-induced activation of the sympathetic nervous system, with increased circulating noradrenaline affecting the erectile tissue, and more likely that some specific noradrenergic mechanism focused on the erectile tissues is involved. One could go further, and in those situations in which the occurrence of an erection might provoke anxiety, its specific inhibition by such central mechanisms could be seen as a way of avoiding or reducing anxiety (Bancroft 1980).

Another type of evidence comes from recent pharmacological studies testing the effects of a new alpha-2 adrenoceptor antagonist on erectile response in normal volunteers and men with erectile dysfunction. An alpha-2 antagonist, of which yohimbine is a well-known example, is believed to act principally on presynaptic autoreceptors. By blocking these, such a drug effectively increases the amount of noradrenaline released at the synapse. Now we start to encounter an apparent paradox. So far, we have considered the inhibitory effect of noradrenaline, through alpha-1 receptors, in the periphery. The reason why alpha-2 antagonists are attracting interest is that there is both animal and human evidence that they can enhance sexual response, perhaps by increasing central sexual arousal (Bancroft 1995). What happens, therefore, when such a drug is administered systematically, when it is not possible to restrict its action to either the central nervous system or the periphery? Studies of its effects on NPT when intravenously infused during sleep (Bancroft *et al.* 1995) showed a curvilinear dose response; low doses of the drug increased erections during sleep, although the effect was only significant during non-REM, whereas higher doses inhibited erections, mainly during REM. One possible explanation for these complex findings is that there are both excitatory and inhibitory systems in the central nervous system, which are selectively affected by varying the dosage of the drug. The concept of parallel excitatory and inhibitory systems both involving noradrenergic mediation is perfectly feasible, but it certainly makes it difficult to predict the effects of a systemically administerd drug. For the present discussion, the main point is that this is evidence of a central inhibitory system, which may well have peripheral inhibitory manifestations.

Further evidence of relevance was obtained from the effects of intravenous administration of this same alpha-2 antagonist on erectile response studied in the waking state, in both functional and dysfunctional men (Munoz *et al.* 1994*a*, *b*). Of particular interest was the finding that in younger dysfunctional men, blood pressure and heart rate responses to erotic stimuli were blunted during placebo administration and normalized by the alpha-2 antagonist. This suggests that there is central inhibition of autonomic response to erotic stimuli in psychogenic erectile dysfunction which is based, at least in part, on increased central alpha-2 tone. The partial normalization of the erectile response by the drug in these subjects was consistent with this explanation. The lack of such effects in the older dysfunctional subjects raises the interesting possibility that these central inhibitory mechanisms (and presumably their excitory counterparts) decline with advancing age. If so, we should be looking at other explanatory models in older men with 'psychogenic' erectile dysfunction.

Although these ideas are new and the evidence preliminary, they raise some crucial issues relevant to psychological treatment. If there is a central inhibitory mechanism which, together with its peripheral manifestations, can effectively block sexual response, how do cognitive mechanisms recruit such inhibitory effects? Clearly, there must be some information-processing involved to lead to such inhibition in psychogenic cases. Is the connection based on learning, or does it reflect constitutionally based individual differences? Are the mechanisms age-related? If the recruitment of such inhibitory mechanisms can be induced in an experimental setting, will this lead to more effective therapeutic interventions? The possibility remains that such interventions will depend on cognitive behavioural principles to be effective, but such efficacy will probably require a clearer understanding of the interface between information-processing and central neurophysiological response. If there was a non-invasive technique for identifying and quantifying such central or peripheral inhibitory mechanisms, the ingenious experimental paradigms used by Barlow, Everaerd, and others would provide excellent opportunities for studying this interface.

Experimental evidence in women

There is even less experimental evidence from women, but there are a number of pointers suggesting potentially important gender differences in the interface between cognitive and physiological aspects of sexual response. It has been known for some time that, compared with men, women show less concordance between subjective and physiological manifestations of sexual arousal (Rosen and Beck 1988). Furthermore, whereas in men, as discussed above, the elicitation of general arousal (e.g., by inducing anxiety) enhances the positive sexual responses of functional men and further impairs the responses of dysfunctional men, in women pre-exposure to anxiety-eliciting stimuli enhances genital responses to erotic stimuli in both functional and dysfunctional subjects (Palace and Gorzalka 1990). More recently, Palace (1995a) found that genital responses to erotic stimuli in dysfunctional women could be increased by combining non-specific autonomic arousal with false positive feedback of vaginal response. Furthermore, the positive effect of the false feedback apparently depended on cognitive mediation as it only occurred in those women who also reported increased *expectation* of sexual response. Although this particular paradigm has not yet been tested in men, such a response pattern would probably not be predicted from the evidence available so far, even if it proved possible to deceive them with false feedback. Palace (1995b) has proposed that this type of manipulation might form the basis for therapeutic intervention, but this remains to be tested. In view of these preliminary but interesting results, further direct comparison of dysfunctional men and women, and their patterns of autonomic arousal in response to erotic stimulation, is warranted. It is conceivable that central inhibition, as discussed above, may play a different role in the two sexes.

Conclusions

Modern sex therapy, while starting with great promise, has not shown continued improvement of efficacy; in fact, practitioners are less optimistic about outcome than they used to be. Although this, in part, reflects a general tendency for cases presenting to the clinician to increase in complexity over time, there are other explanations, some of which have been discussed in this chapter. In particular, it is proposed that cognitive behavioural approaches are effective in dealing with certain aspects of the therapeutic process (e.g., improving communication, restructuring sexual meaning, etc.), and that in some cases this will result in improvement in sexual responding for reasons which are not clear. However, direct attempts to modify the sexual responses, when this proves to be necessary, are much less predictable in their effects. Whereas information processing is clearly fundamental and cognitive behaviour techniques will probably remain the mainstay of effective treatment, predictable efficacy will probably only be achieved when we have clarified the interface between the cognitive processes and the central physiological mechanisms that underlie sexual response. Even then we should expect that both problems and individuals will vary in their responsiveness to treatment, and there may be differences between men and women which have important therapeutic implications,

Although research addressing such issues has hardly started, a number of promising leads to studying the cognitive physiologic interface have been discussed in this chapter and the research agenda is becoming increasingly clear.

When the evolution of cognitive-behaviour methods of treatment is considered in general, the influence of Michael Gelder on the field has been considerable. Personally, I am also indebted to him for his encouragement and wise guidance throughout my career and particularly during my formative years in his department.

References

Bancroft, J. (1970). Disorders of sexual potency. In *Modern Trends in Psychosomatic Medicine* — 2 (ed. O. W. Hill), pp. 246–61. Butterworths, London.

Bancroft, J. (1980). Psychophysiology of sexual dysfunction. In *Handbook of Biological Psychiatry, Part II. Brain mechanisms and abnormal behavior* — *psychophysiology* (ed. H. M. van Praag, M. H. Lader, O. J. Rafaelsen, and E. J. Sachar), pp. 359–92. Dekker, New York.

Bancroft, J. (1989). *Human sexuality and its problems.* Churchill Livingstone, Edinburgh.

Bancroft, J. (1995). Are the effects of androgens on male sexuality noradrenergically mediated? Some consideration of the human. *Neuroscience and Biobehavioral Reviews*, 19, 325–30.

Bancroft, J. and Malone, N. (1995). The clinical assessment of erectile dysfunction: a comparison of nocturnal penile tumescence monitoring and intracavernosal injections. *International Journal of Impotence Research*, 7, 123–30.

Bancroft, J., Munoz, M., Beard, M., and Shapiro, C. (1995). The effects of a new alpha-2 adrenoceptor antagonist on sleep and nocturnal penile tumescence in normal male volunteers and men with erectile dysfunction. *Psychosomatic Medicine*, 57, 345–6.

Barlow, D. H. (1986). Causes of sexual dysfunction the role of anxiety and cognitive interference. *Journal of Clinical and Consulting Psychology*, 54, 140–8.

Buvat, J., Buvat-Herbaut, M., Lemaire, A., Marcolin, G., and Quittelier, E. (1990). Recent developments in the clinical assessment and diagnosis of erectile dysfunction. *Annual Review Sex Research*, 1, 265–308.

Clark, D. M. (1989). Anxiety states; panic and generalised anxiety. In *Cognitive behaviour therapy for psychiatric problems* (ed. K. Hawton, P. M. Salkovkis, J. Kirk, and D. M. Clark). Oxford University Press.

Cranston-Cuebas, M. A. and Barlow, D. H. (1990). Cognitive and affective contributions to sexual functioning. *Annual Review Sex Research*, 1, 119–61.

Granata, A., Bancroft, J., Del Rio, G., and Carani, C. (1995). Stress and the erectile response to intracavernosal prostaglandin E1 in men with erectile dysfunction. *Psychosomatic Medicine*, 57, 336–44.

Hawton, K. (1985). *Sex therapy: a practical guide*. Oxford University Press, Oxford.

Hawton, K. (1989). Sexual dysfunctions. In *Cognitive behaviour therapy for psychiatric problems* (ed. K. Hawton, P. M. Salkovkis, J. Kirk, and D. M. Clark). Oxford University Press.

Hawton, K. (1992). Sex therapy research: has it withered on the vine? *Annual Review Sex Research*, 3, 49–72.

Hawton, K., Salkovkis, P. M., Kirk, J., and Clark, D. M. (1989). The development and principles of cognitive-behavioural treatments. In *Cognitive behaviour therapy for psychiatric problems* (ed. K. Hawton, P. M. Salkovkis, J. Kirk, and D. M. Clark). Oxford University Press.

Janssen, E. and Everaerd, W. (1993). Determinants of male sexual arousal. *Annual Review Sex Research*, 4, 211–45.

Janssen, E. (1995). Provoking penile responses; activation and inhibition of male sexual response. D.Phil.Thesis, University of Amsterdam.

Kaplan, H. S. (1974). *The new sex therapy*. Bailliere Tindall, London.

Kim, S. C. and Oh, M. M. (1992). Norepinephrine involvement in response to intracorporeal injection of papaverine in psychogenic impotence. *Journal of Urology*, 147, 1530–2.

Masters, W. H. and Johnson, V. E. (1970). *Human sexual inadequacy*. Churchill, London.

Masters, W. H. and Johnson, V. E. (1979). *Homosexualtiy in perspective*. Little Brown, Boston.

Munoz, M., Bancroft, J., and Beard, M. (1994a). Evaluating the effects of an alpha-adrenoceptor antagonist on erectile function in the human male. 2. The erectile response to erotic stimuli in men with erectile dysfunction, in relation to age and in comparison with normal volunteers. *Psychopharmacology*, 115, 471–7.

Munoz, M., Bancroft, J., and Turner, M. (1994b). Evaluating the effects of an alpha-2 adrenoceptor on erectile function in the human male. 1. The erectile response to erotic stimuli in volunteers. *Psychopharmacology*, 115, 463–70.

Palace, E. N. (1995a). Modification of dysfunctional patterns of sexual response through autonomic arousal and false physiological feedback. *Journal of Clinical and Consulting Psychology*, 63, 604–15.

Palace, E. M. (1995b). A cognitive-physiological process model of sexual arousal and response. *Clinical Psychology; Science and Practice*, 2, 370–84.

Palace, E. M. and Gorzalka, B. B. (1990). The enhancing effects of anxiety on arousal in sexually dysfunctional and functional women. *Journal of Abnormal Psychology*, 99, 403–11.

Parmeggiana, P. L. and Morrison, A. R. (1990). Alterations in autonomic functions during sleep. In *Central regulation of autonomic functions* (ed. A. D. Loewy and K. M. Spyer), pp. 367–86. Oxford University Press, New York.

Roseu, R. C. and Beck, J. G. (1988). *Patterns of sexual arousal. Psychophysiological processes and clinical applications*. Guilford Press, New York.

11

Depression

J. Mark G. Williams

This chapter summarizes some of the ways in which psychological theory has contributed to our understanding of depression and how best to treat it. My own interest in depression started with my doctoral research on learned helplessness in Michael Gelder's Department at Oxford between 1976 and 1979. Later, in Newcastle with Jan Scott, and in Cambridge with Fraser Watts, John Teasdale, and Andrew MacLeod, I sought to develop this work, investigating the cognitive processes involved in suicidal depression, with particular reference to deficits in autobiographical memory.

The nature of the problem

Depression remains such a challenging mental health problem that there is still much work to be done. Of course, depression as a normal mood state is a common experience. In minor depressive states, the person ruminates on negative themes. He or she feels resentful, irritable or angry much of the time, self-pitying, and constantly needs reassurance from others. Often, this need for reassurance concerns various physical complaints which do not seem to be caused by any physical illness. The mildly depressed person finds him/herself brooding about past unpleasantness and feeling pessimistic about the future.

However, as depression deepens, more symptoms are drawn in. These symptoms include further emotional changes (feelings of extreme sadness and hopelessness); cognitive changes (low self-esteem, guilt, memory, and concentration difficulties); changes in behaviour and motivation (feeling agitated or slowed down, reduced interest in social or recreational activities), and bodily changes (sleep, eating and sexual problems, loss of energy). If the depression is intense enough to include five or more of these symptoms for more than a two-week period, a major depression is diagnosable. Lifetime risk for major depression remains around 12% for males and 20% for females (Sturt *et al.* 1984). At any one time, there are some 5% of the population who are suffering depression of this severity: 25% of these episodes of depression last less than a month; a further 50% recover in less than three months.

However, a chronic clinical course often develops; 15–39% of cases may still be depressed (i.e., meet criteria for major depressive disorder) one year after symptom onset (Berti Ceroni *et al.* 1984; VanValkenburg *et al.* 1984), and 22% of cases remain depressed two years later (Keller *et al.* 1984).

The most commonly administered treatment for such depression is antidepressant medication. It is relatively inexpensive, and easy for family practitioners (who treat the majority of depressed people) to use. However, depression tends to return, and within two years of recovering from one episode, between a one-half and three-quarters will have suffered another episode of depression (Angst 1988). The current main strategy for preventing this recurrence is the continuation of the acute drug treatment in a maintenance format. A number of studies of maintenance antidepressants supports the effectiveness of this approach (Prien *et al.* 1974; Glen *et al.* 1984; Frank *et al.* 1990) and current practice guidelines emphasize the need to continue treatment for at least five to six months beyond the point of recovery (Prien *et al.* 1984). Recent findings suggest that the lowest recurrence rates require patients to be continued at the dosage used to achieve remission (Kupfer *et al.* 1992).

If drugs are effective in preventing relapse and recurrence, why look for psychological models and treatments for depression? Murphy *et al.* (1984) discussed this issue at the end of their study (which found no difference in the acute phase between antidepressants and psychological [cognitive] therapy). They pointed to several reasons for pursuing psychological alternatives (p. 40):

> First, not every patient is psychologically disposed to accept medication as the appropriate treatment for his/her depression. Some will strongly prefer a psychological approach... Second, some patients tolerate the side-effects of tricylic antidepressants (TCAs) poorly or not at all. Rejection of pharmacotherapy is a recurrent problem in outcome studies that include psychotherapy (Friedman 1975; Rush *et al.* 1977; McLean and Hakstian 1979; Bellack *et al.* 1981). Third, TCAs are potentially dangerous to patients with cardiac conduction defects. In addition, TCAs in overdose are cardiotoxic and therefore dangerous for the unsupervised suicidally depressed patient.

Over the years, a number of psychological models and treatments for depression have been developed. In this chapter, three are discussed: Lewinsohn's learning theory and social skills approach, Rehm's self-control theory approach, and Beck's cognitive approach.

The learning theory and social skills approach

The earliest behavioural speculations about depression had spoken of depression as 'extinction' (behavioural repertoire being weakened due to insufficient reinforcement relative to the effort expended — the response cost). One influential theory focused on *loss of reinforcer effectiveness*. According to this theory (Costello 1972) sufficient reinforcers may be available in the environment and the individual might still be capable of procuring them, but for some reason they have lost their *potency* as reinforcers.

Perhaps the most influential behavioural theory was that of Peter Lewinsohn (Lewinsohn *et al.* 1970). According to Lewinsohn, depression was due to a *low rate of response-contingent positive reinforcement*. This has consequences in terms of the respondent behaviour of the individual (elicits crying, dysphoric mood, etc.), and is itself sufficient explanation for reduced behavioural output in depression. In the early stages of depressive breakdown, symptoms may be maintained by reinforcement from others (the 'secondary gain' phenomenon), but later on close family and friends are more likely to stop rewarding the person's behaviour. They may try to avoid the depressed person altogether, thus further reducing frequency of rewards available in the environment. The treatment of choice within this theory was pleasant-events scheduling and social skills training. It is the latter which has received the most attention theoretically and in treatment outcome research.

One of the interesting debates at this time was whether depressed people do indeed have deficient social skills. Social skills have been assessed in many different ways from 'molecular' to 'molar' aspects: observer ratings of the minutiae of behaviour (e.g., eye contact, head nods, etc.); observer ratings of number of positive and negative actions and reactions; self-monitoring of such positive and negative actions/reactions; structured interviews of interpersonal adjustment; and self-ratings of difficulty with interpersonal situations. Different definitions and different methods of assessment produce different results. Lewinsohn *et al.* (1970) and Libet and Lewinsohn (1973) found that depressed individuals talked less, initiated conversation less, distributed attention in a group unevenly, responded more slowly to others, and 'rewarded' others less when they spoke. On the other hand, Coyne (1976) found that depressed individuals, although they had a marked alienating effect on people to whom they were talking in a 20-minute telephone conversation, showed little evidence of deficits in the molecular measures of social behaviour, a conclusion reinforced by later studies (e.g., Hammen and Peters 1978; Howes and Hokanson 1979).

These suggest that it is the content of the depressed person's conversation (either too much disclosure, or too many self-blameful statements) which is responsible for the alienating effect depressed people have on others. When depressed people attempt to engage in interpersonal relationships, they find their mood deteriorates as others lose interest. In reviewing this literature (Williams 1992), I suggested that these attempts may have gone wrong not because of lack of basic social skills, but because of what the depressed person wants to talk about. Inappropriate disclosure may make the social situation genuinely more difficult for them. Once the other person has been alienated, it may take better social skills than most people have to rescue the situation. Thus, it may not be that depressed people have poor social skills. It may be rather that they find themselves (because of what they talk about) more often in social situations which would exceed most people's capacities. It is hardly surprising that they withdraw altogether from such situations. If this is the case, the important area for therapy to tackle is not social skills, but the person's negative and self-blameful way of talking to others. This focus on the content of communication, to others and to oneself, has been the foundation of two theories of depression: the self-control theory of Rehm, and the cognitive theory of Beck.

In the first, self-blame (or lack of self-reward) is seen as one of three problems in attitudes to the self (the other two being self-monitoring and self-evaluation). In the second, low regard for the self is seen as one component of a negative cognitive triad (a distorted view of the self, world, and future) due to the co-occurrence of external stressors and longer-term, dysfunctional attitudes or schemata. The effect of this combination is to prompt a high frequency of negative automatic thoughts that thereafter maintain and exacerbate depressed mood. Let us turn first to self-control theory.

Self-control theory

Consider the following experiment. An individual performs a task (e.g., attempting to recognize which of three nonsense syllables in an array has occurred in a prior list, set up so that participants will have a 50–60% accuracy rate). Following their choice, subjects are asked whether they succeeded or failed, to *evaluate* their level of success relative to subjective standards of accuracy, and then to give themselves a *reward* in proportion to how deserving they think they are. Participants evaluate each response (on a 0–10 scale) and administer reward to themselves by pressing a button which lights up a lamp. No feedback about a participant's accuracy is provided. Such studies show that there is little correlation either between actual performance and participant's evaluation of their performance, or between their actual performance and the amount of reward that they give to themselves. In one such experiment, the maximum number of self-rewards was 30. Subjects varied between 0 and 20, but those who gave themselves low ratings and low numbers of self-reward had done no worse on the task than those who gave themselves a large amount of self-rewards and evaluated their performance highly.

The self-control model starts from these observations, emphasizing the opportunities for distortion there are in such self-monitoring, self-evaluation, and self-reward processes. Depressed individuals selectively attend to negative aspects of themselves and their world. Self-evaluation is performed on the basis of criteria that are biased, being set too high to achieve, so that overt and covert rewards are rarely awarded. Thus, the basis for normal rates of behaviour (self-regulation) in the relative absence of external control is diminished, and the depressed individual's behavioural repertoire is disrupted.

Evidence consistent with Rehm's 1977 formulation has taken the form of results showing that depressed and non-depressed subjects do indeed differentially reward and punish themselves as predicted by the theory (Rozensky *et al.* 1977; Lobitz and Post 1979). The theory has also led to several successful treatment studies (e.g., Fuchs and Rehm 1977; Rehm *et al.* 1979, 1987), using a group treatment approach, combining instructions in self-reinforcement, thought monitoring, and evaluation and activity monitoring.

The cognitive theory and therapy of depression

There are three main components of Beck's cognitive theory of emotional disorders. The first component is the presence of *negative automatic thoughts*—'automatic' by virtue of their coming 'out of the blue', often seemingly unprompted by events and not necessarily the results of 'directed' thinking. They seem 'immediate' and often 'valid' in the sense that they are often accepted as true by the person without further analysis. Their effect is to disrupt mood, and to cause further thoughts and images to emerge in a downward spiral of despair.

The second component is the presence of *systematic logical errors* in the thinking of depressed individuals. Several categories have been distinguished (although these are not mutually exclusive): arbitrary inference (e.g., 'My friend isn't answering the phone: she must be out enjoying herself with someone else'); over-generalization (e.g., 'This always happens to me'); selective abstraction (e.g., 'The nice things she says are irrelevant, it is the occasional criticism that shows what she really feels about me'); magnification (e.g., 'If I'm late for this meeting, they'll all think I'm not up to the job'); minimization (e.g., 'The boss's compliment was because she was in a good mood'); personalization, when a person attributes bad things to himself despite evidence to the contrary ('It's all my fault'); dichotomous (all or nothing: black/white) thinking ('If he leaves me, I may as well be dead').

The third component of the cognitive model is the presence of *depressogenic schemata*. These general, long-lasting attitudes or assumptions about the world represent the way in which the individual organizes his/her past and current experience, and is suggested to be the system by which incoming information about the world is classified. According to Beck, a schema is a structure for screening, coding, and evaluating impinging stimuli. In terms of the individual's adaptation to external reality, it is regarded as the mode by which the environment is broken down and organized into its many psychologically relevant facets; on the basis of the matrix of schemas, the individual is able to orient him/herself in relation to time and space and to categorize and interpret his/her experiences in a meaningful way. According to the theory, depressive schemata develop over many years and, although they may not be evident, remain ready to be activated by a combination of stressful circumstances.

Following from the theory, Beck's cognitive behaviour therapy (Beck *et al.* 1979) aims to deal with negative thoughts, memories, and beliefs which maintain depression and make the person vulnerable to future episodes. Cognitive techniques aim first at making patients re-conceptualize their thoughts and memories as *simply* thoughts and memories with the use of 'experiments' (homework) to test out the truth of the interpretations and gather more data for discussion.

The major techniques used in cognitive therapy are listed in Table 11.1 together with a brief description of their purpose. As an illustration of these techniques, consider the example of a client who comes to a therapy session distressed about something that happened the previous week. She is a student at college, and is feeling very depressed and homesick. The previous Friday, some friends from her hall of residence called round to see if she wanted to go to a party out of town. She did not feel like going, but they persuaded her that it would 'get her out of herself'. On the journey to the party, she felt less and less like socializing. She remembered previous parties that had gone badly, and felt very low. She knew she would not enjoy it. There would probably be no one there she really knew well. She felt that her friends meant well, but they did not really understand.

When she arrived at the party, she went in to see that 'everyone else was having a good time' and 'everyone else knew each other'. She felt even worse, made her excuses, and left after only 15 minutes. She went back to her room feeling suicidal and hopeless: nothing in her life would turn out right.

Faced with this example, the therapist has a number of options, depending on the stage that therapy has reached. *Thought-catching* would involve tracking some of the emotions she had felt during the evening, and asking 'What went through your mind right then?' The therapist will have explained at the outset that emotional reactions tend to follow on from (often barely

TABLE 11.1. Six core techniques of cognitive therapy

Technique	Purpose
Thought-catching	To teach the person to become aware of depressing thoughts as they occur
Task assignment	To encourage activities which the person has been avoiding (e.g., meeting a certain friend, attending a meeting of a club or society)
Reality testing	To select tasks which help to test out the truth of fixed negative thoughts or beliefs (e.g., phoning friend to test out the idea that no one will talk to me)
Cognitive rehearsal	To get the person to recount to the therapist all the stages involved in an activity they have been avoiding, together with the accompanying thoughts and feelings. The aim is to discover possible 'roadblocks', what can be done about them, and to imagine eventual success.
Alternative therapy	To instruct the person to imagine an upsetting situation and then generate strategies for coping
Dealing with underlying fears and assumptions	To investigate the way in which dysfunctional schemata and assumptions have built up over a lifetime, and how they now influence day-to-day thinking

conscious) automatic thoughts, and that understanding more about such thoughts, making them explicit, writing them down, and practising answering them back will help to decentre from such thoughts. The thoughts will seem more like 'just thoughts' rather than as 'reality'. Of course, such thoughts might be accurate in many respects, and it is the therapist's job to collaborate with the client in determining which correspond to reality, and which are simply being produced by the 'depressive propaganda' of automatic negative thinking.

Task assignment, for such a client, will grow out of the discussion of the Friday night event. The client might say, during the discussion, that she is never any good in any social encounter, or that no-one really wants to know her. Task assignment involves generating experiments that can treat such thoughts as experimental predictions. What might she do before the next session that could test out either idea? The therapist will encourage the client to come up with some suggestions, and then perhaps to predict what might happen when testing them out — what might go wrong, and what would she do if it did. The next session would then check whether the list of difficulties the client foresaw actually happened, or whether other unforeseen difficulties arose. In this way, the spirit of the therapy is always driven by encouraging a gentle curiosity and openness on the part of the client to whatever difficulties and challenges arise.

If there is likely to be a similar situation arising in the near future, the therapist may suggest that *cognitive rehearsal* is used: an imagination exercise in which the client anticipates each detail of trying to carry out a task, such as going out with friends. At each stage, as difficulties arise, so they are gently laid aside for later discussion, and the rehearsal proceeds to the end point, where the client is asked to imagine the feeling of pleasure and achievement at having completed the task. Each of the 'roadblocks' that have become evident during the rehearsal may now be discussed, and each may become the target of its own task assignment. For example, if one of the difficulties was the point at which she was going to get ready and she realized she did not have something she needed, then one task for the next few days may be to buy the things she needs. Each of these sub-tasks, although they appear insignificant, may turn out to be an important block to progress, and should not be minimized.

Because depression often involves feelings of helplessness and a reduced sense of efficacy, *alternative therapy* is used to explore coping options. In the example of our client at the party that had given so much distress, it is likely that careful examination of her self-talk would reveal themes of helplessness: 'I won't enjoy this'; 'There is nothing I can do about it'; 'No one here knows me, so what is the point of staying'. Cognitive therapy sees such thoughts and images not as mere symptoms of the depression, but as critical factors in maintaining it. The client has made pessimistic predictions about how the evening will go, and then taken action which prevents her from contradicting those predictions. Alternative therapy involves generating a number of alternative courses of action, and imagining, in detail, enacting them. Some options may well involve 'running away', it being important not to neglect even apparently maladaptive responses. Encouraging other options that are humorous often leads to more creative solutions being suggested. In the end, it will be important to discuss the positive and negative aspect of the possible options to gauge which are realistic.

Finally, and certainly by later stages of therapy, the therapist will encourage the client to look for patterns in her reactions to social situations that betray *underlying fears* (perhaps a fear of rejection) or *underlying assumptions* (perhaps the assumption that 'Everyone must like me, or I can't be happy'). The history of how such a fear or assumption has grown up and been reinforced through the client's experience of relationships at home, school, and college will be discussed. At each stage, the therapy is collaborative, with the therapist sharing his/her formulation of what has made her vulnerable, what has precipitated the latest depression, what is maintaining it, and what positive and protective factors there are in her life.

Evaluating the efficacy of cognitive therapy

Beck's cognitive therapy has been evaluated in several well-controlled outcome studies. Since these are reviewed extensively elsewhere (Williams

1992; Hollon and Beck 1995), they are not discussed here. Several conclusions emerge from such overviews. First, cognitive behaviour therapy (CBT) is effective with a variety of populations of depressed people — clinical and subclinical, from a fairly wide range of social class, in studies from North America, Australia, and Europe at least. Second, the combination of drugs and CBT sometimes appears more effective (although not significantly so) than CBT alone; CBT alone is mostly comparable to drugs alone; but drugs alone have not so far been found to be superior to CBT. Focusing on out-patients, the mean percentage change across the samples of out-patients who have received CBT alone is 66% (Rush *et al.* 1977; McLean and Hakstian 1979; Blackburn *et al.* 1981; Murphy *et al.* 1984; Beck *et al.* 1985; Elkin *et al.* 1989). This compares with a mean of 63% in samples of out-patients receiving tricyclic antidepressants (TCAs) alone (i.e., excluding Beck *et al.* but including Elkin *et al.*'s TCAs+clinical management group), and 72% for samples of out-patients who have received a combination of TCAs and CBT (Blackburn *et al.* 1981; Murphy *et al.* 1984; Beck *et al.* 1985).

However, as Beck *et al.* (1985) acknowledged, cognitive therapy is not the only psychological treatment which appeared to be effective in treating depression (p. 147):

> those approaches that combine both cognitive and behavioural procedures (e.g. Rehm's self-control or McLean's behavioural-cognitive marital skills training) along with cognitive therapy and the newly refined interpersonal psychotherapy (IPT) seem to be the most efficacious psychotherapy intervention for depression... Yet another report by Bellack *et al.* (1981)... (this referred to social skills training)... presented further evidence of the relative efficacy of structured psychological intervention in comparison to standard antidepressant drugs.

Thus, at least five types of psychotherapy were considered effective by the mid 1980s. Beck *et al.* (1985 p. 147) concluded that: 'the type of psychotherapy may not prove to be nearly so important as the extent to which it is adapted to a specific symptomatic focus'.

The NIMH Treatment of Depression Collaborative Research Program

Elkin *et al.*'s (1989) multi-centre trial found results which reinforced Beck's earlier conclusion. I shall describe these results in some detail, since they have been the cause of much discussion and speculation. A total of 250 patients at three sites were randomly allocated to receive Beckian cognitive therapy, interpersonal psychotherapy (IPT, Klerman *et al.* 1984), antidepressant medication plus clinical management, or placebo plus clinical management. To be included in the trial, patients had to be unipolar, non-psychotic, out-patients (Research Diagnostic Criteria, major depressive disorder), who had a score of at least 14 on the Hamilton Depression Scale. The tricyclic antidepressant used was imipramine (a mean of 185 mg/day with 95% of patients having at least 150 mg/day). Careful guidelines were laid down, not only for the CBT and IPT therapy, but also the clinical management (CM). Experienced psychiatrists conducted these 20–30 minute weekly interviews (after an initial session of 45–60 minutes). The guidelines for CM specified discussion of medication and side-effects, plus a review of the patient's clinical status and provision of support, encouragement, and direct advice if necessary. All treatments were planned to be 16 weeks in length, with a range of 16–20 sessions. The mean number of sessions for patients who completed treatment turned out to be 16.2. Each psychotherapy session lasted 50 minutes.

All treatments made significant gains, although there was a Treatment × Site Interaction for the more severely depressed and impaired patients (global assessment scale score < 50), such that IPT did very well on one site, CBT on another, with TCA+CM being more consistent throughout sites. The similarity of outcome of the four treatments was shown by the fact that of 12 primary statistical analyses, only 4 revealed any statistically significant results. Two of these were analyses of those patients who completed treatment (N=155 in the analysis, although 162 had completed, data not having been obtained for seven subjects). These significant findings concerned the Hopkins Symptom Checklist 90 and the Global Assessment Scale (GAS) and showed tricyclics to be superior to placebo. No other comparison was significant. The two other significant effects were found in their analysis of all patients who had entered treatment (N=239) even if they had dropped out immediately and were found on the Hamilton and Global Assessment Scale. *Post-hoc* tests, however, showed that only on the GAS could any between-group difference be detected; again a significant difference between the TCA+CM group and placebo+CM group. Looking at the final scores (for completers) on the Beck CBT (see p. 269) one can see why the analyses yielded so few differences. Outcome for all treatments (including the placebo+CM) were very similar (see Table 11.2).

Elkin *et al.* (1989, p. 977) themselves conclude: 'in the major analyses in this study, there was no evidence that either of the psychotherapies was significantly less (or more) effective than Imipramine+CM'. And regarding the comparison between IPT and CBT (p. 979): 'there is no evidence in this study of the greater effectiveness of one of the psychotherapies on measures of depressive symptoms and overall functioning (although . . . there was adequate power in the primary analyses for detecting any large effect size differences that might exist)'.

TABLE 11.2. Proportion of patients in remission at the end of treatment

	IPT	TCA+CM	CBT	Placebo+CM
Completer sample (N=155)	55%	57%	51%	29%
Total sample (N=239) (including drop-outs)	43%	42%	36%	21%

(From Elkin *et al.* 1989.)

Although there was limited evidence of this specific effectiveness of IPT and no evidence of the specific effectiveness of CBT when compared to placebo+CM, the authors discuss these findings in the light of the more surprising conclusion that there was only some, but not a great deal of evidence of the superiority of imipramine+CM over placebo+CM. The fact that only 4 out of the 12 primary analyses yielded significance was very puzzling given that it included a straight comparison of active antidepressants against an inactive placebo. Indeed, in some circles this apparent failure of the drug treatment has been the cause of much discussion and correspondence (e.g., see Klein's letter suggesting that different statistical analysis be used, and responses to his letter in *Archives of General Psychiatry*, 47, 1990, 682–8).

Comparing the percentage change scores on the Beck Depression Inventory (BDI, Beck *et al.* 1961) with previous outcome trials, the three active treatments achieved levels of improvement broadly comparable with previous studies (CBT, 62%; IPT, 70%; TCA+CM, 76%; placebo+CM, 61%; with TCA+CM doing better than any previous study of TCA alone — presumably due to the carefully described and supervised 'clinical management' component). What is striking is that the placebo+CM group did as well as active treatments have in previous studies. Elkin *et al.* also noted the fact that their placebo, for some reason, exceeded the performance of placebos in standard drug trials presumably, once again, due to the clinical management. If we had become accustomed to finding that different *active* treatments produced similar outcomes (e.g., Murphy *et al.* 1984), it was unexpected that a *placebo* condition should do so well. This was most surprising for patients with a Hamilton score of less than 20, where there was no advantage at all for TCAs or for the psychotherapies over the placebo+CM (although it is important to note that placebo did *not* do so well for the more severe subsample). This result potentially threatens both advocates of drug treatment and advocates of psychotherapy for less severely depressed patients.

Further work is therefore needed to understand what the therapeutic property of the placebo+CM treatment was. Clearly, something is happening here. Note that further research on these questions needs to move away from a 'horse race' model of psychotherapy, in which outcome trials are seen as a race to the finish line by a number of competitors, each with their own 'colours' and followers. Instead, we need to investigate the means by which any and all of these effective therapies have their effects. Considering the effectiveness of the placebo+CM condition in the NIMH trial, is the effect due simply to increased optimism in the patients? Or increased courage to try and do things that they have been avoiding doing, due either to the pill or to the advice? The theory on which interpersonal psychotherapy is premised would predict that what was happening was that, somehow, this clinical management was allowing the patient to overcome grief, to handle role transitions, to resolve interpersonal disputes, and to make up for interpersonal deficits. The theory on which cognitive therapy is premised would suggest that these patients recovered because they were gaining distance from their negative thoughts, engaging in activities to gain a sense of mastery and pleasure, and thereby being enabled to challenge their dysfunctional attitudes towards themselves.

It is quite possible that all the following were happening: interpersonal, cognitive, and behavioural changes. In the less severe patients, such changes were more easily prompted. The findings for the more severe patients are less clear-cut. There were consistent Treatment × Site interactions for these patients. At one site, cognitive therapy did extremely well, producing results comparable with imipramine. At another, IPT did well in a similar way. So we cannot conclude from the NIMH trial that more severely depressed patients respond better to antidepressants. Other studies (e.g., Hollon *et al.* 1992) have found no evidence of such differential response. There remains much scope for future research on these issues.

The prevention of relapse and recurrence

Estimates of the proportion of people who relapse following initial response to treatment varies depending on the severity of patients in the sample, the length of the follow-up period, and the definition of relapse (see Table 11.3). 'Relapse' implies that patients had responded successfully to the treatment of their acute symptoms. Definition of such successful response varies from study to study, but usually consists of achieving a certain low score on a measure of depression such as the Hamilton Depression Scale (cut-offs of 6 or 7 have been suggested) or the Beck Depression Inventory (BDI), where cut-offs of 15 or less (partial remission) or 9 or less (complete remission) have been used. Relapse is then said to have occurred *either* if a person's score rises above a cut-off on such a scale (e.g., two consecutive weeks of a BDI score of 16 or more, Evans *et al.* 1992*a*), *or* if a patient returns for treatment for their depression. For a review of these issues of relapse and its definition see Belsher and Costello (1988).

Klerman *et al.* (1974) found that 36% of their predominantly neurotically depressed out-patients relapsed within 8 months following initial response to

4–6 weeks of amitriptyline, 100–200 mg/day (if given no further treatment). The UK Medical Research Council Multicentre Trial (Mindham *et al.* 1973) involved more severely depressed out-patients and found that 50% relapsed within 6 months following initial treatment response if given no further treatment. The US National Institute of Mental Health Study (Prien *et al.* 1974) examined more severely depressed patients and found that 92% of a placebo maintenance group relapsed within the 2 years following successful response to initial active treatment. This pattern of results has been replicated in a further MRC trial of maintenance amitriptyline or lithium treatment (Glen *et al.* 1984). 6 months after good response to initial treatment, 56% of patients given no further treatment had relapsed; this figure had increased to 67% after 12 months and 78% after 24 months.

Each of the studies in Table 11.3 also examined to what extent maintenance dosage of antidepressant or lithium can reduce the probability of relapse. Although absolute levels have differed depending on severity of the depression being treated, most have found that relapse rates can be (at least) halved by maintenance medication (from 36% to 12% after 8 months, Klerman *et al.* 1984; from 50% to 22% after 6 months, Mindham *et al.* 1973; from 92% to 48% after 24 months, Prien *et al.* 1974). The estimate from the MRC trial (Glen *et al.* 1984) is more pessimistic, however. They found that relapse rates at 6 months were reduced from 56% to 34%; but at 12 months, 45%; and at 24 months, 59% of patients who remained on maintenance medication had relapsed. Keeping patients well after they have responded during the acute treatment phase remains a major mental health challenge. Relying solely on

TABLE 11.3. Percentage of patients relapsing following initial recovery after antidepressant acute or maintenance treatment

		Follow-up (mths) and relapse (%) among initial responders				
Study	Treatment	6	8	12	18	24
Klerman *et al.* (1974)	TCA[a] (acute)		36			
	TCA (+maintenance)		12			
Mindham *et al.* (1973)	TCA[b] (acute)	50				
	TCA (+maintenance)	22				
Prien *et al.* (1974)	TCA[c] (acute)					92
	TCA+lithium (+maintenance)					48
Glen *et al.* (1984)	TCA[d] (acute)	56		67		78
	TCA+lithium (+maintenance)	34		45		59

[a] 4–6 weeks amitriptyline.
[b] 3–10 weeks imipramine/amitriptyline.
[c] Imipramine.
[d] Amitriptyline.

maintenance medication for such prophylaxis has the disadvantage associated with long-term drug usage. It depends on patients continuing to take their drugs, carries the risk of overdose, may be dangerous for patients with heart complaints, and may involve unpleasant side-effects over a prolonged periods. Can cognitive therapy help?

There have been four outcome studies (see Table 11.4) which, having compared tricyclic antidepressants with cognitive therapy in the initial treatment, have taken patients who initially responded and examined their outcome over subsequent 12 or 24 months (Evans *et al.* 1992*a*; Blackburn *et al.* 1986; Simons *et al.* 1986; Shea *et al.* 1992, which is the 18 month follow-up of the Elkin *et al.* 1989 NIMH trial). Each of these studies has found that patients who have responded to tricyclic antidepressants have a probability of relapse equivalent to the groups who receive no maintenance treatment in the drug trials in Table 11.3 (Evans *et al.* 50% at 24 months; Simons *et al.* 66% at 12 months; Blackburn *et al.* 78% at 24 months; Shea *et al.* 28% at 12 months and 50% at 18 months).

These studies have also found, however, that the proportion of patients relapsing was substantially reduced if cognitive therapy had been added to tricyclic antidepressant medication during the acute treatment—Evans *et al.* from 50% to 15% at 24 months (cognitive therapy alone 20%); this compares with a 27% rate of relapse for medication plus maintenance medication for

TABLE 11.4. Percentage of patients relapsing following initial recovery after acute treatment by antidepressants, cognitive therapy, or the combination

Study	Treatment	Follow-up (mths) and relapse (%) among initial responders			
		6	12	18	24
Simons *et al.* (1986)	TCA[a]		66		
	CBT		20		
	TCA+CBT		43		
Blackburn *et al.* (1986)	TCA[b]				78
	CBT				23
	CBT+TCA				21
Shea *et al.* (1992)	TCA[c]+CM	11	28	50	
	CBT	9	9	36	
Evans *et al.* (1992)	TCA[c]				50
	TCA (+maintenance for 12 mths)				27
	CBT				20
	TCA+CBT				15

[a]Nortriptyline.
[b]Amitriptyline and clomipramine.
[c]Imipramine.

the first 12 months; Simons *et al.* from 66% to 43% at 12 months (cognitive therapy alone 20%); Blackburn *et al.* from 78% to 21% at 24 months (cognitive therapy alone 23%); and Shea *et al.* found that cognitive therapy alone had a relapse rate of 9% compared with the TCA+CM of 28% at 12 months. At 18 months, the relapse rate was 36% for CT alone compared with 50% for TCA+CM at 18 months.

Note that Shea *et al.* (1992) used a more rigorous definition of recovery than other studies. For their patients to have been considered recovered they had to have eight consecutive weeks of symptomatic remission. Only 48% of those completing treatment recovered on this definition (N=78, only one-third of the original sample). Thus, recovered patients in this study were much more likely to be truly well than the recovered patients in other studies. Relapse was defined as meeting criteria for major depressive disorder for at least two consecutive weeks in the follow-up period. If relapse is defined as either meeting this criteria or receiving at least three consecutive weeks' treatment for depression, then 14% of CBT patients relapsed in 12 months versus 50% for TCA (IPT was 43%); by 18 months 41% of the CBT group had relapsed compared with 61% of the TCA and 57% of IPT. In the first 12 months of the follow-up period, of those patients who recovered, only 5% of the CBT group sought further treatment, compared with 38% of the IPT group (χ^2=7.43, $P<0.007$) and 39% of the TCA group (χ^2=7.3, $P<0.007$). The corresponding percentage of those seeking treatment over 18 months is 14%, 43%, and 44% from the CBT, IPT, and TCA groups, respectively ($P<0.03$ for each comparison with CBT). Over the 18-month follow-up period, recovered patients who had received CBT received an average of 4.2 weeks of further treatment. Recovered patients who had received imipramine received an average of 20.3 weeks of further treatment ($P<0.017$).[1]

These studies are particularly interesting in that three of them (Evans *et al.*, Simons *et al.*, and Shea *et al.*) found some evidence of different relapse rates despite having found no difference between tricyclic antidepressant and cognitive therapy or the combination of the two in the acute phase of treatment. If these results are reliable, it will indicate an important advance in the management of chronically relapsing depressive illness.

In discussing the use of CBT to prevent relapse, Hollon and Beck (1995) insert an important caveat. It is possible that those people who respond to

[1]Note that these data from Shea *et al.* 1992 and its analysis is taken from my 1992 book, *The psychological treatment of depression*. The authors had made available to me the preprint of their paper, and I was grateful to both Tracie Shea and Irene Elkin for looking subsequently at the draft of the chapter to check the accuracy of the presentation of their follow-up. When the paper eventually appeared in print in the *Archives of General Psychiatry*, however, although none of the data were different, the statistical analyses showing the tendency for the groups to have differential relapse rates were missing.

cognitive therapy (and therefore go forward to the follow-up part of the trials) are different in some way to those people who respond to antidepressants. In other words, there may be a 'differential sieve' effect. If those who respond to CBT are less likely to relapse anyway, any difference between them and those who responded to antidepressants in relapse rates may be due to this individual difference variable, rather than to the effects of the treatment. However, no study has produced any evidence to support this supposed sieve effect, so it remains speculative.

In conclusion, cognitive therapy has been a pioneer in the empirical validation of structured psychological treatment for depression. No study has found it to be less effective than antidepressants, four have found it more effective in preventing relapse. It remains one of the most valuable contributions to the treatment of depression.

Mechanisms of change

The earlier discussion pointed out that cognitive behaviour therapy is only one among a number of structured psychotherapies which has proved to be effective in the acute treatment of depression. This has led some investigators to suggest that the changes brought about by structured psychotherapies are non-specific; they all share a common core of features which bring about the therapeutic effect. For example, Goldfried (1980) maintains that most therapeutic strategies involve the following: (1) they provide patients with new corrective experiences; (2) they offer patients direct feedback; (3) they induce in patients the expectation that therapy will help them; (4) they create a therapeutic relationship; and (5) they provide patients with repeated opportunities to test reality. Focusing more specifically on depression, Zeiss *et al.* (1979) outline the factors which were common to the therapies which are effective in treating depression. First, they have an elaborate, well-planned rationale which provides an initial structure that guides patients to the belief that they can control their own behaviour and thereby their own depression. Second, they provide training in skills that the patients can use to feel more effective in solving problems in their life. Third, such therapy emphasizes the independent use of these skills by the patient outside the therapy context, and provide sufficient structure so that the patient can attain the independent use of them. Finally, such therapies encourage patients to attribute improvement in their mood to their own increased skilfulness and not that of the therapist.

These accounts all claim that, by some means, different therapies bring about increases in self-efficacy and problem-solving abilities. However, they do not describe the mechanisms that bring about such an outcome. This means that they do not help the therapist who finds that their patient cannot increase his/her feelings of self-efficacy, learn skills, or solve problems. The lack of detail occurs because such accounts are 'final common pathway' explanations. These may be accurate accounts of why change finally occurs in psychotherapy, but if so, they need not imply that the same mechanisms of change are always involved in bringing about the final outcome (Hollon *et al.* 1987). It is equally likely that the same result can be produced by many and various specific factors, all of which may have a final common pathway.

It is important for those investigators who are interested in cognitive therapy to give as coherent an account as they can of the possible cognitive mechanisms which bring about change. Only then will it be sensible to discuss how best to measure these mechanisms.

I want to return to a suggestion made previously (Williams 1992) that mood and cognition are related in two ways in depression. First, mood and cognition spiral at times when there is no contrary information to interrupt the cycle or where the information that would normally interrupt it is accessed in a form which is too abstract or insufficiently detailed or imageable. Second, mood and cognition are related in that, in the absence of sufficiently concrete alternative criteria, mood is itself used as the criterion of truth of a self-statement (cf. Schwarz and Clore 1983). A proposition is taken to be true if it is consistent with the mood being felt at the time, however that mood has been caused.

Following cognitive therapy, a person may experience a depressed mood, but he/she is more likely to have: (1) learned to prevent it from activating negative thoughts and images; and (2) learned to ignore it as a source of information about the validity of current ideas (MacLeod 1989). Common to both changes is the ability to retrieve alternative information in a form which will be useful — that is, specific, imageable, and concrete. I predict that where this cannot be done, a person will respond more slowly to therapy, and will be more likely to relapse. In our own research we have investigated the role of autobiographical memory as the source of such information. I will describe these findings in detail below, focusing on the finding that depressed people find it difficult to retrieve specific information. Deficits in personal memories have several important consequences: they impair the reinterpretation of old memories; they obscure the possible links between mood, thoughts, and behaviour; they prevent the person from generating effective alternative means of coping with current problems.

Depression and the specificity of autobiographical memory

Autobiographical memory in depressed people is not only biased, in the sense that they take longer to remember positive events that happened in their lives compared with negative events. In addition, we have found that depressed people are more likely to be over-general in their memories (see Williams 1996 for review). In a typical experiment patients are given words or phrases to cue their memories. These may be positive (e.g., happy, safe) or negative (e.g., angry, sorry). At the outset, it is explained that after each word, the patients are to try and recall an event that the word reminds them of. It is emphasized that what is required is a specific event, something that happened at a particular place at a particular time. A few practice items are given until the patients understand what is required. A large number of studies has found that depressed patients are more likely to respond to these cues not by giving specific events (e.g., going for a walk last Tuesday) but by giving generic statements that summarize events (e.g., going for walks).

This is a phenomenon similar to that which occurs in cognitive therapy for depression. From time to time, the therapist asks the patient a question about his or her past and the patient responds with a statement such as 'We always used to have such good times together' or 'I've always failed in everything I've done'. If therapists try to ask specific questions about the events on which such general statements are based, it sometimes takes patients a great deal of effort to retrieve the specific events. This is true, not only for negative events (which people may not wish to talk about), but also in the case of positive events.

We have explained these phenomenon in terms of those theories of memory which assume that memory is hierarchically organized, with the 'upper' layers containing general memory information that can act as indices to the more specific and detailed 'lower' layers. Thus, these upper layers act as intermediate stages in the encoding and retrieval of memories. When one tries to retrieve an event, one first generates an 'upper layer' general description. This description is then used to search the 'lower layer' memory 'database' for an appropriate candidate memory. For example, in response to the cue word 'happy', people generate an intermediate description based on the implicit question 'what sort of people, activities, places make me happy'. This 'upper layer' description may be such things as 'gardening' or 'my girlfriend' or 'drinking in pubs with friends'. It appears that depressed patients get stuck at that intermediate stage, and cannot use the general descriptions that they generate to help them retrieve specific examples. We have coined the term 'mnemonic interlock' to describe this phenomenon, making explicit reference to the depressive interlock discussed by Teasdale and Barnard (1993; see also Chapter 4). It appears that mnemonic interlock is most likely where the intermediate description used in the memory search involves self-reference and thus is more likely to generate other general self-descriptions, rather than specific event memories (Williams 1996). One implication of this link with Teasdale and Barnard's account is that a non-depressive 'mind-in-place', needed to prevent relapse in depression (Chapter 4), will be characterized by an ability to retrieve specific memories. Whatever its origins and mechanism, the question arises of what effects such mnemonic interlock has on other psychological functions. Here, I shall consider the effects on the reinterpretation of old memories, on the perception of thought–affect–behaviour connections, on problem-solving, and on the maintenance of depression.

The effect of over-general memory

I suggest that generic encoding and retrieval of events may inhibit reinterpretation and reschematization of the past. For example, if somebody has walked past in the street and ignored the patient, then the patient may have encoded that as an 'upper layer' description of 'people not bothering with me' or 'disliking me'. Only by retrieving 'lower layer' details about what actually happened will other information be retrieved which might lead to a different conclusion and a different interpretation of that event.

Second, generic retrieval style shows up most clearly in the difficulty which patients often experience in using diaries. Since this ability to record aspects of daily life is fundamental to cognitive psychotherapies, difficulty in encoding and retrieving specific events will retard progress because specific links between mood and mental contents will not be observed.

Third, over-general retrieval has implications for problem-solving. Problem-solving involves several steps (D'Zurilla and Goldfried 1971; Goldfried and Goldfried 1975). The first is the general orientation to a problem. People have to be able to recognize that a problem exists and to be able to articulate what the problem is as precisely as possible. The next stage is to generate as many alternative solutions as possible, and then to weigh up the advantages and disadvantages of implementing each one. The one that appears to be most likely to produce the best outcome is then selected, implemented, and its effects evaluated. There is little doubt that depressed patients find such problem-solving difficult. For example, they do not generate as many alternative solutions as non-depressed people do and what alternatives they do generate tend to be less effective (as rated by an independent judge) than those generated by non-depressed individuals (Marx *et al.* 1992).

Problem-solving becomes inhibited because depressed people attempt to use their 'upper layer' memory as a database to generate effective solutions to current problems. But this database is severely restricted because of the lack of specific information. Evans *et al.* (1992*b*) tested these hypotheses directly in a group of suicide attempters measuring both the level of over-generality in autobiographical memory, and measuring the effectiveness of the solutions produced in response to the Means-Ends Problem-Solving task (MEPS) (Platt and Spivack 1975). We found that they were very highly correlated. People who had the most difficulty being specific in their memory produced the least effective solutions to the problems.

Finally, over-general retrieval retards progress in therapy. A study of prediction of recovery and relapse in depression has shown that over-generality in the retrieval of positive memories (assessed at admission) predicts severity of depression seven months later (Brittlebank *et al.* 1993). Similarly, DeRubeis and Feeley (1990) found that more reduction in depression symptoms early in therapy occurred when the therapist used more 'concrete' strategies. All of these data are consistent with the suggestion that the way in which a person recalls events about themselves is very important in determining their mood and problem-solving abilities.

In future research, it will be interesting to examine whether such memory problems predict not only persistence of depression, but also the probability of relapse and recurrence. Current evidence on the prediction of relapse has implicated different thinking styles. Three studies (Eaves and Rush 1984; Simons *et al.* 1986; Hollon *et al.* 1990) have assessed dysfunctional attitudes or attributions when patients are discharged (at which point there is still some mild mood disturbance). In each case, level of dysfunctional attitudes or attributions contributed significantly to the prediction of relapse. The conclusion is that what we are measuring here is the capacity of small amounts of mood disturbance to precipitate large shifts in dysfunctional thinking. If dysfunctional thinking is assessed when a person is not currently depressed, it does not predict relapse. The best evidence for the specific efficacy of cognitive behaviour therapy in producing its effect by changing a cognitive variable comes from the Evans and Hollon group. Hollon *et al.* (1990) found that CBT produced greater change in dysfunctional attributions than did antidepressant treatment. Further, causal modelling showed that the extent to which CBT had a relapse preventative effect was mediated most directly by the amount of change in the attributions during acute treatment.

It is possible that the prophylactic effects of CBT are due to patients learning to 'decentre' from their troubling negative thoughts and prevent further deterioration of their mood (Beck *et al.* 1979; Williams 1992; pp. 264–5; Fennell 1989). In a detailed information-processing analysis of the prophylactic effects of CBT (Teasdale *et al.* 1994), we have indicated how such decentring enables patients to learn to interrupt cycles of depressive ruminative thinking that would otherwise lead to relapse. Such cycles have been shown to be associated with the intensification and prolongation of depressed mood (Nolen-Hoeksema 1991). We are currently investigating whether the specificity of people's autobiographical memory contributes to their ability to escape such cycles.

Concluding remarks

Cognitive therapy provides compensation for the errors and biases which have become enslaved by depressive interpretation of events. In part, this is done by giving patients methods by which they can manage their symptoms, and in part by making them aware of the way in which they are making errors in judgements under conditions of uncertainty. There is a growing literature that suggests that cognitive therapy reduces vulnerability to further depression. It appears to do so by preventing small amounts of mood disturbance from precipitating a large amount of cognitive change. This involves the prevention of large increases in negative thinking, in helplessness, in dysfunctional attitudes and mis-attributions, and in biased information-processing that would normally occur (especially if the person has been depressed before). We already know that levels of dysfunctional thinking and negative self-referent descriptions can predict both relapse and persistence of depression. It is a small step, but an important one, to the hypothesis that the critical aspect of cognitive therapy is the breaking of the association between mood disturbance and elaboration of negative self-referent material and the weakening of mood as a criterion of the truth of negative thoughts, assumptions, and fears. Finally, it has been, and will continue to be important to search for critical cognitive processes (such as those aspects of autobiographical memory that we have identified), which help to explain the information-processing processes underlying the therapeutic power of cognitive therapy to bring about such change.

Acknowledgements

This chapter draws on and develops parts of my 1992 book, *The psychological treatment of depression*. I am grateful to David Clark, John Teasdale, and Zindel Segal for many helpful discussions.

References

Angst, J. (1988). Clinical course of affective disorders. In *Depressive illness: Prediction of clinical course and outcome* (ed. T. Helgason and R. J. Daly), pp. 1–48. Springer, Berlin.

Beck, A. T., Ward, C. H., Mendelson, M., Mock, J. E., and Erbaugh, J. K. (1961). An inventory for measuring depression. *Archives of General Psychiatry*, 4, 561–71.

Beck, A. T., Rush, A. J., Shaw, B. F., and Emery, G. (1979). *Cognitive therapy of depression*. Guilford Press, New York.

Beck, A. T., Hollon, S. D., Young, J. E., Bedrosian, R. C., and Budenz, D. (1985). Treatment of depression with cognitive therapy and amitriptyline. *Archives of General Psychiatry*, 42, 142–8

Bellack, A. S., Hersen, M., and Harmondsworth, J. (1981). Social skills training compared with pharmacotherapy and psychotherapy in the treatment of unipolar depression. *American Journal of Psychiatry*, 138, 1562–7.

Belsher, G. and Costello, C. G. (1988). Relapse after recovery from unipolar depression: a critical review. *Psychological Bulletin*, 104, 84–96.

Berti Ceroni, G., Neri, C., and Pezzoli, A. (1984). Chronicity in major depression: A naturalistic prospective study. *Journal of Affective Disorders*, 7, 121–44.

Blackburn, I. M., Bishop, S., Glen, I. M., Whalley, L. J., and Christie, J. E. (1981). The efficacy of cognitive therapy in depression: a treatment trial using cognitive therapy and pharmacotherapy, each alone and in combination. *British Journal of Psychiatry*, 139, 181–9.

Blackburn, I. M., Eunson, K. M., and Bishop, S. (1986). A two year naturalistic follow-up of depressed patients treated with cognitive therapy, pharmacotherapy and a combination of both. *Journal of Affective Disorders*, 10, 67–75.

Brittlebank, A., Scott, J., Ferrier, N., and Williams., J. M. G. (1993). Autobiographical memory in depression: state or trait marker? *British Journal of Psychiatry*, 162, 118–21.

Costello, C. G. (1972). Depression: loss of reinforcement or loss of reinforcer effectiveness. *Behavior Therapy*, 3, 240–7.

Coyne, J. C. (1976). Depression and the response of others. *Journal of Abnormal Psychology*, 85, 186–93.

D'Zurilla, T. J. and Goldfried, M. R. (1971). Problem solving and behaviour modification. *Journal of Abnormal Psychology*, 78, 107–26.

DeRubeis, R. J. and Feeley, M. (1990). Determinants of change in cognitive therapy for depression. *Cognitive Therapy and Research*, 14, 469–82.

Eaves, G. and Rush, A. J. (1984). Cognitive patterns in symptomatic and remitted unipolar major depression. *Journal of Abnormal Psychology*, 93, 31–40.

Elkin, I., Shea, M. T., Watkins, J. T., Imber, S. D., Sotsky, S, M., Collins, J. F., *et al.* (1989). NIMH treatment of depression collaborative research program: general effectiveness of treatments. *Archives of General Psychiatry*, 46, 971–83.

Evans, M., Hollon, S. D., DeRubies, R. J., Piasecki, J. M., Grove, W. M., Garvey, M. J., and Tuason, V. B. (1992*a*). Differential relapse following cognitive therapy, pharmacotherapy, and combined cognitive-pharmacotherapy for depression. *Archives of General Psychiatry*, 49, 802–8.

Evans, J., Williams, J. M. G., O'Loughlin, S., and Howells, K. (1992*b*). Autobiographical memory and problem solving strategies of individuals who parasuicide. *Psychological Medicine*, 22, 399–405.

Fennell, M. (1989). Depression. In *Cognitive behaviour therapy for psychiatric problems* (ed. K. Hawton, P. M. Salkovskis, J. Kirk, and D. M. Clark), pp. 169–234. Oxford University Press.

Frank, E., Kupfer, D. J., Perel, J. M., Cornes, C., Jarrett, D. B., Mallinger, A. G., *et al.* (1990). Three-year outcomes for maintenance therapies in recurrent depression. *Archives of General Psychiatry*, 47, 1093–9.

Friedman, A. S. (1975). Interaction of drug therapy with marital therapy in depressive patients. *Archives of General Psychiatry*, 32, 619–37.

Fuchs, C. and Rehm, L. P. (1977). A self-control behaviour therapy program for depression. *Journal of Consulting and Clinical Psychology*, 45, 206–15.

Glen, A. M., Johnson, A. L., and Shepard, M. (1984). Continuation therapy with lithium and amitriptyline in unipolar depressive illness: A randomised double-blind controlled trial. *Psychological Medicine*, 14, 37–50.

Goldfried, M. R. (1980). Toward a delineation of therapeutic change principles. *American Psychologist*, 35, 991–9.

Goldfried, M. R. and Goldfried, A. P. (1975). Cognitive change methods. In *Helping people change* (ed. F. H. Kanfer and A. P. Goldstein). Academic Press, New York.

Hammen, C. L. and Peters, S. D. (1978). Interpersonal consequences of depression: responses to men and women enacting a depressed role. *Journal of Abnormal Psychology*, 87, 322–32.

Hollon, S. D. and Beck, A. T. (1995). Cognitive and cognitive behavioral therapies. In *Handbook of psychotherapy and behavior change* (4th edn) (ed. S. L. Garfield and A. E. Bergin), pp. 428–66. Wiley, New York.

Hollon, S. D., DeRubeis, R. J., and Evans, M. D. (1987). Cause or mediation of change in treatment for depression: Discriminability between non-specificity and non-causability. *Psychological Bulletin*, 102, 139–49.

Hollon, S. D., Evans, M. D. and De Rubeis, R. J. (1990). Cognitive mediation of relapse prevention following treatment for depression: Implications of differential risk. In *Psychological aspects of depression* (ed. R. E. Ingram), pp. 117–36. Plenum, New York.

Hollon, S. D., DeRubeis, R. J., Evans, M. D., Wiemer, M. J., Garvey, M. J., Grove, W. M., and Tuason, V. B. (1992). Cognitive therapy and pharmacotherapy for depression: singly and in combination. *Archives of General Psychiatry*, 49, 774–81.

Howes, M. J. and Hokanson, J. E. (1979). Conversational and social responses to depressive interpersonal behaviour. *Journal of Abnormal Psychology*, 88, 625–34.

Keller, M. B., Klerman, G. L., Lavori, P. W., Coryell, W., and Endicott, J. (1984). Long-term outcome of episodes of major depression: Clinical and public health significance. *Journal of the American Medical Association*, 252, 788–92.

Klein, D. F. (1990). NIMH collaborative research on treatment of depression (Letter). *Archives of General Psychiatry*, 47, 682–4.

Klerman, G. L., DiMaschio, A., Weissman, M., *et al.* (1974). Treatment of depression by drugs and psychotherapy. *American Journal of Psychiatry*, 131, 186–91.

Klerman, G. L., Weissman, M. M., Rounsaville, B. J., and Chevron, E. S. (1984). *Interpersonal psychotherapy of depression*. Basic Books, New York.

Kupfer, D. J., Frank, E., Perel, J. M., Cornes, C., Mallinger, A. G., Thase, M. E., *et al.* (1992). Five-year outcome for maintenance therapies in recurrent depression. *Archives of General Psychiatry*, 49, 769–73.

Lewinsohn, P. M., Weinstein, M. S., and Alpere, T. A. (1970). A behavioral approach to the group treatment of depressed persons: a methodological contribution. *Journal of Clinical Psychology*, 26, 525–32.

Libet, J. and Lewinsohn, P. M. (1973). The concept of social skill with special reference to the behaviour of depressed persons. *Journal of Consulting and Clinical Psychology*, 40, 301–12.

Lobitz, W. C. and Post, R. D. (1979). Parameters of self-reinforcement and depression. *Journal of Abnormal Psychology*, 88, 33–41.

MacLeod, A. K. (1989). Anxiety and judgement of future personal events. Unpublished D.Phil. Thesis. University of Cambridge.

Marx, E. M., Williams. J. M. G., and Claridge, G. S. (1992). Depression and social problem-solving. *Journal of Abnormal Psychology*, 101, 78–86.

McLean, P. D. and Hakstian, A. R. (1979). Clinical depression: comparative efficacy of outpatient treatments. *Journal of Consulting and Clinical Psychology*, 47, 818–36.

Mindham, R. H. J., Howland, C., and Shepherd, M. (1973). An evaluation of continuation therapy with tricyclic antidepressants in depressive illness. *Psychological Medicine*, 3, 5–17.

Murphy, G. E., Simons, A. D., Wetzel, R. D., and Lustman, P. J. (1984). Cognitive therapy and pharmacotherapy: singly and together in the treatment of depression. *Archives of General Psychiatry*, **41**, 33–41.

Nolen-Hoeksema, S. (1991). Response to depression and their effects on the duration of depressive episodes. *Journal of Abnormal Psychology*, **100**, 569–82.

Platt, J. J. and Sopivack, G. (1975). *Manual for the means-ends-problem-solving (MEPS): A measure of interpersonal problem solving skill.* Hahnemann Medical College and Hospital, Philadelphia, PA.

Prien, R. F., Clet, C. G., and Caffey, E. M. (1974). Lithium prophylaxis in recurrent affective illness. *American Journal of Psychiatry*, **131**, 198–203.

Prien, R. F., Kupfer, D. J., Mansky, P. A., Small, J. G., Tuason, V. B., Voss, C. B., and Johnson, W. E. (1984). Drug therapy in the prevention of recurrences in unipolar and bipolar affective disorders: A report of the NIMH Collaborative Study group comparing lithium carbonate, imipramine, and a lithium carbonate–imipramine combination. *Archives of General Psychiatry*, **41**, 1096–104.

Rehm, L. P. (1977). A self-control model of depression. *Behavior Therapy*, **8**, 787–804.

Rehm, L. P., Fuchs, C. Z., Roth, D. M., Kornblith, S. J., and Romano, J. M. (1979). A comparison of self-control and assertion skills treatment of depression. *Behavior Therapy*, **10**, 429–42.

Rehm, L. P., Kaslow, N. J., and Rabin, A. (1987). Cognitive and behavioural targets in a self-control therapy program for depression. *Journal of Consulting and Clinical Psychology*, **55**, 60–7.

Rozensky, R. H., Rehm. L. P., Pry, G., and Roth, D. (1977). Depression and self-reinforcement behaviour in hospitalized patients. *Journal of Behavior Therapy and Experimental Psychiatry*, **8**, 35–8.

Rush, A. J., Beck, A. T., Kovacs, M., and Hollon, S. (1977). Comparative efficacy of cognitive therapy and pharmacotherapy in the treatment of depressed out-patients. *Cognitive Therapy and Research*, **1**, 17–37.

Schwarz, N. and Clore, G. L. (1983). Mood, misattribution and judgements of well being: Information and directive function of affective states. *Journal of Personality and Social Psychology*, **45**, 513–23.

Segal, Z. V., Shaw, B. F., Vella, D. D., and Katz, R. (1992). Cognitive and life stress predictors of relapse in remitted unipolar depressed patients: Test of the congruency hypothesis. *Journal of Abnormal Psychology*, **101**, 26–36.

Shea, M. T., Elkin, I., Imber, S. D., Sotski, S. M., Watkins, J. T., Collins, J. F., *et al.* (1992). Course of depressive symptoms over follow-up: Findings from the NIMH treatment of depression collaborative research programme. *Archives of General Psychiatry*, **49**, 782–7.

Simons, A. D., Murphy, G. E., Levine, J. L., and Wetzel, R. D. (1986). Cognitive therapy and pharmacotherapy for depression. *Archives of General Psychiatry*, **43**, 43–50.

Sturt, E., Kumarkura, N., and Der, G. (1984). How depressing life is — Life long morbidity risk for depressive disorder in the general population. *Journal of Affective Disorders*, **6**, 104–22.

Teasdale, J. D. and Barnard, P. J. (1993). *Affect, cognition and change: re-modelling depressive thought.* Erlbaum, Hillsdale, NJ.

Teasdale, J. D., Segal, Z. V., and Williams, J. M. G. (1994). How does cognitive therapy prevent depressive relapse and why should attentional control (mindfulness) training help? An information processing analysis. *Behaviour Research and Therapy*, **33**, 25–39.

Van Valkenburg, C., Akiskal, H. W., Puzantian, V., and Rosenthal, T. (1984). Anxious depression: Clinical, family history, and naturalistic outcome—comparisons with panic and major depressive disorders. *Journal of Affective Disorders*, 6, 67–82.

Williams, J. M. G. (1992). *The psychological treatment of depression: A guide to the theory and practice of cognitive behaviour therapy*. Routledge, London.

Williams J. M. G. (1996). The specificity of autobiographical memory in depression. In *Remembering our past: Studies in autobiographical memory* (ed. D. C. Rubin), pp. 271–96). Cambridge University Press.

Zeiss, A. M., Lewinsohn, P. M., and Munoz, R. F. (1979). Nonspecific improvement effects in depression using interpersonal skills training, pleasant activity schedules, or cognitive training. *Journal of Consulting and Clinical Psychology*, 47, 427–39.

12

Attempted suicide

Keith Hawton

The author's work in this field began more than 20 years ago with the encouragement of Michael Gelder and John Bancroft. Michael Gelder has continued to provide ongoing support for the research programme, for which the author is extremely grateful.

This chapter will mainly address the problem of attempted suicide ('deliberate self-harm', 'parasuicide'), which includes any intentional act of self-poisoning (overdose) or self-injury, irrespective of the intended outcome. Although a substantial proportion of such acts are motivated by significant degrees of suicidal intent, others are not and may include complex multiple motivation (Bancroft *et al.* 1976, 1979; Hawton *et al.* 1982*a*). Most of the work on this problem has been conducted in general hospitals. The majority of general hospital referred cases involve overdoses, and much of the remainder are because of self-cutting (Hawton and Fagg 1992*a*). However, it is clear that much self-poisoning and self-injury occurs in the community (especially in young people) and does not come to medical attention (Kienhorst *et al.* 1990), or only does at a later stage, perhaps following a repeat episode (Hawton *et al.* in press).

In the United Kingdom there was a very marked escalation in the extent of attempted suicide from the mid 1960s onwards. In Oxford, for example, the rates of the behaviour based on general hospital statistics increased fourfold during the 10 years up until 1973 (Bancroft *et al.* 1975). The rates further increased until the late 1970s and early 1980s, declined somewhat during the 1980s (especially in females) and then increased again at the beginning of the 1990s. It has been estimated that there are at least 100 000 cases referred to general hospitals per year in England and Wales alone (Hawton and Fagg 1992*a*), almost 20 000 being teenagers (Hawton and Fagg 1992*b*). Attempted suicide is particularly common in young people, two-thirds of cases being under 35 years of age. In contrast to completed suicide it is more common in females than males, but this imbalance has been steadily diminishing.

Although the epidemiology of attempted suicide has been particularly well documented by centres in the United Kingdom it is now apparent that this problem is found throughout Europe and much of the rest of the western world. In Europe, there is considerable variation in the patterns of the behaviour between countries, both in terms of actual rates and (to a lesser degree) the age distribution (Schmidtke *et al.* 1994). The picture is less well documented for North America but there is evidence of self-harm posing similar problems there (Wexler *et al.* 1978).

The outcome following attempted suicide is variable. There is significant risk of completed suicide, this having been estimated in the United Kingdom as being 1% in the first year following an episode (a risk 100 times that of the general population) and approximately 3% in the eight years after an episode (Hawton and Fagg 1988). In other countries, higher rates of subsequent suicide are often reported (Kreitman 1977), this variation probably reflecting differences in the populations of self-harm patients in different countries.

In contrast to the extensive information we now have about the characteristics of people who harm themselves, rather less attention has been paid to finding effective ways of managing the problem. While there are clearly some reasons for this, as will be apparent later, given the size of the problem as a health issue and the current attention to the prevention of suicide (Jenkins *et al.* 1994), it is surprising that there is a relative paucity of evidence on which to base clinical strategy.

In this chapter, the following aspects of treatment will be addressed:

1. What is known about the characteristics of attempted suicide patients and their behaviour which is relevant to treatment needs.
2. The treatment approaches which have been developed, including the principles on which these have been based.
3. The results of treatment studies and what we can learn from them.
4. Research needs in this area, in relation to further understanding of the behaviour relevant to treatment needs, possible developments in treatments, and issues concerning the evaluation of the effectiveness of treatments.

The characteristics of people who attempt suicide

Their problems

The types of problems faced by attempted suicide patients vary according to their sex and age, but within subgroups the findings of studies are fairly consistent. In a general sample of patients the most frequent problems were difficulties in interpersonal relationships, especially with partners (72%), employment problems (28%), particularly in males (54%), difficulties with children (26%), and financial problems (19%) (Bancroft *et al.* 1977). Life events are very frequent in the months before attempts, being more common than in either matched depressed patients or general population controls (Paykel *et al.* 1975). Often, such events occur in the few days before an attempt and these usually involve disruption in a relationship with a partner. Alcohol problems, and to a lesser extent drug misuse, often complicate the picture. For example, in a comparative study of attempted suicide in Oxford and Edinburgh, between 14.3% and 22.6% of males and between 4.7% and 5.5% of females were found to exhibit alcohol dependence (Platt *et al.* 1988). In addition, alcohol use often immediately precedes self-harm behaviour (Hawton *et al.* 1989).

Newson-Smith and Hirsch (1979) found that symptoms of psychiatric disorders, especially depression, were common among these patients, with up to a third having definite psychiatric disorders according to the Present State Examination. Urwin and Gibbons (1979) reported a very similar finding and also identified a quarter of male patients and 10% of females to have personality disorders.

In older adolescent patients, problems with partners commonly precede the acts, whereas difficulties with parents are especially common in younger adolescents (Hawton *et al.* 1982*b*; Hawton *et al.* in press). However, these more immediate problems often occur against a background of long-term family difficulties (Adams *et al.* 1982; Fergusson and Lynskey 1995).

Thus, the recent problems and life events faced by this population are heterogeneous and often complex and in many cases occur in the setting of longer-term difficulties. This means that there will not be a single universal treatment approach suitable in all cases.

Psychological characteristics

Interpersonal problem-solving skills
There is substantial evidence that many suicide attempters have deficits in problem-solving skills, particularly in relation to dealing with difficulties in interpersonal relationships (e.g., McLeavey *et al.* 1987). One method used to investigate problem-solving is the Means-End Problem-Solving Procedure (MEPS, Platt *et al.* 1975) in which subjects are asked to indicate steps that they think appropriate to complete the gap between the beginning and end of stories, the stories usually being relevant to their age group. Schotte and Clum (1987) found that suicidal psychiatric in-patients showed deficiencies in problem-solving skills compared with non-suicidal but equally depressed in-patients. Thus, they generated fewer steps ('means') to complete the stories, fewer relevant means, and more irrelevant means. Using this and other measures

McLeavey *et al.* (1987) found that while patients who had taken overdoses and psychiatric patients both performed less well than non-patient controls, the overdose patients showed greater deficits in problem-solving in terms of scores on both the MEPS and a self-rated problem-solving questionnaire. Also using the MEPS, Linehan *et al.* (1987) found that in-patient suicide attempters tended to be more passive in their problem-solving than either in-patients with suicidal ideas alone or those without suicidal ideas. Deficiencies in problem-solving are especially significant when viewed in the context of the high incidence of life events and difficulties which confront this population.

One question that has not been fully clarified is whether problem-solving deficits are state or trait phenomena (i.e., whether they are persistent overt characteristics or whether they are only manifest at times of low mood and/or crisis). One uncontrolled study has suggested that these deficits are only apparent at times of crisis (Schotte *et al.* 1990). In a longitudinal study Schmidtke and Schaller (1994) found that differences between suicide attempters and controls in terms of 'dichotomous thinking', 'cognitive rigidity', and 'field dependance' were related to mood rather than the occurrence of suicidal behaviour in the former group. In view of its relevance to treatment, this requires further investigation, particularly with regard to problem-solving skills.

It has been suggested by Williams and Broadbent (1986) that a factor underlying poor problem-solving skills is a deficiency in retrieval of personal memories. Thus, when they gave patients who had taken overdoses a single word and asked them to retrieve a specific memory associated with that word ('auto-biographical memory'), they took longer than controls to retrieve positive memories from their lives and tended to recall things in a summarized over-general way (e.g., the word 'happy' might generate a memory in an overdose patient, such as 'when I am having fun with my friends', whereas a control subject might be more likely to say 'when I went to the cinema last week with my boyfriend'). This finding has been repeated and confirmed in patients matched for intellectual level (MacLeod *et al.* 1992). It seems possible that this tendency is linked to problem-solving deficits because when trying to tackle stressful situations, an individual may not have enough specific information from personal memories from which to identify specific coping strategies. This proposal is supported by the finding in overdose patients of an association between the level of over-generalization in autobiographical memories and the effectiveness of solutions elicited on the MEPS (Evans *et al.* 1992).

Hopelessness
Pessimism about the future (Beck *et al.* 1974) is very important in suicidal behaviour, having been shown to be a key factor linking depression with suicidal acts (e.g., Beck *et al.* 1975; Wetzel 1976; Dyer and Kreitman 1984),

an important predictor of repetition of suicidal behaviour (Petrie *et al.* 1988), and a factor associated with risk of eventual suicide (Beck *et al.* 1985). There is evidence that hopelessness in this population is related more to anticipation of fewer positive events rather than anticipation of more negative events (MacLeod *et al.* 1992). In keeping with this finding, Linehan *et al.* (1983) found that attempted suicide patients endorsed fewer important reasons for living when administered the Reasons for Living Inventory than did either general population or psychiatric controls. These findings could relate to the impoverished circumstances with associated lack of opportunities in which many attempted suicide patients find themselves, although there is also some evidence in this population for a specific bias in cognitive processing in this regard (MacLeod *et al.* 1992).

Self-esteem

Low self-esteem is a well recognized vulnerability factor for depression, but it may play a particularly important role in predisposition to suicidal behaviour. This has been shown, for example, in community samples of adolescents reporting suicidal behaviour (Kienhorst *et al.* 1990; Fergusson and Lynskey, 1995). This association will be in part because of a link between low self-regard and hopelessness about the future. However, Overholser *et al.* (1995) found that while low self-esteem in adolescents was related to higher levels of depression, hopelessness, suicidal ideation, and an increased likelihood of having previously attempted suicide, self-esteem added statistically to the risk of suicidal ideation beyond that explained by depression and hopelessness.

Motivation and compliance with treatment

A major feature complicating the aftercare of many patients who have attempted suicide is the high rates of non-attendance at treatment sessions. In several studies, compliance rates of less than 50% have been reported in terms of attendance at initial out-patient sessions (e.g., Morgan *et al.* 1976; O'Brien *et al.* 1987). This may be related in part to the nature of the treatment offered, with continuity of care being especially important. Thus, as discussed later, patients are more likely to attend if they are due to see the same person who conducted their assessment while in hospital (Möller 1989). Other factors likely to influence motivation for treatment are the enthusiasm of the clinician and the importance he/she appears to attach to the patient attending. Compliance will also be affected by the immediacy and location of treatment (Hawton *et al.* 1981).

Treatment approaches

Before appropriate treatment can be initiated, a careful assessment of the attempted suicide patient is necessary. The areas that need to be covered are the apparent intention behind the act of attempted suicide, including suicidal intent, the current risk of repetition of the behaviour or of the patient committing suicide, the problems, difficulties and precipitant(s) preceding the act, whether or not the patient has a psychiatric disorder, and his or her apparent willingness to accept help (Hawton and Catalan 1987). In this assessment, attention should also be paid to investigating the patient's characteristics in relation to the specific psychological features noted above. Intensive psychiatric treatment, including in-patient care, will be required for a minority of patients, particularly those with severe psychiatric disorder and/or marked suicide risk. For a large proportion of patients, however, less intensive treatment will be appropriate. Most of the rest of this chapter will be focused on this group of patients.

As would be expected from the earlier brief review of psychological characteristics, problem-solving is a common element in most of the treatment approaches which have been developed for suicide attempters. Since problem-solving is the focus of another chapter in this volume (see Chapter 17) and is fully described elsewhere (Hawton and Kirk 1989) it will only be outlined here. Following a thorough assessment, the key elements are: assisting patients to specify their problem in detail, helping them identify goals in relation to specific problems, and then establishing steps that can be taken to begin progress towards the goals. Patients are encouraged to try to take agreed steps between treatment sessions and to evaluate their progress. Considerable psychological work is often required to facilitate problem-solving, especially in terms of helping people explore the (often irrational) reasons why they have difficulty in initiating problem-solving steps. This overall approach can be used in individual, couple, or family therapy.

An important element in treatment of many people in this population is flexibility of timing of treatment sessions, such that the treatment programme is tailored to the temporal needs of each patient. Thus, a patient might be seen two or three times in a week initially so that some early progress can be made and then less frequently as the patient is able to function more autonomously.

A further feature of treatment is that it is often brief. In part this is because many attempted suicide patients will only accept short-term care, and in part because the aim is to help patients take full responsibility for their lives as soon as possible and to avoid over-dependence on clinical carers. Given the large numbers of patients presenting following deliberate self-harm, a further pragmatic reason is that there has be to careful distribution of clinical resources to try to benefit as many people as possible. There are, however, some patients who require far more extensive treatment. This applies particularly to individuals with personality disorders in whom the aims of treatment may extend beyond improving problem-solving skills to try to modify in a more fundamental way how they interpret and hence respond to events and difficulties in their lives. This type of approach is at a relatively early stage of development (Beck and Freeman 1990; Casey 1992).

Further important characteristics of the treatment of suicide attempters concern the continuity of care, as already noted, and the extent to which emergency help is made readily available should the patient feel that he/she needs it. Most treatment programmes have included either the individual patient in sessions or the patient plus a partner (if there is one). There has been some attention to treatment of patients within groups or with a combination of individual and group therapy.

Results of treatment studies

In this section, treatment studies that have been conducted in relation to most of the factors discussed above will be reviewed. This review is in no sense a full systematic review of the kind that is now fashionable in relation to the development of evidence-based medical care (such a study by the author and colleagues is in progress) but includes reference to many of the studies reported in readily accessible journals. Most of the studies are randomized controlled trials in which either one treatment has been compared with routine care (treatment as usual) or another specific form of care.

Problem-solving

Several studies have focused on using problem-solving therapy to help patients deal with their current problems. One of the early studies, conducted in Southampton, compared an experimental social work aftercare service with routine aftercare in general hospital referred patients who had taken overdoses and who did not require immediate psychiatric treatment, were not in current treatment, nor at immediate risk of suicide (Table 12.1; Gibbons *et al.* 1978). The main element in the experimental treatment was home-based treatment utilizing the approach termed task-centred casework (Reid and Epstein 1972), which in essence is problem-solving usually focused on one key problem area for each patient. The treatment lasted up to three months. Patients in the control group received routine care as judged appropriate by the general hospital psychiatric service.

As can be seen from Table 12.1, there was no difference between the rates of repetition of suicidal behaviour in patients in the two treatment groups during the year following entry to the study. Depression scores improved markedly in both groups and there was no difference in the mean scores of the two groups after four months. However, patients in the experimental group more often reported improvement in their social problems. In a separate unpublished report (Gibbons 1979) it was noted that the apparent beneficial effect of the social work intervention on social problems was confined to women. Since the

TABLE 12.1. Task-centred casework by social workers compared with routine care of patients who had taken overdoses

	Social work aftercare Up to 3 months social work treatment at home Task-centred casework Social worker available at times of crisis		Routine care Referral back to GP (54%) Psychiatric follow-up (33%) Other referral (13%)
No. of patients	200		200
Patients repeating within one year of entry to study	13.5%	n.s.	14.5%
Depression after 4 months		n.s.	
Patients reporting improved social circumstances after 4 months (%)	86%	P<0.02	70%

n.s., not significant.
(From Gibbons et al. 1978.)

evaluation of social problems was based solely on the patients' views of their social circumstances, there is the possibility of an attributional effect rather than a true treatment effect in the experimental group, but this seems unlikely since it would only have applied to the female patients. Eighteen months after entry to the study no differences were found between the two treatment groups on any of the measures (Gibbons 1979).

Problem-solving was also evaluated in Oxford in a study of patients who had taken overdoses in which the effects of hospital-based out-patient care with flexibly timed treatment sessions provided by experienced non-medical therapists was compared with the results of referring patients back to their general practitioners with advice to the doctors on subsequent management (Hawton et al. 1987). The patients, 40 in each group, were all thought to be suited to out-patient treatment. The treatment was brief (one to eight sessions) problem-orientated therapy (described in Hawton and Catalan 1987), with conjoint treatment with a partner whenever this seemed appropriate.

Although the repetition rate during the year after entry to the study in patients in the out-patient treated group was half that in the general practitioner group, this difference was statistically non-significant (see Table 12.2). There were also no significant differences during the follow-up period in scores on measures of depression, social adjustment, and target problems, although there were trends with regard to the last two, suggesting greater benefits of the out-patient treatment. There were, however, some other findings of interest. First, rates of attendance for out-patient treatment were

TABLE 12.2. Out-patient problem-orientated therapy compared with general practitioner care of patients who had taken overdoses

	Out-patient treatment Brief, problem-orient- ated counselling Flexible timing of appointments Conjoint treatment where appropriate	General practitioner care GP provided care as thought appropriate following advice from clinical service
No. of patients	40	40
Repetition of attempts during year after entry to study (%)	7%	15%
Depression (2, 4 and 9 months)	n.s.	
Social adjustment (2, 4, and 9 months)	Trends favouring out-patient group	
Target problems (2, 4, and 9 months)		

n.s., not significant.
(From Hawton *et al.* 1987.)

somewhat better in female than male patients. Second, women seemed to benefit more from the out-patient treatment, especially in terms of improvement in target problems. Third, patients with problems in an ongoing relationship with a partner had somewhat better outcome in the out-patient group, especially at the nine-month assessment, with regard to depression scores, target problems, and overall social adjustment scores.

Problem-solving was evaluated in a subsequent study in Leeds, but this time with a more cognitive approach than in the two earlier studies (Salkovskis *et al.* 1990). Twenty patients at moderate or high risk of repetition of attempts were selected, using a risk scale, and randomly assigned to either five sessions of home-based cognitive behaviour problem-solving or routine care. Although there was a significant difference in repetition rates after six months, by one year follow-up the repetition rate in the experimental group was still lower than in the control group but not significantly so (see Table 12.3). Of interest is the fact that in the repeaters the period before the repeats occurred was far longer in the experimental group (9.3 months) than in the control group (3 months). There was also evidence for beneficial effects of the experimental treatment in terms of some other factors, such as depression and problem resolution. This study again offers some evidence that outcome is better with a specially designed treatment, but the small number of individuals precludes more definite conclusions.

The evaluation of problem-solving therapy has been taken a further step forward by McLeavey and colleagues (1994) in Cork. They developed a treatment programme which they called interpersonal problem-solving skills training (IPSST). This aimed to improve generally patients' interpersonal

TABLE 12.3. Cognitive behavioural problem-solving compared with routine care in patients who had taken overdoses and who had relatively high risk of repetition

	Cognitive behavioural problem-solving 5 largely home-based treatment sessions by a community psychiatric nurse over 1 month		Routine care Treatment as usual (details not supplied)
No. of patients	12		8
Patients repeating self-harm:			
after 6 months (%)	0	$P=0.049$	37.5%
after 18 months (%)	25%	n.s.	50%
Problems rated on scaled questionnaire ⎫ Depression ⎬ Hopelessness ⎭	Significant differences showing benefits for patients in experimental groups at 6 months and 12 months		

n.s., not significant.
(From Salkovskis *et al.* 1990.)

problem-solving skills rather than primarily focus on solving just their current problems. The programme was delivered in five- (or six-) weekly, one-hour sessions and included progressive training in problem-solving, utilizing specific instruction, discussion and reflective listening, plus modelling, role playing, sentence completion, and prompting strategies. The comparison treatment was the more usual brief problem-solving approach utilizing the type of approach developed by Hawton and Catalan (1987) and used in the trials of Hawton and colleagues (1981, 1987). On average, patients had just over four sessions of this treatment. Thirty-nine patients who had taken overdoses were included in the study.

One year after entry to the study 10.5% of the IPSST group had repeated their attempts compared with 25% of the control group, a statistically non-significant difference (see Table 12.4). There were, however, quite marked differences between the groups on other measures as assessed two to three weeks after the end of treatment. For example, the patients in the IPSST group showed greater gains than the control group with regard to measures of interpersonal problem-solving, including the MEPS (see above), 'optimal thinking' (in which the patient has to generate various possible means of overcoming hypothetical interpersonal problems), 'awareness of consequences' (which is a measure of the patient's ability to consider the likelihood and possible outcomes of transgressing when faced by temptation [*sic*]), and scores on a self-rated problem-solving scale.

In summary, the studies reviewed so far indicate that brief problem-solving therapy may be beneficial for suicide attempters in terms of specific problems, and may be enhanced if cognitive strategies are a specific component of the

TABLE 12.4. Interpersonal problem-solving skills training compared with brief problem-solving for patients who had taken overdoses

	Interpersonal problem-solving skills training 5 to 6 weekly 1 hour sessions. Training in problem-solving aimed at enhancing general problem-solving skills		Brief problem-solving Aimed primarily at helping patients resolve current problems
No. of patients	19		20
Outcome at 6 months:			
repetition of self-harm (%)	10.5%	n.s.	25%
presenting problems		n.s.	
Means-End Problem-solving Procedure			
'Optimal thinking'	Significant differences all showing greater benefits for patients who received interpersonal problem-solving skills training		
Awareness of consequences			
Self-Rated Problem-Solving Scale			
Hopelessness			

n.s., not significant.
(From McLeavey *et al.* 1994.)

treatment. There is some evidence that the benefits are confined to females and, possibly, patients with problems in an ongoing relationship. Focusing on enhancing problem-solving skills may further improve the effectiveness of treatment. Although possible impact of the specific treatments on repetition of suicidal behaviour have been suggested by three of these studies, none have included sufficient numbers of subjects to allow proper evaluation of the impact of treatment on this most important outcome variable. This point is discussed further below.

Motivation and compliance with aftercare

Some attention has been paid to the question of how the well recognized poor rate of attendance of attempted suicide patients at aftercare sessions can be improved. In Germany, Möller and colleagues have conducted some relevant studies, which have been reviewed (in English) by Möller (1989). Of note, perhaps unsurprisingly, was that patients who had taken overdoses who were given a fixed aftercare appointment at a crisis intervention centre showed a higher attendance rate (62%) than those who were simply given the address of the centre (26%). Subsequently, this group demonstrated that continuity of care, in the sense of the patient being seen by the same therapist for both initial assessment and subsequent treatment, was an important factor improving the rate of attendance. The group went on to see if spending up to 30 minutes with patients trying to address 'motivational deficits', as identified in a questionnaire, would improve attendance at follow-up appointments. The results of this step were disappointing in that it appeared to have little impact on compliance. Rather surprisingly, the patients in the group which received this attention had a significantly higher rate of repetition of self-harm than did patients in the control group. This finding was probably due to the fact that more patients in the experimental group had characteristics associated with repetition (e.g., being divorced, living alone, and having employment problems).

Hawton *et al.* (1981) tried to address the problem of poor attendance by developing a home-based treatment programme for attempted suicide patients. They compared the provision of brief problem-solving therapy at home and flexible timing of appointments with treatment provided by the same therapists in a weekly hospital-based out-patient clinic. The patients in this study had all taken overdoses. Patients in the home-treatment group showed far better compliance with treatment sessions than those in the out-patient group, with almost twice as many in this condition completing treatment (see Table 12.5). In spite of this, there were no major differences in outcome between the two groups. There was, however, evidence of better outcome with home-based treatment for patients with problems in an ongoing relationship. No differential effect between the two treatment approaches was found for the two sexes when analysed separately (Hawton 1989). As a result of this study the more expensive home treatment programme in Oxford was terminated in favour of out-patient care. However, the out-patient programme was modified to include flexible timing of appointments rather than being restricted to a weekly out-patient clinic. This, plus continuity of care, appears to be associated

TABLE 12.5. Home-based compared with out-patient treatment of patients who had taken overdoses

	Home-based treatment Problem-solving with flexible timing of appointments in patients' homes		Out-patient treatment Problem-solving in weekly out-patient clinic
No. of patients	48		48
Patients completing treatment (%)	83%	$P < 0.001$	42%
Repetition of attempts within 1 year (%)	10%	n.s.	15%
Mood Social adjustment Target problems	No difference between groups at end of treatment and at 6-months follow-up		

n.s., not significant.
(From Hawton *et al.* 1981.)

with improved compliance with out-patient care (Hawton *et al.* 1979) although this approach has not been subjected to controlled evaluation.

Intensive efforts were made to improve the treatment compliance of patients who had attempted suicide as well as to provide a pragmatic treatment approach in a study by Allard *et al.* (1992) in Montreal. In the experimental treatment, patients were involved with the therapist and family members, where appropriate, in drawing up a treatment plan. The treatment was provided in weekly sessions for the first month, every two weeks for the next three months, and then monthly for eight months. There was at least one home visit by a social worker and written or telephone reminders about appointments for patients who missed appointments. The content of the therapy was very eclectic, and the specific content depended on the needs of the patient. Unfortunately, the nature of the control treatment was not described at all but presumably was treatment as usual. Seventy-six patients were randomly assigned to the intensive intervention group and 74 to the control group. In spite of apparently reasonable compliance with the experimental treatment protocol by a substantial proportion of patients, two years after entry to the study 35% of the patients in this group had made at least one further attempt compared with 30% in the control group, a non-significant trend contrary to the original prediction.

A recent study in Belgium was focused specifically on trying to improve motivation for treatment (van Heeringen *et al.* 1995). The study used a pragmatic approach whereby attempted suicide patients who were offered out-patient treatment and who did not attend their first appointment were visited at home by a community nurse. The nurse assessed the reasons for non-compliance and tried to improve the patients' attitude to attending the out-patient clinic, by pointing out the relevance of this to their problems. These home visits were repeated twice if the patient was not at home or if the first visit was not followed by attendance at the out-patient clinic. In this study, 516 patients who had taken overdoses or deliberately injured themselves were randomly assigned to either this treatment condition or to a control group where out-patient appointments were offered as usual but without the home visits for patients who failed to attend.

Approximately 40% of patients in each group attended their first out-patient sessions. There was, however, a significant increase in attendance in the experimental group following the home visits (see Table 12.6). Patients in the experimental group tended to have a lower rate of repeat suicidal behaviour (including fatal episodes) but when account was taken of potential confounding factors (gender, marital status, and history of suicide attempts) the difference was statistically non-significant. This was a large study but the number of patients included was probably still not sufficient to achieve the statistical power to test fully the effects of the special intervention on repetition.

TABLE 12.6. Home visits to encourage compliance with out-patient care compared with out-patient care only for attempted suicide patients

	Experimental group Out-patient treatment. Home visits(up to 3) by community nurse for patients not attending out-patient care: work on trying to encourage attendance		Control group Out-patient care Non-attenders not pursued
No. of patients	258		258
Patients attending first out-patient appointment			
initially (%)	42.5%	n.s.	39.8%
after home visits (%)	51.2%	Adjusted odds ratio 1.48 (95% CI=1.12–2.26)	39.8%
Repetition of suicidal behaviour after 12 months (%)	10.7%	Adjusted odds ratio 1.58 (95% CI = 0.84–2.78)	17.4%

n.s., not significant; CI, confidence interval.
(From Van Heeringen *et al.* 1995.)

Another approach to try to improve motivation of patients to seek help is to give them a card which provides details of how to get emergency help from the psychiatric services. A preliminary investigation comparing this condition with routine aftercare where no card was provided produced promising results, although again the lower repetition rate in the experimental group (5.0%) compared with that of the control group (10.8%) was not statistically significant (Morgan *et al.* 1993).

In summary, it appears that continuity of care for people who have attempted suicide is important for attendance at treatment sessions. Work on motivation can probably improve compliance. Similarly, home-based treatment results in better compliance. Although none of these measures has so far been shown to have specific benefits in terms of repetition of self-harm there have been encouraging trends in some studies. Limitations in the number of patients included in their studies has probably been the main factor precluding a statistically significant difference being obtained.

Specific subgroups of patients

Patients with a history of repeat attempts
Patients who repeat attempted suicide comprise a group for whom there is a particular need for the development of effective treatment because of their risk

of further episodes, including of completed suicide (Ovenstone and Kreitman 1974; Hawton and Fagg 1988). The patients included in the study by Salkovskis *et al.* (1990), which was discussed earlier, were all at relatively high risk of repetition. In an early study in Edinburgh, patients who had made at least two attempts were randomly assigned to receive help from either an experimental aftercare service or through routine care (Chowdhury *et al.* 1973). In the aftercare service, patients were offered regular and frequent out-patient appointments, non-attenders were visited at home, an emergency telephone call service was available, and home visits were made in response to emergency calls. The actual content of the treatment was not specified. Patients in the control group were offered routine follow-up from the hospital psychiatric service (usually as out-patients) but none of the special facilities of the experimental aftercare programme. There was no difference between the repetition rates of the two groups during the first six months after entering the study (see Table 12.7). However, according to interviewer ratings, the social circumstances (finance, housing, employment) of more patients in the experimental group improved than of those in the control group. This effect was more noticeable in the women (76% improved compared with 36%) than the men (42% improved compared with 26%).

A very different approach to the treatment of attempted suicide patients who repeat was taken by Liberman and Eckman (1981) in Los Angeles. They included only patients with at least one prior act of attempted suicide in the previous two years before the episode which brought them into the study. Twenty-four patients were randomly assigned to either of two treatment

TABLE 12.7. Evaluation of an experimental aftercare service for patients who had made repeat suicide attempts

	Experimental after-care service *Regular and frequent out-patient appoint-ments.* *Domiciliary visits.* *24-hour emergency call service*		*Control treatment* *Out-patient appointments (non-attenders not pursued)*
No. of patients	71		84
Repetition of suicidal behaviour during 6 months after entry to study (%)	24%	n.s.	23%
Improved social circumstances after 6 months (%)	63%	P < 0.001	31%

n.s., not significant.
(From Chowdhury *et al.* 1973.)

groups, both of which received treatment in the same in-patient clinical research unit where four hours of therapy per day was provided for eight days. In this setting both groups were exposed to the general milieu of the unit, which included a token economy programme in which patients earned tokens for self-care and daily living skills. One group received behaviour therapy, which included: (1) social skills training for 17 hours (including role playing, prompting, cuing, modelling and feedback), which was aimed at improving verbal and non-verbal expressive skills; (2) anxiety management training for 10 hours, especially in relation to anxiety cues and symptoms; and (3) family negotiation and contingency contracting for 5 hours, aimed at improving communication between the patient and family members. The other group received insight-orientated therapy, including: (1) individual therapy for 17 hours; (2) psychodrama and group therapy for ten hours; and (3) family therapy for 5 hours. After discharge from the treatment unit patients in both groups were offered aftercare by community agencies, as planned between the therapist, patient, and his/her family.

Follow-up interviews took place at discharge, and 2, 6, 12, 24, and 36 weeks later (at which time all the original assessment measures were repeated) and also after two years (when only suicidal ideation and behaviour were reassessed). After treatment, both treatment groups showed very marked changes on all the measures. However, depression scores were significantly lower in the behaviour therapy group at the follow-up assessments (see Table 12.8). The rate of repetition of suicidal behaviour was also lower in this group, but the difference was not statistically significant. At the 24- and 36-week follow-up assessments, however, significantly fewer people in the behaviour therapy group reported having had suicidal thoughts. It should be noted that there were a couple more female patients in the behaviour therapy group than in the insight-orientated group.

Patients with borderline personality disorder

Self-harm behaviour is a significant characteristic of patients with borderline personality disorder. It is usually acknowledged that such patients are difficult to treat effectively (Casey 1992). Any intervention with a chance of succeeding will probably need to be intensive. Linehan and colleagues (1991) in Seattle developed a programme which combined individual and group treatments and included considerable cognitive behavioural work. They called it 'dialectical behaviour therapy'. The approach was based on a model which assumes that individuals with borderline personality have deficient skills in relation to interpersonal interactions, regulation of emotions, and tolerance of distress. The individual treatment sessions, which occurred weekly, were focused mainly on addressing problems of motivation and strengthening behavioural skills in relation to the specific deficits noted above. The group sessions, which

TABLE 12.8. Behaviour therapy vs. insight-orientated therapy for repeat suicide attempters

	Behaviour therapy	Insight-orientated therapy
	10-day in-patient programme for both groups, 4 hours therapy/day for 8 days	
	Social skills training, anxiety management, family negotiation, and contracting	Individual therapy, psychodrama, and family therapy
No. of patients	12	12
Depression scales	Significant differences favouring behaviour therapy at all follow-up assessments to 36 weeks	
Repetition of self-harm after 2 years (%)	16.6% n.s.	25%
Suicidal ideation	Significant differences favouring behaviour therapy at 24- and 36-week assessments	

n.s., not significant.
(From Liberman and Eckman 1981.)

were also weekly, were mainly 'psychoeducational' and also focused on acquisition of behavioural skills. This treatment programme was primarily, although not solely, targeted on reducing the frequency of deliberate self-harm, which in most of the patients had occurred on many occasions prior to their entry to the study. In a randomized controlled study, Linehan and her colleagues compared the effect of one year of this treatment with that of treatment as usual whereby individuals could receive any type of available therapy.

The results for the one year treatment period were presented in the initial paper from the study (Linehan *et al.* 1991). During this year there were significantly fewer episodes of self-harm among the patients in the dialectical behaviour therapy group than in those in the control group (statistically significant according to 2-tailed test, although the authors presented a 1-tailed result) (see Table 12.9). Patients in the experimental group also had fewer medically treated severe episodes of self-harm and spent fewer days as psychiatric in-patients than patients in the treatment as usual group. There were also benefits with regard to other social, psychological, and performance measures. When followed up at six months and one year after the intensive treatment programme was completed, during which time sizeable proportions of patients in both treatment groups continued to receive therapy, the benefits of the programme with regard to repetition of self-harm persisted, but only for the first six months (Table 12.9; Linehan *et al.* 1993). On other measures, including social adjustment, employment performance, and number of days

TABLE 12.9. Dialectical behaviour therapy compared with routine care of 'chronically parasuicidal' patients with borderline personality disorder

	Dialectical behaviour therapy Weekly 1-hour session of problem-orientated therapy. Weekly group therapy focused on behavioural skills related to specific skill deficits. Emergency telephone contact with therapist		Routine care Treatment as usual
No. of patients	22		22
Patients repeating 'parasuicidal behaviour' in first year (%)	63.6%	P<0.01	95.5%
Mean numbers (SD) of acts per person:			
in first 6 months of follow-up	0.1 (0.32)	P<0.001	2.1 (2.69)
in second 6 months of follow-up	0.72 (1.56)	n.s.	1.06 (1.55)

n.s., not significant; SD, standard deviation.
(From Linehan *et al.* 1991, 1993.)

spent in hospital, there was evidence of persistence of benefits of the programme for the whole of the follow-up year, while on some (e.g., anger) the effect was only found during the first six months.

This study is clearly a landmark investigation in being probably the first to demonstrate a significant effect of a specific psychological intervention on repetition of self-harm when compared with a control condition. However, the intervention was extremely intensive and focused on a particular subgroup of patients and therefore may not be of direct relevance to usual clinical practice. In future work with this specific patient population it is desirable, nonetheless, that lessons be learned from the programme, even if implementation of the full approach is not feasible.

Adolescents

In view of the high prevalence of suicidal behaviour in adolescents (Hawton and Fagg 1992*b*), it is surprising that very little attention appears to have been paid to evaluation of specific interventions in this population. The only randomized controlled trial known to the author was one in which, after general hospital admission because of self-poisoning or self-injury, adolescents were offered access to an emergency service which allowed them to walk into or telephone the hospital at any time to get emergency help (Deykin *et al.* 1986). This was in addition to their routine care. A control group was not offered this facility, only routine care. There was no difference in rates of repetition of suicidal behaviour between the two groups in spite of evidence of far greater help-seeking behaviour in the experimental group.

Given the specific characteristics of adolescents who take overdoses or injure themselves, an appropriate treatment would appear to be one which combines individual help, including development of problem-solving skills, with family therapy (again problem-orientated), whenever the latter is relevant.

People who cut themselves

There has been very little evaluation of treatments for people who cut themselves (although many of the patients in the study of Linehan *et al.* 1991, 1993, would have shown this behaviour). Cutting is usually notable for the frequency with which it is repeated. Evaluation of the effects of therapy on the behaviour would therefore be somewhat easier than is the case for self-poisoning, where repetition, although common, is less frequent. Some success has been reported using a strategy whereby the patient repeatedly squeezes a rubber ball when experiencing feelings of tension, the usual precursor of self-cutting (Rosen and Thomas 1984). However, on pragmatic grounds it would seem that an effective treatment package for this problem would have to combine strategies to help gain control of the cutting, relaxation techniques, work to assist with ventilation of emotions, physical exercise (possibly), and help with underlying problems, including vulnerable self-esteem, mood disturbance, and communication problems (Hawton 1990). The approach used by Linehan and colleagues (1991, 1993) included several of these components.

Conclusions concerning the results of recent treatment studies

In spite of the limitations in terms of the extent and design of the studies of the treatment of attempted suicide patients reviewed here, it is possible to reach some conclusions which are directly relevant to clinical practice. It appears that continuity of care, in terms of the same person who conducted the original assessment of a patient also being the one to provide treatment, is an important factor in determining attendance at treatment sessions. While there is some uncertainty about the effectiveness of trying to motivate patients to comply with treatment, making special efforts to follow-up those who do not attend an initial appointment may improve subsequent attendance and might, although this has not been shown definitively, have an effect on the rate of repetition of self-harm. The majority of studies of problem-solving therapy have shown benefits in terms of subsequent psychosocial adjustment, but where the sexes have been studied separately this has only been apparent in females. It also appears that patients with problems in an ongoing relationship with a partner (most of whom are, in fact, women) may be helped by specific problem-focused therapy. Where the treatment includes attention to problem-solving skills in general, rather than just solution of current difficulties, this may further improve the outcome. Specific cognitive strategies may also improve the impact of treatment.

No study of suicide attempters in general, however, has demonstrated an impact of therapy on rates of repetition, although the delay before repetition may be extended. The main drawback in this respect of nearly all the studies conducted so far is that the sizes of the study samples have been far too small to detect an effect of the magnitude which might be expected and be clinically relevant (see below).

One way of studying smaller numbers of subjects is to focus on patients at high risk of repetition. Linehan *et al.*'s (1991, 1993) study of women with borderline personality disorders has given encouragement that very intensive treatment utilizing cognitive and behavioural strategies can have a significant impact on repetition of self-harm (and on other indicators of psychosocial well-being) in this very difficult to treat patient population. The intensity of this approach probably precludes its use in routine clinical practice, but elements of it may be directly applicable.

The results in the treatment studies where the two genders have been examined separately have not provided encouraging results for males who attempt suicide. It may be that a very different type of strategy needs to be explored such as one in which a very practical approach (e.g., offering a chance for practical manual work in a workshop setting) can facilitate involvement in a therapeutic process. Attention to the problem of substance abuse, including its role in facilitating suicidal behaviour, will also be a necessary component of treatment for many male attempted suicide patients.

We also lack information about effective treatment strategies for people who cut themselves. A logical approach to this problem might include treatment which focuses on the psychological deficits (especially low self-esteem) which make individuals vulnerable to this behaviour, identification of key factors that precipitate the cognitive processes which lead to individual acts of cutting, and both the identification and rehearsal of alternative ways of dealing with negative thoughts and affect (Hawton 1990).

Research needs in the development and evaluation of treatments

The psychological characteristics of patients

The development of potentially effective treatments would benefit from further understanding of the specific characteristics and deficits of attempted suicide patients. More work needs to be done to determine the extent to which problem-solving deficits, pessimism, and other characteristics are either persistent (i.e., trait) phenomena, apparent at any time, or episodic (i.e., state) phenomena that are only apparent during crisis and/or depressed mood. This is important since trait characteristics will be more accessible during treatment whereas state phenomena may require patients to be challenged in some way (such as by mood induction) in order to elicit the deficits so that they can be addressed in treatment. If, as has been proposed, the role of autobiographical memories are important, it would be valuable if studies could be conducted to determine if it is possible to modify these in a way that makes them more specific and hence more useful for generation of problem-solving strategies at times of stress.

Treatment approaches

It is unlikely that a single general treatment approach will be appropriate for all attempted suicide patients, although there may be certain common elements that are helpful for many patients. These are likely to include problem-solving and work on self-esteem. So far, rather little is known about the efficacy of treatments focused on low self-esteem. In a trial comparing cognitive behaviour therapy with antidepressants in the treatment of depression, negative self-concept seemed to improve more with cognitive behaviour therapy (Rush *et al.* 1982). The treatment of people who have attempted suicide is likely to benefit from evaluation of specific treatments directed at low self-esteem.

Family therapy would seem to be the treatment of choice for many younger patients. This approach requires evaluation. Such treatment may need to include attention to the attitude of family members to psychological treatment since negative attitudes of parents have been found to be a key factor associated with poor compliance with treatment (Taylor and Stansfield 1984).

The tendency to repeat attempted suicide also requires particular attention. It seems that altough people who repeat their acts may not differ greatly from non-repeaters in their general improvement in social adjustment following a previous act (Sakinofsky *et al.* 1990), they do appear to differ in terms of the psychological characteristics which probably explain the ease with which they resort to this method of coping at times of distress (Sakinofsky and Roberts 1990). It would seem appropriate, therefore, to incorporate some type of stress-inoculation training in treatment, with specific attention to alternative strategies which might be employed if thoughts of attempted suicide occur.

Lastly, there is a major need for the evaluation of treatments for people who repeatedly cut themselves. A model on which such treatment could be based has been proposed (Hawton 1990) but not subjected to evaluation.

Methodological issues in evaluation of treatments

Several of the methodological issues associated with treatment studies in this field are those that have to be faced in evaluation of psychological therapies for other conditions but some are particularly important with regard to studies of attempted suicide patients (Hawton 1994).

Repetition of self-harm as an outcome variable

If repetition of self-harm is to be used as an indicator of outcome, this has important implications for the size of treatment groups. As already noted, virtually none of the studies reviewed here have included sufficient numbers of patients to have the power to detect the sort of impact on repetition rates which might reasonably be expected. [For example, to detect at a statistically significant level a difference in repetition rates of 20% between the two treatment groups where the usual rate of repetition, and therefore that expected in the control group receiving standard care, is 15% would require (with alpha set at 0.05 and beta at 0.2) inclusion of a total of 4092 subjects in a study (Pocock 1983).] This means that a multi-centre study is likely to be necessary.

An alternative or complementary strategy is to restrict the patient sample to people at high risk of repetition. This can be done, for example, by specifically studying people who have repeated the behaviour, as was the case in the studies of Chowdhury *et al.* (1973) and Linehan *et al.* (1991, 1993), or people who score in the high range on a risk of repetition scale (Buglass and Horton 1974; Kreitman and Foster 1991), as was the case in the study by Salkovskis *et al.* (1990). However, even if the likely repetition rate of a group of patients is, say, 40% in a year, a substantial number of patients (1130) will be required to detect a 20% reduction in repetition in an experimental group, and even a sizeable number (261) to detect a reduction by 40%.

Other outcome variables

In the light of these difficulties it may be considered more appropriate to employ other indicators of outcome as the principal dependant variables. A list of some possible outcome measures is provided in Table 12.10. Most of these are obvious from what has already been noted about the characteristics of this population of patients. The evaluation of outcome on specific or 'target' problems poses some difficulty. The main problem is that problems are not directly comparable across patients in terms of their severity and susceptibility to change. Kiresuk and Sherman (1968) developed Goal Attainment Scaling as a method to address this issue. Specific values are allocated to problems in terms of their severity and a range of outcomes defined at the outset. However, this is a highly subjective approach. It may be better to accept the variation in the quantitative and qualitative nature of problems between patients and to assume that random allocation of patients will mean that there is matching of

TABLE 12.10. Possible outcome measures that may be used in the evaluation of treatments for attempted suicide patients

• Repetition of self-harm, including timing of repeats
• Suicidal ideation
• Hopelessness
• Target problems
• Mood
• Social adjustment
• Self-esteem
• Problem-solving skills
• Alcohol use
• Compliance with treatment: include acceptability, initial attendance and drop-outs
• Attitudes towards treatment

the range of severity of problems between the treatment groups. Then a fairly simple method of evaluating change or improvement in problems can be used (e.g., Hawton *et al.* 1981; Salkovskis *et al.* 1990).

Investigation of the intended effect of treatment on psychological and behavioural characteristics of patients would be invaluable. This could be based on responses to questionnaires, more 'projective' techniques such as the Means-End Problem-Solving Procedure which was discussed earlier, and enquiry of the patient and significant others about actual functioning in the face of adversity.

Conclusions

While the extent and importance of the problem of attempted suicide is all too obvious, the evaluation of psychological treatments for these patients has been surprisingly limited. The results of the studies have, nevertheless, provided pointers relevant to the provision of effective clinical care. Thus, there is evidence that continuity of care, work on motivation for treatment, and specific problem-solving therapy can be effective elements in treatment. Although we are beginning to develop a better understanding of the psychological difficulties that characterize many of these patients, there is clearly a need for further work in this regard. This should help in the design of more effective treatments. The evaluation of treatments for these patients faces particular problems, especially with regard to determining the effects of treatment on the repetition of the behaviour. Large multi-centre studies, focusing on the high risk of repetition patients, or placing dependence on other outcome measures are ways of addressing this problem. The recent attention in the United Kingdom and elsewhere regarding strategies for prevention of suicide is likely to result in welcome further efforts being made to develop and evaluate effective treatments for this large and important population of patients.

Acknowledgements

Jane Rowland and Susannah Mulholland are thanked for their assistance with the preparation of the manuscript.

References

Adam, K. S., Bouckoms, A., and Streiner, D. (1982). Parental loss and family stability in attempted suicide. *Archives of General Psychiatry*, **39**, 1081–5.

Allard, R., Marshall, M., and Plante, M. (1992). Intensive follow-up does not decrease the risk of repeat suicide attempts. *Suicide and Life-Threatening Behavior*, **22**, 303–14.

Bancroft, J., Skrimshire, A., Reynolds, F., Simkin, S., and Smith, J. (1975). Self-poisoning and self-injury in the Oxford area: epidemiological aspects 1969–1973. *British Journal of Preventive and Social Medicine*, **29**, 170–7.

Bancroft, J. H. J., Skrimshire, A. M., and Simkin, S. (1976). The reasons people give for taking overdoses. *British Journal of Psychiatry*, **128**, 538–48.

Bancroft, J., Skrimshire, A., Casson, J., Harvard-Watts, O., and Reynolds, F. (1977). People who deliberately poison or injure themselves: their problems and their contacts with helping agencies. *Psychological Medicine*, **7**, 289–303.

Bancroft, J., Hawton, K., Simkin, S., Kingston, B., Cumming, C., and Whitwell, D. (1979). The reasons people give for taking overdoses: a further enquiry. *British Journal of Medical Psychology*, **52**, 353–65.

Beck, A. T. and Freeman, A. (1990). *Cognitive therapy of personality disorders*. Guilford Press, New York.

Beck, A. T., Weissman, A,, Lester, D., and Trexler, L., (1974). The measurement of pessimism: The Hopelessness Scale. *Journal of Counselling and Clinical Psychology*, **42**, 861–5.

Beck, A., Kovacs, M., and Weissman, A. (1975). Hopelessness and suicidal behavior. *Journal of the American Medical Association*, **234**, 1146–9.

Beck, A. T., Steer, R. A., Kovacs, M., and Garrison, B. S. (1985). Hopelessness and eventual suicide: a 10-year prospective study of patients hospitalised with suicidal ideation. *American Journal of Psychiatry*, **142**, 559–63.

Buglass, D. and Horton, J. (1974). A scale for predicting subsequent suicidal behaviour. *British Journal of Psychiatry*, **124**, 573–8.

Casey, P. R. (1992). Personality disorders: do psychological treatments help? In *Practical problems in clinical psychiatry* (ed. K. Hawton and P. Cowen), pp. 131–40. Oxford University Press.

Chowdhury, N., Hicks, R. C., and Kreitman, N. (1973). Evaluation of an aftercare service for parasuicide (attempted suicide) patients. *Social Psychiatry*, **8**, 67–81.

Deykin, E. Y., Chung-Chen, H., and Joshi, N. (1986). Adolescent suicidal and self-destructive behaviour: results of an intervention study. *Journal of Adolescent Health Care*, **7**, 88–95.

Dyer, J. A. T. and Kreitman, N. (1984). Hopelessness, depression and suicidal intent in parasuicide. *British Journal of Psychiatry*, **144**, 127–33.

Evans, J., Williams, J. M. G., O'Loughlin, S., and Howells, K. (1992). Autobiographical memory and problem-solving strategies of parasuicide patients. *Psychological Medicine*, **22**, 399–405.

Fergusson, D. M. and Lynskey, M. T. (1995). Childhood circumstances, adolescent adjustment and suicide attempts in a New Zealand birth cohort. *Journal of the American Adacemy of Child and Adolescent Psychiatry*, **34**, 612–22.

Gibbons, J. S., Butler, P., Urwin, P., and Gibbons, J. L. (1978). Evaluation of a social work service for self-poisoning patients. *British Journal of Psychiatry*, **133**, 111–8.

Gibbons, J. L. (1979). *The Southampton parasuicide project*. Report to the DHSS. Southampton University Department of Psychiatry, Southampton.

Hawton, K. (1989). Controlled studies of psychosocial intervention following attempted suicide. In *Current research on suicide and parasuicide* (ed. N. Kreitman and S. D. Platt), pp. 180–95. Edinburgh University Press,.

Hawton, K. (1990). Self-cutting: can it be prevented? In *Dilemmas and difficulties in the management of psychiatric patients* (ed. K. Hawton and P. Cowen), pp. 91–103. Oxford University Press.

Hawton, K. (1994). Evaluation of intervention and prevention programmes related to suicidal behaviour: methodological and practical problems. In *Intervention and prevention: Proceedings of the 4th European Symposium on Suicidal Behavior* (ed. U. Bille-Brahe and H. Schiødt), pp. 187–203. Odense University Press, Denmark.

Hawton, K. and Catalan, J. (1987). *Attempted suicide: A practical guide to its nature and management*. Oxford University Press.

Hawton, K. and Fagg, J. (1988). Suicide and other causes of death following attempted suicide. *British Journal of Psychiatry*, **152**, 259–66.

Hawton, K. and Fagg, J. (1992a). Trends in deliberate self-poisoning and self-injury in Oxford, 1976–1990. *British Medical Journal*, **304**, 1409–11.

Hawton, K. and Fagg, J. (1992b). Deliberate self-poisoning and self-injury in adolescents: a study of characteristics and trends in Oxford, 1976–1989. *British Journal of Psychiatry*, **161**, 816–23.

Hawton, K. and Kirk, J. (1989). Problem-solving. In *Cognitive behaviour therapy for psychiatric problems: A practical guide* (ed. K. Hawton, P. Salkovskis, J. Kirk, and D. M. Clark), pp. 406–26. Oxford University Press.

Hawton, K., Gath, D., and Smith, E. (1979). Management of attempted suicide in Oxford. *British Medical Journal*, **2**, 1040–2.

Hawton, K., Bancroft, J., Catalan, J., Kingston, B., Stedeford, A., and Welch, N. (1981). Domiciliary and out-patient treatment of self-poisoning patients by medical and non-medical staff. *Psychological Medicine*, **11**, 169–77.

Hawton, K., Cole, D., O'Grady, J., and Osborn, M. (1982a). Motivational aspects of deliberate self-poisoning in adolescents. *British Journal of Psychiatry*, **141**, 286–91.

Hawton, K., O'Grady, J., Osborn M., and Cole, D. (1982b). Adolescents who take overdoses: their characteristics, problems and contacts with helping agencies. *British Journal of Psychiatry*, **140**, 118–23.

Hawton, K., McKeown, S., Day, A., Martin, P., O'Connor, M., and Yule, J. (1987). Evaluation of out-patient counselling compared with general practitioner care following overdoses. *Psychological Medicine*, **17**, 751–61.

Hawton, K., Fagg, J., and McKeown, S. (1989). Alcoholism, alcohol and attempted suicide. *Alcohol and Alcoholism*, **24**, 3–9.

Hawton, K., Fagg, J., and Simkin, S. Deliberate self-poisoning and self-injury in children and adolescents under 16 years of age in Oxford, 1976–1993. *British Journal of Psychiatry* (in press).

Jenkins, R., Griffiths, S., Wylie, I., Hawton, K., Morgan, G., and Tylee, A. (1994). *The prevention of suicide*. HMSO, London.

Kienhorst, C. W. M., de Wilde, E. J., Broese van Groenou, M. I., Diekstra, R. F. W., and Wolters, W. H. G. (1990). Self-reported suicidal behavior in Dutch secondary education students. *Suicide and Life-Threatening Behavior*, 20, 101–12.

Kiresuk, T. J., and Sherman, R. S. (1968). Goal attainment scaling: a general method for evaluating comprehensive community mental health programs. *Community Mental Health Journal*, 4, 443–53.

Kreitman, N. (ed.) (1977). *Parasuicide*. Wiley, London.

Kreitman, N. and Foster, J. (1991). Construction and selection of predictive scales, with special reference to parasuicide. *British Journal of Psychiatry*, 159, 185–92.

Liberman, R. P. and Eckman, T. (1981). Behavior therapy vs insight-oriented therapy for repeated suicide attempters. *Archives of General Psychiatry*, 38, 1126–30.

Linehan, M. M., Goodstein, J. L., Neilsen, S. L., and Chiles, J. A. (1983). Reasons for staying alive when you are thinking of killing yourself: the reasons for living inventory. *Journal of Consulting and Clinical Psychology*, 51, 276–86.

Linehan, M. M., Camper, P., Chiles, J. A., Strohsal, K., and Shearin, E. N. (1987). Interpersonal problem-solving and parasuicide. *Cognitive Therapy and Research*, 11, 1–12.

Linehan, M. M., Armstrong, H. E., Saurez, A., Allman, D., and Heard, H. L. (1991). Cognitive-behavioral treatment of chronically parasuicidal borderline patients. *Archives of General Psychiatry*, 48, 1060–4.

Linehan, M. M., Heard, H. L., and Armstrong, H. E. (1993). Naturalistic follow-up of a behavioral treatment for chronically parasuicidal borderline patients. *Archives of General Psychiatry*, 50, 971–4.

MacLeod, A. K., Williams, J. M. G., and Linehan, M. M. (1992). New developments in the understanding and treatment of suicidal behaviour. *Behavioural Psychotherapy*, 20, 193–218.

McLeavey, B. C., Daly, R. J., Murray, C. M., O'Riordan, J., and Taylor, M. (1987). Interpersonal problem-solving deficits in self-poisoning patients. *Suicide and Life-Threatening Behavior*, 17, 33–49.

McLeavey, B. C., Daly, R. J., Ludgate, J. W., and Murray, C. M. (1994). Interpersonal problem-solving skills training in the treatment of self-poisoning patients. *Suicide and Life-Threatening Behavior*, 24, 382–94.

Möller, H. J. (1989). Efficacy of different strategies of aftercare for patients who have attempted suicide. *Journal of the Royal Society of Medicine*, 82, 643–7.

Morgan, H. G., Barton, J., and Pottle, S. (1976). Deliberate self-harm: a follow-up of 279 patients. *British Journal of Psychiatry*, 128, 361–8.

Morgan, H. G., Jones, E. M., and Owen, J. H. (1993). Secondary prevention of non-fatal deliberate self-harm: the green card study. *British Journal of Psychiatry*, 163, 111–12.

Newson-Smith, J. G. B. and Hirsch, S. R. (1979). Psychiatric symptoms in self-poisoning patients. *Psychological Medicine*, 9, 493–500.

O'Brien, G., Holton, A. R., Hurren, K., Watt, L., and Hassanyeh, F. (1987). Deliberate self-harm and predictors of out-patient attendance. *British Journal of Psychiatry*, 150, 246–7.

Ovenstone, I. M. K. and Kreitman, N. (1974). Two syndromes of suicide. *British Journal of Psychiatry*, 124, 336–45.

Overholser, J. C., Adams, D. M., Lehnert, K. L., and Brinkman, D. C. (1995). Self-esteem deficits and suicidal tendencies among adolescents. *Journal of the American Academy of Child and Adolescent Psychiatry*, **34**, 919–28.

Paykel, E. S., Prusoff, B. A., and Myers, J. K. (1975). Suicide attempts and recent life events: a controlled comparison. *Archives of General Psychiatry*, **32**, 327–33.

Petrie, K., Chamberlain, K., and Clarke, D. (1988). Psychological predictors of future suicidal behaviour in hospitalized suicide attempters. *British Journal of Clinical Psychology*, **27**, 247–57.

Platt, J. J., Spivack, G., and Bloom, W. (1975). *Manual for the Means-End Problem-Solving Procedure (MEPS): A Measure of Interpersonal Problem Solving Skill.* Hahnemann Medical College and Hospital, Department of Mental Health Services, Hahnemann Community MH/MR Center, Philadelphia, PA.

Platt, S., Hawton, K., Kreitman, N., Fagg, J., and Foster, J. (1988). Trends in parasuicide in Edinburgh and Oxford, 1976–1984: a tale of two cities. *Psychological Medicine*, **18**, 405–18.

Pocock, S. J. (1983). *Clinical trials: A practical approach.* Wiley, Chichester.

Reid, W. and Epstein, L. (1972). *Task-centred casework.* Columbia University Press, New York.

Rosen, L. W. and Thomas, M. A. (1984). Treatment techniques for chronic wrist cutters. *Journal of Behavior Therapy and Experimental Psychiatry*, **141**, 520–5.

Rush, A. J., Beck, A. T., Kovacs, M., Weissenburger, J., and Hollon, S. D. (1982). Comparison of the effects of cognitive therapy and pharmacotherapy on hopelessness and self-concept. *American Journal of Psychiatry*, **139**, 862–6.

Sakinofsky, I. and Roberts, R. S. (1990). Why parasuicides repeat despite problem resolution. *British Journal of Psychiatry*, **156**, 399–405.

Sakinofsky, I., Roberts, R. S., Brown, Y., Cumming, C., and James, P. (1990). Problem resolution and repetition of parasuicide: a prospective study. *British Journal of Psychiatry*, **156**, 395–9.

Salkovskis, P. M., Atha, C., and Storer, D. (1990). Cognitive-behavioural problem-solving in the treatment of patients who repeatedly attempt suicide: a controlled trial. *British Journal of Psychiatry*, **157**, 871–6.

Schmidtke, A. and Schaller, S (1994). The role of cognitive factors in suicidal behaviour; fact or fiction. In *Intervention and prevention. Proceedings from the 4th European Symposium on Suicidal Behavior* (ed. U. Bille-Brahe and H. Schiødt), pp. 104–24. Odense University Press, Denmark.

Schmidtke, A., Bille-Brahe, U., DeLeo, D., Kerkhof, A., Bjerke, T., Crepet, P., *et al.* (1994). Rates and trends of attempted suicide in Europe 1989–1992. In *Attempted suicide in Europe: Findings from the multicentre study on parasuicide by the WHO Regional Office for Europe* (ed. A. J. F. M. Kerkhof, A. Schmidtke, U. Bille-Brahe, D. DeLeo, and J. Lönnqvist), pp. 209–29. DSWO Press, Leiden University, The Netherlands.

Schotte, D. E. and Clum, G. A. (1987). Problem-solving skills in suicidal psychiatric patients. *Journal of Consulting and Clinical Psychology*, **55**, 49–54.

Schotte, D. E., Cools, J., and Payvar, S. (1990). Problem-solving deficits in suicidal patients: trait vulnerability or state phenomenon? *Journal of Consulting and Clinical Psychology*, **58**, 562–4.

Taylor, E. A. and Stansfield, S. A. (1984). Children who poison themselves II. Prediction of attendance for treatment. *British Journal of Psychiatry*, **145**, 132–5.

Urwin, P. and Gibbons, J. L. (1979). Psychiatric diagnosis in self-poisoning patients. *Psychological Medicine*, **9**, 501–7.

van Heeringen, C., Jannes, S., Buylaert, W., Hendrick, H., De Bacquer, D., and Van Remoortel, J. (1995). The management of non-compliance with referral to out-patient after-care among attempted suicide patients: a controlled intervention study. *Psychological Medicine* 25, 963–70.

Wetzel, R. D. (1976). Hopelessness, depression and suicidal intent. *Archives of General Psychiatry*, 33, 1069–73.

Wexler, L., Weissman, M. M., and Kasl, S. V. (1978). Suicide attempts 1970–75: updating a United States study and comparison with international trends. *British Journal of Psychiatry*, 132, 180–5.

Williams, J. M. G. and Broadbent, K. (1986). Autobiographical memory in attempted suicide patients. *Journal of Abnormal Psychology*, 95, 144–9.

13

Hypochondriasis

Paul M. Salkovskis and Christopher Bass

Research into the cognitive behavioural approach to the understanding and treatment of severe health anxiety (hypochondriasis) has its origins in several areas, particularly work on obsessional problems (see Chapter 8) and panic (see Chapter 6). Michael Gelder has both encouraged the development of and directly contributed to the understanding and treatment of somatoform disorders and health anxiety. He recognized the importance of these problems not only to psychiatry but also to medical practice in general, and he was one of the earliest to realize how cognitive behavioural treatment approaches could usefully be applied to them.

Definitions

The essential feature of *hypochondriasis* is preoccupation with a belief in or fear of having a serious illness. This occurs without adequate organic pathology to account for the degree of psychological response, and 'despite medical reassurance'. Such fears are associated with the perception of bodily signs and sensations which are misinterpreted as evidence of serious illness. It has been proposed that hypochondriasis represents the extreme end of a continuum of health-focused anxiety (Salkovskis 1989; Warwick and Salkovskis 1989b). *Health anxiety* also occurs in a range of non-psychiatric subjects, including the physically ill.

Patients suffering from health anxiety are a drain on resources in every area of medical practice (Katon *et al.* 1984; Kellner 1985; Mayou 1976; Warwick and Salkovskis 1989). For many years it was believed that hypochondriasis was always secondary to other disorders, particularly depression (Kenyon 1965). More recent studies indicate that the primary form of the disorder is common. This distinction is important because it has major implications for the assessment and management of patients presenting with hypochondriacal symptoms.

The duration and course of hypochondriasis are uncertain. The DSM–IV definition of hypochondriasis has a minimum duration criterion of six months (APA 1994), but we know little about the relationship between this chronic disorder and more transient forms. There does seem to be a subset of patients with a favourable prognosis whose hypochondriasis is of short duration.

Prevalence

The prevalence of hypochondriacal concerns in the general population is unknown. Since most measures are based on continuous scales, the distinction between cases of hypochondriasis and non-cases is a matter of degree. Kellner (1985) estimated that hypochondriasis ranged from 3% to 13% in different communities and that illness worries, varying from rational concerns to constant, incapacitating fears, occurred in 10–20% of normal people. Barsky *et al.* (1990*a*) reported a six-month prevalence of DSM–III–R (APA 1987) hypochondriasis in a sample of general medical out-patients of between 4.2% and 6.3%.

We have remarked that hypochondriasis can be a transient or relatively enduring phenomenon, and Tyrer *et al.* (1990) have argued that some hypochondriacal patients have a personality disorder rather than a mental state disorder. Using a standardized research instrument, they found that 8.6% of a group of patients with affective disorders had this type of personality disorder. Clearly, more longitudinal data are required to establish the risk factors for these different types of hypochondriasis.

Comorbidity

As described above, hypochondriacal symptoms are common in depression (as secondary hypochondriasis); by the same token, depressive symptoms and intense demoralization are common in hypochondriasis. There is emerging evidence that there are high rates of comorbidity with both panic and obsessional problems (Noyes *et al.* 1986; Salkovskis *et al.* 1990; Salkovskis and Clark 1993). Barsky *et al.* (1990*b*) compared patients with 'transient hypochondriasis' with those with DSM–III–R hypochondriasis (symptoms present for at least six months). He found that the 'transient' group had less psychiatric disorder and more medical morbidity than those with hypochondriasis, and compared with a comparison sample of non-hypochondriacal controls the transient group had more psychiatric disorder, more personality disorder, reported heightened awareness of bodily sensations, and more medical disorder.

The evolution of treatment

A multitude of psychotherapeutic strategies have been used for hypochondriasis in the past, although it was regarded by many as an untreatable chronic condition. When treatment was attempted it was based on the prevailing theories of hypochondriasis which included subconscious motivation, primary or secondary gain, and the need to remain ill (Kellner 1986). More recent uncontrolled studies of modern methods of treatment have shown, however, that the outcome is far better than once believed (Kellner 1983; Pilowsky 1968; Salkovskis and Warwick 1986; Warwick and Marks 1988).

In the last 15 years one of the recurring themes in the treatment of hypochondriasis has been the role of offering reassurance on the one hand and of reducing avoidance (and therefore the use of exposure and belief change strategies) on the other. These two seemingly imcompatible strategies have both been advocated in the treatment of hypochondriasis. The case for reassurance had been argued by many authors in the past including Gillespie (1928) and Kellner (1982); whereas the case for exposure (particularly when accompanied by a specific demonstration to the patient that alleviation of anxiety produced by reassurance is *transient*) is a more recent development derived from the treatment of obsessive–compulsive disorder (see below; Salkovskis and Warwick 1986; Warwick and Marks 1988).

In a paper addressing this issue, Kellner (1992) acknowledged that exposure was likely to be the most effective treatment in patients with pure or predominantly disease phobia (people who are mostly troubled by being afraid of becoming ill). In those with disease conviction (people who believe that they are ill) he advocated a process of 'persuasion', which involved symptom reattribution, explanation, education, and cognitive techniques. Kellner went on to say, however, that: 'treatment strategies include repeated physical examination when the patient fears he has acquired a new disease . . . and repeated reassurance'. It seems most unlikely that this will be a useful strategy in patients fulfilling DSM–III–R criteria, since by definition these patients' 'fear or belief persists despite medical reassurance and causes impairment in social or occupational functioning'.

Warwick (1992) has suggested the possibility that Kellner used reassurance that consisted of primarily new information for the patient, and was more detailed and better delivered than standard medical reassurance. This debate highlights the urgent need for a careful definition of *reassurance*. As outlined above, reassurance can be offered in a variety of ways, some of which should be helpful, others which may actually increase anxiety. It is even possible that health anxiety might be maintained *because* of reassurance.

As part of a study reporting successful treatment of two cases employing elements of exposure and response prevention, Salkovskis and Warwick

(1986) demonstrated a functional similarity between reassurance seeking and obsessional ritualizing (cf. Rachman *et al.* 1976). In another case series of patients with fears concerning AIDS (Miller *et al.* 1985), seven cases showed significant improvement after cognitive behavioural treatment. This study and more recent work on cognitive behavioural approaches to panic and obsessive-compulsive disorder suggest that cognitive behavioural treatments may be useful in hypochondriasis given an appropriate theoretical foundation. Some of the key differences between obsessional ruminations and morbid preoccupations have already been identified by Rachman (1974); many of these considerations can be applied to hypochondriasis, which often takes a form similar to obsessional thinking without the perception of senselessness.

Theories of health anxiety and hypochondriasis

There is no empirical evidence to support the numerous psychodynamic conceptualizations of hypochondriasis; these are of historical interest only (Kellner 1985). Closely related to and currently more influential than psychoanalytic concepts is the notion of 'somanization' as a process. It has been suggested that some people are unable to express distress in personally and socially acceptable ways, and that the distress therefore emerges as somatic symptoms.

The mechanism usually implied in somatization as a process is similar to the hydraulic model central to psychoanalysis. The idea of an implicit underlying psychological disease process is not supported by research findings however: somatizing patients do report psychological distress (Simon and von Korff 1991). Most importantly, this 'hydraulic' view distracts clinical and research attention away from the person's reaction to the symptoms they *actually* experience and on to some presumed but undetected 'deeper' level of distress. This contrasts sharply with the cognitive view, where the interpretation and misinterpretation of symptoms are seen as central to the *experience* of distress and anxiety, and processes, such as selective attention, psychophysiological arousal, and belief-driven changes in behaviour, are viewed as crucial to the *maintenance* of distress (see below).

Misinterpretation of bodily sensations is assumed to be of importance not only because of the development of the cognitive theory, but also because it forms part of the definition of hypochondriasis. There is now experimental evidence showing that hypochondriacal patients differ from normal and anxious patients in both their *perception* and the tendency to *misinterpret* normal bodily sensations (Salkovskis and Clark 1993; Salkovskis 1990). A further set of cognitive factors concern the checking and reassurance seeking behaviours so prominent in many patients with severe hypochondriasis.

A cognitive behavioural approach to understanding and treatment

The cognitive hypothesis of health anxiety and hypochondriasis is based on the central notion that bodily signs and symptoms are perceived as more dangerous than they really are, and that a particular illness is believed to be more probable and/or serious than it really is (Salkovskis 1989*b*; Salkovskis and Warwick, 1986; Warwick and Salkovskis 1989). At the same time, the patient is likely to perceive him/herself as unable to prevent the illness, and unable to affect its course (i.e., as having no effective means of coping with the perceived threat). The general cognitive analysis of the relationship between perceived threat and the experience of anxiety can be readily applied here; that is.

$$\text{Anxiety} = \frac{\text{Perceived likelihood of illness} \times \text{Perceived cost, awfulness, and burden of the illness}}{\text{Perceived ability to cope with the illness} + \text{Perception of the extent to which external factors will help (rescue factors)}}$$

A crucial implication of this breakdown of cognitive factors is that it is possible to be highly anxious about health with relatively low perceived likelihood of illness, given a relatively high perception of the awfulness of being ill (e.g., people who believe that having cancer would result in being crippled by pain, disabled, becoming physically repulsive, being rejected and abandoned by those they love, and generally being dehumanized). Furthermore, a pattern of this kind coupled with a high perceived likelihood of illness is likely to result in very extreme levels of anxiety. All four factors need to be taken into account both in the formulation and in any treatment interventions.

In terms of the *development* of health anxiety as a severe problem, it is proposed that knowledge and past experiences of illness (in self or others) leads to the formation of specific assumptions about symptoms, disease, and health behaviours. These are learned from a variety of sources, particularly from early experience and from events in the patient's social circle and the mass media. Previous experience of physical ill health in patients and their families and previous experience of unsatisfactory medical management may be important (see Bianchi 1971). A further factor is the information carried by the media. A striking example is provided by the influx of cases of 'AIDS phobia' (Miller *et al.* 1985, 1988) noted after the massive publicity campaign on this topic.

Examples of potentially problematic assumptions are 'bodily changes are usually a sign of serious disease, because every symptom has to have an identifiable physical cause'; 'if you don't go to the doctor as soon as you notice anything unusual then it will be too late'. Other beliefs relate to specific personal weaknesses and particular illnesses; for example, 'there's heart trouble in the family', 'I've had weak lungs since I was a baby'. Such beliefs may be a constant source of anxiety and/or may be activated in vulnerable individuals by critical incidents.

Assumptions can also lead the patient to attend selectively to information which appears to confirm the idea of having an illness, and to ignore selectively or discount evidence indicating good health. Thus, particular assumptions often lead to a *confirmatory bias* in the patient's thinking once a critical incident has resulted in the misinterpretation of bodily symptoms and signs as being indications of serious illness. Situations which constitute critical incidents and activate previously dormant assumptions include unfamiliar bodily sensations, hearing details of illness in a friend of a similar age, and new information about illness. Further bodily sensations may then be noticed as a consequence of increased vigilance arising from anxiety. In patients who become particularly anxious about their health, such situations are associated with thoughts which represent personally catastrophic interpretations of the bodily sensations or signs. Catastrophic interpretations can in turn lead to one of two patterns of anxiety. If the sensations or signs are *not* those which increase as a result of anxiety (as a consequence of autonomic arousal), or the patient does not regard the feared catastrophe as immediate, then the reaction will be hypochondriacal anxiety about health, with the cognitive, behavioural, physiological, and affective correlates as detailed in Fig. 13.1 (e.g., 'the pains in my stomach mean I have an undetected cancer'). On the other hand, if the symptoms that are misinterpreted are those which occur as part of anxiety-induced autonomic arousal and the interpretation is that the symptoms are the signs of *immediate* catastrophe (e.g., 'these palpitations mean that I am having a heart attack right now'), a further immediate increase in symptoms will result. If this process continues, then a panic attack is the more likely response (Clark 1988; Salkovskis 1988). Despite the differences in type of symptoms and time course of feared illness, the ideation in panic and hypochondriasis is similar and the two presentations often overlap (see Noyes *et al*. 1986).

Factors that maintain health anxiety

Once anxiety about health has developed, other mechanisms may be involved in the *maintenance* of the problem.

1. Anxiety about health matters and symptoms themselves is likely to result in physiological arousal. Patients then may misinterpret increased autonomic symptoms as further evidence of a physical disease.

2. Selective attention to illness-related information, such as the perception of normal bodily changes (e.g., gastric distention after eating) or previously unnoticed bodily features (e.g., blotchy complexion) is often important. Focusing prompted by worries about health brings slight bodily variations to awareness at times when ideas about illness are already present, leading to a bias towards noticing information that is consistent with the worries about illness, and with a pre-existing confirmatory bias.

3. Behaviour designed to avoid, check for, or totally exclude physical illnesses (e.g., avoiding physical exertion or contact with disease; reading medical textbooks; frequent medical consultations; bodily checking, manipulation, and inspection) will maintain anxiety by increasing symptoms and preoccupation (the latter in a similar way to that seen in obsessional problems; see Chapter 8). However, unlike the more immediate misinterpretations of panic patients, hypochondriacal misinterpretations allow the patient more scope to seek safety by attempts to obtain a medical resolution of the perceived threat to health.

Behaviour occurring as a consequence of anxiety can increase anxiety in a variety of ways. For example, it keeps attention focused on fears about health and can therefore result in the elaboration of these fears, it can increase the range and scope of catastrophic interpretations, and it can prevent disconfirmation of feared catastrophes (Salkovskis 1991, 1996; Salkovskis et al. 1995).

These mechanisms can sustain preoccupation with health and exacerbate hypochondriacal symptoms as shown in Fig. 13.1. Consistent with a dimensional approach based on cognitive vulnerability augmented by cognitive and behavioural mechanisms, transient examples of these processes are seen in any individual gaining access to new information regarding health risks (e.g., medical students perceiving symptoms of diseases under study, public reaction to media coverage of new medical dangers, patients undergoing or waiting for the results of diagnostic tests). The selective attention and checking behaviour serve to sustain long-term anxiety in the same way as neutralization in obsessional disorder (Salkovskis and Warwick 1986).

Cognitive behavioural treatment

Overview

It follows from this cognitive behavioural model that treatment of hypochondriasis needs to involve reaching a shared understanding with

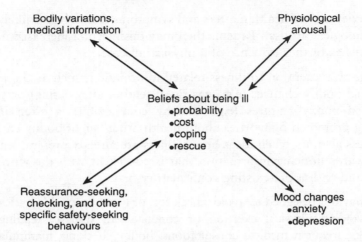

FIG. 13.1. Factors hypothesized as involved in the maintenance of severe health anxiety.

patients concerning the psychological basis of their problem. This is crucial because at the beginning of therapy, these patients believe that they are likely to be suffering from a serious or life-threatening illness. If this belief is held very strongly, patients are unlikely to engage in psychologically (or psychiatrically) based treatment. It is not surprising that the hypochondriacal patient who believes that he/she has heart disease or cancer is reluctant to deal with this by psychological means. Rather, patients seek to solve their problem by strategies such as obtaining the appropriate medical help. It is therefore necessary that, in the early stages of treatment, patients are helped to see that there may be an alternative explanation for the difficulties they are experiencing. Patients are introduced to an idiosyncratically based cognitive model which offers a quite different and less threatening account of their problems. That is, it is not that they have cancer but that they are *worried about and believe* that they might have cancer. For treatment to be effective, it follows that it is crucial that patients agree that therapeutic strategies should be aimed at reducing such worries rather than the fruitless attempts to reduce risk.

At this stage of treatment (engagement) the two possible explanations for the patient's problems are considered alongside each other rather than as mutually exclusive alternatives. The patient is invited to consider how the two alternative views match up to his/her experience. Once the therapist and patient agree on the two alternatives, therapy proceeds as an evaluation of the relative merits of these two views. Evidence for and against each is reviewed and discussed in detail.

Often, discussion reaches the point where further information, which is not currently available to the patient, has to be sought. This is where behavioural experiments come in; these are information-gathering exercises which help the patient reach conclusions about the beliefs which he/she holds. For example, a patient may have noticed that his chest pain tends to worsen around the time that he exercises. During the discussion he is not certain whether this is before, during, or after exercise. In order to test this out therapist and patient go for a brisk walk around the hospital, taking repeated ratings of chest pain intensity. There is a constant interplay between the cognitive behavioural formulation drawn up by patient and therapist, discussion of how the patient's experience fits with that formulation, and generation of new and informative experience using behavioural experiments to further illuminate the model. Cognitive and behavioural elements are interwoven but the guiding principle is always to enable patients to consider and adopt more helpful and less frightening beliefs than the one they have been stuck with previously.

In the treatment of health anxiety, it is considered that the factors which previously triggered anxiety and discomfort may continue to occur. However, therapy has the effect of modifying the meaning of physical variations to the level experienced by most other people who do not suffer from an anxiety disorder of this type. No direct attempt is made to decrease the number of bodily sensations or variations experienced, and any intention on the part of the patient to bring about such a reduction is challenged on the basis of the beliefs which drive it. However, a fortunate and desirable side-effect of cognitive therapy is that there is usually an actual decrease in such symptoms. Note that the 'normal' person does not constantly seek to control symptoms; control tends to be indirect, because there are no serious negative consequences of failing to control symptoms.

The aim of treatment is to help patients identify how their problem works rather than to rule out physical illness. This process requires an early acknowledgement by the therapist that the symptoms experienced by the patients really exist, and that the treatment aims to provide a satisfactory explanation for these symptoms. To achieve this goal, treatment sessions should never become combative; questioning and collaboration are the key techniques. The achievement of this goal is greatly simplified if the therapist remembers that patients' beliefs are invariably based on evidence which they find convincing. The good cognitive behavioural therapist begins the process of challenging beliefs by discovering the observations which the patient believes to be evidence of illness and then working collaboratively with the patient on that basis. Finally, given that, by definition, hypochondriacal patients tend to misinterpret information relevant to their health, it is crucial that the therapist checks patients' understanding about what has been said during the treatment sessions by asking them to summarize what has been said and its implications for them.

Assessment for psychological treatment

Introducing and facilitating the assessment

Introducing the assessment and its purpose is of particular importance in patients who believe that they have been wrongly referred for psychological treatment because their problems are entirely physical (and therefore require physical treatment). These beliefs can make the initial interview particularly difficult, especially when the patients have only agreed to attend with the intention of convincing the therapist that they are physically unwell and that assessment and treatment should be medical rather than psychological. One of the therapist's initial tasks is to discover the patient's attitude to the referral, concentrating particularly on any thoughts the patient may have about its implications. For instance, the patient might be asked, 'When your doctor told you that he was referring you for a psychological opinion, what was your reaction?', then, 'How do you feel about it now?' Quite frequently the response will be something like, 'The doctor thinks the problem is imaginary', or, 'He thinks I'm crazy'. If the patient has worries of this type, it is important to allay these fears before proceeding to further assessment. A helpful way of eliciting the patient's co-operation is to explain:

I work to help people with a variety of problems that are not obviously psychological, but which may involve psychological factors. For instance, I am often asked to help people who have very severe migraine headaches, people who have stomach ulcers, people who have high blood pressure, people who are worried about their health, and so on. In each of these problems, there is often a real physical problem involved, but psychological treatment can be helpful by reducing stress which contributes to the problem, helping with extra stress arising from the problem itself, or helping people adjust to having the problem. Actually, it is very unusual to find someone who isn't at least a little worried about their problem, whatever caused it in the first place.

A further useful tactic is to to tell the patient:

I only know a small amount about your problems at this stage. The purpose of this interview is for me to find out more about your problems and the way they have been affecting you. It may be that psychological help is or is not right for you — you don't have to decide that at this stage. What I would like to do is for us to discuss your problem, then see if there might be anything which we could work on. Then we could discuss whether my kind of treatment would be helpful to you.

Sometimes it may be necessary to devote 15–20 minutes to a discussion of this type. The therapist's aim is to engage the patient sufficiently to be able to assess the problem collaboratively; engaging the patient in treatment is a later goal (see below), but this is neither necessary nor desirable at this stage. No treatment should be offered until the therapist has reached a positive psychological formulation of the patient's problems. A small proportion of patients resist discussing anything other than physical symptoms despite the techniques described above. With these patients, engagement in assessment has to be carried out along the lines used to begin treatment.

General assessment

The assessment interview emphasizes the physiological concomitants of the problem and the patients' beliefs about their physical state. Attention is paid to any events, thoughts, images, feelings, or behaviours which precede or accompany the problem. For instance, in patients where headache is a key complaint, patients are asked whether they have noticed anything which makes the problem worse or better. Have they ever noticed any patterns according to the day of the week, time of the month, or time of the year? When the symptoms are at their peak, what does the patient think is the *worst things that could happen*? Is there anything which, in their particular case, makes this feared possibility particularly frightening or awful?

Patients who are very anxious are often preoccupied with thoughts about what will eventually happen to them, although such thoughts can be very difficult to elicit. This difficulty is especially marked when patients are actively trying not to dwell on their fears. In this type of cognitive avoidance the attempts to suppress thoughts of disaster (sometimes through frantic reassurance seeking about the symptoms experienced) can result in frequent and unpleasant breakthroughs of terrifying thoughts or images. The effects of this cognitive avoidance is therefore a paradoxical increase in preoccupation with vague fears of 'the worst'. An example of this was a patient who noticed that she became very tense when worried; her doctor told her not to worry, and that it was possible to become tense to the point of rigidity and yet still be able to breathe. She interpreted this as meaning that this was what was going to happen to her, and sought a medical solution to her stiffness, believing it to be the sign of a serious wasting disease. An alternative, more helpful line of enquiry is to ask, 'What do you think is the cause of your problems?'; 'How do you think that would work to produce the symptoms you get?'

The therapist should enquire about *visual images* related to the problem. For example, a patient who complained of pain in her legs was able to identify a visual image of her legs being amputated every time she noticed a twinge in her knees; this image was associated with an increase in both anxiety and perceived pain. Assessment of the perceived cost of illness usually involves the therapist probing patients' beliefs about what would happen *if they did develop the disease which they feared.* For example, the therapist might say: 'You are obviously very afraid of cancer. To find out more about this fear, can you remember the last time you felt it was very likely that you did indeed have cancer? At that particular time, when you were worrying about cancer, how did you see it developing? What seemed to you, at that particular time, to be especially awful about having cancer? What would it be like for you and for the people you love?'

Further probes obviously depend on the specific answers given by the patient. The perceived consequences of illness are particularly upsetting for patients, who are often reluctant to describe their fears in great detail. Throughout the assessment and treatment, empathy is crucial, particularly at this stage. Frequent summarizing of both the information and its emotional impact is helpful in encouraging patients to focus on this material, and also has the effect of normalizing the reactions and reinforcing the formulation which is being developed. For example, the therapist might summarize by saying:

> So, it's really not surprising that you are so upset about these lumps under your arms. Not only do you think that they mean you have cancer, but you also believe that cancer will kill you slowly and painfully, that you will lose your humanity, and that your family will suffer terribly both before and after your eventual death. You believe that your young daughter's life will be totally destroyed. These are really terrifying ideas. How do you think that someone else who had these beliefs would react? Do you think that the person might behave in the same way as you?

Exaggerated dysfunctional beliefs about health and illness which may convince patients that they are suffering from a serious illness should be assessed. Examples are: 'Physical symptoms are always a sign that there is something wrong with your body'; 'It is possible to know, with absolute certainty, that you are not ill'. Some patients believe that they will get ill if they do *not* worry about their problems. This can work in at least two ways: first, not worrying can be seen as 'tempting fate', giving an obsessional type of pattern. Alternatively, patients may feel that worry ensures that they remain vigilant for the occurrence of potentially dangerous symptoms; thus, failure to worry might result in missing such symptoms.

Another frequent problem occurs in patients who believe health professionals are likely to make errors of diagnosis with potentially serious consequences. Such beliefs may occur as a result of personal experience or because of examples publicized in the media. Assessing these beliefs is an important part of the initial assessment; later in treatment, they can be challenged using cognitive techniques. Some beliefs may not be problems in themselves, but become problematic in combination with other related beliefs. For example, it is common to find that patients strongly agree both with the notion that 'the only way to really rule out serious illness is for my doctor to send me for medical tests', and with the idea that 'if my doctor sends me for tests, this means that he is convinced that there is something seriously wrong with me'. Clearly, if someone holds both beliefs, then the physician they consult is between a rock and a hard place; if the patient is sent for tests, this is interpreted in a particularly negative way, as is not being sent for tests. These issues need to be addressed in the course of therapy if it is hoped to secure enduring changes in health anxiety in the face of occasional future appropriate medical consultations.

Behaviours which are consequences of patients' symptoms or anxiety are assessed in detail. They include what patients actually do (e.g., go home, lie down, take tablets), but also other less obvious voluntary actions (focusing on their body, distraction, asking for reassurance from others, reading medical textbooks). Anything patients *make themselves do or think* is inquired about. The patient is asked: 'When the problem starts to bother you, is there anything you tend to do because of the problem?' 'Are there any things you try to do when the problem is there?'; 'How would your behaviour be different if the problem were to clear up tomorrow?' Reassurance-seeking from medical or non-medical sources should be specifically assessed.

Assessment should also include enquiry about avoidance which *anticipates* symptoms and anxiety and any associated thoughts. For example, patients often report that they habitually avoid a particular activity, although they cannot identify an associated thought. The therapist could ask: 'If you had *not* been able to avoid that activity . . . what was the worst thing that could have happened then?' Patients with pain, hypochondriasis, irritable bowel, and headache often have anticipatory behaviours of this type, and therefore report few immediately identifiable negative thoughts. Avoidance functions in a similar way to that observed in phobic anxiety and is assessed in similar ways. For instance: 'Are there things that your problem prevents you from doing?'; 'What is the worst that could happen if you did/didn't do these things?'

Once a general account of the problem has been gained, a more detailed description of recent episodes is elicited. This is best done as a narrative progression through a recent occasion which the patient vividly recalls: 'The last time your pain was so severe that it stopped you from walking was on Tuesday. What was the first sign that it was getting bad?'; and as the description progresses, useful questions are, 'What went through your mind when you noticed that the pain was worse?'; 'What happened next?'; 'At that time, what did you think was the worst thing that could happen?'; 'Did you try to do anything to stop that happening?'; 'What did you want to do then?'

Self-monitoring

A full formation is seldom possible immediately after the first assessment session; further assessment should include a period of self-monitoring (which is also useful as a baseline against which to measure the effectiveness of treatment) and the completion of self-report questionnaires. When self-monitoring is begun, the patient is asked to keep records about the relevant variables (e.g., the target problem, thoughts associated with episodes, general mood, and behaviours). The therapist should stress that at this stage patients should describe the thoughts and behaviours associated with the problem, rather than attempt to establish any links between them.

At least one further assessment session is helpful, usually after the therapist has reviewed the medical and psychiatric notes where these are available. The intervening period also allows time for self-monitoring data to be gathered and discussed. Aspects of the patient's history which may intensify the degree of distress the patient experiences should be considered. For example, an outstanding competitive runner developed chronic pain and obesity following a fall in which he damaged his legs so badly that he was never able to walk properly again. Whenever he noticed pain, he had the thought, 'Life isn't worth living if I can't run again; nothing else is worthwhile'.

Physicians and other professionals (e.g., the general practitioner currently involved in the patient's care) should be contacted for their opinion, and to indicate the therapist's involvement. It is important to establish and agree the medical limits which may be imposed on treatment. Treatment often includes medication reduction, exercise programmes, and so on, and these should be conducted in co-operation with the physicians involved. In the second session, the results of self-monitoring are examined and the process of engaging the patient in treatment starts.

Self-monitoring can be either individualized or standardized. Self-monitoring is usually on the basis of a daily diary. This would include the variables which the initial assessment suggested may be important. Although criterion measures (e.g., headache intensity) are kept constant, other details recorded in the diary (e.g., thoughts of brain tumours, stressful events, coping behaviours) may vary as treatment progresses and the formulation is refined. Later in treatment, the application and effectiveness of coping techniques learned in therapy may also be recorded. For example,

In a patient with chronic pain the assessment suggested that he was restricting his physical activities, spending most of his mornings in bed. An activity diary revealed that his afternoon and evenings were usually spent lying on a couch in one position. Extension of the diary to include his thoughts and mood every time his clock struck the hour (so that he had an identifiable signal for his self-recording) revealed gloomy thoughts centred on the hopelessness of the future. This led into a discussion of the role of *mental* as well as physical inactivity, and ways in which he could try to improve his situation *regardless of his medical condition*. He was asked, 'All right, supposing for the moment that the pain were never to improve. How would you want to set about coping with that?'

Medication use should be included in self-monitoring, and can be regarded as an illness behaviour which fosters preoccupation, sometimes because of side-effects. For example,

A patient with mild asthma was experiencing several attacks of anxiety each day, and was constantly in a state of some agitation. She was asked to monitor her breathlessness, general anxiety, anxiety attacks, and use of inhalers. It emerged from these records that episodes of anxiety in the afternoon were five times more likely after she had used her inhaler on three or more occasions. Restricting her use of the inhaler resulted in a dramatic reduction in anxiety, as a preliminary to a fuller programme of treatment.

Intervention

Engagement in treatment

Establishing engagement usually follows from assessment. If the patient has been engaged in treatment, the therapist summarizes what the patient has said, emphasizing the role of the patient's *symptoms*, *thoughts*, *beliefs*, and *behaviours*, and presents the conceptualization in these terms. The acceptability of this conceptualization is discussed with the patient.

Before treatment can proceed beyond this stage, the therapist and patient must agree on treatment goals. Many patients are willing to attend for a psychological assessment, but have a different set of goals from therapist, who is attempting to arrive at a psychological formulation for treatment of the patient's problem. Patients, on the other hand, may regard the therapist as a potential ally in their attempts to rule out physical illnesses or to have their beliefs about the medical basis of their problems accepted as true. For instance, they may intend to prove to the therapist that they are not 'mad', or regard the therapist as a new source of expert reassurance. Unless these different expectations of treatment and how it should proceed can be reconciled, therapy is unlikely to be effective. However, the therapist should not expect patients to 'admit' that their problems are 'just anxiety' when they are seeking treatment for what they believe is an undiagnosed physical illness, or one which is more severe or handicapping than has been recognized.

This impasse is resolved by careful discussion in which the therapist neither rejects the patient's beliefs nor adds weight to them. The therapist first indicates full acceptance that the patient *experiences* physical symptoms and believes that these symptoms are due to a serious physical illness. The therapist can explain that people generally base such beliefs on particular observations which seem to be convincing evidence that they are ill. However, it is also possible that there may be alternative explanations of the observations which they have made. Further assessment and treatment then involve the examination of the evidence and possible alternative explanations, and includes the use of specific tasks designed to test out alternative explanations. The patient is explicitly informed that, in this new way of dealing with the problem, physical tests and checks will not be a part of treatment, nor will reassurance and lengthy discussions of symptoms be useful. Ways in which these could be counter-productive are discussed, where possible with reference to the patient's past experience.

Before patients decide about the acceptability of this new approach to the problem, the usefulness of the two alternative ways (new and old) of tackling the problem should be considered. How long have they been trying to solve their problem and rid themselves of symptoms by exclusively medical means? How effective had this been? Had they ever properly tested the alternative psychological approach suggested by the therapist? It is then proposed that patients commit themselves to work with the therapist in this new way for four months, and the dates are specified. If they were able to do all the things agreed with their therapist and the problem had not improved at all at the end of that time, then it would be reasonable to come back to their original way of tackling the problem, and the therapist would then be happy to reconsider the problem from a more physical perspective. In this way, patients are not asked to give up their view of their problems, but to consider and test an alternative perspective for a limited period. In patients who believe that they may have a physical illness which is being neglected this is an attractive proposition. The transcript below illustrates this approach in the second session with a 57-year-old woman.

Th: So you believe that you have a serious physical problem that the doctors haven't picked up. Is that right?

P: Yes, that's right.

Th: So that thought is very upsetting, and makes you unhappy in a variety of ways. The main ways it affects what you do is it interferes with you being on your own, and it stops you doing things you enjoy such as tennis. It also has stopped you from eating very much, which might be making eating still more difficult. Is that right?

Pt: Yes. Sometimes I will be on my own, but I won't if I can help it.

Th: Right. In general, when people have fears, they usually have reasons for those fears. In your instance, the reason for your fear about your health are the pains you get, your loss of weight, difficulty eating and swallowing, and bowel problems. These all sugget to you that you are ill, especially as they come every day. Is there any other evidence that makes you think you are ill?

Pt: Yes, it's not a lump, it's a horrible feeling in the throat, tight, when it gets to here it's sore. My doctor checked me, but this has only got worse since I had the X-rays, not before; then it didn't stop me from eating. My waterworks are a problem too. It's very frightening, I can't deal with it. These are the main things, they make me think I have the same as my mother.

Th: Right; so these all make you think the worst; you think you have cancer, like your mother.

Pt: Yes.

Th: There are also some things which make you think you have anxiety as well; for instance, towards the end of our last meeting, you said that the sleep problem was anxiety about dying in your sleep, that you fight sleep. So your sleeping problem is explained by being worried?

Pt: Yes, I think so.

Th: Now, you also have problems with pain, eating, waterworks, and bowels. These make you think you are ill. One worry about these is that the doctors would not take these seriously because you've had similar problems in the past.

Pt: How would they know if I had something seriously wrong with me organically? This is different from the past. I can't work through it now.

Th: The doctor has listened to the symptoms, but you are worried that he pays too much attention to your previous problems. [Briefly discusses the way diagnoses are made]. He thinks you have a kind of phobia about your health, and the symptoms come from anxiety. [Discusses symptoms of anxiety, asks patient to identify whether she experiences any of these, describes effects of anxiety on pain and appetite . . .]. What's your reaction to this kind of idea?

Pt: I can say to you that when my symptoms are starting to lift, then I'll believe I'm all right.

Th: OK. I have a proposition for you. Your worry is that there is something physically wrong with you, and I understand why the things we have discussed make you think that. We've also gone over things which make me think you have a type of phobia of being ill. So, there are two possibilities, and we need to consider both of them. The two possibilites are the one you believe and I doubt, which is that there is something physically wrong with you. The other possibility I believe and you doubt; this is that you are getting very anxious and having upsetting thoughts. These thoughts make you do things which focus you more on your worries, and can produce symptoms in your body, and change your eating. Is that a good summary?

Pt: Yes, that's just it.

Th: Recently, how much have you tried to act as if you were ill and deal with the problem in that way?

Pt: Like going to my GP? Yes, he's checked up on me a lot.

Th: Has that been a help in making the symptoms less?

Pt: No, because . . . he gave me medicals, nothing was found. I'm saying, what am I to do?

Th: It sounds like you have tried to put the problem right by dealing with it as if it were a physical problem. I've been suggesting that anxiety might be a big part of your problem. How much have you tried to deal with in that kind of way, as if the problem were anxiety? Have you given that a try?

Pt: Em . . . [long pause] I can't say I have.

Th: You haven't tried to deal with it like anxiety?

Pt: No.

Th: You've tried dealing with it as a physical problem. How about making a bargain for just three months; in those three months, to deal with it is as an anxiety problem. You try to deal with it as anxiety. If you are able to do all the things we work out together to deal with your anxiety, and at the end of three months the problem is not improving, then we will look at it again from a physical angle.

Pt: I understand.

Th: It seems like a sensible way of doing it; if you do this and it works then the problem's gone If it doesn't help, then that's also good, because you can turn round and say 'Ah ha, I got my anxiety down, and the problem is still there; you need to look at it again.' Does that seem all right?

Pt: I see. Where do we start?

A summary and consolidation would then follow. The sessions should be audiotaped; the patient can then listen afterwards and summarize the important points.

Changing beliefs about the nature and consequences of the problem

Anxiety about health involves the interpretation of bodily sensations, physical changes, or medical communications as more dangerous than they really are.

Commonly, the *future development* of a medical condition (real or imagined) may be perceived as more threatening than is truly the case. In problems with a substantial basis in anxiety, treatment involves changing the way in which patients evaluate the meaning of symptoms. Changing beliefs initially involves identifying negative thoughts and the evidence on which they are based; subsequent intervention tends to depend on helping the patient to consider alternative explanations, both in terms of the origin of specific symptoms and the anxiety which symptoms elicit.

Other consequences feared by the patient include a deteriorating course of illness leading to pain, loss of mobility, becoming a burden on one's family, loss of dignity, and painful death. Challenging beliefs about just how bad an illness would be (and could get) is used both to decrease negative preoccupation and to reinforce the formulation.

The combination of discussing the basis of negative beliefs, self-monitoring, and behavioural experiments described above is applicable to a wide range of reactions involving anxiety or depression as a response to physical symptoms or fears. Ratings indicate to the therapist and patient how successful belief change has been. Dual ratings of belief are often helpful; for example: 'I would like you to rate the thought "the symptoms will become so intense as to drive me to suicide" on a 0–100 scale, where 0 is "I don't believe this at all " and 100 is "I am completely convinced that this is true". Right now, how much do you believe this?' Then: 'When the symptoms are particularly severe, what would the rating be then?' Often, the presence of the symptom produces substantial differences in belief ratings; accordingly the negative thoughts should be identified and challenged for situations when beliefs are at their strongest, because this disconfirmation has the biggest impact on the patients' behaviour. Behavioural experiments are a very powerful way of changing patients' beliefs about the origin and nature of their symptoms. In a behavioural experiment the aim is to demonstrate to the patients that their symptoms can be influenced by factors other than the ones they believe are responsible.

For example, a patient who believed that difficulty swallowing was a sign of throat cancer was asked to swallow repeatedly and describe the resulting effects. She was surprised to discover that she found it increasingly difficult to swallow, and that the therapist experienced the same thing when he swallowed repeatedly. The importance of this observation was that she would frequently check her throat by swallowing a number of times. The behavioural experiments used in panic are helpful, particularly when the patient experiences occasional panic attacks (see Clark and Salkovskis in press).

Sometimes, the very sensitivity of the patient to misinterpretation can be used to good effect in therapy. At the end of each therapy session, the patient is asked to summarize the main things that he/she has learned. It is not unknown for the patient to say things like: 'You told me that I have an undetected serious illness'. Rather than denying this directly, the therapist replies by saying: 'I am completely certain that I did not mean to say anything of that kind at any point. However, this is obviously something you understood me to have said. What I would like you to do before the next treatment session is to review the audiotape of today's session and find where you believe I told you this. Listen again to this section very carefully, make notes and bring the tape back, then next time we can find out what happened and what we can learn from it'. Invariably the patient returns and says that he/she had misunderstood and misinterpreted what was discussed. Having clarified the nature of the misunderstanding, the therapist asks 'What do you make of that?'; the discussion then focuses on whether this type of misinterpretation might be common for this person, and whether it might have affected past medical consultations and so on. The aim is to have the patient make allowances for this type of misinterpretation.

Changing behaviour

The majority of behaviours involved in somatic problems are perceived by the patient as serving a preventative function, and are therefore relatively difficult to modify without attention to the underlying beliefs.

Behaviours directly related to the problem

When illness behaviour is prominent, treatment strategies aim to elicit and demonstrate the role of behaviours in maintaining anxiety, preoccupation, and physiological disturbance. The use of questioning as part of guided discovery can be helpful. Direct demonstration is particularly convincing when changing behaviour can be shown to have an effect on symptoms. The patient and therapist design experiments to: (1) test the patient's belief that the behaviour is 'keeping him/herself safe' from serious harm; and (2) to see if behaviours which the patient believes relieve symptoms really do so. For example,

A patient believed that she had developed Hodgkin's disease because she noticed lumps and pain in her neck and armpits. As a result of this fear, she frequently prodded and manipulated these areas, resulting in worsening of the pain, some superficial inflammation, and swelling. She and the therapist carried out an experiment in which both prodded their necks in the same way for three periods of five minutes during a session. The increase in pain and inflammation was sufficient to convince her that her behaviour was implicated in the production of the symptom.

In many instances, avoidance behaviours maintain the patients' preoccupation with disease by preventing them access to information which contradicts negative interpretations of symptoms.

A patient believed that he had prevented himself from having a stroke by focusing his attention on trying to 'make the blood flow more freely', by the exertion of willpower, and that should he stop this he would then have a stroke (belief rated 95/100). He was obviously reluctant to stop doing this so the therapist suggested that he try to *bring on* a stroke in the session by effort of will. Surprised by this suggestion, he said after some discussion that it was not possible; he was able to generalize this to his efforts to prevent a stroke (belief rating dropped to 10/100). He was then able to prevent his efforts at control outside the session, with the result that his belief dropped to 0/100, and he ceased to worry about having a stroke.

Further examples of the specific application of techniques to change pain behaviours and beliefs are described in detail by Philips (1988).

Reassurance

In patients anxious about their health, a variety of behaviours can occur which have the same effect as obsessional checking (see Chapter 8). These reassurance-seeking behaviours focus attention on patients' worries, reduce their anxiety in the short term, but increase preoccupation and other aspects of the problem in the longer term (Salkovskis and Warwick 1986; Warwick and Salkovskis 1985). Such behaviours include requests for physical tests, physical examinations, and detailed discussion of symptoms in an attempt to *rule out* possible disease. Although most non-anxious patients seeking medical help respond to properly delivered reassurance in which illness is 'ruled out', patients anxious about their health respond differently; repeated and 'stronger' reassurance quickly becomes counter-productive as the patients selectively attend to and misinterpret the reassurance itself. For example, a patient was told, 'These headaches are certainly caused by tension; if they persist, then I'll send you for a skull X-ray to put your mind at rest'. The patient interpreted this as a sign that the doctor believed that he might have a brain tumour. Repeated attempts to 'prove' to patients that they are *not* ill, either through medical tests or verbal persuasion, are likely to increase anxiety.

The role of reassurance-seeking in maintaining patients' problems must be explained to them in a way which they clearly understand. For example, a patient who wanted to discuss his symptoms repeatedly in case he had developed cancer asked why the therapist would not discuss the symptoms.

The therapist was aware that the interview was developing into an unproductive argument:

Th: Do you think that you really need this?

P: Well, it would make me feel better.

Th: OK. I guess that if that's what will help I ought to go over the symptoms with you. And I think I really ought to do it properly. I have a lot of time now, which I'm happy to spend with you, so long as it deals with the problem properly. How many times would I have to reassure you to last until the end of the year?

Pt: Until the end of the year?

Th: Yes: there seems little point in doing something like this, which you have done lots before, unless it's really going to work this time. Is three hours enough for the rest of the year?

Pt: But . . . it won't last for the rest of the year.

Th: I see. How long will it last?

Pt: Probably for the rest of the day. Then I'll probably get worried again.

Th: So however much reassurance you get it never lasts?

Pt: No. Sometimes the more I get the more I want.

Th: You are saying that however much reassurance I give you, it isn't going to last very long before you are going to get worried again, and it might even make you more worried. As we have already identified anxiety about your health as one of your major problems, do you think that reassurance is an effective treatment, or should we look for alternatives?

Where reassurance-seeking is a major feature of a patient's difficulties, it is helpful to devise a behavioural experiment demonstrating the effects of reassurance (Salkovskis and Warwick 1986). This experiment can also function as an engagement strategy in patients who are reluctant to start treatment without a 'final test'. For example, a last physical investigation before psychological treatment starts is discussed and arranged on the strict understanding that it is regarded as unnecessary for the patient's physical health, but may be helpful in the psychological assessment. Self-monitoring of anxiety about health, belief in specific illness-related thoughts, and need for reassurance are all regularly rated on a 0–100 scale over the period prior to and after the test. If anxiety is reduced in an enduring way, then this is helpful in any case. If, as is much more common, anxiety is reduced only briefly, this is used as the basis for discussion about the way in which reassurance keeps anxiety going. The demonstration also engages the patient in treatment and establishes a collaborative relationship. It provides a clear rationale for controlling reassurance-seeking and thereby helps the patient to tolerate the initial anxiety caused by behaviour change. A similar strategy is to ask patients to specify exactly what procedures would *fully* convince them that they are *not* suffering from the feared illness. The therapist then adopts the role of the interested sceptic, asking things like: 'Yes, but would that *really* be convincing? How could you be sure that the doctor was properly aware of how to use the test?', and so on; this is to illustrate that it is *never* possible to be certain that illness is not present, in the same way as it is never possible to be sure that a satellite will not fall on their heads as they walk down the street. This discussion is related to the importance of reassurance in maintaining anxiety, preoccupation, and illness belief.

Families and others involved with the patient must be included in such discussions and shown how to deal with requests for reassurance. A role-play may be used, in which the patient asks the relative for reassurance and the relative answers (without non-verbal criticism) in previously agreed terms. For example, a relative might reply: 'As we agreed at the clinic, it does not help you if I give you reassurance. I'm not going to respond at all after this.' The relative then either leaves or talks about unrelated things. Except as a stopgap at times when the patient is *especially* stressed, this type of strategy is of little use without the patient's agreement.

Review of outcome of research

Despite the fact that hypochondriasis has been identified as a distinct syndrome for over a century, there has previously been no evidence from controlled trials for the effectiveness of any kind of treatment. Over the past two decades, a number of case reports, single-case experiments, and case series have been reported, indicating that treatment can be effective in some instances. For example, Salkovskis and Warwick (1986) reported the treatment of two patients who erroneously believed themselves to be suffering from life-threatening illnesses; in both patients, a baseline was established, during which evidence for the anxiogenic effects of medical reassurance was gathered through diary recording. This information was presented to the patient as the outcome of a behavioural experiment (see p. 321), indicating the possible role of reassurance-seeking and associated checking behaviours. This information was presented to the patient and a cognitive account of the patients' problems agreed with them. The patients showed substantial and sustained improvement once they engaged in treatment. In a larger case series, including both illness phobics and patients with high levels of disease conviction, Warwick and Marks (1988) used a strategy based on exposure, response prevention, and belief change with good effect. More recently, a similar cognitive behavioural treatment delivered in the context of group therapy was found to be effective in an uncontrolled study with general hospital patients (Stern and Fernandez 1991).

Two controlled trials of cognitive therapy, as described in the present chapter, have now been conducted. In the first, Warwick *et al.* (in press) compared 16 sessions of cognitive behavioural treatment with a waiting list control of comparable duration. On 23 of 24 measures, the treated group improved significantly more than the waiting list group, with a mean assessor rated improvement of 5% in the waiting list group as opposed to 76% in those treated with cognitive behaviour therapy. Treatment gains were mostly maintained at three-month follow-up. In a second study, cognitive behavioural treatment was compared with a carefully devised stress-management package and a waiting list control. At the time of writing, full results are not available for this trial, but preliminary data analysed for a conference presentation (with a small number of patients not having completed therapy and therefore not included in the analysis) indicate that both active treatments do significantly better than the waiting list condition (Salkovskis 1995). This result is not unexpected as behavioural stress management provides patients with a detailed alternative explanation for their symptoms (e.g., stress) and a comprehensive package of management techniques based on this alternative explanation. The final analysis will allow us to determine the relative efficacy of the two treatments in short and longer term, and the role of cognitive variables in predicting relapse.

New directions

Now that the efficacy of cognitive behavioural treatment for severe hypochondriasis has been established in controlled trials, future developments lie in at least two connected areas. First, the effective components of the treatment need to be identified, particularly in the light of the effectiveness of behavioural stress-management treatment. Developments in this direction should lead to briefer and more efficient interventions. Second, it seems likely that it will be possible to extend this work to the understanding and treatment of anxiety as a reaction to medical testing and screening. This type of development is likely to be increasingly important as population-based screening becomes more widely available and applied. This is especially so with the development of new genetic screening techniques for common multi-factorially determined diseases. When used as population screening, people who may have no inkling that they are at risk for life-threatening disease may be informed that they have somewhat increased risk. It is known anecdotally that some individuals experience major negative psychological reactions to such information. Measures derived from the cognitive behavioural hypothesis should be able to allow prediction of negative psychological reactions to such screening. Previous interventions in such situations have been confined to genetic counselling, which is clearly not necessarily a form of psychological help. The use of a cognitive behavioural model in understanding and predicting the psychological reaction to testing offers the possibility of specific and directed pre-test counselling designed to prevent negative reactions and the adoption of cognitive treatments for health anxiety and depression in the alleviation of post-test psychological distress.

A great deal of work remains to be carried out to clarify the psychological processes involved in health anxiety; an adequate classification and definition of the range of problems and syndromes within the area cannot be successfully achieved until this has been done. In the past, too much emphasis has been placed on the use of drug-treatments in the absence of evidence for their efficacy; cognitive behavioural methods of treatment are promising and require evaluation.

References

APA (American Psychiatric Association) (1987). *Diagnostic and Statistical Manual of Mental Disorders* (3rd edn, revised). APA, Washington, DC.

APA (American Psychiatric Association) (1994). *Diagnostic and Statistical Manual of Mental Disorders* (4th edn), Washington, DC.

Barsky, A. J., Wyshak, G., Klerman, G. L., and Latham K. S. (1990a). The prevalence of hypochondriasis in medical outpatients. *Social Psychiatry and Psychiatric Epidemiology*, 25, 89–94.

Barksy, A. J., Wyshak, G., and Klerman, G. L. (1990b). Transient hypochondriasis. *Archives of General Psychiatry*, 47, 746–52.

Becker, M. H., Maiman, L. A., Kirscht, J. P., Haefner, D. P., Drachman, R. H., and Taylor, D. W. (1979). Patient perceptions and compliance; recent studies of the health belief model. In *Compliance in health care* (ed. R. B. Haynes, D. W. Taylor, and D. L. Sackett), pp. 78–109. Johns Hopkins University Press, Baltimore, MD.

Bianchi, G. N. (1971). The origins of disease phobia. *Australia and New Zealand Journal of Psychiatry*, 5, 241–57.

Clark, D. M. (1988). A cognitive model of panic attacks. In *Panic: psychological perspectives* (ed. S. Rachman, and J. D. Maser), pp. 71–90. Erlbaum, Hillsdale, NJ.

Gillespie, R. D. (1928). Hypochondria: Its definition, nosology and psychopathology. *Guy's Hospital Reports*, 8, 408–60.

Katon, W., Ries, R. K., and Kleinman, A. (1984). The prevalence of somatization in primary care. *Comprehensive Psychiatry*, 25, 208–11.

Kellner, R. (1982). Psychotherapeutic strategies in hypochondriasis: a clinical study. *American Journal of Psychiatry*, 36, 146–57.

Kellner, R. (1983). The prognosis of treated hypochondriasis; a clinical study. *Acta Psychiatrica Scandinavica*, 67, 69–79.

Kellner, R. (1985). Functional somatic symptoms and hypochondriasis. *Archives of General Psychiatry*, 42, 821–33.

Kellner, R. (1986). *Somatization and Hypochondriasis*. Praeger, New York.

Kellner, R. (1992). The treatment of hypochondriasis: to reassure or not to reassure? *International Review of Psychiatry*, 4, 71–5.

Kenyon, F. E. (1965). Hypochondriasis: A survey of some historical, clinical and social aspects. *British Journal of Psychiatry*, **119**, 305–7.

Mayou, R. (1976). The nature of bodily symptoms. *British Journal of Psychiatry*, **129**, 55–60.

Miller, D., Green, J., Farmer, R., and Carroll, G. (1985). A "pseudo-AIDS" syndrome following from fear of AIDS. *British Journal of Psychiatry*, **146**, 550–1.

Miller, D., Acton, T. M. G., and Hedge, B. (1988). The worried well: their identification and management. *Journal of the Royal College of Physicians*, **22**, 158–65.

Noyes, R., Reich, J., Clancy, J., and O'Gorman, J. W. (1986). Reduction in hypochondriasis with treatment of panic disorder. *British Journal of Psychiatry*, **149**, 631–5.

Philips, H. C. (1988). *The psychological management of chronic pain: a manual*. Springer, New York.

Pilowsky, I. (1968). The response to treatment in hypochondriacal disorders. *Australian and New Zealand Journal of Psychiatry*, **2**, 88–94.

Rachman, S. J. (1974). Some similarities and differences between obsessional ruminations and morbid preoccupations. *Canadian Psychiatric Association Journal*, **18**, 71–3.

Rachman, S. J., de Silva, P., and Roper, G. (1976). The spontaneous decay of compulsive urges. *Behaviour Research and Therapy*, **14**, 445–53.

Salkovskis, P. M. (1988). Phenomonology, assessment and the cognitive model of panic attacks. In *Panic: psychologial views* (ed. S. J. Rachman, and J. Maser). Erlbaum, Hove, UK.

Salkovskis, P. M. (1989a). Obsessions and compulsions. In *Cognitive therapy: a clinical casebook* (ed. J. Scott, J. M. G. Williams, and A. T. Beck). Routledge, London.

Salkovskis, P. M. (1989b). Somatic problems. In *Cognitive-behavioural approaches to adult psychological disorder: a practical guide* (ed. K. Hawton, P. M. Salkovskis, J. W. Kirk, and D. M. Clark). Oxford University Press.

Salkovskis, P. M. (1990). The nature of and interaction between cognitive and physiological factors in panic attacks and their treatment. Unpublished Ph.D. thesis. University of Reading.

Salkovskis, P. M. (1991). The importance of behaviour in the maintenance of anxiety and panic: a cognitive account. *Behavioural Psychotherapy*, **19**, 6–19.

Salkovskis, P. M. (1995). *Treatment of hypochondriasis*. Paper presented at the World Congress of Behavioural and Cognitive Therapies, Copenhagen.

Salkovskis, P. M. and Clark, D. M. (1993). Panic disorder and hypochondriasis. *Advances in Behaviour Research and Therapy*, **15**, 23–48.

Salkovskis, P. M. and Warwick, H. M. C. (1986). Morbid preoccupations, health anxiety and reassurance: a cognitive-behavioural approach to hypochondriasis. *Behaviour Research and Therapy*, **24**, 597–602.

Salkovskis, P. M., Warwick, H. M. C., and Clark, D. M. (1990). *Hypochondriasis*. Paper for DSM IV working groups.

Simon, G. E. and von Korff, M. (1991). Somatization and psychiatric disorder in the NIMH Epidemiologic Catchment Area Study. *American Journal of Psychiatry*, **148**, 1494–500.

Tyrer, P., Fowler-Dixon, R. T., and Ferguson, B. (1990). The justification for the diagnosis of hypochondriacal personality disorder. *Journal of Psychosomatic Research*, **34**, 637–42.

Warwick, H. M. C. (1992). Provision of appropriate and effective reassurance. *International Review of Psychiatry*, **4**, 76–80.

Warwick, H. M. C. and Marks, I. M. (1988). Behavioural treatment of illness phobia. *British Journal of Psychiatry*, 152, 239–41.

Warwick, H. M. C. and Salkovskis, P. M. (1985). Reassurance. *British Medical Journal*, 290, 1028.

Warwick, H. M. C. and Salkovskis, P. M. (1989). Hypochondriasis. In *Cognitive therapy in clinical practice* (ed. J. Scott, J. M. G. WIlliams, and A. T. Beck). Gower, London.

Warwick, H. M. C., Clark, D. M., Cobb, A., and Salkovskis, P. M. (in press). A controlled trial of cognitive-behavioural treatment of hypochondriasis. *British Journal of Psychiatry*.

14

Cardiovascular disease

Derek W. Johnston

Disease is rooted in behaviour. There would be little lung cancer if people did not smoke cigarettes or cirrhosis of the liver if they did not consume alcohol. Heart disease would be dramatically reduced if western industrialized nations consumed the diet of parts of Italy or China, or even the diet of their own forefathers. Diseased individuals would recover more quickly from illness and reduce the risk of recurrence if they adhered to medical advice and altered their lifestyles in ways that few dispute. There would also be less disease if doctors and others in the health professions altered their own behaviour, implemented treatment guidelines, screened for disease, and carried out hygienic practices that have been recommended for decades.

'Behavioural medicine' is the term generally used for the efforts of a number of health disciplines to apply the methods of behavioural science to the understanding of disease-inducing behaviours and their modification. It is grounded jointly in psychosomatic medicine, which is traditionally concerned with aetiology, and cognitive behaviour therapy, which is primarily concerned with treatment. This combination has proved potent and in the 20 years since behavioural medicine was recognized there have been great advances, particularly in our understanding of the role of psychological processes in the aetiology of disease and in the development of psychological interventions to treat disease and to improve patients' welfare after major diseases such as heart disease and cancer.

This chapter concentrates on the role of behavioural medicine in the treatment of cardiovascular disease. This is one of the most common causes of morbidity and mortality in adults and has been the subject of critical and vigorous research. Those interested in learning about the many other areas in which behavioural medicine have had an impact should consult Pearce and Wardle (1989) on the practice of behavioural medicine, M. Johnston and Wallace (1990) on the stressfulness of medical procedures, Winnett et al. (1989) on behavioural applications in public health, Glaser and Kiecolt-Glaser (1994) on the burgeoning area of psychoimmunology and Chapters 13, 15, and 16 in this volume. In this chapter, treatments are discussed that attempt to alter psychological states, such as heightened arousal, coronary-prone behaviour, and the pain and distress associated with disease since that is where cognitive behaviour therapy has had the most impact. There are obviously other behavioural ways of reducing the risk of disease and its recurrence, such as by altering diet, not smoking, and exercise, and their exclusion from this chapter does not mean that they are of lesser importance. In many, instances altering these behavioural risk factors is as important, and as challenging, as altering the psychological states mentioned above.

Stress management in the treatment of primary hypertension

Although stress has been implicated in the elevation of several risk factors for coronary heart disease, the only substantial work carried out has been on primary hypertension. Primary hypertension (i.e., raised blood pressure of no clearly identified origin), is found in up to 20% of the adult population and is associated with an increased risk of myocardial infarction and a greatly increased risk of cerebral stroke. The aetiology of primary hypertension is complex but it appears at least plausible that psychological stress plays a part, probably in combination with biological vulnerability. Studies in animals have shown that stress can lead to persistent elevations in blood pressure in genetically susceptible rats (Lawler *et al.* 1981); and dogs made vulnerable through a high-salt diet (Anderson *et al.* 1983). The teenage offspring of parents with hypertension, who are at increased risk of developing hypertension in later life, show increased blood pressure responses to acute stress, despite their resting blood pressure being normal (Fredrikson and Matthews 1990). It is currently quite uncertain if the blood pressure rise to acute stress predicts the development of hypertension. Some find that it does (e.g., Menkes *et al.* 1989; Light *et al.* 1992), however a recent analysis of a substantial data set from the Whitehall study failed to confirm this (Carroll *et al.* 1995).

If stress plays a role in the aetiology and maintenance of hypertension it is attractive to attempt to reduce blood pressure by teaching patients to manage stress. In treating high blood pressure stress management is essentially a form of applied relaxation training. The therapies with some record of success have the following characteristics: (1) they are based on live (rather than tape-recorded) relaxation training; (2) they include regular home practice; (3) patients apply relaxation in stressful situations; and (4) they include some form of counselling, often simple and informal. The prototypic application was been developed by Patel (Patel and North 1975). In addition to the above elements Patel uses skin conductance biofeedback to aid relaxation. It is unlikely that this is necessary and few other workers have adopted it. Stress management is usually given on an individual basis over a course of approximately eight sessions. Patel, however, has used the treatment successfully with groups of up to 10 patients (Patel *et al.* 1981).

Despite almost 25 years of study and many randomized controlled trials, it is not clear if stress management is effective in treating primary hypertension. Various summaries and meta-analyses of these trials have been published, and although they reach slightly different conclusions (see Jacob *et al.* 1991; Johnston 1991) most have been positive, until recently. A more recent summary analysis (Eisenberg *et al.* 1993) appears to suggest that the effects of stress management are little different from non-specific interventions or even that of repeated blood pressure measurement. However, 25 five years of investigation would not have been pursued if there was not some basis for believing that stress management was a useful treatment. In the early studies stress management appeared to lead to persistent decreases in blood pressure and even a reduction in the incidence of myocardial infarction and related heart conditions (e.g., Bali 1979; Irvine *et al.* 1986; Patel and Marmot 1988; Patel *et al.* 1981, 1985; Patel and North 1975; Taylor *et al.* 1977). However more recent studies have been predominantly negative. Agras *et al.* (1987), who had published some of the earliest positive studies, and Chesney *et al.* (1987) found that at best stress management had only a temporary advantage and at the end of a two-year follow-up period there was no difference in blood pressure between those receiving stress management and those receiving a control condition in which blood pressure was measured regularly. When these results are compared with the more positive studies, such as Patel *et al.* (1985), it is apparent that the main difference is in the blood pressure of the control subjects. In Patel *et al.* (1985) the controls' blood pressure does not drop while in Agras *et al.* (1987) and Chesney *et al.* (1987) it drops substantially. Irvine and Logan (1991) also failed to find any advantage of relaxation-based stress management over a psychotherapy control in a substantial study of men recruited from a worksite screening programme.

Concern has often been expressed that stress management might simply enable the patient to reduce their blood pressure at the time of measurement. This was addressed by van Montfrans *et al.* (1990) who examined the effects of relaxation on blood pressure measured continuously over a 24-hour period using the highly accurate and reliable intra-arterial method. Pressure did not differ between subjects receiving relaxation and an untreated control group. Finally, Johnston *et al.* (1993), following-up an earlier study in which relaxation was more effective than a control treatment (Irvine *et al.* 1986), compared relaxation and an exercise-based control condition in almost 100 unmedicated hypertensives. Outcome was assessed by clinic blood pressure, ambulatory blood pressure, and a measurement of the left ventricle of the heart. This is often enlarged in patients with raised blood pressure and reduces when pressure drops over a prolonged period. It can therefore be regarded as an indicator of a sustained drop in pressure. Johnston *et al.* (1993) could find no difference on any measure between the relaxation and the control condition either over the six months of treatment or a six-month follow-up period. Additionally, and most unusually, there was no reduction in blood pressure in either group.

It is clear that the apparent promise of stress management in the treatment of primary hypertension has not been fulfilled. Why? Jacob *et al.* (1991) have identified two important factors: (1) the starting level of blood pressure, and (2) the length of the baseline period over which it was measured before treatment started. They have shown that blood pressure drops more following relaxation in studies in which initial pressure is high and in which the baseline period is short. Compared to earlier studies, recent investigations have been conducted on patients with only mild elevations in pressure. Furthermore, assessment periods have lengthened in an attempt to deal with the instability of blood pressure. These results therefore suggest that stress management is most effective in patients with the higher ranges of mild hypertension and in whom blood pressure has not stabilized. These are, of course, the conditions most likely to lead to regression to the mean and this has led to some concern that relaxation may be doing absolutely nothing. This conclusion may be premature. Such errors in experimental design or measurement would mean that there would be a drop in blood pressure irrespective of treatment. That is not the finding in the positive studies. A comparison of two studies from the same research group, initially based in Oxford, Irvine *et al.* (1986) and Johnston *et al.* (1993), may be instructive. These studies used virtually identical designs, patient recruitment procedures, measurements, and methods of treatment. Irvine *et al.* (1986) found reductions in pressure that were significantly greater in patients receiving stress management. Johnston *et al.* (1993) obtained no evidence of a reduction in pressure in either the relaxation or the control group. The most obvious difference between these two studies is in the time of randomization. Irvine *et al.* (1986) randomized before collecting baseline blood pressure and patients received therapy irrespective of their blood pressure at the end of the three-month baseline. Johnston *et al.* (1993) randomized the end of a similar baseline and excluded patients who were no longer hypertensive. The differences in the outcomes suggests that the patients who show a substantial reduction in pressure during repeated blood pressure measurement (which happened during the baseline period) are also the patients who benefit from relaxation training. By not offering them treatment, Johnston *et al.* (1993) may have excluded those patients who had contributed to the apparent benefits of relaxation training in previous studies. These patients may include those who are particularly sensitive to the measurement of blood pressure (the 'white coat' hypertensives) and they may not be at heightened risk for cardiovascular disease. Hence, the health benefits of relaxation to such patients are unknown (although it may reduce their likelihood of receiving unnecessary antihypertensive medication).

On balance, the effect of stress management on blood pressure is disappointing as the effect appears weak, variable, temporary, and limited to a subset of patients who may not be at great risk from their elevated pressure. However, since the effects of measurement are so profound and may interact with relaxation, there may well be scope for a cost-effective intervention based on self-measurement of blood pressure, relaxation, and advice on other behavioural risk factors for hypertension, such as obesity and excessive alcohol consumption.

Coronary heart disease

This is a disease of the heart that results from the altered functioning of the coronary arteries. The most important of such diseases are angina, acute myocardial infarction, and sudden cardiac death. These conditions are primarily the consequence of atherosclerosis, a process in which atheromas plaques develop on the walls of the arteries and obstruct the flow of blood. Angina, a powerful pain in the chest and, on occasion, down the left arm develops when blood flow in the coronary arteries is sufficiently compromised to starve the heart muscle (myocardium) of oxygen. An acute myocardial infarction occurs when myocardial ischaemia is severe enough to lead to the destruction of myocardial tissue. It is now thought that this usually occurs when a thrombus, resulting from the rupture of an atheromas plaque, further restricts blood flow in an artery already compromised by atheroma. Sudden cardiac death, which is normally defined in terms of rapidity of death following collapse, may be due to an acute myocardial infarction or result from a fatal arrhythmia in the absence of an infarction. This typically occurs in patients with diseased arteries or a damaged heart following an earlier myocardial infarction. In addition to atheroma restricting coronary arteries, coronary arteries can constrict, possibly under sympathetic influence, sufficiently to cause angina, or even infarction, in patients with little evidence of arterial disease. If stress has a role to play in the causation of coronary heart disease it is most likely to operate through one of the processes described above. That is, stress most probably influences the development of atheroma and thrombi, plaque rupture, the constriction of the coronary arteries, or the electrical stability of the diseased heart, or a combination of theses factors.

As indicated in the section on hypertension, stress may increase blood pressure. Stress also appears to have direct effects on the coronary arteries and the myocardium. Manuck and colleagues (Kaplan *et al.* 1983) have shown that, in monkeys, social stress has a profound effect on the development of atheroma in the coronary arteries in the absence of differences in cholesterol. Blockade studies show that this effect is sympathetic in origin (Kaplan *et al.* 1987). Related effects may operate in humans. For example, there is a whole class of stress-related behaviours which appear to predispose individuals to coronary heart disease independently of the main classical risk factors. By far the best known is Type A behaviour, a pattern of behaviour characterized by extreme time pressure, hostility, and aggression (Rosenman *et al.* 1964). The literature on Type A behaviour is complex and contradictory. It is now clear that it is not appropriate to regard Type A as a unitary pattern of behaviour and that it can usefully be split into components, such as hostility and speech styles like fast explosive speech. Some of these components have been shown to predict coronary heart disease independently of what is now called global Type A (see Johnston 1993). Hostility is currently receiving most attention (see Siegman and Smith 1994). The psychological precursors of an acute myocardial infarction have also been studied extensively by Appels and colleagues (Appels and Mulder 1989) who have shown that a combination of fatigue and depression (which they call 'vital exhaustion') is common in the year prior to a myocardial infarction. Depression has also been shown to be a powerful predictor of re-infarction (Frasure-Smith *et al.* 1993).

As well as the effects of stress on the medium- to long-term risk of coronary heart disease, stress also effects the acute risk. A useful, integrative theory of the acute precipitants of manifest cardiovascular disease has been proposed by Muller, Tofler, and colleagues (Muller *et al.* 1989, 1994) who suggest that clinically manifest disease, such as a myocardial infarction, is the product of two related processes. One determines the development of stenosis in the coronary, carotid, or cerebral arteries, and the other the conversion of the stenotic plaque into the critical events causing myocardial infarction and thrombotic stroke. The end-point is, they hypothesize, a product of at least three sub-processes:

(1) the development of an unstable stenotic plaque;
(2) the processes that cause such a plaque to rupture; and
(3) the processes that lead such a rupture to produce an occlusive thrombus.

Muller and Tofler argue that the actual moment of occurrence of a myocardial infarction, sudden cardiac death, and thrombotic stroke is not random. All have clear diurnal variation and are much more likely in the morning shortly after rising and for the next few hours (Muller *et al.* 1985). They suggest that many processes that could affect the likelihood of such events follow the same time course. These include processes that might make plaque rupture more likely, including haemodynamic factors, such as rises in blood pressure and heart rate, and haemostatic processes related to platelet aggregability and blood viscosity. Although the variation in end-points and putative mediators is diurnal, it is likely that they reflect changes in activity, such as changing posture on rising (Tofler *et al.* 1990), and are not solely the product of some endogenous biological process. They also suggest that many of these processes could be triggered by factors that are not time-linked and that could determine the occurrence of myocardial infarction at other times of day. They postulate that stress is one of these factors and have recently shown that patients are likely to have undertaken heavy physical activity or been psychologically aroused prior to their myocardial infarction (Tofler *et al.* 1990). If, after plaque rupture, stress plays a part in the development of an occlusive thrombus in the coronary or cerebral arteries, it is likely to do so through alterations in the coagulant and adhesive properties of the blood so that it is more likely to form a thrombus or to adhere to the endothelium. Although the literature is still scanty and not entirely consistent, it appears that stressors, such as giving an important oral presentation, and cognitive laboratory stressors can increase platelet aggregation and lead to increases in measures of platelet activation (e.g., Jern *et al.* 1989; Grignami *et al.* 1991; Larsson *et al.* 1989; Malkoff *et al.* 1993). Acute effects on the myocardium can also be seen. Lown and Verrier (see Verrier 1987) have shown that in dogs with experimentally induced ischaemia, stress, such as electric shock or anger, reduces the threshold for the induction of potentially fatal arrhythmias. In humans, it is hard to demonstrate such effects; however, it has become clear from studies using radionuclide ventriculography to study ventricle wall abnormalities that apparently innocuous laboratory stressors, such as mental arithmetic or simulated public speaking, can induce substantial myocardial ischaemia in patients with arterial disease (Rozanski *et al.* 1988).

Type A behaviour change

There appears no doubt that comprehensive cognitive behaviour stress reduction programmes can produce a lessening of Type A behaviour as assessed either by questionnaire or the more satisfactory Structured Interview (Rosenman *et al.* 1964). All the components so far reliably identified as predictive of coronary heart disease can be changed (see Nunes *et al.* 1987, for a review of the early studies). Perhaps the most satisfactory study of Type A change in a healthy population is the Montreal study of Type A executives (Roskies *et al.* 1986). Three treatments were compared in 120 middle-aged executives with marked Type A behaviour and excessive cardiovascular responses to laboratory stressors. These were a comprehensive stress-management package (Roskies 1987), and either aerobic exercise (mainly jogging) or weight training. The stress-management package sought to teach coping skills, including relaxation, and train the client to identify stress and modify inappropriate responses. While both forms of physical training had the expected effects on fitness and strength only the cognitive behaviour intervention lead to substantial reductions in Type A behaviour. Most importantly, virtually all aspects of Type A were changed including global Type A, hostility, and the various speech styles characteristic of Type A behaviour.

The main study in patients is undoubtedly the Recurrent Coronary Prevention Project (RCPP, Friedman *et al.* 1982, 1984, 1986) and the intervention methods used will surely influence future developments in this field although the current uncertainties over the exact status of Type A behaviour appear to have dampened enthusiasm for such work. The clearest brief account of the intervention is given by Burell *et al.* (1994, p. 41) who conducted a small replication of the RCPP in Sweden. They summarized the treatment goals as:

1. Reduction and better control of time-urgent behaviours such as fast eating, walking, and talking; interruption of others; and polyphasic activities.
2. Less display of aggressive behaviour such as in traffic, competitive situations, and situations of social conflict.
3. Reduction of muscle tensions and hostile facial expressions.
4. Changes of hostile attitudes towards self and others.
5. Improved ability to relax.
6. Improved positive social skills such as attention, active listening, and problem-solving skills.
7. Increased tolerance and acceptance of others.
8. Promotion of self-enhancing and self-reinforcing thoughts.

The content of treatment was summarized as:

1. Education about coronary heart disease, risk factors, medical treatment, health behaviour, and Type A behaviour, with the goal being to promote a feeling of self-control and an improved sense of personal responsibility.
2. Learning to recognize one's own Type A behaviour by studying written, audiotaped, or videotaped material; by studying specific behaviours in everyday situations, and by systematic self-observation, the goal of this self-observation being to provide a baseline for behaviour change.
3. Changing behaviour by daily behavioural drills, role-playing, modelling, and group processes, with the goal being to decrease time-urgent and hostile behaviours and enhance coping behaviours.
4. Relaxation.
5. Cognitive restructuring by self-monitoring and discussing experiences from behavioural changes, by learning specific cognitive techniques, reviewing thought patterns, and evaluating basic attitudes and beliefs associated with

Type A behaviour pattern, with the goal being to change negative and hostile attitudes.

In the RCPP, patients meet in groups of around 10, initially weekly, at increasing intervals for the 4.5 years of the intervention. Burell *et al.*'s (1994) patients met 35 times over one year.

In the RCPP, almost 1000 patients who had experienced at least one myocardial infarction were randomly allocated on a 2:1 ratio into either the cognitive behaviour Type A reduction programme plus cardiological care or high quality cardiological care alone. In the cardiological care condition the group sessions concentrated on the medical management of coronary heart disease, although some time was spent on the psychological effects of heart disease but not its prevention.

Behavioural outcome was assessed using a videotaped version of the Structured Interview (the best method of measuring Type A behaviour) and a specially constructed questionnaire completed by the patient, and, in the behaviour change condition, by the patient's spouse and an informant at their work place. Questionnaire assessments were carried out annually and the Structured Interview used on three occasions. Although patients in both conditions showed reductions in Type A behaviour, this was reliably greater in the behaviour change group. During the programme 17.5% of the behaviour change group displayed a marked reduction in Type A behaviour compared to only 3.7% of the control group (Friedman *et al.* 1984). Both global Type A and hostility were affected, as were participant's Type A behaviour as assessed by spouse and informant. The behaviour change persisted for at least one year after the end of the intervention (Friedman *et al.* 1987). In a subsidiary study Friedman, *et al.* (1987) showed that patients in the previous control group showed a substantial reduction in Type A behaviour when they received a behavioural change programme lasting one year. Burell *et al.* (1994) essentially replicated the main behavioural findings from the RCPP.

The RCPP is the only adequate study of the effect of type A change on coronary heart disease. In an 'intention to treat' analysis patients were followed-up for 4.5 years. The average annual re-infarction rate was 5% in the control condition and 3% in the behaviour change condition (Friedman *et al.* 1986). Following treatment, the Type A change condition and the control group did not differ on potentially confounding variables such as medication, arrhythmias, and serum cholesterol. Subsidiary analyses showed that the Type A intervention was ineffective in reducing re-infarction in patients with severe pre-treatment myocardial infarctions (Powell and Thoresen 1988). In a subsequent small study a proportion of the control subjects took part in a behavioural change programme and showed an apparent reduction in re-infarction rate (Friedman *et al.* 1987). The study by Burell *et al.* (1994) was on less than 50 subjects and thus little detectable effect on cardiovascular disease was expected. Nevertheless, there was some evidence of health benefit in the Type A change condition.

Life stress monitoring

The RCPP was directed specifically at patients with marked Type A behaviour. Many patients who experience a myocardial infarction will not display such behaviour but may well be experiencing marked stress and related distress. Frasure-Smith and Prince (1985, 1987, 1989) have evaluated a practical individualized form of stress reduction co-ordinated by a cardiac nurse. In the 12 months following discharge from hospital, post-myocardial infarction patients were contacted monthly and a brief measure of psychological distress, the General Hospital Questionnaire (GHQ, Goldberg 1978), was administered by telephone. Respondents who were above a cut-off on the GHQ, or were re-admitted to hospital, were then contacted by the nurse and the specific sources of stress explored. Approximately 230 patients were randomly allocated to stress monitoring and a similar number to routine care. Slightly more than half the patients in the experimental group were seen by the nurse during the 12 months and, of these, 79% had elevated GHQ scores. Almost half were dealt with entirely by the nurse, while other health care professionals, usually physicians, saw the remainder of cases. Most of the problems related to the effects of heart disease on the patient's life and associated distress. Interventions by the nurse most frequently centred on providing information about heart disease and encouraging the patient to seek other forms of help themselves. Frasure-Smith and Prince (1985) consider that the monthly telephone calls may in themselves be an important form of intervention. It was found that GHQ scores were reliably reduced by the intervention while there were rather complex effects on the patients' subsequent cardiovascular health. Over the first two years of the study cardiac deaths, particularly sudden cardiac death, were reliably less common in the stress monitoring condition. The effect peaked approximately six months after the intervention ceased. The intervention had no apparent immediate effect on acute myocardial infarctions but differences favouring stress monitoring emerged during the second year of follow-up and remained significant until the end of the study, seven years post myocardial infarction. The pattern of results is consistent with stress management having an immediate, but possibly temporary, effect on the acute factors that induce a myocardial infarction or fatal arrythmia in patients with coronary artery disease, as well as a more enduring effect that took some time to be manifest, on limiting further deterioration of the patients' arteries.

In the Frasure-Smith and Prince study, an inadequate randomization procedure resulted in blue collar workers being under-represented in the stress monitoring condition (e.g., 53.1% of the control group were blue-collar workers compared to only 35.4% of the experimental subjects). As socioeconomic status is predictive of coronary heart disease this could have improved the prognosis of the experimental group quite independently of the effects of the stress-monitoring programme. In addition, it was found that the effect of the intervention on cardiac death was greatest in those prescribed β blocking medication, which reduces mortality after a myocardial infarction (Frasure-Smith and Prince 1987). Since medication was not closely monitored, this suggests that adherence to medication may have favoured the stress management group. This study is therefore flawed but nevertheless of great importance since it uses resources that are widely available in general hospitals. It is understood that a substantial replication is underway.

Angina pectoris

This, like all pain, is the function of a physical cause of the pain and of the physical and psychological factors which influence pain experience and reporting. Ambulatory electrocardiogram (ECG) studies have shown that many episodes of ischaemia are not accompanied by reports of pain (Deanfield et al. 1983) and angina is often not accompanied by ECG evidence of ischaemia (Krantz et al. 1994), and, instead, may relate to anger or neuroticism (Smith et al. 1984). This suggest that stress- or pain-management techniques, or both, might well reduce angina pectoris. Two recent studies have attempted to use stress management to reduce the pain, anxiety, and disability associated with angina. Bundy et al. (1994) compared a group form of stress management and routine treatment and found some evidence that stress management reduced the duration of pain in daily life and the use of medication. Lewin et al. (1995) have described a more substantial study of 77 patients in which stress management was found to reduce pain, medication use, and a questionnaire measure of disability, compared to normal care. Perhaps more critically, many of the patients in this study were awaiting coronary artery bypass surgery and it was found that 50% were removed from the waiting list since, in the judgement of their surgeons, they no longer needed this surgery. It should not be assumed that this means that the patients were experiencing less ischaemia or that their atherosclerosis had reduced, since elective coronary artery bypass grafting is usually carried out to reduce pain. There is, as yet, no compelling evidence that stress management affects the occurrence of ischaemia. However, in a small early study, Johnston and Lo (1983) demonstrated that relaxation and cardiovascular biofeedback was associated with an apparent reduction in pain in some patients and this appeared to relate to a reduction in the cardiovascular response to exercise. Whatever the mechanism, this novel application of stress management is a potentially valuable method for treating stable angina pectoris. It may be worth mentioning that Ornish has claimed that stress management can actually reduce the extent of coronary atherosclerosis (Ornish *et al*. 1990) However, as his interesting and influential study combined stress management with exercise and a very rigorous low fat diet, it is impossible to isolate the contribution of stress-management.

Rehabilitation

Many of the behavioural interventions in patients with coronary heart disease, or at high risk for such disease, are directed at altering the risk factors for the condition, the actual risk of the condition, or at reducing the symptoms such as anginal pain. While cardiac rehabilitation is also directed at all these things it is also concerned with altering the distress and functional limitations resulting from a myocardial infarction. In clinical practice most cardiac rehabilitation is exercise-based and is directed primarily at reducing re-infarction, which it may do (Oldridge *et al*. 1988). However, such exercise regimes have very little effect on psychological distress (Kugler *et al*. 1994). Early attempts to use various forms of counselling were of very limited value (see Johnston 1985, for a review of the early studies) but more recent work is much more encouraging. Lewin *et al*. (1992) have shown that a comprehensive manual supplemented with relaxation tapes and infrequent telephone calls from a cardiac nurse is much more effective than routine care in reducing anxiety and depression in the year following a myocardial infarction. Thompson and Meddis (1990*a,b*) showed that a brief educational intervention delivered to the patient and his/her spouse while the patient was in hospital led to reductions in anxiety and depression in both parties that persisted for six months. In a very recent study, M. Johnston *et al*. (submitted) compared an in-patient intervention with a more extensive in- and out-patient intervention. Both interventions were offered to patients and their spouses. The intervention, which was carried out by specially trained nurses, was designed to increase the patients' control over their recovery and focused on five topics: explanation of a heart attack; risk factors and their modification; emotional effects of a heart attack; the recovery period; and investigations and treatment. The patients and spouses decided the topics on which they wished to receive advice. The interventions were more effective than routine care in increasing knowledge about coronary heart disease, reducing anxiety, and depression in the patient and spouse, and in reducing the limitations in the patients' life. The more extensive intervention was marginally more effective than the in-patient programme, especially in reducing the distress of the spouses. The reductions in distress were still apparent 12 months after the infarction (and 10 months after the extensive intervention ceased). It is therefore quite clear that cost-effective behavioural interventions can reduce the distress and disability associated with a myocardial infarction in patients and members of their family.

Overview and future developments

In this chapter, the author argues that there is considerable evidence that psychological processes play a role in the aetiology and clinical manifestation of cardiovascular disease and how patients cope with the disease. In addition, treatments based on cognitive behaviour practice and principles have been applied with considerable success. The most successful applications are in patients with symptomatic disease (e.g., angina pectoris); in those who are experiencing distress as a result of disease (e.g., post-myocardial infarction patients); and in those where there is clearly identifiable behaviour that can serve as the focus for therapy, the Type A behaviour pattern being an obvious example. With the growing realization of the critical role that psychological processes play in the clinical manifestation of arterial disease we can expect further developments in the application of cognitive behaviour methods in patients at high risk because of manifest arterial disease. The situation is less positive in conditions such as in primary hypertension where there is no obviously related behaviour, distress, or symptom. This may not be surprising since most of the methods of cognitive behaviour therapy are derived from treatments for problems, such as anxiety or depression, where the behaviour to be altered or the distress to be reduced are all too obvious. With comparatively low-risk asymptomatic conditions like primary hypertension, social cognition models such as the Theory of Planned Behaviour (Ajzen 1992), which locate the determinants of individual's behaviour more firmly in their interaction with their external as well as their internal world, may offer a way forward. This would encourage researchers to incorporate in their interventions the patient's beliefs concerning the causes of their raised blood pressure, the associated risks, and the views of those important to them.

On a personal note

I was in Michael Gelder's Department at the Warneford Hospital from 1970 until 1985. My interest in behavioural medicine developed during that time. It arose out of my research on biofeedback, a topic that was causing great excitement in the early 1970s. Biofeedback did not generate useful therapies or theoretical insights. However, it raised new questions about the possibilities of psychological interventions with the physically ill, questions that are now being addressed using a different methodology. My work on biofeedback, hypertension, and my collaborative work with Michael Gelder, Andrew Mathews, and others on agoraphobia would not have been possible without Michael's preparedness to let researchers go in the direction that they felt was most likely to be productive and exciting and to support them (critically) for long enough for *the researcher* to decide if he or she was working along the right lines. I am exceedingly grateful for the scope I was allowed in Oxford during these years and the opportunities afforded me.

References

Agras, W. S., Taylor, C. B., Kraemer, H. C., Southam, M. A., and Schneider, J. A. (1987). Relaxation training for essential hypertension at the worksite: II. the poorly controlled hypertensive. *Psychosomatic Medicine*, 49, 264–73.

Ajzen, I. (1992). From intentions to actions; a theory of planned behavior. In: *Action control: from cognition to behaviour* (ed. J. Kuhl, J. and J. Beckman), pp. 11–39. Springer, New York.

Anderson, D. E., Kearns, W. D., and Better, W. E. (1983). Progressive hypertension in dogs by avoidance conditioning and saline infusion. *Hypertension*, 5, 286–91.

Appels, A. and Mulder, P. (1989). Fatigue and heart disease. The association between vital exhaustion and past, present and future coronary heart disease. *Journal of Psychosomatic Research*, 17, 15–24.

Bali, L. R. (1979). Long-term effect of relaxation on blood pressure and anxiety levels in essential hypertensive males: A controlled study. *Psychosomatic Medicine*, 41, 637–646.

Bundy, C., Carroll, D., Wallace, L., and Nagle, R. (1994). Psychological treatment of chronic stable angina pectoris. *Psychology and Health*, 10, 69–77.

Burell, G., Ohman, A., Sundin, O., Strom, G., Ramund, B., Cullhead, I., and Thoresen, C. E. (1994). Modification of the Type A behaviour pattern in post-myocardial infarction patients: a route to cardiac rehabilitation. *International Journal of Behavioural Medicine*, 1, 32–54.

Carroll, D., Davey Smith, G., Sheffield, D., Shipley, M. J., and Marmot, M. G. (1995). Pressor reactions to psychological stress and prediction of future blood pressure: data from the Whitehall II study. *British Medical Journal*, 310, 771–6.

Chesney, M. A., Black, G. W., Swan, G. E., and Ward, M. M. (1987). Relaxation training for essential hypertension at the worksite: I. the untreated mild hypertensive. *Psychosomatic Medicine*, 49, 250–63.

Deanfield, J. E., Maseri, A., Selwyn, A. P., Ribeiro, P., Chierchia, S., Krikler, S., and Morgan, M. (1983). Myocardial ischaemia during daily life in patients with stable angina: its relation to symptoms and heart rate changes. *Lancet*, i, 753–58.

Eisenberg, D. M., Delbanco, T. L., Berkey, C. S., Kaptchuk, T. J., Kupelnick, B., Kuhl, J., and Chalmers, T. C. (1993). Cognitive behavioural techniques for hypertension: are they effective?. *Annals of Internal Medicine*, 118, 964–72.

Frasure-Smith, N. and Prince, R. (1985). The Ischemic Heart Disease Life Stress Monitoring Program: Impact on mortality. *Psychosomatic Medicine*, 47, 431–45.

Frasure-Smith, N. and Prince, R. H. (1987). The Ischemic Heart Disease Life Stress Monitoring Program: Possible therapeutic mechanisms. *Psychology and Health*, 1, 273–85.

Frasure-Smith, N. and Prince, R. (1989). Long-term follow-up of the Ischemic Heart Disease Life Stress Monitoring Program. *Psychosomatic Medicine*, 51, 485–513.

Frasure-Smith, N., Lesperance, F., and Talajic, M. (1993). Depression following myocardial infarction: impact on 6-month survival. *Journal of the American Medical Association*, 270, 1819–25.

Fredrikson, M. and Matthews, K. A. (1990). Cardiovascular responses to behavioral stress and hypertension: a meta-analytic review. *Annals of Behavioral Medicine*, 12, 30–9.

Friedman, M., Thoresen, C. E., Gill, C. E., Ulmer, D., Thompson, L., Powell, L., et al. (1982). Feasibility of altering Type A behaviour patterns after myocardial infarction: Recurrent coronary prevention project study: methods, baseline results and preliminary findings. *Circulation*, 66, 83–92.

Friedman, M., Thoresen, C. E., Gill, J. J., Powell, L. H., Ulmer, D., Thompson, L., et al. (1984). Alteration of Type A behaviour and reduction in cardiac recurrences in post-myocardial infraction patients. *American Heart Journal*, 108, 237–48.

Friedman, M., Thoresen, C. D., Gill, J. J., Ulmer, D., Powell, L. H., Price, V. A., et al. (1986). Alteration of Type A behaviour and its effect on cardiac recurrences in post myocardial infarction patients: Summary results of the recurrent coronary prevention project. *American Heart Journal*, 112, 653–65.

Friedman, M., Powell, L. H., Thoresen, C. E., Ulmer, D., Price, V., Gill, J. J., et al. (1987). Effect of discontinuance of type A counselling on Type A behaviour and cardiac recurrence rate of post myocardial infarction patients. *American Heart Journal*, 114, 483–90.

Glaser, R. and Kiecolt-Glaser, J. (ed.) (1994). *Handbook of human stress and immunity*. Academic Press, San Diego.

Goldberg, D. (1978). *Manual of the General Health Questionnaire*. NFER, Oxford.

Grignami, G., Soffiantino, F., Zucchella, M., Pacchiarini, L., Tacconi, F., Bonomi, E., et al. (1991). Platelet activation by emotional stress in patients with coronary artery disease. *Circulation*, 83(suppl. II), II128–36.

Irvine, J., Johnston, D. W., Jenner, D., and Marie, G. V. (1986). Relaxation and stress management in the treatment of essential hypertension. *Journal of Psychosomatic Research*, 30, 437–50.

Irvine, M. J. and Logan, A. G. (1991). Relaxation behavior therapy as sole treatment for mild hypertension. *Psychosomatic Medicine*, 53, 587–97.

Jacob, R. G., Chesney, M. A., Williams, D. M., Ding, Y., and Shapiro, A. P. (1991). Relaxation therapy for hypertension: design effects and treatment effects. *Annals of Behavioral Medicine*, 13, 5–17.

Jern, C., Wadenvik, H., Mark, H., Hallgren, J., and Jern, S. (1989). Haematological changes during acute mental stress. *British Journal of Haematology*, 71, 153–6.

Johnston, D. W. (1985). Psychological interventions in cardiovascular disease. *Journal of Psychosomatic Research*, 29, 447–56.

Johnston, D. W. (1991). Stress management in the treatment of mild primary hypertension. *Hypertension*, 17 (suppl. III), III63–8.

Johnston, D. W. (1993). The current status of the coronary prone behaviour pattern. *Journal of the Royal Society of Medicine*, 86, 406–409.

Johnston, D. W. and Lo, C. R. (1983). The effects of cardiovascular feedback and relaxation on angina pectoris. *Behavioural Psychotherapy*, 11, 257–264.

Johnston, M. and Wallace, L. (ed.) (1990). *Stress and medical procedures*. Oxford University Press.

Johnston, D. W., Gold, A., Kentish, J., Smith, D., Vallance, P., Shah, D., *et al.* (1993). Effect of stress management on blood pressure in mild primary hypertension. *British Medical Journal*, 306, 963–6.

Johnston, M., Foulkes, J., Johnston, D. W., Pollard, B., and Gudmundsdottir, H. (submitted). A comparison of inpatient and extended rehabilitation in patients following a myocardial infarction.

Kaplan, J. R., Manuck, S. B., Clarkson, T. B., Lusso, F. M., Taub, D. M., and Miller, E. W. (1983). Social stress and atherosclerosis in normocholesterolemic monkeys. *Science*, 220, 733–4.

Kaplan, J. R., Manuck, S. B., Adams, M. R., Weingand, K. W., and Clarkson, T. B. (1987). Inhibition of coronary atherosclerosis by propranolol in behaviorally predisposed monkeys fed an atherogenic diet. *Circulation*, 76, 1364–72.

Krantz, D. S., Hedges, S. M., Gabbay, F. H., Klein, J., Falconer, J. J., Merz, C. N. B., *et al.* (1994). Triggers for angina and ST-segment depression in ambulatory patients with coronary artery disease: evidence for an uncoupling of angina and ischemia. *American Heart Journal*, 128, 703–12.

Kugler, J., Seelbach, H., and Kruskemper, G. M. (1994). Effects of rehabilitation exercise programmes on anxiety and depression in coronary patients: a meta-analysis. *British Journal of Clinical Psychology*, 33 401–10.

Larsson, P. T., Hjemdahl, P., Olsson, G., Egberg, N., and Hornstra, G. (1989). Altered platelet function during mental stress and adrenaline infusion in humans: evidence for an increased aggregability *in vivo* as measured by filtrometry. *Clinical Science*, 76, 369–76.

Lawler, J. E., Barker, G. F., Hubbard, J. W., and Schaub, R. G. (1981). Effects of stress on blood pressure and cardiac pathology in rats with borderline hypertension. *Hypertension*, 3, 496–505.

Lewin, B., Robertson, I. H., Irving, J. B., and Campbell, M. (1992). Effects of self-help post-myocardial-infarction rehabilitation on the psychological adjustment and use of health services. *Lancet*, 339, 1036–40.

Lewin, B., Cay, E., Todd, I., Soryal, I., Goodfield, N., Bloomfield, P., *et al.* (1995). The angina management programme: a rehabilitation treatment for chronic angina pectoris. *British Journal of Cardiology*, 1, 221–6.

Light, K. C., Dolan, C. A., Davis, M. R., and Sherwood, A. (1992). Cardiovascular responses to an active coping challenge as predictors of blood pressure patterns 10 to 15 years later. *Psychosomatic Medicine*, 54, 217–30.

Malkoff, S. B., Muldoon, M. F., Zeigler, Z. R., and Manuck, S. B. (1993). Blood platelet responsivity to acute mental stress. *Psychosomatic Medicine*, 55, 477–82.

Menkes, M. S., Matthews, K. A., Krantz, D. S., Lundberg, U., Mead, L. A., Qaquish, B., *et al.* (1989). Cardiovascular reactivity to the cold pressor test as a predictor of hypertension. *Hypertension*, 14, 524–30.

Muller, J. E., Tofler, G. H., and Stone, P. H. (1989). Circadian variation and triggers of onset of acute cardiovascular disease. *Circulation*, 79, 733–43.

Muller, J. E., Abela, G. S., Nesto, R. W., and Tofler, G. H. (1994). Triggers, acute risk factors and vulnerable plaques: the lexicon of a new frontier. *Journal of the American College of Cardiology*, 23, 809–13.

Muller, J. E., Stone, P. H., Turi, Z. G., Rutherford, J. D., Czeisler, C. A., Parker, C., *et al.* (1985). Circadian variation in the frequency of onset of acute myocardial infarction. *New England Journal of Medicine, 313*, 1315–22.

Nunes, E. V., Frank, K. A., and Kornfeld, D. S. (1987). Psychologic treatment for the Type A behaviour pattern and coronary heart disease: A meta-analysis of the literature. *Psychosomatic Medicine, 48*, 159–73.

Oldridge, N. B., Guyatt, G. H., Fischer, M. E., and Rimm, A. A. (1988). Cardiac rehabilitation after myocardial infarction: combined experience of randomized trials. *Journal of the American Medical Association, 260*, 945–50.

Ornish, D., Brown, S. E., Scherwitz, L. W., Billings, J. H., Armstrong, W. T., *et al.* (1990). Can lifestyle changes reverse coronary heart disease. *Lancet, 336*, 129–33.

Patel, C. and North, W. R. S. (1975). Randomised controlled trial of yoga and biofeedback in the management of hypertension. *Lancet, ii*, 93–5.

Patel, C., Marmot, M. G., and Terry, D. J. (1981). Controlled trial of biofeedback-aided behavioural methods in reducing mild hypertension. *British Medical Journal, 282*, 2005–8.

Patel, C., Marmot, M. G., Terry, D. J., Carruthers, M., Hunt, B., and Patel, M. (1985). Trial of relaxation in reducing coronary risk: Four year follow-up. *British Medical Journal, 290*, 1103–06.

Patel, C. and Marmot, M. G. (1988). Can general practitioners use training in relaxation and management of stress to reduce mild hypertension? *British Medical Journal, 296*, 21–4.

Pearce, S., and Wardle, J. (ed.) (1989). *The practice of behavioural medicine.* British Psychological Society, Oxford.

Powell, L. H. and Thoresen, C. E. (1988). Effects of Type A behavioral counselling and severity of prior acute myocardial infarction on survival. *American Journal of Cardiology, 62*, 1159–63.

Rosenman, R. H., Friedman, M., Strauss, R., Wurm, M., Kositchek, R., Hahn, W., and Werthessen, N. T. (1964). A predictive study of coronary heart disease. *Journal of The American Medical Association, 189*, 15–26.

Roskies, E. (1987). *Stress management for the healthy Type A.* Guilford Press, New York.

Roskies, E., Seraganian, P., Oseasohn, R., Hanley, J. A., Collu, R., Martin, N., and Smilga, C. (1986). The Montreal type A intervention project: Major findings. *Health Psychology, 5*, 45–69.

Rozanski, A., Bairey, C. N., Krantz, D. S., Friedman, J., Resser, K. J., Morell, M., *et al.* (1988). Mental stress and the induction of silent myocardial ischemia in patients with coronary artery disease. *New England Journal of Medicine, 318*, 1006–12.

Siegman, A. R., and Smith, T. W. (ed.) (1994). *Anger, hostility and the heart.* Erlbaum, Hillsdale, NJ.

Smith, T. W., Follick, M. J., and Korr, K. S. (1984). Anger, neuroticism, Type A behaviour and the experience of angina. *British Journal of Medical Psychology, 57*, 249–52.

Taylor, C. B., Farquhar, J. W., Nelson, E., and Agras, W. S. (1977). Relaxation therapy and high blood pressure. *Archives of General Psychiatry, 34*, 339–42.

Thompson, D. R. and Meddis, R. (1990a). A prospective evaluation of in-hospital counselling for first time myocardial infarction men. *Journal of Psychosomatic Research, 34*, 237–48.

Thompson, D. R. and Meddis, R. (1990b). Wive's responses to counselling early after myocardial infarction. *Journal of Psychosomatic Research, 34*, 249–58.

Tofler, G. H., Stone, P. H., Maclure, M., Edelman, E., Davis, V. G., Robertson, T., *et al.* (1990). Analysis of possible triggers of acute myocardial infarction (the MILIS study). *American Journal of Cardiology*, 66, 22–7.

van Montfrans, G., Karemeker, J., Wieling, W., and Dunning, A. J. (1990). Effect of relaxation therapy on the 24-hour continuous ambulatory blood pressure: one year follow-up. *British Medical Journal*, 300, 1368–72.

Verrier, R. L. (1987). Mechanisms of behaviourally induced arrhythmias. *Circulation*, 76 (suppl. I), I48–56.

Winett, R. A., King, A. C., and Altman, D. G. (1989). *Health psychology and public health: an integrative approach*. Pergamon, New York.

15

Atypical chest pain

Richard Mayou

Atypical (or non-cardiac) chest pain is, at first sight, a more specialist and restricted topic than others in this book. It is, however, an important and common clinical problem in both primary and specialist care which is generally accepted as being difficult to treat (Assey 1993); its management raises general issues which are applicable to many other specific functional somatic symptoms (Mayou *et al.* 1995). The discussion will centre on atypical chest pain as a presenting symptom in primary care and in general hospitals, but it is important to be aware that chest pain is both a prominent symptom of general anxiety disorder and panic and a common form of health anxiety and, therefore, it is also discussed in Chapters 6, 7, and 13. The chapter brings together themes which Michael Gelder has promoted and encouraged from the first days of the Department of Psychiatry at Oxford; psychiatry as part of medicine, the development of research and clinical care within the general hospital, and the evaluation of psychological treatments.

Atypical chest pain is defined in terms of its *presentation*, rather than as an operational clinical syndrome or in terms of aetiology, and is heterogeneous (Table 15.1). The definition excludes recognizable cardiac and other major physical causes. There are no specific characteristics apart from the presenting symptom, but persistent pain is often accompanied by complaints of palpitations and breathlessness and by concern or conviction that it is due

TABLE 15.1. Characteristics of atypical chest pain

Defined in terms of the presenting symptoms
Occurs as single symptom or accompanied by other non-specific symptoms
Managed in primary and specialist cardiac care
Many proven physical and psychiatric causes
May be acute and transient, recurrent, or persistent
Associated with panic, anxiety, and other psychiatric disorders
Frequently due to interaction of physical and psychological factors
Management should combine physical and psychological elements
Need for 'stepped' care for large numbers of patients

to heart disease. Psychological symptoms are common but also heterogeneous; they include panic, general anxiety, major depression, and somatoform disorders.

Discussion of treatment must take account of the wide range of possible contributory causes and also of cost-efficient delivery within routine clinical settings, especially primary care and cardiological out-patient clinics. Management is likely to require flexible use of a number of components that can largely be provided by non-specialists. Care must be designed to be acceptable to patients who are reluctant to accept psychological explanations and treatment. Therefore, treatment is considerably more complex than for research trials of specialist treatment of highly selected homogeneous patient groups with a clearly defined psychiatric disorder.

History

Atypical chest pain has had a long and complex history in medical practice and literature under a wide range of names (Mayou 1989). Its causes have been disputed and there have always been arguments about the role of physical and psychological (or functional) explanations. During the nineteenth and early-twentieth century unexplained chest pain was seen as a central feature of a syndrome which was particularly associated with military service (e.g., soldiers' heart, effort syndrome). Da Costa, who in 1871 published a classic account of soldiers he had treated during the American Civil War, regarded 'the irritable heart' as being due to 'disordered innervation'. Chest pain was also seen as a feature of neurasthenia. William Osler, in the first edition of his *Textbook* (1892), wrote that in the diagnosis of angina: 'the chief difficulty, however, arises in the cases of hysterical and pseudo-angina. This is a common affection in women, it may also occur in neurasthenic men.' He believed that 'treatment was directed to the general nervous condition. Electricity is sometimes very beneficial, particularly the "Franklinic form".' Freud, on the other hand, included it as a symptom of his newly identified syndrome of anxiety neurosis.

During the First World War, 'soldiers' heart' was the third most common cause of invalidism in the British army. Sir Thomas Lewis, who reported on 100 cases in 1917, believed it was a 'functional disorder' with 'exaggerated manifestations of healthy responses to effort'. Between the wars, the syndrome attracted less interest; in contrast, anxiety disorders were increasingly being recognized and seen as being characterized by numerous physical symptoms including chest pain and breathlessness. The syndrome again became conspicuous in the Second World War. A definitive cardiological study of patients in a military hospital was presented in three classic papers (Wood

1941) by Dr Paul Wood who concluded that 'a proper psychiatric diagnosis is nearly always available'. Wood studied 175 patients, comparing them with heart disease patients and normal controls. He provided a clear account of the symptoms, writing: 'Da Costa's syndrome is characterized by a certain group of symptoms which underlie the subject's capacity for effort, and by a number of signs depending upon disturbance of the autonomic system, when such signs are not due to any known organic disease. The cardinal symptoms are breathlessness, palpitations, fatigue, left infra-mammary pain, and dizziness; the cardinal signs are functional disturbances of the respiratory, vasomotor and sudomotor systems' (Wood 1941).

Since the Second World War, research has substantially clarified the numerous causes of chest pain: (1) anginal and other ischaemic heart disease; (2) general and phobic anxiety and panic; (3) oesophageal disorders; and (4) a variety of minor physical conditions. Even so, many of the patients now presenting to general practitioners and cardiologists with chest pain and worries about heart disease continue to cause diagnostic difficulty and argument about aetiology (Mayou 1989). It is these patients, and especially those with persistent symptoms and disability, despite negative investigations, who are the subject of this chapter.

The size of the problem

Studies of the general population have consistently found that chest pain is frequent and that it is often persistent (von Korff et al. 1988; Murabito et al. 1990). Although only a minority of those suffering chest pain consult doctors, both chest pain and the commonly associated symptom of palpitations are frequently reported in all surveys of patients in primary care (Kroenke and Mangelsdorff 1989).

There is also much evidence that non-cardiac chest pain is a frequent cause of attendance at emergency departments (Kisely et al., 1992) and cardiac clinics. For example, in a study of 94 consecutive referrals to a cardiac clinic with chest pain and palpitations, more than half the patients were diagnosed as not having any significant physical disorder (Mayou et al. 1994).

In the general population it is probable that most chest pain is transient, although the Framingham study found that 32% of their subjects with 'non-anginal chest discomfort' reported symptoms at follow-up two years later (Murabito et al. 1990). Studies of patients attending emergency departments or referred to cardiologists for non-cardiac chest pain show that many continue to report symptoms and disability despite medical reassurance.

Patients with chest pain who have been investigated by coronary angiography and found to have normal coronary arteries have a particularly poor symptomatic social and psychological outcome (Mayou 1989; Potts and Bass 1995). Expectation of life and cardiac morbidity is the same as for the general population (Lichtlen *et al.* 1995); but around three-quarters report continuing pain, disability, and emotional distress and continue to make much use of medical resources. A recent long-term follow-up study found much of the psychosocial morbidity described one year after angiography was little changed 11 years later (Potts and Bass 1995).

Aetiology

Although the major causes of chest pain, such as ischaemic heart disease and anxiety disorders, have been clearly described in recent years, there are still many patients in which the cause of their pain remains partially or wholly unexplained. Numerous physical causes (see Table 15.2) are well established, but in clinical practice differential diagnosis is often restricted to angina or atypical pain. It is also apparent that single causes are often inadequate to account, *by themselves*, for the patient's distress and disability. Thus, clear recognition of a chest wall muscular syndrome may be only partially reassuring so that the patient who continues both to suffer symptoms, worries about heart disease, and restricts activities.

In addition to the many generally accepted causes of non-cardiac chest pain, several *non-ischaemic cardiac* mechanisms have been proposed. Some, such as cardiomyopathy and aortic valve disease, are well established. There are occasional instances of undoubted infarction which are reasonably attributed to 'spasm' of angiographically normal coronary arteries (Chambers and Bass 1990). Other mechanisms are more dubious. Mitral valve prolapse has frequently been maintained to have an association with panic disorder and to be a cause of chest pain, but the weight of evidence suggests this is spurious (Katerndahl 1993). Recently, there has been considerable interest in

TABLE 15.2. Possible physical causes of chest pain

Cardiac	Non-cardiac
Ischaemic heart disease	Chest infection
Coronary spasm	Pulmonary embolus
Micro vascular angina	Post thoracotomy
Chest wall: muscular, costochondritis	Mitral valve prolapse
Valvular heart disease	Hyperventilation
Cardiomyopathy	Cervical spine
Aortic valve disease	Oesophageal reflux and spasm
Pericarditis	

microvascular angina (Cannon 1993). Claims for this alleged mechanism seem to be overstated at the very least, and are best seen as the latest of the long history of cardiac explanations that have been put forward with confidence but without any convincing support.

Oesophageal spasm has been widely proposed by gastroenterologists as the cause of non-cardiac chest pain, being viewed as motility disorder or as abnormal sensitivity. However, it is impossible to establish any clear relation between oesophageal motility and chest pain. It would seem unlikely in the absence of evidence of oesophageal reflux that this is an explanation for atypical pain.

There is a strong association with *psychiatric disorder*, with the prevalence being greatest in specialist care. The most common psychiatric diagnoses of these are panic disorder, general anxiety, and depression. Somatoform disorders are also frequent. Although specific psychiatric explanations in terms of panic or general anxiety are common, it is important that they are not over-stated as primary causes. For example, anxiety is often secondary to a physical condition, and with a complex history it may be difficult to establish what is cause and effect. There are also a considerable number of patients in whom *psychological factors* appear to be significant but in whom psychiatric diagnosis is not possible. For example, a middle-aged patient with a bad family history of heart disease may suffer chest wall pain and seek reassurance. Over-cautious diagnosis by a doctor of probable angina, prescription of cardiac drugs, and discussion of referral to a specialist may lead to anxiety and to a worsening of symptoms. Such a patient may be disabled but without suffering anxiety disorder and not being diagnosable as suffering from any form of somatoform disorder (in which patients have been given clear reassurance by doctors).

Although this chapter is mainly concerned with atypical chest pain in those who have no evidence of heart disease, it is very important to be aware that patients recovering from myocardial infarction or cardiac surgery also frequently suffer atypical pains, palpitations, and breathlessness which are, in fact, attributable to medically insignificant causes.

We can conclude that there continues to be substantial argument about aetiology, with rival experts putting forward explanations within their own particular field of interest, for example, gastroenterology, cardiology, rheumatology, and psychiatry (Mayou 1989; Chambers and Bass 1990; Hutchinson *et al.* 1988). At the same time there is increasing acceptance that claims for particular physical mechanisms have been generally over-stated. It would seem that aetiology is often multi-causal and that there is an interaction of physical and psychological factors, as discussed below in a description of a psychological model (Mayou 1989; Bass and Mayou 1995).

History of treatment

Early accounts of the treatment of soldiers' heart and effort syndrome describe many physical manoeuvres for what is largely seen as a functional cardiac disturbance. Rest and reassurance were often seen as all that the doctor had to offer, a view which remains widely held to this day. An early account of the value of psychological treatment is provided by Paul Wood (1941) who stated that: 'patients should be informed of the nature of their illness and treated as psychoneurotics; their distaste for this label may prove helpful. The psychotherapy required is simple in its object and extremely difficult in practice. The patient must be induced to believe that he is suffering from the effects of emotional disturbance; reassurance can only be coupled with adequate explanation in terms he can understand.'

Although Paul Wood was the author of the standard cardiological textbook of his day, his views had relatively little impact and cardiologists have largely remained unwilling to consider any treatment other than reassurance (Assey 1993). Atypical chest pain is seen as being difficult to manage in primary care and in specialist cardiac clinics. Accounts by cardiologists give little guidance on treatment. Recently, a number of psychiatrists and psychologists have promoted the role of psychological treatment. In part this reflects the interest in panic disorder and generalized anxiety; in part an increased presence of psychiatrists and psychologists in general hospitals who are willing to assess and treat patients who were formerly seen as having 'no treatable psychiatric disorder'. These treatments are discussed in the remainder of the chapter.

A psychological model

Paul Wood (1941) demonstrated the associations with family and emotional factors. He believed the cause was usually psychological due to: 'misinterpretation of emotional symptoms, certain vicious circular patterns, the growth of a conviction that the heart is to blame, consequent fears of sudden death on exertion, conditioning and hysteria.' We have posed the model shown in Fig 15.1, a specific form of a model which we believe is applicable to all functional somatic symptoms (Mayou 1989; Bass and Mayou 1995). The central component of the model is the emphasis on attribution or cognitive appraisal of symptoms, whereby physiological or minor pathological symptoms are misinterpreted by patients as evidence of heart disease. Hypochondriacal personality, psychiatric disorder, and illness beliefs and experience all predispose to misinterpretation (see Table 15.3). It is notable that many patients presenting to doctors with persistent chest pain have histories of previous episodes of chest pain or other functional symptoms, and

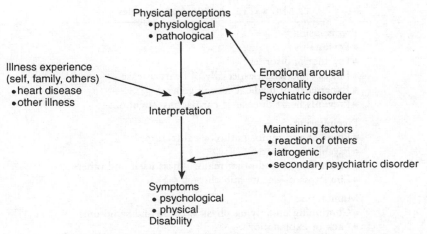

FIG. 15.1.   A psychological model of atypical chest pain.

that family history or other experience of heart disease is common. Once established, increased anxiety may lead to chest pain and to other physical symptoms. Panic is frequent.

The evidence for the model is largely descriptive and it includes the evidence for the cognitive models of panic and health anxiety (see Chapters 6 and 13). In addition, it is clear there are strong associations with illness experience (especially of heart disease), psychiatric disorder, and with previous episodes of health anxiety. As previously noted, non-cardiac chest pains are especially frequent in those with definite heart disease (e.g., those recovering from myocardial infarction or cardiac surgery). Unsurprisingly, such patients find it difficult to distinguish between anginal infarct pain and minor muscular and other aches and pains. Iatrogenic factors, including the prescription of cardiac drugs, are frequent.

Abnormal awareness of cardiac rate has been shown in patients with panic (Ehlers and Breuer 1992). There is clear experimental evidence of unusual cardiac awareness in those who have atypical chest pain (Tyrer *et al.* 1980) and palpitations (Barsky *et al.* 1994), and in those who have chest pain as a feature of an anxiety disorder (Ehlers and Breuer 1992). The model is strongly supported by the success of psychological treatments derived from it (as described below).

Maintaining factors

The principal maintaining factors are listed in Table 15.3 and are best considered in terms of factors in the patient and those relating to the responses

TABLE 15.3. Aetiological variables

Predisposing
- Personality
- Psychiatric disorder
- Illness experience: especially of heart disease
- Experience of medical care in general
- Previous heart disease or cardiac investigations

Precipitating
- Physical and minor pathological factors
- Psychiatric disorder
- Heart disease and other major illness itself and others
- Life stresses — acute and chronic

Maintaining
- Continuing underlying physical cause and symptoms
- Lack of explanation
- Psychiatric disorder
- Attitude of others
- Medical care

of other people. Among the former, the most important variables are the persistence of the symptoms, anxiety or other psychiatric disorder, and continuing belief that the chest pain is due to heart disease or other serious physical disorder. It is unsurprising that negative investigations and reassurance by and authoritative specialist opinion often have little impact if the patient continues to suffer severe distressing pain which makes it difficult to believe that there is not an unrecognized ominous physical cause. The concern of friends and relatives is often important in reinforcing worry about heart disease and scepticism about alternative minor physical or psychological explanations.

Iatrogenic factors are prominent. General practitioners, emergency clinic doctors, and cardiologists all tend to be cautious and to make provisional diagnoses of heart disease and resort to medication. For example, in our studies of consecutive out-patient attenders and those with normal coronary angiograms, many patients had already been told by doctors that they had heart disease before the eventual conclusion that their pain was non-cardiac (Mayou *et al.* 1994). Indeed, in research on patients who have had normal coronary angiograms for chest pain it is surprisingly common to find that patients have been treated as having angina for long periods and that it is not unusual for them to say that specialists, including cardiologists, have often told them that they have typical symptoms of angina and that surgery should be considered. In these circumstances it is to be expected that a single negative investigation without any further explanation and without specific advice is ineffective.

One should not underestimate the diagnostic difficulties. This is particularly true for the general practitioner confronted with many patients who complain of chest pain, a proportion of whom may have angina. In a recent Oxford general practice series one-third of those provisionally diagnosed as having angina were eventually thought to be suffering from non-cardiac chest pain (Dawes *et al.* submitted). Two years later their symptoms and disability remained very similar to those of patients whose diagnosis of angina had been confirmed by further investigation.

Approaches to management

The heterogeneous nature of atypical chest pain as a condition defined by its presenting symptom means that rather varied treatments need to be considered. It may be necessary to combine several treatment elements and frequently both psychological and physical interventions. The interactive model of aetiology described above suggests the value of specific physical treatment of underlying causes and of psychological treatment of either psychological cause of symptoms or of misinterpretation. In practice, some form of psychological treatment is required for most of those whose symptoms have persisted despite initial reassurance.

This section summarizes the main treatment approaches (see Table 15.4); the evaluation of psychological treatments is discussed in the next section.

Negative investigations

Doctors tend to assume that a report of negative findings on clinical examination or specialist investigation will be reassuring to their patients. A proportion of patients are indeed reassured and recover without further symptoms or disability following negative clinical assessment in the emergency department (Kisely *et al.* 1992) or by a cardiac out-patient clinic (Mayou *et al.* 1994), or following negative investigation, such as oesophageal testing (Rose *et al.* 1994), exercise testing (Channer *et al.* 1987), or angiography (Faxon *et al.* 1982). However, these same studies show that despite initial relief many patients are not permanently reassured and continue to suffer symptoms and disability.

Reassurance and explanation

Cardiologists and other doctors tend to see reassurance in terms of an authoritative opinion about the lack of a serious medical cause, rather than

TABLE 15.4. Treatments

1. Negative investigations
2. Reassurance
3. Explanation
4. Treatment of specific physical causes
5. Psychotropic medication
6. Beta blockers
7. Breathing retraining
8. Cognitive behavioural treatment
    Individual specialist
    Group specialist
    Routine non-specialist
    Self-help

discussion about symptoms, their causes, and the practical implication. In general, patients report satisfaction immediately after seeing a cardiologist but later are likely to complain that they have had no adequate explanation for the continuing symptoms. Some continue to worry about heart disease; others may accept they do not have a cardiac condition but remain concerned about the lack of an explanation and treatment. In our recent trial of a self-help intervention following normal coronary angiography (see below) we found many patients were angry about being given the negative result and discharged after what was often months or years of definite diagnosis of heart disease (Bass *et al.* submitted).

Treatment of specific physical causes

It has repeatedly been claimed that treatment of minor causes, such as chest muscle pain (Epstein *et al.* 1979), costochondritis (Scott and Scott 1993; Disla *et al.* 1994), hyperventilation and oesophageal spasm (Clouse 1992), is effective. However, the few systematic reports are unconvincing. Where figures are given, specific intervention seems little more successful than reassurance or negative cardiac investigation. This ineffectiveness may be due to misdiagnosis, but perhaps more probably to a failure to deal with patients' individual concerns and fears which are as important as the underlying physical aetiology.

Psychotropic medication

A variety of psychotropic drugs have been used either as the only method of treatment or in conjunction with psychological treatment. The choice has depended on the underlying psychiatric disturbance.

Tricyclic antidepressants. These are clearly indicated in the small proportion of patients with evidence of depressed mood and can be a valuable treatment for panic disorder. A multi-national study has shown that imipramine is useful for patients with panic attacks in which cardiac respiratory symptoms are prominent. Cannon and his colleagues (Cannon 1993; Cannon *et al.* 1994), who have made claims that angina is due to cardiac microvascular disease, have shown that imipramine can reduce the frequency of chest pain in patients with normal coronary arteries by 50%. This improvement is apparently independent of effects on psychological morbidity and the authors suggested that it might be due to a visceral analgesic effect.

Tricyclic antidepressants (and indeed selective serotonin reuptake inhibitors) should be used in the standard manner and for standard psychiatric indications. However, patients may be unduly aware of and sensitive to side-effects. It may be advisable to start with a small dose and to pay particular attention to encourage patients to persevere.

Monoamine oxidase inhibitors. Frequent occurrence of panic attacks in association with atypical chest pain suggest an important role for this group of antidepressants. There have been no controlled trials, but there is considerable evidence that patients with anxiety and somatic symptoms have a good response to phenelzine compared with placebo.

Benzodiazepines. The problems of tolerance, dependance, and withdrawal mean that these drugs must be used with considerable care. A small study of alprazolam has suggested a reduction in chest pain and panic (Beitman *et al.* 1988). Further evidence is required about efficacy, but at present there seem no good reasons for favouring this method of treatment when there are clearly better alternatives.

Beta blockers

Although sympathetically mediated symptoms such as chest pain, palpitations, trembling, and sweating all respond to beta blockers, clinical impressions suggest that they have rather little role in patients presenting with chest pain. There may be a small proportion of patients who also suffer from palpitations in which beta blockers are useful. However, in what can be a chronic problem it would seem more satisfactory to choose another method of treatment.

Breathing retraining

Hyperventilation is a common accompaniment of chest pain and would appear to be a contributory factor to aetiology. While the contribution of breathing retraining to the treatment of patients with panic attacks remains somewhat uncertain, there is some evidence that this can play an important part in the management of some patients with non-cardiac chest pain whether or not they also have symptoms of panic (Salkovskis 1992). A recent study demonstrated the efficacy of breathing retraining in patients with functional cardiac symptoms (DeGuire *et al.* 1992). It appeared that three methods of guided breathing retraining accompanied by physiological monitoring of varying degrees of complexity were effective.

Cognitive behavioural treatment

There have been encouraging clinical reports of psychological treatments using cognitive and behavioural concepts and procedures. The cognitive element of treatment is based on the observation that patients have a tendency to misinterpret chest pain as a sign of serious illness. Behavioural elements are directed towards anxiety management and graded increase in activities. These general methods have been used in a number of ways in research studies:

1. individual cognitive behavioural treatment by an experienced specialist therapist;
2. group treatment based on cognitive behavioural principles; and
3. a brief educational programme based on cognitive behavioural principles but delivered by a cardiac nurse.

The details of the procedures and their efficacy are discussed below. It is also necessary to consider major service issues:

1. The ways in which patients can be engaged in psychological treatment.
2. How resources can be most appropriately used for the large numbers of patients.

These questions are important for all methods of treatment but especially for psychological approaches since these are time-consuming, dependent on skilled therapists, and may be less acceptable to patients, relatives, and other doctors involved.

Delivery of care

The heterogeneous nature of patients with chest pain means that it is essential to deliver care in a flexible manner, so that individuals receive the treatment they require in a cost-efficient manner. It would seem sensible to aim for some form of 'stepped' care so that those who require relatively little intervention do not use excessive resources, whereas those who require considerable help are able to receive it. Although such extra care requires increased resources it is likely to result in significant savings in long-term health care and other costs.

Practical guidelines for psychological treatment

1. *Explanation.* Initial assessment must consider all the specific causes of chest pain and also define disability and elicit patients' attitudes and beliefs. It

TABLE 15.5. The components of effective reassurance

Chest pain is a common and important clinical symptom for which there are many causes,
  mostly non-cardiac
Full assessment is sensible and allows a clear diagnosis and treatment plan
The investigations have been negative and exclude serious medical causes
Explanation of a probable physical cause
Explain that tension, over-breathing, and other factors may contribute
Exercise is not dangerous; gradual return to normal activities is possible and beneficial
Advice about symptom management and return to normal activities
Offer a follow-up review

---

is essential to avoid over-hasty concentration on cardiac causation. Once
cardiac and other major physical causes are excluded it is appropriate to
reassure the patient. This should be clear and indicate that the condition is
real, common, and known to be of good physical prognosis (Table 15.5). The
patient should be given an explanation of the probable non-cardiac causes and
then have an opportunity to discuss the investigations and diagnosis and be
given guidelines on management. It is often helpful to involve a relative. Such
full reassurance and advice may be all that is required, but the patient should
be encouraged to return if there are further symptoms or problems.

2. *Persistent symptoms.* If symptoms persist, there may be an indication
for further investigation. A specialist cardiological opinion which provides
clear information, an explanation and advice may be valuable in providing
truly effective reassurance to the patient and, indeed, to the primary care
doctor. At an early stage further simple discussion and behavioural advice
may be appropriate and effective. However, it may also be necessary to
consider specialist psychiatric or psychological referral. The success of such
referral depends substantially on providing the patient with an explanation.

3. *Referral for specialist care.* An explanation about the reasons for
further advice is best given in terms of referral to a close colleague who has
particular experience of management of chest pain and of the value of
methods to deal with tension, stress, and decreased activity which are known
to contribute to the problems of atypical chest pain. Many patients are very
open to the idea that tension and stress are important contributory factors, but
others may remain convinced that there is a serious physical cause. It is
essential not to argue about the role of physical factors but to concentrate on
suggesting that the proposed treatment can very frequently alleviate
symptoms.

There are substantial arguments for providing extra treatment in a medical
setting. The more the psychological explanation is seen as part of standard

medical care, the more likely it is to be acceptable and effective to patients and to their relatives.

Evaluation of psychological treatment

Evidence from randomized controlled trials are of two types:

1. Specific trials for patients presenting with chest pain. There have been relatively few specific evaluations of psychological treatment, three carried out in Oxford and one in Edinburgh, as described below.
2. Evaluations of cognitive behavioural treatment for panic attacks and anxiety disorders in which atypical chest pain is a usual symptom, provide valuable information (Salkovskis 1992).

There is consistent evidence of efficacy of these treatments from published and unpublished trials. However, as yet these encouraging findings about a symptom which is widely seen as common, disabling, and difficult to treat have had little impact on routine care.

The conduct of these clinical trials has been generally similar to the principles outlined elsewhere in this book. However, the nature of the presentation in medical settings and the difficulties of ensuring that delivery is both acceptable and cost-efficient mean that there is a special requirement to keep in mind applications to routine practice. Demonstration that intensive specialist treatment is effective is unlikely to be seen as useful in the care of very large numbers of patients.

Treatments should be shown to be effective in terms of relief of the symptoms of chest pain, associated emotional distress, other physical symptoms, and quality of life. Other significant measures are changes in beliefs about the cause of the chest pain and reduction in use of resources.

Treatment of panic disorder and anxiety

Chest pain often accompanies panic attack and anxiety. Evidence discussed elsewhere in this book suggests cognitive treatment is highly effective and substantially superior to pharmacotherapy both in the short and long term (see Chapters 6 & 7). Relapse rates are lower in cognitive therapy since patients learn skills which they can continue to use (Salkovskis 1992).

Treatment of hypochondriasis (see Chapter 13)

A recent controlled trial has shown substantial improvements with cognitive therapy as compared with a control treatment. Patients with long histories of

TABLE 15.6. The four Oxford randomized controlled trials

---

1. Referrals from general practitioners
   • Chronic pain despite negative investigation
   • Cognitive behaviour therapy by an experienced practitioner
2. Specialist treatment following reassurance by cardiologist
   • Consecutive referrals to the out-patient department and consecutive normal coronary angiography
   • Review 6 weeks after reassurance
   • Cognitive behaviour therapy by an experienced practitioner
3. Advice and self-help following normal coronary angiography
   • Consecutive patients with normal angiogram
   • Advice and explanation cassette by cardiac nurse
   • Telephone follow-up
4. Consecutive out-patient referrals with benign palpitations
   • Pre-clinic assessment
   • Randomization by cardiologist
   • Flexible intervention by cardiac nurse
   • Close collaboration with cardiologist

---

disabling symptoms were largely free of health anxiety at the end of treatment and gains were largely maintained at follow-up (Warwick 1995).

The Oxford randomized controlled trials

Three completed studies of patients (Table 15.6) with persistent disabling non-cardiac chest pain have addressed the following issues:

1. Demonstration of the efficacy of psychological treatment.
2. Delivery of specialist psychological care within routine cardiac clinic.
3. Evaluation of a brief self-help intervention designed for patients who have been shown to have normal coronary arteries.

All these treatments have been based on the cognitive model presented earlier, but we have been concerned to seek ways of applying the general principles in cost effective ways. The efficacy of specialist treatment with motivated patients is proven; the challenge is to treat large numbers of patients in primary care settings.

1. *Referrals from general practice.* This first Oxford study demonstrated the effectiveness of specialist cognitive behavioural techniques (Klimes *et al.* 1990). Thirty-one patients with persistent non-cardiac chest pain were referred by general practitioners. They had a mean duration of pain of 4.7 years and had all been assessed by cardiologists and reassured that their pain was non-cardiac. Subjects were randomized to treatment by a clinical psychologist or to a waiting list control.

The main components of the treatment (introduced consecutively over 4–11 sessions) were:

1. functional analysis of complaints, an explanation of the rationale for psychological treatment, an introduction to progressive muscular relaxation;
2. discussion of the role of breathing; forced voluntary breathing was used to demonstrate how easily 'real' unpleasant sensations can be induced. Learning of slow-paced breathing control was introduced;
3. an introduction to distraction (focusing attention away from symptoms and associated worry) and to monitoring the relationship between chest pain and physical activity;
4. learning to apply skills (relaxation, slow paced breathing, and distraction) and to monitor effects on pain; and
5. review and management of any maintaining factors (e.g., morbid health beliefs). Use of exposure to counteract avoidance of exertion, response prevention methods to counter checking (e.g., repeated pulse taking) and other reassurance-seeking behaviours, pacing activities to control unrealistic expectations, cognitive challenge of any persistent beliefs about organic illness, and problem-solving of social problems.

All the patients found the treatment acceptable, even those who initially were somewhat sceptical about the significance of psychological factors as contributing to their complaints. They were reassured that their physical status would, if necessary, be reassessed on completion of treatment.

There were significant reductions in chest pain, limitation of daily life, and psychological morbidity. The assessment only control group were subsequently treated and showed comparable changes. Improvements in both groups were maintained at follow-up four to six months later.

2. *Out-patients study.* A second Oxford trial aimed to replicate the findings within the setting of normal out-patient care. Consecutive subjects, reassured by cardiologists after out-patient assessment or normal coronary angiogram, were invited to attend a follow-up assessment six weeks later. Subjects with continuing pain and disability were invited to enter the treatment trial.

At the end of treatment, the intervention group had a substantially better outcome in terms of symptoms, mood, quality of life, and reduced concern about heart disease. During a further three-month follow-up there was little change in the treated subjects, but evidence of slower improvement in the control group. Although differences in frequency and severity of symptoms were less striking at follow-up, the treated group continued to have significantly better outcome in terms of the effects of symptoms on important everyday activities and were much less likely to be concerned about heart disease. A number of clinically important clinical difficulties were apparent:

1. patients were unenthusiastic about attending for follow-up;
2. a number of patients found the assessment and description of treatment too psychological and were reluctant to take part in the trial;
3. several more patients dropped out during treatment because they thought the treatment was paying too much attention to psychological factors; and
4. a number of patients found the assessment useful but declared that the assessment and general information was adequate in itself and there was no need for further treatment.

A major finding was that many patients felt dissatisfied and uncertain with the didactic medical reassurance they had been given and wanted more opportunity for discussion, explanation of their symptoms, and advice on how to return to full activities. They were less interested in specialist care and would have preferred simple help at, or soon after, the clinic assessment. We concluded that the offer of cognitive behaviour treatment at follow-up was seen as separate to cardiac care and as generally less acceptable. It was also apparent that in the out-patient setting it might have been more appropriate to offer 'stepped care' in which some patients received brief extra help while others moved on to the full intervention.

3. *Self-help following coronary angiography.* A recent Oxford controlled trial has evaluated a brief intervention for patients with chest pain who have had negative coronary angiograms. The intervention, administered by a cardiac nurse immediately following the results of the angiogram and before discharge from hospital, included a verbal explanation, a handout and cassette, and telephone follow-up. The content of the brief intervention was based on the cognitive behavioural principles of the earlier treatment and was designed to meet the particular complaints of patients about the lack of explanation and information.

The intervention was welcomed by a proportion of patients but disappointingly seemed to be less acceptable to others. Overall, there were no differences at follow-up between treatment and control subjects.

We have concluded that the intervention was too early for patients who had previously been treated as having heart disease and who were surprised and disconcerted by being given the results of the angiogram together with a general injunction to return to normal activities. The uncertainty, dissatisfaction, and occasional anger meant that patients were hardly receptive to a sudden change to a vastly different clinical approach. It is probable that the patients who were not reassured by the angiogram would have been helped by a selective and more intensive intervention a week or two later. As in the previous out-patient Oxford study, the separation of the psychological treatment from cardiac care is likely to have diminished acceptability and effectiveness.

Group treatment

A recent Edinburgh study of subjects with chest pain and normal coronary arteries evaluated a group cognitive behavioural treatment (Potts, personal communication). The subjects were 54 patients who had had normal results on coronary angiography and whose chest pain continued at least twice a week. Patients were approached after obtaining permission from general practitioners and consultants and asked to attend for initial assessment. Those who agreed to take part in the trial were randomly allocated to waiting list control or to treatment. Groups of up to six subjects attended for six two-hour sessions over eight weeks. Each session began with feedback and involved education, mutual support, teaching relaxation and breathing training, and some light physical exercise. In addition, there was goal setting and pacing, and cognitive work using thought diaries. The treatment was effective compared with randomized controls. Again, there were difficulties in co-ordination with medical care and recruitment.

This study confirms the finding of the first Oxford study that psychological treatment based on cognitive behavioural principles is effective. It raises, but does not answer, the same questions about implications for delivery to patients in routine care. There are many practical reasons why, even if patients are interested in psychological treatment, it may be difficult to recruit them for groups which they may not find acceptable or may find inconvenient to attend. Despite these reservations, the study does suggest that, at least in hospitals serving nearby city populations, it may be possible to establish groups.

New directions

The findings of the controlled trials and clinical experience support the value of psychological treatment involving both cognitive and behavioural elements. However, it is evident that it is difficult to deliver such treatment within ordinary medical settings, such as the out-patient clinic or as an in-patient following angiography. It is also difficult to provide treatment in a flexible enough pattern so that individual subjects receive the treatment they need but no more.

It would seem that more effective treatment will depend on greater flexibility and on integration of psychological treatment with the cardiological assessment. The involvement of the cardiologist in beginning and recommending further treatment and being available as necessary during treatment could be expected to be of substantial benefit.

If treatment is to be more cost-efficient and therefore suitable for the treatment of patients in primary care or in out-patient clinics, then it will need to be available in a simple format making maximum use of self-help materials and suitable for administration by those who are not experts in cognitive behaviour treatment. We need treatment procedures designed by experts but suitable to be used by doctors and nurses in busy clinical settings.

An out-patient trial for benign palpitations

We are currently attempting to devise and evaluate such a treatment in the out-patient setting (see Table 15.6). This treatment will be concerned with patients presenting with symptoms of palpitations but we expect that many will also describe chest discomfort. The intervention will be fully integrated with cardiac care and will be delivered by cardiac nurses supervised by psychiatrists. The content of the intervention will be based on previous experience and will be available in a therapist's manual. The treatment elements are:

1. Introductory explanation by the cardiologist which emphasizes that palpitations are a common complaint which frequently result in referral to a cardiac clinic. They are usually not due to significant cardiac or other physical disease, but to an unusual degree of awareness or sensitivity to normal heart rate and to the irregularities of heart rate which are found in substantial proportion in the general population. Although palpitations may be unpleasant and a nuisance, they are not a sign of cardiac weakness and expectation of life is normal. There are a number of well-tried procedures which are valuable in controlling the palpitations, making them less upsetting and promoting a return to normal activities. The experience of palpitations does not indicate that activities should be limited; on the contrary, exercise is beneficial.
2. Brief description of the follow-up appointment with the cardiac nurse and provision of a handout.
3. Follow-up appointment one to two weeks later. Review of palpitations diary kept since cardiac clinic, discussion questions arising from the cardiologist. Discussion of an explanation of palpitations, introduction to anxiety management, and graded practice.
4. Hand out appropriate questionnaires on graded practice and elements of anxiety management. Agree any plans for any further follow-up
5. Further appointment or telephone follow-up.

The intervention will be tailored to the patient's needs and progress. In addition to the cognitive and behavioural elements, ambulatory cardiac monitors will be used to record episodes of palpitations as part of further behavioural experiments and as a means of further reassurance.

The trial is designed not only to show that cognitive behaviour therapy is effective for such patients, but that a treatment informed by cognitive and behavioural principles can be modified and delivered by cardiac nurses working together with cardiologists. The results of this trial should help us to develop further a treatment procedure and treatment materials which can be widely used for chest pain as well as palpitations.

Implications for primary care

Descriptions of the characteristics and course of non-cardiac chest pain in a variety of settings and the accounts of randomized controlled trials all indicate the significance of early management as a determinant of treatment. Over-cautious preoccupation with the possibility of heart disease may reinforce symptoms and disability and it may become difficult to change direction and offer an alternative formulation of cause and a very different approach to treatment. At the same time, it is essential to recognize the initial diagnostic difficulties of identifying angina and the further problems that may be created by equivocal findings on clinical assessment, routine electrocardiogram, and on exercise testing. The answer may lie in a management approach which is initially open-minded and conveys to the patient the range of causes of chest pain. Further investigation and trials of treatment can be decided in terms of the distress, disability, and possible indications for more specialist cardiological intervention.

It should be possible to convey to the patient with chest pain that this is a common and real problem which has many causes. It is often transient, but if it does not improve, further assessment may be helpful. The management of non-cardiac chest pain can then be a logical development from initial care rather than an abrupt and bewildering change of direction. Provided in primary care or in medical clinic it should be possible to see psychological treatment as a part of ordinary clinical care.

The role of specialists

An approach to treatment which stresses the importance of improved care largely delivered by non-specialists does not imply that there will be no role for psychiatrists, psychologists, and others with specialized training in psychology. Indeed, the role of such services will need to be much greater than at present. Some patients will undoubtedly require specialist treatment, but psychologists and psychiatrists may well spend more of their time training and supervising general practitioners, medical specialists, and others involved in care. In view of the very large numbers of patients involved, they will undoubtedly need to work closely with specialist cardiac nurses on wards, in clinics, and in rehabilitation settings as well as in primary care.

References

Assey, M. E. (1993). The puzzle of normal coronary arteries in the patient with chest pain: what to do? *Clinical Cardiology*, **16**, 170–80.

Barsky, A. J., Cleary, P. D., Barnett, M. C., Christiansen, C. L., and Ruskin, J. N. (1994). The accuracy of symptom reported in patients complaining of palpitations. *American Journal of Medicine*, **97**, 214–21.

Bass, C. and Mayou, R. A. (1995). Chest pain and palpitations. In *Treatment of functional somatic symptoms* (ed. R. A. Mayou, C. Bass, and M. Sharpe), pp. 328–52. Oxford University Press.

Bass, C., Saunders, D., Mayou, R. A., Bryant, B., and Tyndel, S. *Non-cardiac chest pain: Why is a brief intervention ineffective?* Submitted.

Beitman, B. D., Basha, I. M., Trombka, L. H., *et al.* (1988). Alprazolam in the treatment of cardiology patients with atypical chest pain and panic disorder. *Journal Clinical Psychopharmacology*, **8**, 127–30.

Cannon, R. O. (1993). Chest pain with normal coronary angiograms. *New England Journal of Medicine*, **328**, 1706–8.

Cannon, R. O., Quyyumi, A. A., Mincemoyer, R., Stine, A. M., Gracely, R. H., Smith, W. B., *et al.* (1994). Imipramine in patients with chest pain despite normal coronary angiograms. *New England Journal of Medicine*, **330**, 1411–17.

Chambers, J. and Bass, C. (1990). Chest pain with normal coronary anatomy: a review of natural history and possible etiologic factors. *Progress in Cardiovascular Disease*, **33**, 161–84.

Channer, K. S., James, M. A., Papouchado, M., and Russell Rees, J. (1987). Failure of a negative exercise test to reassure patients with chest pain. *Quarterly Journal Medicine*, **240**, 315–22.

Clouse, R. E. (1992). Psychopharmacologic approaches to therapy for chest pain of presumed esophageal origin. *American Journal of Medicine*, **92**, S106–S13.

Dawes, M., Mayou, R. A., Mart, D., Fuller, A., and Eeley, D. *Identification and management of ischaemic heart disease in general practice*. Submitted.

DeGuire, S., Gevirtz, R., Kawahara, Y., and Maguire, W. (1992). Hyperventilation syndrome and the assessment of treatment for functional cardiac symptoms. *American Journal of Cardiology*, **70**, 673–7.

Disla, E., Rhim, H. R., Reddy, A., Karten, I., and Taranta, A. (1994). Costochondritis: A prospective analysis in an emergency department setting. *Archives of Internal Medicine*, **154**, 2466–9.

Ehlers, A. and Breuer, P. (1992). Increased cardiac awareness in panic disorder. *Journal of Abnormal Psychology*, **101**, 371–82.

Epstein, S. E., Gerber, L. H., and Borer, J. S. (1979). Chest wall syndrome: a common cause of unexplained cardiac pain. *Journal of the American Medical Association*, **241**, 2793–7.

Faxon, D. P., McGabe, C. H., Kreigel, D. E., and Ryan, T. J. (1982). Therapeutic and economic value of a normal coronary angiogram. *American Journal of Medicine*, **73**, 500–5.

Hutchinson, S. J., Poole-Wilson, P. A., and Henderson, A. H. (1988). Angina with normal coronary arteries: a review. *Quartely Journal of Medicine*, 268 (NS, 72), 677–88.

Katerndahl, D. A. (1993). Panic and prolapse: Meta-analysis. *Journal of Nervous and Mental Disease*, 181, 539–44.

Kisely, S. R., Creed, F., and Cotter, L. (1992). The course of psychiatric disorder associated with non-specific chest pain. *Journal of Psychosomatic Research*, 36, 329–35.

Klimes, I., Mayou, R. A., Pearce, M. J., Coles, L., and Fagg, J. R. (1990). Psychological treatment for atypical non-cardiac chest pain: a controlled evaluation. *Psychological Medicine*, 20, 605–11.

Kroenke, K. and Mangelsdorff, D. (1989). Common symptoms in ambulatory care: incidence, evaluation, therapy and outcome. *American Journal of Medicine*, 86, 262–66.

Lichtlen, P. R., Bargheer, K., and Wenzlaff, P. (1995). Long-term prognosis of patients with angina-like chest pain and normal coronary angiographic findings. *Journal of the American College of Cardiology*, 25, 1013–18.

Mayou, R. A. (1989). Invited review: atypical chest pain. *Journal of Psychosomatic Research*, 33, 373–406.

Mayou, R. A., Bryant, B., Forfar, C., and Clark, D. M. (1994). Non-cardiac chest pain and benign palpitations in the cardiac clinic. *British Heart Journal*, 72, 548–53.

Mayou, R. A., Bass, C., and Sharpe, M. (1995). *Treatment of functional somatic symptoms*. Oxford University Press.

Murabito, J. M., Anderson, K. M., Kannel, W. B., Evans, J. C., and Levy, D. L. (1990). Risk of coronary heart disease in subjects with chest discomfort: The Framingham heart study. *American Journal of Medicine*, 89, 297–302.

Potts, S. G. and Bass, C. M. (1995). Psychological morbidity in patients with chest pain and normal or near-normal coronary arteries: a long-term follow-up study. *Psychological Medicine*, 25, 339–47.

Rose, S., Achkar, E., and Easley, K. A. (1994). Follow-up of patients with noncardiac chest pain: value of esophageal testing. *Digestive Diseases and Sciences*, 39, 2063–8.

Salkovskis, P. (1992). Psychological treatment of non-cardiac chest pain: the cognitive approach. *American Journal of Medicine*, 92, S114.

Scott, E. M. and Scott, B. B. (1993). Painful rib syndrome — a review of 76 cases. *Gut*, 34, 1006–8.

Tyrer, P., Lee, I., and Alexander, J. (1980). Awareness of cardiac function in anxious, phobic and hypochondriacal patients. *Psychological Medicine*, 10, 171–4.

von Korff, M., Dworkin, S. F., Le Resche, L. L., and Kruger, A. (1988). An epidemiologic comparison of pain complaints. *Pain*, 32, 173–83.

Warwick, H. M. C. (1995). Treatment of hypochondriasis. In *Treatment of functional somatic symptoms* (ed. R. Mayou, C. Bass, and M. Sharpe), pp. 163–74. Oxford University Press.

Wood, P. (1941). Da Costa's syndrome (or effort syndrome). *British Medical Journal*, 767–72; 805–11; 845–51.

16

Chronic fatigue

Michael Sharpe

Although not his own area of research, my studies into chronic fatigue have been fostered and supported by Professor Michael Gelder in a number of ways. His careful and compassionate clinical practice has taught me how to make clinical progress with patients who are often difficult to help; his wise and sceptical clinical perspective has encouraged me to look beyond their diagnosis and to value a clinically useful formulation; his consistent encouragement and incisive criticism have been important in enabling me to turn clinical curiosity into answerable research questions. Finally, it is largely because of his work over many years in developing the Oxford Department of Psychiatry into a centre of excellence for psychological therapies that the intellectual environment and colleagueship, that have been the basis of the development of the cognitive behavioural approach to fatigue, were available to me.

This chapter will describe the cognitive behavioural approach to the problem of chronic fatigue and chronic fatigue syndrome. The nature and definition of fatigue as a symptom and chronic fatigue syndrome as an illness will be discussed, and the various diagnoses to which fatigue has been attributed examined. An historical perspective on the aetiology and treatment of chronic fatigue is taken because this both highlights the long-standing competition between physical and psychological theories of its aetiology, and places current ideas in the context of changing fashions in the treatment of fatigue.

The modern cognitive behavioural perspective on chronic fatigue syndrome involves an expansion of the medical approach to fatigue with its focus on somatic complaints and physiological mechanisms to include an examination of cognition, behaviour, mood, and social situation. These additional factors are considered to interact in ways that serve to perpetuate the illness. This approach is represented by the 'generic' cognitive behavioural model. Specific cognitive behavioural models for fatigue have also been proposed.

Cognitive behavioural treatment of chronic fatigue syndrome has much in common with the treatment of depression, but requires a much greater emphasis on patients' beliefs about the illness. The evidence for the efficacy of the approach has been strengthened by the findings of two recent randomized controlled trials in which cognitive behaviour therapy was shown to be considerably more effective than alternative treatments. Despite the many years of interest in fatigue states and their treatment many questions remain unanswered. In the final section of this chapter, suggestions for future research will be proposed and the developments in services required to meet the needs of patients with chronic fatigue and related syndromes outlined.

The nature of the problem

Before considering the cognitive behavioural approach to chronic fatigue it is necessary to review the nature and history of the problem of chronic fatigue.

Fatigue as a symptom

Fatigue has been defined in a variety of ways, many of which focus on objectively measurable reductions in the performance of a task (Kennedy 1988). Here, however, we are concerned with fatigue as a *subjective feeling* of weariness, lack of energy and exhaustion, that is typically exacerbated by even minor exertion (Berrios 1990). The feeling of fatigue is a common human experience and at any one time is regarded as a problem by as many as a quarter of the adult population (Chen 1986; Hannay 1978). Often the fatigue is readily explicable in terms of life stresses, overwork, or interrupted sleep. In others it appears disproportionate in severity and may be regarded as an illness.

Fatigue as an illness

Although only a minority of people experiencing chronic severe fatigue consult a physician, it is still one of the most common presenting symptoms in primary care (Kroenke *et al.* 1988; David *et al.* 1991). While it can be a symptom of almost any organic disease, in most cases the fatigue remains unexplained after rigorous medical assessment (Kroenke *et al.* 1988). The diagnosis and management of chronic fatigue as an illness unexplained by definite organic disease has been described in medical writings for more than a hundred years (Wessely 1991). In the last century patients would be likely to receive a diagnosis of neurasthenia, a concept that became an umbrella term for many symptoms, but especially chronic fatigue (Costa e Silva and De Girolamo 1990). By the early years of this century, however, neurasthenia was becoming less acceptable as a diagnosis, and its usage declined. Although it is uncertain whether the prevalence of fatigue showed a corresponding decline, it did not go away. It seems likely that patients still presented with severe chronic fatigue, but rather than being labelled as neurasthenic, they received diagnoses according to the speciality of the doctor that they were consulting (Wessely 1994). Psychiatrists tended to attribute chronic fatigue to the broad diagnostic category of depression, and when it did not readily fit regarded it as 'atypical' or 'masked' (Greenberg 1990). Physicians were more likely simply to describe the symptom (Wilbur 1949) or to attribute the fatigue to hypothetical disease processes such as chronic brucellosis, hypoglycaemia, myalgic encephalomyelitis, or chronic Epstein–Barr virus infection (Costa e Silva and De Girolamo 1990).

In recent years an illness characterized by a predominant complaint of fatigue and often profound disability has been the focus of renewed attention. This interest has been partly driven by non-psychiatric physicians for whom neither the previously proposed disease processes, nor the syndrome of depression, were plausible explanations for the majority of cases they saw. A need for a new, aetiologically neutral name arose, and the term 'chronic fatigue syndrome' (CFS) was coined (Holmes *et al.* 1988). Despite considerable interest and research effort both the cause and treatment of this syndrome remain uncertain and it has achieved widespread notoriety as a 'clinical conundrum' (Kyle and deShazo 1992).

Chronic fatigue syndrome

This syndrome was initially defined by a consensus meeting in 1988 (Holmes *et al.* 1988). The term has been generally accepted, although the original definition has not and alternatives have been proposed (Sharpe *et al.* 1991; Lloyd *et al.* 1988; Schluederberg *et al.* 1992; Fukuda *et al.* 1994). All describe a syndrome characterized by fatigue as the predominant complaint. It must have been present for at least six months, and associated with significant disability, but unexplained by organic disease. Descriptions of the syndrome typically include symptoms of poor concentration and muscle pain as well as fatigue (Beard 1869; Abbey and Garfinkel 1991). The definitions all refer to these symptoms but differ in the precise number required for the diagnosis to be made and the types of psychiatric syndromes which lead to exclusion.

The latest definition is based on an international consensus of researchers and takes a broader approach to the problem than its predecessors. It requires only a small number of symptoms in addition to fatigue, and the exclusion of only a limited number of specified psychiatric syndromes (Fukuda *et al.* 1994). These diagnostic criteria are summarized in Table 16.1. However, even this

TABLE 16.1. Definition of chronic fatigue syndrome

Inclusion criteria:
1. Clinically evaluated, medically unexplained fatigue of at least six months duration that is:
   - of new onset (not life long)
   - not resulting from ongoing exertion
   - not substantially alleviated by rest
   - a substantial reduction in previous level of activities

2. The occurrence of four or more of the following symptoms:
   - Subjective memory impairment
   - Sore throat
   - Tender lymph nodes
   - Muscle pain
   - Joint pain
   - Headache
   - Unrefreshing sleep
   - Post-exertional malaise lasting more than 24 hours

Exclusion criteria:
   - Active, unresolved or suspected disease
   - Melancholic or bipolar depression (but not uncomplicated major depression)
   - Psychotic disorders
   - Dementia
   - Anorexia or bulimia nervosa
   - Alcohol or other substance misuse
   - Severe obesity

(Fukuda *et al*, 1995.)

new definition remains controversial. Chronic fatigue syndrome overlaps with other medically unexplained somatic syndromes (Straus 1992), especially fibromyalgia, a syndrome characterized by fatigue and muscle pain and tender points in the muscles (Goldenberg 1989*b*). Furthermore, if existing psychiatric classifications such as DSM–IV or ICD–10, are applied to patients meeting criteria for CFS most can be accommodated into one or other of the diagnostic categories. Many patients meet criteria for depression and anxiety syndromes (Greenberg 1990), some report a sufficient number of symptoms to meet criteria for somatization disorder and others express sufficient concern about the cause of their illness to suggest a diagnosis of hypochondriasis. However, the fit of the patients' symptoms to the diagnostic criteria for these syndromes is often poor, and the validity of the diagnoses therefore uncertain. Finally, it is interesting to note that neurasthenia persists as a category among the psychiatric diagnoses specified in ICD–10 (but not DSM–IV) and most patients with CFS satisfy the criteria for this diagnosis (Farmer *et al.* 1995).

Status of chronic fatigue syndrome as a diagnosis

The category of CFS has the advantage of describing patients according to their predominant complaint. Although most can be given an alternative syndromal diagnosis, it is less certain how useful it is to do this (Ray 1991). At present, therefore, it remains a reasonable strategy to describe patients whose clinical presentation is dominated by the complaint of chronic disabling fatigue as suffering from CFS, and also to specify any other diagnostic criteria they meet (Sharpe 1996). This way of approaching the problem is analogous to that used in the study and management of patients with chronic unexplained pain (APA 1994).

Once the broad category has been defined, patients can be further described according to a number of clinically relevant factors including illness beliefs, mood, coping behaviour, physiological state, and social situation. This approach has been advocated for other functional somatic syndromes (Mayou *et al.* 1995) and may provide the basis for a more useful subclassification of fatigue states (Vercoulen *et al.* 1994).

The aetiology of chronic fatigue syndrome

Many factors have been championed as the cause of chronic medically unexplained fatigue, but none established. Indeed, CFS is unlikely to have a single cause, and is more likely to involve an interplay between physiological, psychological, and social factors. Such considerations have not prevented hypotheses, research, and treatment into chronic fatigue being dominated by often heated and polarized debate about whether the condition is physical or psychological in nature (Sharpe 1996).

Physical causes

Neurasthenia as described by Beard in the 1860s was considered a physical disease resulting from a depletion of nerve force. This depletion was seen as a consequence of overwork (Beard 1869). Freud also considered chronic fatigue to be a physical condition due to energy depletion (an actual neurosis rather than a psychoneurosis) although resulting from excessive masturbation rather than work (Freud 1896/1924). Both these views fell out of favour in the early years of the twentieth century (Wessely 1994).

In the decades that followed, physical causes of chronic fatigue continued to find a voice. Those proposed included chronic infection, chemical imbalance, and metabolic problems (Wessely 1994). More recently, new hypotheses have been added to the list including chronic immune dysregulation, muscle dysfunction, and neuroendocrine abnormalities. Although each of these ideas has some evidence to support them, none have been convincingly established (Manu *et al.* 1992).

Psychological factors

Against the backdrop of an assumed physical cause for chronic fatigue, a role for psychological factors in its perpetuation was being hypothesized as early as the turn of the century. Most of these early hypotheses envisaged psychological and physiological factors to be operating in conjunction. Writing in 1909, Waterman, a Harvard neurologist, identified a subgroup of patients with fatigue in whom attitudes and behavioural avoidance were identified as important perpetuating factors '. . . [they] have the psychological element of fatigue developed out of all proportion to the physical, and every attempt at a departure from their life of rest and quiet is made under protest, with the firm conviction that disaster is sure to follow.' Psychological factors were also clearly described by Jamieson Hurry who identified both disordered ideation and physiological processes as components in the 'vicious circles' which he proposed perpetuated the illness called neurasthenia (Hurry 1915). This type of model of fatigue can be seen to be a precursor of more modern cognitive behavioural formulations.

As time went by more exclusively psychological models of fatigue began to be proposed (Wessely 1994). Much of the psychological theorizing about chronic fatigue subsumed it into the notion of depression, combined with an ill-defined process of somatization (Stewart 1990). A number of accounts have, however, focused on the symptom of fatigue itself. In the 1930s and 1940s, although fatigue was regarded by many clinicians as psychogenic in nature, the precise mechanism was only vaguely specified (Alvarez 1935; Wilbur 1949). The psychodynamic perspective filled the gap and portrayed chronic fatigue to be a consequence of chronic conflict and frustration (Bartley 1943).

Alexander devoted a section of his famous textbook of psychosomatic medicine specifically to fatigue states, and highlighted the role of conflict between the belief one should do something and (unconscious) emotional resistance to doing it (Alexander 1950). Shands and Finesinger further elaborated these ideas, and saw fatigue not only as a consequence of such conflict, but also as a self-protective reaction that defended the sufferer's self-image. They further postulated that whereas depression was the result of blaming impaired function on oneself, fatigue resulted when it was attributed to external factors (Shands and Finesinger 1952).

In one of the most recent and interesting psychodynamic analyses, McCranie hypothesized that chronic fatigue is often brought on by overwork, itself a result of attempts to compensate for low self-esteem. This disabling fatigue state can become chronic if it becomes an acceptable explanation for an inability to meet demands or for failure (McCranie 1980). Although never empirically tested, these observations serve as a valuable source of hypotheses for modern cognitive behavioural formulations.

The psychological versus physical debate

Thus, it can be seen that the competition between physical and psychological schools of thought has long been a feature of thinking about chronic fatigue. A recent skirmish in this ongoing battle involved an epidemic of unexplained symptoms including disabling fatigue that occurred at the Royal Free Hospital in 1955 (Wessely 1994). This was initially interpreted as a purely neurological disease resulting from an infectious cause, and gave rise to the term myalgic encephalomyelitis (ME) (Anonymous 1956). It was later interpreted as being more consistent with the purely psychological mechanism of epidemic hysteria (McEverdy and Beard 1970). The debate was acrimonious, and despite important clinical differences between this epidemic of illness and individual cases of chronic fatigue (Wessely 1990), polarized thinking has continued to dominate and even distort the aetiological debate. An important advantage of the cognitive behavioural approach described below is that it can transcend such dualistic thinking and integrate psychological, social, and physical factors into a coherent model and a rational treatment.

Treatments for chronic fatigue

Many treatments have been proposed over the years with most being based on the advocate's own particular aetiological theory. Despite brief enthusiasms, however, few of these treatments have been systematically evaluated, and none generally accepted as effective (Wilson et al. 1994b).

Physical therapies

Those advocating a physical model of chronic fatigue have tended to favour rest as the mainstay of therapy. Thus, in Victorian times Beard (Beard 1869) and Mitchell (Mitchell 1904), both of whom regarded chronic fatigue as due to depletion of nervous energy, were advocates of the application of electricity, rest, and modification of diet as a means of regaining it.

In a similar way more recent biological theories have led to large numbers of corresponding physical therapies. Therefore, the idea that the illness may be a consequence of chronic viral infection led to a trial of antiviral drugs (Straus et al. 1988), the theory of immune dysfunction to treatment with immunoglobulin (Straus 1991), and the hypothesis that the problem was deficiency of various biochemical factors to the administration of substances such as magnesium (Cox *et al.* 1991). Perhaps more plausibly the conceptualization of chronic fatigue as resulting from the biological processes associated with a depressive syndrome (or a related neuroendocrine disturbance) has prompted the use of antidepressant agents (Lynch *et al.* 1991).

Psychotherapies

Psychotherapy in one form or other has long been advocated in the treatment of chronic fatigue by those who considered psychological factors to be important in its aetiology. In its earliest form, as expounded by Dubois toward the end of the last century and fully described in his later book as the psychotherapy of rational persuasion (Dubois 1909), it consisted only of encouragement and persuasion by the physician. By the early years of this century psychotherapy was well established as one of a number of treatments for neurasthenia (Proust and Ballet 1902). As the years passed and the role of psychological factors became increasingly accepted, treatment by prolonged rest and the administration of tonics and medications was increasingly replaced by psychotherapy and graded increases in activity (Wessely 1994).

Once psychotherapy had a secure place in the treatment of fatigue, it developed from the principle of simple suggestion based on the physician's authority into more sophisticated treatments which clearly presage modern cognitive behaviour therapy. As early as 1909 Waterman emphasized the use of a collaborative relationship to achieve necessary changes in the patients' attitudes (Waterman 1909). His techniques included both the provision of information and the use of a behavioural experiment. The latter consisted of a course of gradually increasing activity to challenge the patient's belief that fatigue was an inevitable accompaniment of activity.

The rise of psychodynamic psychotherapy and its radical psychogenic stance led to an eclipse of this pragmatic approach, and in its place psychoanalysis was substituted. However, the potential benefit that an increasingly sophisticated psychological appreciation of the problem may have offered was consequently offset by reluctance on the part of patients to accept this approach. Many found a purely psychological approach to a complaint they regarded as somatic both implausible and unacceptable, and continued to vote with their feet by displaying a preference for a more medical type of treatment (Shorter 1992). So today we find that almost all the patients included in studies of chronic fatigue syndrome have been recruited from medical not psychiatric services.

A cognitive behavioural approach to chronic fatigue syndrome

The more recent psychological approaches to chronic fatigue began with the application of a cognitive behavioural formulation to patients attending a specialist neurology service with medically unexplained chronic fatigue and disability, most of whom believed that they had a physical disease (Wessely *et al.* 1989). In an attempt to overcome the impasse imposed by the physical versus psychiatric dichotomy a pragmatic approach was pursued that focused on the factors perpetuating the illness. Borrowing their model from that pioneered by specialists in the treatment of chronic pain (Philips 1988), an attempt was made to identify and modify both the psychological and physical factors that appeared to perpetuate the problem (Wessely *et al.* 1989). Although considered novel at the time, this approach can now be seen as a rediscovery of ideas that had been described some 90 years earlier.

The modern cognitive behavioural approach to chronic fatigue is based on: (1) an expansion of the medical perspective to include not only the patients' somatic symptoms and physiological state but also factors including cognitions, mood, behaviour and circumstances; and (2) the adoption of a model in which the factors identified interact to perpetuate the illness.

Components of the clinical presentation

Both clinical experience and systematic descriptions allow us to discern many common characteristics among patients who present with chronic fatigue syndrome. These factors do not present equally in all patients and therefore lend themselves to a dimensional assessment. They are considered under the categories listed in Table 16.2.

Thoughts beliefs and attitudes

Although attributions for fatigue in the general population are predominantly psychosocial (McDonald *et al.* 1993), patients with chronic disabling fatigue seen in secondary care almost invariably regard their fatigue as caused by a physical disease. In the United Kingdom, patients frequently adhere to a self-diagnosis of myalgic encephalomyelitis (ME), and may have joined a patient organization, membership of which is based on a belief in this diagnosis (Sharpe *et al.* 1992). Patients are also frequently reluctant to consider a role for psychological factors in the aetiology of their illness, as these are considered to imply that the illness is not real, or that they brought it on themselves (Ware 1992). Belief in a disease explanation of the symptoms is not only associated with greater disability (Sharpe *et al.* 1992), but also predicts a worse outcome (Wilson *et al.* 1994*a*). Furthermore, there is some evidence to support the suggestion that patients who attribute incapacity and failure to a

TABLE 16.2.   Clinical characteristics of patients with chronic fatigue syndrome

Thoughts, beliefs, and attitudes
- Organic not psychological cause
- Symptoms indicate depletion of energy
- Concern with performance
- Vulnerable self-esteem

Behaviour
- Avoid activity
- Oscillation in activity

Mood frustration
- Depression and anxiety
- Reluctance to express distress

Physiology
- Sympathetic arousal
- Deconditioning
- Poor sleep

Interpersonal and social factors
- Occupational problems
- Beliefs of others
- Self-help literature and media
- Iatrogenic influences

physical disease, rather then to their own shortcomings, are able to maintain a more positive self-view (Powell *et al.* 1990).

Exacerbations of symptoms are seen by patients as evidence of further depletion of their limited energy supply (Petrie *et al.* 1995). Exploration of these concerns usually reveals that patients' main fear about the illness is not that it will lead to death or deterioration, but that it interferes with their ability to do things (Surawy *et al.* 1995). Typical thoughts include 'I'm making myself worse', 'This will cause a relapse'. Patients who interpret exercise-induced symptoms in a catastrophic way (e.g., 'If I carry on I will be in bed for weeks'), are more disabled (Petrie *et al.* 1995).

It has also been noted by many clinicians that patients often hold rigid perfectionistic attitudes about performance and feel that they should always cope (Ware 1993; Lewis *et al.* 1994; Puffer and McShane 1992). Common thoughts include 'I should try harder', 'I must not complain'. It seems likely that these attitudes may in many cases be a compensation for vulnerable self-esteem—a hypothesis that has important implications for how they are dealt with in treatment.

Behaviour

The definition of chronic fatigue syndrome requires that patients have significant disability (Fukuda *et al.* 1994). Although many patients can function for brief periods, they find themselves unable to sustain their activity because it leads to an exacerbation of fatigue and other symptoms. Their understandable response is to avoid further activity (Vercoulen *et al.* 1994; Sharpe *et al.* 1992). The idea that limited energy is being used up leads patients to adopt rest as their principal way of coping (Surawy *et al.* 1995). The more avoidant the strategies employed, the greater the disability (Sharpe *et al.* 1992).

Many patients do not, however, maintain a constant low level of activity, but instead punctuate this with intermittent attempts to act normally. These attempts are abandoned when fatigue recurs and the result is a chronic oscillation in activity level from one extreme to the other (Nielson *et al.* 1992; Surawy *et al.* 1995).

Mood

The predominant mood reported by patients is one of frustration (Surawy *et al.* 1995) which they explain as resulting from a conflict between their strong desire to get on with activities, and feeling blocked by 'the illness'. Depressive and anxious mood may be also reported, although rarely emphasized by patients (Kendell 1991; Greenberg 1990). Depressive and anxiety syndromes can be diagnosed in more than half of most samples (David 1991). Patients, however, are often very reluctant to consider the possibility that they may be depressed, and even when acknowledged, depression tends to be regarded as a response to, rather than cause of the illness (Kendell 1991).

Physiology

The precise physiological mechanisms that cause the feeling of fatigue are unknown, although many contributory processes have been identified (Sharpe and Bass 1992). Many, if not all of the symptoms considered typical of CFS also occur in patients suffering from anxiety and depression, and may result from the physiological processes (including sympathetic nervous system arousal) associated with these syndromes (Mathew *et al.* 1981; Sainsbury and Gibson 1954). Disturbed and unrefreshing sleep is an almost universal complaint, and may contribute to daytime fatigue (Morriss *et al.* 1993). Prolonged inactivity is likely to have produced profound physiological deconditioning and reduced tolerance of exercise (Riley *et al.* 1990). Related physiological changes in muscle may at least in part explain exercise-associated muscular pain (Edwards 1986). The common factor about all these processes is that they are understandable and reversible.

Interpersonal and social factors

There is often a history of chronic work stress before the onset of the illness and, in many cases, patients have allowed themselves to accept excessive work demands over a prolonged period, without protesting or seeking help (Surawy *et al.* 1995). It is possible to speculate that this is evidence of a greater susceptibility to pervasive social and cultural pressures to behave in this way (Ware 1993).

Another potentially important interpersonal factor concerns the beliefs of others about the cause of the illness. As with chronic pain (Benjamin *et al.* 1992), friends and relatives may hold strong beliefs in physical causation. In addition, the patient may have received self-help literature or be a member of a patient group that emphasizes a disease causation and the need for rest (Macintyre 1992). Being a member of a patient group (which is itself associated with a belief in physical causation and in rest as a coping strategy) has been found to be associated with greater disability (Sharpe *et al.* 1992).

Media coverage of the illness may also do much to shape patients' beliefs about the nature and cause of the syndrome. In general it is biased towards physical causes (MacLean and Wessely 1994). Finally, doctors can play an important, and sometimes unwitting role in shaping patient's illness beliefs in unhelpful ways.

A *cognitive behavioural conceptualization of chronic fatigue syndrome*

The cognitive behavioural approach assumes that the factors considered above may all be relevant to the perpetuation of the syndrome and may interact in mutually reinforcing ways. This interaction can be depicted both in the form of a 'generic' cognitive behavioural model, and also in more specific models that emphasize the most important pathways. Figure 16.1 illustrates the generic model.

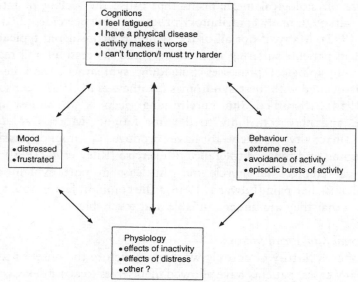

FIG. 16.1. A generic cognitive behavioural conceptualization of chronic fatigue syndrome.

A *specific model of chronic fatigue*

A more specific model of chronic fatigue syndrome which highlights those interactions that are of greatest importance may be a better guide to therapy. The cognitive behavioural model of CFS proposed by Wessely and colleagues employs a simple vicious circle to highlight particular interactions between psychological and physiological factors. Here, the psychological components are the patients' misinterpretation of the symptom of fatigue as a disease worsened by activity and the resulting behavioural avoidance, helplessness, and depressed mood. The physiological components are the changes associated with emotional disorder and deconditioning consequent on chronic inactivity. These components are hypothesized to form a self-perpetuating vicious circle as illustrated in Fig. 16.2.

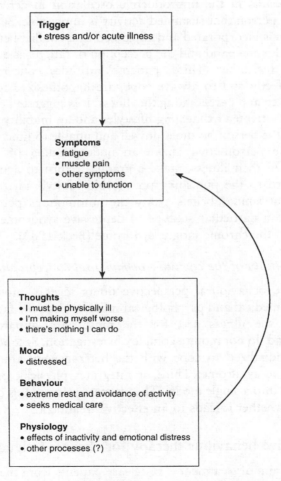

FIG. 16.2. A simple specific cognitive behavioural model of chronic fatigue syndrome.

This simple model has important limitations, however. First, it does not adequately explain some aspects of the clinical presentation such as oscillations in activity levels and the complaint of frustration. Second, it does not include thoughts or beliefs about performance and coping. Third, it offers no explanation why certain persons should be vulnerable to developing a chronic fatigue syndrome. We have recently proposed a more complex model (illustrated in Fig. 16.3) that aims to rectify these deficiencies (Surawy *et al.* 1995).

This model includes several important additions. First, it is based on not one, but two interacting cycles: one of these is based on a catastrophic misinterpretation of symptoms leading to distress and to avoidance of activity; the other is based on 'should' statements that lead to frustration and to brief, but unsustainable, bursts of activity. The alternating dominance of these cognitions results in the unproductive oscillation in activity that serves to convince the person that sustained activity is impossible. Second, the emotion of frustration is incorporated and explained by a conflict between the desire to perform on the one hand and the perception of fatigue as an unsurmountable obstacle on the other. Third, patients' attitudes concerning the need to perform perfectly and to always cope, are hypothesized to be important in predisposing to and perpetuating the illness. It is suggested that these attitudes lead to work-oriented exhausting lifestyles and an inability to seek help or to complain. If the person becomes unwell and unable to function these attitudes also bias the person away from an understanding of the psychological components of their illness, make a gradual return to activity difficult, and make a return to the punishing pre-morbid lifestyle unattractive. Beck has suggested that similar beliefs typify the automonous personality type and predispose to a particular subtype of depressive syndrome which has many similarities to the chronic fatigue syndrome (Beck 1983).

Utility of the cognitive behavioural conceptualization

The cognitive behavioural perspective offers several important advantages over simpler medical and psychological models. First, the factors important in perpetuating the illness are, for the most part, apparent from clinical assessment and do not require complex investigation. Second, the formulation can be individualized to cope with the heterogeneity among patients with chronic fatigue syndrome. Third, it integrates physical, psychological, and social factors into a single model. The ultimate value of this conceptualization, however, is whether it leads to an effective treatment.

Cognitive behaviour therapy for chronic fatigue syndrome

The primary aim of treatment is to release patients from the self-perpetuating cycles described above by helping them to reappraise their understanding of

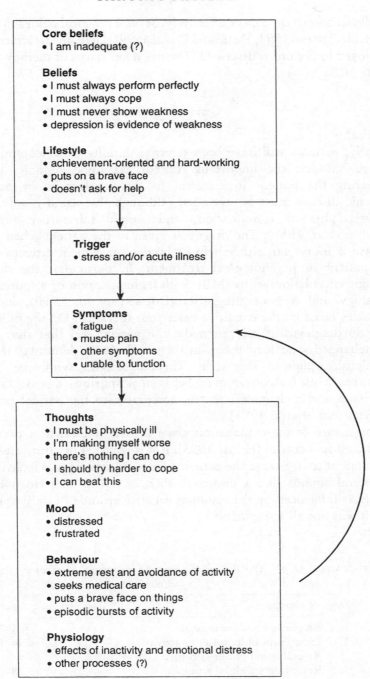

FIG. 16.3. A complex specific model of chronic fatigue syndrome.

the illness and to cope more effectively. Several practical guides to therapy are available (Sharpe 1994; Deale and David 1994). Here, the treatment approach employed in Oxford is described. The five main stages of therapy are listed in Table 16.3.

General assessment

Medical

Usually, patients will have been referred initially to a hospital physician. He or she has the important role of excluding organic disease and preparing the patient for referral to the psychiatrist or psychologist. Organic disease must be excluded, although this usually only requires a history, physical examination, and simple laboratory investigations (Valdini *et al.* 1989). The diagnosis given to the patient when no organic disease is found can either help or hinder subsequent attempts to engage the patient in psychological treatment. In particular, the diagnosis of myalgic encephalomyelitis (ME), with its implication of a 'purely physical' aetiology and a poor prognosis (Dowsett *et al.* 1990), increases the obstacles faced by the cognitive behaviour therapist. On the other hand, to give no diagnosis at all can make the patient feel that they have been shortchanged, and lead them into a search for a definitive, if ultimately unhelpful, opinion. The term 'chronic fatigue syndrome' offers the physician a useful compromise between a spurious disease label on the one hand and a diagnosis that is acceptable to the patient on the other (Mayou and Sharpe 1995).

The nature of the explanation given for the referral to a psychiatrist or psychologist is crucial (House 1995). If it is couched in positive terms it may be sufficient to overcome the patient's initial reluctance to pursue this avenue. If referral sounds like a dismissal, there is a risk that treatment will be adversely influenced by the resulting negative attitude ('I only went to prove that it was not all in my mind').

TABLE 16.3. The five main stages of treatment of chronic fatigue syndrome

Stage of therapy	Sessions
1. Assessment and formulation	1–3
2. Experiment of increases in activity Re-evaluation of illness beliefs	4–10
3. Reviewing unhelpful attitudes	8–12
4. Problem-solving practical difficulties	10–14
5. Review and planning for future	12–16

Psychiatric

The general assessment should include an examination of the patient's mental state. The aim is to seek evidence of major psychiatric disorder and suicidal intent, and to diagnose depressive and anxiety syndromes. A structured interview may be helpful in eliciting symptoms that are not readily volunteered by the patient (Spitzer *et al.* 1992).

Cognitive behavioural assessment

The purpose of this part of the assessment process is to elicit detailed information about the patient's presenting problems, his/her cognitions, emotions, behaviour, and physiological state, as relevant aspects of his/her life situation. Sources of information include:

1. an interview with the patient and his/her significant other(s);
2. patient-completed questionnaires; and
3. patient-completed diaries.

Current problems. Assessment should begin by eliciting an exhaustive list of the patient's current problems. This list will include both symptoms and life difficulties. Self-report scales may be used to quantify the severity of fatigue (Chalder *et al.* 1993) and the current level of disability (Ware and Sherbourne 1992). Having covered the physical symptoms to both the therapist's and the patient's satisfaction, it is then appropriate to move on to psychological and social factors. A *bridge* between physical and psychological matters can be made by enquiring about the effect that the illness has had on the patient's life. Specific examples are most useful.

Cognitions. Patients' beliefs about the illness must be elicited. These include their understanding of the cause of the symptoms, the significance of exercise-induced exacerbations and also their 'worst fears'. It is also appropriate to ask patients how they believe the illness should be managed and, in particular, their hopes and fears concerning cognitive behavioural treatment. The therapist should also be alert to evidence of attitudes such as perfectionism, a belief that the expression of emotion is evidence of weakness, and vulnerable self-esteem.

The recording of thoughts in a diary format is a useful way of eliciting cognitions about symptoms and performance. Questionnaires may supplement the interview in eliciting both illness beliefs (Schweitzer *et al.* 1994) and more general attitudes such as perfectionism (Frost *et al.* 1994).

Emotion. Patients who present with chronic fatigue are often reluctant to express emotions and may habitually present 'a brave face' or cope with their feelings by ignoring them. It therefore requires both a trusting relationship and some sensitivity to elicit feelings of distress. An expression of empathy about the effect that the illness has had on the patient's life is one way to encourage expression of emotion. Questionnaires, such as the Hospital Anxiety Depression Scale (HAD) are useful in quantifying the severity of emotional distress (Zigmond and Snaith 1983).

Behaviour. It is important to find out how the patient copes with fatigue. Useful questions include: 'What do you do to prevent it?', 'What do you do to prevent the worst happening?', and 'What do you do to relieve it?' A detailed behavioural account of the patient's current life should also be obtained. This can then be examined in more detail by going through a typical day, hour by hour, or by asking the patient to keep a diary for a week or so. This record is useful both to provide a baseline and to identify patterns of activity, rest and, sleep. Oscillations in activity provide opportunities to identify relevant cognitions.

Physiology. Physiological changes are usually inferred from the patient's symptoms. Thus, decreased exercise tolerance may suggest deconditioning due to prolonged inactivity and shakiness, and sweaty palms may be indicative of increased sympathetic nervous system activity. Specific provocation tests, such as voluntary hyperventilation, may reveal whether this process causes an exacerbation of symptoms. Laboratory investigations of these parameters, if available, may contribute to the assessment and to the education of the patient, but are not essential for treatment.

Interpersonal and social factors. Occupational and financial factors that pose potential blocks to a return to normal activity must be elicited. Asking the patient if recovery would raise any problems may produce surprisingly candid responses. As well as interviewing patients to find out about their beliefs, emotions, and coping behaviours, interviewing the patient's cohabitee or family is equally important in order to elicit their understanding of the illness. Friends and relatives often hold surprisingly extreme beliefs about the nature of the illness. Finally, it is essential to know whether the patient is attending other doctors or alternative practitioners, and his/her views about these other forms of treatment.

The initial formulation

The next step is to construct a provisional cognitive behavioural formulation. Although the cognitive behavioural conceptualization as described above (Fig. 16.3) provides a guide, an individualized formulation is required if therapy is to be most effective for that particular patient. This formulation is not fixed but is a hypothesis that may be modified or elaborated as new information is discovered.

General issues

A positive and collaborative therapeutic relationship is a prerequisite to effective therapy. This may be difficult to establish since some patients may suppose that acceptance of a psychotherapeutic approach will lead to their problems being interpreted as 'psychiatric', 'all in the mind', or 'their own fault'. A sensitivity to these perceived implications is all the more understandable if they are seen as major threats to the patients' view of themselves. It is therefore essential that the therapist is seen to take the patients' physical complaints seriously before moving on to more psychological issues.

Engaging the patient in therapy

An important part of the collaborative approach to treatment is to share this initial formulation with the patient. The way in which this is done will depend on the patient's willingness to consider an interpretation of his/her difficulties that includes psychological factors. Patients who are mystified by their symptoms may be presented with the formulation in a fairly direct way, while making it clear that this is an initial hypothesis to be modified in the light of new evidence, and that their active collaboration will be sought in developing it.

For patients who believe moderately strongly that their fatigue is purely physical in nature, the formulation may need to be presented more slowly. One strategy is to ask them to present their own initial formulation and then, using the information that they have provided in the assessment, to add additional elements. The physical disease explanation need not be discarded but some doubt cast about whether it provides an adequate explanation of the illness.

For patients who hold very strong beliefs concerning a fixed physical causation, setting up their explanation and the cognitive behavioural formulation as alternative hypotheses may be useful. The therapist can then say that it is not possible to know which is the best explanation but that they need to find out. If they reject the more optimistic formulation out of hand, they may have missed an opportunity to improve their quality of life. The initial aim of therapy is then to collect observations (such as exacerbations of fatigue before starting a task) and test predictions (such as increased capacity for activity as a result of graded increases) which discriminate between the two theories.

Planning therapy

It is useful at this point to consider how much treatment the patient needs. Some patients find the initial formulation not only acceptable but a revelation.

They may immediately start making suggestions about how they could change their attitudes, behaviour, and lifestyle in a way that will unlock them from the vicious circles they now perceive. These patients may only need encouragement and follow-up to check that they remain on course. I have known patients who have recovered after a single telephone conversation that enabled them to reconceptualize their illness, reduce their fear of symptoms, and overcome their avoidance.

The difficulties of other patients are so long-standing and rooted in intractable social or personality difficulties that brief cognitive behaviour therapy may not be appropriate. For these patients, one strategy is to manage them within a cognitive behavioural framework but to do it in a 'slow motion' way, seeing them intermittently for months or even years.

Most of the patients will fall into a middle group. These are patients who had a good level of pre-morbid functioning but who need help in re-evaluating their understanding of their illness, improving their coping behaviour, and perhaps also making occupational, social, and lifestyle changes. This is the group we will focus on in the following account of therapy.

Setting goals

An important early task is the negotiation of therapeutic goals. It is important that the goals are, as far as possible, operationally defined. So, for example 'feeling better' is less useful than being able to walk five miles twice a week. It is also important that the goals are realistic. If someone has been severely disabled for several years, the regaining of normal sporting activities within several months is not a realistic target. Nor is it realistic to aim for complete absence of fatigue whatever their level of activity. Indeed, an important aspect of therapy may be to help patients to adopt more realistic expectations of themselves, and to change excessively demanding pre-morbid lifestyles.

The process of treatment

Assuming that the patient is at least willing to consider the cognitive behavioural formulation, has identified realistic goals, and is willing to attend for a course of therapy, treatment can proceed. The aim is to work with the patient in a collaborative way in order to help him/her to attain a more realistic and useful formulation of his/her illness, and to develop ways of coping most conducive to recovery.

As far as possible therapeutic interventions should be based on and guided by the formulation. It is often useful to start with a focus on coping behaviour, and then to move on to cognitive aspects of the problem. The other components of the cognitive model (physiology, mood, and social environment) may not require any direct intervention. Sometimes, however, additional interventions in these realms may also be necessary. The components of treatment are described below.

Behavioural interventions

The principal behavioural intervention used to treat fatigue is to stabilize and then to gradually increase activity. When used as part of a cognitive behavioural approach this strategy is intended not only to change behaviour, but also to influence the other components of the model. Thus, a planned increase in activity can be used to evaluate beliefs that the patient may hold about the illness such as 'activity always makes me worse'. By increasing the patient's confidence and range of activities, mood can also be improved. Finally, behavioural change is an important means by which the effects of inactivity on physiological functioning can be reversed.

It is useful for the patient to keep activity records for several weeks. Once his/her level and pattern of activity have been identified, a behavioural experiment may be set up. This requires the patient first to stabilize his/her level of activity and then to make a small increase. The effects on mood, symptoms, and progress towards goals are monitored. The activity should be: (1) at a reasonable and tolerable level for the patient; (2) consistent day-to-day; (3) aimed at the attainment of realistic goals; and (4) gradually increased. A temporary increase in fatigue should be anticipated. For a minority of patients such a simple behavioural regimen may be sufficient to achieve recovery, for the majority, other behaviours, cognitions, and social factors need to be addressed more explicitly.

For patients who exhibit intermittent bursts of activity, the exacerbation of symptoms that accompanies these reinforces the belief that activity makes the illness worse. In these cases curbing the excesses is as important as increasing the baseline. Pointing out the pattern may be sufficient for some. In others the bursts of activity reflect 'all or nothing' beliefs about performance which must be addressed using cognitive techniques.

Some patients may adopt safety behaviours that interfere with the experiment of increasing activity. These include walking very slowly, carrying a walking stick, and telling others that they are ill and not to expect too much. If they are to regain their belief in their own ability to function normally, these behaviours need to be dropped.

Cognitive interventions

The principal cognitive interventions are designed both to enable patients to see that improvement can be achieved by their own efforts and to build confidence in their ability to function. Throughout this process the therapist must be sensitive to potential threats to the patient's self-esteem. The idea that they are physically ill may (as described in psychodynamic approaches) be defending their self-image from self-criticism. The therapist needs therefore to help them to take responsibility for their recovery without implying that they are to blame for their current predicament. A distinction between perpetuating factors and initial causes can be helpful in this respect.

The behavioural experiment of increasing activity levels provides valuable evidence on which patients can evaluate their beliefs about the insurmountable nature of the illness and their ability to influence its course. However, other important cognitive factors are likely to be revealed in the execution of this simple experiment which require attention in their own right.

First, the programme itself is likely to provoke task-interfering cognitions that are best captured by having the patient record his/her thoughts before and during activity. Some beliefs may prevent the patient even beginning. These include the belief that 'I've tried an increase in activity before and it didn't work' and that 'activity is harmful for people with my disease'. In both cases the therapist needs to review the cognitive behavioural formulation with the patients, and to ask them whether they have previously tried a graded activity programme in the context of cognitive behaviour therapy. Most often patients will have tried sudden large increases in activity, unaccompanied by a review of their understanding of the illness and symptoms. Examination of what happened usually reveals why the attempt failed.

The second problem is likely to occur after patients have started to increase their level of activity, and become increasingly concerned about the significance of increasing fatigue and/or muscle pain. If they interpret these as heralding a major relapse, they will understandably back-off from activity, or maintain a pattern of oscillating bursts of activity and avoidance. In order to deal with this difficulty, it is important to review with patients the evidence for and against the belief that the symptoms have sinister significance. They should be encouraged to persist with the behavioural experiment of a gradual and consistent increase in activity and to examine their interpretation of the symptoms. Alternative interpretations include the idea that an increase in symptoms is to be expected, and is a positive sign of progress. Persistent recording of activity-associated thoughts and the challenging of these may be required.

The third group of cognitions that interfere with rehabilitation are more general attitudes. Common ones include perfectionism with an 'all or nothing' approach to activities and the view that 'I should always do what other people ask of me'. Both these attitudes lead to large swings in activity, and make it difficult to carry out the behavioural experiment of a graded consistent increase. If the effect of these attitudes are disruptive to the therapy they need to be tackled. The patient may be encouraged to review the advantages and disadvantages of holding them, and to consider less extreme alternatives. However, major attitude change is a potentially difficult and long-term therapeutic task. A simpler method is repeatedly to encourage the patient (and their significant others) to make rehabilitation, rather than meeting external demands, the highest priority in his/her daily life.

Reducing distress and depression

One factor driving these patients' continuing emotional arousal is worry about their symptoms and distress at their inability to function. Therefore, a more benign understanding of the illness and evidence of improvement usually results in a resolution of distress. It is common, however, for other issues, such as unresolved grief and chronic relationship conflicts, to emerge in the therapy. If these are prominent they may have to be dealt with during treatment. Often, however, they can be deferred until the patient has reached an adequate level of rehabilitation. Antidepressant medication may also have a place where the patient is clearly depressed.

Normalizing physiology

This is achieved as a result of the reduction in emotional distress and the adoption of an increasing and consistent level of physical activity. Other interventions that may help patients' physiological status include normalizing of the sleep pattern using simple sleep hygiene techniques, ensuring an adequate balanced diet, and reducing the number of medications they are taking.

Overcoming external obstacles

As patients recover, chronic difficulties and obstacles to recovery may become apparent. In particular, a conflict between patients' aspirations and their current lifestyle, as described by psychodynamic theorists (McCranie 1980), often becomes apparent. The task then becomes one of helping the patients to use more effective coping methods for resolving the difficulty. This often entails both a modification of unrealistic work standards and, not uncommonly, a change of occupation.

Another issue that often emerges when patients start increasing activity is the impact of this change on other people. It is hoped that the therapist will have anticipated reactions from family or others who may tell the patient that they should persist with rest. In these cases it is highly desirable to involve the relatives in the therapy and use similar cognitive techniques to persuade them of the potential benefits of the cognitive behavioural approach. In a few cases, the patient's family may strongly resist their efforts to rehabilitate. Such cases can be very difficult to manage and may require that concerns of other family members are dealt with directly.

Consolidating gains and planning for the future

By the end of therapy, the therapist and patient should have a final collaboratively generated formulation on which they can agree. At this point it is useful for the patient to produce a written document which includes both the formulation and a list of the things that he/she has learnt from the therapy. Practical guidelines on how the patient can continue their rehabilitation and cope with 'relapse' are especially valuable and are often subsequently referred to by the patient.

Administration of therapy

Individual or group

Most research on the cognitive behaviour therapy of chronic fatigue has involved individually administered treatment. Group therapy offers a potentially more potent and efficient alternative, and has been used in related conditions (Stern and Fernandez 1991). Interaction with other patients has the potential advantage of allowing the more effective challenging of beliefs and behaviour, but it also has the potential for reinforcing unhelpful illness beliefs.

How many sessions?

Some patients can benefit greatly from simple assessment and advice, others require 20 sessions or more, and a minority may require long-term therapy and follow-up. An average number would be between 10 and 20 individual sessions over a four- to six-month period, with one or two follow-up or 'booster' sessions.

Informational aids

There are a variety of ways in which patients can be helped to get the most out of their therapy sessions. One that we use is for all the therapy sessions to be tape recorded and for the patient to be given the 'homework' task of listening to the tape at home. It is also useful to give patients written summaries outlining certain components of the therapy. Topics might include an outline of cognitive behaviour therapy (CBT), the cognitive behavioural conceptualization of chronic fatigue syndrome, and also detailed sheets explaining how to record and evaluate unhelpful thoughts and beliefs. Other written material, including books and articles, may occasionally be useful. These include a patient's guide to a cognitive behavioural approach to fatigue (Chalder, 1995), and self-help books on the cognitive behavioural approach to problematic attitudes such as perfectionism (e.g., Burns 1980).

Outcome studies

The cognitive behavioural approach to chronic fatigue syndrome is plausible and leads to a rational treatment approach, but is it effective? At the time of writing, five studies (two non-randomized comparisons and three randomized trials) have been completed. These are summarized in Table 16.4.

The first systematic evaluation of CBT for chronic fatigue syndrome was an uncontrolled evaluation based on the simple cognitive behavioural model. It was important because, although there was a high rate of patient refusal, many achieved a marked improvement that was sustained at long-term follow-up (Butler *et al.* 1991; Bonner *et al.* 1994), a result that challenged the prevailing idea that nothing could be done for such patients.

A second study used a non-randomized controlled design that compared CBT with a waiting list condition. The therapy had a cognitive emphasis but differed from the previous study in accepting a disease model of the illness and aiming to achieve adjustment rather than rehabilitation (Friedberg and Krupp 1994). Therapy was administered in a group format. At the end of treatment a greater reduction in depression but not in disability was observed in the patients treated with CBT.

The first randomized trial of CBT for chronic fatigue syndrome compared a rehabilitative behavioural treatment with standard medical care. The therapy in this study was brief (only six sessions) and the average duration of patients' illness relatively long (mean of 5.5 years, and maximum of 28 years). The effect of therapy may also have been unintentionally diluted by the study methodology, which attempted to evaluate immunotherapy as well as CBT in a factorial design (Sharpe 1995). No difference was found in the effect of the treatments on disability at the three-month final follow up evaluation (Lloyd *et al.* 1993).

The second randomized trial was conducted in Oxford and compared medical care with medical care plus CBT (Sharpe *et al.* 1996). The CBT comprised 16 individual treatment sessions over four months. It had a rehabilitative aim and a cognitive emphasis, and was similar to the treatment described above. Only two patients declined to enter the study and all completed therapy. The patients were followed up for eight months after the four-month treatment period, and disability was the principal outcome measure. Patients who received CBT showed a far greater improvement than patients who had received only medical care. This superiority of CBT was also reflected in a greater improvement on subjective ratings of general state, fatigue, and depression. A notable observation was a slow improvement in disability which continued during the follow-up period. At the final evaluation 73% of patients who received CBT attained normal daily functioning, compared with only 27% of those given medical care alone.

TABLE 16.4. Overview of outcome studies of cognitive behaviour therapy for patients with chronic fatigue syndrome

Authors	Study Design	Treatment Cognitive behaviour therapy	Comparison	Patients No.	Mean length of illness (yrs)	Outcome at final assessment Main variables	Follow-up	Comments
Butler et al. 1991	Case series	Rehabilitative with behavioural emphasis (mean 8 sessions) also used antidepressants	None	32	3.2	Fatigue, disability, and depression all improved from baseline	4 yrs	18 patient refusals and five drop-outs
Lloyd et al. (1993)	Randomized controlled trial	Rehabilitative (6 individual sessions)	Medical care	41+49	5.5	No difference	3 mths	Complex design including immunotherapy
Friedberg and Krupp (1994)	Non-randomized comparison	Non-rehabilitative (6 group sessions)	Waiting list	22+22	3	Greater reduction in depression only	None	Emphasis on accommodation to illness
Sharpe et al. (1996)	Randomized controlled trial	Rehabilitative with cognitive emphasis (16 individual sessions)	Medical care	30+30	2.6	Greater reduction in disability, fatigue, and depression	8 mths	Difference increased during follow-up
Deale et al. (in press)	Randomized controlled trial	Rehabilitative with behavioural emphasis (13 individual sessions)	Relaxation therapy (13 sessions)	30+30	3.5	Greater reduction in disability, fatigue, and depression	6 mths	Difference increased during follow-up

The most recent study to be completed was conducted at King's College Hospital, London (Deale *et al.* in press) by the same group who conducted the original case series. The CBT evaluated was similar to that used in the Oxford trial although with more emphasis on early behavioural change. This study also differed by comparing CBT with relaxation therapy, rather than simple medical care. The patients in each treatment condition received therapy for a similar amount of time, thereby controlling for non-specific effects. The results of this study were remarkably similar to those obtained in Oxford, except that they had some drop-outs (four from relaxation and three from CBT). An analysis of treatment completers showed that 70% of patients who received CBT and only 20% given relaxation were substantially improved at final evaluation. As in the Oxford study, continuing improvement during the follow-up period was observed in the patients who received CBT.

An examination of the results of these studies suggests that in order to achieve patient compliance the therapy should address illness beliefs in a collaborative manner, and in order to reduce disability it should be intensive and aim for rehabilitation. The most recent studies show that intensive CBT that incorporates these aspects can be an acceptable and effective therapy for many patients with chronic fatigue syndrome.

New directions

There remain many controversies and uncertainties about chronic fatigue syndrome, and much to be learned. The current definition has important shortcomings. If further progress is to be made, a useful subclassification of the syndrome will be needed. One approach would be to define subcategories or dimensions that specify beliefs, mood disturbance, and behaviour, as well as physiological findings. This approach has been proposed but requires further evaluation (Vercoulen *et al.* 1994).

Cognitive model

As well as obtaining a definition that more effectively specifies the clinical phenomena, we need more research into the cognitive and behavioural aspects of the syndrome. Specific topics requiring investigation include: (1) the role of attitudes and assumptions in perpetuating the syndrome; (2) the potential role of cognitive avoidance in modifying the presentation of depression and anxiety, (3) the mechanisms underlying symptom production and the exacerbation that occurs with activity.

Cognitive behavioural treatment

We need both a brief treatment for more widespread use in primary care and a more effective treatment for resistant cases. We also need predictors of response to brief therapy. At present, we have to be guided largely by clinical impression. This experience suggests that some patients can benefit from a very brief therapy (several sessions only) in which they are helped to shift from a disease model to a cognitive behavioural formulation, and jointly to produce an action plan. It also suggests that patients who have never coped well or who are in difficult occupational circumstances do not do well. The new 'schema-based' therapies (Young 1990) may be appropriate for this group. All these issues require empirical evaluation.

Services

Chronic fatigue is just one example of the large range of medically unexplained syndromes that are poorly managed by existing services (Kroenke *et al.* 1990). This is part of the wider problem created by a split of specialist service provision into psychiatry devoted to 'mental health' and medical services that focus on 'organic disease' (Kirmayer 1988). As in Victorian times, patients with fatigue prefer to see their problem as physical and to use medical rather than psychiatric services. Although the general principles of cognitive behaviour therapy can, in principle, be applied by any clinician, more complex or difficult cases require the skills of a trained cognitive behaviour therapist. Unfortunately, such practitioners are rare and this may be a major impediment to the development of effective services. It has also been our experience that therapists used to working with patients who present with psychological problems often have difficulty engaging and working with patients who present with predominantly somatic complaints such as chronic fatigue. The provision of appropriately skilled therapists and the development of integrated medical/psychiatric services presents us with a considerable challenge.

Conclusions

Fatigue is one of the most common complaints in medical practice and is a symptom of almost every disease. As the main symptom of a medically unexplained illness it has a long and chequered history. Perhaps because of its ambiguous nature the predominant view of its aetiology has fluctuated over the years from the purely physical to the purely psychological and back again, with fashions in treatment following. The modern cognitive behavioural approach offers an integrative perspective on the problem. Like chronic fatigue this approach is not new but largely a re-invention of theories and treatments described almost a century ago. The significant development in recent years has been the demonstration of the efficacy of this approach in randomized clinical trials. Much remains to be done in characterizing the problem of fatigue, researching its aetiology, and further developing approaches to treatment. Nonetheless, the development of a cognitive behavioural treatment for chronic fatigue further increases the number of somatic problems for which this form of therapy has a role. It also reinforces the case for an integration of psychological therapies into general medical practice.

Acknowledgements

I wish to thank my colleagues in the Oxford University Department of Psychiatry and Nuffield Department of Medicine for their support of my research into this often difficult topic. The Oxford treatment trial was funded by a grant from the Wellcome Trust.

References

Abbey, S. E. and Garfinkel, P. E. (1991). Neurasthenia and chronic fatigue syndrome: the role of culture in the making of a diagnosis. *American Journal of Psychiatry*, **148**, 1638–1646.

Alexander, F. (1950). *Psychosomatic medicine: its principles and applications*, Norton, New York.

Alvarez, W. C. (1935). What is wrong with the patient who feels tired, weak and toxic? *New England Journal of Medicine*, **212**, 96–104.

APA (American Psychiatric Association) (1994). *Diagnostic and Statistical Manual of Mental Disorders* (4th edn). APA, Washington, DC.

Anonymous (1956). A new clinical entity? *Lancet*, i, 789–790.

Bartley, S. H. (1943). Conflict, frustration and fatigue. *Psychosomatic Medicine*, **5**, 160–162.

Beard, G. (1869). Neurasthenia or nervous exhaustion. *Boston Medical and Surgical Journal*, **3**, 217–221.

Beck, A. T. (1983). Cognitive therapy of depression: New perspectives. In *Treatment of depression: old controversies and new approaches* (ed. P. J. Clayton and J. E. Barrett), pp. 265–90. Raven, New York.

Benjamin, S., Mawer, J., and Lennon, S. (1992). The knowledge and beliefs of family care givers about chronic pain patients. *Journal of Psychosomatic Research*, **36**, 211–17.

Berrios, G. E. (1990). Feelings of fatigue and psychopathology: a conceptual history. *Comprehensive Psychiatry*, **31**, 140–151.

Bonner, D., Ron, M., Chalder, T., and Wessely, S. (1994). Chronic fatigue syndrome: a follow up study. *Journal of Neurology, Neurosurgery and Psychiatry*, **57**, 617–21.

Burns, D. D. (1980). *Feeling good: the new mood therapy*. William Morrow, New York.

Butler, S., Chalder, T., Ron, M., and Wessely, S. (1991). Cognitive behaviour therapy in chronic fatigue syndrome. *Journal of Neurology, Neurosurgery and Psychiatry*, **54**, 153–8.

Chalder, T. (1995). *Coping with chronic fatigue*. Sheldon, London.

Chalder, T., Berelowitz, G., Pawlikowska, T., Watts, L., Wessely, S., Wright, D., and Wallace, E. P. (1993). Development of a fatigue scale. *Journal of Psychosomatic Research*, **37**, 147–53.

Chen, M. K. (1986). The epidemiology of self-perceived fatigue among adults. *Preventative Medicine*, **15**, 74–81.

Costa e Silva, J. A. and De Girolamo, G. (1990). Neurasthania: History of a concept. In *Psychological Disorders in General Medical Settings* (ed. N. Sartorious, D. Goldberg, G. de Girolamo, J. Costa e Silva, Y. Lecrubier and U. Wittchen), pp. 69–81. Hogrefe & Huber, Toronto.

Cox, I. M., Campbell, M. J., and Dowson, D. (1991). Red blood cell magnesium and chronic fatigue syndrome. *Lancet*, **337**, 757–60.

David, A. S. (1991). Postviral fatigue syndrome and psychiatry. *British Medical Bulletin*, **47**, 966–88.

David, A. S., Pelosi, A. J., McDonald, E., Stephens, D., Ledger, D., Rathbone, R., and Mann, A. (1991). Tired, weak, or in need of rest: fatigue among general practice attenders. *British Medical Journal*, **301**, 1199–1202.

Deale, A. and David, A. (1994). Chronic fatigue syndrome: Evaluation and management. *Journal of Neuropsychiatry and Clinical Neurosciences*, **6**, 189–94.

Deale, A., Chalder, T., Everitt, B., Marks, I., and Wessely, S. Cognitive behaviour therapy for chronic fatigue syndrome: a randomized controlled trial. *American Journal of Psychiatry* (in press).

Dowsett, E. G., Ramsay, A. M., McCartney, R. A., and Bell, E. J. (1990). Myalgic encephalomyelitis—a persistent enteroviral infection? *Postgraduate Medical Journal*, **66**, 526–30.

Dubois, P. (1909). *The psychic treatment of nervous disorders* (6th edn). Funk and Wagnalls, New York.

Edwards, R. H. T. (1986). Muscle fatigue and pain. *Acta Medica Scandinavica*, **711**(suppl.), 179–88.

Farmer, A., Jones, I., Hillier, J., Llewellyn, M., Borysiewicz, L., and Smith, A. (1995). Neurasthenia revisited. *British Journal of Psychiatry*, **167**, 496–502.

Freud, S. (1924). *Heredity and the aetiology of the neuroses*, Collected Papers, volume 1. The International Psycho-analytic Press, London. (Original work published 1896.)

Friedberg, F. and Krupp, L.B. (1994). A comparison of cognitive behavioural treatment for Chronic Fatigue Syndrome and primary depression. *Clinical Infectious Diseases*, **18**(suppl. 1), s105–9.

Frost, R. O., Marten, P., Lahart, C., and Rosenblate, R. (1994). The dimensions of perfectionism. *Cognitive Therapy and Research*, **14**, 449–68.

Fukuda, K., Straus, S. E., Hickie, I., Sharpe, M. C., Dobbins, J. G., and Komaroff, A. L. (1994). Chronic Fatigue Syndrome: a comprehensive approach to its definition and management. *Annals of Internal Medicine*, **121**, 953–9.

Goldenberg, D. L. (1989*b*). Fibromyalgia and its relation to chronic fatigue syndrome, viral illness and immune abnormalities. *Journal of Rheumatology*, **19**, 91–3.

Greenberg, D. (1990). Neurasthenia in the 1980s: Chronic mononucleosis, chronic fatigue syndrome, and anxiety and depressive disorders. *Psychosomatics*, **31**, 129–37.

Hannay, D. R. (1978). Symptom prevalence in the community. *Journal of the Royal College of General Practitioners*, **28**, 492–9.

Holmes, G. P., Kaplan, J. E., Gantz, N. M., Komaroff, A. L., Schonberger, L. B., Straus, S. E., *et al* (1988). Chronic fatigue syndrome: a working case definition. *Annals of Internal Medicine*, **108**, 387–9.

House, A. (1995). The patient with medically unexplained symptoms: making the initial psychiatric contact. In: *Treatment of functional somatic symptoms* (ed. R. Mayou, C. Bass, and M. Sharpe), pp. 89–102. Oxford University Press.

Hurry, J. B. (1915). *The vicious circles of neurasthenia and their treatment*. Churchill, London.

Kendell, R. E. (1991). Chronic fatigue, viruses and depression. *Lancet*, **337**, 160–2.

Kennedy, H. G. (1988). Fatigue and fatiguability. *British Journal of Psychiatry*, **153**, 1–5.

Kirmayer, L. J. (1988). Mind and body as metaphors: hidden values in biomedicine. In *Biomedicine examined* (ed. M. Lock and D. Gordon), pp. 57–92. Kluwer, Dordrecht.

Kroenke, K., Wood, D. R., Mangelsdorff, D., Meier, N. J., and Powell, J. B. (1988). Chronic fatigue in primary care; prevalence, patient characteristics and outcome. *Journal of the American Medical Association*, **260**, 929–34.

Kroenke, K., Arrington, M. E., and Manglesdorff, D. (1990). The prevalence of symptoms in medical outpatients and the adequacy of therapy. *Archives of Internal Medicine*, **150**, 1685–9.

Kyle, D. V. and deShazo, R. D. (1992). Chronic fatigue syndrome: a conundrum. *American Journal of the Medical Sciences*, **303**, 28–34.

Lewis, S., Cooper, C. L., and Bennett, D. (1994). Psychosocial factors and chronic fatigue syndrome. *Psychological Medicine*, **24**, 661–71.

Lloyd, A. R., Wakefield, D., Boughton, C. R., and Dwyer, J. (1988). What is myalgic encephalomyelitis? *Lancet*, i, 1286–7.

Lloyd, A. R., Hickie, I., Brockman, A., Hickie, C., Wilson, A., Dwyer, J., and Wakefield, D. (1993). Immunologic and psychologic therapy for patients with chronic fatigue syndrome: a double-blind, placebo-controlled trial. *American Journal of Medicine*, **94**, 197–203.

Lynch, S., Seth, R., and Montgomery, S. (1991). Antidepressant therapy in the chronic fatigue syndrome. *British Journal of General Practice*, **41**, 339–42.

Macintyre, A. (1992). *M.E. post-viral fatigue syndrome and how to live with it* (2nd edn). HarperCollins, London.

MacLean, G. and Wessely, S. (1994). Professional and popular views of chronic fatigue syndrome. *British Medical Journal*, **308**, 776–7.

Manu, P., Lane, T. J., and Matthews, D. A. (1992). The pathophysiology of chronic fatigue syndrome: confirmations, contradictions, and conjectures. *International Journal of Psychiatry in Medicine*, **22**, 397–408.

Mathew, R. J., Weinman, M. L., and Mirabi, M. (1981). Physical symptoms of depression. *British Journal of Psychiatry*, **139**, 293–6.

Mayou, R. and Sharpe, M. (1995). Diagnosis, illness and disease. *Quarterly Journal of Medicine*, **88**, 827–31.

Mayou, R., Bass, C., and Sharpe, M. (1995). *Treatment of functional somatic symptoms*. Oxford University Press.

McCranie, E. J. (1980). Neurasthenic neurosis: psychogenic weakness and fatigue. *Psychosomatics*, **21**, 19–24.

McDonald, E., David, A., Pelosi, A. J., and Mann, A. H. (1993). Chronic fatigue in primary care attenders. *Psychological Medicine*, **23**, 978–98.

McEverdy, C. and Beard, A. (1970). Royal Free Epidemic of 1955: a reconsideration. *British Medical Journal*, 1, 7–11.

Mitchell, S. W. (1904). The evolution of the rest treatment. *Journal of Nervous and Mental Diseases*, 31, 368–73.

Morriss, R., Sharpe, M. C., Sharpley, A., Cowen, P., Hawton, K. E., and Morris, J. (1993). Abnormalities of sleep in patients with chronic fatigue syndrome. *British Medical Journal*, 306, 1161–4.

Nielson, W. R., Walker, C., and McCain, G. (1992). Cognitive behavioural treatment of fibromyalgia syndrome: preliminary findings. *Journal of Rheumatology*, 19, 98–103.

Petrie, K., Moss-Morris, R., and Weinman, J. (1995). The impact of catastrophic beliefs on functioning in chronic fatigue syndrome. *Journal of Psychosomatic Research*, 39, 31–8.

Philips, H. C. (1988). *The psychological management of chronic pain: a manual*. Springer, New York.

Powell, R., Dolan, R., and Wessely, S. (1990). Attributions and self-esteem in depression and chronic fatigue syndromes. *Journal of Psychosomatic Research*, 34, 665–73.

Proust, A. and Ballet, G. (1902). *The treatment of neurasthenia*. Henry Kimpton, London.

Puffer, J. C. and McShane, J. M. (1992). Depression and chronic fatigue in athletes. *Clinical Sports Medicine*, 11, 327–38.

Ray, C. (1991). Chronic fatigue syndrome and depression: conceptual and methodological ambiguities. *Psychological Medicine*, 21, 1–9.

Riley, M. S., O'Brien, C. J., McCluskey, D. R., Bell, N. P., and Nicholls, D. P. (1990). Aerobic work capacity in patients with chronic fatigue syndrome. *British Medical Journal*, 301, 953–6.

Sainsbury, P. and Gibson, J. G. (1954). Symptoms of anxiety and tension and the accompanying physiological changes in muscular system. *Journal of Neurology, Neurosurgery and Psychiatry*, 17, 216–24.

Schluederberg, A., Straus, S. E., Peterson, P. K., Blumenthal, S., Komaroff, A. L., Spring, S. B., et al. (1992). Chronic fatigue syndrome research: definition and medical outcome. *Annals of Internal Medicine*, 117, 325–31.

Schweitzer, R., Robertson, D. L., Kelly, B., and Whiting, J. (1994). Illness behaviour of patients with chronic fatigue syndrome. *Journal of Psychosomatic Research*, 38, 41–9.

Shands, H. and Finesinger, J. E. (1952). A note on the significance of fatigue. *Psychosomatic Medicine*, 14, 309–14.

Sharpe, M. (1994). Cognitive behavioural therapy and the treatment of chronic fatigue syndrome. In *Chronic fatigue syndrome* (ed. S. E. Straus), pp. 435–54. Marcel Dekker, New York.

Sharpe, M. (1995). Cognitive behavior therapy for chronic fatigue syndrome. *American Journal of Medicine*, 98, 420–1.

Sharpe, M. (1996). Chronic fatigue syndrome. *Psychiatric Clinics of North America* (in press).

Sharpe, M. C. and Bass, C. (1992). Pathophysiological mechanisms in somatization. *International Reviews in Psychiatry*, 4, 81–97.

Sharpe, M. C., Archard, L. C., Banatvala, J. E., Borysiewicz, L. K., Clare, A. W., David, A. S., et al. (1991). A report—chronic fatigue syndrome: guidelines for research. *Journal of the Royal Society of Medicine*, 84, 118–21.

Sharpe, M. C., Hawton, K. E., Seagraott, V., and Pasvol, G. (1992). Patients who present with fatigue: a follow up of referrals to an infectious diseases clinic. *British Medical Journal*, 305, 147–52.

Sharpe, M., Hawton, K., Simkin, S., Surawy, C., Hackmann, A., Klimes, I., *et al.* (1996). Cognitive behaviour therapy for chronic fatigue syndrome: a randomized controlled trial. *British Medical Journal*, 312, 22–6.

Shorter, E. (1992). *From paralysis to fatigue: a history of psychosomatic illness in the modern era.* Free Press, New York.

Spitzer, R. L., Williams, J. B. W., Gibbon, M., and First, M. B. (1992). The structured clinical interview for DSM-III-R (SCID). 1: History, rationale and description. *Archives of General Psychiatry*, 49, 624–9.

Stern, R. and Fernandez, M. (1991). Group cognitive and behavioural treatment for hypochondriasis. *British Medical Journal*, 303, 1229–31.

Stewart, D. E. (1990). Emotional disorders misdiagnosed as physical illness: environmental hypersensitivity, candidiasis hypersensitivity, and chronic fatigue syndrome. *International Journal of Mental Health*, 19, 56–68.

Straus, S. E. (1992). Defining the chronic fatigue syndrome. *Archives of Internal Medicine*, 152, 1569–70.

Straus, S. E. (1991). Intravenous immunoglobulin treatment for the chronic fatigue syndrome. *American Journal of Medicine*, 89, 551–2.

Straus, S. E., Dale, J. K., Tobi, M., Lawley, T., Preble, O., Blaese, M., *et al.* (1988). Acyclovir treatment of the chronic fatigue syndrome; lack of efficacy in a placebo controlled trial. *New England Journal of Medicine*, 319, 1692–8.

Surawy, C., Hackmann, A., Hawton, K., and Sharpe, M. (1995). Chronic fatigue syndrome: a cognitive approach. *Behaviour Research and Therapy*, 33, 535–44.

Valdini, A. F., Steinhardt, S., and Feldman, E. (1989). Usefulness of a standard battery of laboratory tests in investigating chronic fatigue in adults. *Family Practice*, 6, 286–91.

Vercoulen, J. H., Swanink, C. M., Fennis, J. F., Galama, J. M., Van der Meer, J. W., and Bleijenberg, G. (1994). Dimensional assessment of chronic fatigue syndrome. *Journal of Psychosomatic Research*, 38, 383–92.

Ware, N. C. (1993). Society, mind and body in chronic fatigue syndrome: and anthropological view. In *Chronic fatigue syndrome* (ed. G. R. Bock and J. Whelan), pp. 62–73. Wiley, Chichester, UK.

Ware, N. C. (1992). Suffering and the social construction of illness: the deligitimation of illness experience in chronic fatigue syndrome. *Medical Anthropology Quarterly*, 6, 347–61.

Ware, J. E. and Sherbourne, C. D. (1992). The MOS 36-item short-form health survey. *Medical Care*, 30, 473–81.

Waterman, G. A. (1909). The treatment of fatigue states. *Journal of Abnormal Psychology*, 4, 128–39.

Wessely, S. (1990). Old wine in new bottles: neurasthenia and 'M.E.'. *Psychological Medicine*, 20, 35–53.

Wessely, S. (1991). History of postviral fatigue syndrome. *British Medical Bulletin*, 47, 919–41.

Wessely, S. (1994). The history of chronic fatigue syndrome. In *Chronic fatigue syndrome* (ed. S. E. Straus), pp. 3-44. Marcel Dekker, New York.

Wessely, S., David, A. S., Butler, S., and Chalder, T. (1989). Management of chronic (post-viral) fatigue syndrome. *Journal of the Royal College of General Practitioners*, 39, 26–9.

Wilbur, D. L. (1949). Clinical management of the patient with fatigue and nervousness. *Journal of the American Medical Association*, 141, 1199–204.

Wilson, A., Hickie, I., Lloyd, A., Hadzi-Pavlovic, D., Boughton, C., Dwyer, J., and Wakefield, D. (1994*a*). Longitudinal study of outcome of chronic fatigue syndrome. *British Medical Journal*, 308, 756–9.

Wilson, A., Hickie, I., Lloyd, A., and Wakefield, D. (1994*b*). The treatment of chronic fatigue syndrome: science and speculation. *American Journal of Medicine*, 96, 544–50.

Young, J. E. (1990). *Cognitive therapy for personality disorders: a schema focussed approach*. Professional Resource Exchange Inc, Florida.

Zigmond, A. S. and Snaith, R. P. (1983). The hospital anxiety and depression scale. *Acta Psychiatrica Scandinavica*, 67, 361–70.

17

Problem-solving treatment in primary care

Dennis Gath and Laurence Mynors-Wallis

In the United Kingdom, about 98% of people in the general population are registered as patients with general practitioners (GPs). About three-quarters of these patients consult their GP in the course of a year (Goldberg and Huxley 1992). Among these consulting patients, one-fifth (about 300 patients per year per GP) are given a psychiatric diagnosis by the GP (Fry 1982).

A highly important finding is that nearly all (95%) of these patients with a psychiatric diagnosis are treated by their GP, whereas only a few (5%) are seen by a psychiatrist (Shepherd 1974). Given this distribution of care between family doctors and psychiatrists, it is important to ensure that GPs are well trained in psychiatric assessment, diagnosis, and treatment.

The skills of assessment and diagnosis of psychiatric disorders in primary care have been identified and effectively taught by Goldberg, Gask, and their colleagues in Manchester (Gask 1990), and will not be detailed here. This chapter will focus on one particular psychological treatment in primary care, namely, problem-solving. This treatment has been evaluated previously for other psychiatric conditions, such as in the treatment of patients after deliberate self-harm (Hawton *et al.* 1981, Salkovskis *et al.* 1990). It has been shown that problem-solving techniques have also been used to improve coping skills of schizophrenic patients (Falloon *et al.* 1984).

Among patients who present psychiatric problems in primary care, most are in the age range 45–64, and about two-thirds are women. Compared with other patients consulting in primary care, those with psychiatric disorders consult their GP twice as often, have more physical illnesses, and take more time off work (Wilkinson *et al.* 1988). The financial cost of these disorders is high: Croft-Jefferies and Wilkinson (1989) estimated that psychiatric disorders in primary care totalled £5.6 billion in 1985, when account was taken of the costs of treatment and lost production.

Many of these patients are diagnosed as having minor emotional disorders. There are few published descriptions of these disorders, but a study by

Goldberg and Huxley (1980) provided an illuminating account. In this study of 88 patients diagnosed as having mental disorder in general practice, it was found that the frequencies of psychiatric symptoms in these patients were: anxiety and worry (82); despondency, sadness (71); fatigue (71); somatic symptoms (52); sleep disturbance (50); irritability (38); excessive concern with bodily function (27); depressive thoughts, inability to concentrate (27); obsessions and compulsions (19); phobias (11); depersonalization (6).

Against this background, the authors and their colleagues in Oxford have undertaken a series of studies of the treatment of emotional disorders in primary care. The overall aim of this research has been to evaluate a brief psychological treatment as an alternative to medication. The central aims have been to discover whether psychological treatments in primary care are effective (compared with medication), feasible, and acceptable to patients.

With these aims in view, all the studies have been carried out in primary care, and not in the more rarefied atmosphere of the hospital.

Study 1: The effects of not prescribing anxiolytic medication for emotional disorders

The first study (Catalan *et al.* 1984*a*,*b*) was carried out when the scale of prescribing of anxiolytic medication for emotional disorders was causing widespread unease among medical and related professions (*Lancet* 1973). The aim of this first study was straightforward: to discover whether anxiolytic medication could be withheld from patients without causing untoward consequences. To examine this question, two treatments were compared for emotional disorders in which anxiety was predominant: (1) anxiolytic medication; (2) brief counselling given by the GP, with no medication.

The study was carried out with the help of six GPs who worked in two local health centres. The GPs had not received any special training in psychiatry. Patients were selected by these doctors on two criteria: (1) the patients were presenting with new episodes of emotional disorder for which the GP would normally prescribe an anxiolytic drug; (2) the patients had taken no psychotropic medication in the preceding three months. Patients meeting these conditions were randomly allocated to one or other of the two treatments—anxiolytic medication or brief counselling. The contents of these two treatments were stipulated: (1) medication should consist of a benzodiazepine (usually diazepam), which could be prescribed for a calming action by day, or as a hypnotic at night; (2) brief counselling should consist of four stages: (i) *listening* to the patient, and *assessing* the patient's symptoms; (ii) *explaining* the symptoms to the patient; (iii) *reassuring* the patient; (iv) *advising* the patient. No specialized treatment was to be given. From standardized records kept by both the GPs and patients, it was clear that these guidelines were observed. It should be emphasized that the GPs were given no specific training in the techniques of brief counselling; instead they were encouraged to use their own skills in a clear and focused way. No stipulations were made as to the frequency or duration of consultations. In practice, the mean duration of the initial consultation was 10.5 minutes for the drug group and 12 minutes for the counselled group. The mean number of consultations during the subsequent six months was 4.6 for the drug group and 4.5 for the counselled group.

Assessments of the patients' mental state were made at three stages: at the initial consultation; after one month; and after seven months. The assessments included self-ratings by patients, and a comprehensive assessment by trained research assessors.

The characteristics of the sample indicated that the GPs had complied well with the selection criteria. Thus, 85% of the patients were high scorers (that is, scoring above 11) on the General Health Questionnaire (GHQ) 60-item scale (Goldberg 1972). The symptoms were predominantly anxiety and somatic symptoms, as shown by the subscales of the GHQ (Goldberg and Hillier 1979).

Outcome was judged in terms of four questions: does withholding anxiolytic medication (1) worsen clinical outcome? (2) increase consumption of tobacco, alcohol, and non-prescribed drugs? (3) increase demands on GPs' time? (4) dissatisfy patients?

In answer to question (1) (clinical outcome), there were no significant differences between the two treatment groups on any measure of psychiatric or social outcome at any time. In the two treatment groups there were significant improvements, which occurred in parallel and at the same rate. These improvements were found on the Present State Examination (PSE) (Wing et al. 1974), the Profile of Mood States (McNair and Lorr 1964), the modified Social Adjustment Scale (Cooper et al. 1982), and the patients' ratings of their satisfaction with treatment.

The findings on question (2) were that withholding anxiolytics did not increase consumption of tobacco, alcohol, or non-prescribed drugs.

The findings on question (3) were that withholding anxiolytics did not result in increased demands on GPs' time in either the frequency or the length of consultations (as measured with stop-watches during consultation).

Finally, the answer to question (4) was that withholding anxiolytics did not cause dissatisfaction to the patients.

The conclusion from this first study was that, in the treatment of emotional disorders, anxiolytic medication was no more beneficial than the brief counselling techniques used by the GPs in the course of a usual consultation (Catalan et al. 1984a, 1984b). There was, however, a substantial proportion of patients who remained unwell six months after the initial consultation. Patients of this kind provided the focus for the next study.

Study 2: The feasibility and efficacy of problem-solving for emotional disorders of poor prognosis treatment

In Study 1 (described above) it was found that 60% of patients with anxiety/depressive disorders had recovered within four weeks of starting treatment. After 28 weeks, the proportion of recovered patients had increased to 70%, but 30% of patients were still psychiatrically unwell as shown by high scores on the PSE (Wing *et al.* 1974) and the GHQ (Goldberg and Hillier 1979). This finding was consistent with a later report by Mann *et al.* (1981) that among patients presenting with neurotic disorders in general practice, about one-third had disorders that persisted for six months or longer. In the second study, our group evaluated a psychological treatment designed specifically for these patients (about 30%) who were likely to have a poor prognosis. The procedures for selecting these 'poor prognosis' patients are described later.

The psychological treatment chosen for evaluation was problem-solving, for three reasons. First, this treatment was likely to be effective because it focuses on the personal and social problems that are important determinants of emotional disorders in primary care (Sireling *et al.* 1985). Second, the treatment was brief and non-specialized and therefore likely to be feasible in general practice. Third, from earlier Oxford work on the treatment of deliberate self-harm (Hawton *et al.* 1981), it had been established that problem-solving treatment could be learnt in a relatively short time. The main components of problem-solving are summarized below:

1. Assess the patient's symptoms, and any practical and social problems.
2. Give the patient an explanation of the emotional symptoms, and how they are caused.
3. Reassure the patient that problem-solving will be appropriate and effective for the symptoms.
4. Carry out problem-solving in the following stages:

(a) The patient's problems are clarified in detail.
(b) For each problem, one or more achievable goals are identified.
(c) The patient is asked to think of as many solutions as he/she can.
(d) The patient chooses the most suitable solution.
(e) The patient and therapist devise a plan of action to be carried out before the next treatment session.
(f) In subsequent sessions, progress is evaluated.

These steps were followed in a course of four treatment sessions over six weeks. A summary of the process of problem-solving treatment is given on pp. 425–429.

As this was a first evaluative study of problem-solving treatment in primary care, it was decided that the treatment should be given by a research psychiatrist in the health centre. The control treatment was the GP's usual treatment, whether psychological, pharmacological, or both.

From Study 1 it had been established that, if a patient had a PSE total score under 12 when assessed four weeks after the initial consultation with the GP, then the likelihood of the patient being a PSE case at 28 weeks was only 10%. If the patient's PSE total score at four weeks was 12 or over, then the likelihood of the patient being a PSE case at 28 weeks was 66%. This finding was valuable as it provided a method of selecting 'poor prognosis' patients for treatment, while withholding treatment from 'good prognosis' patients who would mostly recover without further treatment.

The selection of patients was initially made by the GP using the same criteria as in Study 1. Four weeks later, a member of the research team visited the patient at home, took a history, and administered the PSE. Patients were then selected for the study if their total score was 12 or more on the PSE.

In this study, 113 potentially suitable patients were referred by GPs. The PSE was administered to all 113 patients four weeks after referral. Of the 113 patients, 66 had a PSE total score under 12 at four weeks, while 47 had a PSE total score of 12 or more. These 47 patients with high scores at four weeks were randomly allocated to problem-solving treatment (21 patients) or to the GP's usual treatment (26 patients). All patients in the trial were assessed at 4, 12, and 28 weeks after the initial referral by their GP. These assessments were carried out by trained research assistants. The assessments included the PSE and two self-rated scales, the 28-item GHQ (Goldberg and Hillier 1979) and the modified Social Adjustment Scale (SAS-M) (Cooper *et al.* 1982).

Before treatment the two patient groups were found to be well matched on PSE total scores (problem-solving group 16.6, SD 3.3; control group 17.7, SD 4.4; no significant difference). After seven weeks, both treatment groups had improved significantly ($P < 0.001$ for both), but the reduction in scores was significantly greater for the problem-solving group than for the control group ($P < 0.01$).

At the final assessment (28 weeks), the problem-solving group showed slight further improvement, but this improvement was not significant as against the earlier findings at 11 weeks. At 28 weeks, the reduction in PSE total score since the start of treatment was significantly greater in the problem-solving group than the control group ($P < 0.01$). The pattern of improvement shown with the GHQ and the SAS-M was essentially the same as the pattern shown with the PSE as reported above.

At the end of treatment, patients were given a check-list on which to identify elements of the treatment that they found helpful. Compared with control patients, significantly more problem-solving patients endorsed elements of problem-solving such as: problems were pin-pointed; problems were broken into steps; help was given in deciding what to do; advice was given on tackling problems; plans were made on what to do between meetings.

The conclusion from this study was that problem-solving, given by a psychiatrist, was a feasible and effective treatment for emotional disorders of poor prognosis in primary care (Catalan *et al.* 1991). The next step was to evaluate problem-solving treatment for major depression. This was the aim of the third study.

Study 3. Problem-solving treatment for major depression in general practice

So far, the research had provided evidence that problem-solving treatment was effective for the mixed anxiety and depressive disorders seen in general practice. At this stage, a salient question arose: would problem-solving treatment be effective for depressive disorders (major depression) presenting in general practice? This is an important question because 1 in 10 patients consulting in primary care suffers from a depressive disorder, and 1 in 20 meets the diagnostic criteria for major depression (Blacker and Clare 1988). These depressive disorders cause both psychological distress and impaired social functioning.

In an important trial in general practice, it had been found that amitriptyline was more effective than drug placebo for most depressive disorders, but not the mildest disorders (Paykel *et al.* 1988). Although convenient and effective, antidepressant medication has certain disadvantages in primary care. First, antidepressant drugs may have unpleasant side-effects. Second, medication may seem irrelevant to many patients who are beset with psychological and social problems. Both these factors may result in poor compliance. Third, there is good evidence that depressive disorders in general practice are related to psychological and social problems (Sireling *et al.* 1985). These disadvantages point to the need for a psychological treatment as an effective alternative to antidepressant drugs.

Several psychological treatments may be considered for the treatment of depressive disorders in primary care. For example, there is some evidence that cognitive therapy is effective for depressive disorders in general practice. In the working conditions of primary care, however, time constraints and the limited availability of trained psychologists are likely to prohibit a full course of this treatment. Interpersonal psychotherapy is also an effective treatment for depression (Klerman *et al.* 1984) but it has not been evaluated specifically in primary care.

There were good reasons for evaluating the efficacy of problem-solving treatment for depressive disorders in primary care. These reasons were that problem-solving treatment is brief, readily learnt, acceptable to patients, free from drug side-effects, and directed at likely causative problems.

Against this background a controlled clinical trial was carried out in Oxford to evaluate problem-solving treatment for major depression in primary care. The aim of this study was to answer two questions: (1) is problem-solving treatment *effective*? (2) is problem-solving treatment *feasible*?

The design was a randomized controlled clinical trial to compare three treatments: (1) problem-solving treatment; (2) amitriptyline with standard clinical management; (3) drug placebo with standard clinical management.

Patients were recruited into the study by GPs and were screened to meet the following selection criteria: (1) a diagnosis of Research Diagnostic Criteria major depression (Spitzer *et al.* 1978); (2) a Hamilton depression rating score of 13 or more (Hamilton 1967); (3) a minimum duration of two weeks.

Each of the three treatments was given in six sessions over 12 weeks. The first session was scheduled to last 60 minutes, and the five subsequent sessions to last 30 minutes each. The three treatments were given in primary care health centres or in patients' homes. The treatments were provided by three therapists (one research psychiatrist and two research GPs). The therapists received systematic training in all three treatments.

The problem-solving treatment was similar to that given in Study 2. A threefold explanation of the treatment was given to the patients: (1) symptoms (such as low mood, poor sleep, and tiredness) are caused by problems of living (e.g., problems with work, social relationships, family, or finances); (2) if these problems can be resolved, then the symptoms will improve; (3) problems can be resolved with problem-solving treatment. Most patients readily accepted this formulation, and many readily agreed that their depressive symptoms were related to psychological and social problems.

As explained above, the drug treatment was either amitriptyline or drug placebo. The administration of these substances was double-blind. All capsules were prescribed as for amitriptyline, the dose being increased to 150 mg over 10 days. The same amount of therapist's time was given to patients receiving drug treatment as to those receiving problem-solving treatment.

In order to structure the drug treatment sessions, and in order to avoid problem-solving techniques during these sessions, a manual was written for the drug treatments. This manual was based on the manual used in the NIMH Treatment of Depression Collaborative Research Program (Fawcett *et al.* 1987). The therapist and patient spent the allocated time in discussing, for example: how the medication might be expected to work; what side-effects might be experienced; how these effects could be minimized; and how the patient's symptoms were progressing from session to session.

Assessments of the patients were carried out by independent research interviewers who were blind to the treatment given. These assessments were made at week 0 (pre-treatment), week 6 (halfway through treatment), and week 12 (completion of treatment). The main measures were the Hamilton Rating Scale for Depression (Hamilton 1967), the Beck Depression Inventory (Beck *et al.* 1961), and the modified Social Adjustment Scale (Cooper *et al.* 1982).

Of 174 patients referred to the trial by GPs, 107 (61%) met the entry criteria. Of these 107 eligible patients, 91 agreed to enter the study. On random allocation 30 patients received problem-solving, 31 amitriptyline, and 30 placebo. Among these patients the median duration of symptoms before treatment was six months. On admission to the study the patients' mean score on the Hamilton depression scale was 19, and their mean score on the Beck Depression Inventory (BDI) was 26. Just under half of the patients had previously had one or more episodes of depression requiring treatment.

On entry to the study (week 0) the three treatment groups did not differ significantly in mean scores on the Hamilton depression scale (problem-solving group 19.4, SD 4.9; amitriptyline group 19.1, SD 4.8; placebo group 18.4, SD 3.6). At week 6 the scores were problem-solving group 8.5, SD 6.2; amitriptyline group 10.3, SD 6.5; placebo group 13.8, SD 5.7. Problem-solving was significantly more effective than placebo, but not significantly different from amitriptyline. Findings with the BDI were similar, at weeks 6 and 12 of the trial, problem-solving was significantly more effective than placebo, but not significantly different from amitriptyline. A similar outcome was found with the Social Adjustment Scale.

It was of interest to know not only the overall outcome for the whole group of patients but also how many patients had fully recovered by the end of treatment. For this purpose predetermined recovery criteria were used, as recommended by Frank *et al.* (1991). Thus, patients were categorized as recovered if they had end-of-treatment scores of 7 or less on the Hamilton rating scale. When this criterion was used, the proportions of patients who had recovered were problem-solving 60%, amitriptyline 52%, placebo 27% ($P = 0.03$).

Another important question was whether problem-solving treatment was feasible in primary care. To answer this, three issues were evaluated: (1) Was the duration of problem-solving treatment practicable? (2) Could members of a primary health care team deliver the treatment effectively? (3) Was the treatment acceptable to patients?

With regard to duration of treatment, for the patients who completed all six treatment sessions, the mean overall therapy times were: problem-solving, 3 h

24 min; amitriptyline, 3 h 3 min; placebo 2 h 55 min. In comparison with most other psychological treatments, the duration of problem-solving was very brief.

Question (2) was concerned with the efficacy of problem-solving treatment given by GPs. In this study, two GPs were given a brief course of training in two parts, - theory and practice. During theoretical training, the GPs were provided with a problem-solving manual and a series of illustrative case-vignettes. They also watched a training videotape, and participated in role play of doctor–patient treatment sessions. Each GP then carried out supervised treatments of five patients.

For patients treated by research GPs the outcome was as good as the outcome for patients treated by the research psychiatrist. It is important to be cautious in interpreting this result because of the small number of therapists involved. The result, however, suggests that interested GPs can be trained to use problem-solving therapy effectively.

The final question was whether problem-solving treatment was acceptable to patients. The low drop-out rate (2 of 30 patients) suggested that the patients found the treatment acceptable. This suggestion was reinforced by the patients' answers to a self-report questionnaire. For example, among patients who completed treatment, the treatment was regarded as helpful by 100% of patients receiving problem-solving and by 83% receiving amitriptyline. When asked whether they were given help with problems, 96% of problem-solving patients answered positively, compared with 56% of amitriptyline patients.

Overall, the findings indicated that problem-solving was: (a) as effective as amitriptyline and more effective than drug placebo; (b) feasible in practice; and (c) well accepted by patients and family doctors (Mynors-Wallis et al. 1995).

Study 4: Further evaluation of problem-solving treatment for major depression in primary care

Two questions arose from the findings of Study 3: (1) Is the combination of problem-solving treatment and medication more effective than either treatment alone? (2) Can problem-solving treatment be given effectively by non-medical members of the primary care team?

These two questions are currently being examined by using a single design, namely a randomized controlled clinical trial designed to last three years. Four treatments are being compared: (1) paroxetine given by research GPs; (2) problem-solving treatment alone given by research GPs; (3) problem-solving treatment alone given by research community nurses; (4) a combination of problem-solving treatment given by research community nurses and paroxetine given by research GPs.

Community nurses have been chosen to deliver the problem-solving treatment because they are widely employed in most primary health care teams, and may well have more time available than GPs to offer a psychological treatment. Also, employing community nurses is cost-effective and we have shown that they can be trained to use problem-solving treatment. This current study will determine how effective these trained nurses are in treating major depression.

Future research

Building on the studies described so far, it is planned to develop the research programme in two new directions.

The first new direction will be to evaluate problem-solving as a treatment for depressive disorders in the elderly. In primary care, depressive disorders in the elderly are common and often disabling. Frequently, these disorders do not receive appropriate treatment either with antidepressant medication or with psychological treatment. We have planned a controlled clinical trial in which elderly patients with major depression will be treated either with paroxetine alone or with problem-solving treatment alone.

The second new direction will be to evaluate problem-solving treatment in communities that are culturally different from Oxford. Problem-solving treatment for depressive disorders is being evaluated in four centres in the United States: Dartmouth, Pittsburgh, San Antonio, and Seattle. In this way, we hope to evaluate the feasibility, efficacy, and acceptability of problem-solving treatment in societies with different values, different social structures, and different health care systems.

On a personal note

This chapter has focused on a programme of research in primary care, in which both authors have taken part. Two other research programmes have been carried out by the first author (DHG), the one focusing on the evaluation of psychiatric community care, and the other on psychiatric aspects of obstetrics and gynaecology. In all three research areas, we have received generous and invaluable advice from Michael Gelder. On many occasions we have benefited from his exceptional research wisdom and enthusiasm. To give but one example, our work on problem-solving treatment (reviewed in this chapter) originated directly from the stimulus of an informal lunchtime conversation with Michael. For these and many other reasons, we are constantly indebted to Michael Gelder's great contribution to Oxford psychiatry.

Summary of problem-solving treatment

Problem-solving consists of seven stages.

Stage 1: *Explanation of the treatment and its rationale.*
Stage 2: *Clarification and definition of problems.*
Listing the problems in a clear and concrete form and breaking down large problems into smaller and more manageable parts.
Stage 3: *Choice of achievable goals.*
Specific goals are set to be achieved both quickly (before the next treatment session), and more slowly (over the course of treatment).
Stage 4: *Generating solutions.*
Consider any relevant solutions to achieve the goals set (brainstorming).
Stage 5: *Choice of a preferred solution.*
Stage 6: *Implementation of the preferred solution.*
Any steps required to implement the preferred solution should be listed clearly and precisely. The therapist and patient should agree homework tasks for the patient to carry out before the next session.
Stage 7: *Evaluation.*
The patient and therapist evaluate the patient's success or lack of success in the assigned homework tasks.
The course of a typical problem-solving treatment is detailed below.

SESSION ONE

Introduction
The *aims* of this session are:

(a) to list the patient's symptoms and problems, and to establish a link between them;
(b) to explain the rationale and principles of problem-solving treatment;
(c) to illustrate the stages of problem-solving by using a specific problem as an example.

In this first session the most important task is to motivate the patient to comply with treatment. This motivation can be achieved if the patient recognizes that the therapist has listened to and understood the patient's difficulties, and has used this understanding to explain the principles of problem-solving clearly and simply.

Stage 1: *Explanation of treatment and its rationale*
There are three steps:
(1) *Recognition of emotional symptoms*
The first step is to obtain a full account of the patient's *symptoms*. Common emotional symptoms include low mood, tearfulness, loss of enjoyment in life, worries, hopelessness, poor concentration, and irritability. Physical symptoms include appetite change, tiredness, sleep disturbance, headaches, and non-specific aches and pains.
(2) *Recognition of problems*
The second step is to list the patient's *problems*. This list can be compiled by enquiring about potential problem areas such as relationships, work, money, housing, health, and leisure activities.
(3) *Acceptance of a link between emotional symptoms and problems*
A link should be made between the patient's symptoms and problems. The patient should understand that his/her symptoms are an emotional reponse to his/her problems. The therapist then explains that the patient can tackle his/her problems during treatment, and that successful resolution of the problems will lead to resolution of the symptoms. Although unrealistic expectations should not be fostered, some optimism should be encouraged in order to motivate the patient. At this point it is important to emphasize that the patient will play an active part in the treatment.

Stage 2: *Clarification and definition of problems*
There are two steps:
(1) *Listing the problems in a clear and concrete form*
A list of problems should already have been drawn up. The next step is to choose one particular problem which is important to the patient, and which the therapist considers feasible for problem-solving.
  This problem should be defined as clearly as possible. In specifying the problem it may help if the patient considers four questions:

  (i) What is the problem?
 (ii) When does the problem occur?
(iii) Where does the problem occur?
 (iv) Who is involved in the problem?

(2) *Breaking down large problems into smaller and more manageable parts*
Usually a patient presents several related problems. The therapist and patient should review these problems carefully, and then select one or two problems to tackle initially.
  A housewife may say that her problem is the family. On further enquiry, the therapist may establish that the patient has several problems. Thus, she may

be distressed because her husband stays in the pub four nights a week, she may be criticized by her mother about poor housework, and she may have to support a sister in hospital.

Stage 3: *Choice of achievable goals*
Once the problems have been clarified and defined, the next stage is to choose one or more achievable goals. In making this choice it is important to take into account the balance between the patient's resources and obstacles. The patient's resources may include:

 (i) Personal strengths and assets.
 (ii) Education; leisure activities; social and financial resources.
(iii) Support from other people, such as the spouse or other relative a friend, or a professional person such as a social worker or clergyman.
(iv) Self-help groups: direct advice about the availability of self-help groups may be appropriate.

It is important that the patient develops a sense of achievement early in treatment; for this purpose goals should be identified that can be achieved quickly, for example, before the next session. Medium-term goals can be attained in stages over the course of treatment.

Stage 4: *Generating solutions*
Once an achievable goal has been set, the patient is asked to list as many solutions as he/she can generate. Potential solutions should not be discarded or prejudged, even if initially they seem to be silly or unworkable.

Stage 5: *Choice of a preferred solution*
The therapist encourages the patient to draw up a list of the pros and cons for each potential solution. It may be useful to ask the patient to prepare this list as a homework task.
    The patient should select a preferred solution, that is, a solution that best achieves the stated goals with the least personal and social disadvantages. Some patients find this stage of problem-solving the most difficult to achieve alone; such patients may ruminate about possible solutions without being able to choose one.

Stage 6: *Implementation of the preferred solution*
It is important not to rush this stage because the patient may lack the confidence to implement the preferred solution. The steps needed to achieve the solution may have to be broken down into simpler sub-steps. There should

be clear specifications of the sub-steps and when they should be carried out. For example:

Preferred solution: Obtain a part-time job in a shop.
Sub-steps:

(a) go to jobcentre on Monday and speak to staff there;
(b) buy a local paper each day and read the advertisements, respond to at least two;
(c) go to the local high street and look for any jobs advertised in the window on Monday, check specifically the high street stores.

The patient should have a clear set of tasks that need to be completed between therapy sessions. These tasks are referred to as homework.

The session concludes with three important 'take home' messages:

(1) symptoms are related to problems;
(2) if the problems can be tackled, symptoms will improve; and
(3) specific tasks need to be completed before the next session.

Towards the end of the session, time should be allowed for the patient to ask questions and clarify issues.

SESSION TWO

Session Two should start with Stage 7 of the problem-solving treatment, evaluation.

Stage 7: *Evaluation*
At the start of this session (and subsequent sessions) the patient's progress should be assessed. The patient should have completed or attempted to complete the homework tasks agreed in the previous session.

The therapist should begin by praising any progress and success. The therapist can then discuss problems and difficulties, bearing in mind that patients may selectively attend to failures. It is important to praise all successes, however small.

If difficulties have arisen, the reasons should be examined:

(a) Should the goal be defined more clearly?
(b) Are the goals unrealistic?
(c) Have new obstacles arisen?
(d) Are the implementation steps difficult to achieve? If so, why?

If the first problem proves very difficult, another problem may be tackled. This change does not mean that the original problem is unimportant but in solving one problem the patient may gain a sense of control over his/her life that alters his/her perception of other problems.

If the patient has not completed the homework tasks, he/she may not have understood what was expected. It should be emphasized that any progress occurring between treatment sessions may be more important than progress achieved within a session. A patient's motivation is likely to be greater if he/she is striving to achieve his/her own goals with his/her own solutions. If patients are not completing homework tasks, the therapist should stress that the goals and solutions were chosen by the patient and not by the therapist.

After the review of progress, the rest of the session should be spent on planning tasks to be undertaken before the next session. These tasks may be linked to the initial problem, or to a new problem.

SESSION THREE *and subsequent sessions*

The patient and therapist should review the original problems and should consider progress. Should efforts be focused on new problems or should work continue developing goals for the original problems? At this point, the patient may be working through a series of intermediate goals to achieve a final goal. For example, if the final goal is to obtain a new job, the intermediate goals may be to:

(i) obtain information about the qualifications required;
(ii) send application forms; and
(iii) attend an interview.

In session one, the therapist will have explained that treatment will probably be limited to a specific number of sessions over a specific number of weeks. Both therapist and patient should bear this point in mind during treatment. In later sessions, once the patient has grasped the principles of treatment, the therapist should emphasize that problem-solving can be used not only for current problems, but also for future problems. It may be valuable to rehearse the use of problem-solving to resolve future hypothetical problems.

In the penultimate session it is often useful to review the original problem list, and to identify any problems that should be considered in the final session. Later sessions may be briefer than early sessions. In the later sessions, the therapist should become less active in the problem-solving, and this change should be emphasized to the patient. If treatment has been successful, patients should feel convinced that they have contributed to their own recovery, with the use of common sense techniques.

References

Beck, A. T., Ward, C. H., and Mendelson, M. (1961). An inventory for measuring depression. *Archives of General Psychiatry*, 4, 561–71.

Blackburn, I. M., Bishop, S., Glen, A. I. M., Walley, L. J., and Christie, J. E. (1981). The efficacy of cognitive therapy in depression. *British Journal of Psychiatry*, 139, 181–9.

Blacker, C. V. R. and Clare, A. W. (1988). The prevalence and treatment of depression in general practice. *Psychopharmacology*, 95, S14–17.

Catalan, J., Gath, D., Edmonds, G., and Ennis, J. (1984a). The effects of non-prescribing of anxiolytics in general practice: I. Controlled evaluation of psychiatric and social outcome. *British Journal of Psychiatry*, 144, 593–602.

Catalan, J., Gath, D., Bond, A., and Martin, P. (1984b). The effects of non-prescribing of anxiolytics in general practice: II. Factors associated with outcome. *British Journal of Psychiatry*, 144, 603–10.

Catalan, J., Gath, D. H., Bond, A., Day, A., and Hall, L. (1991). Evaluation of a brief psychological treatment for emotional disorders in primary care. *Psychological Medicine*, 21, 1013–18.

Cooper, P., Osborn, M., Gath, D., and Feggetter, G. (1982). Evaluation of a modified self-report measure of social adjustment. *British Journal of Psychiatry*, 141, 68–75.

Croft-Jefferies, C. and Wilkinson, G. (1989). Estimated costs of neurotic disorders in UK general practice in 1985. *Psychological Medicine*, 19, 549–58.

Falloon, I. R., Boyd, J. L., and McGill, C. W. (1984). *Family care of schizophrenia*. Guilford Press, New York.

Fawcett, J., Epstein, P., Fiester, S. J., Ellan, I., and Autry, J. (1987). Clinical management—imipramine/placebo administration manual. *Psychopharmacology Bulletin*, 23, 309–24.

Frank, E., Prien, R. F., Jarrett, R. B., Keller, M. B., Kupfer, D. J., *et al.* (1991). Conceptualization and rationale for consensus definition of terms in major depressive disorder: remission, recovery, relapse and recurrence. *Archives of General Psychiatry*, 48, 851–5.

Fry, J. (1982). Psychiatric illness in general practice. In *Psychiatry and general practice* (ed. A. Clare and M. Lader), pp. 43–9. Academic Press, London.

Gask, L. (1990). Teaching psychiatric interview skills to GPs. In *The prevention of depression and anxiety—the role of the primary care team* (ed. R. Jenkins, J. Newston, and R. Young). HMSO, London.

Goldberg, D. (1972). *The detection of psychiatric illness by questionnaire*. Oxford University Press.

Goldberg, D. and Hillier, V. F. (1979). A scaled version of the General Health Questionnaire. *Psychological Medicine*, 9, 139–45.

Goldberg, D. and Huxley, P. (1980). *Mental illness in the community*. Tavistock, London.

Goldberg, D. and Huxley, P. (1992). *Common mental disorders—a biosocial model*. Routledge, London.

Hamilton, M. (1967). Development of a rating scale for primary depressive illness. *British Journal of Social and Clinical Psychology*, 6, 278–96.

Hawton, K., Bancroft, J., Catalan, J., Kingston, B., Stedeford, A., and Welch, N. (1981). Domicilary and out-patient treatment of self-poisoning patients by medical and non-medical staff. *Psychological Medicine*, 11, 169–77.

Klerman, G. L., Weissman, M. M., Rounsaville, B. J., *et al.* (1984). *Interpersonal psychotherapy of depression*. Basic Books, New York.

Lancet (1973). Benzodiazepines: use, over-use, misuse and abuse? 1, 1101–2.

Mann, A. H., Jenkins, R., and Belsey, E. (1981). The 12 month outcome of patients with neurotic illness in general practice. *Psychological Medicine*, II, 535–550.

McNair, D. M. and Lorr, M. (1964). An analysis of mood in neurotics. *Journal of Abnormal and Social Psychology*, 69, 620–7.

Mynors-Wallis, L. M., Gath, D. H., Lloyd-Thomas, A. R., and Tomlinson, D. (1995). Randomised controlled trial comparing problem-solving treatment with amitriptyline and placebo for major depression in primary care. *British Medical Journal*, 310, 441–5.

Paykel, E. S., Hollyman, J. A., Freeling, P., and Sedgwick, P. (1988). Predictors of therapeutic benefit from amitriptyline in mild depression: a general practice placebo-controlled trial. *Journal of Affective Disorders*, 14, 83–95.

Salkovskis, P., Atha, C., and Storer, D. (1990). Cognitive–behavioural problem-solving in the treatment of patients who repeatedly attempt suicide. *British Journal of Psychiatry*, 157, 781–876.

Shepherd, M. (1974). Social practice, mental illness and the British National Health Service. *American Journal of Public Health*, 64, 230–2.

Sireling, L.-I., Freeling, P., Paykel, E.-S., and Rao, B.-M. (1985). Depression in general practice: clinical features and comparison with out-patients. *British Journal of Psychiatry*, 147, 119–26.

Spitzer, R. L., Endicott, V., and Robins, E. (1978). Research diagnostic criteria: rationale and reliability. *Archives of General Psychiatry*, 36, 773–82.

Teasdale, J. D., Fennell, M. J. V., Hibbert, G. A., and Amies, P. L. (1984). Cognitive therapy for major depression in primary care. *British Journal of Psychiatry*, 144, 400–6.

Wilkinson, G., Smeeton, N., Skuse, D., and Fry, J. (1988). Consultation for physical illnesses by patients diagnosed and treated for psychiatric disorders by a GP: 20 year follow-up study. *British Medical Journal*, 297, 776–8.

Wing, J. K., Cooper, J. E., and Sartorius, N. (1974). *The measurement and classification of psychiatric symptoms*. Cambridge University Press.

Index